MW00561352

GROUP COUNSELING AND GROUP PSYCHOTHERAPY

Theory and Application

GEORGE M. GAZDA

*University of Georgia
and Medical College of Georgia*

EARL J. GINTER

University of Georgia

ARTHUR M. HORNE

University of Georgia

Allyn and Bacon

Boston ■ London ■ Toronto ■ Sydney ■ Tokyo ■ Singapore

Senior Editor: Virginia C. Lanigan
Vice President, Editor in Chief: Paul A. Smith
Editorial Assistant: Jennifer Connors
Marketing Manager: Kathleen Morgan
Editorial-Production Administration: Annette Joseph
Editorial-Production Coordinator: Susan Freese
Editorial-Production Service: TKM Productions
Electronic Composition: Omegatype Typography, Inc.
Composition Buyer: Linda Cox
Manufacturing Buyer: Suzanne Lareau
Cover Administrator: Brian Gogolin
Cover Designer: Suzanne Harbison

Between the time website information is gathered and then published, it is not unusual for some sites to have closed. Also, the transcription of URLs can result in unintended typographical errors. The publisher would appreciate being notified of any problems with URLs so that they may be corrected in subsequent editions. Thank you.

Library of Congress Cataloging-in-Publication Data

Gazda. George Michael.
    Group counseling and group psychotherapy : theory and application / George M. Gazda, Earl J. Ginter, Arthur M. Horne.
       p.   cm.
    Includes bibliographical references and index.
    ISBN 0-205-30630-6
    1. Group counseling. 2. Group psychotherapy. I. Ginter, Earl J. II. Horne, Arthur M. III. Title.

BF637.C6 G37 2000
158'.35—dc21

                                          00-063949

Printed in the United States of America

10 9 8 7 6 5 4 3 2 1   05 04 03 02 01 00

To Our Mentor and Dear Friend:
Dr. Merle M. Ohlsen

CONTENTS

PART II   THEORIES AND APPLICATIONS

CHAPTER TWELVE

Psychoanalytic-Based Group Theories: Applications   248

CHAPTER FIFTEEN

Life-Skills Training: A Psychoeducational Model   318

CHAPTER SIXTEEN

Self-Help/Mutual Support Groups   344

PREFACE

■ ■ ■ ■ ■

Group Counseling and Group Psychotherapy: Theory and Application was written with a twofold purpose, as the subtitle suggests. However, the text goes beyond the presentation of basic theories and issues related to the applications of group counseling and group therapy in general, as it addresses the needs of those professionals who will be working in educational and mental health (institutional) settings *as well as* those who will be self-employed in private practice. We have also extended the scope of the book by including chapters on psychoeducation (life-skills training groups) and self-help/mutual support groups because we recognize the increasingly strategic role that these group approaches are assuming in the group treatment arena. Current and future group specialists will need to be involved in each of these areas of group work.

The book is divided into two parts for convenience of presentation; however, other than Chapters 1 and 2 on the introduction, definitions, and history of group counseling and group psychotherapy, the remainder of the chapters in Parts I and II could be assigned at the pleasure of the instructor without any loss of intended subject mastery. Including the "applications" chapter with the "theory" chapter for each of four basic theories presented is highly recommended, of course. The four appendices are included for the convenience of the student and instructor and to supplement the chapters on multicultural issues and ethical issues. Depending on the professional path chosen by the student, the code of ethics for the Association for Specialists in Group Work and for the American Group Psychotherapy Association will guide him or her in training as well as in practice.

The Instructor's Manual with Test Items provides useful suggestions for teaching.

ACKNOWLEDGMENTS

The following individuals contributed to earlier authored or edited publications of George M. Gazda from which liberal use was made: John K. Wood, James S. Simkin, David A. Williams, Joseph Fabry, and Walter M. Lifton (Chapters 7 and 8 of this book, "Existential-Humanistic Group Theories" and "Existential-Humanistic Group Theories: Applications"). Malcolm Pines, Lisbeth E. Hearst, and Harold Behr's work was used in Chapters 11 and 12 of this book ("Psychoanalytic-Based Group Theories" and "Psychoanalytic-Based Group Theories: Applications"). Inese Wheeler's work was used in Chapter 16 of this book ("Self-Help/Mutual Support Groups").

Permission was granted from the American Counseling Association and the American Mental Health Counselors Association to use portions of previously published works by Earl J. Ginter and Arthur M. Horne—specifically, Earl J. Ginter and Warren Bonney (Chapter 11 of this book, "Psychoanalytic-Based Group Theories" and Chapter 12, "Psychoanalytic-Based Group Theories: Applications"), Linda L. Lawless, Earl J. Ginter, and Kevin R. Kelly (Chapter 1 of this book, "Group Counseling and

Group Psychotherapy: Origins, Comparisons, and Directions"), and Arthur M. Horne and Robin Rosenthal (Chapter 5 of this book, "Groups That Work: Research and Evaluation Considerations in Group Counseling and Group Psychotherapy").

We also wish to acknowledge the typing assistance of Alicia Dellinger and the library research of Christi Bartolomucci and Ryan Scott.

Thanks, too, to our editors and their assistants—Ray Short, Virginia Lanigan, Karin Huang, and Jennifer Connors—for their support and patience. Special thanks to Lynda Griffiths of TKM Productions for adding clarity and precision to our text. To the external reviewers of our material, we express our appreciation and thanks for their critical and thoughtful reviews.

CHAPTER ONE

GROUP COUNSELING AND GROUP PSYCHOTHERAPY

Origins, Comparisons, and Directions

One need only to look to the early years of the twentieth century for the initial stirrings of what is now recognized as traceable precursors to group counseling and group psychotherapy. In 1905, Joseph Pratt used a group format to work with patients suffering from an infectious disease that at the time was incurable. Quoting Pratt (1922) directly,

> I originally brought the patients together as a group with the idea that it would save my time, that of my associates and of the social worker. It was planned as a labor saving device. I did not have the time to instruct or encourage the patients individually. Advice, encouragement or admonition given to one I hoped would be heeded by all. (p. 403)

These "helping" groups were perceived by members as a valuable adjunct to treatment because sessions were devoted to sharing personal experiences and information. Due to the interpersonal focus of Pratt's groups, a valuable sense of mutual support was created and recognized as an important adjunct to medical treatment (Hadden, 1955).

Outside of medical settings, one may also point to educational environments as a direct contributor to the beginnings of so-called helping groups. According to Glanz and Hayes (1967), as early as 1907, Jesse B. Davis, principal of Cedar Rapids High School in Iowa, devoted weekly sessions in certain classes to the topic of " 'Vocational and Moral Guidance,' and George Boyden in 1912 introduced a course in vocations at the Beauport, Connecticut, high school. So 'group guidance' was 'born' " (p. 3). Glanz and Hayes (1967) cautioned that these first group guidance courses were instructional groups and that the techniques used were devoid, for the most part, of systematic use of group dynamics principles and specific group techniques. It is important to note that around the same period, a means was established to disseminate information pertaining to vocational topics. A predecessor to the National Vocational Guidance Association published the *Vocational Guidance News-Letter.* A line of subsequent publications followed, leading directly to the American Counseling Association's (ACA) *Journal of Counseling & Development* and other publications historically tied to ACA, such as the *Journal for Specialists in Group* (personal communication, Sylvia Nisenoff, July 6, 1999).

Although Pratt is generally credited for being the precursor of group psychother-apy, there is less agreement as to the person or persons to credit with the origination of group counseling. However, Gazda (1968) has traced the early, if not earliest, use of the term to Richard D. Allen (1931). In an article published in *Education,* Allen used the term interchangeably with *case conference* and *group guidance* but the descriptions of the process would more accurately describe what is now defined as *group guidance.*

In this chapter, a general overview to group counseling and group psychotherapy is provided. Specifically, a discussion of the most common descriptors used, as revealed in the group work research literature, is discussed; contributing factors lead-ing up to definitions for group counseling and group psychotherapy that are used in this text are covered, distinctions between group counseling and group psychotherapy are made, and a discussion of managed care and how it might affect the future of practice is presented. (A comprehensive presentation of the definitions and historical develop-ment of group counseling and group psychotherapy is presented in the next chapter.) Finally, a brief description of the contents of the textbook is provided.

GROUP WORK LITERATURE

Table 1.1 represents a summary of the group work research literature dating from 1970 through 1995. This summary was obtained by a careful review of Lubin, Wilson, Petren, and Polk's (1996) work *Research on Group Treatment Methods: A Selectively Anno-tated Bibliography.* Lubin and colleagues (1996) assimilated and compiled a listing of 1,793 sources, research articles, and books in the field of group work, many of which are annotated. This comprehensive annotated listing was reviewed to obtain an indication of the most frequently used group methods across various age groups. We classified the articles and books according to the type of group method used for each of the following developmental periods: childhood, adolescence, young adults (i.e., college students), adults, and older adults (the term *elderly* was frequently used in the literature). Some liberty was taken in categorizing group methods (i.e., group descriptors reported by Lubin et al.). For example, group methods listed by Lubin and colleagues included such terms as *group treatment, group process, group approaches,* and the like. The descrip-tors used by us to categorize what was reported by Lubin and coauthors are listed at the bottom of Table 1.1 and are organized in the table according to frequency of use.

Although there were 1,793 references included in the Lubin resource book, only 1,041 contained a group word descriptor that could be reasonably classified (concur-rent agreement). In addition, it is important to point out that sometimes a reference's annotation contained several group descriptors; for example, a study might compare the effects of several different group methods on a given population.

Having described the basis on which Table 1.1 was developed, what information may be abstracted that would promote better understanding the field of group work? What is obvious from Table 1.1 is that *group counseling* and *group psychotherapy/ther-apy* are, by far, the descriptors most frequently employed. Also, there seems to be a slight trend revealed in terms of a group member's age; that is, the younger the group member, the less likely he or she will be a member of a psychotherapy group but the

TABLE 1.1   Number of References to a Certain Group Descriptor

	GC	GT	GI	ST	M/C	PD	PE	EN	MA	SG	GG	SH	AT	GU	PT	ROW TOTALS
POPULATION (*n* = 1793)																
CHILDREN (*n* = 203)	89	65	6	10	5	0	1	0	0	0	0	0	2	3	2	**183**
ADOLESCENTS (*n* = 278)	138	63	8	7	3	3	1	0	0	0	0	0	2	2	0	**227**
COLLEGE (*n* = 114)	57	19	1	4	0	1	1	1	5	1	5	0	3	0	0	**98**
ADULTS (*n* = 1110)	60	200	64	26	34	12	5	11	10	12	8	12	10	0	0	**464**
OLDER ADULTS (*n* = 88)	14	44	7	0	0	1	0	0	0	2	0	1	0	0	0	**69**
COLUMN TOTALS	**358**	**391**	**86**	**47**	**42**	**17**	**8**	**12**	**15**	**15**	**13**	**13**	**17**	**5**	**2**	

Note: GC = Group Counseling, GT = Group Psychotherapy/Therapy, GI = Group Intervention, ST = Social Skills Training Groups, M/C = Marriage & Family Therapy/Counseling, PD = Psychodrama, PE = Psychoeducational Groups, EN = Encounter Groups, MA = Marathon Groups, SG = Support Groups, GG = Growth Groups, SH = Self-Help Groups, AT = Assertiveness Training Groups, GU = Group Guidance, PT = Play Therapy

more likely he or she will be a member of a counseling group. Also, based on the Lubin resources, one may conclude that *group therapy* and *group psychotherapy* are used synonymously in the literature. Specifically, *group therapy* has become the shortened or colloquial version of *group psychotherapy*. (Note: The particular term used in the various sections and chapters in this textbook is intended to reflect the body of literature being discussed at the time; for example, authors reporting on a psychodynamic approach to group work tend to use the term *psychotherapy*. In cases where there may not be a clear preference, the term *group counseling* will be used.)

DELINEATION OF GROUP COUNSELING AND GROUP PSYCHOTHERAPY

Even though a study of the Lubin and colleagues' (1996) resource book clearly leads a reviewer to conclude that the terms *group counseling* and *group psychotherapy* are frequently used interchangeably, we believe each term has a distinctive quality that can serve a useful purpose. In other words, although there is overlap between group counseling and group psychotherapy, there are qualities possessed by each that allows each to be used independent of the other. Figure 1.1 illustrates each term's distinctive but overlapping nature. Group counseling possesses qualities of growth engendering, prevention, and remediation (to a lesser degree than the other two qualities); group psychotherapy, in a sense, operates in the "opposite direction"—it starts by being remediation oriented and "therapeutically" spills over into the areas of prevention and growth engendering. Examples of groups are provided in Figure 1.1, with each example being placed along a continuum that depicts how areas of prevention, growth engendering, and remediation overlap, and thus how group counseling and group psychotherapy relate to one another in a conjoint manner but are still able to maintain a separate "therapeutic personality."

Let us now elaborate on what is illustrated in Figure 1.1. Group counseling is *prevention oriented* in the sense that the group members are capable of functioning in society but may be experiencing some "rough spots" in their lives. If group counseling is successful, these rough spots are successfully smoothed out, with no serious personality defects incurred. Group counseling is *growth engendering* insofar as it provides the participants with incentive and motivation to make changes that are in their best interests (i.e., the participants are motivated to take actions that maximize their human potential through self-actualizing behaviors). Group counseling is *remedial* for those individuals who have entered into a spiral of self-defeating behavior but who, nevertheless, may be capable of reversing the spiral without counseling intervention. How-

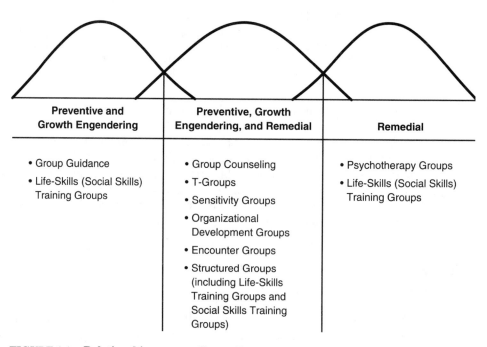

Preventive and Growth Engendering	Preventive, Growth Engendering, and Remedial	Remedial
• Group Guidance • Life-Skills (Social Skills) Training Groups	• Group Counseling • T-Groups • Sensitivity Groups • Organizational Development Groups • Encounter Groups • Structured Groups (including Life-Skills Training Groups and Social Skills Training Groups)	• Psychotherapy Groups • Life-Skills (Social Skills) Training Groups

FIGURE 1.1   Relationships among Group Processes

ever, with counseling intervention, the group member is more likely to recover, recover more quickly, and recover with fewer lingering emotional effects.

Finally, as suggested earlier, although the content and focus of group counseling is somewhat similar to what has been termed *group guidance*—including educational, vocational, personal, and social concerns—a number of factors that comprise each are quite different. First, group guidance is typically judged to be relevant for everyone on an intermittent basis (at certain points during the educational process). Regardless of the exact schedule of delivery, group counseling is generally judged to be relevant only for those experiencing a continuation of what was expected to be a "temporary problem"—information alone will not resolve the persistent problem. Second, traditional group guidance makes an *indirect* attempt to change attitudes and behaviors through accurate information or an emphasis on cognitive or intellectual functioning; group counseling makes a *direct* attempt to modify attitudes and behaviors by emphasizing extensive interpersonal involvement (i.e., member to counselor, member to member, member to members, etc.). Third, traditional group guidance was applicable to groups of 15 to 30, whereas group counseling is dependent on the development of strong group cohesiveness and the sharing of personal concerns, which are most applicable to small, intimate groups of 3 or 4 (children) or 8 to 12 (adolescents or adults).

Brammer and Shostrom (1960) characterized the differences between counseling and psychotherapy by the following series of adjectives, in which counseling is best described as

> educational, supportive, situational, problem-solving, conscious awareness, emphasis on "normals," and short-term. Psychotherapy is characterized by supportive (in a more particular sense), reconstructive, depth analysis, analytical, focus on the unconscious, emphasis on "neurotics" or other severe emotional problems, and long-term. (p. 6)

Based on Brammer and Shostrom's distinction, one may conclude that group psychotherapy can certainly be thought of as remedial based and that members of a psychotherapy group, relatively speaking, are more seriously emotionally disturbed than members of a counseling group. It could also be inferred that the training of group psychotherapists includes longer years of clinical experience, and thus psychotherapists differ in type of degree program, special certifications, and type of licenses. (These differences reflect the "depth" approach taken in psychotherapy group work.) But times are changing, and managed care, more than any other current force, is causing all practice related fields to reconsider how approaches differ from one another. Professionals are learning that some past distinctions are really not very relevant today. The best example of this is length of treatment—*short-term* treatment no longer relegates an approach automatically to the arena of "counseling." Even the type of technique is not a reliable demarcation. For instance, transference is a useful way to conceptualize certain types of interactions for both counselors and psychotherapists. This technique was once confined solely to the realm of a classic psychoanalytic approach with protracted treatment that could extend over many years of several sessions a week.

Managed Care

Any existing body of literature in a field of study and practice reveals trends or various necessary points of interests that have emerged over the profession's history. Such reviews are undertaken so one can learn where the field has been, where it is going, and where it is likely to go next, but any prediction of the future based on a literature review must now consider the effect that managed care is having on the delivery of mental health services. Otherwise, the significance of the information distilled could be misunderstood, or worse, the information might serve as a poor indicator of a field's future needs.

Undeniably, the scope of managed care is such that it is having a profound effect on practice and therefore has implications for training and career opportunities in group counseling and group psychotherapy. In this section, we review issues of concern about managed care and make general recommendations concerning how group practitioners may better prepare themselves to work in a world increasingly dominated by managed care. Finally, it is important to keep in mind two things when considering the effect that managed care has on the practice of group counseling and group therapy. First, although the influence of managed care is widespread, its influence is less for some groups of practitioners than others (e.g., one may assume that school counselors are being affected less than private practitioners). Second, the whole area of managed care is currently undergoing change and one cannot predict with total accuracy what form it may take in the future (e.g., many constituents of politicians are now asking for the legal right to sue managed care organization for losses).

According to Lawless, Ginter, and Kelly (1999), "The advent of managed care has caused dramatic changes in the provision and financing of treatments. These changes have required counselors and therapists to develop new knowledge and skills in order to establish and maintain economically viable practices" (p. 50). Lawless and colleagues surveyed professionals using open-ended questions about managed care—a procedure that allowed these professionals to identify current and future trends related to managed care. Professionals representing the following roles were surveyed: a managed care employee, a managed care publication publisher, a private practitioner (member of a group practice), a professional counseling association leader, a counselor educator, and a managed care consultant. The questions used by Lawless and associates that follow were altered slightly to serve as headings and are followed by a representative sample of participants' responses.

1. *How Does Managed Care Currently Affect the Practice of Counseling and Therapy?*

> Managed care is going to kill private practice, as we know it. Third-party payments will only be accessible through integrated groups. There is a strong private pay market, but there are too many mental health professionals for the money that is available. Clinicians will be working harder for less income. Practitioners will need to provide the kinds of services that the industry is asking for. Decisions about treatment goals will be shaped by the payers.
>
> The field has become very competitive with a lot of control over therapy being taken away from counselors. Claims are paid slowly by managed care organizations

[MCOs] with little recourse for the clinician. There is a compromise of confidentiality [in relation to client information].

Managed care affects the number and types of counseling sessions a consumer receives. There is a revolution in therapy with two roads, one dealing with the current problems and the other looking at a model of community health and wellness. When working with current problems the field is moving from a psychodynamic treatment model to a developmental counseling model dealing with life problems. There is a move towards the use of master's prepared therapists and there is less need for specialty providers [i.e., providers with doctorates]. MCOs tend to develop relationships with integrated groups, paying case rates and capitation. There is a lot of pressure for outcomes and clinicians are being profiled on how effective they are based on the MCOs' standards of practice.

2. How Do You Foresee the Future of Managed Care?

Managed care is "ever changing" and is here to stay. We are moving towards working more and more with large group practices or large delivery care systems. There will be innovative contracting arrangements in the areas of subcapitation and case rates. MCOs will move from a micro-management style to a macro-management system with providers that have documented records of a cost-effective management system. There will always be a place for private practitioners, but they will be needed because of geographical location and clinical specialties. Quality assurance will be a growing field due to national standards needed for accreditation. There will be internal quality measures as well as client satisfaction tracking.

The private practitioner will need to adopt a style of clinical practice that fits the health care system to which he/she is providing services. Boundaries between insurers and providers will disappear with insurers backward integrating and hiring providers. The biggest challenge will be the regulation. It is currently in the provider's best interest to not provide services. This will need to be watched and regulated.

The future lies in being part of a group practice.

The future of psychotherapy as a profession will need to be protected as managed care becomes the definer of the profession. The health care industry will grow to be a larger financial source within the culture. We are looking at a defining moment of the nature of the field and what our profession will evolve into.

3. What Advice Do You Have for Practitioners Regarding Managed Care?

Educate yourself and learn about managed care. What are some of the things they are attempting to do? How do they go about it? If you are looking at contracting with an MCO, ask them: What are your guidelines in terms of how you make decisions about the number of visits or type of treatment you authorize? What are your denial and appeal processes if we have a disagreement about coverage? What is your clinical philosophy that you are looking for and how do you partner with a provider? Differentiate yourself in terms of the type of services you provide. Attend training programs in solution-oriented brief treatment.

Ask yourself, what kind of professional life do you want to have? Do you want to be part of an integrated delivery system? This will mean you are no longer truly financially or operationally independent but you will have tremendous assets and resources you would never have as a [lone] private practitioner. Build strategic alliances with referring resources. Be highly specialized and find a small arena to become an expert. Look to funding outside of managed care such as education, child welfare or the criminal justice system. Tell your professional association to focus on exerting more control over the profession by being involved in practice protocol development.

Get on as many managed care panels as you can. Then follow up with whomever makes the referrals. Don't just sit back and wait for referrals. Maintain a wide referral base—network, network, network. Make professional outreach a lifestyle.

Subcontract with groups. Have a specialty or niche that is managed care oriented. Belong to and use your regional and national professional organization. Be creative and innovative in a cost efficient manner, offering services that are backed up with the proper training and credentialing.

4. *What Skills and Strategies Are Needed to Work Successfully with Managed Care?*

Understand health care financing. Have business skills such as accounting and practice costs. Be computer literate.

Be well versed in group therapy. Be well organized. Know brief therapy strategies.

Learn to speak the language of managed care. For many, it is a foreign language. Learn the "tongue of the land." Be aware of current legislation that is driving the industry and be proactive.

Understand the managed care need for treatment planning.

Use a developmental model. Understand when a problem is situational or self-growth and when it is a medical necessity.

5. *Frequently Managed Care Organizations Limit the Number of Client Sessions. What Is Your Opinion Concerning Such Limits?*

I believe that the job of managed care is to match the treatment needs of the individual. To not over-treat or under-treat. It is the clinician's responsibility to understand his/her guidelines and his/her clinical philosophy and keep them in mind as you plan your treatment. If there is a dispute, discuss it with the case manager in a cooperative, problem-solving manner and reach an agreeable level for both parties. If this is not possible there should be an appeals process. You might also consider consulting for a second opinion. The most important thing is that this be done in a cooperative manner rather than an adversarial one.

There are two kinds of limits. One is beyond the control of the MCO; those are the limits set by the health care contract. Those limits need to be addressed through parity legislation. The other is the interpretation of the MCO regarding best practice criteria, medical necessity, and clinical appropriateness. The therapist needs to understand the MCOs decision making process—this is an arena for professional associations. There needs to be a dialogue regarding standards. Currently the largest MCOs are setting mental health policies through practice standards, quality guidelines, and credentialing guidelines. They are eclipsing the professional associations.

Benefit structures vary tremendously. Some have unlimited visits per year and others have five allocated at a time. When health care contract benefits are exhausted . . . negotiate future sessions at another rate. Most people stop going to therapy anywhere after three to six days [i.e., sessions]. They simply drop out and then call some time in the future if they have problems arising again.

A number of conclusions may be reached as a result of Lawless, Ginter, and Kelly's (1999) study. First, it appears that although independent practitioners will continue to profit in a managed care environment, this particular avenue of practice will continue to shrink. Group practitioners who deliver services that match the needs of managed care organizations are likely to prosper. The interviewees did provide specific suggestions for making oneself more marketable.

One suggestion seems particularly relevant. There was a general recognition among the interviewees that working with clients is best thought of as a *business* that requires *business shrewdness.* Development of business operations and marketing skills is not currently an integral part of most counselor education curricula; counselors and therapists in training must develop business acumen if they are to survive in a competitive business environment. Through a series of encounters, the need for these business skills became clear to one of the authors of this textbook. I (Ginter) know of several doctoral graduates who had difficulty finding employment. All of these graduates were essentially equal in training, experiences, and achievements, with one exception. One of the graduates who possessed a degree in business was hired before the others; he was told by members of the group responsible for his hiring that the degree in business mattered more to them than his clinical skills.

Second, it can be expected that a growing demand for master's degree practitioners will occur. Training institutions should be devoting more energy to creating or strengthening master's programs (Cummings & Hayes, 1996). Training programs that continue to focus solely on the doctorate, as *the degree of practice,* might encounter significant challenges in the future. Just as managed care organizations have asked counselors to demonstrate the efficacy of their treatments, prospective doctoral students will begin to demand assurances that doctoral training leads to compensatory employment. Additional emphasis in training on group work competencies may help create a much-needed distinction—the type of distinction that enhances the person's range of therapeutic skills as well as his or her marketability.

Based on the results of the Lawless study and others (e.g., Cummings, Budman, & Thomas, 1998, Cummings & Hayes, 1996), too many training programs are lagging behind what is actually occurring in practice settings. It is reasonable to assume that the practice arena will increasingly drive the configuration of successful training programs.

Third, for those practitioners who have not received the *requisite knowledge* and *requisite skills* from their training programs or for those students currently in training who want specific advice about relevant preparation, we suggest that the following items be viewed as constituting a set of necessary tools. Acquiring these listed necessities will directly relate to a practitioner's degree of success for establishing a viable practice. Lawless, Ginter, and Kelly (1999) list these necessities under one of two categories: requisite knowledge and requisite skills. We have added to their list.

Requisite knowledge includes *understanding* the following:

- Diagnostic categories of the *Diagnostic and Statistical Manual of Mental Disorders* (APA, 1994)
- Standards of practice for various clinical problems (see Beamish, Granello, Granello, McSteen, & Stone, 1997)
- Language of the managed care environment
- Factors related to client satisfaction

- Multicultural group interventions (Robinson & Ginter, 1999)
- Procedures for receiving reimbursement for services
- Procedures for providing treatment when a client's designated counselor or therapist is not available
- How to balance legitimate information needs of managed care organizations against client confidentiality
- Availability of Internet-related sources of information (e.g., International Association for Group Psychotherapy <www.psych.mcgill.ca/labs/iagp/IAGP.html> and American Group Psychotherapy Association <www.social.com/health/nhic/data/hr01000/hr0119.html>)

Requisite skills include *developed ability* in

- Use of the *DSM-IV;* treatment plan writing
- Record-keeping procedures consistent with professional standards and managed care organization expectations
- One's stated specialty area (evidence of formal training must also be available)
- Brief and solution-focused treatment skills
- Multicultural group skills
- Implementation and maintenance of a practice management program in relation to managed care billing and reporting
- Collection of treatment outcome and effectiveness data
- Basic accounting procedures
- Provision of a clear and thorough description of one's group treatment philosophy to both clients and managed care organizations
- Ability to work with managed care personnel in a cooperative manner, and working with other service providers as part of a team
- Accessing information via the Internet

No longer can a group counselor or group therapist afford to enter practice in a naive fashion. Certainly, group counseling and group psychotherapy have a place in this time of managed care. An abundance of research, reviewed throughout this text, supports their effectiveness and that each format is well suited for the brief, solution-focused types of interventions increasingly required in today's world of managed care. Interestingly, a group work approach may enable counselors and therapists to work longer with clients since added sessions, it could be argued, can be offered at a lower rate of cost per client compared to individual sessions with each client (MacKenzie, 1997).

We agree with Bion (1961), who succinctly captured why a group approach to working with clients has an advantage over individual forms of counseling and psychotherapy. According to Bion, "No individual, however isolated in time and space, can be regarded as outside a group or lacking in active manifestation of group psychology" (p. 54). Simply stated, clients treated by means of individual counseling or individual psychotherapy must ultimately return to "some group" and carry with them the gains achieved through self-exploration and skills acquired. Working with a client, from the start, using a group approach has the potential to offer a cost-effective treatment that more closely parallels the context in which a client must apply his or her gains if he or she hopes to "live fully" in today's interpersonal world.

ORGANIZATION OF THIS BOOK

The remainder of this book is organized in a manner to provide a history of group counseling and group psychotherapy; an overview of group dynamics; a discussion of diversity issues; a summary of both group work research and methods for practitioner evaluation; relevant ethical, professional, and legal issues; detailed discussion of several theoretical approaches and examples of application; an overview of developmental group counseling and group psychotherapy; an overview of psychoeducational group counseling, self-help, and mutual support groups; and appendices that list the standards for training, best practice guidelines, and principles for diversity competence for the Association for Specialists in Group Work and the ethical standards for the American Group Psychotherapy Association.

Also, at various points in the text, multicultural considerations are introduced and discussed in light of what has been learned about group counseling and group psychotherapy. In addition, we focus in detail on those group approaches that are among the most frequently relied on to work with clients. Certainly, there exist other group approaches that have made their own lasting contribution to both group counseling and group psychotherapy, but we have decided to focus primarily on those group approaches that have a rich and well-documented history of theoretical, practice, and research support. These are the approaches that group practitioners are very likely to hear the most about and rely on the most in working with clients.

SUMMARY

This chapter briefly traced the development of group counseling and group psychotherapy and summarized the findings of a large body of professional literature compiled by Lubin and colleagues. In addition, persons responsible for coining terms and the related disciplines contributing to the growth and development of group counseling and group psychotherapy were presented, along with definitions for both *group counseling* and *group psychotherapy*. The chapter concluded with a discussion of managed care and the effect it is having on the practice of counseling and psychotherapy. The intent of this chapter is to set the stage for subsequent chapters, which provide a practical foundation of theory, research, and application. The triad of theory, research, and application are necessary points of mastery if a student of group work hopes to meet the challenges of the twenty-first century.

REFERENCES

Allen, R. D. (1931). A group guidance curriculum in the senior high school. *Education, 52,* 189–194.

American Psychiatric Association. (1964). *Diagnostic and statistical manual of mental disorders* (4th ed.). Washington, DC: Author.

Beamish, P. M., Granello, D. H., Granello, A. F., McSteen, P. B., & Stone, D. A. (1997). Emerging standards for the diagnosis and treatment of panic disorders. *Journal of Mental Health Counseling, 19,* 99–113.

Bion, W. (1961). *Experiences in groups and other papers.* New York: Basic Books.

Brammer, L. M., & Shostrom, E. L. (1960). *Therapeutic psychology.* Englewood Cliffs, NJ: Prentice-Hall.

Cummings, N. A., Budman, S. H., & Thomas, J. L. (1998). Efficient psychotherapy as a viable response to scarce resources and rationing of treatment. *Professional Psychology: Research and Practice, 29,* 460–469.

Cummings, N. A., & Hayes, N. A. (1996). Now we're facing the consequences (an interview with Nick Cummings by S. C. Hayes). *The Scientist Practitioner, 6* (1), 9–13.

Gazda, G. M. (1968). *Basic approaches to group psychotherapy and group counseling.* Springfield, IL: Charles C. Thomas.

Gazda, G. M., Duncan, J. A., & Meadows, M. E. (1967). Group counseling and group psychotherapy—Report of a survey. *Counselor Education and Supervision, 6,* 305–310.

Glanz, E. C., & Hayes, R. W. (1967). *Groups in guidance* (2nd ed.). Boston: Allyn and Bacon.

Hadden, S. B. (1955). Historical background of group psychotherapy. *International Journal of Group Psychotherapy, 5,* 162–168.

Lawless, L. L., Ginter, E. J., & Kelly, K. (1999). Managed care: What mental health counselors need to know. *Journal of Mental Health Counseling, 221,* 50–65.

Lubin, B., Wilson, C. D., Petren, S., & Polk, A. (1996). *Research on group treatment methods: A selectively annotated bibliography.* Westport, CT: Greenwood.

MacKenzie, K. R. (1997). *Time-managed group psychotherapy: Effective clinical applications.* Washington, DC: American Psychiatric Press.

Pratt, J. H. (1922). The principles of class treatment and their application to various chronic diseases. *Hospital Society Services Quarterly, 6,* 401–411.

Robinson, T. L., & Ginter, E. J. (1999). Introduction to the *Journal of Counseling and Development*'s special issue on Racism. *Journal of Counseling and Development, 33,* 3.

CHAPTER TWO

GROUP COUNSELING AND GROUP PSYCHOTHERAPY

Definitions and Historical Development

Inasmuch as group psychotherapy can trace its origin in the United States to 1905, and because the earliest use of the term *group counseling* dates back to the early 1930s, we shall first present the historical development of group psychotherapy. Group counseling theory and practice has also borrowed heavily from its forerunner group psychotherapy.

GROUP PSYCHOTHERAPY

It may seem paradoxical that the group psychotherapy movement is indigenous to a country where the individual and the rights of the individual are extolled. Nevertheless, it is probably *because* of the respect for the individual and the favorable political climate that group psychotherapy would come to fruition in the United States. Although there is general agreement (Corsini, 1957; J. L. Moreno, 1962; Z. T. Moreno, 1966; Rosenbaum & Berger, 1963) that group psychotherapy in its present form is a product of the United States, there is considerably less than a consensus regarding who deserves to be called the father or founder of group psychotherapy.

If one accepts July 1, 1905 (Hadden, 1955), or the introduction of Pratt's "class method" as the beginning of group psychotherapy, rather than some ancient ritual such as Mesmer's treatment through suggestions, then the history of group psychotherapy covers approximately 95 years. Corsini (1957) has described group psychotherapy as "a conglomerate of methods and theories having diverse multiple origins in the past, resulting inevitably from social demands, and developed in various forms by many persons" (p. 9). J. L. Moreno (1966) has described scientific group psychotherapy as having its roots in medicine, sociology, and religion.

It is not our intent to present an exhaustive historical account of group psychotherapy, since several accounts (Corsini, 1957; Hadden, 1955; Meiers, 1945; Z. T. Moreno, 1966; Mullan & Rosenbaum, 1962; Rosenbaum & Snadowsky, 1976; Rosenbaum, Lakin, & Roback, 1992; Scheidlinger, 1993; Scheidlinger & Schames, 1992) are readily available. However, an outline of significant figures and events will be presented.

Before this tracing of the development of group psychotherapy is presented, it is necessary first to define group psychotherapy, or at least present what we believe to be the boundaries and ingredients of the current definition.

Definition

Group therapy and group psychotherapy have been defined by several writers (Corsini, 1957; Gibb, Platts, & Miller, 1951; Harms, 1944; Z. T. Moreno, 1966) since the term *group therapy* was introduced by J. L. Moreno in 1931 (Z. T. Moreno, 1966) and *group psychotherapy* in 1932 (Corsini, 1957). These writers have attempted to interpret Moreno's use of the two terms, but their interpretations lack agreement (Z. T. Moreno, 1966). J. L. Moreno's (1962) general and brief statement that "group psychotherapy means simply to treat people in groups" offers little assistance in clarifying the issue. Gibb and colleagues (1951) contend that Moreno used *group therapy* to represent "personality change which is a by-product of more primary group activities carried on for other purposes than therapy" and *group psychotherapy* to designate "the process by which a professional therapist guides a group in which the immediate and primary objective is the therapeutic welfare of the group" (p. 14).

The distinction made by Gibb and associates (1951) between Moreno's group therapy and group psychotherapy is seldom adhered to in current parlance; however, there are some limited and specific meanings assigned to the two different terms. Contemporary group therapies frequently represent adaptations of all individual psychotherapies plus some varieties that may not have their counterparts in the individual psychotherapies.

In general, *group therapy* and *group psychotherapy* are used synonymously in current discourse; *group therapy* has become the shortened or colloquial version of group *psychotherapy. Group therapy* also is used, on occasion, to represent a more inclusive category of group procedures, including physical therapy, recreational therapy, psychotherapy, and the like. In this sense, group psychotherapy represents a special type of group therapy, and thus has created a problem in communication.

Much of the disagreement over the historical development of group psychotherapy apparently stems from variations in the definition given to group psychotherapy. Slavson (1959) would not agree that Pratt or anyone else before 1930 was practicing group psychotherapy, because the groups of these practitioners did not meet the following criteria: small group size (approximately eight people), permissive group leadership (catalytic rather than authoritative or didactic), grouping of clients on the basis of some diagnostic classification (rather than indiscriminate collections of individuals), and freedom and spontaneity of action of group members (rather than recipients of advice, information, etc.). Many would agree that Slavson makes a strong case, many others would not agree.

Corsini (1957) has defined group psychotherapy in a parsimonious but satisfactory manner. It is not as detailed as it might be, but it is more specific than J. L. Moreno's definition. We shall therefore use Corsini's definition to illustrate definitions given to group psychotherapy today:

Group psychotherapy consists of processes occurring in formally organized, protected groups, and calculated to attain rapid ameliorations in personality and behavior of individual members through specified and controlled group interactions. (Corsini, 1957, p. 5)

Building on and updating Brammer and Shostrom's (1960) distinction and the Gazda, Duncan, and Meadows (1967) definition of group counseling, we would define *group psychotherapy* as a dynamic interpersonal process focusing on conscious and hidden patterns of thought (e.g., unconscious) and behavior that are relatively pervasive in the member's life. Group psychotherapy involves functions such as mutual trust, support, caring, understanding, reality testing, catharsis, and action-oriented insight. These functions are created and nurtured in a small group through an in-depth exploration of concerns with other group members and the group therapist. The group members are individuals with concerns that are debilitating to the degree that personality change is often a general aim. The group experience provides members with an opportunity to unlearn certain persistent attitudes and behaviors as well as learn new attitudes and patterns that will alter the behavior of the members' general approach to life.

SIGNIFICANT CONTRIBUTORS

Although it can be demonstrated that nonprofessional forms of group therapy have existed since the beginning of recorded history, the basic approaches to group psychotherapy presented in this volume have their roots in the more recent history of the 1900s. Therefore, only the most significant contributors and their contributions to this period of history will be cited. This brief tracking of the significant contributors to group therapy will be divided into the early period from 1905 to 1932 and the period of expansion from 1932 to the present.

Early Period: 1905 to 1932

The early period is perhaps best represented by the contributions of six men: Pratt, Lazell, Marsh, Burrow, Adler, and Moreno. This period begins with Joseph H. Pratt's application of his "class method" to the treatment of tubercular patients and ends with Moreno's introduction of the terms *group therapy* in 1931 and *group psychotherapy* in 1932.

J. H. Pratt.   As early as 1905, Pratt held group meetings with tuberculosis patients for the purpose of saving time in instructing them in hygienic practices (Hadden, 1955). It is generally accepted that Pratt did not at first understand the psychological impact on his patients of this group procedure. It is quite likely that he began to understand and appreciate the psychotherapeutic effects of one person on another in his "class" or "thought control" approach to group therapy only *after* he had read Dejerine's work (perhaps as early as 1913). Slavson (1959) characterized Pratt's approach as authoritative-inspirational.

E. W. Lazell.   Lazell, a psychiatrist, was one of the first to use group procedures, mainly didactic (inspirational) lectures ("lecture method"), to hospitalized schizophrenics. The first published accounts of Lazell's work appears to have been in 1921, at least two years following his first application of it.

L. C. Marsh.   First an Episcopal minister, Marsh entered the field of psychiatry at middle age. Along with Lazell, Marsh was one of the first to use group psychotherapy in mental hospitals. He used an inspirational, revival-like method of lectures, group discussions, music, art, dance, and other media to involve the patients with each other, and he met with all segments of the hospital staff to develop a therapeutic team—the forerunner of the milieu therapy approach. Perhaps Marsh can best be characterized by his famous motto: "By the crowd they have been broken; by the crowd they shall be healed."

T. Burrow.   Like several other well-known followers of Freud, Burrow became dissatisfied with the lack of concern of psychoanalysis with the social forces affecting behavior. Thus, he developed group analysis, which was his most significant contribution to group psychotherapy. Burrow's group analysis stressed the importance of studying humans in relation to the group of which they are a part. After 1932, Burrow's efforts were devoted to the study of biological principles of group behavior, which he named *phyloanalysis.* Phyloanalysis did not achieve widespread popularity, and Burrow's contributions to group psychotherapy after 1932 were minimal.

A. Adler.   The form of group therapy that Adler initiated in Vienna about 1921, according to Seidler (1936), would best fit the description of individual counseling/therapy *within* the group setting. Adler counseled children in front of a group, including doctors, social workers, teachers, and psychologists. His purpose was to teach the audience how to do individual therapy. However, in the process, he noticed that the group was positively affecting the patient instead of interfering with the patient-doctor relationship. When the group members responded, they did so as quasitherapists and therefore the situation was more akin to "multiple therapy" (i.e., the use of more than one therapist with a single patient). Today, Adlerians continue to interview clients/patients in front of others, and usually, but not always, other clients/patients. Current Adlerians consider this practice to be group counseling/therapy. Part of their rationale, like Adler's, is to teach, but they are simultaneously treating as well as teaching.

J. L. Moreno.   Moreno was very likely the most colorful, controversial, and influential person in the field of group psychotherapy. Moreno immigrated to the United States in 1925, but while still in Vienna he worked with prostitutes in groups. He stated, "Modern group psychotherapy started in the sexual ghetto of Vienna, in a natural setting in situ" (J. L. Moreno, 1966, p. 156).

Moreno introduced psychodrama into the United States in 1925; in 1931, he coined the term *group therapy* and in 1932, *group psychotherapy;* in 1931, he began to publish *Impromptu,* a journal concerned with dramatics and therapy. In 1936–37, he founded the journal *Sociometry; Sociatry* was founded in 1947, but was changed to

Group Psychotherapy in 1949; *Group Psychotherapy and Psychodrama* in 1970; *Group Psychotherapy, Psychodrama, and Sociometry* in 1976; *Journal of Group Psychotherapy, Psychodrama, and Sociometry* in 1981; and *The International Journal of Action Methods: Psychodrama, Skill Training, and Role Playing* in 1997. In 1941–42, Moreno founded the Sociometric and Psychodramatic Institutes and the first society of group psychotherapy (the American Society of Group Psychotherapy and Psychodrama) and became its first president; he organized the First International Committee on Group Psychotherapy in 1951, and was instrumental in organizing the First International Congress of Group Psychotherapy in 1954. He was elected president of the Second International Congress of Group Psychotherapy in 1957, the International Council of Group Psychotherapy in 1962, and the Third International Congress of Group Psychotherapy in 1963. He was Honorary President of the International Congress of Psychodrama and Sociodrama. In addition to these accomplishments, Moreno has written numerous books and journal articles in the field of group psychodrama, group therapy, and sociometry. His more recent works include the editing of the *International Handbook of Group Psychotherapy* (1966) and the authoring of Volume 3 of *Psychodrama* (1969) and *Group Psychotherapy: A Symposium* (1972). Moreno provided leadership to the group psychotherapy movement, although he was best known for his championing of psychodrama. After Moreno died in 1974, Zerka Moreno, his wife, continued to provide leadership to the psychodrama movement.

Period of Expansion: 1932 to the Present

The total number of books, articles, and dissertations in the group psychotherapy literature for the 25-year period preceding 1931 was only 34, but the increase was steady and rapid. For example, for the five-year period, 1931–35, the total was 20; in 1936–40, 69; in 1941–45, 203; and in 1946–50, 536 (Corsinsi, 1957). The annual review of group psychotherapy references published in the *International Journal of Group Psychotherapy* listed 199 references for the year 1965 (MacLennan, Morse, & Goode, 1966), 481 references for 1970 (MacLennan & Levy, 1971), and 500 references for 1972 (Lubin & Lubin, 1973). These figures represent a rapid increase for many years in the growth of interest and contributions to the field of group psychotherapy.

In their 1978 and final review of group psychotherapy literature, Lubin, Lubin, and Taylor (1979) stated:

> The identified overall output has increased to 531 in 1978 as compared to 349 in 1977 and 293 in 1976. A large part of this increase is due to the substantially larger number of books, book reviews, and articles in the area of family therapy, marital therapy, and couples therapy that appeared in 1978. (p. 523)

Silver, Lubin, Silver, and Dobson (1980) prefaced their 1979 review as follows:

> Although the output identified for 1979 was 538 items, surpassing the peak of 531 reached in 1978, it appears that something of an output plateau may now have been reached. Output continued at a high level, but absent was evidence of past 20 to 50 percent

annual increases. Again, the sustained high level of productivity is attributal to continued high output in both the group therapy and the family therapy literatures. (p. 491)

The plateau in publications that appeared to have been reached in 1979 held for 1980, with 569 publications, but there was a 35 percent increase in 1981, bringing the total to 748. Much of this increase was attributed to the increase in the family therapy area. There were no more annual reviews after the 1981 review, so no further comparable data are available.

"The boundaries between group therapy and the intensive small group experience that have developed in recent years are not clear" (Lubin & Lubin, 1973, p. 474). Therefore, the references include related literature from group counseling, T-groups, encounter groups, growth groups, and so on. The significant year-to-year increase in the group psychotherapy literature has been reflected in the number of different contributors to the field. For the sake of brevity, only some of the most significant contributors will be cited for the period of expansion.

Paul Schilder and Louis Wender were two group therapists who were practicing during the latter part of the so-called Early Period but did not publish their results until the middle and late 1930s. Both of these psychiatrists pioneered the applications of psychoanalytic procedures to psychotic, hospitalized, adult patients. Schilder also pioneered the use of group therapy with prison inmates, and Wender discovered the value of group meetings for discharged patients, although A. A. Low had earlier recognized the possibility of self-help groups when he organized Recovery, Inc., in Chicago. Wender also recognized the similarity of the group experience to the family and included different generations in the outpatient groups that he conducted.

Samuel R. Slavson, originally trained as an engineer, was one of the leading figures to emerge in the early 1930s. Slavson, an analytically oriented group therapist, is probably best known for his development of *activity group therapy* and other play therapies for children.

In 1934, Slavson introduced a child-guidance clinic that featured a "creative recreational program for small groups of socially maladjusted latency-aged girls" (and later boys). These groups became known as *therapeutics of creative activity* and finally *group therapy.* Betty Gabriel and later Fanny Amster also pioneered group therapy with children (Durkin et al., 1971, p. 410). Slavson also organized the American Group Psychotherapy Association in 1943 and was a leader of that organization as well as editor of its journal, *The International Journal of Group Psychotherapy.* Slavson was one of the most prolific early writers in the field of group psychotherapy.

Among the leaders in the application of group therapy techniques to play therapy with children have been F. Redl, Lauretta Bender, Gisela Konopka, W. Klopfer, Betty Gabriel, Henriette Glatzer, Helen Durkin, Lawson Lowrey, A. G. Woltman, Virginia Axline, Haim Ginott, and Sheldon Rose. Ginott was instrumental in implementing new techniques in activity and play group therapies. He authored a very useful book on play therapy, *Group Psychotherapy with Children.* Rose developed a cognitive-behavioral approach and is still making significant contributions to the field (see, for example, *Treating Children in Groups: A Behavioral Approach, Group Therapy: A Behavioral Approach,* and *Group Therapy with Troubled Youth*).

Nathan Ackerman was a New York psychiatrist and a member of the group with Slavson who formed the American Group Psychotherapy Association. He utilized analytic techniques with a wide variety of clientele and was particularly noted for group therapy with adolescents and for his pioneer work with family group therapy.

Following in the tradition of Schilder and Wender, Alexander Wolf became one of the leading spokespersons for psychoanalysis in groups in the United States. E. K. Schwartz collaborated with Wolf in producing numerous publications dealing with psychoanalysis in groups in England. S. H. Foulkes developed group analytic psychotherapy and his work has been elaborated by E. J. Anthony and Malcomb Pines, among others. Others who have contributed significantly to the group psychoanalytic literature are H. Spotnitz, S. Scheidlinger, A. Stein, E. Fried, M. Rosenbaum, A. Kadis, and H. Durkin.

Rudolf Dreikurs, who was a Chicago psychiatrist trained by Adler, applied Adlerian principles to group therapy. He is known especially for his work with family groups, child guidance, and the development of group therapy training centers. One of his collaborators is Manford Sonstegard, who with Dreikurs has applied Adlerian principles to group counseling in the school setting with children, parents, teachers, and other school personnel.

George Bach, a clinical psychologist in private practice, was a leader in innovations in group psychotherapy. His book *Intensive Group Psychotherapy* represents one of the most complete treatments of the application of concepts of group dynamics to group therapy. Bach, a former student of Lewin's, was also one of the pioneers of marathon group therapy and marital therapy. Martin Lakin has also utilized Lewinian theory with Bion's in his approach to group therapy. One of the more successful applications of group dynamics concepts and research to group therapy has been that of Irvin Yalom in *The Theory and Practice of Group Psychotherapy*. This text has become a classic in group psychotherapy and Yalom is one of the most significant contributors to the field in the past 20 years.

The followers of Carl Rogers have not been without interest in the application of phenomenological psychology and person-centered principles to groups—witness the work of Thomas Gordon, Nicholas Hobbs, Walter Lifton, William Coulson, Bruce and Betty Meador, Jerold Bozarth, John Wood, and Eugene Gendlin (see Chapter 7 in this text). Gendlin, perhaps more than any of the others of the group cited, and perhaps more than Rogers himself, has championed the experiential approach to group psychotherapy. Gendlin's applications of Rogerian principles appear to incorporate some of the principles of certain elder statesmen of experiential group therapy such as Carl Whitaker, Thomas Malone, and John Warkentin. This approach includes a greater involvement of the therapist; his or her values and feelings are expressed and become a significant part of the treatment. Hugh Mullan and Max Rosenbaum's *Group Psychotherapy* presents a variation of the experiential approach advocated by Whitaker, Malone, and Warkentin; Mullan was one of the more articulate spokesmen for the existential-experiential approach to group therapy. Millton Berger has also become identified as an exponent of existential group therapy. Thomas Hora, like Mullan, a New York psychiatrist, is also an advocate of existential group psychotherapy. Hora combined his psychoanalytic training with communications theory and has produced a system of group psychotherapy similar to his counterparts in Europe.

A promising addition to the existential literature has been the application of Viktor Frankl's logotherapy to groups. Joseph Fabry (1980), in *The Pursuit of Meaning,* has made a very functional translation of logotherapy to logotherapy and logoeducation groups. These translations hold great promise for application to individuals suffering from lack of purpose or meaning in life and those with identity problems (see Chapter 7 in this text).

Behavior theory applied to group therapy made its impact primarily through the efforts of Arnold Lazarus. His books, *Behavior Therapy and Beyond* and *The Practice of Multimodal Therapy,* and his cassettes and films represent significant additions to the group therapy literature. Alan Goldstein's and Joseph Wolpe's chapter in *Comprehensive Group Psychotherapy* adds a behavioral position that will permit a comparison and contrast with the Lazarus model.

Several other individual therapies have been adapted to group therapy. These positions have large followings and are not likely to be passing fads. They include Eric Berne's transactional analysis (TA), Fritz Perls's Gestalt therapy (see Chapter 7 in this text), William Glasser's reality therapy, Albert Ellis's rational-emotive-behavioral therapy (see Chapter 9 in this text), and various structured group therapies.

Perhaps the greatest current movement in therapy/counseling groups is the rapid rise of structured group therapy/counseling. The models that represent this movement are generally eclectic in that they utilize interventions from a variety of theories. They have elements of the early practices of Pratt, Marsh, and Allen insofar as they take a didactic, educational approach. They also contain elements of behavioral group therapy and the human resource development (HRD) models of Robert Carkhuff. Some representative models are Gazda's life-skills training (see Chapter 15 in this text), Goldstein's structured learning therapy, Adkins's life-skills education, and Mosher and Sprinthall's psychoeducation model.

By now, the reader's head is probably buzzing with names and the list of significant contributors to group psychotherapy seems endless. Yet it would seem unfair to omit some individuals who have made recent significant contributions to the field, especially through their publications: Clifford Sager and Helen Kaplan's *Progress in Group and Family Therapy;* Harold Kaplan and Benjamin Sadock's *Comprehensive Group Psychotherapy;* Morton Lieberman, Irvin Yalom, and Matthew Miles's *Encounter Groups: First Facts,* and Max Rosenbaum and Alvin Snadowsky's *The Intensive Group Experience.* Kaplan and Sadock's several editions of *Comprehensive Group Psychotherapy* have provided a comprehensive and developmental picture of the field for 30 years and the recent Furhiman and Burlingame's *Handbook of Group Psychotherapy* complements Kaplan and Sadock's classic.

There are many others who have made and are making a significant contribution to specialized areas of group psychotherapy. For example, Harris Peck's and Mansell Pattison's contributions to community psychiatry; Irvin Kraft, Beryce MacLennan, and Naomi Felsenfeld's contributions to group therapy with children and adolescents; Bernard Lubin's and Robert Dies's literature summaries and research reviews; and Arthur Teicher's leadership in founding Division 49 of the American Psychological Association are but a sampling of more recent contributors to specialized areas of group therapy.

Several leading English group therapists are included in the tracing of the history of group psychotherapy because of their influence on American group therapists. Joshua Bierer has been one of the most significant proponents of group psychotherapy in England. Bierer is probably best known for his development of the therapeutic social club, a type of self-help therapy group.

W. R. Bion and a colleague, H. Ezriel of the Tavistock Clinic, promoted the concept of the therapy group as an entity, as has J. D. Sutherland. Bion, in particular, has been the advocate of this concept. He is also well known for his concept of the "leadership by default" group approach to psychotherapy and his use of Kleinian concepts in group therapy. Bion's work has stimulated the interest of Herbert Thelen and his students at the University of Chicago. Dorothy Stock-Whitaker and Morton Lieberman have combined the theory of Bion, Ezriel, and Foulkes with the focal conflict model of Thomas French and produced an intriguing book, *Psychotherapy Through the Group Process.*

A review of the history of group psychotherapy and contributions on an international scope has been written by Zerka Moreno, a leader in the field of group psychodrama and group psychotherapy in the United States. Her account can be found in Part II of *The International Handbook of Group Psychotherapy* (1966). S. B. Hadden is also known for his careful historical account of the group psychotherapy movement. More recent comprehensive publications on the history of group psychotherapy include K. Roy Mackenzie's edited *Classics in Group Psychotherapy;* Donals K. Freedheim's edited *History of Psychotherapy,* especially Rosenbaum, Lubin, and Roback's chapter on "Psychotherapy in Groups"; and, finally, Mark Ettin's *Foundations and Applications of Group Psychotherapy.* Figure 2.1 highlights some of the most significant early contributors as well as the names and dates of the beginning of the most significant professional associations and their journals.

The list of significant contributors to the field of group psychotherapy is so lengthy that this book cannot do justice to any of them; worse yet, some important contributors have not been cited. Aside from the British and Canadian group psychotherapists, no attempt was made to cite the contributions of the growing number of other foreign group psychotherapists.

GROUP COUNSELING[1]

The origin of the term *group counseling* is somewhat obscured. Its historical antecedent was most likely *group guidance* or *case conference.* In other words, much like its counterpart, group psychotherapy, group counseling in its inception was very likely a class method similar to what is referred to today as *group guidance.* The earliest use in print in the United States of the term *group counseling* appears to have been in 1931. Dr. Richard D. Allen (1931), in an article entitled "A Group Guidance Curriculum in the Senior High School" published in *Education,* used the term in the following context:

> *Group thinking and the case-conference method* usually take the place of the recitation. . . . Problems of educational and vocational guidance require teachers who are

FIGURE 2.1 Group Procedures Historical Time Line

GROUP PSYCHOTHERAPY	T-GROUPS	GROUP GUIDANCE
J. H. Pratt ("class method") (1905) Boston	K. Lewin, L. Bradford, R. Lippitt, and K. Benne (Connecticut Laboratory, 1946)	G. Boyden (1912)
J. L. Moreno (1910) Vienna	L. Bradford, R. Lippitt, and K. Benne (Gould Academy [Bethel, Maine] "Basic Skill Training Groups," 1947)	A. Adler (1921) Vienna
A. Adler (1921) Vienna	"T-group" name change from BST Group (1949)	*Group Counseling*
L. C. Marsh and E. W. Lazell (1921) U.S.A.	National Training Laboratory in Group Development of the National Education Association with Leland Bradford 1st. Executive Director (1950)	R. D. Allen (1931) Providence
T. Burrow (1925) U.S.A.		Interest Group for Group Procedures—A group of the American Personnel and Guidance Association (APGA). APGA Convention, Washington, DC, Dwight Arnold, Chairman (1966)
L. Wender (1929) U.S.A.		Interest Group for Group Procedures of APGA, G. M. Gazda, Chairman (1968)
P. Schilder (1930s) U.S.A.		
S. R. Slavson (1930) U.S.A.		
J. L. Moreno coined term *group therapy* (1931)		
J. L. Moreno coined term *group psychotherapy* (1932)		
J. L. Moreno founded the American Society of Group Psychotherapy and Psychodrama (ASGPP) (1941–1942)		
First Annual Meeting of ASGPP at the Sociometric Institute, New York City, 1943		
S. R. Slavson founded the American Group Psychotherapy Association (AGPA) (1942)		
First Annual Conference of AGPA held at Russell Sage Foundation, January 14 and 15, 1944		

Sociatry (Group Psychotherapy and Psychodrama) founded by J. L. Moreno (1947)

International Journal of Group Psychotherapy founded by S. R. Slavson (1949–1951)

J. L. Moreno organized the First International Committee on Group Psychotherapy (1951)

First International Congress of Group Psychotherapy (1954)

International Association of Group Psychotherapy founded (1973) Zurich

Division of Group Psychology and Group Psychotherapy became the 49th Division of the American Psychological Association in February of 1991. Arthur Teicher was the first President. Division 49's journal, *Group Dynamics: Theory, Research and Practice*, was published in March of 1997. Donelson R. Forsyth was the first editor.

"Family Oriented"

The term *development group* used as early as 1956 by Blake and Mouton

"Stranger Oriented"

I. Weschler, F. Massarik, R. Tannenbaum, J. Reisel, etc. Sensitivity Training (Therapy for Normals) Graduate School of Business Administration, U.C.L.A. and Western Training Laboratory (late 1950s and early 1960s, especially 1962)

Growth Groups (Encounter Groups) Mid-1960s

International Association of Applied Social Scientists (1971)

G. M. Gazda, J. A. Duncan, and K. E. Geoffroy founded the Association for Specialists in Group Work (ASWG)—a Division of the American Personnel and Guidance Association, Washington, DC (1973) and Gazda was appointed its first president.

Together: A Journal of the Association for Specialists in Group Work (1976) (Now *Journal for Specialists in Group Work*)

specially selected and trained for the work, who understand problems of individual differences and are continually studying them. These teachers require continuous contacts with the same pupils for several years, a knowledge of occupations and occupational problems, and special training in methods of individual and group counseling.

All of these considerations draw attention to the class counselor as the logical teacher of the new unit. There is much similarity between the techniques of individual guidance and group guidance. When the counselor finds by individual interviews that certain problems are common to most of the pupils, such problems become units in the group guidance course. The class discussions of these problems should reduce the length and number of individual interviews with a saving of considerable time and expense. In fact, the separation of *group counseling* (emphasis ours) from individual counseling would seem very short-sighted. . . .

If the above principle prevails, the next serious problem concerns its practical application in the time schedule of the school. Ideally, such a course should be *extensive* rather than *intensive* in its nature, in order to accomplish its objectives effectively. Its purpose is to arouse interests in current educational, vocational and social problems, to develop social attitudes, and to build up a background of occupational information. Such objectives require considerable *time extended over several years.* (p. 190)

This lengthy quotation is included to show that what Allen described as *group counseling* in 1931 today is generally referred to as *group guidance.* Also, it should be noted that Allen used the terms *case-conference, group guidance,* and *group counseling* interchangeably.

Although Allen's use of *group counseling* appeared in print in 1931, it is very likely that he had used the expression before 1931. For example, John M. Brewer (1937), writing the Introduction to *Allen's Organization and Supervision of Guidance in Education,* published in 1937, wrote, "For more than a decade his colleagues in the Harvard Summer School have urged Dr. Allen to put his ideas into permanent form" (p. xxi).

Jones, as early as 1934, in his second edition of *Principles of Guidance,* stated "It [group guidance] is a term that has come into use chiefly through the excellent work of Richard D. Allen in Providence, RI. It includes all those forms of guidance activities that are undertaken in groups or in classes" (1934, p. 284). Jones (p. 291) also referred to the "Boston Plan for Group Counseling in Intermediate Schools" and cited the source as two circulars[2] developed by the Committee on Guidance of the Boston Public Schools. Although group counseling is used in the title of the Boston publication, the description of the nature of the process described by Jones places it squarely in the realm of group guidance and not group counseling as it is defined today.

In his fifth edition of *Principles of Guidance,* published in 1963, Jones had this to say about Allen's case conference procedures: "A technique that combined the techniques of 'counseling in groups' and 'group counseling' was used by Allen and practiced in the public schools of Providence, Rhode Island more than twenty-five years ago" (1963, pp. 218–219). Jones contended that the purpose of the case conference was to provide the counselor with a means for students to discuss their personal and social relationships. Common problems of group members were used as the basis for discussion. A case was presented to the group to illustrate the problem, and each student was expected to compare his or her own experiences with those revealed through the case. The leader encouraged the group to seek the more permanent values exposed rather than the more immediate temporary ones, and he or she also encouraged the participants to consider the effect on others of their proposed action before performing it. Conclusions were summarized to formulate generalizations for other situations. Jones stated that Allen believed his method worked best when "each case represented a common, usual, or typical situation that concerned most of the group. The case should involve persons and personal or social relations" (1963, p. 219).

According to Jones, Allen characterized the case conference leader as one who never expressed approval or disapproval of any opinion or attitude and never stated opinions of his or her own. In addition, the leader was impartial and open-minded and encouraged the expression of all points of view; he or she would occasionally restate and summarize the group's thinking, and organize the group so that it was large enough to guarantee a diversity of opinions, but not so large as to prevent each member the opportunity to enter into discussion.

The goals and procedures of Allen's case conference approach described by Jones are similar to those of contemporary group counselors. Most contemporary group counselors, however, do not structure their groups around specific cases.

Definition

Although group counseling is very likely here to stay—witness its inclusion in the *Review of Educational Research, Psychological Abstracts, Education Index* and similar indexes and references—it was not without substantial opposition. A brief tracing of the resistance to its acceptance is outlined here through the use of selected quotations. In his second edition of *Principles of Guidance,* Jones (1934) wrote,

> Counseling has such an intimate sound that it would seem advisable to limit it to that intimate, heart-to-heart talk between teacher and pupil. It is frankly admitted that it is difficult to draw the line sharply between the essence of what is done in the personal interview and what is done in small groups. But it is even more difficult to make any distinction between group counseling and the more modern forms of class work." (p. 274)

Almost 20 years later, in his fifth edition of the same text, Jones (1963) wrote,

> The values of group guidance are generally accepted, but the term "group counseling" is still rejected by many guidance authorities. Some believe that group counseling is an "anomaly" and say that it is as silly to speak of "group counseling" as "group courtship." (pp. 217–218)

In the thirty-seventh yearbook of the National Society for the Study of Education, *Part I Guidance in Educational Institutions,* Gilbert Wrenn (1938) wrote, "First of all, counseling is personal. It cannot be performed with a group. 'Group counseling' is a tautology; counseling is always personal" (p. 119). In 1942, Brewer, also a highly respected guidance authority, wrote, " 'Group guidance' was invented, apparently, as a term to mean classroom study, recitation, or discussion; is it any longer needed? 'Group counseling' is a similar term, but might it not be best to confine the word counseling to work with individuals?" (p. 294).

Slavson (1964), too, resisted the use of the term *group counseling*. He stated, "Counseling should be done on a one-to-one relation" (p. 102). He also believed that there are different treatments for different levels of the person's psyche. On the continuum from least to most in terms of depth and intensity of treatment and level of psyche reached, Slavson placed group counseling at the level of least depth and intensity and most superficial level of psyche dealt with and group psychotherapy at the level of greatest depth and intensity and deepest level of psyche reached. Group guidance was in the middle of this continuum. In terms of duration of treatment, the order from shortest to longest was group counseling, group guidance, and group psychotherapy. Slavson's conception of group counseling and his placement of it on the continuum is not in accord with the majority of group counselors.

Lifton (1966) also has dealt with the confusion of "group" terminology (including group counseling) and concluded "that although some nine years have passed since the earlier edition of this text [his first edition] was written, confusion and disagreement over the meaning of terms still exist" (p. 13). A "group procedures" interest group of some 30 members of the American Personnel and Guidance Association met at the Association's 1966 Convention in Washington, DC, and appeared to confirm Lifton's conclusion when they had difficulty differentiating between group guidance and group counseling.

The term *multiple counseling* was introduced by Froehlich (n.d.). Froehlich's use of the term is consistent with the generally accepted use of *group counseling;* however, Helen Driver (1958) introduced *multiple counseling* to mean the conjunctive use of individual counseling with group counseling. Still others frequently used *multiple counseling* when they were referring to the use of more than one counselor. The term is rarely used today to refer to group counseling.

Given the early confusion over the definition of group counseling, there is evidence that it has abated. A survey of 54 of the more prominent contributors to the field of group counseling for the period from 1960 to 1965 revealed that 80 percent preferred the term *group counseling* to *group guidance, multiple counseling, group therapy, psychodrama,* and *sociodrama* when they were asked to select the term they preferred to use to describe "counseling with more than one individual simultaneously" (Gazda, Duncan, & Meadows, 1967). This appears consistent with a conclusion reached by Bennett as early as 1963, who stated, "The term group counseling has become very popular, and practices under this name have been introduced rather widely in school systems. One might almost call it an epidemic" (p. 136).

The 43 respondents to the survey by Gazda and colleagues (1967) who preferred the term *group counseling* were asked to define it. From their definitions, a composite definition was generated:

> Group counseling is a dynamic interpersonal process focusing on conscious thought and behavior and involving the therapy functions of permissiveness, orientation to reality, catharsis, and mutual trust, caring, understanding, acceptance, and support. The therapy functions are created and nurtured in a small group through the sharing of personal concerns with one's peers and the counselor(s). The group counselees are basically normal individuals with various concerns which are not debilitating to the extent

requiring extensive personality change. The group counselees may utilize the group interaction to increase understanding and acceptance of values and goals and to learn and/or unlearn certain attitudes and behaviors. (Gazda, Duncan, & Meadows, 1967, p. 305)

MOVEMENTS CONTRIBUTING TO GROUP COUNSELING

The previous reference to R. D. Allen's use of the term *group counseling* suggests that Allen may have coined the expression; however, we do not contend that we have discovered the missing link. More likely than not, several individuals were using the term in Allen's era. Several movements have contributed to the group counseling movement. The most significant of these contributing movements, in addition to group psychotherapy described earlier in this chapter, were child guidance, vocational guidance, social casework, group work, group dynamics, and the human potential movement.

Child Guidance

Group counseling possibly originated in Europe. According to Dreikurs and Corsinsi (1954), between 1900 and 1930, major steps were being made in Europe toward a systematic use of the group method called *collective counseling*. They believed that Alfred Adler, in his child guidance clinics in Vienna, was likely the first psychiatrist to use *collective counseling* formally and systematically. According to Ansbacher and Ansbacher (1956), Adler was conducing group procedures—perhaps collective counseling—as early as 1922.

In 1942, Brewer described the child guidance movement "as yet largely dissociated from the work of the schools" (p. 263). Nevertheless, because of its many similarities, the child guidance movement has influenced, directly or indirectly, the group counseling movement. Currently, Adlerian-oriented counselors are making a very significant contribution in elementary school guidance programs and in parent and child guidance clinics not unlike those originated by Adler in Vienna.

Vocational Guidance

Frank Parsons has been recognized as the father of the vocational guidance movement because of his founding of the Vocational Bureau of Boston in 1908 (Brewer, 1942). Just when, where, and by whom the word *group* was added to the word *guidance* is not known; however, according to Brewer (1942), Charles L. Jacobs of San Jose was one of the first to suggest a wider use of the term *guidance* when, in the October 1915 issue of *Manual Training and Vocational Education,* he stated that his work included three departments: educational guidance, vocational guidance, and avocational guidance.

The vocational guidance movement was instrumental in the introduction of classes in occupational information, homeroom guidance, and certain extracurricular activities that were forerunners of current group guidance and group counseling.

Classes in Occupational Information.   As early as 1908, William A. Wheatley was instrumental in introducing a course in occupational information for freshmen boys at Westport (Connecticut) High School. Similar courses were offered in Boston and New York City soon after Wheatley's (Brewer, 1942).

Homeroom.   McKown (1934) authored a text, *Home Room Guidance,* as early as 1934. The content of the text and the fact that McKown proposed the director of guidance as the director of homeroom guidance suggests its close association to group guidance and counseling. In fact, some schools referred to the homeroom as "the 'guidance hour,' or 'guidance room' " (McKown, 1934, p. 53). In a publication of approximately the same vintage, Strang (1935) cited the contribution of the homeroom teacher as being fourfold: "to establish friendly relationships, to discover the abilities and needs, and to develop right attitudes toward school, home, and community"(p. 116). Once more, the group guidance and counseling "flavor" was expressed in the work of the homeroom teacher.

Extracurricular Activities.   C. R. Foster authored a book, *Extra Curricular Activities,* in 1925, in which he recognized guidance as an extracurricular activity. In the same text, Foster also urged the counselor to "hold many group conferences with the students on the subject of future educational or vocational plans" (p. 182). Foster cited Pittsburgh as including instructional guidance taking "the form of tenth-grade group conferences which were held for the purpose of discussing Pittsburgh's industrial life and the opportunities it affords the young people" (p. 183).

Social Casework

In reviewing the history of the Marriage Council of Philadelphia, Gaskill and Mudd (1950) stated that group counseling and family life education had been part of the "Marriage Council's service from the agency's inception in 1932" (p. 194). Whether the term *group counseling* itself was actually used by the Council as early as 1932 and whether the treatment was similar to current group counseling is not indicted. However, Gaskill and Mudd (1950) gave the following definition of group counseling for which they express their indebtedness to Hazel Froscher, Margery Klein, and Helen Phillips:

> [Group counseling is] a dynamic relationship between a counselor and the members of a group, involving presentation and discussion of subjects about which the counselor has special knowledge, which is of general or specific concern to the group, and around which emotions may be brought out and attitudes developed or changed. The relationship between the group members themselves and the counselor's use of this is essentially important in the total process. (1950, p. 195)

The definition implies that the counselor gives a presentation and encourages discussion of it. Gaskill and Mudd (1950), in their description of the group counseling sessions, indicate that the group size ranged between 35 and 50 people, and they further described the group sessions as a *course,* including speakers other than the group counselor. This approach to group counseling seems more closely related to group guidance or a family living class rather than the typical small, 8- to 10-member counseling groups where leader-imposed content is absent or minimal.

Group Work

Sullivan (1952) described a group in the following manner:

> The group must be a small stable one which feels itself as an entity and which the individual can feel close identification. Membership . . . is voluntary. There is a group leader, who is consciously making constructive use of the process of personality interaction among the members. The leader utilizes the desire of a normal person to be accepted by his fellows. He establishes the dignity of the individual and teaches acceptance of differences in race, creed, and nationality. Group work stresses programs evolved by the group itself, in consultation with the leader who guides toward socially desirable ends. Creative activities are encouraged to provide legitimate channels of self-expressions and to relieve emotional stress. . . . The atmosphere is friendly, informal, and democratic. (p. 189)

This description of group work contains many of the ingredients that are present in definitions of group counseling, and the possible influence on group counseling of the group work specialists becomes readily apparent.

Group Dynamics

The group dynamics movement, according to Bonner (1959), had its beginning in the late 1800s, notably in Europe. Contribution to the group dynamics discipline came from sociology, psychology, philosophy, and education, but primarily from sociology and psychology. Bonner was careful not to give major credit to a single individual or discipline; however, he cites Kurt Lewin and J. L. Moreno for making significant, but dissimilar, contributions during the contemporary phase of development—1930s to the present.

The National Training Laboratories (NTL) was established in Bethel, Maine, in 1947; "it was not until the middle to late 1950s before the tools and techniques of good dynamics really found their way into education and more specifically, into guidance" (Glanz & Hayes, 1968, p. 4). Durkin and associates (1971), after a careful survey of group dynamicists and group therapists wrote:

> In spite of the general impression to the contrary, there was almost no therapy actually being conducted on solely group dynamics principles by group dynamicists. From private correspondence with some of the leading social scientists, I learned that they did not acknowledge group dynamics therapy as an identifiable approach and that they were meticulous in distinguishing between their work and group therapy. (p. 4)

One can conclude from the earlier Glanz, Hayes, and Durkin statements that group dynamics principles and concepts had begun to affect the field of *group guidance* only since the 1960s. Also, Durkin emphasized that, although group dynamics had begun to influence the field of group therapy, as late as 1964, there was still no complete application of group therapy based primarily on group dynamics principles. In 1966, the senior author began to assemble a book, *Innovations to Group Psychotherapy* (Gazda, 1968), and was able to secure a contribution from some group dynamicists, Jack and Lorraine Gibb, of a theory of group dynamics applied to group therapy. They referred to their theory as *Emergence Therapy: The TORI Process in an Emergent Group*. This theory really represents a leaderless approach to group therapy as well as to small and large groups in general.

The application of group dynamics principles to *group counseling* has a rather recent history. The explication of these applications can be found in the early writings of Bonney (1969), Fullmer (1969), Gazda (1969, 1971, 1978), and Mahler (1969).

Human Potential Movement

The human potential emphasis began to be felt in the early and middle 1960s. Its origin is multiple and diverse. The disciplines of psychology, education, and management have made significant contributions. Some of the more influential early contributors have been Carl Rogers, Abraham Maslow, Herbert Otto, Jack Gibb, and William Schutz. The more practical elements of the movement are being applied to classroom instruction and, in that sense, are *group guidance* oriented.

Association for Specialists in Group Work

In 1966, Dwight Arnold assumed a leadership role in developing an interest group among the American Personnel and Guidance Association (now ACA) members for the purpose of defining the field, sharing information on training programs, and establishing communication among practitioners to provide some form of organization to the loose-knit group counseling movement. The senior author assumed Dr. Arnold's coordinator role in 1968 and developed this interest group from approximately 100 to over 1,500. On December 8, 1973, the senior author, with Jack Duncan and Kevin Geoffrey, succeeded in establishing the Association for Specialists in Group Work (ASGW) as the eleventh division of the then American Personnel and Guidance Association (the parent organization). With the establishment of this new division for group work, of which group counseling was the core, the continued growth and impact of group counseling seemed assured.

SUMMARY

This chapter traced the history and development of group psychotherapy and group counseling and defined each. Significant contributors and a brief summary of their contributions were included. The contributions of related disciplines to the development of group counseling were outlined. A historical time line was developed to illustrate the interrelationship in the development of the small group field.

REFERENCES

Allen, R. D. (1931). A group guidance curriculum in the senior high school. *Education, 2,* 189.

Ansbacher, H. L., & Ansbacher, R. R. (Eds.). (1956). *The individual psychology of Alfred Adler.* New York: Basic Books.

Bonner, H. (1959). *Group dynamics.* New York: Ronald Press.

Bonney, W. C. (1969). Group counseling and developmental processes. In G. M. Gazda (Ed.), *Theories and methods of group counseling in the schools.* Springfield, IL: Charles C. Thomas.

Brammer, L. M., & Shostrom, E. L. (1960). *Therapeutic psychology.* Englewood Cliffs, NJ: Prentice-Hall.

Brewer, J. M. (1937). Introduction. In R. D. Allen (Ed.), *Organization and supervision of guidance in public education.* New York: Inor.

Brewer, J. M. (1942). *History of vocational guidance.* New York: Harper.

Corsini, R. J. (1957). *Methods of group psychotherapy.* Chicago: William James Press.

Dreikurs, R., & Corsini, R. J. (1954). Twenty years of group psychotherapy. *American Journal of Psychiatry, 110,* 567.

Driver, H. I. (1958). *Counseling and learning in small-group discussion.* Madison, WI: Monona.

Durkin, H., et al. (AGPA Committee on History). (1971). A brief history of the American Group Psychotherapy Association. *International Journal of Group Psychotherapy, 21* (4), 406.

Fabry, J. A. (1980). *The pursuit of meaning.* San Francisco: Harper and Row.

Foster, C. R. (1925). *Extra-curricular activities in the high school.* Richmond, VA: Johnson.

Froehlich, C. P. (n.d.). *Multiple counseling—A research proposal.* Berkeley: University of California, Department of Education.

Fullmer, D. W. (1969). Family group consultation. In G. M. Gazda (Ed.), *Theories and methods of group counseling in the schools.* Springfield, IL: Charles C. Thomas.

Gaskill, E. R., & Mudd, E. H. (1950). A decade of group counseling. *Social Casework, 31,* 194.

Gazda, G. M. (Ed.). (1969). *Theories and methods of group counseling in the schools.* Springfield, IL: Charles C. Thomas.

Gazda, G. M. (1971). *Group Counseling: A developmental approach.* Boston: Allyn and Bacon.

Gazda, G. M. (1978). *Group counseling: A developmental approach* (2nd ed.). Boston: Allyn and Bacon.

Gazda, G. M., Duncan, J. A., & Meadows, M. E. (1967). Counseling and group procedures—Report of a survey. *Counselor Education and Supervision, 6,* 305.

Gibb, J. R., Platts, G. N., & Miller, L. F. (1951). *Dynamics of participative groups.* St. Louis: John Swift.

Glanz, E. C., & Hayes, R. W. (1968). *Groups in guidance* (2nd ed.). Boston: Allyn and Bacon.

Hadden, S. B. (1955). Historic background of group psychotherapy. *International Journal of Group Psychotherapy, 5,* 62.

Harms, E. (1944). Group therapy—Farce, fashion, or sociologically sound? *Nervous Child, 4,* 186.

Jones, A. J. (1934). *Principles of guidance* (2nd ed.). New York: McGraw.

Jones, A. J. (1963). *Principles of guidance* (5th ed.). New York: McGraw.

Lifton, W. M. (1966). *Working with groups* (2nd ed.). New York: Wiley.

Lubin, B., & Lubin, A. W. (1973). The group psychotherapy literature: 1971. *International Journal of Group Psychotherapy, 23* (4), 474.

Lubin, B., Lubin, A. W., & Taylor, A. (1979). The group psychotherapy literature: 1978. *International Journal of Group Psychotherapy, 29,* 523–576.

MacLennan, B., Morse, V., & Goode, P. (1966). The group psychotherapy literature, 1965. *International Journal of Group Psychotherapy, 16,* 225.

MacLennan, B., & Levy, N. (1971). The group psychotherapy literature, 1970. *International Journal of Group Psychotherapy, 21* (3), 345.

Mahler, C. A. (1969). *Group counseling in the schools.* Boston: Houghton Mifflin.

McKown, H. C. (1934). *Home room guidance.* New York: McGraw.

Meiers, J. L. (1945). Origins and development of group psychotherapy. *Sociometry, 8,* 499.

Moreno, J. L. (1962). Common ground for all group psychotherapists. What is a group psychotherapist? *Group Psychotherapy, 15,* 263.

Moreno, J. L., et al. (Eds.). (1966). *The international handbook of group psychotherapy.* New York: Philosophical Library.

Moreno, J. L. (1969). *Psychodrama* (Vol. 3). Beacon, NY: Beacon House.

Moreno, J. L. (1972). *Group psychotherapy: A symposium.* Boston: Beacon House.

Moreno, Z. T. (1966). Evolution and dynamics of the groups psychotherapy movement. In J. L. Moreno et al. (Eds.), *The international handbook of group psychotherapy*. New York: Philosophical Library.

Mullan, H., & Rosenbaum, M. (1962). *Group psychotherapy*. New York: Glencoe Free Press.

Rosenbaum, M., & Berger, M. (Eds.). (1963). *Group psychotherapy and function*. New York: Basic Books.

Rosenbaum, M., Lakin, M., & Roback, H. B. (1992). In D. K. Freedharm (Ed.), *History of psychotherapy: A century of change*. Washington, DC: American Psychological Association.

Rosenbaum, M., & Snadowsky, A. (1976). *The intensive group experience*. New York: Free Press.

Scheindlinger, S. (1993). History of group psychotherapy. In H. I. Kaplan & B. J. Sadock (Eds.), *Comprehensive group psychotherapy* (3rd ed.). Baltimore: Williams & Wilkins.

Scheidlinger, S., & Schames, G. (1992). Fifty years of American Group Psychotherapy Association 1942–1992: An overview. In K. R. MacKenzie (Ed.), *Classics in group psychotherapy*. New York: Guilford.

Seidler, R. (1936). School guidance clinics in Vienna. *Journal of Individual Psychology, 2*, 75.

Silver, R. J., Lubin, B., Silver, D., & Dobson, N. H. (1980). The group psychotherapy literature: 1979. *International Journal of Group Psychotherapy, 30,* 491–538.

Slavson, S. R. (1959). Parallelisms in the development of group psychotherapy. *International Journal of Group Psychotherapy, 9,* 451.

Slavson, S. R. (1964). *A textbook in analytic group psychotherapy*. New York: International U. P.

Strang, R. (1935). *The role of the teacher in personnel work*. New York: Bureau of Publications, Teachers College, Columbia University.

Sullivan, D. F. (Ed.). (1952). *Readings in group work*. New York: Association Press.

Wrenn, C. G. (1938). Counseling with students. In G. M. Whipple (Ed.), *Guidance in educational institutions, part I, National Society for the Study of Education*. Bloomington Public School Publishing.

ENDNOTES

1. See also G. M. Gazda, "Comparison of Group Counseling and Group Psychotherapy" in H. I. Kaplan & B. J. Sadock (Eds.), *Comprehensive Group Psychotherapy,* 3rd ed. (Baltimore: Williams and Wilkins, 1993).

2. Boston Public Schools, *Guidance—Educational and Vocational, A Tentative Plan for Group Counseling,* *Board of Superintendents' Circular No. 2, 1928–1929,* and *Board of Superintendents' Circular No. 17, 1928–1929, First Supplement to Board of Superintendents' Circular No. 2.* Boston: Printing Department, 1929.

CHAPTER THREE

GROUP DYNAMICS

Prevailing Group Forces

A counseling group is marked by continuous interactions, although at times the inter-actions are subtle and may even appear to have come to a complete standstill—such as, when members of a mature group are saying little of significance for one or two con-current sessions. Even when such a "therapeutic pause" manifests itself, the unspoken thoughts of the group members can be furiously active, turbulent, and powerful. The dynamics can be powerful enough to prevent achievement of a necessary step to reach a goal, whether that goal is relatively minor or major, such as breaking down a barrier preventing the group from moving into a new phase in its functional capacity.

It is difficult to imagine anyone responsible for leading a group over a period of time (whether it is an eating disorder group or a social group such as a scouting troop) who has not soon come to realize the strong interpersonal forces that reside within the group. Groups are dynamic entities. It is equally difficult to imagine that, early in the study of groups, several prominent figures argued whether groups were real or an aca-demic exercise of little import—that is, that groups were simply collections of individ-uals and nothing special or unusual. Obviously, the winning argument was that groups are real entities with their own set of defining features and influences. Kurt Lewin, the recognized "parent" of *group dynamics,* who used the term to refer to the study of groups (Forsyth, 1990), also used the term *dynamic* to refer to the powerful forces that make a group just that—a group.

Counseling was not the only field drawn to the study of groups. According to Forsyth (1990), disciplines such as anthropology, business and industry, criminal jus-tice, education, general psychology, speech and communication, sports and recreation, sociology, political science, and various mental health specialties other than counseling have all found this area of study too fascinating and pertinent to resist. Each of these disciplines continues to contribute findings in the area of group dynamics, and even though the topics are field-specific topics (topics are grounded in a field's own concep-tual language [Forsyth, 1990]), many are applicable to working with counseling groups. The specific terms preferred by each discipline will have a certain recognizable quality to any experienced group leader, which hints of the generalizability of findings—terms such as *attitude change, deviance, groups in cross-cultural contexts, political influence or power, networks, productivity, systems, team teaching, gangs, jury deliberations,* and *team performance*. These are just a few of the areas associated with specific disciplines that have cross-discipline implications. Although terminology may differ (e.g., *team teaching* vs. *co-leaders* in a psychoeducational group), clearly, the area of group dynamics is an area of study that has wide applicability. Simply stated, group dynamics is a necessary subject of concern for all group counselors.

Admittedly, for the novice counselor, the forces captured by the term *group dynamics*, in all their complexity, eventually can be reduced to the concern expressed at some point by every novice group counselor, "I must lead my first group." To effectively confront this training challenge requires investigating what may seem to the novice to be a myriad of factors affecting the complexity level of a counseling group. Certainly, the complexity of any group will rise or fall due to decisions and actions taken by the counselor. For example, one of these factors is group size. Once the number of members in a counseling group exceeds seven or eight, any attempt by the group counselor to structure or intervene during a group session becomes increasingly difficult to initiate as well as bring to fruition. Recognizing that working with any number of clients in a group context can prove challenging for even the most seasoned group counselor, there are certain key aspects of a counseling group, in addition to size, that should be kept in the forefront of consideration by all counselors. When preparing to run a group, altering any of these key aspects can be expected to have a noticeable effect on the group and thus the counselor's ability to effectively deal with content and processes in a way that leads to effective treatments.

IS GROUP DYNAMICS *THE* THERAPEUTIC LEVER?

An understanding of and reliance on group dynamics provide the counselor the necessary therapeutic tools to be an effective group counselor. Group dynamics represent the very essence of what constitutes group counseling, and these dynamics are analogous to interpersonal markers that enable the counselor to find his or her way even during difficult periods. Group dynamics can be thought of as the interpersonal glue that links and binds unfolding group events that occur over time—these unfolding group events in total denote the stages (or phases) through which groups move. Interestingly, although group dynamics are stage related, one would be mistaken to assume group dynamics are easily characterized by some sort of linear progression. Groups can advance, regress, or plateau and stay stagnated at a stage. Groups can flounder, revive, "awaken" only to "fall asleep" again—the term *dynamic* even applies when the group takes these unwanted twists and turns.

Before reviewing the stages that groups move through or the "parts" of the group counseling process that result in moving through those stages, it is necessary to decide what the term *group dynamics* exactly refers to. A number of writers have offered definitions or explanations for the term. Forsyth (1990, p. 12) wrote that the term "refers not only to the powerful processes that occur within groups but also the scientific study of these processes." Another explanation offers the following: "Group dynamics is a field of inquiry dedicated to advancing knowledge about the nature of groups, the laws of their development, and their interrelations with individuals, other groups, and large institutions" (Cartwright & Zander, 1968, p.19). Specifically, Knowles and Knowles (1959) captured the spirit of the term *group dynamics* when they claimed that beyond certain set aspects of any particular group (e.g., closed, co-led, solution-focused group), the group "is always moving, doing something, changing, becoming, interacting, and reacting" (p. 12).

Two comments are warranted. First, any term that encompasses as much as group dynamics is intended to encompass will be fully understood only when tested and experienced in an actual group counseling context. Moore (1997) illustrated how confidence in what we understand at an intellectual level about group dynamics can easily be lost by discussing the experience of "holding a fish for the first time." If one relies totally on what one is told about holding a fish, one is likely to find that the ready-made explanation conflicts with the reality. Holding too tight to the fish (i.e., clinging tightly to preconceptions) simply leads to the fish slipping through one's grasp back into the water. It is not only the concepts learned via textbooks, articles, and supervisors' shared wisdom, it is also the "experience of fishing" (actually conducting groups) that enables the counselor to truly "hold on" and achieve the level of full awareness of group dynamics that is necessary to be an effective group counselor.

Second, it should be pointed out that not everyone agrees as to the importance of group dynamics in terms of utility. Slavson's (1957) theoretical perspective guided how he interpreted behavior within a group. He applied classic psychoanalytic concepts acquired from working with individuals to group work which, it could be argued, prevented him from seeing the group, as a whole, as having significant therapeutic value. We disagree with such a restrictive perspective—although individual therapy tactics are applicable to groups (Wolf & Schwartz, 1962), groups have their own set of characteristics and interpersonal forces, as stated earlier, that are different from what a counselor will encounter when facing an individual client.

For our purposes, we will rely on Dagley, Gazda, and Pistole's (1986) explanation of what constitutes group dynamics as a point of reference from here on. According to these authors, *group dynamics* refers to the internal and external forces that unfold over the life of a group's evolution—those internal and external forces that affect counseling outcome and process. A group counselor aware of the internal and external forces that comprise group dynamics will find that he or she is much better prepared to influence those dynamics, interpret them, and predict what will occur next during the course of counseling. Certainly, it is essential to keep in mind that the group leader is part of the dynamics and cannot fully stand apart from whatever aspect of group dynamics is manifesting itself at any particular time during the life of a group.

Also, once activated, the dynamics of a group take on a life of their own. Group dynamics are not something that a counselor can conveniently store on a shelf between sessions. It is best to think of group dynamics as something that permeates an upcoming group from its inception to its termination and, to a certain degree, beyond termination (e.g., each member will carry memories of that group experience that have a persistent dynamic force). Group dynamics even have a life prior to the first group session, since each member, upon knowing he or she will be in a group, begins to think "group"; preconceptions about the group experience will affect, at least initially, the role he or she plays.

Exactly what are the internal and external forces alluded to by Dagley, Pistotle, and Gazda? The following contributing factors to group dynamics are generally recognized as key points of understanding, experiencing, and utilization: leadership variables, structure, goal setting, cohesion, group norms, roles, multicultural dynamics, curative elements, and stages or phases of development. Although each point is isolated for discussion in this chapter so as to distill its contribution to the group dynamics mix, group dynamics represent a system of interconnecting points that function as a whole—a sort of kaleidoscope of interpersonal forces that result in client change. Again, affecting any one of these points will affect the entire system making up the group dynamics.

LEADER VARIABLES

The leader is the therapeutic fulcrum point in the process. The manner in which the leader achieves therapeutic efficacy can take several forms: being active or nonactive in the leadership role, transparent or opaque about self, past focused or present focused to facilitate members' insight, affective oriented or cognitive oriented, process or content focused, or a seemingly limitless combination of forms. In reviewing the works of researchers and theorists (e.g., Berenson & Mitchell, 1974; Bergin, 1975; Conyne et al., 1990; Couch & Childers, 1987; Delucia-Waack, 1999; Ginter & Robinson, 1999; Hersey & Blanchard, 1982; Hurley & Pinches, 1978; Lieberman, Yalom, & Miles, 1973; Russell, 1978; Stockton & Morran, 1982; Truax & Carkhuff, 1967), one may reasonably conclude that a group counselor's effectiveness encompasses but extends well beyond what has been found to be effective in working with a single client in an individual counseling context. The effective leader can be expected to display the following:

1. The leader expresses a high degree of caring and warmth; that is, he or she is supportive, encouraging, protective, nonaggressive, and nonauthoritarian regardless of the theoretical approach used. The leader is sensitive to the needs of the group body.
2. The leader reframes and processes group data in a manner to enhance members' understanding and ability to clarify their own behavior and thoughts as well as to develop the ability to interpret interpersonal and intrapsychic interactions without the leader's assistance.
3. The group leader utilizes an appropriate level of setting group rules, group limits, and time-management techniques. Although strictly adhering to a policy is generally warranted, the effective leader places therapeutic gain before rigid adherence to any policy that has become a block to therapeutic gain (e.g., in certain cases, it may be therapeutically sound to go beyond the preestablished time limit for one session).
4. An appropriate level of emotional stimulation is called forth by the leader—for example, having members disclose feelings. Challenging comments or behaviors of members, confronting members, is done in an artful way that leads to growth

or, at a minimum, that helps position members to move to a higher level of awareness and readiness for growth.

5. The leader clearly displays evidence of being self-accepting, psychologically
   integrated, and able to interact with others in a nondefensive manner and, as a
   result, serves as a model for all. For example, the leader sees criticism from group
   members in "therapeutic terms," not as a personal attack.

6. The leader displays an appropriate level of self-disclosure that is oriented toward
   the group as a whole rather than a single member. Even when the disclosure is
   evoked because of some member's comment, the leader's disclosure should have
   a quality that allows all to get the message. Self-disclosure is not only to be
   gauged according to its effect on an individual member but on every member of
   the group; thus, what may prove effective in an individual counseling context
   may not be appropriate to disclose in the group setting.

7. The leader displays low ego needs. He or she is there for members and does not
   use members as an audience or followers to inflate his or her view of self.

8. The leader is a good judge of when to intervene—that is, to "therapeutically
   intrude" in what is occurring. Thus, appropriate timing of techniques is a hallmark feature of the effective leader.

9. Allowing group members to pace themselves is characteristic of the leader's
   behavior. Enough therapeutic anxiety is maintained in the group to achieve therapeutic goals for each member and the group-as-a-whole.

10. The leader is genuine in what is verbally and behaviorally expressed to the group.
    Different avenues of expression are congruent and are perceived so by the group
    members; for example, the leader's body language and spoken word match.

11. Empathic understanding permeates all stages of group work beginning with the
    first session through termination of the group. The intellectual and emotional
    understanding of each member rests on a foundation of accurate perception.

12. Groups benefit from leadership that is congruent with the needs of the group
    members. Although this has generally been tied to the leader being relationship
    oriented and task oriented it is not limited to just these orientations. Other factors
    may play a primary role. For example, the general learning style of the group
    members should match what the leader is doing (e.g., members of a group who
    predominantly process information in a visual manner may have difficulty with a
    leader who focuses solely on verbal exchange).

The role of leader may seem daunting to the beginning group counselor, but it
should be remembered that from a group dynamics perspective, it is more than mastery
of counseling techniques that creates the effective group counselor. Rather, it is acquiring a type of wisdom that denotes a trusting of the dynamics—trusting that allows one
to use any emerging dynamic therapeutically. Finally, although group counseling cannot take place without a counselor (a leader), a group counselor should not view his or
her leadership role as the indispensable catalyst resulting in all client change. Inflation
of the leader's self-importance is likely to occur when the counselor perceives himself
or herself to be "the transformational figure" for client growth rather than an observer-
participant in a "transformation process" (Ginter, 1996, 1999).

GROUP STRUCTURE: UNAVOIDABLE TASK
OF THE LEADER

The group counselor can be expected to take a central role in developing group structure. Typically, group structure is of special interest to the group counselor in the early stages of a group (Couch & Childers, 1987). Setting goals, reviewing what typically occurs in a group setting, and delineating rules and procedures falls under the category of structure (e.g., Forsyth, 1990; Gazda, 1976; Wilborn & Muro, 1979). The term *structure* has also been applied in other ways—for example, to refer to activities designed to facilitate skill development (Drum & Knott, 1977; Picklesimer, Hooper, Ginter, 1999).

Even if the issue of group structure is not of utmost importance to a group counselor, the counselor will be confronted with the issue of structure in some manner or form. As pointed out by Dagley, Gazda, and Pistole (1986), creating structure in a group is unavoidable, since even when a group leader makes a decision to refrain from establishing stated goals, expectations, and rules, that counselor introduces another type of structure but a structure nonetheless. According to Ettin (1992), "The nondirective leader, by his or her silence or seemingly unpredictable, quixotic, punctuation remarks, often stimulates formless anxiety, in fighting, and a mad dash toward any semblance of order or consensus, however irrational" (p. 213). In a sense, members abhor a vacuum left unfilled by a leader and will rush in to fill the vacuum with structure.

Summarizing literature (i.e., Bednar & Battersby, 1976; Bednar, Melnick, & Kaul, 1974; Evensen & Bednar, 1978; Gazda, 1976; House, Schuler, & Levanoni, 1983; Lee & Bednar, 1978; Muro & Dinkmeyer, 1977; Stockton & Morran, 1982; Wilborn & Muro, 1979) pertaining to the interaction of structuring and risk taking by the group members as well as the effect that structuring has on group behavior, in general, leads to the following conclusions:

1. Instruction along the behavioral dimension has been positively linked to greater levels of cohesion, a perceived value of the group experience, the amount of time devoted to goal focused communication, and a lower degree of conventional patterns of communication. Interestingly, instruction from a leader focused on goal clarification and persuasion is less likely to elicit these outcomes than the specific behavioral instructions.

2. Message specificity from the leader is directly related to target behaviors in low risk-taking persons. It appears that for low risk-taking members of a group, instructions that are enumerated, definite, explicit, and described in detail free the low risk-taking members to explore concerns. A reason for such an occurrence was aptly captured by Lee and Bednar (1978), who stated, "Structure reduces personal responsibility, thereby increasing the freedom to engage in higher risk interpersonal behavior. . . . The high-structure condition dramatically increased the level of relevant, and presumably risky, communications of the low risk-taking subjects. In fact, the observed behavior of the low risk-taking subjects in the high-structure conditions was virtually identical to that of the high risk-taking subjects" (p. 198).

3. The combination of high structure and low risk-taking predisposition results in a high frequency of interaction, which is perceived as meaningful but also painful. Interestingly, this combination of meaningful exchange but troublesome feelings coalesce in a manner that leads members to perceive the situation as one where there is less cohesiveness than desired.

4. High risk-takers who are exposed to behavioral structuring report the highest level of cohesion and positive attitudes, whereas the combination of cognitive and behavioral components creates the most favorable conditions for members of a low risk-taking orientation.

5. Building group structure using a positive approach is supported by the professional literature. A positive approach that recognizes members' individual concerns is much more likely to lead to a thought that the group structure created applies both to "me" and the "group-as-a-whole." Thus, members feel invested in the group work to be done.

6. Stressing that effort is required to achieve a counseling goal results in less resistance, in general, when members are later confronted with their lack of effort. Also, such an emphasis in the beginning can simply be expected to lead to greater effort on the part of members.

7. Emphasizing to members that group members have been screened for inclusion in the group affects perceived attractiveness between members. Attractiveness contributes to group cohesion and willingness among members to help each other achieve change.

8. Differentiating group norms from social norms will increase the likelihood of greater self-disclosure and discussion of problems. Some basic instructions and examples of appropriate self-disclosure in a counseling group will facilitate certain types of disclosure and shorten the length of the initial stage that all members must travel through to achieve a genuine therapeutic environment.

9. Discussing a member's role in terms of helping self and others will reduce role ambiguity for the member, which in turn reduces needless stress and group floundering and thus expedites goal attainment.

Although not exhaustive, the preceding list indicates that it is advantageous to both the group counselor and the members themselves to pay close attention to structuring tactics because of the positive effect such tactics can be expected to have on the content and process of group counseling. The positive outcomes associated with structuring were stated by Stockton and Morran (1982), who wrote,

> Findings show that the establishment of structure in the early meetings of the group tends to facilitate the development of cohesion and risk-taking by members in performing selected behaviors, such as self-disclosure and feed-back exchange. In addition, direct instruction also appears to facilitate this group development, particularly in its formative stages. The most salient finding from research on structure suggests that the effects of structure on behavioral performance, perceived cohesion, and attitudes toward the group tend to vary as a function of members' personal characteristics, including their risk-taking. (p. 45)

Pretraining and Games

Some factors will always lie outside the control of the group counselor, but there are specific types of actions that are at the discretion of the leader that affect the group dynamics and can be said to fall into the category of group structure. Two important examples are pretraining and the use of games. Obviously, pretraining activities come before the first group meeting, and games can be introduced at any point once the group meets.

Pretraining runs the gamut of communication channels beyond simply speaking to each member; that is, the counselor may prepare each member before the first meeting via printed sheets, books, recorded testimonies of previous members, e-mail exchanges from former members (if necessary, evolving from the counselor's office to protect anonymity of former members), videotapes, and audio recordings. Any possible medium to communicate information falls here. The creative approach of pretraining procedures knows no bounds in an increasingly technologically oriented world, as long as ethical standards and legal precedence are followed (Ginter, 1984).

Bednar and Lawlis (1971) have addressed the significant role that pretraining can play in effective group counseling: discussing what each member can generally expect in terms of counseling; outlining principles that determine the predetermined course of group counseling (this includes goals and what can be expected based on stages of development); and stipulating the types of interactions that represent effective behaviors that can be expected to result in members achieving their goals.

Based on research (e.g., Stockton & Morran, 1982), one may conclude that specific pretraining tactics are related to specific outcomes. Handouts or written instructions, although not effective in relation to group cohesion, have been found to reassure members about the group experience, stimulate group interactions, enhance acquisition of knowledge or skills, facilitate the process of entry into a group, and cause treatment goals to be achieved sooner. Pretraining interviews have been positively associated with affecting communication patterns; that is, the level of communication increases and the exploration of self-related issues occurs more frequently. Audiotapes used for the purpose of vicarious therapy pretraining accelerates self-exploration, improves self-concept, and increases social awareness and self-disclosure (when communication openness is emphasized). The use of audiotapes relates to higher satisfaction with group relations, goals completed, and improvement achieved. Finally, pregroup experiential skill building to confront anxiety will result in changes in level of extroversion; that is, there will be fewer inhibition behaviors and an increase in approach behaviors.

In general, groups are likely to achieve greater progress (greater depth in less time) when members are taught basic skills in attending, perceiving, and responding. Such communication skills are related to less frequency of hurtful responses and increases in accurate, empathic types of responses. Simply stated, time invested in pretraining members in basic skills and in to what to expect from participation in a group will increase overall efficiency. Stockton and Morran (1982) provided a key consideration in relation to effective utilization of pretraining tactics when they wrote, "Successful pre-training includes both a cognitive and a behavioral component. Studies have consistently shown that groups receiving both instructions and modeling do better than those receiving one treatment or neither" (p. 53).

Games (structured activities) have a long history and certainly have a place in working with clients, but we believe in their judicious use. In general, the basic rule we advocate is: A game should be used only if the group counselor has full knowledge of the game's intent and when he or she can be reasonably accurate in predicting how the game will affect the group at any particular stage in the group's development. Schutz (1967), whose name is associated with the game-laden encounter group movement, introduced many different types of exercises to facilitate group process but was careful to indicate that the structured activity should match what is occurring in the group. Because the use of games can potentially affect a large number of interacting group forces (e.g., cohesion, trust, self-disclosure), games are best used when there is a clear tie to counseling theory and stages of group development (Ginter, 1996). A cookbook approach to introducing games without careful consideration of group dynamics is, at best, very questionable and, at worst, can be expected to have an adverse affect on the group's members. Possible negative outcomes from poorly grounded game use can be that the peace is upset, distance results between the members and the group counselor, and the sensitivity and responsibility levels for members and the counselor are impaired.

Games inappropriately injected into the group process by the counselor can have a strong negative effect. At times, games have an inappropriate group-as-a-whole quality that is therapeutically questionable and possibly unethical. For example, to have everyone write a secret on a slip of paper and then to "surprise" members by collecting and randomly distributing the papers to play a guessing game of "Who Is the Discloser?" is not only poor group counseling but harmful and unethical. Simply stated, the use of games in a counseling group deserves careful consideration and monitoring in terms of their effects when they are used. Yalom (1985) stated, "Group workers agree that proper timing is essential in the use of exercises; a poorly timed exercise will 'bomb out,' be puzzling or harmful to the group. Such exercises are best used to clarify some shared, but dimly conscious group concern or problem" (p. 334).

GOAL SETTING, COHESION, AND GROUP NORMS

Reasons for participating in the group should be stated by each potential member before sessions begin, and it is advantageous to have each member, with the help of the counselor if necessary, state these in behavioral terms, since "observable" change is the true test for group counseling's effectiveness. Even if a member is mostly concerned about his or her affects (e.g., overcoming depression), the member is to express how the achieved goal will be noticeable to others. Also, we recommend that all members repeat what their perceived goals are in the first group session. If these goals lack specificity (e.g., "I want to be in this group to see what I can get out of it"), the counselor should have the member clarify and concretely state what his or her goals are. Finally, while each member's goal is to be thoughtfully enumerated, there is another type of overarching goal—the metagoal—that deserves to be mentioned (Thoresen & Potter, 1975). A metagoal represents the "therapeutic net" that gathers members together to form a particular group, such as managing stress, overcoming feelings of loneliness, building communication skills, or developing skills to combat an eating disorder. Personal goals contribute to maximizing cohesion and trust as well as contribute to norm setting, but the metagoal serves as an obvious reason and reminder why the group exists.

Thoresen and Potter (1975) offered a suggestion that is still relevant today. The group counselor "must conceptualize and relate to the group on two levels: as a collection of discrete persons and as an entity itself. The leader's goals are aimed at the person within the group; interaction goals are focused on the group as a whole" (p. 455). In this latter case, one could apply the term *process goals.*

The central contribution that goals and, of course, tasks related to achieving those goals make was recognized by Lakin (1976), who stated that group cohesiveness is demonstrated by a binding together to each other and the metagoal, greater stability that can withstand frustration, and a group frame of reference that tolerates differing paths taken to meet the group and individual goal. It becomes clear that cohesion is inseparable from accomplishing tasks and achieving end goals. According to Forsyth (1990), cohesion is associated with a sense of "we-ness," greater participation, (e.g., less absences and more involvement in the group's activities), effective communication, satisfaction (e.g., less anxiety, elevations in self-esteem, rise in feelings of security), and "greater acceptance by members of group's goals" (p. 83). Of course, cohesion must be carefully monitored by the group counselor, since the sense of we-ness can reach a level that it "decreases the quality of group performance and increases hostility and interpersonal rejection" (p. 85).

In all groups, completion of the composite of individual goals and the overarching group goal rests on the establishment of group norms (the linkage between cohesiveness and norms is unbreakable). Simply stated, group norms are what is expected and allowable in a group—these are the principles of action that bind members together and serve to guide, control, and regulate what takes place in and, to a certain degree, outside the group (e.g., confidentiality). Violation of norms are usually followed by some form of punishment, but whether this outcome actually occurs is directly related to the magnitude and frequency of occurrence.

Some norms are explicit and some are implicit. Implicit norms are somewhat fluid; that is, they should not be expected to remain the same over time as the group evolves and travels through stages of development. Implicit norms contribute positively to the group but can also interfere with the group achieving goals. Subgroups may develop for a number of reasons (e.g., outside threat, internal threat), and these subgroups may openly or in a subtler manner affect the group adversely. When this takes place, the leader must intervene and review what has occurred in light of earlier stated goals.

Explicit norms are those norms that are openly discussed and mutually decided on—forced unanimity only hinders progress and goal attainment (Shiffer, 1983). The group counselor is expected by members to be active in helping the group develop appropriate goal-directed norms. In the early sessions, it is not just what is said but also what is done; what is modeled by the counselor helps form the set of explicit norms. The stated norm of "being sensitive to others, allowing ourselves to listen in a way that we fully understand the other member both emotionally and intellectually" is best modeled by the counselor who provides evidence of empathic responding.

It is important to emphasize that norm setting should not be the sole responsibility of the counselor. It should be a collaborative effort that involves all the members. Of course, the manner in which this is done will differ from group to group. Norm setting in a group of adolescents diagnosed with conduct disorder will not be the same as a support group formed for adolescents with a learning disability. According to Bonney (1969), the leader

> should assume an active though not highly directive part in the formation of the group's norms. Ideally the setting of norms should emanate from the group itself. . . . The eventual acceptance of a group norm should . . . be left to the consensus of the group and not forced by the leader, particularly in the early stages of the group's development. (p. 167)

Contributing directly to the norms allows members to claim norm ownership. It has been our experience that this type of ownership contributes to the overall therapeutic atmosphere as well as a type of psychological hardiness that enables the group to withstand pressures that can be expected to occur during group counseling. Lakin and Carson (1966) contributed further to our understanding of this dynamic when they wrote, "The pressures to adhere to group norms and to facilitate task and maintenance functions of the group generally operates to 'socialize' the individual within the particular group culture" (p. 30).

ROLES

To define the term *group member* "as a member of a counseling/therapy group" does little to capture the reality of role complexity (Moxnes, 1999). Roles can be described as task, growth/vitalizing, or even antigroup oriented (Benne & Sheats, 1948; Kottler, 1994; Lifton, 1972; Moxnes, 1999). Of course, these can be even further elaborated and differentiated. *Task roles* include recorder, procedural technician, energizer, evaluator, orienter, coordinator, information giver, opinion giver, elaborator, opinion seeker, information seeker, and initiator. *Growth/vitalizing roles* include encourager, gatekeeper/expediter, harmonizer, compromiser, standard setter, group observer/commentator, and follower. *Antigroup roles* include aggressor, blocker, recognition seeker, self-confessor, pleasure-seeker (e.g., "playboy"), dominator, help seeker, and special-interest pleader.

Obviously, the category of antigroup roles is of most concern to group counselors because of their therapeutic inhibitor quality. To establish or reestablish effective counseling when confronted with one or more antigroup roles, the counselor should use himself or herself as a means to assess the group situation. In co-led groups, the two counselors can serve to validate one another's assessment. The following set of questions are intended to guide the group leader in determining the most appropriate intervention:

1. What feelings am I experiencing? (For example, am I feeling blue, empty, angry, agitated, isolated, alienated, dejected, agitated, violated, or some other feeling?)
2. What is this prominent feeling linked to? (For example, is it associated with a particular member or is it related to a topic that I cannot handle because of a personal experience? If the link is a group member, then a series of questions should be answered).

3. Is the group member:
   - Inappropriately questioning my role as leader?
   - Distracting the group from either the metagoal or a member's personal goal because of resistance to his or her own growth or change?
   - Drawing attention to himself or herself to feed a false self-need for interpersonal attention?
   - Dueling with me to assert superiority because of personal self-doubt?
   - Resisting the therapeutic process because maintaining his or her unpleasant but safe functional disorder is less threatening than growth or change?
   - Pulling me into a contest to "win" and receive recognition (to receive a "psychological trophy" that recognizes the member for being the brightest, toughest, most insightful)?
   - Using a group format to strengthen or build nontherapeutic defenses? ("Group frequenters" join groups with a false, stated reason that is *near* the truth. The real goal is to develop skills and create a layer of defenses so that the current psychological self, perceived as shocking and frightful, will never be seen. Sometimes the degree of compulsive defense building [repeatedly becoming involved in therapy] is directly linked to the degree of past trauma experienced by the member.)
   - Eliciting me to take on a pathogizing role to replicate an earlier interpersonal role experienced by the member, a type of role reenactment that is central to the member's concerns or symptoms? (For example, "I am here in this group because I keep remarrying the same type of person." In this case, the group member symbolically marries the group leader and thus replicates his or her interpersonal problem with the cooperation of the counselor, who is not initially aware of the nontherapeutic role he or she is filling.)
4. What is the payoff for this member?
   - What is the member receiving—what is the reward?
   - Does this person require and seek punishment?
   - Is it primarily a matter of seeking to have all others focus their energy on him or her?
   - Is the member searching for safety?
5. What is the overriding quality of the antigroup role?
   - Review the following list of descriptors (Leary, 1957) to assist you in determining the role's interpersonal quality: submitting, displaying weakness, being over-respectful, conforming, clinging to others, depending on others, smoothing, being obsequious, being soft-hearted, displaying over-responsiveness, displaying dogmatic actions, dominating, being boastful, exploiting, rejecting, withholding, being punitive, being sarcastic, attacking, threatening, displaying bitterness, acting treacherous, complaining, hurting, being suspicious, being distrustful, displaying anxiety, acting guilty, or displaying self-condemning.
   - Possible healthy counterparts to these unhealthy qualities may be qualities such as the ones listed next. These qualities offer reframing possibilities to assist the member to see the hidden strength in his or her behavior: obliging, obeying, respecting, admiring, asking for help, trusting, cooperating, being friendly, supporting, helping, guiding, leading, displaying confidence, competing appropri-

ately, asserting, being firm, displaying strength, being forthright, acting/thinking in an unconventional but appropriate way, being realistic, acting in an appropriately skeptical manner, being sensitive, and acting modest.

6. Do other members of the group appear to experience this particular member as I do? What is the evidence?
   - Is there verbal evidence?
   - Is there nonverbal evidence?
     (*Note*: At this stage, if no reliable and valid evidence is isolated, then the counselor should consider whether the reaction to this member is actually a case of projection on the part of the counselor and thus countertransference.)
7. Does the problem require action? If action is warranted, then from whom?
   - The group counselor?
   - Another member?
   - The member himself or herself?
   - A co-counselor?
   - A nonpresent other (i.e., a person outside the group—living or not—present or past)? (In this case, the member may be requested to speak to and have this nonmember speak back, using the "empty chair" technique.)

Following this assessment procedure, the group counselor may find it helpful to use the solution-decision tree. Once the primary interaction antigroup pattern is identified, the counselor selects the most appropriate action associated with that pattern. In all cases, one should avoid negative confrontation—that is, being pulled into a complimentary role that can be predicted only to fuel the role being played out by the member. Likely behaviors from this negative confrontation will be escalation of defensiveness, greater withdrawal, or other reactions that are at the core of the member's problem behavior (reactions that may have laid dormant until the negative confrontation—for example, the threatening quality identified earlier now becomes an actual physical attack). Assuming this problem pattern is pervasive and appears in other interpersonal settings, reframing techniques and focusing on strengths may serve as an "intervention wedge" to "dislodge" a defective pattern. Finally, it is important to keep in mind that these patterns may represent the manifestation of defense mechanisms on the part of a group member, and, as such, potentially represent a rich source of therapeutic material to explore with the group.

AGGRESSOR INTERPERSONAL PATTERN
- Encourage the member to be specific about personal feelings.
- Have the member take part in a role-playing situation that requires self-disclosure, which allows the group counselor to search for clues that reveal the nature of the aggressiveness.
- Request a private conference (not to be confused with an individual counseling session). Share your feelings and thoughts in an assertive, nonaccusatory manner and indicate expectations. It is important to point out how the aggressive role that is manifested in group sessions is counterproductive to each member's individual goals and the metagoal that served as an impetus to form the group.
- Have the member leave if these measures fail. The member should be referred.

RECOGNITION SEEKER/ATTENTION-GETTER
- Respond to the member's feelings of insecurity, if such feelings are evident and at the core of the behavior.
- Avoid eye contact.
- Do not respond to off-task comments/behavior.
- Ask for a private conference, and evaluate the member's reasons for the group behavior.

HOSTILE/ACTING OUT
- Respond to a possible negative transference phenomenon.
- Carefully observe nonverbal behavior and respond appropriately (verbal and nonverbal responses should be consistent).
- Remind the member of explicit rules related to hostile/acting-out behavior in a nonangery confrontational manner.
- If in-group interventions fail, meet privately with the member to resolve feelings toward the group counselor or other member(s). In utilizing this tactic, the counselor should take necessary precautions to protect himself or herself in case the tactic elicits a stronger hostile reaction that endangers the leader or others.
- If interventions fail, the member should be referred.

ADVICE GIVER
- Seek evidence of feelings and thoughts related to insecurity and, if present, act accordingly.
- Encourage the member to self-disclose directly in relation to the advice given.
- Have the advice giver role-play in a restricted manner—that is, to get out of the "ready-made solution finder mode," have the member only respond to the other in the role-play along an affective dimension.
- Do not reinforce the advice giver's inappropriate solution solving.

SILENT/WITHDRAWN
- Respect the silence in general, but recognize those times the member has something to say and pull the member out, with the goal of building on each increment of sharing that does occur.
- Rather than respond to the verbal, recognize that the member speaks a different language (e.g., nonverbal) and speak to this language.
- Use positive confrontation when confrontation is used.
- Make a direct request for members comprising the group to respond to comments and behaviors of other group members—offering opinions and sharing feelings.

SPLITTING PATTERN (SEE AGAZARIAN, 1989; GINTER & BONNEY, 1993)
- Recognize the pattern as one of inner turmoil that prevents the person from integrating certain aspects of his or her personality. The member is projecting these aspects onto and into other members.
- Meet with the member to determine if this pattern is suitable for group intervention or a situation where the individual should be referred to another group or individual counseling.

MONOPOLIZER
- Respond to feelings of insecurity, if present.
- Make specific suggestions about appropriate group behavior in the context of this member's actions in the group, and model appropriate behaviors. Time and place of intervention (during a group session or outside the group) should be based on the disruptive level of the antigroup role.

THERMOSTAT SETTER (ANXIETY BAROMETER AND ADJUSTER)
- Acknowledge the interaction pattern (the member is driven to lower the group's anxiety below what is necessary for therapeutic change to occur), which may be "recognized" by the member but one which the member has never discussed.
- Discuss with the member the necessary contribution made by anxiety in relation to growth and change.

UNDIFFERENTIATED PROBLEM MEMBER
- Avoid eye contact during irrelevant conversation.
- Respond only to relevant statements.
- Ask for a private conference, and explore and identify what exact effect the member's actions have on the group. Refer the member to individual counseling if the member cannot alter his or her current role.

MULTICULTURAL DYNAMICS

Culturally related dynamics are powerful forces that can have a profound effect on group interactions and outcomes (Rao & Stewart, 1999; Robinson & Ginter, 1999). Members can achieve their personal goals (and the metagoal) only if they share experiences and test those experiences against the scrutiny of the "community of inquirers." Conflicting versions of reality that occur may be due to cultural differences and a lack of trust toward some members of the group. Culturally based pathology, such as racism, can take a searing form in groups but is much more likely to take a less obvious form, which is no less damaging. Oppressive images, thoughts, and feelings are frequently relegated to the unconscious but reside there as dynamic forces that affect what can occur in counseling (Elliott & Frosh, 1995).

Leong, Wagner, and Pirashaw (1995) emphasized the need for counselors to be culturally responsive. This responsiveness can span a wide range and certainly involves preventive measures (Robinson & Ginter, 1999). Leong and associates have advocated being active, going beyond typical conceptualizations of counseling, and creating situations that allow for certain oppressed groups to have counseling opportunities that were not previously open to them, such as group counseling. To better understand the oppressive forces that affect the world and the microcosm world of the group, Robinson's (1999) depiction of the various areas of oppression serves as an example (see Figure 3.1). Robinson's (1999) model on dominant U.S. discourses indicates that identities are "socially constructed, 'statuses,' and have particular meanings" (p. 75). According to her model, a type of stratification of identities occurs (visible and invisible levels), which in turn results in an oppressive hierarchy. Simply stated, individuals who deviate from a preferred standard are valued less than those who reflect the standard.

VISIBLE AND INVISIBLE IDENTITIES

Race	Sex	Sexual Orientation	Physical Ability	Class

DOMINANT U.S. DISCOURSES

Whites	Males	Heterosexuals	Able-bodied	Middle-Class

People of Color	Females	Gay Men Lesbians Bisexuals	Persons with Disabilities	Poor People

CONSEQUENCES OF DOMINANT DISCOURSES

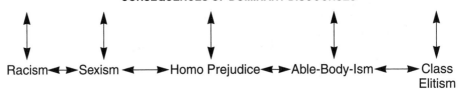

Racism◄►Sexism ◄——►Homo Prejudice◄►Able-Body-Ism◄——►Class Elitism

FIGURE 3.1   The Robinson Model of Discourses: Identities in the United States Are Socially Constructed, "Statused," and Have Specific Meanings

Source: T. L. Robinson, "The Intersections of Dominant Discourses across Race, Gender, and Other Identities," *Journal of Counseling & Development, 77* (1999): 73–79. © ACA. Reprinted with permission from the American Counseling Association to use this figure. No further reproduction authorized without written permission of the American Counseling Association.

It is probably impossible for any group formed not to be made up of members that have been affected one way or another by the areas listed by Robinson. Certainly gender issues (sexism) are a frequent topic encountered in counseling. Okum (1992) and Miller (1981) provide support for the position that hidden role assumptions affect women's ability to deal with conflict. As such, group counseling sessions that harbor these unstated assumptions can further fuel oppression and be dangerous to a member's mental health. The group counselor is responsible for revealing such hidden assumptions and placing them under the scrutiny of a therapeutic "light."

In addition to being aware of the oppressive forces that affect many members, it is necessary for the group counselor to be open to nontraditional avenues of therapy (e.g., herbalists and mystics) that may have significant cultural meaning for some members. Further, various cultural perspectives can provide individual members with new "ways of seeing"—increasing awareness as well as opportunities for a positive therapeutic response—and enhance the group-as-a-whole. As supported by Lee (1996), listening to what is culturally important to another may open a door for assisting the member in a way previously unknown to the group counselor. For example, in Islamic culture, one may find that certain verses from the Koran have a healing potential, and this material may be effectively incorporated into the group process.

Basically, the group counselor should maintain a high level of *cultural elasticity,* allowing himself or herself to be pulled in various cultural directions. In the final analysis, a group counselor, throughout the life of a group, must stay aware of the multicultural dynamics present. This awareness is indispensable in a world that increases its diversity quotient. The shrinking world exposes all peoples to the rich tapestry of diversity that has always been present but frequently unacknowledged or unappreciated.

THE GROUP MATRIX: CURATIVE ELEMENTS AND STAGES OF DEVELOPMENT

A number of writers (Corsini & Rosenberg, 1955; Dagley, Gazda, & Pistotle, 1986; Yalom, 1975, 1985) have listed the ingredients of the experiences that contribute to change. Yalom specifically mentions instillation of hope, universality, imparting of information, altruism, the corrective recapitulation of the primary family group, the development of socialization techniques, imitative behavior, interpersonal learning, group cohesiveness, catharsis, and experiential factors. According to Yalom (1985), "Their [therapeutic factors] interplay and differential importance can vary widely from group to group. Furthermore, [members] in the same group may be benefited by widely differing clusters of therapeutic factors" (p. 4).

Obviously, the field of counseling is ultimately interested in group dynamics because of its relation to client change. Research based on 300 articles on group work (Corsini, 1957; Corsini & Rosenberg, 1955) revealed that positive change attributed to group counseling and group psychotherapy is due to well over 100 reasons cited by authors. Further analysis, specifically a system of cluster analysis, reduced these elements to nine therapeutic or curative ingredients that can be further reduced to one of three categories: cognition, behavior, and emotion (see Long, 1988). The nine key aspects may be summarized as follows:

- Observational learning of "healthy" behaviors
- Universality of concerns, which causes a therapeutic reframing of each client's concerns
- Opportunities to understand the inner nature of things that leads to meaningful insight
- Experiencing "acceptance" by others and accepting others for simply being
- Basking in and reciprocally providing unselfish concern
- Experiencing the "we-ness" atmosphere found to exist in appropriately functioning groups, which buffers against alienation
- Opportunities to test the validity of both self-defeating thoughts and untapped inherent strengths
- Opportunities to ventilate and release what has blocked healthy change
- Exposure to an environment of social nurturing that fulfills a basic human need that can be satisfied only by interacting with others

For Winnicott (1971, 1986), the group serves as a group container capable of holding what the client confronts daily in life and confronts therapeutically in the group. The counselor who is mindful of these key ingredients and the various derivatives that originate from these curative ingredients crafts successful counseling outcomes.

Possibly the most intriguing aspect of such curative factors is how the counselor fosters their occurrence. Using the geometric analogy of a point, line, and sphere, Ettin (1992) graphically painted a picture of the varying levels on which a counselor may skillfully intervene in a therapeutic manner. The counselor can facilitate certain group occurrences by interacting with an individual member (i.e., point interaction), interacting with two members (i.e., line interaction), or interacting with several members or even the entire group (i.e., sphere interaction). Ettin provided examples of each interaction level. Point interactions may involve counselor-client transference, member resistance, member frustration, or narcissistic vulnerabilities. Line interactions occur when a counselor's comments are focused on cooperation, competition, complementary roles, commonalties, attractions, repulsions, affiliations, or peer transference. At the greatest level of complexity, sphere interactions involve issues pertaining to group themes, group conflicts, group atmosphere, boundaries, group tasks, developmental sequences, universals, group defenses, and subgroup dynamics. It is clear that counselors utilizing a group format to assist clients are relying on a rich, organic mix of counseling strategies.

As mentioned earlier, groups are not static entities nor do the curative factors mentioned occur randomly. Stages of group development place everything else into perspective—stages are like mileposts that measure how far the group has traveled on its therapeutic journey. A large number of theorists and researchers have contributed to the understanding of these stages or phases (e.g., Bach, 1954; Bonney, 1969; Gendlin & Beebe, 1968; Mahler, 1969). Although the actual number of stages or phases discussed by different authors varies (e.g., three to seven), it is generally recognized that the group counselor should base intervention timing on consideration of the stage or phase dimension of the group. Gazda has conceptualized counseling groups as going through four distinct stages: exploratory, transition, action, and termination. Others have used similar labels: Bonney (1969) refers to the exploratory stage as the establishment stage, and Mahler (1969) calls it the involvement stage. Both Bonney and Mahler have a second, or transition, stage. Finally, the action stage matches Mathler's working stage. The fourth stage, termination, is essentially equivalent to Mahler's ending stage.

Gazda's Four Developmental Stages

Exploratory Stage. During the exploratory stage, the group members introduce themselves and each member describes the goals he or she hopes to achieve. The members also agree on some basic ground rules. Following the initial session, the members usually engage in social and superficial discussions about themselves, each parrying with the other to present himself or herself in an acceptable fashion. Bonney (1969) has referred to this as the "process by which the group, consciously and unconsciously, assigns power and influence, in varying degrees to each member of the group" (p. 166). It is also a means of establishing various roles that each member will first assume in the group. Members' hidden agendas also begin to emerge, and the group begins to establish norms that will eventually become the explicit and implicit controlling ground rules.

It is especially important that group counselors are actively helpful during the exploratory stage. They show their helpfulness by clarifying both the goals for the group and the group means for achieving them, by telling the group something about themselves, and, most important, by modeling the facilitative dimensions of empathy, respect, warmth, and genuineness. In the Carkhuff (1969a) sense, counselors consistently give responses to each member that are similar to those of the members—the responses are interchangeable, especially in respect to affects expressed by the members and to the content or messages expressed. It is during this initial or exploratory stage that a facilitative base of mutual trust and caring is built. Without this, the group fails to reach the next stage in its development.

Transition Stage.   The transition stage occurs at a point when one or more members begin to self-disclose at a level significantly deeper than the "historical" type of disclosures (commonly given outside the group) heretofore given in group. At this point, the group members can be expected to experience a feeling of threat, since the typical social group does not usually function in this manner. The members may attempt to block the self-disclosures with overly supportive responses or by attempts to change the subject—more precisely, to revert to the superficial conversation of the historical type of disclosures that occurred in the group at the previous stage.

To facilitate movement of the group, as a whole, through the transition stage to the action stage (work phase) requires high levels of discrimination or sensitivity in timing of counselor responses. Counselors must be able to encourage members to self-disclose at a level that gives them a sense of involvement; simultaneously, counselors must be able to hold the anxiety level of the more threatened group members to a level that will not force their defense systems to overact. Following the Carkhuff model of moving from client exploration to understanding to action, counselors must be able to give responses that are at least minimally action oriented (i.e., responses up to this point have embodied empathy, warmth, and respect for members; the action-oriented phase is hastened by responses that exemplify genuineness, concreteness, and reflect suitable self-disclosure to match the new phase). The counselor, too, should be willing to self-disclose, when appropriate, at a depth equal to that of the most advanced member. In that way, the counselor serves as a model for members who are beginning to involve themselves in the action-oriented dimensions of problem resolution—that is, goal-related work.

Action Stage.   The action stage is synonymous with the work or productive stage of a group. It invokes the implementation of the action-oriented dimensions, illustrated in Carkhuff's model, of confrontation and immediacy, plus it facilitates the action dimensions of genuineness, concreteness, and appropriate self-disclosures aimed at problem solving.

The group counselor must orient the members toward adopting a therapeutic-driven belief, if not present, that their condition will not be altered until they take steps to initiate in-group and out-of-group actions to modify their lives. Frequently, the first step in goal achievement is modifying the interaction patterns (behaviors, cognition, and affects) in the group itself; members should be encouraged to do so and "rewarded" when they do.

In this phase of the process, members talking about how they are planning to change is no longer defensible; commitment to change must be demonstrated in the here-in-now context of the group experience. Counselors use appropriate confrontation and share with the members their own here-and-now feelings and thoughts about the members' in-group behavior. They also encourage other group members to interact in a similar manner.

In this stage, members' action must be goal related and dependent on behavioral modifications to be employed outside of the group sessions. It is encouraged in the form of homework to be done and then reported on to the group at the next session. Attempts that fail to achieve the desired goal can be appraised and modified, even role-played in the group.

If group counselors involve all group members in the action stage of group counseling, they will seldom need to confront members themselves. Rather, the group members will confront each other, and the counselors will become gatekeepers of group safety. Counselors must be the most "expert timing devices" in the group process—the ones who can best predict when a given member is ready to be confronted with decision making and/or action. They not only confront but they also solicit confrontation by the members through their openness to such confrontation.

Termination Stage.   The termination stage is marked by a tapering off of member self-disclosure, especially in new areas of concern that arise. In a closed group with a preset termination date, the tapering off usually begins automatically two or three sessions before the preset date of termination. This may be evidenced by half-hearted attempts by some members to continue the sessions beyond the deadline. It is not uncommon during the termination stage for members to display a general need to spontaneously tell how much other group members and the group experience meant to them. Members can be expected to show reluctance to see the group terminate and may even suggest a plan for a group reunion in the future.

The group counselor's responsibility at termination is to reinforce the growth made by group members and to make sure that all group members have had the opportunity to work out their differences with the counselor and other group members before taking leave of the group. If any member of the group, for whatever reason, continues to require counseling, the counselor must assume responsibility or assist the member in a mutually satisfactory referral.

SUMMARY

This chapter contained a summary of group dynamics theory, research, and practice. It began with leadership research and outlined those leadership characteristics that have proven to be effective in group work. Also, leadership characteristics that are not effective were cited.

Group structure was discussed in detail. Research findings indicate that the effects of structure on behavioral performance, perceived cohesion, and attitudes toward the group tend to vary as a function of members' personal characteristics, including their risk taking. Research pertaining to pretraining procedures shows that groups receiving both instruction and modeling do better than those receiving only one treatment and those receiving neither. The value of goal setting for group members was also outlined.

The core processes of a group were summarized, including goal setting, norms, roles, multicultural dynamics, and curative elements. Suggested counselor interventions in relation to antigroup roles or "problem" members were offered. Finally, the chapter concluded with a detailed description of Gazda's four stages of group development: exploratory, transition, action, and termination.

REFERENCES

Agazarian, Y. (1989). Group-as-a whole systems theory and practice. *Group, 13* (3 & 4), 131–154.

Bach, G. R. (1954). *Intensive group psychotherapy.* New York: Ronald Press.

Bednar, R. L., & Battersby, C. P. (1976). The effects of specific cognitive structure on early group development. *Journal of Applied Behavioral Sciences, 12,* 513–522.

Bednar, R. L., & Lawlis, G. F. (1971). Empirical research in group psychotherapy. In A. E. Bergin & S. L. Garfield (Eds.), *Handbook of psychotherapy and behavior change: An empirical analysis.* New York: Wiley.

Bednar, R. L., Melnick, J., & Kaul, T. (1974). Risk responsibility and structure: Conceptual framework of initiating group counseling and psychotherapy. *Journal of Counseling Psychology, 21,* 31–37.

Berensen, B. G., & Mitchell, K. M. (1974). *Confrontation: For better or worse.* Amherst, MA: Human Resource Development Press.

Bergin, A. E. (1975). Psychotherapy can be dangerous. *Psychology Today, 9,* 96, 98, 100, 104.

Benne, K. D., & Sheats, P. (1948). Functional roles of group members. *Journal of Social Issues, 4,* 41–49.

Bonney, W. C. (1969). Group counseling and developmental processes. In G. M. Gazda (Ed.), *Theories and methods of group counseling in the schools.* Springfield, IL: Charles C. Thomas.

Bonney, W. C., & Foley, W. J. (1963). The transition stage in group counseling in terms of congruity theory. *Journal of Counseling Psychology, 10,* 136–138.

Carkhuff, R. R. (1969a). *Helping and human relations. Vol. 1. Selection and training.* New York: Holt, Rinehart and Winston.

Carkhuff, R. R. (1969b). *Helping and human relations. Vol. 2. Selection and training.* New York: Holt, Rinehart and Winston.

Cartwright, D., & Zander, A. (1968). *Group dynamics: Research and theory* (3rd ed.). New York: Harper and Row.

Conyne, R. K., Harvill, R. L., Morganett, R. S., Morran, D. F. K., & Hulse-Killacky, D. (1990). Effective group leadership: Continuing the search for greater clarity and understanding. *Journal for Specialists in Group Work, 15,* 30–36.

Corsini, R. (1957). *Methods of group psychotherapy.* Chicago: William James Press.

Corsini, R., & Rosenberg, B. (1955). Mechanisms of group psychotherapy: Processes and dynamics. *Journal of Abnormal Social Psychology, 51,* 406–411.

Couch, R. D., & Childers, J. H. (1987). Leadership strategies for instilling and maintaining hope in group counseling. *Journal for Specialists in Group Work, 12,* 138–143.

Dagley, J., Gazda, G. M., & Pistole, M. C. (1986). In M. O. Lewis, R. Hayes, & J. A. Lewis (Eds.), *The counseling profession.* Itasca, IL: Peacock.

DeLucia-Waack, J. L. (1999). Supervision for counselors working with eating disorder groups: Countertransference issues related to body imager, food, and weight. *Journal of Counseling and Development, 77,* 379–388.

Drum, D. J., & Knott, J. E. (1977). *Structured groups for facilitating development: Acquiring life skills, resolving life themes, and making life transitions.* New York: Human Sciences.

Elliot, A., & Frosh, S. (Eds.). (1995). *Psychoanalysis in contexts.* New York: Routledge & Kegan Paul.

Ettin, M. F. (1992). *Foundations and applications of group psychotherapy: A sphere of influence.* Boston: Allyn and Bacon.

Evensen, E. P., & Bednar, R. L. (1978). Effects of specific cognitive and behavioral structure on early group behavior and atmosphere. *Journal of Counseling Psychology, 25,* 66–75.

Forsyth, D. R. (1990). *Group dynamics* (2nd ed.). Pacific Grove, CA: Brooks/Cole.

Gazda, G. M. (Ed.). (1976). *Theories and methods of group counseling in the schools* (2nd ed.). Springfield, IL: Charles C. Thomas.

Gendlin, E. T., & Beebe, J. (1968). Experiential groups: Instructions for groups. In G. M. Gazda (Ed.), *Innovations of group psychotherapy.* Springfield, IL: Charles C. Thomas.

Ginter, E. J. (1984, February). Ethics and computer usage. *Louisiana Lagniappe: Newsletter of the Louisiana Association for Counseling and Development, 4,* 3.

Ginter, E. J. (1996). The three pillars of mental health counseling—Watch in what you step. *Journal of Mental Health Counseling, 18,* 99–108.

Ginter, E. J. (1999). David K. Brooks's contribution to the developmentally based life-skills approach. *Journal of Mental Health Counseling, 21,* 191–202.

Ginter, E. J., & Robinson, T. L. (1999). Racism: Healing its effects [Special issue]. *Journal of Counseling & Development, 77* (1).

Ginter, E. J., & Bonney, W. (1993). Freud, ESP, and interpersonal relationships: Projective identification and the Mobius interaction. *Journal of Mental Health Counseling, 15,* 150–169.

Hersey, P., & Blanchard, K. H. (1982). *Management of organizational behavior* (4th ed.). Englewood Cliffs, NJ: Prentice-Hall.

House, R. J., Schuler, R. S., & Levanoni, E. (1983). Role conflict and ambiguous scales: Realities or artifacts. *Journal of Applied Psychology, 68,* 334–337.

Hurley, J. P., & Pinches, S. K. (1978). Interpersonal behavior and effectiveness of T-group leaders. *Small Group Behaviors, 9,* 529–539.

Knowles, M., & Knowles, J. (1959). *Introduction to group dynamics.* New York: Association Press.

Kottler, J. A. (1994). Working with difficult group members. *Journal for Specialist in Group Work, 19,* 3, 10.

Lakin, M. (1976). The human relations training laboratory: A special case of the experiential group. In M. Rosenbaum & A. Snadowsky (Eds.), *The intensive group experience.* New York: Free Press.

Lakin, M., & Carson, R. C. (1966). A therapeutic vehicle in search of a theory of therapy: *Journal of Applied Behavioral Science, 2,* 27–40.

Leary, T. (1957). *Interpersonal diagnosis of personality.* New York: Ronald Press.

Lee, C. (1996). Implications for indigenous healing systems. In D. Sue, A. Ivey, & P. Pederson (Eds.), *Children of color.* San Francisco: Jossey-Bass.

Lee, F., & Bednar, R. L. (1978). Effects of group structure and risk-taking, disposition on group behavior, attitudes, and atmosphere. *Journal of Counseling Psychology, 24,* 191–199.

Leong, F., Wagner, N., & Pirashaw, T. (1995). Racial and ethnic evaluations in help-seeking attitude. In J. Ponterotto, M. Casas, L. Suzuki, & C. Alexandria (Eds.), *Handbook of multicultural counseling.* Thousand Oaks, CA: Sage.

Lieberman, M. A., Yalom, I. D., & Miles, M. B. (1973). Encounter: The leader makes the difference. *Psychology Today, 6,* 69ff.

Lifton, W. M. (1972). *Groups: Facilitating individual growth & societal change.* New York: Wiley.

Long, S. (Ed.). (1988). *Six group therapies.* New York: Plenum.

Mahler, C. A. (1969). *Group counseling in the schools.* Boston: Houghton Mifflin.

Miller, A. (1981). *The drama of the gifted child.* New York: Basic Books.

Moore, D. W. (1997). *The accidental Buddhist.* New York: Doubleday.

Moxnes, P. (1999). Understanding roles: A psychodynamic model for role differentiation in groups. *Group Dynamics: Theory, Research, and Practice, 3,* 99–113.

Muro, J. J., & Dinkmeyer, D. (1977). *Counseling children in the elementary and middle schools.* Dubuque, IA: Wm. C. Brown.

Okum, B. (1992). Object relations and self-psychology: Overview and feminist perspective. In L. Brown & M. Ballou (Eds.), *Theories of personality and psychotherapy: Feminist reappraisals.* New York: Guilford.

Picklesimer, B. K., Hooper, D. R., & Ginter, E. J. (1998). Life-skills, adolescence, and career choices. *Journal of Mental Health Counseling, 20,* 272–282.

Rao, N., & Stewart, S. M. (1999). Cultural influence on sharer and recipient behavior: Sharing in Chinese and Indian preschool children. *Journal of Cross-Cultural Psychology, 30,* 219–241.

Robinson, T., (1999). The intersection of dominant discourses across race, gender, and other identities. *Journal of Counseling and Development, 77,* 73–80.

Robinson, T., & Ginter, E. J. (1999). Racism: Healing its effect [Special Issue]. *Journal of Counseling and Development, 77* (1).

Russell, E. W. (1978). The facts about encounter groups: First facts. *Journal of Clinical Psychology, 34,* 130–137.

Schutz, W. (1967). *Joy.* New York: Grove Press.

Shiffer, M. (1983). S. R. Slavson. In L. Wolberg & M. Aronson (Eds.). *Group and family therapy.* New York: Brunner/Mazel.

Slavson, S. R. (1957). Are there dynamics in therapy groups? *International Journal of Group Psychotherapy, 7,* 131–154.

Slavson, S. R. (1964). *A textbook in analytic group psychotherapy.* New York: International Universities Press.

Stockton, R., & Morran, D. K. (1982). Review and perspective of critical dimensions in therapeutic small group research. In G. M. Gazda (Ed.), *Basic approaches to group psychotherapy and group counseling* (3rd ed.). Springfield, IL: Charles C. Thomas.

Thoresen, C. E., & Potter, B. (1975). Behavioral group counseling. In G. M. Gazda (Ed.), *Basic approaches to group psychotherapy and group counseling* (2nd ed.). Springfield, IL: Charles C. Thomas.

Truax, C. B., & Carkhuff, R. R. (1967). *Toward effective counseling and psychotherapy: Training and Practice.* Chicago: Aldine.

Wilborn, B. L., & Muro, J. J. (1979). The impact of structuring technique on group functions. *The Journal for Specialists in Group, 4,* 193–200.

Winnicott, D. W. (1971). *Playing and reality.* New York: Basic Books.

Winnicott, W. D. (1986). *Holding and interpretation: Fragments of an analysis.* New York: Grove Press.

Wolf, L. A., & Schwartz, E. (1962). *Psychoanalysis in groups.* New York: Grune and Stratton.

Yalom, I. D. (1975). *The theory and practice of group psychotherapy* (2nd ed.). New York: Basic Books.

Yalom, I. D. (1985). *The theory and practice of group psychotherapy* (3rd ed.) New York: Basic Books.

CHAPTER FOUR

DIVERSITY ISSUES IN GROUP COUNSELING AND GROUP PSYCHOTHERAPY

Much of the writing in early group texts described group processes and interventions as though there was a standard person who would be appropriate for all group approaches described. There often seemed to be an assumption that people who partook of group counseling and therapy had characteristics that included being mainstream American, probably White or at least middle class, and who would resemble the characteristics of the group leader. Exceptions to this expectation were generally described in more detail in chapters that defined and explained how to work with those who were different: treating troublesome group members, working with low-income group members, treating special populations such as alcoholics and habitual offenders, and so on.

Over the last two decades, tremendous changes have occurred in U.S. and world cultures, with the rich array and complexity of the diversity of people becoming more recognized, acknowledged, and attended to by counselors and therapists. Everyone in the field of mental health services today—students, faculty, practitioners, and clients/patients—is familiar with the increased emphasis on being aware of and sensitive to diversity issues in training and treatment approaches. The American Counseling Association (ACA) has a long history of commitment to training and service delivery related to diversity, as does the American Psychological Association (APA). Within these two organizations various divisions have been created that emphasize diversity issues. Specialty divisions, such as the Association for Specialists in Group Work (ASGW), the Association for Multicultural Counseling and Development (AMCD) of ACA, and the Division of Counseling Psychology of the APA, have endorsed training guidelines and moved toward identifying principles for the development of diversity-competent mental health workers. Additionally, the Council on the Accreditation of Counseling and Related Educational Programs (CACREP) has incorporated multicultural issues into their training standards.

There is considerable overlap among the various professional organizations' guidelines regarding developing culturally competent counselors and psychologists. Among the competencies generally endorsed are a sensitivity to the inherent diversity of people and the uniqueness of clients with whom counselors and therapists work.

There must be an awareness of the impact of race and ethnicity on the theory, training, and practice of counseling and therapy, and the culturally competent therapist must be cognizant of the various dimensions of identity, including race, ethnicity, gender, age, sexual orientation, and socioeconomic class. Further, there must be an awareness of the impact of social influence—power—in people's lives, particularly those who have experienced less power in their cultural experiences. Finally, counselors and therapists are expected to be cognizant of their influence in the lives of their clients and their role in society as agents of public change.

The tremendous changes in the cultural and ethnic makeup have presented challenges as school populations, communities, and even major sections of states and regions have experienced changing demographic composition. Richard Suinn, as president of the American Psychological Association, has reported, "The rapidly changing demography of the United States represents one of the most unprecedented challenges this country has ever faced" (reported in D'Andrea & Arredondo, 1999, p. 16). The United States is shifting from a nation where the majority of people are White and of European ancestry to becoming a country in which most people come from non-White, non-European backgrounds. This dramatic change, this demographic shift, is requiring extensive reexamination of the nature of counseling and therapy, and demanding an increased knowledge and awareness on the part of mental health practitioners to become more aware and skilled relative to the cultural backgrounds of the clientele with whom they work.

Today, it is recognized that all mental health practitioners must be more knowledgeable, have increased skills, and have greater appreciation for the diversity of people. A recent study reported by Holcomb-McCoy and Myers (1999) addressing counselors' self-perceived multicultural competence and the adequacy of the multicultural training found that most professional counselors perceive themselves to be competent in relation to the three core components of multicultural training: awareness, knowledge, and skills. However, they reported feeling less competent in knowledge related to racial identity dimensions and believing that they are more familiar with their own personal worldviews than they are about their client's cultures. Overall, practitioners found their level of training to have been less than adequate, with most of their current knowledge coming from professional development experiences. Finally, the counselors who were ethnic minorities reported greater sensitivity and awareness of multicultural issues than did White counselors.

Although many practitioners and trainers have endorsed the changing emphasis on diversity, others have not been as involved. For some, this has been a function of the timing of training, because many educators and practitioners were trained in a time where there was little acknowledgment or education related to the diversity of populations. For many, the training that occurred identified those whose backgrounds were dissimilar, or who had experienced environments that were less empowering, as well as those whose educational and economic experiences were deficient or lacking. Practitioners often applied diagnostic categories to people who entered counseling or therapy with different behaviors, using labels implying illness or mental incapacitation, perhaps sick, definitely not fitting the middle-class American mold. For persons coming from other countries, and at times for persons within less visible cultures in America, their beliefs and practices were often identified as pathological or disturbed. Many mental health practitioners often saw as peculiar and in need of therapy Japanese who practiced ancestor worship, for example, or Native Americans who embraced a spiritual naturism. Even women of middle-class backgrounds were often diagnosed with depression as a result of the social circumstances they encountered in their daily lives, including lack of access to acceptable employment and social restraints on education. The standard diagnostic procedure for most mental health workers, the *Diagnostic and Statistical Manual (DSM)* provided little accommodation for people who failed to be mainstream in their behavior.

While some have not embraced multiculturalism because of lack of training or opportunity for increased exposure to a more diverse population, others have been critical of the emphasis for an entirely different reason: that the focus on differences moves one from identifying common components of effective therapy to attempting to develop specific techniques for every different cultural group. Patterson (1996), for example, believes that the focus on differences ignores the interconnectedness of a global world and that when emphasis is placed on how people are different, the common ground of people is overlooked. The conflict between addressing differences and commonalties is referred to as *the etic versus the emic debate. Etic* refers to identifying the universal, the common ground, the similarities (of people, cultures, theories, strategies, principles), whereas the *emic* refers to those characteristics that are specific (specific to the culture, the ethnic group, the treatment). The etic approach places emphasis on the similarities people have, the sameness, and not on their differences, their uniqueness. The emic approach focuses on how people are unique and different, and on the singular rather than the common.

Patterson (1996) reviewed the developing emphasis on diversity over the last two decades. He reported that the initial focus of texts in the late 1970s and early 1980s was on particular minority groups within the United States. Books addressed the predominant minority cultural groups in the country at that time—African Americans, Asian Americans, Hispanics, and Native Americans—and authors attempted to define and clarify the cultural and ethnic characteristics of these four groups. Some authors identified specific counseling or therapy approaches to be used with each group discussed, and some authors advocated the development of unique theories and interventions for each cultural group identified. Pederson (1976, p. 26), for example, reported that "each cultural group requires a different set of skills, unique areas of emphasis, and specific insights for effective counseling to occur." This clearly represented a strong commitment to the Emic approach.

During the 1980s, writers began to expand their discussions of cultural groups to include not only the predominant four racial/ethnic groups but also topics of gender, economics, and sexual orientation, as well as lesser recognized ethnic groups. At the same time, attention was paid to why mainstream counselors were less effective with diverse populations. Explanations included understanding that the majority of counselors were White and of the majority culture, lacked bilingual/multilingual skills, failed to appreciate the values and backgrounds of many clients, and perhaps practiced prejudice or discrimination. Mays and Albee (1992) reported that there was "a failure of the profession of psychology to develop and promote relevant and adequate mental health services for this population" (p. 554).

A considerable number of publications were developed that attempted to provide extensive information and knowledge about ethnic, racial, and cultural groups. As the number of identified groups increased, so did the numbers of theories, methods, and techniques. Extensive research on racial identity development also focused attention on the need for increased awareness not only of the ethnic identity of a particular person, but of that person's stage of racial consciousness or racial identity (Cross, Parham, & Helms, 1991; Helms, 1984, 1990). Recognizing the role of gender and sexual orientation (straight, gay/lesbian, bisexual) added additional dimensions to the mix. Thus, with the proliferating emphasis on an emic approach, differing knowledge about and interventions with specific populations became increasingly complex. Knowing the specifics of working with an African American male, at the encounter stage of racial identity, from a middle-class background, with a straight sexual orientation would demand different knowledge and skills than other combinations of counselees from other ethnic/gender/racial identity/socioeconomic/sexual orientations. Added to that, the counselor or therapist then had to incorporate the diverse treatment possibilities: individual, group, couples, or family. Finally, the counselor's own racial identity, gender, sexual orientation, socioeconomic level, and stage of racial awareness had to be considered in relation to the interactions possible among the group members, the model of intervention selected, and even the theoretical orientation of the counselor.

One problem that became evident with the emic approach was that even though groups could be broadly identified by ethnic characteristics, such as Hispanics, there was often as much "within differences" as "between differences." That is, not all Hispanics were similar; they differed in where they came from (Puerto Rico, Mexico, Spain), their educational and income levels, their religious or family orientations, and so on. So, often, people who appeared physically to be Hispanic may have more resemblance to a non-Hispanic-looking person than to another person who had the physical characteristics of Hispanics but different learning and living experiences.

With the great variations of members of groups, generalizations presented in texts provided an introduction to cultural characteristics of groups of people, but failed to provide information about the specific individuals entering counseling or therapy. Further, this process contributed to stereotyping, treating people as like the group from which they came, rather than as individuals with unique characteristics. Sue (1983) was one of the first to discuss the wide variation that occurs within cultural groups and to caution that although it is important to increase one's general knowledge of the various ethnic groups, counselors should use caution in their attributions of those generalizations to all members of the group. Sue and Zane (1987) went on to report that a counselor's knowledge of the culture does not necessarily lead to more effective therapy: "Recommendations that admonish therapists to be culturally sensitive and to know the culture of the client have not been very helpful" (p. 37) and "the major problem with approaches emphasizing either cultural knowledge or culture-specific techniques is that neither is linked to particular processes that result in effective psychotherapy. . . . Recommendations for knowledge of culture are necessary but not sufficient for effective treatment" (p. 39).

The concern over the difficulties of defining appropriate theories and interventions for each of the multitude of possible diverse treatment populations has led to an increased focus of the balancing of the emic with the etic approaches. There is increased recognition that knowledge, awareness, and skills related to the cultural, ethnic, and social groups of people worked with in counseling and therapy is important; likewise, understanding the importance of an approach that is inclusive, respectful, and helpful is crucial. Patterson (1996) identified the basic counselor qualities developed by Carl Rogers—respect, genuineness, and empathic understanding—as being crucial for working with clients of diverse backgrounds and orientations. He stated that these conditions are necessary, though they will not be sufficiently effective unless the conditions are perceived and recognized by the client. With clients from varying cultures, ages, genders, sexual orientations, and socioeconomic statuses the counselor must have an understanding and appreciation of the verbal and nonverbal behaviors of the participants. There must be a balance of the etic and the emic, and this comes about through the openness to learning about new and different cultural groups and experiences, appreciating the humanness of all people, and having a commitment to help bring about social changes that will lead to respect and dignity for all people.

This is a book on group counseling and therapy. Yet, the culturally sensitive counselor recognizes that group counseling and therapy do not address all the concerns of the people with whom he or she works. A culturally sensitive counselor also recognizes the alternative applications of group work that can lead to beneficial change for people. Parham, a leader in the multicultural arena, has advocated that counselors must move beyond individual and group counseling to become more effective in bringing about change in clients' environments. He advocated (described in D'Andrea & Arredondo, 1999) that counselors must be activists for change so that rather than only treating clients who have experienced racism, violence, and homophobia, actions be taken to reduce or eliminate the problems. In schools, this may involve working with teachers and parents to help them become more sensitive to issues of race, gender, and power imbalances. In communities, an activist stance may involve working with larger groups to address problems of housing, availability of resources, and laws—both written and unwritten—that work contrary to the healthy development of people. The skills used in individual and group counseling and therapy are useful, but become applied in a very different way. They are used to help people encounter their biases and their prejudices, and to move toward the common goal of preventing the hurt that comes to those less empowered.

DIVERSITY AND GROUP WORK

Gladding (1999) reported that groups are an important way for addressing problems of racism, sexism, religious intolerance, and homophobia. There was not an extensive focus on diversity in group work for some time, because many group workers operated as though all group members were similar and did not differ much from the dominant culture. More currently, though, there is greater recognition of the impact diverse members have on how groups function, and group leaders today have to be much more cognizant of how cultural forces play out in groups. As Baca and Koss-Chioino (1997, p. 130) stated, "Culture becomes the foreground rather than the background in group processes."

For groups to be effective in meeting Gladding's (1999) goal of addressing racism, sexism, and other cultural issues, counseling and therapy models and methods are going to have to pay greater attention to the way in which group process is impacted by the members of the group. For many years, group leaders have focused on the difference of doing group counseling and therapy, versus doing counseling and therapy in a group. The former implies that the curative effect of the group is powerful and that the interactions of the members of the group effects change and outcome. The later has the members of the group as incidental to the therapy process and is not properly considered group counseling or therapy. Not only does group counseling/therapy expect group interaction to occur for the group to be powerful and impact change of the members but it *demands* the member-to-member interaction and influence. When the members of the group come from diverse backgrounds and orientations, the differences may be powerful for influencing change, or may bring progress to a halt as conflicting cultural standards come into play. Thus, the leadership skills of the counselor are tested more completely as the diversity of the group increases. This potential shortcoming of group work may easily be reframed as a strength and a desired aspect of group work.

We have described in Chapters 1, 2, and 3 the advantages and benefits of working in groups, of doing group counseling and therapy. Yet, group work remains a very underutilized intervention in schools, community agencies, and hospitals. Explanations have been offered for the underutilization of groups, including difficulties in initiating and maintaining in practice, scheduling, and lack of availability of space. Sciarra (1999) cited a fundamental difficulty with doing group work—that groups create anxiety, for the group member as well as the group leader. When a leaders says "We will now break down into groups," participants begin immediately wondering about the process and the participants. Part of the concern with the question of who the other participants will be is directed to diversity: Who will be in my group? What will they be like? What will they say and do? How will I compare to them? The leader has similar questions, because there may be a concern about the ability to be therapeutic in a public "group" setting, as compared to an individual approach, and being unsure about the possibilities of working with the diversity of people and problems that may be present in the group. The group is a microcosm of society and may provide the opportunity for members to become familiar with and less resistant to people from diverse backgrounds.

An assumption of group work is that the group functions as a social microcosm, that members of the group will eventually behave as they do out of the group, and that the group is "a miniaturized representation of each patient's social universe" (Yalom, 1995, p. 42). As group members accommodate to the group setting, they develop the interactional patterns and styles that are evident outside the group, and they learn to encounter each other as they do people outside the group. This interaction provides the opportunity, under the leadership of the group counselor or therapist, to experience others and learn how others experience them.

One of the earliest applications of T-groups, a model developed by Kurt Lewin, was in the 1940s and early 1950s with community leaders attempting to reduce interracial tensions (Merta, 1995). With the beginning applications of group work applied to diverse populations, the stage was set for groups to be powerful settings for addressing both problems and solutions of diversity and multicultural concerns.

Developing the Group

Group counseling and therapy, as practiced in the United States, developed from mainstream therapy models in the United States, most often by practitioners and academics who were of European ancestry. It is important to differentiate the European ancestry of the developers of many of the theories and therapies from the more common expression, *Eurocentric,* because the *Eurocentric* term implies that the therapies practiced are also descended from and similar to the practices of Europe. Counselors and therapists who have studied European approaches to counseling and therapy are aware, first, that there are many different models (therapy in Spain hardly resembles therapy in England, yet both are European), and, second, that there are extensive differences in the European and American practices. Having said that, there are a number of commonalties of the therapies, and these were identified by DeLucia-Waack (1996) when she reported that there are common tenets: a focus on the individual, a heavy emphasis on the verbal language, the importance of unstructured interaction, a value on risk taking and autonomy, and a focus of the importance of the role of the leader. These characteristics of a group as most commonly practiced may result in groups not being appropriate for all people.

It is important to be aware of the general group expectations and determine whether potential members will be able to participate and benefit from the group as presented. Variations on groups are possible and encouraged, particularly when aspects of the group do not fit the potential members. Groups may need to be changed from unstructured to structured, high levels of interaction may need to be modified to accommodate less verbal members, and a focus on risk taking and autonomy may need to be lessened.

Some concerns that have to be addressed early on in establishing a group are: What need will it meet? Why is it necessary? Who will benefit from the group? As soon as these decisions are considered, the group leader must be aware of both the obvious applications for group work as well as subtle implications. The obvious may include the importance of reducing a problem. A middle-school counselor, for example, may initiate a group to help students who are bullies learn less coercive and more adaptive ways of behaving at school. Clearly, there is a need to reduce violence and aggression in schools and all should benefit from the experience, but what is the subtler message that goes with the decision? Will this be a group that is comprised only of boys, in which case it is not a general group but one that focuses on males? Who will be in the group—will the participants be from a particular racial group or ethnic background? If so, what is the message being communicated in the membership of such a group—that students from that cultural background are believed to be trouble-makers? This is a complex issue, and it is important that counselors explore the obvious and the subtle messages being sent when establishing the group.

A second issue is whether the group will be homogeneous or heterogeneous in membership makeup. The more similar group members are (homogeneous), the more likely they are to form an earlier cohesive group that appears to be productive and progressive. Groups comprised of members from diverse backgrounds (heterogeneous) are considerably less likely to cohere early and move toward productive steps as quickly as the homogeneous group.

The homogeneous group provides the opportunity for the group to establish a strong feeling of being connected, offers immediate support, and generally has few conflicts (Yalom, 1995). A number of group models embrace a homogeneous model, including groups for African Americans (Brown, 1984), Native Americans (Edwards & Edwards, 1984), Hispanics (Acosta & Yamamoto, 1984), and Asian Americans (Chu & Sue, 1984). Although no group can be completely homogeneous, the leader has the opportunity of selecting members and may move toward having more or less similarity among the members. There are problems, though, with having a highly similar number of members in a group. Generally, homogeneous groups tend to think similarly, resulting in a "groupthink" approach in which there is little dissent or independent thinking related to activities. They are less prone to taking risks and may result in joining together against the leader if the leader challenges a position that the group takes. This tends to be an intensified problem if the leader is of a different cultural background than the membership.

Heterogeneous groups, on the other hand, are more difficult for developing cohesion and a sense of group. Members are generally more cautious in the beginning because they recognize the other members of the group are "not like me" and there is little common ground or identity. The lack of similarity poses a threat for early termination of group members and for failure of the group to cohere and move toward a common goal. Heterogeneous groups, though, have the advantage of having differences among members be a positive force that can lead to higher functioning among members. Jackson (1992) reported that homogeneous groups are more effective on performance and decision-making tasks.

Sciarra (1999) has described difficulties and advantages of working with racially heterogeneous groups. He has recommended that when forming a racially diverse group, the leader should plan the formulation carefully. There should not be only one member of a racial category in a group, because that presents two problems: the isolation of the member and the expectation that the member will not only be a member of the counseling group but also a representative for the racial group. Sciarra stated that racially mixed groups result in anxiety for group members, particularly for White members of the group. Minority members are accustomed to the experiences of their presence around majority members; Whites are less accustomed to the interactions, particularly if the Whites are in the minority of racial/ethnic makeup of the group. Sciarra reported research by Davis (1979) (reported in Sciarra, 1999) in which Davis stated that Whites prefer groups to be 80 percent White, and 20 percent Black, whereas Blacks are comfortable in groups that are half White and half Black.

Sciarra (1999) recommended directly addressing issues of racial diversity with groups: "If the group leader is comfortable dealing with issues of gender, race, and sexual orientation, then the underlying dynamics of projective identification can be exposed. If the group is racially diverse, it would be appropriate for the group leader in early stages to facilitate a discussion of the groups racial composition" (p. 111).

Sciarra also reported that issues of the group that are not addressed directly have a way of either subtly encroaching into the group discussion or of becoming the focal point of discussion. It is therefore better to take a leadership position and address the topics than to avoid them. This requires, of course, that the group leader is confident in his or her abilities, is aware of diversity issues and has developed a knowledge of stages of cultural identity development both for group members and for himself or herself, and is sensitive to the level of development of group members.

When developing and conducting counseling or therapy groups, it is important to go back to the basics of the steps of the group and be certain that in each stage of group preparation and implementation, diversity issues have been considered and influence each aspect of the group. The steps are briefly described here.

Defining the Focus/Goals.   When considering the focus of the group or the goals that are established for the group, what diversity issues need to be considered? What is the focus of the group and will that be appealing and applicable to a diverse population? If no, should it be? If yes, then how is that message going to be conveyed and how will diversity issues be incorporated into the focus of the group? Are the goals that are established consistent with values and beliefs of the cultural groups for whom the group will be offered? When will the group be conducted and how will that contribute to or detract from a diverse group of participants? What level of consultation with others needs to occur to ensure that the group and the leadership will be sensitive to issues of diversity? Are there leadership characteristics that will influence group participation, either positively or negatively, and how might a coleader contribute to better group facilitation regarding diversity issues?

Selecting Members.   The selection of members, which is a crucial component in group work, strongly influences the success or problems that may occur for the counseling or therapy group. Following the admonition to be setting up for success, one aspect of ensuring success is to consider issues of diversity among the membership, and how the factor of diversity influences who is in the group, who stays in the group, and to what extent members are supportive and facilitative of one another. Discussions of the advantages and disadvantages of homogeneity and heterogeneity of group membership have been discussed earlier (see Chapter 3). Discussions of homogeneity generally refer to member problems or concerns, but it can also refer to the makeup of the group. Selecting members includes not only identifying those who may benefit from the group and contribute to the benefit of others but it should also include the importance of having members of diverse backgrounds together so that they may come to better understandings of each other in a social environment that is founded on support, member communications, and personal growth and development through social learning opportunities. Unless the purpose of the group is to bring disputing parties together to engage in conflict resolution, it is important to recognize that some people simply should not be in a group together. If members have histories that go beyond the present situation—such as members of differing gangs, or groups with traditional histories of animosity or discrimination—they may best be served in another group format until the time they are able to come together to work cooperatively.

Questions to examine when selecting new members include: At what level of racial identity development is the leader, and how will that characteristic interact with membership? Should the group selection process have racial identity development as a criterion for selection in or out of the group? What is the history of people in the pool being considered for participation and how well will they work together? What goals do the potential members have and are those consistent with the goals of the leader and the group?

Establishing Norms.   Other chapters describe the importance of establishing norms for the group (see, for example, Chapter 3). One aspect of norm setting is the level of openness to discussion of diversity issues, such as race and ethnicity, socioeconomic status, sexual orientation, and other factors that group members may be uncomfortable addressing openly. DeLucia-Waack (1996) encourages the discussion of racial or cultural differences within the groups. She has reported that some counselors are hesitant to allow the discussion because some group members may be offended. Rather than that being the case, though, DeLucia-Waack has said, "In reality, the acknowledgement of cultural differences may increase group cohesion" (p. 219). When a subject is made public rather than private, members do not perceive the topic as taboo in other discussions. The ability of the leader to model openness in discussion and objectivity in approaching issues that members may find uncomfortable is crucial to the development of group cohesiveness and openness about diversity issues.

Managing the Process.   It is crucial that the group leader or leaders have training and awareness of diversity issues. Having a leader who is unaware of diversity issues results in a leader missing much of the possible communication and conflict that may occur in a group. When leaders have a rich background and understanding of the problems people have experienced because of their race, ethnicity, gender, sexual orientation, age, or physical restraints, they are sensitive to how the process of the group influences both the openness of the member-to-group experiences as well as the interactions between members. It is the responsibility of the group leader to serve as the conscience of the group by being sensitive to interactions among the members and to recommendations members make to one another.

Questions to consider include: Are members cognizant of the impact their comments have on one another? Should the leader provide more reflection or interpretation of interactions to help the members become more aware and sensitive? Do members have the strength to address other members who are not as sensitive as need be? Are diversity issues slowing down the progress of the group, and would the group work better with the leader taking a more active role in defining issues related to diversity? Are members interacting with respect, treating each other with dignity—and if not, why and what might the leader do? As a leader, is there a conscious awareness of the impact of the group on the values and beliefs of the diverse membership, and what needs to be done to help the group members address these values and beliefs?

Evaluating Outcome.   Although it is important to examine the outcome of the group from the perspective of whether the overall goal of the group was achieved and whether individual members showed growth and problem resolution, it is also important to examine whether the group achieved all it could in relation to diversity. This means going beyond the basic points of achieving behavior change for specific problems, and asking: Was this a successful group? In what ways? Did it result in people feeling better about themselves and others? Was there evidence of respect and dignity for self and others becoming more obvious by the end of the group? Can the leader, with clarity of expression and a clear conscious, share with community leaders and employers the outcome of the group and know that there will be acceptance that diversity issues were incorporated and addressed?

By taking the time to address these questions with concerns of diversity in the foreground, it is possible to become a more effective group leader. If a period of time ever existed when diversity issues were not important and need to be considered, that time is long passed. Leaders have a professional and ethical mandate to incorporate sensitivity to diversity into their training, practices, and program evaluations. Following are discussions of two particular areas of diversity in groups.

WOMEN IN GROUPS

A quiet revolution began in the late 1960s and early 1970s with the advent of gatherings in kitchens and living rooms around the country: The consciousness-raising group revolutionized the way women thought of themselves, interacted with their friends and families, and viewed the world. Consciousness-raising groups were leaderless in terms of professional counselors or therapists; rather, they were organized and facilitated by women who were interested in the opportunity of exploring the meaning of their lives and the roles they had been ascribed and had accepted. With the development of feminist therapy there came an examination of power and responsibilities in life and between females and males. There was a demand for equality, as more and more women became aware of the extent to which social forces shaped the life experiences women had. They began addressing issues of discrimination and subordination, as well as means toward autonomy and empowerment. The focus was on women's strength and resources rather than on the "experts" who relied on authority and tradition, providing for empowerment of women's identity rather than focusing on the pathology many therapists observed. (As an anecdote: When I [Arthur Horne] attended a training program in 1970, a psychiatrist at an internship site explained that all women experienced depression, that it was a biological characteristic of being female. The feminist movement demonstrated it was not a biological condition but rather an artifact of the social roles ascribed to women at the time.)

Today, many counseling and therapy groups are de facto women's groups because of the nature of the concerns addressed in the groups, such as groups addressing concerns of incest survivors, battered spouses, and those with eating disorders. The topics of many earlier consciousness-raising groups have become the core of issues addressed in these groups: violence against women, unrealistic expectations for how women should look and behave, inequality in the workplace and family decision making, and others.

Bernardez (1996) has taken a strong position that women should be treated in women-only groups led by women therapists because of the extent of the devaluing of women and the failure of male therapists and male clients to understand, appreciate, and support the circumstances women experience. Bernardez stated,

> It has taken an unusual amount of time to discover and acknowledge that the oppression of women is universal. Yet oppression of women has been with us for millennia and has been viewed as natural law. The shades and nuances of oppression may vary with the culture, but there is no known society where women are the equals of men. (p. 243)

She continued,

> Any therapist who disregards the social determinants in these disorders or who continues to treat women and men alike as if the hurdles they encounter are no different is reacting with a "traditional bias." (p. 244)

Since acknowledging the victimization of women would require massive changes in both personal and professional relationships, as well as accepting alternative theoretical models, Bernardez posited that many—perhaps most—therapists do not acknowledge the disempowering social circumstances of women, and therefore cannot provide adequate services to them. The alternative, and the position she has advocated, is that women should be treated by women therapists in all-women groups.

The female group counselor or therapist must be one who has the clinical skills both to facilitate insight and interaction and to help group members through the stages of group development. The therapist must also, though, be one who understands the circumstances of social influence in women's lives, yet can model both personal and therapeutic expectations of leadership, strength, caring, and self-assertion. There must be counselor or therapist knowledge of new theories of female development, combined with a healthy awareness of her own strengths and abilities, and an understanding of her own experiences wrestling with the socialization process so that there is congruence in her self-view and her clinical skills.

Bernardez (1996) presented several advantages of a women's group. She has indicated that although women in groups are assertive and can be autonomous and independent, they are also caring and listen well, making them good group members. Most women have experienced cultural bias and have a shared experience of insecurity and fear, and the group provides them with an opportunity of sharing their experiences as they move to overcome the oppression. There is a safety and security in sharing the common universal experience of all women with others in a group setting, while at the same time providing support and encouragement for moving beyond the oppression of the societal role.

Women's groups, conducted by women therapists, may be more powerful for helping women deal with anger, because women have often not been as socialized to experience and express anger as men have. Women have been more likely than males to experience negative consequences for anger outbursts, and have experienced disapproval for expressions of anger or for engaging in angry behaviors. This has often been true even when the behavior engaged in is assertive rather than aggressive, but still challenging or perceived as threatening, by spouses, bosses, and others in power relationships. Women in a group may be more supportive of identifying and demonstrating the assertive responses that may be discouraged in a mixed-gender group. A group composed of all women is likely to be more effective in helping to identify members' propensity to avoid conflict and engage in cooperation and support rather than conflict and confrontation. A female leader who has awareness of this characteristic may be more likely than a male group leader to bring the topic to the forefront in group work. An emphasis on conflict, competition, and dealing with rivalry and ambition may also be more effectively facilitated by a female leader who is aware of the extent to which women have experienced disapproval from peers and partners for expressing these characteristics.

Bernardez (1996) has described another characteristic of women-only groups that may be very facilitative of members' growth. She has described the harmful socialization of sexual attitudes and behaviors women have learned as a function of the double standard of sexual behavior and repression of women's natural sexual interests and desires. Further, many women have had traumatic sexual abuse experiences and male therapists may be less sensitive to the extent of damage that may have been done. Women, whether victims of sexual abuse or not, have a stronger identity with the experience than most men.

Another area that may be especially appropriate for all-women group treatments is addressing eating disorders and body image distortions. Although more and more men are presenting for therapy with eating disorders, still the largest majority are women, and women have had to deal with the idealization of the female body in the media, films, and general society. Helping women come to terms with the victimization of double standards for weight and fitness, the impossible standards of beauty, and the shame that goes with body concerns may be better accomplished in the all-women group. Although many men may be understanding and supportive, most men have not experienced the level of negative identity development and accompanying shame that women have to contend with in relation to body image.

Bernardez (1996) has also described the importance of a women's group for examining issues related to mothering. The issue takes several forms, including mother-daughter relationships, mother responsibility, and mother choice. Mother choice involves recognizing that the current generation for mothers is the first in history to have a choice of whether to become a mother. Male leaders may be less sensitive to the full importance of this historical event, and may not be able to help women in a group openly discuss the meaning and responsibility of choice that is placed on women today. Mother responsibility refers to the societal responsibility placed on women for the state of the culture, from child rearing to keeping the family together, to providing the nurturance and peace making to the conflicts of families and communities. Women who elect not to become mothers, who choose to have employment out of the home, or who do not provide nurturing may experience considerable guilt. Few men are criticized for failing to be home and to nurture, but women who select alternative directions are often criticized and feel great guilt about their choices. The third area, mother-daughter conflicts, also are situations not experienced by men, but are common to women, and therefore may be more appropriately addressed within a group setting that provides understanding and empathy for the experience. The women's group may be much more facilitative of each of these three areas of mothering concerns than groups led by men or groups that have men as clients, because the level of acceptance and support needed may be unavailable from men who have not shared in the common situation that women have.

An alternative position to the all-women's groups has been taken by Schoenholtz-Read (1996), who has identified the mixed-gender therapy groups as the treatment of choice for women. She has acknowledged the potential benefits of an all-women group, including providing warmth and support and being more facilitative in developing a greater consciousness of women's issues and problems of sex-role stereotyping that has occurred in their lives. On the other hand, Schoenholtz-Read has reported that there is no research in the literature that clearly demonstrates this superiority or benefit. Instead, Schoenholtz-Read has suggested that the focus should be not on the gender of the leader or the members, but on the ability of the group to provide benefit, to confront gender issues in the group, and have group leaders who can be feminists and work in mixed-gender groups.

Schoenholtz-Read (1996), in her review of literature addressing gender-role research in small groups, has reported that the results are mixed on the impact of the sex of the group members as an influence of the members' behavior in groups. If a group is comprised of several men and a few or only one woman, for example, the woman is disadvantaged, because rather than being responded to as an individual, she more likely will experience role entrapment. The opposite was found to be true for men, because when they are in the minority or the only male, they do better on tasks and become more independent and autonomous. Schoenholtz-Read reported that when gender balance occurs, there is little impact of the group on members' sex-role stereotype behavior, but that each gender exaggerates their stereotype when they are in the minority. The important consideration may be the leader's sensitivity to gender issues, the leader's level of skill development and credentials, and the members' sex-role identity and characteristics (feminine, masculine, or androgynous).

In addressing gender issues in group counseling and therapy, Schoenholtz-Read (1996) indicated that an understanding of gender and the implications that go with the concept of gender is an important consideration for group leaders: "If we view the psychotherapy group as a place where members bring their own personal history, conflicts, and suffering as well as the place where members bring social role issues associated with gender, one of the major tasks in group psychotherapy is to identify those conflicts related uniquely to the individual and those patterns based on culture" (p. 227). As new social roles have developed, counselors and therapists encounter women dealing with many of the same issues that in the past were the focus of males, including competition and aggression, achievement and satisfaction concerns related to work and employment, and changes in family structure. Since gender identity is also a power issue, it is necessary for group counselors and therapists to attend to power imbalances within the group setting and to be sensitive to how relationships within the group, as well as outside, impact the members. Yalom (1995) has identified the importance of the group to provide an opportunity for a corrective recapitulation, and Schoenholtz-Read has indicated that the therapy group may provide for the restructuring—the correcting—of culturally embedded responses to learned gender roles. By having a mixed-gender group, the participants have the opportunity, under the skillful leadership of a gender-sensitive counselor or therapist, to have more learning experiences that will more closely mirror real-life situations. This will allow for a greater use of the group membership for discussions, modeling, role-playing, and other more natural opportunities to develop new and rewarding gender role characteristics.

The mixed-gender group provides a number of advantages for women who are dealing with issues related to gender identity. One is the opportunity for women to be able to "confront interpersonal conflicts and dilemmas related to gendered behavior and sex-role stereotypes" (Schoenholtz-Read, 1996, p. 229) by having men and women in a safe environment where there is an opportunity to discuss concerns and issues. Members can be themselves, express their problems and desires, and explore their confusion about sex-role identity concerns. Although Schoenholtz-Read was mostly attending to the issues of women's gender issues in the group format, the same safe environment would allow men to describe their concerns and the difficulties they have in the changing world of roles and responsibilities. Men are also impacted by changing social roles, and the opportunity to express fears of economic responsibility, changing parenting roles, and corporate demands and expectations can be helpful to men in a mixed-gender group that provides for safety in discussing gender issues.

MEN IN GROUPS

Goldberg (1979) has reported that therapy is an unmasculine process and one that is foreign to most males, because it more closely mirrors traditional female gender characteristics than it does male gender characteristics. Therapy requires that those seeking the service acknowledge they cannot manage their own problems. Also, men are taught to be tough and invulnerable to protect themselves from those who would take advantage of their weaknesses, but in therapy they must present their weaknesses and expose their vulnerabilities. Therapy clients must be dependent on another person, for an extended period of time, and they will be encouraged—demanded—to use affective language and explore emotional contexts of their being, rather than rely on rational problem solving. They will learn that therapy requires personal review, contemplation, and consideration rather than action and immediate answers; it also involves spending money on an intangible product. Many men have been taught that they are responsible for knowing what direction is the correct one to take, that taking action resolves problems, that being in charge is the manly/responsible thing to do, and that staying emotionally distanced allows for greater control over situations. In therapy, all these issues become topsy-turvy and unbalanced. Men may have to explore ways in which their cherished beliefs are founded on distorted premises and motivations, learn that action often is not what is called for, and accept that emotional intimacy may develop between the client and the therapist, as well as other members of the group. Such prospects are potentially scary for men considering therapy.

Group counseling and therapy have been identified as being perhaps the most helpful and appropriate way to facilitate men's entry into the therapeutic arena (Andronico,

1996). Andronico has reported that groups—therapeutic, educational, supportive—are particularly facilitative as men face issues of transition, stress, and identity, and that group therapy is the treatment of choice for today's male. The group provides the opportunity to have support, learn the universality of problems men experience, have a network of experiences that allow for exploring new ways of being and doing, and even have a safe environment for developing intimacy without it leading to misunderstanding or confusion. Groups have been used to help men get in touch with their spiritual side, to be in a community in which they will not be shamed or ridiculed for how they are or what they think, to be a place where they can express vulnerability without fear of attack, and to experience mentoring and learning opportunities not available to men in general social settings. Further, since group work is cost efficient, it appeals to the practical side of men. Groups provide the opportunity for men to experience the therapeutic factors described by Yalom (1995): the instillation of hope, the recognition of the universality of problems men experience, the development of sources for information, the discovery of a place where altruism may be enacted and the corrective recapitulation of early learning experiences can be reenacted, and the development of cohesion, commitment, and self-disclosure.

Men experience a high level of alienation, and the community that can develop for men in a group is very powerful. The group can provide support for exploring the damages of addictions—such as alcohol, work, gambling, and sex—and also help redefine value systems that may be unhealthy or self-defeating, such as a commitment to materialism and wealth. To do all this, the group leader and members must be therapeutically flexible and modify traditional approaches to group counseling or therapy in such a way as to be sensitive to men's needs and abilities in the groups.

Jolliff and Horne (1996) have reported there are two major requirements for engaging a man in group counseling and therapy: an invitation to join and tell his story (present his problems) and an assurance there will be no shame or disgrace involved. Group leaders for men's groups should talk straight, demonstrate that they are trustworthy, and not reinforce the intellectualization of feelings. Jolliff and Horne described the male counseling or therapy group as one that helps members become aware of male socialization issues and the potential effects these have on men in general. Leaders should be willing to share the power of the group, rather than expect to dominate it, and should demonstrate self-confidence, competence, and expertise—all characteristics men seek in other men they trust. Usually, men's groups have a focus on short-term and action therapies, such as brief therapy, cognitive-behavioral techniques, and behavior management programs.

Leaders of men's groups should be sensitive to the need to do work around shame, guilt, abandonment, grief, fear, dependency, and anger, but not be afraid of any of these emotional states. New leaders often worry about the expression of anger, but soon come to realize that the leader and the members of the group can, should, and will take care of themselves, and that with the exploration of anger, most often what is uncovered is grief and fear. Masculine nurturing is important for men in groups, and leaders need to know how to help members find the support and encouragement as well as the mentors and role models necessary for mature masculinity to develop.

Male leaders must assess and be cognizant of their own beliefs about males. This includes empowering male clients, because much of male hostility and violence comes from feelings of powerlessness—a particularly important topic, as men have been told they "have all the power" but yet don't feel powerful themselves. Also, leaders need to know how to validate the self-sacrifices men have made, because there is often little recognition today for their contributions. What men originally thought of as responsibility and sacrifice, such as working long hours in a job that may not be fulfilling, may now be redefined as a fault, such as being called a "workaholic" instead of a responsible breadwinner and husband. Related to this is the importance of emphasizing self-care, including physical, mental, spiritual, and emotional areas. The work should be wholistic.

Men in groups show great growth and awareness when they are invited to "tell their stories," particularly as they describe times when they decided it was important to push feelings away, to stop experiencing life emotionally. This often ties back to family of origin issues, and in particular to father-son relationships, which are important to explore. It is important to help men realize that their strengths, their gifts, come from their wounds; this reframe is powerful and allows members to move from grief to pride.

If there is a commitment to working with men, to having the process of group work be invitational rather than blaming, then there are ample opportunities. Men's groups may be operational through other services, including correctional/prison work, Alcoholics Anonymous, employee assistance programs through business and industry, church and community groups in local settings, and college and university settings. It is important to be aware that most often, men do not go to the groups—the groups need to come to men, to be offered where they are and when they can attend.

Once the group is offered and operational, it is important for the leader to avoid stereotypical or sexist attitudes toward men and, instead, recognize that men can become supportive, nurturing, and open. It is often the leader who blocks the development of the group by assuming men will behave in a stereotypical way rather than with authenticity and honesty. To help the therapeutic work proceed, the leader and members need to model mature male relationships. An ongoing group, with some men coming as others are leaving, provides the opportunity for men who have been in the group longer to model appropriate communications of thoughts and feelings.

A male group changes when a woman or women enter the group. It is our experience that men can develop mature and clear communication patterns, but if women are introduced to the group, the men often resort back to competitiveness and direct an inappropriate amount of their attention to the women. Men have the opportunity of being more genuine in an all-male group. Men's groups present a special type of group, but one that is rewarding and enjoyable to conduct.

PERSONS OF COLOR: THE MULTICULTURAL GROUP

Whites, Asians, African Americans, Latinos, and Native Americans enter a counseling or therapy group as unique individuals as well as members of a unique culture. In working with groups in which the members are from a culture other than the group leader's culture, the leader is likely to discover the experience to be rewarding and challenging. As discussed earlier in this chapter, multicultural groups can be expected to mirror the

larger society (i.e., relationship patterns common to the larger society will surface during the life of the group and become apparent in the behavior of group members, such
as issues that surround the dominant-subordinate relationship experiences encountered
by those group members who have been marginalized in society).

To be an effective group leader, one must recognize various cultural factors (e.g.,
degree of emotional expressiveness, views about gender and age, and time orientation)
that appear during the course of group work. These factors can have a profound effect
on the dynamics of the group, which in turn may determine whether the group can
achieve its expressed goals. It is equally if not more important for the group leader to
operate from the perspective of viewing multicultural groups as offering each member
as well as the leader himself or herself an opportunity to personally grow in ways that
can only be achieved because these groups possess a wealth of interpersonal resources.
Too often, the novice White group leader enters a multicultural group with a sense of
dread, fearing that he or she will not be "sensitive enough," rather than tempering such
concerns with the understanding that each member, beginning with the first session,
injects into the group cultural beliefs that potentially make a strong, positive contribution to the curative factors inherent in the group process. For example, common middle-
class White values of individuality and competition may be balanced by common
African American values that reflect an interest in communal work (Sue & Sue, 1999).
Such "cultural positives" are the rule rather than the exception in group work.

Several models exist that can be used to better understand both the cultural
dynamics of multicultural groups and to serve as a guide in terms of relevant issues to
look for during the course of group work. One such model was developed by Jones
(1985), who suggested that in working with oppressed group members, four factors
should be kept in mind: members' reactions to the oppression, influences that members' culture has had on them, influences that the majority culture has had on them, and
each member's personal experience and endowment. It is important to note that this last
factor may prove more significant to any or all members of the group than the other
three factors and may turn out to play a more significant role in the effectiveness of the
group counseling or therapy than the individual's racial identity.

Recently, Arredondo (1999) and colleagues (Arredondo et al., 1996) listed several premises that support the need for multicultural competencies. The following represents an adaptation of four of these premises to group work:

- All group counseling and therapy is cross-cultural.
- Group counseling and therapy occurs in an interpersonal context affected by
  institutional and societal biases and norms.
- Group members that White group leaders are least prepared to serve are from
  Asian, African American, Latino, and Native American cultures.
- Group counseling and therapy are culture-bound fields.

Finally, Arredondo and Glauner (1992) presented a global means by which to
conceptualize the multicultural group (i.e., Personal Identity Model: A, B, C Dimensions). According to Arredondo (1999), the model "describes multiple fixed and flexible dimensions that may contribute to an individual's sense of identity and worldview

within a sociopolitical and historical context" (p.105). The model is made up of three dimensions. The *A Dimension* pertains to a group member's age, culture, ethnicity, gender, language, physical/mental well being, race, sexual orientation, and social class. The *B Dimension* is made up of educational background, geographic location, hobbies/recreational interest, military experiences, relationship status, religion/spirituality, work experience, and health care practices/beliefs. The *C Dimension* pertains to historical moments/era.

According to Arredondo and colleagues (1996), the model offers advantages to a group leader working with any counseling therapy group. First, the large number of factors comprising the dimensions allows a group leader to "connect" with members via numerous topics of importance. Second, the dimensions provide the leader with a means to reframe the typical view of cultural differences. Using this model to facilitate group processing, the novice leader comes to realize that Asians, African Americans, Latinos, and Native Americans, who are culturally different from Whites, are in fact different from one another. Simply stated, the lesson to be learned and profited from in mastering multicultural group work skills is that all group counseling and therapy is cross-cultural.

SUMMARY

There appear to be two positions on the issue of why persons with backgrounds that are diverse from the majority population participate less in counseling and therapy, including group counseling and group therapy. One of the positions is that potential clients are resistant to therapy and do not appreciate the opportunity they have to benefit from counseling services. This approach places responsibility on the potential client for fitting into counseling or therapy and assumes that all clients have the potential to benefit from services if they will avail themselves of it. The clients, from this perspective, often are "thrown out with the bath water" because they cannot benefit from a service to which they do not apply or comply.

The second approach is often an attack on traditional counseling and therapy as being insensitive to and irrelevant for persons of diverse backgrounds. If counseling and therapy require attendance, talking, responding to the affective, moving toward risk taking and independence, and the sharing of intimate information among strangers, then many, if not most, of the culturally different will refuse to participate. More and more, the question arises: Why is therapy not more adaptive to the needs of the people most in need of help? The answers range from criticism that providers lack sensitivity, to prejudice and bias, to the unsuitability of the techniques, including language barriers, setting problems, and differences in value systems.

We are encouraging a coming together of the positions—a recognition that most providers and trainers are very committed to helping and to service, for they have devoted their lives to being helpful and therapeutic to people in need. On the other hand, they do need to be sensitive to the ways in which persons from other cultures and background experiences do not benefit from some of the traditional offerings of service. It behooves both sides to work toward identifying the most effective ways of being helpful, to learn what of the current models works best, and then make adaptations and considerations that will result in therapy being more facilitative for all involved.

REFERENCES

Acosta, F. X., & Yamamoto, J. (1984). The utility of group work practice for Hispanic Americans. *Social Work with Groups, 7*, 63–73.

Andronico, M. (1996). *Men in groups: Insights, interventions, psychoeducational work.* Washington, DC: American Psychological Association.

Arredondo, P. (1999). Multicultural counseling competencies as tools to address oppression and racism. *Journal of Counseling & Development, 77*, 102–108.

Arredando, P., & Glauner, T. (1992). *Personal dimensions of identity model.* Boston: Empowerment Workshops, Inc.

Arredando, P., Toporek, R., Brown, S. P., Jones, J., Locke, D. C., Sanchez, J., & Standler, H. (1996). Operationalization of the multicultural counseling competencies. *Journal of Multicultural Counseling and Development, 24*, 42–78.

Baca, L. M., & Koss-Choino, J. D. (1997). Development of a culturally responsive group counseling model for Mexican American adolescents. *Journal of Multicultural Counseling and Development, 25*, 130–141.

Bernardez, T. (1996). Women's therapy groups as the treatment of choice. In B. DeChant (Ed.), *Women and group psychotherapy.* New York: Guilford.

Brown, J. A. (1984). Group work with low-income Black youths. *Social Work with Groups, 7*, 111–124.

Chu, J. & Sue, S. (1984). Asian/Pacific-Americans and group practice. *Social Work with Groups, 7*, 23–26.

Cross, W. E., Parham, T. A., & Helms, J. E. (1991). The stages of Black identity development: Nigrescence models. In R. L. Jones (Ed.), *Black psychology* (3rd ed.). Hampton, VA: Cobbs & Henry.

D'Andrea, M., & Arredondo, P. (1999, March). Promoting human dignity and development through diversity. *Counseling Today, 16*, 22.

DeLucia-Waack, J. (1996). Multiculturalism is inherent in all group work. *Journal for Specialists in Group Work, 21*, 218–223.

Edwards, E. D., & Edwards, M. E. (1984). Group work practice with American Indians. *Social Work with Groups, 7*, 7–21.

Gladding, S. T. (1999). *Group work: A counseling specialty.* Upper Saddle River, NJ: Prentice-Hall.

Goldberg, H. (1979). *The new male.* New York: William Morrow.

Helms, J. E. (1984). Toward a theoretical explanation of the effects of race on counseling: A Black and White model. *The Counseling Psychologist, 21*, 487–513.

Helms, J. E. (1990). *Black and White racial identity: Theory, research and practice.* Westport, CT: Greenwood.

Holcomb-McCoy, C., & Myers, J. (1999). Multicultural competence and counselor training: A national survey. *Journal of Counseling and Development, 77*, 294–302.

Jackson, S. (1992). Team composition in organizational settings: Issues in managing an increasingly diverse workforce. In S. Worchel, W. Wood, & J. Simpson (Eds.), *Group process and productivity.* Newbury Park, CA: Sage.

Jolliff, D. L., & Horne, A. (1996). Group counseling for middle-class men. In M. Andronico (Ed.), *Men in groups: Insights, interventions, psychoeducational work.* Washington, DC: American Psychological Association.

Jones, A. C. (1985). Psychological functioning in Black Americans: A conceptual guide for use in psychotherapy. *Psychotherapy, 22*, 363–369.

Mays, V. M., & Albee, G. W. (1992). Psychotherapy and ethnic minorities. In D. K. Freedheim (Ed.), *History of psychotherapy.* Washington, DC: American Psychological Association.

Merta, R. (1995). Group work: Multicultural perspectives. In J. G. Ponterotto, J. M. Casas, L. A. Suzuki, & C. M. Alexander (Eds.), *Handbook of multicultural counseling.* Thousand Oaks, CA: Sage.

Patterson, C. H. (1996). Multicultural counseling: From diversity to universality. *Journal of Counseling and Development, 74*, 227–235.

Pederson, P. (1976). A model for training mental health workers in cross-cultural counseling. In J. Westmeyer & B. Madday (Eds.), *Culture and Mental Health.* The Hague, The Netherlands: Mouton.

Schoenholtz-Read, J. (1996). Sex-role issues: Mixed-gender therapy groups as the treatment of choice. In B. DeChant (Ed.), *Women and group psychotherapy.* New York: Guilford.

Sciarra, D. T. (1999). *Multiculturalism in counseling.* Itasca, IL: Peacock.

Sue, D. W., & Sue, D. (1999). *Counseling the culturally different: Theory and practice.* New York: Wiley.

Sue, S. (1983). Ethnic minorities in psychology: A reexamination. *American Psychologist, 38,* 583–592.

Sue, S., & Zane, N. (1987). The role of culture and cultural techniques in psychotherapy. *American Psychologist, 42,* 37–45.

Yalom, I. (1995). *The theory and practice of group psychotherapy* (4th ed.). New York: Basic Books.

CHAPTER FIVE

GROUPS THAT WORK

Research and Evaluation Considerations in Group Counseling and Group Psychotherapy

Group counseling and therapy are a mainstay of mental health services, making up an integral part of treatment programs in hospitals and prisons. Similarly, group counseling is a primary component of school counseling services. Many private practitioners or health service personnel in community service agencies turn to group work as an important therapeutic tool and one that provides a needed treatment alternative to individual therapy or pharmacological approaches to helping people.

Clearly, we are advocates for group work; we would not have undertaken a project such as the completion of this book without a belief in the power and effectiveness of group. Yet, we still must ask the question: Does group work really work? Is group counseling and therapy an effective means for providing needed help to persons experiencing emotional and behavioral problems? Is it on a par with individual treatments? Are group approaches to mental health treatment cost efficient? Do managed care companies, insurance and other third-party payers, and taxpayers who underwrite community and school counseling and therapy services get their money's worth? How is one to know?

It is very important to ask questions about group counseling and therapy effectiveness, cost efficiency, and efficacy, primarily from an ethical stance but also from an economic approach. Ethically, human service providers are expected to use interventions that have a demonstrated ability to provide help to those in need. Group counselors and therapists are obligated to understand not only theory and clinical interventions but also how well the various alternative models of treatment work to maximize personal development and to alleviate the pain and suffering of the clients served. To be familiar with the current knowledge base about treatment effectiveness is simply expected of all professionals. Additionally, third-party payers—whether insurance companies, managed care facilities, hospitals, or taxpayers—have a right to expect that the services they are

Note: An earlier version of the first half of this chapter appeared as an article by A. Horne and R. Rosenthal entitled "Research in Group Work" in the *Journal for Specialists in Group Work, 22* (1997): 228–240. © ACA. Used with permission from the American Counseling Association. No further reproduction authorized without written permission of the American Counseling Association.

paying for are being evaluated and that the services are helping as well as, or better than, alternative interventions.

This chapter presents a brief history of research in group work, followed by an overview of some of the current research knowledge of group counseling and therapy. It concludes with recommendations for program evaluation that group counselors and practitioners may apply to their own practices.

RESEARCH IN GROUP WORK: A BRIEF HISTORICAL REVIEW

Examples of the importance of working with groups can be traced back to earliest civilization. On the other hand, group work as a form of mental health service to be practiced by recognized counselors and therapists is a fairly recent phenomenon, dating back to the beginning of the 1900s. Since the beginning of group work as a human development and mental health service, research has comprised but a small part of the attention given to the overall field of group counseling and therapy. In fact, at a recent meeting of the American Psychological Association, Rex Stockton, the president-elect of the Division of Group Psychology and Group Psychotherapy, noted that there has been more written about the lack of research in group therapy than has been written about the actual research itself.

Horne and Rosenthal (1997) began their review of the history of research in group counseling and therapy with the period from 1900 to 1920, and described Joseph Pratt's early experiences with group work. Pratt, a Boston physician, initiated a treatment group for patients with tuberculosis. The initial goal of the group was efficiency, with the expectation that treating several patients at once would be more economical than treating them individually. Pratt soon recognized, however, the power of the group, and as Fuhriman and Burlingame (1994, p. 4) reported, "He attributed the success of the classes to patients' sense of identification with one another, their hope of recovery and faith in the class, the methods, and the physician." Although Pratt did not develop a research program to evaluate the effectiveness of the group, other than patient self-report of improvement and physician-observed changes, he did make a major contribution to the development of group work. Pratt was able to identify several of the curative factors of group work—hope, identification with others (universality), self-disclosure, and acceptance—which are still at the core of effective group therapy today (Yalom, 1995).

Almost a decade after Pratt's original group work in 1907, the first recorded application of a group approach to the school environment was described by Jesse B. Davis, a school principal in Grand Rapids, Michigan. Davis conducted groups in the school that were designed to assist students in making educational, vocational, and moral decisions, but, like Pratt's work, there was not an evaluation component involved, other than Davis's contention that the groups were helpful to young students in making decisions about their lives. Another proponent of group work in schools was Frank Parsons, often cited as the founder of the modern counseling profession because of his advocacy of guidance and counseling services for public school students in

Boston. He introduced career and vocational development groups that were prominent in his lifetime, and continued well after his death in 1908. Parsons's goal was the efficient delivery of career development services, and though he advocated the group approach, he did not conduct evaluations of the effectiveness of the intervention.

Psychiatrist Cody Marsh began offering "inspirational" sessions for his inpatient population in 1909. Scheidlinger (1993, p. 2) reported that Marsh said, "By the crowd they have been broken, by the crowd they shall be healed." His work developed into what would today be referred to as psychoeducational groups for hospital personnel. Like others before him, Marsh believed in the power of the group interaction to serve as a healing force, but as others before him—and after him as well—there was no attempt to evaluate the outcome of his group services beyond his personal observations that change occurred.

Throughout the remainder of the early 1900s, educational and vocational groups continued to be offered in schools and some applications occurred in medical settings. However, attention to group work as a treatment approach diminished with the advent of World War I, except that in the military community there was an expanded emphasis on teamwork in the form of work and task groups (Gladding, 1995).

The period from 1920 to 1930 saw an increased use of group counseling and therapy and the beginnings of some measurement of group impact. Edward Lazell, for example, presented lectures on Freudian psychology to groups of schizophrenic patients. Apparently there was a powerful impact on the patients, some of whom had been considered untreatable previously. Fuhriman and Burlingame (1994) described the therapeutic factors of universality and social interaction being core to Lazell's treatment, and, anecdotally, there was a report by the medical and nursing staff of a reduction in the use of sedatives by the patients. Thus, an outcome measurement of a group treatment had occurred. In an effort to determine whether the group had an effect on patients, researchers began observing behavioral changes as well as medication reduction, with the finding that patients did, indeed, progress rather than regress and did become more autonomous in their behavior. These findings led to further development of observations by practitioners to measure the impact of group interventions. There was a period of descriptions of group case studies and qualitative descriptions of change that occurred when patients were treated in groups. The anecdotal records expanded from physicians to include observations by other medical staff, such as nurses, as well as family member reports and patient self-reports.

During the decade of the 1920s, Alfred Adler began conducting groups for families and children (Dagley, 2000; Gladding, 1995). He used a group approach to help families identify relationships between children's problems and family experiences and history. Adler emphasized the social nature of people to support a group treatment model, and his approach was followed by one of his students, Rudolph Dreikurs, who applied Adler's group approach to alcoholics (Dagley, 2000; Fuhriman & Burlingame, 1994). The Adlerian group approach did not rely on carefully controlled research programs for the external validation of the effectiveness of their treatment. Such external evaluation was considered unnecessary because it was believed that change was clearly observable to the group leader. During the same time period that Adler was developing group treatments for families in Vienna, Jacob Moreno, also in Vienna, was working with groups to develop what would later become known as *psychodrama* (Scheidlinger, 1993). Again, no measurement of the impact of the group, beyond leader observation and reporting, was conducted.

A growing interest in small groups occurred during the 1920s, but the interest was from scholars in the social sciences area instead of the therapeutic community. All-port (1924), for example, studied small groups to determine how individual behavior changed from solitary events to group events, and concluded that group interaction impacted the quantity of people's behaviors, but not the quality.

The contributions of Allport and other social science researchers continued and increased in the period of from 1930 to 1945. Considerable laboratory research was conducted to examine the impact of social influence on people's behavior, and methods of influencing people through social involvement and group persuasion was examined. Attempts were made to explore the level of conviction people had regarding beliefs, and the extent to which those beliefs could be influenced by peer group pressure. In part, these investigations were tied to the development of war propaganda. Research in both Europe and the United States, although not being oriented toward group counseling and therapy, was investigating how group influence could change people's opinions on matters of prejudice, anti-Semitism, and war.

Moreno moved from Austria to the United States and in 1932 wrote the first book on group psychotherapy (reported in Fuhriman & Burlingame, 1994). In the same time period, Paul Schilder was conducting research on the impact of the universality of the group on the individual member. The focus was the impact on the individual and how that person changed, rather than on the group process that led to the change. In both Moreno's and Schilder's work, the object of study was the individual within the group, not the dynamics of the group (reported in Scheidlinger, 1993). The focus on studying the dynamics of the group to impact change and the use of group resources as a therapeutic factor would have resulted in different research than was accomplished during this period.

Also during this period, S. R. Slavson, an educator and self-taught therapist, began offering activity therapy groups for children and adolescents. He did attempt to measure the impact of the group experience and reported that young people could demonstrate as much change through activity group sessions as they could through individual therapy treatments. Scheidlinger (1993) reported that Slavson's work was quite impressive and resulted in the increased application of group procedures for treatment of children and adolescents. Although there was considerable interest in group applications of treatments to children and adolescents, the focus was still on individual change of group participants rather than on the dynamics of the group that influenced the change.

One area that did experience increased interest in the power of group dynamics occurred in the work of Kurt Lewin (1940), who began the study of *intragroup relations,* later called *training groups,* or just *T-groups.* Lewin studied the impact and characteristics of the group leader that influenced change and growth on the part of group members. Further, by maintaining descriptions of groups, Lewin came to describe predictable stages of the group, as well as markers of group change that could be studied. Finally, he examined how specific interventions within the group format resulted in change for specific types of group members, demonstrating that the leadership style of a group member could influence particular members' behavior.

Toward the end of this period of group development, Moreno founded the American Society for Group Psychotherapy and Psychodrama, and Slavson founded the American Group Psychotherapy Association, with the association publishing the *International Journal of Group Psychotherapy*. The two movements, and particularly the publication of the journal, resulted in expanded growth in interest in group work as well as a considerable increase in the quantity and quality of group research (Scheidlinger, 1993).

The next era of group work, from 1945 to 1960, saw extensive growth in the use of groups. World War II resulted in a significant increase in the use of groups, and William Menninger, who was the U.S. Chief of Military Psychiatry, implemented a group format for working with large numbers of military personnel requiring treatment. Although still not conducting research on the effectiveness of the group work done, Menninger cited his use of group practice as one of the military's major contributions to civilian psychiatry (Scheidlinger, 1993).

During the 1950s, there was a proliferation of empirical research, particularly regarding group structure, group climate, leadership variables, and group setting conditions. Experimental control group research increased, and the study of institutional populations increased dramatically (Fuhriman & Burlingame, 1994).

There was also a trend toward greater applications of group work in schools, as counseling began replacing guidance as a primary function of school personnel (Gazda, 1989). Educators continued to recognize the importance of assisting students in selecting careers but also began to focus more on applying knowledge from group psychotherapy and individual therapy to the school setting. Research on group counseling in schools demonstrated that counseling could lead to students' increased satisfaction with school, help students obtain higher academic achievement, and facilitate improved family relationships as a result of school counseling focusing on family issues (Ohlsen, 1971, 1974).

Beyond the schools, group therapy became a model of intervention in veterans' hospitals. Not only was treatment offered but there were also ongoing attempts to evaluate the effectiveness of treatment programs, resulting in an increase in research sponsored by the federal government. Both in veterans' hospitals and schools attempts were made to determine what forms of groups provided what types of responses, as group leaders sought group interventions that were more effective. This was particularly important, given the extent of emotional and physical trauma the military personnel had experienced in war, and that was requiring rehabilitation after the war.

Interactional dynamics of group work were still to be studied, as well as the counseling and therapeutic models being explored in the schools and hospitals. Lewin's work at the National Training Laboratories in Bethel, Maine, resulted in research examining training groups (T-groups). One aspect of their research demonstrated that group discussions were superior to individual interaction for changing people's ideas and behaviors (Gladding, 1995), demonstrating, in part, that the whole (the group) is greater than the sum of its parts (the individual). The group dynamics research led to further applications and evaluations of treatment programs as knowledge of how social interactions in groups could influence behavior change.

During the next era, from 1960 to 1980, the level of research in group treatment actually decreased from the previous period. Although there was extensive use of groups in societal settings, such as the use of encounter groups and T-groups in many communities (often without leaders having received relevant training to conduct the groups), the evaluation of group work declined. There was a period of antiscience sentiment in many universities and training centers and a period of endorsement of experiential activity over a focus on empirical study. Some have attributed the decrease in the emphasis on research and the increasing focus on experiential learning and participation to the social unrest that led to questioning of authority related to Viet Nam, the development of civil rights and desegregation, and the growth of the women's movement in the United States (Gladding, 1995).

In 1963, the Community Mental Health Act provided funding for 500 community mental health centers. This act took several years to move from a legislative action to actually providing services, but eventually it did lead to an increased demand for mental health services, including group treatment. Scheidlinger (1993) reported that this increased demand, combined with a shortage of well-trained group therapists, resulted in fewer long-term psychotherapy and more short-term psychoeducational outpatient groups being established. The focus of the new mental health centers was on behavioral control rather than personality reconstruction. With this change came a more focused examination of clearly defined outcome measures, examining specific behavioral change as a function of group involvement, and a turning away from exploring unconscious contributors to pathology, focusing more on developing behavioral change expectations.

During the 1970s, there was an increase in the amount of writing about group intervention and group counseling and therapy research. In the 1970s, 20 percent of the articles contained in the counseling literature were about group work, whereas in the 1950s, only 5 percent of the articles had been group related (Stockton & Morran, 1982). Yalom (1970) defined the curative factors of group work and described them and investigated the way in which leadership style in groups positively influenced group participants. He reported that individuals who were casualties of group treatments—those who not only failed to benefit but who also suffered losses—were responding to leaders who were authoritarian, confrontational, and aggressive. Ohlsen, another major contributor to research on group work in the 1970s, initiated a series of investigations documenting the rationale and importance of developmental group counseling as well as a model of teaching skills enhancement for developmental problems that had a major influence on group counseling in the United States (Ohlsen, 1971).

During the last era of group work, from 1980 through the present, Gazda (1989) continued to advance the developmental model of group counseling and therapy. The model asserts that there are stages of group work, and that these stages follow a prescribed pattern of development across groups and settings. Furthermore, there are skills that group leaders may use that are developmental in that they approach the group with specific interventions, depending on the needs and expectations of the group membership. Applied research on group factors affecting productivity increased during the 1980s.

In the 1980s, two books were published (Shaw, 1981; Steiner, 1986) that criticized group research as being too bound by the controls of the research laboratory—at best an artificial environment for studying group behavior that fails to reflect group practices in the real world. The settings where the groups took place (university research programs) and the past emphasis on artificially controlled conditions and experimental studies were seen as major limitations of group work. It was assumed that much of the earlier group work research was therefore not applicable to naturally occurring groups. There was a call for more field studies, and a set of problems were identified regarding resources (i.e., funding, time, and access to groups) that were to be incorporated into applied group studies (Wheelan, 1994). The plea for more research, field initiated and environmentally based, began to raise the consciousness of group researchers that, indeed, more research and evaluation was needed.

Research on group treatments over the past 10 years has been increasingly focused on very specific applications. There have been group studies on a wide range of problem areas, including group treatment of depression, eating disorders, couples therapy, behavioral change programs for children, support groups for specific disabilities, and bereavement groups for people of different ages. Outcome studies have included multiple comparison groups, comparing different group techniques for specific problem areas, thus allowing evaluation regarding "both general and differential efficacy of the groups format" (Fuhriman & Burlingame, 1994, p. 515). This means that group researchers learned more about what type of group interventions and techniques worked with what type of client under what conditions. Although these efforts are especially helpful in narrowing assumptions of generalized efficiency to a more limited population, much less effort is now concentrated on gaining a basic understanding of group dynamics and composition (Fuhriman & Burlingame, 1994; Wheelan, 1994). Researchers have moved from studying general characteristics of group dynamics to focusing much more on specific interventions related to limited group memberships. The focus of study has shifted from an emphasis on process research to an examination of outcome studies.

Following the trend toward examining specific groups in particular settings, there has been a notable increase in psychoeducational and counseling groups in the school setting, dealing with children's and adolescents' adjustment to divorce as well as study and social skills (Dagley, Gazda, Eppinger, & Stewart, 1994; Gladding, 1995). This increase in group work in schools has not necessarily been accompanied by increased research productivity, and the work is often performed with little evaluation. School evaluations often focus more on the level of satisfaction of the group leader and the members of the group than on evaluating whether change occurred.

Perhaps the clearest lesson from the group research over the past century is an acknowledgment of its complex nature. Group treatment effectiveness seems to have less to do with specific theoretical persuasion than to finding an optimum combination of pregroup training, patient characteristics, therapeutic factors, group structure, group stage of development, and appropriateness of the interventions selected. The problem that remains is that therapeutic factors are complex and hard to control, experimental comparisons are difficult, and there is a lack of research in group work in which clear definitions of constructs or of treatment methods are provided. Methodological problems in group work are rather widespread, with few studies defining their constructs, a paucity of research projects that include long-term follow-ups, and considerable inconsistency in the dependent variables being studied, thus providing less opportunity for comparability of research (Burlingame, Kircher, & Taylor, 1994; Gazda, 1989).

ARE GROUP TREATMENTS EFFECTIVE?

Over the past 30 years, a number of studies and reviews of studies have shown, in general, that individuals treated in groups experience change that is superior to no-treatment control group members and that when the group treatment is appropriate to the problem being examined, the group treatment is at least comparable to individual therapy (Emrick, 1975; Kaul & Bednar, 1986; Lieberman, 1976). Toseland and Siporin (1986), reviewing 32 studies comparing individual and group formats, found the two modalities equally effective in 75 percent of the cases, with groups being more effective in 25 percent of those studied. Although there have been exceptions associated with these findings, Fuhriman and Burlingame (1994) suggested that individual treatment has been shown to be more effective only in studies in which the group format was used because it simply provided a convenient and economical way to present material. Although the specific strengths of groups were not measured in the studies cited, the basic efficiency and effectiveness of groups has been established across an array of disorders and treatment models.

Piper (1994) pointed out, however, that group work is not always the best choice for each client, as there may be circumstances that require one-on-one interventions. Likewise, not all group members are as powerfully influenced by group dynamics and group process. Thus, although the overall effectiveness of group work may be beneficial on most members, some may benefit considerably more than others. According to Bostwick (1987) and Freeman and Munro (1988), a combination of individual and group therapy often produces better outcomes than either one alone. This combined approach has been found especially effective for those diagnosed with eating disorders (Bohanske & Lemberg, 1987; Franko, 1987; Hendren, Atkins, Sumner, Calvin, & Barber, 1987) and for persons diagnosed with borderline personality disorders (Slavinsky-Holey, 1983). Recent studies have concentrated on different aspects of groups and how to create more effective groups. Several of the recent findings are described next.

Pregroup Training

Pregroup training means providing some type of preparation for members about to enter a group. The training may be in the form of written materials or audio- or videotaped presentations by the staff or by the individual counselor or therapist describing what to expect from the group. Pregroup training has been demonstrated to be effective for both group process and outcome. Using questionnaires at the end of each session, Yalom, Houts, Zimberg, and Rand (1967) found greater faith in therapy and more group and interpersonal interaction (using the Hill Interaction Matrix) for clients who had received pretraining compared to controls. Hilkey, Wilhelm, and Horne (1982) found progress toward goals improved with pregroup training, and France and Dugo (1985) reported that pretraining predicted better attendance in groups of psychiatric outpatients. In a quasiexperimental collaborative study between researchers and social workers who were trying to reduce dropout rates in groups for physically abusive men found that a single more extensive pregroup experience resulted in better attendance than shorter pregroup exercises that were spaced over a period of time.

Muller and Scott (1984) varied five pregroup training procedures and found written materials to be the most effective, whereas Lawe, Horne, and Taylor (1983) found verbally taped sessions to be preferable. Bowman and DeLucia (1993) reported that a cognitive-vicarious-experiential program of preparation is useful for skill building and providing information about therapy. Their research also supported the notion that pregroup preparation may assist beginning group leaders in understanding and developing confidence in their leadership abilities.

Yalom (1995) suggested that there does not seem to be unanimity about the best method for pregroup training, with written material, practice, role-plays, and watching videos all suggested as effective.

Structure

Rohde and Stockton (1994) have reported that structure can be introduced to a group either through pregroup training or through an in-group process using specific activities and leader management of the group process. Although structure was once thought to inhibit the natural developmental process of groups, Rohde and Stockton have suggested that structure early in the group's life offers an opportunity to slowly build safety and trust and to define boundaries. Caple and Cox (1989) found group cohesion increased in later group sessions when groups began with a structured exercise.

Stockton, Rohde, and Haughey (1992) demonstrated the effectiveness of group exercises to build early cohesion and to decrease the likelihood of members becoming avoidant as group time wears on. An interaction between developmental stages and context was found when structured interventions involving anger and intimacy were matched or mismatched with "storming and norming" stages. When content was matched with the stage of the group, anger and intimacy were seen as more appropriately expressed (Kivlighan, McGovern, & Corazzini, 1984).

Increased structure may mediate the effects of group composition and of leadership styles. For example, Hilkey and colleagues (1982) reported that providing increased structure early in the group experience resulted in experienced and inexperienced group leaders working at a similar pace. When working with unstructured groups, experienced leaders outpaced experienced group leaders in the stages of group development and in the behavioral gains made by group members. Horne and Matson (1977) found that providing an audio or video modeling experience similar in sound and appearance to the group membership and providing examples at the skill level of development of group members at the beginning of sessions for reducing speech and test anxiety resulted in superior change compared to four other models of group intervention. The interaction between structure, group composition, leader characteristics, and group stage is always complex. These will continue to be important variables in future research efforts.

Therapeutic Factors

Yalom (1970) proposed 11 curative or therapeutic factors in the group process: instillation of hope, universality, imparting information, altruism, corrective recapitulation of the primary family group, development of socializing techniques, imitative behavior, interpersonal learning, group cohesiveness, catharsis, and existential factors. Bloch, Reibstein, Crouch, Holyroyd, and Theman (1979), using critical incident questionnaires, offered additions to the curative factors that included acceptance (cohesion) and interpersonal action, vicarious learning, guidance, insight (self-understanding), and self-disclosure. Researchers examining the effectiveness of group treatments have confirmed that the factors identified by Yalom and by Bloch and associates are, indeed, important factors for change in group work.

Fuhriman and Burlingame (1994) suggested that the early pioneers of group work alluded to these curative factors in their own groups: hope (Pratt and Marsh), universality (Lazell), cohesion (Adler and Dreikurs), and recapitulation of the family (Wenders). The notion of the special factors creating the potential for healing in group work has been explored in a number of contexts.

Group cohesion is often considered the most important factor in predicting group success and individual goal attainment, although the term is not always clearly defined or understood, which leads to difficulty in conducting group research. Stokes, Fuehrer, and Childs (1983) and Yalom (1995), for example, have offered different definitions for *group cohesion*. Although it is a useful theoretical concept, research examining the construct has left questions about the nature or function unanswered.

Indications are that different therapeutic factors may be differentially important in different disorders and populations (Kaul & Bednar, 1986) and within different stages of group development. Kivlighan and Mullison (1988) found universality to be more important in early stages, whereas interpersonal learning was more important in later stages. More research is necessary to obtain clearer definitions and measurements of these constructs and to discern how they can be specifically introduced or enhanced in group work (Stockton et al., 1992).

Summary of Review of Research on Group Work

Throughout the review of group literature over the century, one observes repeated comments regarding the relative "youth" of the field of group work and related research. Kaul and Bednar (1986), however, took the position that group interventions have been around for close to 100 years and that the methodology selected for conducting research should be appropriate to the developmental level of group work; they promoted all levels of research in group work. The focus of research on group counseling and group therapy should include approaches ranging from descriptive to highly empirical controlled random research studies. Conducting research that addresses both group process and outcome, through more sophisticated qualitative methods of evaluating group work, is supported by Wheelan (1994) and Blythe and Rodgers (1993), and Chwalisz (1999). Kivlighan (1999), although supporting the call for increased use of qualitative methods in group therapy research, has also been developing increasingly sophisticated statistical measurement procedures for conducting group research—processes that could be accomplished only by the use of today's high-speed computers. Brower and Rose (1990) cited the need for more field and descriptive research, whereas Fuhriman and Burlingame (1994) have recommended that group leaders become familiar with Polkinghorne (1991) and Miles and Huberman (1984) as examples of rigor in qualitative methodology. More recently, Chwalisz (1999) has provided a newly developed qualitative method of studying process and outcome in groups, using the event phenomena approach.

Kaul and Bednar (1986) have indicated that experimental control and manipulation, which are essential for determining causation, are currently difficult or impossible to achieve in group counseling and therapy research. Piper (1994), however, requested that outcome studies not be abandoned in response to Kaul and Bednar's comments, but that both process and outcome factors, and their interactions, be investigated. Both approaches are necessary.

Some of the most complete and helpful assessments of both clinical and statistical significance are offered in Zimpfer's (1989, 1990a, 199b, 1991) topical reviews of group counseling and therapy treatments of midlife career change, divorce and separation, bulimia, and bereavement, and in Gazda's (1989) comprehensive analysis of group counseling research from 1938 to 1987, which included 641 studies. Helgeson and Cohen (1996) have discussed the contradictory findings on psychoeducational groups versus support groups, and have suggested directions for future research. Vandervoort and Fuhriman (1991) reviewed a variety of group treatments for depression across different populations with a variety of measures and reported the differential effectiveness of the different treatments. Group research has evolved in qualitative and quantitative ways, and provides for excitement and enthusiasm for future investigations.

PRACTITIONER-GENERATED RESEARCH

For too long there has been an artificial separation of research and practice, with the majority of group counseling and therapy research being conducted by university faculty in academic settings, and the practice being conducted by counselors, social workers, psychologists, and other mental health practitioners in applied settings. There are a number of factors currently operating to help change this dichotomous approach to group work.

First, there is a significant reduction in support for research in many academic institutions, as more administrators require faculty to find external funding for research. With less "in-house" financial support available, and with few opportunities for external funding for group research, faculty are seeking other ways of gaining access to groups for research purposes.

A second factor contributing to change is a greater focus on accountability in the workplace. As mental health services have come under greater influence of accountability by external funding sources, such as managed care and third-party insurance companies, there is a greater need to document the effectiveness of the treatments offered. Also, in school counseling programs there has been a reduction of support for counseling services, as schools have required increasing resources to meet the ever larger student population demands.

A third factor contributing to researchers and practitioners working more closely together is the growing recognition that research conducted in artificial settings, and practice conducted without evaluation, serve neither sector well. Thus, there is a growing national movement to have greater researcher and practitioner collaboration.

Riva (1999) and Kalodner (Kalodner & Riva, 1997) have described why researchers and practitioners should engage in greater collaboration. Riva described two methods used to conduct therapy research: the efficacy method and the effectiveness method. *Efficacy* involves having manualized treatments—the intervention carefully described in a manual, along with step-by-step procedures for each part of the intervention process. The sessions are limited to the number defined in the manual, and the exercises are carefully scripted. The efficacy method ensures that the delivery of the treatment is consistent, controls for extraneous variables, and reduces the influence of the group leader. The problem? There is very little generalizability to the real world, since very few practitioners conduct groups as they are spelled out in manual form. Also, it is difficult to identify group members who exactly fit the treatment specified in manual form, and group leaders lose interest very quickly in such a structured approach.

The alternative model described by Riva is the *effectiveness* model. The approach examines group treatments exactly as practitioners in the real world, using true group interventions, conduct them. Studies of effectiveness, however, are difficult for researchers because there is little control over extraneous variables. There is little control for what happens in the group, the orientation or leadership style of the group leader, the exercises that may—or may not—happen in session, the characteristics of the membership of the group, as well as the presenting problem of group members.

Riva has pointed out that both approaches are valuable for increasing the knowledge of how groups work. Although researchers prefer the more easily controlled and managed experimental approach of the efficacy model, few practitioners practice that way. And so Riva has recommended that researchers move toward greater collaboration with practitioners in order to develop, conduct, and examine group research that is more applicable and useful than some of previous efforts.

Group research conducted as practitioners practice it needs to go beyond just demonstrating effectiveness of the intervention, as measured by an outcome assessment. Although it is important to know whether persons experiencing anxiety report a reduction of symptoms, it is also crucial to know what happens in the group that leads to that reduction. Riva has recommended studying fewer groups in more detail, but this intensity requires a close working relationship between the practitioner and the researcher, because rather than completing brief "snapshots" of therapy, it is important to get the full picture of the process. By participating as colleagues on group projects, practitioners and researchers may bring together more and better ideas on how to conduct the research and also how to conduct the practice of group work—allowing a reciprocal benefit in the process.

Collaboration involves more than just having permission from the practitioner to evaluate components of the group. It also means working together closely to develop the appropriate questions to ask about how groups work, to design the study in order to address the problems and incidental events that may influence the outcome, to address how to recruit membership, to conduct analyses of data generated, and to write and edit manuscripts (Kalodner & Riva, 1997; Riva, 1999).

To bring about collaboration such as this will require that researchers leave the comfort of the university setting and reach out to practitioners to establish ongoing relationships. The focus should be on long-term collaboration, not brief one-shot experiences together, and moving toward more longitudinal and programmatic research studies rather than single-group approaches. Many agencies and practices will appreciate such involvement because they recognize the need to evaluate their work, yet usually lack the resources to maintain a research component of their own. Further, by working collaboratively in the agency or practice setting, the researcher will be able to share information about current knowledge and practice, perhaps conduct seminars and training sessions for staff, and in general be a facilitative resource rather than an "outsider" trying to get publishable data.

TRAINING RESEARCHERS

To develop researchers with the skills that Riva has advocated, it is important that the training programs that prepare group practitioners and researchers have this as an agenda in their academic programs. Stockton (1999) and Toth (Stockton & Toth, 1997) have discussed the negative images graduate students seem to have of research, reporting that many approach research training as something that has to be done and should be gotten through as quickly as possible so that students may then get about the important part: learning about practicing therapeutic skills.

Research often lags behind practice because research—with an empirical model and goal of controlling variables influencing therapy—attempts to carefully analyze and evaluate what occurs in clinical settings instead of generating new knowledge to share with practitioners (Hill & Corbett, 1993). Stockton (1999), though, has recommended that training in graduate school could take a very different approach. For starters, recognizing group research approaches along the continuum that Fuhriman and Burlingame (1994, p. 28) have suggested would help: "From descriptive (case study and survey), through relational (correlation), to more controlled methods of investigation (quasi-experimental and experimental)."

According to Stockton (1999) environmental factors—what goes on in the research community—influences graduate students' attitudes toward research training. He has therefore recommended that faculty serve as role models and demonstrate positive research skills and attitudes. This is difficult if the faculty perceive research as "something that has to be done to be promoted" rather than as a function of their work and a reason for being in the field. One way to address this issue is through the use of research teams.

Stockton (1999) has described efforts to incorporate several faculty and graduate students to work together on problems of group research. By giving team members developmentally appropriate roles on the research team, sharing with them the excitement and enthusiasm of the work, and having students experience the close contact with faculty as they work out the details of conducting research can be a powerful learning opportunity. As Stockton and Hulse (1983, p. 304) have described, "Unless students have active contact with role models whose efforts exemplify research as a dynamic process subject to revisions, false starts, and intuitive hunches, it will be difficult to view it as the extremely pleasurable process it can be."

Research teams at the University of Georgia follow the model advocated by Stockton. One or more faculty members identify research areas of interest and invite students to be on the team, beginning with entry-level master's degree students, and including graduate students at all levels of experience. The team meets weekly, reviews the current state of knowledge of the field, identifies questions and problems to be addressed, develops relationships with appropriate agencies (as recommended by Riva), and collaboratively develops the research design. All members of the team contribute at the level of their knowledge and experience, and all share in the work and recognition that goes with the project. A recent example has included two faculty (John Dagley and Andy Horne) working with students to review two decades of research on prevention groups to be used with children and adolescents. Further, we have been working collaboratively with two faculty (Robert Conyne and Robert Wilson) and their students at the University of Cincinnati who are studying prevention groups with adults. The two teams have examined more than 30,000 articles and the students and faculty have presented several papers for publication and at four national conventions. We have also experienced a positive mentoring relationship, learned about real-world research through collaboration and teamwork, and developed an exciting positive attitude toward applied group research.

MEASURING GROUP PROCESS AND OUTCOME

One of the difficulties of conducting group research is finding appropriate measures of the process and outcome of group work. Fuhriman and Burlingame (1994) edited the *Handbook of Group Psychotherapy: An Empirical and Clinical Synthesis,* an excellent resource for identifying both methods and measures of evaluating group outcome and process. The chapters address conceptual and methodological foundations of group work as well as examine specific components of group counseling and therapy: client variables, therapist variables, structure, interactional analyses measures, group development assessment, examination of therapeutic factors, and work with special populations. By using this excellent text as a reference source, readers will be able to identify measurement methods for almost all evaluation projects in group counseling and group therapy.

DeLucia-Waack (1997, 1999) has identified measures of group outcome and process that have been examined for reliability and validity and that have good psychometric qualities. She has suggested that researchers selecting the measures should pay attention to the construct being measured by the instrument, for there are differing definitions of the constructs (see the earlier discussion of cohesion), how the information will be gathered, who will provide the information, whether the measure of the construct is based on perceptions of the leader or members or outside observers, and whether the theory is based on a theoretical framework or an established research program. DeLucia-Waack then recommended reviewing instruments that measure these and similar constructs, using such sources as the Fuhriman and Burlingame text described earlier and the Psychlit and Social Science Index searches. After identifying appropriate instruments, she suggested checking the reliability and validity, the population for which it was designed, and whether the measure can show change over time (since members of groups are expected to change as the group progresses).

DeLucia-Waack's review describes instruments that are useful for screening potential group members for their appropriateness in the group, for identifying group leadership characteristics and styles, for evaluating the group environment and the use and role of therapeutic factors in the group, for conducting in-session behavior ratings of both group members and the leader(s), and for evaluating postgroup assessment instruments. Although there is still a pressing need for more and improved group evaluation instruments, researchers should not shy away from conducting group research for lack of instrumentation (DeLucia-Waack, 1997, 1999).

An alternative to the use of standardized instruments, as described by DeLucia-Waack, is to have evaluations of group work that are tailored by the group leader to the specific focus of the group being offered. Smead (1995, p. 27) has suggested that each group should be evaluated, and in the process the following questions should be asked:

1. How do you plan to determine whether a member has changed due to the group experience?
2. How are you going to determine whether your goals and objectives have been met?
3. What follow-up procedures do you anticipate?
4. Who will receive evaluation data about the group?
5. How will evaluation data be stored?
6. Who will have access to the data?
7. How do you plan to evaluate leader performance?

Smead (1995) next described ways of conducting the evaluation of the group to answer the preceding questions. She recommended that the evaluation be tailored to the specific group. Although the process may not address the concerns over research methodology that have been discussed by Fuhriman and Burlingame and others, it will provide direction to the group leader, as he or she develops the group and considers how the group will function, and the methods that will be used to determine whether the group goals were achieved. This level of accountability is very important for practitioners and those providing support services and should be a basic component of all group work. Finally, a recent comprehensive, selectively annotated bibliography of 1,793 group treatment research articles from 1970 to 1995 by Lubin, Wilson, Petren, and Polk (1996) provides an excellent recent resource of the past 25 years of group research.

SUMMARY

This chapter began with the question of whether groups work, and if so, how? With almost a century of clinical practice, followed by research and evaluation for most of the history of group work, answers are available. Groups do work. They are often as effective as individual therapy and, when the group process and experience is appropriate, may be even more beneficial than individual therapy. Several researchers have documented that individual and group therapy combined are likely to be the most powerful intervention of choice.

Research in group work is difficult because there are so many potential influences on the group: theory, leader style, membership, structure, and length of time. All of these may have an interactional effect such that leader style may be congruous with some members but not with others, and result in interpersonal dynamics that are helpful for some but not for others, thereby creating measurement problems for those wishing to evaluate the process and outcome of research. At the same time, excellent research has been conducted and models exist for those entering the field. There is a movement toward collaborative research between researchers and practitioners, and there is a recommendation that the training of graduate students should focus on collaboration and teamwork to address important questions while also providing mentoring and quality education. A number of instruments exist for evaluating group work, and it is recommended that all persons involved in group counseling and group therapy become familiar with measurement of the group experience, both process and outcome, in such a way as to be able to document the effectiveness of their work, both for ethical and professional purposes.

REFERENCES

Allport, F. (1924). *Social psychology*. Boston: Houghton Mifflin.

Bloch, S., Reibstein, J., Crouch, E., Holyroyd, P., & Theman, J. (1979). A method for the study of therapeutic factors in group psychotherapy. *British Journal of Psychiatry, 134*, 257–263.

Blythe, B. J., & Rodgers, A. Y. (1993). Evaluating our own practice: Past present and future trends. *Journal of Social Service Research, 18*, 101–119.

Bohanske, J., & Lemberg, R. (1987). An intensive group process-retreat model for the treatment of bulimia. *Group, 11*, 228–237.

Bostwick, G. J. (1987). Where's Mary? A review of the group treatment dropout literature. *Social Work with Groups, 10*, 117–132.

Bowman, V., & DeLucia, J. L. (1993). Preparation for group therapy: The effects of preparer and modality on group process and individual functioning. *Journal for Specialists in Group Work, 18*, 67–79.

Brower, A. M., & Rose, S. D. (1990). The group work research dilemma. *Journal of Social Service Research, 18*, 1–7.

Burlingame, G. M., Kircher, J. C., & Taylor, S. (1994). Methodological considerations in group psy-

chotherapy research: Past, present, and future practices. In A. Fuhriman & G. M. Burlingame (Eds.), *Handbook of group psychotherapy: An empirical and clinical synthesis*. New York: Wiley.

Caple, R. B., & Cox, P. L. (1989). Relationships among group structure, member expectations, attraction to group, and satisfaction with the group experience. *Journal for Specialists in Group Work, 14*, 16–24.

Chwalisz, K. (1999). *The event phenomena: A qualitative method for studying process and outcome in groups*. Paper presented at the American Psychological Association Convention, Boston.

Dagley, J. C., Gazda, G. M., Eppinger, S. J., & Stewart, A. E. (1994). Group psychotherapy research with children, preadolescents, and adolescents. In A. Fuhriman & G. M. Burlingame (Eds.), *Handbook of group psychotherapy: An empirical and clinical synthesis* (pp. 340–369). New York: Wiley.

Dagley, J. C. (2000). Adlerian family therapy. In A. Horne (Ed.), *Family counseling and therapy* (3rd ed.). Itasca, IL: Peacock.

DeLucia-Waack, J. L. (1997). Measuring the effectiveness of group work: A review and analysis of process and outcome measures. *Journal for Specialists in Group Work, 22,* 277–293.

DeLucia-Waack, J. L. (1999). *Group psychotherapy and outcome measures.* Paper presented at the annual convention of the American Psychological Association, Boston.

Emrick, C. (1975). A review of psychologically oriented treatment of alcoholism. *Journal for the Study of Alcoholism, 36,* 88–108.

France, D. L., & Dugo, J. M. (1985). Pretherapy orientation as preparation for psychotherapy groups. *Psychotherapy, 22,* 256–261.

Franko, D. L. (1987). Anorexia nervosa and bulimia: A self-help group. *Small Group Behavior, 18,* 398–407.

Freeman, C. P., & Munro, J. K. (1988). Drug and group treatments for bulimia/bulimia nervosa. *Journal of Psychosomatic Research, 32,* 647–660.

Fuhriman, A., & Burlingame, G. M. (1994). *Handbook of group psychotherapy: An empirical and clinical synthesis.* New York: Wiley.

Gazda, G. (1989). *Group counseling: A developmental approach* (4th ed.). Boston: Allyn and Bacon.

Gladding, S. (1995). *Group work: A counseling specialty* (3rd ed.). Upper Saddle River, NJ: Prentice-Hall.

Helgeson, V. S., & Cohen, S. (1996). Social support and adjustment to cancer: Reconciling descriptive, correlational, and intervention research. *Health Psychology, 15,* 135–148.

Hendren, R. L., Atkins, D. M., Sumner, F., Calvin, R., & Barber, J. K. (1987). *International Journal of Group Psychotherapy, 37,* 589–602.

Hilkey, J., Wilhelm, C., & Horne, A. (1982). Comparative effectiveness of videotape pretraining versus no pretraining on selected process and outcome variables in group therapy. *Psychological Reports, 50,* 1151–1159.

Hill, C. E., & Corbett, M. M. (1993). A perspective on the history of process and outcome research in counseling psychology. *Journal of Counseling Psychology, 40,* 3–24.

Horne, A. M., & Matson, J. L. (1977). A comparison of modeling, desensitization, flooding, study skills and control group for reducing test anxiety. *Behavior Therapy, 8,* 1–8.

Horne, A. M., & Rosenthal, R. (1997). Research in group work: How did we get where we are? *Journal for Specialists in Group Work, 22,* 228–240.

Kalodner, C. R., & Riva, M. T. (1997). Group research: Encouraging a collaboration between practitioners and researchers—A conclusion. *Journal for Specialists in Group Work, 22,* 297–298.

Kaul, T., & Bednar, R. (1986). Experimental group research: Results, questions, and suggestions. In S. L. Garfield & A. E. Bergin (Eds.), *Handbook of psychotherapy and behavior change* (3rd ed.). New York: Wiley.

Kivlighan, D. M. (1999, August). *Measuring change in groups.* Presented at the American Psychological Association annual convention, Boston.

Kivlighan, D. M., McGovern, T. V., & Corazzini, J. G. (1984). Effects of content and timing of structuring interventions on group therapy process and outcome. *Journal of Counseling Psychology, 31,* 363–370.

Kivlighan, D. M., & Mullison, D. (1988). Participants' perceptions of therapeutic factors in group counseling: The role of interpersonal style and stage of group development. *Small Group Behavior, 19,* 452–468.

Kivlighan, D. M., & Schwenn, H. (1999). *Methodological and statistical issues in group counseling research.* Paper presented at the annual convention of the American Psychological Association, Boston.

Lawe, C. F., Horne, A., & Taylor S. (1983). Effects of pretraining procedures for clients in counseling. *Psychological Reports, 53,* 327–334.

Lewin, K. (1940). Formulation and progress in psychology: University of Iowa studies. *Child Welfare, 16,* 9–42.

Lieberman, M. (1976). Change induction in small groups. *Annual Review of Psychology, 22,* 217.

Lubin, B., Wilson, C. D., Petren, S., & Polk, A. (1996). *Research and group treatment methods: A selected bibliography.* Westport, CT: Greenwood.

Miles, M., & Huberman, A., (1984). *Qualitative data analysis.* Beverly Hills: Sage.

Muller, E. J., & Scott, T. B. (1984). A comparison of film and written presentations used for pregroup training experiences. *Journal for Specialists in Group Work, 9,* 122–126.

Ohlsen, M. M. (1971). *Group counseling.* New York: Holt, Rinehart and Winston.

Ohlsen, M. M. (1974). *Guidance services in the modern school.* New York: Harcourt Brace Jovanvich.

Piper, W. E. (1994). Client variables. In A. Fuhriman & G. M. Burlingame (Eds.), *Handbook of group psychotherapy: An empirical and clinical synthesis.* New York: Wiley.

Polkinghorne, D. (1991). Qualitative procedures for counseling research. In C. Watkins, Jr. & L. Schneider (Eds.), *Research in counseling.* Hillsdale, NJ: Erlbaum.

Riva, M. T. (1999). *Researcher and practitioner collaboration in group process and outcome studies.*

Paper presented at the annual convention of the American Psychological Association, Boston.

Rohde, R. I., & Stockton, R. (1994). Group structure: A review. *Journal of Group Psychotherapy, Psychodrama, and Sociometry, 46,* 151–158.

Scheidlinger, S. (1993). History of group psychotherapy. In H. I. Kaplan & B. J. Sadock (Eds.), *Comprehensive group psychotherapy,* (3rd ed.). Baltimore: Williams & Wilkins.

Shaw, M. E. (1981). *Group dynamics: The psychology of small group behavior.* New York: McGraw-Hill.

Slavinsky-Holy, N. (1983). Combining homogeneous group psychotherapies for borderline conditions. *International Journal of Group Psychotherapy, 33,* 297–312.

Smead, R. (1995) *Skills and techniques for group work with children.* Champaign, IL: Research Press.

Steiner, I. D. (1986). Paradigms and groups. In L. Berkowitz (Ed.), *Advances in experimental social psychology.* Orlando, FL: Academic.

Stokes, J. P., Fuehrer, A., & Childs, L. O. (1983). Group members' self-disclosure: Relation to perceived outcome. *Small Group Behavior, 14,* 63–76.

Stockton, R. (1999). *Research training for group work.* Paper presented at the annual convention of the American Psychological Association, Boston.

Stockton, R., & Hulse, D. (1983). The use of research teams to enhance competence in counseling research. *Counselor Education and Supervision, 22,* 303–310.

Stockton, R., & Moran, D. K. (1982). Review and perspective of critical dimensions in therapeutic small group research. In G. M. Gazda (Ed.), *Basic approaches to group psychotherapy and group counseling* (3rd ed.). Springfield, IL: Charles C. Thomas.

Stockton, R., Rohde, R. I., & Haughey, J. (1992). The effects of structured group exercises on cohesion, engagement, avoidance, and conflict. *Small Group Research, 23,* 155–168.

Stockton, R., & Toth, P. L. (1997). Applying a general research training model to group work. *Journal for Specialists in Group Work, 22,* 241–252.

Toseland, R., & Siporin, M. (1986). When to recommend group treatment: A review of the clinical and group literature. *International Journal of Group Psychotherapy, 36,* 172–201.

Vandervoort, D., & Fuhriman, A., (1991). The efficacy of group therapy for depression. *Small Group Research, 22,* 320–338.

Wheelan, S. A. (1994). *Group process: A developmental perspective.* Boston: Allyn and Bacon.

Yalom, I. (1970). *Theory and practice of group psychotherapy.* New York: Basic Books.

Yalom, I. (1995). *Theory and practice of group psychotherapy* (4th ed.). edition. New York: Basic Books.

Yalom, I., Houts, P., Zimerberg, S., & Rand, K. (1967). Predictions of improvement in group therapy. *Archives of General Psychiatry, 17,* 159–168.

Zimpfer, D. G. (1989). Groups for persons who have cancer. *Journal for Specialists in Group Work, 14,* 98–104.

Zimpfer, D. G. (1990a). Group work for bulimia: A review of outcomes. *Journal for Specialists in Group Work, 15,* 239–251.

Zimpfer, D. G. (1990b). Groups for divorce/separation: A review. *Journal for Specialists in Group Work, 15,* 51–60.

Zimpfer, D. G. (1991). Groups for grief and survivorship after bereavement: A review. *Journal for Specialists in Group Work, 16,* 46–55.

CHAPTER SIX

ETHICAL, PROFESSIONAL, AND LEGAL ISSUES IN GROUP COUNSELING AND GROUP PSYCHOTHERAPY

Above all else, do no harm.

The basic moral principle of "do no harm" is at the core of professional and ethical standards of group work. Group workers are expected to focus on learning theories of personality and behavior change and to have a thorough grasp of theories and strategies of group work, but there must also be a core appreciation for and understanding of ethical, professional, and legal principles governing the practice of group work, for, as Van Hoose (1980, p. 2) has said, "Ethics lies at the heart of the counseling profession."

Involvement in group counseling or group therapy is often the first experience people have with the counseling process. Not only will it provide a unique opportunity for members to be in a social interaction that allows open and honest involvement with others but it is also expected that they will be able to share with others as they seek assistance with their concerns and, at the same time, provide support and encouragement for others to change. The process involves considerable honesty and trust, and with the potential for tremendous growth, there is also the possibility of harm if the group leader lacks the necessary skill, expertise, and ethical and professional guidance for the responsibility of leading the group.

Although ethical behavior and professional standards are expected of all counselors and therapists, there are special considerations that need to be addressed for those who work with groups, because, as the Association for Specialists in Group Work (ASGW) notes in the preamble to the ASGW Ethical Guidelines for Group Counselors (now referred to as the ASGW Standards of Best Practice):

Group counselors, by their very nature in being responsible and responsive to their group members, necessarily embrace a certain potential for ethical vulnerability. It is incumbent upon group counselors to give considerable attention to the intent and context of their actions because the attempts of counselors to influence human behavior through group work always have ethical implications. (Association for Specialists in Group Work, 1989, p. 1)

It is expected that readers of this chapter will be familiar with the ethical standards governing their professional associations, such as the American Counseling Association (ACA), the American Psychological Association (APA), the National Association of School Psychologists (NASP), and the National Association of Social Workers (NASW). The material presented in this chapter builds on the ethical standards of the professional associations by addressing concerns specific to group work.

ETHICS AND LEGAL ISSUES

It is important to understand the difference between ethical issues and legal issues. Gladding (1999, p. 216) reported, "A code of ethics is a set of standards and principles that organizations create to provide guidelines for their members to follow in working with the public and each other. Codes of ethics are constantly evolving, however, and do not refer to all possible situations." Note that the ethical code is developed by members of an organization, such as the American Counseling Association or the American Psychological Association, to provide guidance for the behavior and practice of the membership of that organization. Van Hoose and Kottler (1985) reported that a code of ethics helps counselors by setting a standard of care and provides some protection to clients by having professionals function in accordance with professional standards, a level of self-regulation, and ethical decision making.

The standards of the association are binding for the membership of that association, but they are not laws established by a community. Legal acts, or laws, are a "body of rules recognized by a state or community as binding on its members" (Shertzer & Stone, 1980, p. 386). Although there is considerable overlap between ethical standards and legal requirements, the two are not the same. A person may commit an ethical violation, such as violating confidentiality, which in most cases would be considered inappropriate behavior but not necessarily illegal. Or a person may violate a law, such as speeding in a car, which would be illegal but generally would not result in charges of being unethical. Often, though, there is a close tie between ethical standards and legal actions, such as improper billing for client services that may be both unethical and illegal (fraudulent). Further, some states accept selected professional organizations' ethical standards as legal guidelines for the governance of those licensed as professionals in the state; therefore, a violation of an ethical code may also be considered in that state as an illegal act.

It is imperative that group workers are cognizant of not only the professional standards to which they subscribe by virtue of being a member of a professional association and being licensed or certified to practice but also the community standards and state laws that govern the professional practice (Ohlsen, Horne, & Lawe, 1988). The best source for information about laws governing the practice of group work is usually the licensing or certification office of the state, generally identified as a professional board. Fellow professionals within the community are often the best source of guidance for understanding community standards and practices. Generally, within a state there are university faculty who are current on standards of professional practice at the national, state, and local levels and may be a very good resource for becoming familiar with expected professional behavior of group leaders. Finally, professional associations usually have easy access to information concerning their code of ethics and standards of professional practice, often through easy-to-use interactive websites. Some associations provide ongoing training sessions for members or work in conjunction with a professional liability insurance company to provide continuing education opportunities for training in risk management and practice standards, for it is in the best interests of the individual practitioner, the professional association, and the liability insurance company to have practitioners well acquainted with best practice standards. As Robinson and Gross (1989) have demonstrated, those trained in ethical standards are better equipped than those less trained to identify ethical issues and to take appropriate action on those issues.

Development of an Ethical Orientation

Knowledge of ethics codes and legal mandates is necessary but not sufficient for conducting an effective group practice that adheres to high standards of respect and care for the clients served. In addition, group leaders need to continue to examine their own standards of moral commitment and understanding. This may come from a combination of continuing education and a continuous examination of the personal life and values of the clinician.

Continuing education may take the form of ongoing supervision of one's practice, which has been recommended by a number of contributors to the group literature, including Gazda (1989), Gladding (1999), and Ohlsen, Horne, and Lawe (1988). Supervision provides the opportunity of continuing to learn about the effectiveness of current practice, allows for expanding skills and expertise under the supervision and guidance of professionals, and holds a mirror to one's practice that helps show how one interacts and conducts oneself in a more objective manner than the unexamined practice allows for.

An examination of one's personal life also provides the opportunity of developing a higher level of moral and ethical behavior. An exercise that is very helpful for facilitating this examination of one's personal life is called "Understanding Our Needs to be a Counselor or Therapist." The exercise involves having the student or practitioner begin to write out or discuss with a supervisor why he or she wants or needs to be a group counselor or therapist. Generally, when students engage in this activity, early responses center on external issues ("I had a great counselor when I was in school and I want to be helpful like that person was to me" or "I've been blessed with good mentors and I want to repay the debt I feel to those who have helped me)." With further prompting from a supervisor, though, the discussion often becomes more internalized, making it possible to explore the very personal aspects of the work that one finds fulfilling but that may not always be as helpful to clients as one wishes. A need to be admired and respected is positive, but when fulfilling that personal need leads to continuing a group beyond a point where it is helping the members, even though the members report admiration and appreciation to the leader, the group begins to meet the needs of the leader and not the members, which then moves toward unprofessional behavior.

It is very important for group leaders to examine their lives, their needs, their goals, and then to put those personal needs in perspective to the needs of the members of the group and to be certain that the group is serving the membership at a high level of professional and ethical practice. Although the example we have used refers to students engaging in this very personal examination, it is also important for practitioners, regardless of age, to engage in the exercise on an ongoing basis, for as practitioners go through their personal developmental stages of life and profession, their needs change, and the changing needs may result in a need for changing the practice, as well.

THE PURPOSE OF A CODE OF ETHICS

A code of ethics goes beyond rules and regulations; rather, it is based on principles of behavior for practitioners. Practitioners must have a knowledge and familiarity with the moral principles upon which the code is established, and then use those principles to establish standards of practice that serve the group and individual members well. Training programs that emphasize the rules of ethical behavior without going into the values behind the rules do students a disservice, for it is the understanding of the principles that provides the foundation for effective ethical decision making in future situations. An ethical dilemma occurs when a decision must be made, when rules or regulations conflict, or when an original situation occurs for which the group leader has no rule and must make a decision. The decision should be based on a principle or a human value, which is at the core of ethical decision making.

Kitchner (1984), Koocher and Keith-Spiegel (1998) and Meara, Schmidt, and Day (1996) have discussed some of the primary values that are at the core of ethical decision making:

■ *Nonmaleficence.* Do no harm. No group leader intends to do harm to clients, but through acts of omission or commission, such may happen. It is the obligation of the group leader to prevent or minimize any harm that may come through group work. Leaders must be aware that harm may come from within the group if undue influence is given to certain members of the group over other members. Likewise, change that occurs and that may be valued within the group setting may result in difficulties for the member outside of the group. Group leaders should not avoid facilitating change that may be healthy, but it is necessary to help group members consider the impact of change on others in their lives, such as family members, coworkers, and peers.

■ *Autonomy.* Autonomy is the right to choose one's direction, to have the independence and power to determine what is best for oneself, to have the right to make one's own decisions without the undue influence of others. In group work, autonomy for the individual requires that the group leader recognizes the potential of the group to attempt to influence members, perhaps leading to a group consensus regardless of the wishes of the individual. It is the responsibility of the leader to help the group provide a balance of caring suggestions and recommendations versus an undue influence on the individual member to conform to the expectations of the other group members. At the same time, a major focus of much group counseling and therapy is an increase of autonomy for group members.

■ *Beneficence.*   Beneficence includes doing good for others, being kind, and showing charity toward others. In group work, it is expected that all members will come to work on their own personal issues, but will also be available to help others in their work on their concerns. It includes being open and sharing in the group, appreciating that others are struggling and need support.

■ *Justice.*   The concept of justice or fairness is imperative in group work. It involves treating all members of the group fairly, with respect and dignity, and with equity toward all. Members are not treated differently because of race, ethnicity, gender, religious orientation, age, or other factors. Justice also involves having the leader exert influence over all group members to enforce fairness and just treatment to all.

■ *Faithfulness and Fidelity.*   Group leaders must demonstrate loyalty to group members and do so in an honest, straightforward manner. Ethical behavior includes not deceiving or misleading people, and providing the services that were promised. A group leader will behave consistent with the nature of the group and not, for example, attempt to recruit group counseling members for individual and group counseling.

■ *Dignity.*   All members of the group are treated with respect and dignity. The group leader models interactional processes with group members that allows for the open discussion of concerns and problems, but in a dignified manner so that there is no shame or humiliation from the leader or group members as a function of what is shared in the group.

■ *Care and Compassion.*   It is necessary to maintain professional boundaries when relating to clients in groups. Group leaders must therefore be familiar with group leadership roles and the boundaries and responsibilities that go with the role of leader, but at the same time leaders must demonstrate care and compassion for the members of the group.

■ *Professional Performance.*   The group leader must strive for excellence in group work and although this may be aspirational rather than realized, group leaders must demonstrate competence and ability in group counseling and therapy skills. Group workers should have pride in their work and their competencies in conducting groups, and work to ensure that the professional services provided are of high quality.

■ *Accountability.*   Group leaders must work to deliver quality services and to accept responsibility for the work provided as well as the selection and involvement of clients in a group, and to be accountable for the outcome of the group experience.

All of these characteristics described should be inherent qualities of a counselor or therapist who elects to engage in group work, for activities such as treating group members with care and respect are expected to be innate characteristics of a person in the helping fields. At the same time, if all of the characteristics are not part of the fabric of the group leader, they may still be adhered to as a function of responding to the demands of ethical principles. Accountability, for example, may be a trait that is not part of the personality of a group leader, but that may occur even if the leader would prefer not to be accountable and would not do so unless it was specified as an ethical principle.

Making Ethical Decisions

In 1984, Kitchner presented the principles of moral decision making and discussed the five characteristics of moral decision making (autonomy, justice, beneficence, nonmaleficence, and fidelity—the first five from the list of nine characteristics just listed). She indicated that the principles are all of primary importance but that at times the principles will be in conflict with one another. For example, the concept of fidelity—loyalty and faithfulness to the client—may be in conflict with the construct of nonmaleficence—do no harm—if the leader becomes aware that a group member is in danger of harming himself or herself or another person. In such a circumstance, it is difficult to maintain loyalty and confidentiality while needing to break confidentiality to ensure the safety of the client or others. In this case, there is an ethical conflict because two (or more) of the principles are contradictory, thus creating an ethical dilemma.

Kitchner (1984) suggested a decision-making model that includes steps to take to make effective decisions regarding dilemmas. Since her original contribution, others have added and expanded on the decision-making criteria, at times applying it to specific areas. Forester-Miller (1998), for example, applied the decision-making model to examples of group work using the ethical standards of the Association for Specialists in Group Work and the American Counseling Association. Treppa (1998, p. 27), building on the work of others who have examined ethical decision-making models over the last decade, proposed the following model:

1. Consider the context and setting.
2. Define the obligations owed.
3. Identify and challenge assumptions.
4. Consult resources.
5. Generate potential solutions.
6. Evaluate each proposed solution.
7. Decide on a course of action.
8. Make and implement the decision.

The first point of Treppa's model requires understanding the work setting (school, community agency, hospital, private practice, etc.), the population treated (children, adults, incarcerated adolescents, military personnel, etc.), whether the participants are voluntarily participating or are coerced into treatment, the interventions available (long-term group therapy, brief time-limited group interventions, encounter or growth groups, psychoeducational training groups, etc.), and the rules and expectations that go with each of the possible approaches to group work.

The second feature, defining the obligations owed, involves considering who is affected by the work being done. In a school setting, for example, the group counselor must consider the clientele of the group (children), the person(s) referring the client (perhaps a teacher or administrator), and the legal guardians (parents or other adults). In these considerations the counselor must identify to whom she or he is obligated. Whose agent is the counselor: the child, the school administrator, or the parent? In considering this, one must also ask Who pays the bill? For whom does the counselor work? Once these questions are answered, the counselor must then address what responsibilities are owed to each party.

When the conflict has been identified and the obligations considered, it is then necessary to identify and examine the assumptions under which the counselor or therapist operates. What is the value system, the belief system, and the theoretical model of the counselor and how are those similar or dissimilar to the client and organization with which the counselor works? How are those values and beliefs problematic now? Often, this is the time for external consultation—that is, having to have someone else step in and assist in examining values and beliefs and how those are interacting to contribute to the ethical dilemma that has developed.

Consultation, the next step of ethical decision making, involves reviewing relevant professional standards and ethical guidelines, such as those published by the American Counseling Association, the American Psychological Association, the American Group Psychotherapy Association, and the Association for Specialists in Group Work. Further, consulting with respected colleagues, regional members of professional organizations, or local university faculty may be helpful. Many states provide free phone consultations to professional licensing boards. If the problem has been determined to be a legal dilemma instead of, or in addition to, an ethical one, it is time to consult with a legal advisor.

At the stage of generating potential solutions, it is best to have an open mind and engage in brainstorming activities. This includes deferring making a judgment about the value or potential of a possible solution, considering all possibilities, developing as many possible alternatives as is feasible, and pulling potential solutions into additional new solutions.

When evaluating each proposed solution, it is crucial that the counselor return to the professional standards and guidelines to be certain that the solutions are consistent with the ethical standards of the profession. The evaluation of solutions should include consideration of the potential outcome if the solution is implemented: What will happen in a week, in a month, in a year, for each possible solution? What are the consequences of these short- and long-term solutions in terms of emotional costs and personal finances to all involved? How much time will be required to implement the outcome? At this point, it is important to review the principles of ethical decision making (beneficence, nonmaleficence, autonomy, justice, fidelity) to consider the extent to which the proposed solution upholds the principles. Treppa (1998, p. 35) has suggested that (1) the process and outcome will be uncertain, (2) it is riskier to implement an outcome when there is no evidence to support the estimates regarding consequences, (3) outside consultation is crucial for more objective decision making, and (4) the greater the risk of harm, the more the choice should be a conservative solution.

After the solution is selected, a course of action is taken. At this point, one must consider the strengths and weaknesses of the selected action and perhaps incorporate changes. For risk-management purposes, it is also important to have alternative actions available should the first choice not work. When an ethical dilemma occurs, it is almost always necessary to explain why the action taken was selected; therefore, it is crucial to have a rationale for the action. It is best that this be written out or at least outlined on paper for future reference. It is also wise to present the rationale to one or more respected colleagues and to those who have an interest in the outcome of the dilemma (school administrators, parents, etc.).

The implementation of the solution is the final stage of ethical decision making and one that often results in anxiety and tension, because steps are being taken that may not be recalled. It is important to review, again the moral principles and one's personal values and beliefs. The implementation of the decision must be consistent with professional standards, appropriate within the community and state legal framework, consistent with moral principles that underlie ethical guidelines, and congruous with the individual beliefs and values of the counselor or therapist.

ETHICAL ISSUES IN GROUP WORK

Having reviewed the moral principles that provide the basis of ethics standards, and presenting a decision-making model for understanding how to address ethical dilemmas, we will now review some of the ethical dilemmas that may develop that are specific to group work.

Training

The majority of people doing group work are trained professionals with high standards of practice and an extensive knowledge of interventions. However, there are many people conducting groups who have had little or no training in group work. Most often, these are young professionals who are employed in settings that require the delivery of group services, but identify such services as ancillary to the primary therapy offered. This would be the case, for example, in a medical setting where the primary mode of treatment is medical, pharmacological, or individual psychotherapy, and group involvement is seen as supportive. In this situation, there is often a failure to regard the group work as therapeutic and on a par with other methods of intervention. In other situations, groups are led by minimally trained individuals who do not perceive group work as requiring special expertise or knowledge. Their naiveté of their own lack of understanding and skill level prevents them from seeking increased knowledge and skills or appropriate consultation. In either case—through employment that requires counselors or therapists to work beyond their skill level with groups, or through naiveté on the part of the group leader—there is an ethical dilemma, for the standard of care is below the professional level and jeopardizes the welfare of the clients involved as well as the practice in which the services are delivered.

Appendix A presents the Association for Specialists in Group Work (ASGW) *Professional Standards for the Training of Group Workers* (1991). These standards provide guidelines for minimum training in four areas of group work: Task or work groups, psychoeducational or guidance groups, counseling groups, and psychotherapy groups. The standards include recommended knowledge competencies, skill competencies, and recommended clinical practice guidelines for each of the four types of group work. The ASGW has also contributed to professional standards by the publication of the *ASGW Best Practice Guidelines for Group Workers* (Appendix B) and the *ASGW Principles for Diversity-Competent Group Workers* (Appendix C). Additionally, the American Group Psychotherapy Association (AGPA) (1978) has published *Guidelines for Ethics* (Appendix D). These training guidelines should be perceived as the beginning point for persons preparing to be group counselors or therapists. Each set of training standards (ASGW, AGPA) recommends personal experience in a group as part of the training program for those aspiring to be group leaders.

Purpose of the Group

Smead (1995) has described steps to be taken in establishing groups. She has indicated that a needs survey should be conducted, followed by a written proposal for conducting a group if there is a sufficient need for one to be offered. The written proposal should include a description and rationale for the group, objectives or outcomes expected, logistics and procedures for conducting the group, and an evaluation process to examine the effectiveness of the group. Following the written description, the group leader should then advertise the group, obtain parent or guardian consent for young people or informed consent for adults, conduct a pregroup interview to select members for the group, evaluate potential members' readiness for the group, conduct the sessions, and then complete a postreatment evaluation of the group.

Consistent with Smead's recommended steps for beginning a group, Gazda (1989), Ohlsen, Horne, and Lawe (1988), Yalom (1995) and others have advocated that a first step in beginning a group should be a clear understanding of the purpose of the group—that is, why it is being initiated. In defining the purpose, the group leader needs to assess the need for the group, the purpose for the group, and the specific goals and objectives of the group. In terms of ethical dilemmas, when group leaders have clearly identified the need, purpose, and goals, members are more likely to recognize how the group will meet their needs, resulting in fewer complaints later about misrepresentation of or misunderstanding about the group, for the group goals will be compatible with the individual members' goals. Providing clear information about a group allows potential members to self-select into the group, and by providing an ongoing re-presentation of group goals, members stay focused on the purpose and expectations of the group. Since it is expected that group members will have provided informed consent to be in the group, their understanding of the group at the beginning will remain consistent and will provide the leader with a focus for the group.

One aspect of member selection that must be considered early in the development of a group is whether membership is voluntary or involuntary. A voluntary group is one in which the members elect to participate and are free to leave the group if they decide it is not meeting their needs or expectations. An involuntary group is one in which members are required to attend and their presence is not an option, nor may they withdraw freely. Generally, voluntary groups provide for greater involvement, commitment, and growth, though the outcome of the group depends on many factors, including the leader's skills and the purpose of the group. In an involuntary group, it is very important that members be allowed and encouraged to share their thoughts and feelings about the mandatory nature of the experience. Incarcerated youth, hospitalized patients, mandatory disciplinary groups at schools, court-ordered parent training groups, and spouse-abuse treatment groups are examples of involuntary groups.

With members of involuntary groups, the leader is obligated to inform the members that participation is elective. We have worked with court-ordered family treatment programs with a group focus on parent counseling. Even in those situations, we always informed the parents they had other options than being in our groups, even though the options were not positive (removal of children from the home, incarceration of the parents, hospitalization of parent with forced treatment, etc.). We respected the parents rights to elect to not be in the group. We further assured them that we understood the difficulty they were experiencing and would do all we could to facilitate movement out of the group as they demonstrated the parental roles and responsibilities the courts sought.

Intake Interviews

Some groups require no screening or intake procedures. Work or task groups, for example, may function as groups but have a very specific focus, such as a departmental committee assigned to develop alternative scheduling procedures. Most psychoeducational groups are provided to a universal population—that is, all members in a group receive the group intervention, such as an anger control training session provided by a school counselor to an entire classroom of children. With universal populations it is generally not necessary to conduct intake interviews, because all members of the group are selected for participation. When groups are organized for counseling or therapy purposes, though, there is greater need for intake procedures in order to screen those who may be particularly appropriate or inappropriate for the group (Ohlsen, Horne, & Lawe, 1988).

Screening involves providing potential members with a description of the group to be offered, with attention to making sure the group is not misrepresented to potential members. It is important to clarify group goals, define membership expectations, describe leader activities, explain how members are expected to participate and what they are to do, and discuss any potential risks that may be involved as a function of the group. Once potential members are apprised of the opportunity to participate in the group, individual or small-group interviews are conducted to evaluate the appropriateness of the group for the individuals. It is important to have an alternative referral source for those for whom group participation is deemed inappropriate. The intake interview provides the potential member with increased information about the group, begins to establish rapport between the leader and the potential member, and provides the leader an opportunity to begin helping the member prepare for active participation once the group begins. The intake interview should provide the leader with information about other services the potential member may be participating in, such as medical treatment or previous or ongoing treatment by another counselor, and whether the member may benefit more from group or individual treatment (Gazda, 1989).

Informed Consent

During the intake procedure, informed consent or parental/guardian permission to participate in a group should be obtained. If participants are adults, they should provide an informed consent form agreeing to participate in the group. To reach this stage, it is important to have a written description of the group and expectations spelled out for group participants. This clears confusion and allows for potential members to make an informed choice about whether to be in the group. Further, if the leader adheres to the written description, it provides support for the leader if an ethical or legal issue should arise after the group has commenced.

Counselors must take the steps necessary to obtain parental or guardian permission for the underage member to participate in group treatment. School counselors should be familiar with school and community policies regarding permission, because the standards vary a great deal for states, communities, and even schools within a given community.

An informed consent form should contain the following information:

1. Name of the participant
2. Acknowledgment that group work involves being open and sharing one's concern with others in the group in an effort to achieve personal goals
3. Agreement to share one's own concerns but also to be open to concerns or problems of others and work with them to help them achieve their personal goals
4. Awareness that both positive and negative outcomes are possible from the group experience
5. Acknowledgement that the group participation is voluntary (if it is) and that the member has the right to discontinue the group at any time (if he or she does)

Another aspect of the intake procedure that ties in with informed consent is to be certain group members know in advance the rights they have as members of a group. All members are to be treated with respect and dignity, by both the leader and by other members of the group. It is the leader's ethical responsibility to ensure that the respect is provided, even if that means becoming confrontational in the group setting with members who fail to provide the level of support needed for the group to function effectively. Members have the right to follow recommendations and solutions to problems that are proposed by other members of the group, but by being respected and valued people, they also have the right to reject other members' suggestions, and still be a valued member of the group.

Confidentiality in Groups

All people expect counseling and therapy to be supportive and to provide an opportunity to share concerns and problems, with confidence that the information will not be shared with others, unless required by law or to protect the health and safety of one or more people. In individual therapy, this expectation may be fulfilled by having the therapist maintain a confidential relationship; if information about therapy is shared, it is because the client involved elected to share it with others, not because the therapist violated client confidence.

Confidentiality is not as easy to ensure with a group. The leader will explain, during the intake interview, the importance of trust and respect, and how that involves each member maintaining the confidences of information and experiences shared by others in the group. On the other hand, although the leader can promise confidentiality on his or her part, no such assurances may be guaranteed on the part of other group members. Information may be inadvertently or purposefully shared by other group members. Thus, as part of the intake interview, and later as part of the initial session of the entire group, it is necessary to explain confidentiality, give examples, and make it clear that the rule of the group is not to violate the confidences of others.

Members of a group must be able to trust one another, and they must have confidence that the leader may be relied on to encourage and support the trust, to model effective interactions that are therapeutic but also supportive, and to take action to protect group members from one another should that be necessary. This involves having a plan for what to do if a group confidence is violated. It also means having the leader explain to the group the conditions under which he or she will violate confidentiality (e.g., threat of harm to oneself or someone else or information about child abuse and neglect) and what he or she will do upon learning that the trust has been broken.

Generally, it is helpful if the leader can provide examples of inadvertently a member breaking the trust. Examples may include a person talking to friends about what is presented in the group and, although not mentioning other members by name, describing some of the problems others have presented. This can be a violation because people outside the group may be familiar with other members of the group and be able to make the connections between the incidents told about and the other group members.

If the leader or another member of the group suspects that the confidence of the group has been violated, the problem should be attended to, in the group, immediately, because from that point on, there will be no further trust or open sharing of problems and emotions until the issue is resolved. The leader will want the group to discuss the issue. He or she should demonstrate effective skills in conflict resolution and problem solving to move the group to address the problem, explore ramifications and the impact on the group, and develop a solution that will be acceptable to all group members. Our experience is that there is seldom malicious breaking of confidentiality; rather, a problem will more likely arise as a function of a group member being enthusiastic about what is happening in the group and, in the process of sharing the enthusiasm with others, shares more information than intended. Members must be reminded of what a small world it is in terms of relationships and knowledge of peers and friends, so that what may seem to be an innocuous disclosure can become a serious breach of confidence.

The leader must attend to the environment and setting when addressing issues of confidentiality. Once, in doing group work at a large juvenile correctional institution, one of us was amazed to find that in the brief time it took for the juveniles to return from the group session and reenter the school, word would already be out in the school about the topics of the group for the day and who had talked. After several years of attempting to instill a sense of confidentiality within the groups of the correctional center, it was finally agreed that there simply would be no such attempt. The culture of the institution was such that confidentiality—even in therapy groups—was not a norm and could not be established as one, and this was a choice by both the adolescents and the correctional personnel who ran the institution.

Coercion in Groups

Coercion in groups may take several forms, and in each situation it is the responsibility of the leader to be aware of the potential for coercion to harm members. One form of coercion may occur when the counselor elects to offer a group. In an effort to get membership, group leaders will often seek out potential members and encourage them to join the group. When this happens, the leader must examine several issues: Why does the leader think the group should be offered—is there really a need in the setting or community, or is it a need of the counselor to use a newly obtained technique or process? Why does this person need to be in the group? Is it really appropriate for this person, or is the leader simply wanting to be certain the group has sufficient members? How does the leader benefit from the group—is there a financial incentive to induce more members to join the group, and is that the guiding force, or is the group truly an appropriate avenue for helping potential members, or both?

Further, once the group is operating, do members have the option of participating at their level of comfort? Often, in an attempt to have greater participation, either the leader or members of the group will encourage—or coerce—quieter members to become more involved, to become greater risk-takers, and perhaps to be more disclosing. Is this encouragement an attempt to be more helpful to the individual member, or is it a result of the leader or other group members' curiosity? Is the encouragement in the best interests of the client or the best interests of the group, or can it be both?

When activities are offered in the group, do members truly have a choice of whether to participate? Often, members are reticent to engage in interactional activities with other members of the group, and this may be particularly true for shy and withdrawn members or members from differing cultural backgrounds than the majority. The counselor plays a major role in determining the comfort level of the reticent group member and is ethically bound to ensure the emotional safety of the member when others place undue demands on him or her. Lakin (1988) reported that there are heightened expressions of emotion inherent in the group process, resulting in an intensified push toward conformity. This conformity may potentially limit the early opportunity for individual differences to be expressed within the group, because there may be group pressure for premature or inauthentic self-disclosure. With the pressure to disclose, whether members are ready or not, may come a tacit agreement to talk, but to be inauthentic in the process. It is the leader's responsibility to guard against this coercive process.

Dual Relationships

All professional association ethics guidelines address the issue of *dual relationships*, defined as when two people have more than one relationship. Dual relationships in everyday experiences may not be problematic—two coworkers, for instance, may enjoy attending sports events outside of work or having family dinners together on weekends. Although there may be two relationships—worker relationships and social/friend relationships—these are unlikely to cause problems or conflicts. In counseling and therapeutic relationships, however, there is considerable potential for difficulties to develop (Donigian, 1993).

The reason dual relationships are problematic in counseling and therapy is that there is almost always an imbalance of power in the relationship, and any imbalance of power provides the opportunity for the more powerful individual to have influence over the less powerful one. If a school counselor also teaches a course at the high school, for example, and a student in the course is engaged in a counseling relationship with the counselor, there is a dual-role relationship in that the counselor—who is expected to be open, trusting, accepting, and encouraging—may carry a different role as a teacher. If the counselor learns of an extreme level of stress that has led the student to cheating, for instance, or the use of drugs to reduce the anxiety, the teacher role may require disciplinary action or even retaliation against the student for having cheated in class. The two roles—counselor and teacher—are conflictual, and create a dual relationship with the student. Although people attempt to put the imbalance of power in perspective, and strive to be fair and just, when there are dual relationships, there is a powerful potential for abuse. That is why the ethical guidelines of professional associations admonish that counselors and therapists attend to the potential for abuse of all dual roles and attempt to avoid any relationships that will result in an abuse of power of one person over another.

Schoener and Luepker (1996) described the issue of dual-role relationships in terms of establishing clear boundaries. According to them, ethical dilemmas occur when boundaries are not clear and confusion develops. Boundaries in group settings, between the leader and group members as well as among the group participants, provide the safety necessary for clients to achieve constructive change. Clear boundaries also provide protection for the counselor or therapist in dealing with issues of transference and countertransference. (See Chapter 11 for a discussion of transference and countertransference.)

In setting boundaries for group practices, the group leader must be clear on the point that he or she is the one who is providing the service. As the service provider, he or she should be healthy, have an understanding of personal values and how those impact his or her performance in group work, and able to deliver services with a high degree of integrity. The client, on the other hand, is the one with a problem and is seeking services. Thus, a boundary issue that has to be addressed is that the group is not present to provide therapy for the leader, nor is the group member present to be a therapist but is there for the benefit of interacting with other members seeking solutions to real problems.

Dual relationships may take several forms, which are discussed next.

Academic Settings.   Faculty members have a responsibility for selecting students for programs, teaching them and providing supervision of their learning and clinical skill development, and evaluating their progress toward becoming independent practitioners. If a faculty member also becomes the leader of a group, or even an individual therapist, with students in the program, there is the possibility that he or she will become aware of information about the members that may be detrimental to their progress in the program. For example, say a faculty member, in the role of a group leader, promises to provide a secure and safe environment for sharing personal information, and he or she learns information about group members that may be detrimental to their progress in the program. Either the faculty member must maintain the confidentiality—which could be harmful to the program—or violate the confidentiality and share with other faculty the concerns that have been raised. Thus, group members have not been provided with the safety that had been assured them in the group. Examples of student topics that could arise include alcohol or drug abuse; antagonism toward values of the program, such as appreciation for diversity; sexual orientation that may be in conflict with the values of the institution; or other topics.

The admonishment not to provide services to students creates a dilemma for faculty, for the training guidelines for students in counseling and therapy programs who aspire to be group leaders recommends experience in a group during the training experience. How does one not provide groups for students, yet expect them to be in one? Forester-Miller and Duncan (1990) have suggested a number of alternative ways of providing the experiences, including:

> Requiring students to participate in groups external to the program, such as through a university counseling center or through arrangements with other agencies or private practitioners in the community;
>
> Having experienced graduate students who have no input into student selection or evaluation conduct sessions and provide supervision of groups.

Dual Relationships between the Group Leader and a Group Member.   This situation may present an ethical dilemma in several ways:

1. A group leader may be developing a new group and a person who wishes to be a member of the group may have a previous relationship with the leader, or during the intake interview, the leader may become aware of a possible dual-role relationship. If, for example, the leader has previously treated another member of the family of the potential group member, the knowledge and information from that other family member may influence the relationship that develops between the leader and the group member. Or, if the leader has worked with the member in another capacity—a coworker, a teacher-student relationship, or some other relationship—there may be a conflict.

2. After the counseling group has begun, a dual-role conflict may develop as information is shared with the group, or as the leader and member come to know each other better. In some situations, information may emerge that was not known or shared during the intake interview. We know of a situation in which the leader of a group for members who had experienced painful couples breakups became aware that two of the women in the group were—unknown to each other—dating a man whom the leader was seeing in individual therapy. Further, the man had left a ministerial role and had accepted a new position in the practice in which the therapist worked. It was not until the fifth session that the multiple relationships became known to the leader, who then had to deal not only with dual relationships but also with multiple roles with three clients, all unknown in their relationships to each other.

3. A physical attraction may develop between the leader and a group member. Although this may be handled the same as it would in individual therapy, there are other considerations when it happens in a group setting. Members of a counseling or therapy group are generally very attuned to the relationships that emerge within the group. Other members are often aware of the development of a special relationship between a leader and a member even before the leader recognizes it. For the group, this raises multiple issues, including fairness (not all members are being treated the same), justice (members may see the behavior as not appropriate or just), and fidelity (the relationship is probably secretive and therefore the leader is not being honest to and with the members).

4. Traditionally, practitioners have functioned in two relationships with clients or patients: individual and group. A therapist will often believe that individual therapy is appropriate for issues being addressed, but also believe that a patient may benefit from the social support and group dynamics available in a group setting. In that case, the therapist may serve the client in two roles, and often will be seeing several patients or clients similarly, so that in a group of eight members, there may be eight individual clients as well. Although counselors and practitioners will attempt to compartmentalize the information received in individual treatment from that obtained during the group sessions, it is sometimes difficult, if not impossible, to keep all of the known information assigned to the model of intervention in which it was received. Information from individual sessions often finds its way into the group sessions. This may be accidental, such as the leader may not remember whether the information was learned individually or in the group session. Or, at times, the leader may believe that the information, although obtained in an individual session, may need to be shared with the group in order to provide peer feedback and group support, whether the individual member believes that or not. There is considerable opportunity for a breach of confidentiality if the counselor or therapist maintains the two roles of serving the individual client and the group member.

Another aspect of the dual-role relationship issue between the leader and group members centers on the issue of the counselor's values and expectations for working with particular people. Although counselors and therapists should be open to all issues and concerns that people have, and should strive to provide a safe environment and one that provides equitable treatment to all involved, inevitably there are some people with whom the counselor or therapist just does not work well. This may perhaps be a function of skill level, for not all counselors have the skills to work with all people. Also, some counselors have their own unresolved issues and those issues will influence the degree to which a group leader is open to addressing certain problems. A counselor having marital conflicts, for example, may not be emotionally available to helping others experiencing those problems.

Finally, when a counselor has personal conflicts with certain characteristics of clients—such as sexual orientation, lifestyle, religious, gender, or age conflicts—the counselor must be aware of his or her value system and how the negative reactions will affect the group if certain individuals are admitted. When this happens, it is the counselor's responsibility to seek supervision and consultation to gain insight and awareness into his or her own issues. On the other hand, there are times when a counselor needs to admit he or she cannot serve all clients, in which case the counselor must refer the client to a different professional. Counselors cannot be expected to be able to work with all clients, but they still must show respect and fairness and help provide alternative services as appropriate.

Related to this topic is the duty of the counselor to warn and report issues to proper authorities. Certainly many incidents are clear-cut and endorsed by group counselors and therapists, such as referrals for child abuse and neglect and warning potential victims. Another area, however, is more difficult: the need to report impaired professionals, particularly those who have brought harm to clients. Learning about the misbehavior/unprofessional practice of another professional is very difficult, yet it occurs, and when it does, one must be prepared to take action to stop the unprofessional behavior. Ethical practitioners must know relevant state laws, including knowing when mandatory reporting is necessary. Some states do not have clear guidelines on this matter, whereas others take the position that a therapist who fails to take action when knowing of unprofessional behavior is also engaging in unprofessional behavior and is liable as an accomplice to the misdeeds. It is the professional's responsibility to help keep the profession professional.

Relationships between Group Members.   Members of groups share in a trusting and meaningful relationship. Some group leaders take the position that the sharing should be limited strictly to the group, that outside contact and interaction is inappropriate because it works against the cohesiveness of the group and may result in cliques, special friendships, or violation of the rule of confidentiality that says material shared in the group stays in the group. Other leaders are much less forceful on this issue and are more flexible in allowing, and at times even encouraging, outside contacts and the development of friendships beyond the confines of the group.

The context of the group plays a large role in determining the extent to which outside group contact may occur. If the group members reside in a large city and commute to the group, or if they participate in an outpatient treatment facility at a large medical center, there may be little opportunity for outside contact. On the other hand, in schools, correctional facilities, work settings, or small communities, outside contact is very likely. Although there are no hard and fast guidelines on this issue, it is important that the leader discusses the topic with members and reviews the expectations of the leader and the norms that are established by the group members. Once the norms are established for the group, it is up to the members to adhere to them or to bring back to the group the need to revisit and perhaps revise the group norms. This should be a topic of discussion of the group, though, and not be a decision made independently by individual members.

Some groups lend themselves naturally to having outside contact. Norsworthy and Horne (1994), for example, have described how an ongoing, long-term therapy group for gay men who are HIV-positive may function very differently from other groups. For example, the members of the group shared phone numbers and addresses so that as they became aware of the latest information about AIDS treatment, they could share the information (and they were generally more knowledgeable than their personal physicians on treatments and pharmacology issues). Also, along the model of Alcoholics Anonymous, group members made themselves available to one another for "after-hours" support when it was needed, as happened many times when panic or fear would strike late at night. They also were available to share support and knowledge about safe sex practices, safe places for HIV-infected gay men to congregate and be, and—unlike any group we had worked with before—the members and the leaders were present in hospice situations and attended funerals of deceased members and their partners. The important issue regarding outside contact of group members is the facilitative or harmful impact it has on the membership of the group. It is the ethical responsibility of the group leader to monitor the effect it has on his or her group.

Diversity Issues in Group Work

"Counselors will actively attempt to understand the diverse cultural backgrounds of the clients with whom they work. This includes, but is not limited to, learning how the counselor's own cultural/ethnic/racial identity impacts her/his values and beliefs about the counseling process" (American Counseling Association, 1995, p. 2). It is imperative that the group leader examines his or her cultural background and racial identity and become familiar with the impact that background and identity has on the practices of the leader. Further, the leader must develop an understanding of the backgrounds and experiences that clients bring with them when they enter counseling or therapy. Finally, the leader must be aware of how his or her personal background interacts with the background of the clients, and be able to use this knowledge and awareness in a supportive and therapeutic manner rather than allow it to introduce blocks and conflicts in group work.

Group leaders must attend to how they, as leaders, interact with clients from varying experiences. They must also attend to the dynamics of the group process as potential members from diverse backgrounds come together to share in the group experience. Maintaining commitment to the core principles of ethical group work, the leader must ensure the safety of group members, have the group function in a just and fair way, and be certain that the group does no harm to the members. Therefore, when designing the group, the leader will be cognizant of potential members and how their backgrounds may influence their being accepted into the group and their behavior once in the group. Further, the leader will explore the ability of group members to work together, regardless of their racial, ethnic, or cultural backgrounds. If during the intake process the leader determines the group makeup will not be facilitative for all members, alternative arrangements must be made to best serve the members.

One specific area that is important to address as a diversity issue is the relationship a male leader has with male members and with female members of the group. As described in Chapter 4, when describing working with women's groups, women have experienced more boundary violations than have most men in U.S. society. It is therefore imperative that the group leader, whether female or male, be attentive to the possibility of abuse of boundary violations with women members of the group. Similarly, though, for men, boundary setting may be an important issue for the counseling or therapy group, for many men have had boundary issues themselves, such as setting reasonable boundaries so that there is not an abuse of power or that they do not become victims of power abuse. In short, it is the responsibility of the leader to attend to these issues within the group setting.

One way of addressing boundary issues is through therapist self-disclosure. The leader is responsible for describing boundaries (rules) of the group, and this should occur early in the life of the group. This can provide an added benefit, for by having early self-disclosure from the group leader, the leader begins to model responsible and respectful ways of interacting among the members of the group. This approach is supported by Vinogradov and Yalom (1990, p. 192) who stated that the group is "generally more self-disclosing than the individual therapist. The leader who judiciously uses his or her own person to relate authentically to others in the group creates an atmosphere in which sharing, mutual respect, and interpersonal honesty are modeled." Thus, boundaries are determined in a respectful manner. On the issue of self-disclosure, Yalom (1989) reported that over the years he has probably shared too little rather than too much, because when he *has* shared, patients benefit by learning that he, too, must struggle with the problems of being human.

It is important for group leaders to be familiar with what is appropriate and inappropriate in self-disclosure. The group is for the members, not the leader. Appropriate self-disclosures generally relate to the "then and there" (e.g., "When I had children at home, it was important to provide limits, while still respecting their autonomy. How are you doing that in your family today?") or to the "here and now" (e.g., "My concern now, with what is being presented in the group, is . . ."). Benowitz (1995), who found that inappropriate therapist disclosure occurred in 93 percent of the cases of inappropriate therapist-client involvement, reported the extent of the importance of learning appropriate boundaries, expressed through appropriate self-disclosure. Clearly, for those 93 percent, a lack of clear boundaries, expressed through inappropriate self-disclosure, reflected their lack of professional standards and adherence to appropriate ethical guidelines.

Use of Group Models, Interventions, and Techniques

There are many models of group treatment, ranging from brief, time-limited interventions to long-term analytically oriented group therapy. We have attempted to delineate several of those in this text. Even within models, though, there is considerable variation of methods of interventions and the role of group techniques. An ethical and professionally responsible group leader will have training in group work, understand various modalities of group treatment, and have a strong theoretical stance on which to base the group work. Additionally, the professional group leader will stay current with recent developments in theory and practice of group work, including not only learning new techniques but also becoming familiar with the literature that examines group effectiveness. Professional counselors continue to grow in their practice skills, and they learn newer and better models of group work. Further, they examine the research to become familiar with the literature on what groups work for what population under what conditions and with what membership characteristics.

Regardless of the orientation to group work a group leader adheres to, there are group strategies and interventions that are available and that are often very beneficial for involving members in the group process. Gladding (1999, p. 223) reported that "group techniques or exercises are structured ways of getting members to interact with one another. They can have a powerful impact on group members and positively affect how people work together or change. They can also inhibit the natural ebb and flow of a group when leaders misuse them." The use of techniques and group activities may result in the group operating at a faster pace early in the life of the group, but in doing so, some positive aspects of the group may not have the opportunity to develop, such as greater cohesion of members and trust that evolves from interactional processes and sharing of personal concerns and issues.

If the group techniques are carefully developed in order to illustrate a particular point or to lead members to a specific position, then the techniques may be very beneficial to the group. In describing group techniques, Corey (1995), has advocated that their use be tied to specific goals of the group or to specific members' needs or concerns, but not be used simply to fill time in a group or when the group leader is not sure what to do next.

Often, the use of group exercises occurs when group leaders have not yet developed experience and comfort in leading groups. They might resort to group activities to provide structure to the work they are doing, particularly when they are fearful that the group will contain considerable "dead space" or silence if the leader does not have a strong repertoire of group activities. An example of this occurs when working with groups for men. Students learning group work with men have often heard the stories that men need a lot of structure to participate in a group and that leaders need a cookbook of techniques to apply to keep them involved. Our experience is just the opposite: When men are *invited* to participate in a group and have assurances that there will be no *blame or shame* in the group for whatever they say or present, they have a lot to talk about and are very disclosing and appropriate for the group (Horne, Jolliff, & Roth, 1996).

It is the ethical responsibility of the group leader to be certain that when techniques are used, they are used for a reason. Further, when an activity occurs in a group, it is necessary to provide time to process the activity and determine what meaning it has for the members or how the members may make meaning of the experience. The activity should be based on a theoretical model, be consistent with the goals of the group and appropriate to the needs and developmental level of the participants, and be monitored to be certain that the activities do not draw members away from personal sharing and interacting.

Termination

"Termination and follow-up become ethical issues more because of errors of omission rather than errors of commission" (Gazda, 1989, p. 307). Group counselors and therapists spend considerable time planning their groups, working to make certain the groups form and progress through developmentally appropriate stages of group work, and assuring that group cohesion and intimacy develop among the members. Many members, however, simply stop the group at a designated time—the end of the semester, the end of the contracted 10 sessions—and fail to obtain closure on the group experience. Changes that have occurred during the life of a group are much more likely to be maintained if there is a planned closure to the group, if generalization of learnings from the group to the real world are planned and practiced, and if all the members have a sense of termination that is respectful and dignified.

Regardless of whether it is a long-term group, in which a number of sessions will likely be devoted to closure, or a brief psychoeducational group, in which less time will be spent, it is important for all members that there be closure to the experience. Members are likely to experience a sense of loss, perhaps grief, and certainly sadness as the group comes to an end, for in the period of time the group has existed, members have come to know one another well, they have shared intimate information and experiences, and they have sought support and nurturance from the group. Grief occurs with the loss of all intimate friendships, whether the friend is a person or a group. The ethical group leader will be sensitive to this need for closure and will provide the opportunity for all members to successfully say their good-byes and move on. Gladding (1999) has referred to this as a time for issues of separation and consolidation of changes to be addressed.

Termination activities should occur with the entire group. The group leader, though, should also provide availability for follow-up meetings, either with the group as a whole if necessary, or with individuals as the needs arises. For work we have done with parenting groups, it has been our experience that a scheduled follow-up group, meeting—a booster session—after about six weeks is very powerful for maintaining changes within the family system. This is an example of a group follow-up. If the leader is unavailable to meet with the group at a later date, he or she should be available for meetings with individuals if they are requested and needed. Again, Gladding reported that the follow-up after termination provides the opportunity of consolidating changes and moving toward closure on issues of loss and grief. It also provides the leader with feedback and evaluation information on the effectiveness and impact of the group. Follow-up with group members is expected of professional counselors and therapists.

SUMMARY

As with other areas of practice, preventing problems from happening is more effective than fixing problems after they have developed. It behooves the group counselor and group therapist, then, to be familiar with the ethical standards of the profession, to know the specific applications of ethical standards to group counseling and therapy, and to be knowledgeable of community standards as well as standards of practice within a given state as determined by the state's professional certification or licensing board. Further, for a practice to be successful, the practitioner must be knowledgeable of the theoretical models and therapeutic skills of group work and aspire to high standards of practice. Still, it is necessary for the practitioner to maintain membership in a professional association and to be certified or licensed for practice, for it is through professional associations and state licensing boards that members may stay current on ethical and legal developments impacting their practice. Also, it is important that practitioners maintain professional liability insurance to provide for legal advice and guidance if an ethical or legal charge is filed.

In preparing to present a group offering to potential group members, it is necessary that (1) the goals of the group be clear and explained to potential members, (2) an informed consent or parental/guardian permission is obtained, and (3) the consent include disclosure of the therapist's values, intended activities and plans for the group, a description of benefits and dangers to group members, and a description of what is expected of group members while in the group. All of this information should be provided before the initial session of the group.

REFERENCES

American Counseling Association. (1995). *Code of ethics and standards of practice.* Alexandria, VA: Author.

American Group Psychotherapy Association. (1978). *Guidelines for the training of group psychotherapists.* New York: Author.

Association for Specialists in Group Work. (1991). *Professional standards for training of group work generalists and of group work specialists, revised.* Alexandria, VA: Author.

Benowitz, M. (1995). Comparing the experiences of women clients sexually exploited by female versus male psychotherapists. In J. Gonsiorek (Ed.), *Breach of trust: Sexual exploitation by health care professionals and clergy.* Thousand Oaks, CA: Sage.

Corey, G. (1995). *Theory and practice of group counseling* (4th ed.). Pacific Grove, CA: Brooks/Cole.

Donigian, J. (1993). Duality: The issue that won't go away. *Journal for Specialists in Group Work, 18,* 137–140.

Forester-Miller, H. (1998). Group counseling: Ethical considerations. In D. Capuzzi & D. Gross (Eds.), *Introduction to group counseling* (2nd ed.). Denver: Love.

Forester-Miller, H., & Duncan, J. (1990). The ethics of dual relationships in the training of group counselors. *Journal for Specialists in Group Work, 15,* 88–93.

Gazda, G. M. (1989). *Group counseling: A developmental approach* (4th ed.). Boston: Allyn and Bacon.

Gladding, S. (1999). *Group work: A counseling specialty* (3rd ed.). Upper Saddle River, NJ: Prentice-Hall.

Horne, A. M., Jolliff, D. L., & Roth, E. W. (1996). Men mentoring men in groups. In M. Andronico

(Ed.), *Men in groups: Insights, interventions, psychoeducational work.* Washington, DC: American Psychological Association.

Kitchner, K. S. (1984). Intuition, critical evaluation, and ethical principles: The foundation for ethical decisions in counseling psychology. *The Counseling Psychologist, 12,* 43–55.

Koocher, G. P., & Keith-Spiegel, P. (1998). *Ethics in psychology: Professional standards and cases* (2nd ed.). New York: Oxford University Press.

Lakin, M. (1988). *Ethical issues in the psychotherapies.* New York: Oxford University Press.

Meara, N. M., Schmidt, L. D., & Day, J. D. (1996). Principles and virtues: A foundation for ethical decision, policies, and character. *The Counseling Psychologist, 24,* 4–77.

Norsworthy, K., & Horne, A. (1994). Issues in group work with HIV+ gay and bisexual men. Special issue on counseling men in groups. *Journal for Specialists in Group Work, 19,* 112–119.

Ohlsen, M. M., Horne, A. M., & Lawe, C. F. (1988). *Group counseling* (3rd ed.). New York: Holt, Rinehart and Winston.

Robinson, S. E., & Gross, D. R. (1989). Applied ethics and the mental health counselor. *Journal of Mental Health Counseling, 11,* 289–299.

Schoener, R. G., & Luepker, E. T. (1996). Boundaries in group therapy: Ethical and practical issues. In B. DeChant (Ed.), *Women and group psychotherapy* (pp. 373–399). New York: Guilford.

Shertzer, B., & Stone, S. (1980). *Fundamentals of counseling* (3rd ed.). Boston: Houghton Mifflin.

Smead, R. (1995). *Skills and techniques for group work with children and adolescents.* Champaign, IL: Research Press.

Treppa, J. A. (1998). A practitioner's guide to ethical decision-making. In R. M. Anderson, T. L.

Needels, & H. V. Hall (Eds.), *Avoiding ethical misconduct in psychological specialty areas.* Springfield, IL: Charles C. Thomas.

Van Hoose, W. H. (1980). Ethics and counseling. *Counseling and Human Development, 13,* 112.

Van Hoose, W. H., & Kottler, J. A. (1985). *Ethical and legal issues in counseling and psychotherapy* (2nd ed.). San Francisco: Jossey-Bass.

Vinogradov, S., & Yalom, I. (1990). Self-disclosure in group psychotherapy. In G. Stricker & M. Fisher (Eds.), *Self-disclosure in the therapeutic relationship.* New York: Plenum.

West, M., & Livesley, J. (1986). Therapist transparency and the frame for group psychotherapy. *International Journal of Group Psychotherapy, 36,* 5–19.

Yalom, I. (1989). *Love's executioner, and other tales of psychotherapy.* New York: Harper Perennial.

Yalom, I. (1995). *Theory and practice of group psychotherapy* (4th ed.). New York: Basic Books.

CHAPTER SEVEN

EXISTENTIAL-HUMANISTIC GROUP THEORIES

Existential-humanistic theories represent one of the three major theoretical groupings of group counseling and therapy models presented in this text in addition to the senior author's eclectic developmental model. The existential-humanistic theories are characterized by the placement of responsibility for one's fate with the individual rather than with one's inherited predispositions or environment. It is believed that the individual will choose health and self-actualization over illness or self-destruction if he or she has freedom of choice. There is a strong focus on the immediate situation and on the nature of the relationship between the counselor/therapist and the client(s). Carl Rogers and his colleagues, especially Carkhuff, Truax, and Gendlin, were primarily responsible for the seminal research that isolated the "core" (necessary and sufficient) conditions of a helping relationship.

Three major theories were selected to represent the existential-humanistic theory and practice: person centered, logotherapy, and Gestalt. Each of these theoretical models will be described and in certain areas compared and contrasted in this chapter. Examples of application will follow in the next chapter. Although logotherapy, Gestalt, and person-centered therapy were selected to represent existential-humanistic theory, other individuals have developed variations of existential therapy that should be studied for a more comprehensive understanding. Particularly, as applicable to group therapy, Yalom's (1995) fourth edition of *The Theory and Practice of Group Psychotherapy* (1989) and *Love's Executioner* (1989) as well as his *Existential Psychotherapy* (1980) should be studied. Rollo May's existential applications to existential therapy are explicated in *Existential Psychology* (1961) and in May, Angel, and Ellenburger's (1958) *Existence: A New Dimension in Psychiatry and Psychology*. Bugental's focus on authenticity adds another element to existential theory and therapy. His theory and practice are found in *Psychotherapy and Process: The Fundamentals of an Existential-Humanistic Approach* (1978) and the *Search for Authenticity: An Existential-Analytic Approach to Psychotherapy* (1981).

HISTORY AND DEVELOPMENT

Person-Centered Group Therapy

On the 11th of December, 1940, in a speech at the University of Minnesota, Carl Rogers aroused a furor among scholars and mental health professionals by sketching a radically different therapeutic approach. He tentatively outlined Newer Concepts in Psychotherapy, which relied "much more heavily on the individual drive toward growth, health, and adjustment." Therapy becomes "a matter of freeing (the client) for normal growth and development." This new approach, Rogers announced, "places greater stress upon . . . the feeling aspects of the situation than upon the intellectual aspects." It stresses "the immediate situation" rather than "the individual's past," emphasizing "the therapeutic relationship itself as a growth experience" (Rogers & Wood, 1974, p. 8). In the next 20 years, through empirical studies, the conditions for realizing the ambitions of this "newer therapy" were meticulously formulated in theory and practice. Client-/person-centered therapy is still dedicated to discovering the conditions that favor the activation of healing and growth within the person.

In the 1970s, the term *person centered* won favor over *client centered.* The term is used to reflect the therapist's attitude toward the person. The therapist does not see a patient who is sick nor a client who is a customer. The therapist centers attention not on a theory, nor on himself or herself, but on the other—the whole person.

The person-centered therapy group consisting of 8 to 12 individuals with one or two therapists revolutionized the practice of psychotherapy. With the advent of the encounter group, it was no longer possible to make a sharp distinction between *therapy* and *growth.* In 1968, the La Jolla Program (an institute of the Center for Studies of the Person) began an education program for group facilitators featuring brief groups of 50 to 100 persons. In 1973, Rogers and other colleagues initiated a new form of person-centered group work: More than 100 people live together for about two weeks in a group-directed community for learning; their only planned activity, besides meals, is to gather in one large meeting where all plans and decisions of the group are made. Person-centered approach workshops have been convened in North and South America, Asia, and Europe. Figure 7.1 highlights trends in person-centered group development.

Group Logotherapy

Logotherapy was chosen as representative of existential therapy because it is a direct offshoot of modern existential philosophy, which originated from the Danish theologian Soren Kierkegaard. Although the word *existentialism* did not come into usage until 70 years after Kierkegaard's death, he laid the foundations of a philosophy that was further developed in Germany by Martin Heidegger and Karl Jaspers, and in France by Jean Paul Sartre, Albert Camus, and Gabriel Marcel.

The basic tenet of existential philosophy is contained in the sentence, *Existence precedes essence,* which means that one's essence, one's essential being, is the result of one's existence—namely, what one does with one's life. To put it more succinctly, what people do determines what they are. The emphasis is on choice and responsibility for one's choices. Further, emphasis is placed on personal uniqueness and the importance of meaning.

Although meaning is central for both the German and the French branch of existential philosophy, there is a significant difference. The French existentialists assume that life has no meaning in itself, but that human beings have an innate need to find meaning; therefore, people have to invent meanings that makes sense to them. The

Trends in Half Century of Person-Centered Therapy

1935	Rochester, New York			Patient (Therapist)	Surrender of role of expert.
		Nondirection (two-person)			Take guidance from client.
1940	Ohio				
1945			Two-person group: Psychotherapy		Relationship more personal.
1950				Client (Facilitator)	Surrender of rigid theories.
1955	Chicago, Illinois				
					Trust in own feelings.
1960		Reflection (two-person)			Congruent with own experience.
1965	Wisconsin	Experiencing (two-person) (applications)	Small group: Psychotherapy and social therapy		Therapist experience enters relation.
					Surrender control of intellect.
1970		Encounter (small group)	Large group:		
1975	California (Center for Studies of the Person)	Community for Learning (large group)	Psychotherapy, social therapy, and create, heal, and surpass culture	Person (Convenor)	Trust more intuitive processes.
1980					Surrender theories to rely on experience.
					Greater trust in group for organic decisions, self-knowing beyond the personal.
					Surrender to being more than doing.
	Rogers moves west– organizing radius expands	Increased involvement of therapist as a genuine person with larger numbers of persons–closer to "real" life	Increased complexity of therapeutic effort	"Other" viewed more holistically	Therapist's deepening surrender to increased complexity

FIGURE 7.1   Trends in Person-Centered Group Development

German existentialists assume that life, existence itself, does have meaning, and that it is not up to people to invent their own but to discover the meanings their lives hold.

The first person to use the principles of existential philosophy in therapy and counseling was the Swiss psychiatrist Ludwig Binswanger, who was a follower of Sigmund Freud but broadened Freud's ideas in the direction of existentialism. He called his system *daseinsanalyse.*

Viktor Frankl, the founder of logotherapy, was a student of Alfred Adler, whose individual psychology was in turn an offshoot of Freud's psychoanalysis. Frankl was greatly influenced by the philosophy of the German existentialists Martin Heidegger and Karl Jaspers, and the phenomenologist Scheler. Frankl rejected the French existentialists' contention that life has no meaning and that people have to arbitrarily "give" meaning to their existence.

Frankl's whole life and work is testimony of his attempts to prove that life does have intrinsic meaning. Such proof can be found only existentially, by living as if life had meaning and not as if everything were chance. In his practice, and in the practice of his followers, Frankl found proof that the assumption of a meaningful life is the precondition of health. The therapy he developed was originally (in the 1920s) called *logotherapy;* later (in the 1930s), the alternative term *existential analysis* was used. When his book began to be translated into English, the confusion with Binswanger's *daseinanalyse,* which also was translated as "existential analysis," prompted Frankl to change the name of his therapy to *logotherapy* to avoid confusion. The Greek word *logos,* which signifies "the unifying principle of the universe," was translated by Frankl as "meaning," thus logotherapy is "therapy through meaning."

Logotherapy differs from other existential treatment modes in that it alone has successfully developed what can properly be called *psychotherapeutic techniques* (Ungersma, 1961). Logotherapy also differs from other current existential modes in that it places more emphasis on what Frankl calls objective meanings to be fulfilled in the world. The other existential modes are much more subjectively based.

Gestalt Group Therapy

Gestalt is a German word meaning whole or configuration. As one psychological dictionary puts it, "Gestalt is an *integration* of members as contrasted with a summation of parts" (Warren, 1934, p. 115). The term also implies a unique kind of patterning. *Gestalt therapy* is a term applied to a unique kind of psychotherapy as formulated by Frederick S. Perls, his coworkers, and his followers.

Perls began, as did many of his colleagues in those days, as a psychoanalyst, after having been trained as a physician in post–World War I Germany. In 1926, he worked under Professor Kurt Goldstein at the Frankfurt Neurological Institute for brain-injured soldiers, where he was first exposed to the tenets of Gestalt psychology but "was still too preoccupied with the orthodox approach to assimilate more than a fraction of what was offered" (Perls, 1947, p. 5). Later, Perls was exposed to the theories and practice of Wilhelm Reich and incorporated some of the concepts and techniques of character analysis into his work.

While serving as a Captain in the South African Corps, Perls wrote his first manuscript in 1941–1942, outlining his emerging theory and application of personality integration, which later appeared as the book *Ego, Hunger and Aggression.* The term *gestalt therapy* was first used by him and two coauthors, Ralph Hefferline of Columbia University and Paul Goodman of New York City.

In 1952, the New York Institute for Gestalt Therapy was formed and soon began to offer workshops and courses for professionals. The New York Institute was housed in the apartment of Fritz and Laura Perls, with their living room serving as the group or seminar room. The initial faculty consisted of Frederick S. Perls, M.D., Laura Posner Perls, D.Sc., Elliot Shapiro, M.A., Paul Goodman, Ph.D., and Paul Weisz, M.D.

Intensive courses for non–New York City residents were offered beginning in 1953, and some of the faculty began to commute to Cleveland following the formation of a Gestalt therapy study group there in 1953. This study group formed the Gestalt Institute of Cleveland in 1955. The Cleveland Institute was instrumental in the development of Gestalt theory in groups and communities (Greve, 1993).

Simkin, who was among the original students studying at the New York Institute (1952–1955), moved to Los Angeles in 1958. When Fritz Perls came back to the West Coast in 1960, Simkin arranged a Gestalt therapy study group for Perls that fall. Walter Kempler, M.D., Robert Gerard, Ph.D., Everett Shostrom, Ph.D., as well as Simkin and some six to eight other psychotherapists were among those who participated.

Fritz Perls returned from a trip around the world in 1963 and resumed training Gestalt therapists in the Los Angeles area. In 1964, Simkin, Kempler, and Perls began training psychotherapists in Gestalt therapy at the Esalen Institute. Some of these psychotherapists were from the San Francisco area and an Institute was formed there in the late 1960s by Jack Downing, M.D., Cynthia (Werthman) Sheldon, M.S.W., and others. The Los Angeles Gestalt Therapy Institute was organized in 1969 by three of Simkin's trainees: Robert L. Martin, D.S.W., Robert W. Resnick, Ph.D., and Eric H. Marcus, M.D.

In addition to the New York Institute, two are in the San Diego area: one primarily organized by Tom Munson, M.D., and the other organized by Erving Polster, Ph.D., and Miriam Polster, Ph.D., in 1973. The Simkin Training Center in Gestalt Therapy opened in Big Sur in 1972. Since the early 1970s, Gestalt therapy institutes have been multiplying rapidly.

THEORETICAL RATIONALE

Person-Centered Group Therapy

By the early 1960s, a theory for what is now known as *person-centered group therapy* was well established. A basic axiom of the theory (a corollary of the "formative tendency") states that each person is capable of experiencing the incongruence between the *self-concept and his or her total organismic reality;* also within the person is a natural tendency to *reorganize the self-concept to a closer congruence with the totality of experience.*

Running through the development of person-centered group therapy from the beginning has been an increasing willingness (without denying the destructive forces of life) to trust and follow formative events in others, in oneself, and in groups of persons. The formative tendency may be seen as driving or enhancing the experiencing of a client in the presence of another who is perceived as empathic, genuine, and warm. It can be seen in the process of the small group where the formative tendency sharpens and obscures outlines of individuality and reorganizes the collection into a new complexity. It can be seen in the larger group or community in organic decisions that surpass the group's rational abilities, moving madness toward health, even surpassing the organization of culture itself. In each of these forms, one sees a tendency operating within to awaken the person to a consciousness of his or her own evolution. Surviving the changing forms of therapy over the years, there remains in the person-centered therapist an inner constancy: the desire to be engaged (in a facilitative way) in the client's struggle for liberation and the willingness to be changed by his or her own interaction, or experiencing, in the relationship with the client.

A current theoretical statement that takes into account years of research and clinical observations in two-person groups, small groups, and large groups may now be formulated. The foundations of the theory of person-centered group therapy is the formative tendency of the universe. The fundamental theorem of this theory may be stated: When persons (i.e., therapist, facilitator, convenor and client, group member, participant) bring a certain *readiness* to their meeting, the formative tendency is allowed to reorganize *more complex capacities and perceptions within the individuals and within the collective.*

The *readiness* in the person called therapist is characterized by the ability to translate easily between feelings and ideas, to be congruent in the relationship with others, to experience unconditional positive regard toward others, and to experience an empathic understanding of the others' internal frame of reference and to follow it intuitively without necessarily "understanding." It is further characterized by the capability of living in the moment, in uncertainty and even doubt, to follow intuitively the expressions of the "collective organism," with every expression to be able to follow, to lead, to remain still in cooperation with the creativity of the moment's mysterious dictates. This readiness is also characterized by the willingness to trust the formative tendency as it organizes the other person's experiencing. There is a willingness, in this readiness, to be guided and changed by the therapist's own inner experiencing in the relationship(s).

In the person called client, this *readiness* includes the willingness to be changed by his or her direct experience and to develop the ability to focus within his or her inner world and the inner world of others. Thus, this person allows the operation of the actualizing tendency and perceives the other's unconditional positive regard and empathic understanding for him or her.

More complex capacities and perceptions include the increased awareness and heightened receptivity of the total organismic reality and the reduction of the incongruence between self and experience—becoming a complete person, as an individual and as a member of the human species. These capacities may also include self-healing, "psychic" abilities, and spirituality, as well as practical knowledge by which individual and collective human life may benefit. The small group is believed to possess all the capacities for healing and self-knowing as the dyadic as well as the other significant features. The therapist centers attention not on a theory, nor on himself or herself, but on the other, the *whole person.*

Group Logotherapy

In logotherapy, the human being is seen as a totality in three dimensions: the biological, the psychological, and the spiritual or noëtic. To see human beings only in their biological or psychological dimensions is to see them only as animals, the victims of their drives and instincts, or as machines that can be manipulated. To see a human being as devoid of the spiritual dimension is to reduce the person to a caricature.

The *will to meaning* in logotherapy is the central force in human motivation. The "will to meaning" is seen as stronger than Freud's "will to pleasure" and Adler's "will to power." According to logophilosophy, the human will to meaning is not in vain, for, according to its precepts, life offers a meaning in all circumstances. Whether one chooses to search for the meaning is another matter.

Logotherapy recognizes two types of meaning: the meaning of the moment and ultimate meaning. Fabry (1980) defines *ultimate meaning* as "the premise that order exists in the universe despite apparent chaos; that each person is part of that order and that he can decide whether and how to participate in that order" (pp. 22–23). This definition allows for several interpretations of that order, including God, life, nature, science, the great spirit, and others. The acid test for ultimate meaning is whether it is adequate in the face of tragedy. If it is, then one can presume that the meaning is, indeed, ultimate.

The *meaning of the moment* refers to the transitory meanings that present themselves to the individual literally moment by moment. The significance of the meaning of the moment ranges from the mundane to the heroic, with the former being far more frequent. Crumbaugh (1973) has pointed out that the perception of the moment-by-moment meanings requires a Gestalt process. Frankl thinks that in Gestalt perception, a "figure" is perceived against a "background." In the specific case of meaning perception, one becomes aware of a possibility against the background of reality; that is, one suddenly becomes aware of what one can do about a given situation. In every moment, one chooses from the Gestalt of life—from the totality of all potential choices, one possibility—and makes it a reality.

Logotherapy suggests three major routes to meaning: (1) creativity and achievement, (2) experiential meaning, and (3) attitude. The meaning derived from creativity and achievement is usually obvious; it is equally obvious that this source of meaning is a powerful motivator of human behavior. Experiential meaning refers to the meaning derived through the experience of that which is aesthetically pleasing (e.g., the experience of truth or beauty in nature or art or music) or the experience of love. Attitudinal meaning is most important in logotherapy. It refers to the meaning potential inherent in a situation in which the individual freely chooses an attitude (seeing the opportunity to learn from a crisis, for example) in the face of unavoidable circumstances. One can take a meaningful attitude toward a situation that in itself is meaningless.

Self-transcendence, which occupies a central position in logotherapy, refers to the human ability to reach beyond one's own person toward causes to serve or people to love. Frankl (1978) stated, "I thereby understand the primordial anthropological fact that being human is being always directed, and pointing, to something or someone other than oneself: to a meaning to fulfill or another human being to encounter, a cause to serve or a person to love. Only to the extent that someone is living out this self-transcendence of human existence, is he truly human or does he become his true self " (p. 35). Frankl holds that even one's identity is dependent on self-transcendence; he quotes one of his existential mentors, Karl Jaspers, in support of his position. Jaspers observed that "what man is, he ultimately becomes through the cause which he has made his own" (cited in Frankl, 1967, p. 9). Frankl also takes the position that self-actualization cannot occur except as a consequence of self-transcendence. According to logophilosophy, the more one aims directly for self-actualization, the more one will miss it. Only by investing one's time and energy in causes and people beyond one's self can self-actualization occur. Frankl claims that even Maslow eventually accepted this notion.

Logotherapy places a great deal of emphasis on human freedom. However, it is clearly restricted; human beings are never free *from* conditions, but they are always free to choose their attitude *toward* the conditions. Environment and heredity both have a great impact on one's life but neither influence can ever take away one's freedom to take a stance toward those conditions.

Frankl has referred to logotherapy as education to responsibility. In logotherapeutic terms, *responsibility* refers to the ability and willingness to respond to the meaning potentials offered by life. Responsibility also carries the traditional meaning of owning the outcomes of human choices and behavior. Logotherapy treats freedom and responsibility as if they were a single phenomenon, with freedom constituting the negative portion and responsibility constituting the positive portion.

The issue of choice is most important from an existentialist standpoint. Jaspers (1932) said it poignantly when he stated, "So far as I choose, I am; if I am not, I do not choose" (p. 182). In a sense, then, a person *becomes* his or her choices. Frankl's view of human choice is consistent with Jasper's. In *Psychotherapy and Existentialism* (1967), he stated, "Man makes decisions every moment, even unwittingly and against his will. Through these decisions man decides upon himself. Continually and incessantly he shapes and reshapes himself" (p. 35). In the concentration camps Frankl saw that despite the horror of the conditions, many free choices remained. Through their own choices some inmates behaved "like swine while other behaved like saints" (1967, p. 35).

Meaningful choice implies the implementing of the appropriate action. The existential position has little regard for reflection and intentions that are not followed up with substantive action. Sartre and Frankl are largely in agreement on the issue of action. Sartre (1957) stated, "He [the human being] exists only insofar as he realizes himself. He is, therefore, nothing else but the sum of his actions, nothing else but what his life is" (p. 37). Frankl's emphasis on action is equally clear. In *The Unconscious God* (1975), he stated, "Human existence exists in action rather than reflection" (p. 30).

Logotherapy uses the term *tragic triad* to refer to three inescapable conditions of human life—namely, suffering, guilt, and death. Although the inescapability of these conditions is patently obvious to most people, it does not in any way prevent people from attempting to escape via comforting illusions. Rather than burying the reality under illusions, logotherapy urges that these inescapable conditions be faced and accepted. This acceptance, once it has occurred, becomes the source of great strength.

Logotherapy does not view suffering as the great menace of humankind. According to logotherapeutic doctrine, suffering offers the sufferer the possibility of experiencing the highest value, the deepest meaning. Animals can suffer, but only human beings can perceive a meaning in their suffering. Often, the meaning of the suffering is not readily apparent. In such cases, the sufferers may find meaning in their predicaments by choosing an attitude of courage and resolve in the face of their tragedy. Only because humans are endowed with what Frankl calls "the defiant power of the human spirit" is this attitude of courage possible. The assumption of such an attitude has the effect of ennobling the sufferers, for their suffering has become an achievement. Attitudinal meanings therefore remain as a possibility right up until the last breath. The suffering referred to here is, of course, unavoidable suffering. To suffer needlessly is simply masochism.

Like suffering, guilt should be avoided when possible, but there always remains a profound guilt that is inescapable. Frankl even goes so far as to assert that becoming guilty is a human *right*. Just as it is the right of human beings to feel guilty, it is also their obligation to overcome guilt. The obligation to overcome guilt can serve as a powerful incentive to initiate healthy changes.

Breisach (1962) considered human finiteness to be the central challenge of Sartre and Kierkegaard and the central pillar of Heidegger's philosophy. Frankl is in agreement with this mainstream existential concept. Frankl (1967) spoke of the need of human beings to become reconciled with their finiteness. When they come to grips with their limited time and capacities, they will likely begin to ask what meanings life has to offer in the time remaining. The asking of such questions has the effect of projecting them out of the superficial comfort that life offers and into the more important meanings that remain to be realized.

The most significant aspect of human finiteness is one's own death, and perhaps one most desperately does need to come to terms with this. Frankl (1967) stated that only in the face of death is it meaningful to act. So long as one soothes oneself with the illusion of endless time, decisive action is meaningless or even fanatical. Kaufman (1976) captured this view in the following: "Lives are spoiled and made rotten by the sense that death is distant and irrelevant. One lives better when one expects to die, say, at forty" (p. 214).

The logotherapist's preoccupation with death is in no way morbid. The acceptance of one's own death allows individuals to place the petty concerns of their lives into proper perspective and to begin to take action on those larger issues they have been intending to begin "tomorrow" for the past many years. However, once a person has taken action and actualized a meaning potential, there is no need to be concerned with the transitoriness of life.

The logotherapist considers *commitment* to be an essential life task. Individuals must risk committing themselves to causes even though those causes may, in the end, prove to be unworthy of their commitment. Crumbaugh (1979) considered commit-ment to be the most important and the most difficult step in logotherapy.

Gestalt Group Therapy

Much of what human beings need in order to live in the world is contained outside of the ego boundary. In order to bring what is needed within the organism from the world out-side of the ego boundary, it is necessary for the organism to (1) be *aware* of a need and (2) expend the necessary energy to bring the needed substance through the ego bound-ary. The process of getting something through the ego boundary is called *contact.*

Perls believed that the basic drive in the human organism is *dental aggression.* During the first several months of life, the infant as a suckling is totally dependent on his or her environment for survival. At this early stage, the infant's only self-supportive mechanisms are basic physiological survival systems, such as respiration, metabolism, assimilation, elimination, and so on.

With the eruption of teeth and the development of the ability to crawl and then perambulate, a marked change occurs, or at least potentially can occur, with a gradual switch from almost complete environmental support to more and more self-supportive possibilities. The young child, if permitted, can now begin to explore and discriminate, discover what is nourishing (palatable) and what is toxic (unpalatable).

This developmental phase during which dental aggression allows the child to destructure (primarily food, but also the beginning possibilities of ideas, values, etc.) and, through contact, restructure, integrate, and make part of oneself, is crucial. To the extent that the child is interfered with during this developmental phase, he or she is forced to *introject* (swallow whole) rather than destructure and reintegrate. If the child is continuously forced to take in without chewing and tasting, he or she will form the habit of becoming more and more dependent on environmental support, behaving like an automaton and gradually losing the capacity for creativity.

A human being is considered a total organism functioning as a whole, rather than an entity split into dichotomies such as mind and body. With the philosophical back-ground of humanism, à la Otto Rank, the organism is seen as being born with the capacity to cope with life. This is opposed to the original sin theory of human develop-ment—that the organism must learn to repress or suppress its instinctual strivings in order to become "civilized." The emergence of existential philosophy coincided histor-ically with the development of Gestalt therapy.

Perls, trained as a psychoanalyst and strongly influenced by the philosophy of Sigmund Friedlander, conceptualized personality as being multilayered. The outer layer he described as the *cliché layer.* There is little, if any, genuine self invested in the polite inquiry, "How are you?" or asking others questions about themselves or their families without any real interest. Beneath the cliché layer is a second, which is called the *role-playing layer.* Originally when learning these roles, there was a lot of self invested. However, at present, role-playing is frequently automatized and masks the genuine self. These learned roles may be that of father or mother, son or daughter, teacher or student, and the like. Beneath the role-playing layer, Perls described the *impasse layer.* Sometimes called the death layer by the Russians, this layer is experienced as a feeling of emptiness or no-thing-ness in the Zen sense. For many people, the subjective experience of being without clichés or roles is extremely frightening. If one passes through the impasse, the fourth layer, the *implosive-explosive layer,* is reached. At this level, a person is closely aware of emotions that are either expressed or imploded. The last layer is the genuine personality stripped of all the learned (usually phoney) ways of being in the world (Simkin, 1979).

Perls posited a hierarchical need system in expanding his personality theory. He believed that "from the survival point of view the most urgent situation becomes the controller, the director takes over" (Perls, 1976, p. 33). An example of the hierarchical need system would be an emergency when there is a sudden outbreak of fire. If a person ran from the fire and depleted his or her oxygen supply, the person would stop to breathe because breathing would now take precedence over running (Simkin, 1979).

In summarizing the theory of Gestalt therapy, Yontef (1971) reasoned that organismic needs lead to sensory motor behavior. Once a configuration is formed that has the qualities of a good Gestalt, the organismic need that had been in the foreground is met and a balance, or state of satiation, or no-need is achieved.

> When a need is met, the Gestalt it organized becomes complete and it no longer exerts an influence—the organism is free to form new gestalten [meaningful episode]. When this gestalt formation and destruction are blocked or rigified at any stage, when needs are not recognized and expressed, the flexible harmony and flow of the organism/environment field is disturbed. Unmet needs form incomplete gestalten that clamor for attention and, therefore, interfere with the formation of new gestalten. (Yontef, 1971 p. 3)

As Perls, Hefferline, and Goodman (1951) stated, "The most important fact about the figure-background formation is that if a need is genuinely satisfied, the situation changes" (p. xi).

In order to bring about the possibility of closure, or the completion of earlier unfinished situations, persons are encouraged to deal with events as if they were occurring in the present. A specific technique for bringing past events into the present is asking the person to describe the event in the first-person present tense, as if it were occurring at the moment. The theoretical basis for this technique is rooted in the belief (and experience) that emotions that were overwhelming at the time they occurred were dealt with through the ego defenses of projection, retroflection, and introjection. By encouraging a person to reexperience rather than talk about a past event, the avoided affect may, and frequently does, surface through the support of the patient's adult ego as well as the presence of a sympathetic nonjudgmental Gestalt therapist.

According to Beisser, change occurs paradoxically by continuing a behavioral pattern rather than attempting to alter or change that pattern. "Change can occur when the patient abandons, at least for the moment, what he would like to become and attempts to be what he is. The premise is that one must stand in one place in order to have firm footing to move" (Beisser, 1970, p. 77).

From another theoretical vantage, Perls claimed that all that is needed for behavioral change to occur is *awareness.* The primary therapeutic tool in Gestalt therapy is awareness, which may be defined as being in touch with one's own existence. This ability to focus on what is actual defines a person's immediate subjective reality. Learning to focus one's awareness allows that person to discover that what is, is. There is no right or wrong reality.

Perls suggested the possibility of *universal awareness.* "With the hypothesis of universal awareness we open up to considering ourselves in a living way rather than in the aboutisms of having a mind, ego, superego and so forth" (Perls, 1975, p. 69). In order to establish good contact with the environment, it is necessary to risk discovering one's own contact boundaries through experiencing what is "me" and "not me." Adequate contact requires adequate *support.* Focus in Gestalt therapy frequently is on development of appropriate support for desired contact fullness. Support systems may include knowledge, interest, concern for others, breathing, the undercarriage of one's body, and so on. Invariably, Gestalt therapists become cognizant of faulty support systems as they deal with their patients' inability to be contactful.

Greve (1993) provided a more succinct description of the Gestalt theory and personality development. He described the personality being structured from interactions within the person and between the person and the environment. Gestalts "are formed from the inherent biological processes of human organisms to organize impinging events or emerging sensations into meaningful entities" (p. 229). The formation of Gestalt is a continuous process. Needs emerge into awareness, are acted on and satisfied, and then fade into the background. Motivation comes from the need to complete the emerging Gestalt. "The spontaneous, unconscious contact with the environment gradually creates the *self system,* the inner support structure that is based on experience. That system guides the organism through the awareness of self and the environment . . . functioning without conscious thoughts directing the action" (Greve, 1993, p. 229).

The *ego* is the objective, or reality-oriented, process that can impose limitations on the self and stop the formation of a Gestalt, such as suppressing a thought. It is essential for adapting to the real world.

According to Greve, all people have three zones of awareness through which they develop their level of functioning and personality—the greater the level of awareness the higher the level of functioning. The *interior* zone of awareness is everything that occurs within the body, such as sensations, pain, and needs. The *exterior* zone is that part of the environment within range of the senses, such as what can be seen, felt, smelt, and touched. The *middle* zone is between the other two zones and includes memories, fantasies, wishes, judgments, dreams, and so on. *Thought* controls this zone. People with a highly developed middle zone tend to be highly intellectual but out of touch with themselves and their environments.

According to Greve, the *contact boundary* is the point at which the self touches the environment. It can be psychological or physical. "The *self boundary* is a limiting psychological line beyond which the self does not develop, function, or apply (Greve, 1993, p. 230). It limits the self from the not-self.

The Gestalt cycle described by Greve would resemble Figure 7.2. Zinker (1977) would add centering before sensation. According to Greve, healthy people are authentic and know what they want. They have goal awareness of self and environment, which is characterized

> by the full expression of one's self, by experiencing rather than thinking, by completed expression, and by action taken and full responsibility taken for one's self. . . . Psychopathology occurs when awareness of self is blocked or when contact with the environment is avoided. With loss of awareness, parts of the self are lost; with avoidance of contact, experience is diminished or missed, and growth is impeded. (Greve, 1993, p. 230)

Greve listed and defined five contact boundary disturbances that may lead to psychopathology: confluence, retroflexion, introjection, projection, and deflection. Confluence and retroflexions occur during the awareness phase of the Gestalt cycle; the others occur during the second half or action phase. *Confluence* is when the figure does not form against the background; awareness does not occur. *Retroflexion* occurs when the organism holds back action although awareness is present; conflict with the environment becomes one with self. *Introjection* occurs when values, beliefs, or objects from the environment are taken into the self system but are not assimilated. *Projection* occurs when the person cannot discriminate between self and the environment and part of self is seen as environment. *Deflection* occurs when contact is about to be made but must be avoided and the resultant action misses the mark.

A basic assumption in Gestalt therapy is that the way in which the patient deals with his or her world is reenacted in the way he or she deals with the therapist. Based on this assumption, stress is placed on the I-thou interaction that occurs between therapist and patient. Gestalt therapists aim for transparency of self rather than cloaking themselves in the mantle of therapist and encouraging transference reactions. This is not to say that transference does not occur in Gestalt therapy. Rather, an attempt is made to minimize rather than to maximize transference reactions by dealing with what is ongoing at the moment in the therapist-patient interactive process.

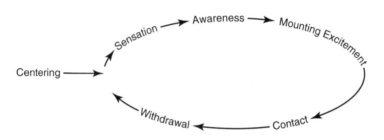

FIGURE 7.2   Gestalt Cycle

THERAPIST'S ROLE

Person-Centered Group Therapy

The role of the facilitator (or therapist) is to be facilitative in the creation of a climate that does not interfere with the potency of natural life focus. An ideal atmosphere is one where the facilitator and each group participant may enter into a creative process, with each participant living his or her own complex wholeness, whether in direct interaction with the designated facilitator, another member, or even in silence.

Participants are asked to bring a readiness and reasonable expectations to the group meeting. For his or her part, the facilitator is asked to bring, first of all, an *alertness* to each other person, to himself or herself, and to the group as a single entity or process. This alertness includes the sensitivity to who might be the most facilitative person at any time in the group. The facilitator listens sensitively, carefully, and as accurately as possible to each person and the feelings on the edge of the person's awareness. He or she listens in such a way as to sense the meaning and feelings aroused by the person's expressions (verbally and nonverbally), in the group and internally. The facilitator accompanies the person, sifting through complications (in the person or within the group), keeping the communication on the track of the significance it has for the person. The goal of this listening is not just to "get in touch with feelings," it is to follow the person's discovery of the moment's rich labyrinth of experiencing and to facilitate the expression of one grand unclear internal "this" in a present meaning.

Gendlin (1974) has advised facilitators to do anything they want, as long as they "stay in touch at all times with the person's directly felt concrete experiential datum— and help the person also to stay in touch with that, and get into it. (If doing that is the baseline, every other procedure and idea can also be tried out, and one returns quickly again to finding out, listening, and responding to where it leaves the person)" (p. 220).

Although, through directing attention to one's inner self, a person may become more self-centered, it is not the purpose of group therapy to bring about a self-preoccupation. The climate of the group is intended to allow the participant to focus inwardly, not to the exclusion of effective life in the world but solely to contact and unite with the formative tendency.

The facilitator is asked to bring to the meeting not an obligation but a *willingness* to live within a creative environment that the group may construct together (at times in ways he or she would not be able to predict or perhaps even understand). Though not blindly acceptant, he or she is asked to trust the group and be willing to "live" the theory, doing what is implicitly demanded of other participants.

Cooperating with the inner forces of his or her own actualization, the facilitator listens within with the same sensitivity and alertness he or she affords others. From the facilitator's point of view, the attention paid toward himself or herself, toward another person in the group, or to the mood or climate of the group is more of an "a-tension," a melting of tension, of role, of analysis, or of evaluative capacities in favor of an intuitive following of his or her inner world, the other's inner world, and the organic wisdom of the group. The facilitator's *willingness* to be changed by the experience characterizes, and perhaps distinguishes, this approach from other approaches to group therapy.

The facilitator trusts his or her own total organism—body, sensations, emotions, reasoning, and intuitive faculties—to live in the moment, to be guided by new principles developed out of increased awareness. The other group members will come to know who the facilitator genuinely is and what he or she is feeling. They know that the facilitator will respond to the moment, not from learned techniques, even if that means saying or doing something risky, unpopular, or even "untherapeutic." Although he or she will not impede the process with personal problems, the character of the group will be influenced by the *person* of the facilitator as much as by the individuality of the group members, to the extent that he or she feels comfortable, just as the others.

Finally, the facilitator is asked to bring an attitude of nonevaluative caring for the group members. This attitude grows out of the trust in the individual's capacity to know himself or herself and to find the pace and direction of personal change. This kind of acceptance applies to the group as well, and the ability of a group of persons together to mobilize a healing capability. Of this trust, Rogers (1970) stated,

> I trust the group, given a reasonably facilitating climate, to develop its own potential and that of its members. For me this capacity of the group is an awesome thing. . . . This is undoubtedly similar to the trust I came to have in the process of therapy in the individual, when it was facilitated rather than directed. To me the group seems like an organism, having a sense of its own direction even though it could not define the direction intellectually. . . . I have seen the "wisdom of the organism" exhibited at every level from cell to group. (p. 44)

Not suffocating everyone with a single approach, the facilitator attempts to understand and (within the limits of existing conditions) operate within the group on its own terms. The facilitator interacts with each other member in an authentic way and keeps in consciousness the whole, paying attention to the overall "music" of the group.

The facilitator is not *trying* to be the best or even, strictly speaking, trying to be empathic, or genuine, or nonpossessively warm. He or she simply *brings* these capacities to the meeting. The designated person does not decide in advance to direct the person or the group in a particular way, as this is not of the creativity of life. The designated facilitator, likewise, does not decide in advance to be nondirective, or unstructured, as this does not come from the creativity of the moment either. The facilitator surrenders impatience and easy answers for a creative state of waiting—alert to follow *or* to lead. He or she is willing to live unattached to a particular form of outcome, to be surprised by the unique creation of each group of persons.

Success is not marked by how well the facilitator shines in presenting the cardinal attitudes but in how well the group's creative, growthful wisdom is released and the benefits of growth afforded its members. *If the group can create a facilitative climate, the formative tendency will do the rest.*

Group Logotherapy

The most important qualification for logotherapy leaders is their familiarity with the basic principles of this therapy so they can impart and apply them to the group. Some leaders spend the first few minutes of each session in a minilecture of some aspect of logotherapy. Others have no set time for "teaching" but explain certain facets of logotherapy whenever an opportunity presents itself, and rely in general on books on logotherapy the group members are expected to read. Books on logotherapy have been termed *bibliotherapy* because their reading itself provides therapy.

Das (1998) has pointed out that "counselors should become thoroughly familiar with the sources of meaning in people's lives: what they receive from life, what they contribute to it, and the stance they take toward what cannot be changed" (p. 209). They should also increase their understanding of the signs and symptoms of psychopathology arising from the absence of meaning and in which meaninglessness is a contributing factor.

Leaders must also be trained in applying the methods of logotherapy, especially the Socratic dialogue, paradoxical intention, and dereflection. They must also be familiar with a variety of supplementary methods they can apply by improvisation when they seem to serve a purpose.

Although leaders of logogroups must be superior in knowledge to the other group members on principles and methods, they must be equals on the human level. They must participate fully in the discussions, relate incidents from their lives, illustrate a point at hand, and share their problems. They must act as role models for the other members of the group. Logoleaders will be most successful in being genuine, caring human beings struggling with the problems of life as everyone else but who have found a philosophy that has helped them and that they are willing to share with the group members.

Robert Leslie (1971), professor of pastoral counseling at the Pacific School of Religion in Berkeley, and a student of Frankl, sees the following as functions of a logoleader:

Structuring: Starting and ending at the appointed time, providing support for each person's contribution, and protecting members against destructive attack

Mirroring: Making observations about what is happening, observing incongruities between words and actions, and pointing out behavior patterns

Focusing: Helping the group move from social chitchat into greater depth, from impersonal, peripheral issues to personal involvement in significant concerns

Modeling: Actively participating as one of the group, according to the agreed rules

Nudging: Encouraging participants toward change: "Where do you go from here? What are you going to do about it?"

Linking: Tying together disconnected statements and picking up unfinished business

Sharing: Not only participating in the group process but also allowing members to participate in leadership

These functions may seem similar to those of other groups, especially those of existential or humanistic hue. But logotherapy group leaders have an additional function: challenging a person from where he or she is to where he or she wants to be, to see the learning opportunity behind a failure, to spot the growing edge of a crisis, to divine meaning possibilities behind frustrations, to be aware of the escape hatches of traps, and to see the chance to reach out beyond the present limitations toward a vision yet unrealized.

Perhaps the most important function of the logoleader is to be aware of the unconscious decisions that become apparent during the group discussions, even though they may not be apparent to the person concerned. Some word, some gesture, some cue may give an indication of a decision that has taken place in the unconscious—a "logo-hook" on which the principles of logotherapy can be attached. The leader is not authorized to *give* meaning to the participants, but once a logohook has become visible, the leader is justified to throw his or her support behind it, to say yes to a direction the group member has chosen, however tentatively and unconsciously. The leader will not automatically say yes to all the decisions of individual members. He or she will say no to decisions that are reductionistic (reducing the person below his or her humanness), pandeterministic (expressing the belief that one's actions are completely determined by forces beyond one's control), or nihilistic (denying that meaning can be found).

A final role of the leader is assistance in the establishment of group norms that are consistent with logophilosophy. The following lists some of the more important norms and some suggestions as to how such norms can be promoted:

1. Norm of assuming responsibility for one's attitude toward unavoidable circumstances: The leader's modeling of this norm is highly desirable, if not essential. To promote this norm, it should be made clear to all that they have the right to gently confront those who may wish to deny that choice exists in the realm of attitude.
2. Norm of self-transcendence: Self-transcendent behavior, especially when evidenced in the group, should be generously rewarded. Further reinforcement of this norm can be obtained by soliciting testimonials of the benefit derived from this behavior.
3. Norm of challenging those who systematically evade making choices. When it becomes obvious that a group member is attempting to keep all of his or her options open in order to avoid decisive choice, the right to challenge this person on this issue should be clear.
4. Norm of disdain for reductionism, pandeterminism, and nihilism: Comments or interpretations that smack of these "isms" should be challenged.
5. Norm of opposing hyperreflection: Catharsis is highly desirable. However, if the focus on one particular problem becomes inordinate (in the subjective judgment of the leader), the group should be encouraged to move on to another issue, perhaps treating the hyperreflected issue via paradoxical intention before doing so.

Gestalt Group Therapy

The Gestalt therapist primarily acts as a facilitator in the group, using his or her awareness to feed back to the group members their perceptions, attitudes, and feelings while interacting within the group. By concentrating on what is going on (the process) rather than what could be (fantasy) or should be (moralizing), each group member is encouraged to take responsibility for what he or she is doing. Assuming members desire to change how they are, they are encouraged to *be* how they are in the present in order to change. All Gestalt therapists, in keeping with the I-thou philosophy, see themselves as models who will relate in a horizontal fashion with the rest of the group members.

In addition to the role of facilitator, some Gestalt therapists will also engage in dyadic exchanges with one member of the group. Frequently, this is perceived as individual therapy within a group setting, even though the other group members may be influenced by witnessing this dyadic interchange.

In co-therapy situations, usually one of the Gestalt therapists is available to work with any member of the group wishing to explore an issue, while the other will attend to the rest of the group members as the work proceeds. Occasionally, co-leaders will agree to be equally available to work with one person within the group or will alternate focusing on the one person.

The early stages of Gestalt therapy as practiced by Perls did not make use of group members or of the group dynamic but was individual Gestalt therapy practiced in a group setting. Basically, the client or patient took the "hot seat" (chair) across from the therapist and the therapist began the therapy, ignoring the other group members. Each member in turn took the "hot seat" and returned to the circle when the therapist terminated the interaction. Through the efforts of the Cleveland Institute (Kepner, 1980) and Zinker (1977) and Frew (1988, 1990), group theory and dynamics were added to Gestalt therapy. The Cleveland Institute emphasized four basic principles in Gestalt group therapy (Greve, 1993):

> (1) the here-and-now experience, (2) group awareness, (3) active contact between the members, and (4) the use of intentional experiments. The group leader [was] seen as the catalyst that transforms the individual members into a community. (p. 229)

New concepts in Gestalt group therapy integrate the intrapersonal, interpersonal, and group process dynamics. As the group progresses through developmental stages of trust and safety, establishing norms, exploration, confrontation, confluence, and working, the group members develop awareness of themselves as individuals as well as members of the group.

GOALS AND OBJECTIVES

Person-Centered Group Therapy

Wood (1982) summed up the goal of person-centered group therapy as follows: "The goal (and the art) of person-centered group therapy is to facilitate the creation of a climate in which the formative tendency may freely express itself in each person and in the group of persons" (p. 239). The person-centered group therapist views the person who comes to therapy as being in a state of incongruence between the self, as perceived, and the actual experience of the total organism. The process whereby a person becomes aware of this incongruence and also the means through which the discrepancy is reduced is called *experiencing* (Gendlin, 1978). Experiencing within group therapy may result from silence, from an encounter with another member or members of the group, or during an interaction with the therapist. Experiencing (moments of inner-movement when a person becomes more completely his or her reality) is not caused by the therapist; it is a manifestation of the natural capacity and tendency for healing and growth within the person—the *formative tendency.*

Group Logotherapy

Williams and Fabry (1982) stated "The goal of the logotherapist is often to bring clients into full awareness of their life task" (p. 191). Nietzsche put it this way: "He who has a *why* to live for can bear almost any *how*" (cited in Frankl, 1963, p. xi). In logotherapy, the facts are not so important as the *attitude* taken toward the facts; likewise, one's symptoms are not so important as the attitude taken toward the symptoms.

Logotherapy focuses on three inescapable conditions of human life: suffering, guilt, and death. Logotherapists view suffering as offering the sufferer the possibility of experiencing the highest value, or the deepest meaning. Only because humans are endowed with what Frankl calls "the defiant power of the human spirit" can they find meaning in their suffering and develop an attitude of courage and resolve in the face of their tragedy.

Guilt, like suffering, should be avoided when possible, but there always remains a profound guilt that is inescapable. One has a right to feel guilty, but one also has the obligation to overcome guilt—or at least to initiate change toward health.

The most significant aspect of human finiteness is one's own death, and people need to come to terms with this. Frankl (1967) stated that only in the face of death is it meaningful to act. The acceptance of one's own death allows individuals to place the petty concerns of their lives into proper perspective and to begin to take action on those larger issues they have been intending to begin "tomorrow" for the past many years.

Logotherapy research has shown that about 20 percent of neuroses are noögenic (i.e., existential frustration caused by competing values within the human spirit). Focusing on the symptoms only intensifies them, according to logotherapy theory. Through *dereflection* clients are encouraged to cease focusing on their symptoms and instead to focus on meaning potentials.

Gestalt Group Therapy

Simkin (1982) described what might be considered the goal of Gestalt group therapy as follows:

> Being in contact with one's own potentially nourishing or toxic behavior enables assimilation or rejection of that behavior. This is also true for being in contact with the behavior of others, experiencing the other at the contact boundary and 'tasting' before chewing up (if nourishing) or 'spitting' out (if toxic). Choice and growth are thus enhanced through organismic self-regulation. (p. 354)

Gestalt therapy is described as a noninterpretive, ahistoric, existentially grounded system in which *awareness* is the primary focus in the here-and-now. Group members are encouraged to *be* how they are in order to change (Simkin, 1982). The group therapist and group members support the "working" client to be who he or she is in the here-and-now of the group interactions.

SELECTION AND GROUP COMPOSITION

Person-Centered Group Therapy

Selection of Group Members.   There are no rules for the selection of group members for a person-centered group. Meetings convened for certain populations, such as women's groups or men's groups, or for specific themes, of course, select members accordingly.

Generally speaking, the person's readiness and his or her own choice are the primary factors in group membership. The congruence between the person's goal in attending and what the convenor believes is possible to achieve from attending the group is assessed by the prospective participant and convenor. Together they decide. The person with realistic expectations who believes he or she may benefit from the group experience and will be able to contribute to the group process is usually accepted. In ongoing therapy, the group members are usually consulted before admitting a new member.

Group Composition.   Doubtless, the attitudes and skills of the facilitator, the attitudes and learning capacities of group members, conditions of the environment, the composition of persons, and the interaction generated all influence the outcomes, for better or worse, of group therapy. It is not known, at present, just what the composition of group members should be for optimum results.

It is customary for group convenors to attempt, if possible, a balance between male and female, old and young, in the composition of groups. In large residential programs, the many small groups are balanced "geographically" as well. Of course, if certain persons, such as married couples, wish to be together or separate, their wishes are respected. In support of this diverse composition for groups, Meador (1980) stated, "We don't feel we are playing god by composing groups as much as possible like the world." Having members whose personal experiences are very different is also thought to increase the creative possibilities of the group in releasing the formative tendency and enriching each person's learning.

Group Logotherapy

Selection of Group Members.   "The patients best suited for an existential approach are those who express a lack of purpose about living and who have a long history of floundering in search of goals" (Rosenbaum, 1993, p. 238). Since the goal of logotherapy is to help people find focus and direction in their lives, logogroups can be helpful to almost anyone and, properly handled, harmful to no one. Nevertheless, there are considerations as far as the selection of group members is concerned.

One consideration pertains to the distinction between logogroups for the mentally ill and those for participants with common human problems. The distinction is not always clear; there is a no-man's-land between the two areas. Some clients could be diagnosed as mentally ill or merely as struggling with problems that are, or seem to be, too large to be borne without outside help. Ideally, a psychiatrist would be the one to make the diagnosis and assign the participant to one type of group or the other. In most cases, however, the selection is made by the group leader, who generally is a psychologist, a counselor, or a social worker trained in the field of logotherapy. The assignment to one type of group or the other can, by itself, have therapeutic effects. Prospective group members who belong to the no-man's-land between the mentally ill and those merely having human problems will, in turn, gain by being admitted to the problem-solving logogroups. If such persons are assigned to therapy groups for the mentally ill, they will consider themselves mentally ill, intensify their hyperreflection on mental illness, and make it more difficult to achieve the first goal of logotherapy: to gain distance from their symptoms.

Most of today's logotherapy groups are problem-solving groups. These groups span a wide range of human problems—career, family, old age, the struggle to find meaning in a chaotic world. In such general groups, participants are accepted who respond to such wordings as "This group is not for the mentally ill but for the mentally searching" or "This group is for those who feel empty, frustrated, trapped, in transition, or in need of direction, purpose." During the past years, logogroups have been established that concentrate on certain problems as just mentioned. Special intergenerational groups have been held and researched in Chicago (Eisenberg, 1980), with members ranging in age from the upper teens to the eighties.

In the volume *Logotherapy in Action* (Crumbaugh, 1979), several logotherapists discuss group therapy for juvenile delinquents, the aged, addicts, and minorities. Elisabeth Lukas has started "dereflective" logogroups, with the purpose of steering the attention of the participants away from their problems and toward goals and commitments. James C. Crumbaugh has for years held logogroups for problem drinkers. Naturally, the selection of members for special type groups has to be geared to their stated purpose.

Group Composition.   Except for groups selected for a specific purpose, and even within the special-purpose groups, logogroups will do best with a variety of participants in age, sex, race, and social and educational backgrounds. This consideration, too, is in line with the logophilosophy that emphasizes the human spirit where most people are similar because they are human.

The universality of the resources of the human spirit becomes evident in a group comprising a variety with their diverse problems and backgrounds. Thus, the lesson of universality of spirit comes across without ever having to be mentioned. By listening to the concerns of others, many participants are surprised that they can identify with so many aspects brought up even though their own situation of age, sex, and background may be different. The unspoken message of the mixed group is: "We are all human beings; let's make use of our human resources."

Gestalt Group Therapy

Selection of Group Members.   According to Simkin (1982) and Greve (1993), a major criterion in the selection of group members is heterogeneity. When forming a group, care is taken to include as wide a range as is practicable of age and type of presenting problem. Attempts are also made to have equal numbers of male and female participants.

All potential group members are first seen in individual therapy (Simkin, 1982) or are oriented individually by the group therapist prior to being admitted to the group (Greve, 1993) to determine the nature and degree of disturbance and to explore the person's attitudes and extent of willingness to participate in a group. Inasmuch as group attendance involves less flexibility as to time of appointment, more time spent during each treatment session, and the reduced cost of each treatment session, these issues are addressed and explicated.

Whenever there is overwhelming evidence that the potential group member is or will become a monopolist within the group, he or she is excluded from consideration. This frequently involves evidence of extreme narcissism and/or severe characterological defects. Although Simkin (1982) has successfully included borderline patients in his groups, he has excluded patients who were actively hallucinating and/or delusional.

An additional criterion used in the selection of group members has been the degree of acceptance by the other group members when introducing a potential new member to an established group. If several members of an ongoing group feel negatively toward the prospective new member, experience has shown that attempting to bring in someone under these circumstances frequently becomes disruptive to both the group process and the therapy of the new member as well.

Group Composition.   Each therapy group is balanced with an equal number of male and female patients. Attempts are made to ensure the heterogeneity of the groups by bringing in as wide a range of age, occupation, presenting problems, and so on, as possible from the sources available. Greve (1993) indicated that Gestalt group therapy is most effective with inhibited and highly intellectual persons out of touch with themselves, but increasing attempts are being made to treat disturbed individuals.

GROUP SETTING

There is general agreement among the three theories on the setting for therapy groups. Each recommends that the room be sufficiently large and comfortable for the group members and be free of distractions. Couches, upholstered chairs, and large pillows used on a carpeted floor are options suggested. Person-centered community groups are often held in any large facility that can accommodate the group, such as hotels, monasteries, residence halls, and the like. Logotherapists differ somewhat from Gestalt therapists inasmuch as they discourage the use of private homes. They also suggest smoking areas and availability of coffee and tea.

GROUP SIZE

For the three theoretical approaches, 8 to 12 appears to be the preferred size for therapy, problem-solving, and couples groups. (Greve [1993] has indicated that Gestalt therapy groups usually have 8 to 10 members.) However, logotherapists may have only 3 or 4 people in their therapy groups, which are usually led by psychiatrists. Person-centered *training* groups run from 50 to 150 and *community* groups from 100 to 250 or more.

FREQUENCY, LENGTH, AND DURATION OF GROUP SESSIONS

The purpose of the group seems to determine the frequency of meetings, length, and duration of the three theoretical approaches. The greatest variation is with person-centered groups. Their typical small therapy groups meet 3 to 4 hours per week, compared to 2½ to 3 hours for logotherapy groups and 1½ to 2 hours for Gestalt groups. For all three theoretical positions, open-ended (new members are added to replace departing members) groups are most common, although certain groups are closed and time limited, especially for logotherapy groups. For example, Eisenberg's (1980) intergenerational groups meet 1½ hours per week for eight weeks. Crumbaugh (1980) has been successful treating problem drinkers for four 2-hour sessions over three weeks. Weekend group training workshops are common in logotherapy (but not marathons) and person-centered therapy. Person-centered community groups meet from 10 days to two weeks in duration.

APPLICATIONS TO VARIOUS AGE GROUPS

The model that has been used most frequently across all age groups is the person-centered model. However, when this model is applied to young children, it is accompanied with play material and activities appropriate to the age group and it becomes somewhat eclectic insofar as the play media include dolls and toys that involves psychodynamic concepts. In a 25-year review (1970–1995) of group treatment in which 1,793 articles in journals and books were analyzed, Lubin, Wilson, Petren, and Polk (1996) reported 26 studies under the following descriptors: nondirective, client-centered, and Rogerion encounter groups. Age groups ranged from young children in nondirective play therapy to the elderly, plus preadolescents, adolescents, college students, and adults. Of the 10 reported studies (Lubin et al., 1996) on Gestalt group therapy, the lowest age level reported in which Gestalt therapy was a treatment was with college undergraduates. No logotherapy studies were reported in the Lubin review, but one will find few applications of logotherapy to others than adult-age groups.

MULTICULTURAL ISSUES

What might be appealing to some cultural groups within the three theoretical positions that illustrate the existential-humanistic point of view may be the same issues that would create problems for other cultures. The emphasis placed on the development of the individual within the group would appeal to most clients of Western and European cultures but may be resisted by cultures where the family group and the community supercede the individual's well-being, such as in Asian, Hispanic, and Native American cultures. A similar split might occur with respect to the encouragement of emotional expression by group members. A third area that could create confusion and resistance on the part of clients from lower socioeconomic classes in the United States and Asian cultures in general is the emphasis placed on the individual's responsibility for developing programs of action for solving his or her problems rather than receiving a prescription from the group leader. Having cited three common areas of multicultural issues that could present problems for clients in existential-humanistic groups, let us focus on some issues unique to each of the three theoretical models.

Clients from cultures where authority figures are expected to lead and provide direction would likely be confused in person-centered groups where the leader trusts co- or multiple leadership to come from the group members themselves. The same phenomenon would likely result with certain social classes where the expectation is similar, especially where adult family members (parents and grandparents) provide leadership. In some cultures and classes, seeking help for mental and emotional problems is not socially sanctioned and clients from these groups are, as Chue and Sue (1984) report about some Asian cultures, seeking help as a last resort. They expect advice and immediate help. Although Japan may be an exception among Asian cultures, Murayama, Nojima, and Abe (1988) reported that client-centered therapy has been very popular in Japan since the 1950s. Many Japanese are now depending more on psychological ties than kinship for mutual help.

With a focus in self-actualization, there is the possibility that the individual will interpret this to mean placing himself or herself above everyone or everything else and move in the direction of self-centeredness. When clients come to person-centered therapy groups with poor social skills, especially those with sociopathic tendencies, self-centeredness could be inadvertently fostered.

As a form of existential philosophy and therapy, logotherapy, especially, has a universal appeal. The focus on the *will to meaning* as the central force of motivation as one struggles with three inescapable conditions of human life—namely, suffering, guilt, and death—may account for the universal appeal of the theory. Insofar as all major religions deal with these issues, people from every culture could identify with the theology. Vontress (1988) confirmed this hypothesis by contending that clients and counselors share the same universal culture and all deal with existential issues. Logotherapy has its roots in western European existential philosophy, and Gould (1993) has described the many similarities between eastern Hindu and Buddhist religions and Frankl's existential psychology.

One basic emphasis in Gestalt therapy is on how the client is dealing with the present. Many cultural groups will bring a stereotyped understanding of therapy to the group. The stereotype, stemming from psychoanalysis, is that clients talk about their past, especially their childhoods. Most clients would likely need to be directed to focus on the present and some would find this awkward and difficult. Being *directed* to focus on certain feelings or body sensations would be alien to most cultures, other than some

Eastern cultures where meditation is a common practice. Similarly, arousing deep emotions of clients, a common outcome of Gestalt therapy (e.g., "directed" expression of anger toward parents, older adults, and authority figures), may be resisted by Asians, certain cultures of South America, and Native Americans.

SPECIAL ETHICAL CONSIDERATIONS

Whenever a group of individuals come together to work toward alleviating or solving personal problems, there is the potential for growth or deterioration. Insofar as the trained professionals take appropriate and reasonable precautions to protect group members, they would be performing ethically. The leader's ethics are in evidence, beginning with his or her advertising literature and continuing with group member selection, orientation and contracting, group process/work, termination, and follow-up.

Whenever group leaders make the effort to develop written contracts and ground rules for group members' participation, most potential avenues for unethical behavior would be anticipated and prevented. Of course, the onus is with the professional leader, since members would not be ethically liable for their behavior although they could be legally liable.

Let us examine the three theoretical positions and leader practices that could lead to potential ethical violations. First, there is no comprehensive treatment of the concept of contracting (in writing) used by leaders of any of the person-centered and logotherapy groups. But that does not mean that group leaders of these theoretical positions do not use written contracts; some most certainly do. Greve (1993) indicated that Gestalt group therapists provide a group contract during orientation.

Regarding selection of group members, the person-centered leaders have the most lenient selection practices, with the decision to accept being made between the leader or convenor and the client. The Gestalt leaders, as described by Simkin (1982), select from individual caseloads, except for training groups of professionals. Logotherapists prefer to have psychiatrists select members for groups to treat the most seriously disturbed. Least restrictive selection practices seem to be with the person-centered approach, and perhaps this would expose this model to more threat for harmful behavior by certain group members even though Wood (1982) points out their ground rules, *generally speaking,* prohibit physical violence.

Leader behavior during the group process would be an occasion for potential claims of unethical conduct. Although all three models admonish the leader to be empathic and to show unconditional positive regard for group members, some Gestalt therapists assume a guru status with its attendant opportunities to abuse the power attributed to the status. Some Gestalt "directives" (exercises) are of questionable therapeutic value, and client harm has been associated with client deterioration.

Very little information can be found in the literature on termination and follow-up of group members for any of the three models representing the existential-humanistic philosophy. One can only hope that appropriate preparation is made for clients terminating their group therapy and that follow-up treatment is available.

RESEARCH

Person-Centered Group Therapy

Research on person-centered therapy occurred primarily while it was known as non-directive counseling and client-centered counseling. In fact, of the 26 studies reviewed by Lubin and colleagues (1996), none were labeled person centered. Of the numerous studies on what has now evolved to person-centered therapy, many if not most, especially in the 1960s and 1970s, were studies on the role of the core conditions of empathy, genuineness, and unconditional positive regard (acceptance) in effecting therapeutic change. These studies were conducted by using scales devised to measure these core conditions and others not necessarily included in the "core." Ratings of recorded interviews (individual and group) were correlated with measures of outcome or change. The degree of the presence or absence of the core conditions was assessed in conjunction with positive and negative change. An unresolved professional dilemma arose among person-centered therapists and those from other persuasions over the contention that the presence of the core conditions in a helping relationship were necessary and sufficient for behavioral/personality change. The almost universal acceptance of these conditions in the practice of therapists from all theoretical persuasions probably answered part of the question—that is, that the core conditions are necessary but the issue of whether they are sufficient remains unresolved. Bozarth (Round Table Discussion, 1990) has raised still another issue: "Are the conditions not necessarily necessary but always sufficient?" (p. 467).

The second type of studies on person-centered therapy focus on the effectiveness of the treatment when compared to control groups and groups treated by other therapies. A sample of the 26 studies reported by Lubin and colleagues (1996) is reviewed here to illustrate the varied results. Schwartz, Kieff, and Winers (1976) reported the effects of a group nondirective, facilitative approach on nonpatient undergraduates with difficulties in making decisions. Group members moved from guarded reactions to revealing themselves, and developed considerable cohesion at the end. All members completed the project and two reported definite increases in self-esteem.

Anderson (1978) did a comparison study of Rogerian encounter, self-directed encounter, and Gestalt therapy groups. All groups experienced significantly decreased feelings of alienation and increased sense of autonomy.

Jensen (1982) studied the relationship of leadership technique and anxiety level in group therapy with chronic schizophrenics. The leadership was either directive and structured or nondirective and nonstructured. No difference in anxiety was found between the two groups. In another comparison study of structured versus nondirective group counseling, Leak (1980) found that the highly structured group counseling approach resulted in significantly greater empathy, in enhanced interpersonal functioning, and in decreased serious infraction of rules of incarcerated felons.

In a comparison study of group cognitive behavioral and group nondirective treatment with a delayed control group, Shaul (1981) found strong support for the effectiveness of group counseling treatment in the management of loneliness and depression in adults. There was no significant difference between the two group treatments.

Braaten (1989) studied nine person-centered therapy groups of graduate students and nonstudent clients and compared them with each other and a control group in Scandinavia. Several objective measures were employed to assess change. Person-centered group therapy resulted in significant personality improvements for nonstudent client groups, but not for students, as compared to normal controls in relation to positive goal attainment, but not with symptom reduction. Maintenance of gains at a 10-month follow-up was 48 percent for clients but only 9 percent for students. Person-centered group therapy was associated with significant increases in group atmosphere/climate from early to late treatment for crucial cohesion dimensions such as affiliation and engagement. Results supported that the application of the core conditions were essential to building a cohesive atmosphere in the treatment groups.

Raskin (1986) provided a comprehensive review of client-centered group psychotherapy beginning in the 1940s and concluding with research of community groups in Central America in 1980s. This review highlights the more prominent studies.

Research on person-centered group therapy and its predecessor group treatments supports the effectiveness of this treatment over no treatment, but in comparison studies the effectiveness varies with the type of clientele treated. Research is now being directed toward identifying who benefits most from which kinds of therapy.

Group Logotherapy

No studies of group logotherapy, per se, were cited in the 25-year review by Lubin and associates (1996). This fact underscores the limited number of research studies of this group treatment modality. Likewise, effectiveness of existential psychotherapies, in general, is not well researched.

Based on Frankl's concept of meaninglessness in life, Crumbaugh and Maholick (1976) developed a Purpose in Life Test that assesses a person's views of life goals, the world, and death. Many studies of existential group treatment use this instrument to assess change, particularly of existential themes. Another test that measures aspects of meaninglessness is the Alienation-Commitment Test of Maddi, Kobasa, and Hoover (1979).

Lantz's (1984) study of curative factors using acute-care patients in group therapy found that the noëtic factor "The group helped me find meaning in my life" was selected most often as the most important curative factor. This finding certainly supports the importance given to this concept by Frankl and group logotherapists.

Opalic (1989) used the Minnesota Multiphasic Personality Inventory (MMPI) to measure change of existential group therapy of both neurotic and psychotic patients. He concluded that existential group therapy can be assessed by the MMPI and other objective instruments. Yalom, one of the most prolific authors and researchers of existential group therapy, and colleagues found improvement of bereaved spouses when they were treated with existential group therapy (see Lieberman & Yalom, 1992; Yalom & Lieberman, 1991; Yalom & Vinogradov, 1988).

Gestalt Group Therapy

The limited research on Gestalt therapy is often attributed to the fact that there are few trained Gestalt therapists in the universities where most research originates and that the treatment is difficult to "standardize" insofar as interventions are often unique to a given client. Nevertheless, 10 studies were cited in the review by Lubin and colleagues (1996). Two research teams were responsible for 5 of the 10 studies. (The Foulds and colleagues' teams focused on nonclinical population of students.) Foulds, Guinan, and Hannigan (1974) used an experiential-Gestalt 24-hour marathon intervention with undergraduates. Compared with a nonparticipating control group, the researchers found significant changes on 11 of 18 scales of the California Personality Inventory (CPI) for the experimental subjects. This suggests that the experiential Gestalt group enhances feelings of intra- and interpersonal adequacy, fosters a stronger sense of values and a greater acceptance of different values, and increases motivation in both academic and social activities.

With a similar population and research design, Foulds and Hannigan (1976) employed a Gestalt marathon workshop with undergraduates and assessed change with the Eysenck Personality Inventory (EPI). Changes were hypothesized in extraversion (increase) and neuroticism (decrease). Significant changes were found in predicted direction.

The Serok and associates' team focused on clinical populations. A sample of their research study results follows. Serok and Bar (1984) examined the effectiveness of Gestalt group therapy in increasing the self-concept of 33 25- to 35-year olds. Compared to control conditions, self-concept and decisiveness significantly improved in the Gestalt therapy group.

Serok, Rabin, and Spitz (1985) assessed the effects of intensive Gestalt group therapy with schizophrenics. Compared to a control group, the treatment group showed some improvement in self- and other-perception and significant improvement in the presentation of body image. Serok and Zemet (1983) studied the effects of Gestalt group therapy on another group of schizophrenics. With this group of hospitalized schizophrenics, Rorschach results showed a significant increase in one measurement of reality perception.

A third research team, headed by Greenberg and involving a variety of clientele, has done considerable research on Gestalt therapy—both individual and group. Two studies of Gestalt group therapy by Greenberg are cited here. Greenberg and Webster (1982) studied the effects of Gestalt group therapy on clients with intrapsychic conflicts. Group members rated as "resolvers" showed significant decreases in anxiety and indecision and also reported greater improvement in behavior when compared with "nonresolvers." Clarke and Greenberg (1986) compared a Gestalt group therapy treatment of individuals with career indecision with a cognitive-behavioral group therapy treatment and an untreated control group. Both treatment groups were superior to the control group, but the Gestalt group was superior to the cognitive-behavioral group in reducing indecision and anxiety.

In a comparison study of short-term Gestalt sensory awareness groups with Rogerian encounter and self-directed encounter groups, Anderson (1978) found that all the treatments significantly decreased feelings of alienation and increased the sense of autonomy. No significant differences were reported on measures of intermember empathy and cohesiveness.

SUMMARY

This chapter has provided a comprehensive overview of three basic models within the existential-humanistic therapies. The three models were selected because they represented unique and distinct treatments that together best illustrated the family of existential-humanistic therapies. The individuals who were most prominent in the development of each of the three models described were Carl Rogers for person-centered therapy, Viktor Frankl for logotherapy, and Fritz Perls for Gestalt therapy. Person-centered therapy was first known as client-centered therapy, which was introduced by Rogers in 1940. Frankl introduced "logo-therapy" in the 1920s, changed it to "existential analysis" in the 1930s and later to "logotherapy" to avoid confusion with Binswanger's *daseinsanalyse*. Perls's first manuscript was written in 1941–1942 and in this manuscript he outlined his emerging theory of Gestalt therapy. The term *gestalt therapy* was first used by Fritz Perls, Ralph Hefferline, and Paul Goodman.

In person-centered therapy, there is a belief in the innate ability of each person to experience incongruence between the self-concept and organismic reality and to reorganize the self-concept to a closer congruence with the totality of experience ("formative tendency"). In logotherapy, will to meaning is the central force in human motivation. In Gestalt therapy, there is a belief that organismic needs lead to sensory motor behavior. Once a configuration is formed that has the qualities of a good Gestalt, the organismic need that has been the foreground is met and a balance or state of satiation is achieved.

The role of the therapist in person-centered therapy is to facilitate the creation of a climate that does not interfere with the potency of natural life focus. This climate is believed to be produced when the therapist brings an attitude of nonevaluative, nonpossessive caring to the group. The basic role of the logotherpist is to assist the group member to find meaning in his or her life and to take action and the responsibility associated with the action congruent with the meaning. The therapist challenges the person to move from where he or she is to where he or she wants to be. Gestalt therapists encourage group members to *be* how they are in the present in order to change and to take responsibility for what they are doing.

The middle section of the chapter compared and contrasted goals and objectives, selection and group composition, group setting, group size, frequency, length, and duration of group sessions of the three models. The final section of the chapter concerned special ethical issues, applications to various age groups, multicultural issues, and research implications for each model.

REFERENCES

Anderson, J. D. (1978). Growth groups and alienation: A comparative study of Rogerian encounter, self-directed encounter, and Gestalt. *Group and Organization Studies, 3*(1), 85–107.

Beisser, A. R. (1970). The paradoxical theory of change. In J. Fagan & I. L. Shepherd (Eds.), *Gestalt therapy now*. Palo Alto, CA: Science and Behavior Books.

Breisach, E. (1962). *Introduction to modern existentialism.* New York: Grove Press.

Braaten, L. J. (1989). The effects of person-centered group therapy. *Person-Centered Review, 4*(2), 183–209.

Bugental, J. F. T. (1978). *Psychotherapy and process: The fundamentals of an existential-humanistic approach.* Reading MA: Addison-Wesley.

Bugental, J. F. T. (1981). *Search for authenticity: An existential-analytic approach to psychotherapy.* New York: Holt, Rinehart and Winston.

Chue, J., & Sue, S. (1984). Asian/Pacific American and group practice. In L. E. Davis (Ed.), *Ethnic-*

ity in social group work practice. New York: Haworth.

Clarke, K. M., & Greenberg, L. S. (1986). Differential effects of the Gestalt two-chair intervention and problem solving in resolving decisional conflict. *Journal of Counseling Psychology, 33,* 11–15.

Crumbaugh, J. C. (1973). *Everything to gain: A guide to self-fullfillment through logoanalysis.* Chicago: Nelson Hall.

Crumbaugh, J. C. (1979). Exercises in logoanalysis. In J. B. Fabry (Ed.), *Logotherapy in action.* New York: Aronson.

Crumbaugh, J. C. (1980). *Logotherapy: New help for problem drinkers.* Chicago: Nelson Hall.

Crumbaugh, J. C., & Maholick, L. T. (1976). *PIL.* Murfreesboro, TN: Psychometric Affiliates.

Das, A. K. (1998). Frankl and the realm of meaning. *Journal of Humanistic Education and Development, 36,* 199–211.

Eisenberg, M. (1980). Logotherapy and the college student. *The International Forum for Logotherapy, 3,* 22–24.

Fabry, J. B. (1980). *The pursuit of meaning: Victor Frankl, logotherapy, and life.* San Francisco: Harper and Row.

Foulds, M. L., Guinan, J. F., & Hannigan, P. (1974). Marathon group: Changes in scores on the California Psychological Inventory. *Journal of College Student Personnel, 15*(6), 474–479.

Foulds, M. L., & Hannigan, P. S. (1976). A Gestalt marathon workshop: Effects on extraversion and neuroticism. *Journal of College Student Personnel, 17*(1), 50–54.

Frankl, V. E. (1963). *Man's search for meaning.* New York: Simon and Schuster.

Frankl, V. E. (1967). *Psychotherapy and existentialism: Selected papers on logotherapy.* New York: Simon and Schuster.

Frankl, V. E. (1975). *The unconscious god: Psychotherapy and theology.* New York: Simon and Schuster.

Frankl, V. E. (1978). *The unheard cry for meaning: Psychotherapy and humanism.* New York: Simon and Schuster.

Frew, J. (1990). Analysis of transference in Gestalt group psychotherapy. *International Journal of Group Psychotherapy, 40,* 189–202.

Frew, J. (1988). The practice of Gestalt therapy in groups. *Gestalt Journal, 11,* 77.

Gendlin, E. T. (1974). Client-centered and experiential psychotherapy. In D. A. Wexler & L. N. Rice (Eds.), *Innovations in client-centered therapy.* New York: Wiley.

Gendlin, E. T. (1978). *Focusing.* New York: Event House.

Gould, W. B. (1993). *Victor E. Frankl: Life with meaning.* Pacific Grove, CA: Brooks/Cole.

Greenberg, L. S., & Webster, M. C. (1982). Resolving decisional conflict by Gestalt two-chair dialogue: Relating process to outcome. *Journal of Counseling Psychology, 29,* 468–477.

Greve, D. W. (1993). Gestalt group therapy. In H. I. Kaplan & B. J. Sadock (Eds.) *Comprehensive group psychotherapy* (3rd ed.). Baltimore: Williams & Wilkins.

Jaspers, K. (1932). *Philosophic.* Berlin: Springer.

Jensen, J. L. (1982). The relationship of leadership technique and anxiety level in group therapy with chronic schizophrenics. *Psychotherapy: Theory, Research and Practice, 19,* 237–248.

Kaufman, W. (1976). *Existentialism, religion and death.* New York: New American Library.

Kepner, E. (1980). Beyond group process. In B. Feder & R. Ronall (Eds.), *Beyond the hot seat: Gestalt approaches to group.* New York: Bruner/Mazel.

Lantz, J. E. The noetic curative factor in group therapy. *International Forum for Logotherapy, 7,* 121–123.

Leak, G. K. (1980). Effects of highly structured versus nondirective group counseling approaches on personality and behavioral measures of adjustment in incarcerated felons. *Journal of Counseling Psychology, 27,* 450–523.

Leslie, R. C. (1971). *Sharing groups in the church.* Nashville, TN: Abingdon.

Lieberman, M. A., & Yalom, I. (1992). Brief group psychotherapy for the spousally bereaved: A controlled study. *International Journal of Group Psychotherapy, 42,* 117–132.

Lubin, B., Wilson, C. D., Petren, S., & Polk, A. (1996). *Research on group treatment methods: A selectively annotated bibliography.* Westport, CT: Greenwood.

Maddi, S. R., Kobasa, S. C., & Hoover, M. (1979). An alienation test. *Journal of Humanistic Psychology, 19,* 73–76.

May, R. (1961). *Existential psychology.* New York: Random House.

May, R., Angel, E., & Ellenberger, H. (Eds.) (1958). *Existence: A new dimension in psychiatry and psychology.* New York: Basic Books.

Meador, B. S. Personal communication, June 20, 1980.

Murayama, S., Nojima, K., & Abe, T. (1988). Person-centered groups in Japan. *Person-Centered Review, 3*(4), 479–492.

Opalic, P. (1989). Existential and psychopathological evaluation of group psychotherapy of neurotic and psychotic patients. *International Journal of Group Psychogherapy, 30,* 389–411.

Perls, F. S. (1947/1969). *Ego, hunger and aggression.* London: Allen and Unwin. New York: Random House.

Perls, F. S. (1975). Resolution. In J. O. Stevens (Ed.), *Gestalt is.* Moab, UT: People Press.

Perls, F. S. (1976). Gestalt therapy verbatim: Introduction. In C. Hatcher & P. Himelstein (Eds.), *The handbook of Gestalt therapy.* New York: Jason Aronson.

Perls, F. S., Hefferline, R. D., & Goodman, P. (1951/1965). *Gestalt therapy.* New York: Julian Press. New York: Dell.

Raskin, N. J. (1986). Client-centered group psychotherapy: Part II: Research on client-centered groups. *Person-Centered Review, 1*(4), 389–408.

Rogers, C. R. (1970). *On encounter groups.* New York: Harper and Row.

Rogers, C. R. (1971). Carl Rogers describes his way of facilitating encounter groups. *American Journal of Nursing, 71,* 275–279.

Rogers, C. R., & Wood, J. K. (1974). Client-centered theory. In A. Burton (Ed.), *Operational theories of personality.* New York: Bruner/Mazel.

Rosenbaum, M. (1993). Existential-humanistic approach to group psychotherapy. In H. I. Kaplan & B. J. Sadock (Eds.), *Comprehensive group psychotherapy* (3rd ed.). Baltimore: Williams & Wilkins.

Round Table Discussion. (1990). *Person-Centered Review, 5*(4), 464–477.

Sartre, J. P. (1957). *Existentialism and human emotion.* New York: Philosophical Library.

Schwartz, L., Kieff, J. S., & Winers, J. A. (1976). Groups experience for nonpatient undergraduates with difficulties making decisions. *Journal of the American College Health Association, 24*(4), 195–197.

Serok, S., & Bar, R. (1984). Looking at Gestalt group impact: An experiment. *Small Group Behavior, 15,* 270–277.

Serok, S., Rabin, C., & Spitz, Y. (1984). Intensive Gestalt group therapy with schizophrenics. *International Journal of Group Psychotherapy, 34,* 431–450.

Serok, S., & Zemet, R. M. (1983). An experiment of Gestalt group therapy with hospitalized schizo-phrenics. *Psychotherapy: Theory, Research, and Practice, 20,* 417–424.

Shaul, S. L. (1981). Loneliness: A comparison of two group counseling strategies with adults. *Dissertation Abstracts International, 42*(4), 1560A.

Simkin, J. S. (1979). Gestalt therapy. In R. J. Corsini & Contributors (Eds.), *Current psychotherapies* (2nd ed.). Itasca, IL: Peacock.

Simkin, J. S. (1982). Gestalt therapy in groups. In G. M. Gazda (Ed.), *Basic approaches to group psychotherapy and group counseling.* Springfield, IL: Charles C. Thomas.

Ungersma, A. J. (1961). *The search for meaning: A new approach in psychotherapy and pastoral psychology.* Philadelphia: Westmoreland Library.

Vontress, C. E. (1988). An existential approach to cross-cultural counseling. *Journal of Multicultural Counseling and Development, 16,* 73–83.

Warren, H. D. (1934). *Dictionary of psychology.* New York: Houghton Mifflin.

Williams, D. A., & Fabry, J. (1982). The existential approach: Logotherapy. In G. M. Gazda (Ed.), *Basic approaches to group psychotherapy and group counseling* (3rd ed.). Springfield, IL: Charles C. Thomas.

Wood, J. K. (1982). Person-centered group therapy. In G. M. Gazda (Ed.), *Basic approaches to group psychotherapy and group counseling* (3rd ed.). Springfield, IL: Charles C. Thomas.

Yalom, I. D. (1980). *Existential psychotherapy.* New York: Basic Books.

Yalom, I. D. (1989). *Love's executioner.* New York: Basic Books.

Yalom, I. D. (1995). *The theory and practice of group psychotherapy* (4th ed). New York: Basic Books.

Yalom, I. D., & Lieberman, M. A. (1991). Bereavement and heightened existential awareness. *Psychiatry, 54,* 334–345.

Yalom, I. D., & Vinogradov, S. C. (1988). Bereavement groups: Techniques and themes. *International Journal of Group Psychotherapy, 38,* 419–446.

Yontef, G. M. (1971). *A review of the practice of Gestalt therapy.* Los Angeles: Trident Shop, California State College.

Zinker, J. (1977). *Creative process in Gestalt therapy.* New York: Bruner/Mazel.

CHAPTER EIGHT

EXISTENTIAL-HUMANISTIC GROUP THEORIES

Applications

This chapter supplements the preceding chapter, describing in greater detail techniques or intervention strategies employed by group therapists who practice person-centered, logotherapy, and Gestalt therapies. Following a description of the basic techniques or intervention strategies, some of these techniques/strategies will be illustrated in the context of a group protocol that will follow for each of the three theoretical models.

PERSON-CENTERED GROUP THERAPY

Techniques

It is probably the *absence* of techniques that is most associated with person-centered group therapy. The therapist in the small group is expected to give up his or her professional role with its attendant authority and instead to become a group member and facilitator who is expected to remain open to his or her unique experiencing in the group and to trust in the formative tendency in the group. The facilitator is expected to bring to the group openness, genuineness or congruence, empathy, nonevaluativeness, and unconditional positive regard for group members, but these conditions are to be *lived,* not "practiced" as techniques. Let us now examine the "core" conditions of a therapeutic relationship as *offered* by the therapist.

Empathy

Rogers was adamant about empathy not being a *technique,* such as "reflection of feeling." He described empathy as much more than that. He viewed it as "the therapist's sensitive immersion in the client's world of experience" (Raskin & Rogers, 1995, p. 143). The therapist tries to communicate his or her understanding of the client in such a way as to communicate a genuine appreciation of the client's world and a willingness to be corrected when it is misunderstood. This process allows the therapist to get closer and closer to the client's feelings and meanings, including those just below the level of awareness.

Unconditional Positive Regard

Synonyms for *unconditional positive regard* are *warmth, acceptance, nonpossessive caring,* and *prizing.* According to Rogers, therapeutic change is more likely when the therapist is expressing a positive, nonjudgmental attitude toward whatever the client is at a given moment (Raskin & Rogers, 1995, p. 143).

Congruence

Sometimes *genuineness* and *immediacy* are used as synonyms for *congruence.* In either case, it refers to the therapist's sharing of his or her feelings with the client that are generated from the relationship. One purpose is to reduce the distance that might be created by the therapist's professional role. Another purpose is to prevent therapeutic fatigue caused by the therapist's attempt to suppress feelings (Raskin & Rogers, 1995).

Client-Offered Conditions

In addition to therapist-offered conditions, Rogers believed that the client needed to bring certain "conditions" to the therapy or be able to develop them during therapy. These conditions were "(1) The client and therapist must be in psychological contact. (2) The client must be experiencing some anxiety, vulnerability, or incongruence. (3) The client must receive or experience the conditions offered by the therapist" (Raskin & Rogers, 1995, p. 143). Rogers considered the first two conditions as preconditions and the third one as essential.

Traditionally, person-centered group therapists have preferred verbal interaction and use no supplements. Some have used video, art, dance, creative writing, and various nonverbal exercises, but most of these have occurred in the community groups, and when they occur it is because the convenors and the members concur on their use.

Group Protocols

Rogers (1970) and Coulson (1970) have described the process movement of the person-centered small group, giving many examples of dialogue taken from group sessions. Examples may also be found in Rogers and Wood (1974).

The shifting expression of an individual's felt meaning is illustrated in this example from the filmed encounter group "Journey into Self" (McGaw, 1968).

Jerry, a middle-aged businessman, makes this comment in the first hour: "We have tremendous fears of insecurity and many times the same things which you are so insecure about you look back . . . and what you were insecure about—thank heavens, you cannot remember, and you would like to get an honest feeling . . . and act this way in all cases. This is where the thing gets off the track because you keep thinking about what other people are expecting."

In the fifth hour, Jerry speaks this way: "As far as people are concerned I . . . I, in a sense, like being around people, but I . . . I only like to go up to a certain point, then, from there I don't like to get too close to people, and it's because of . . . uh . . . it's complicated."

As he comes more and more in contact with his own experiencing, he is beginning to speak for himself. In the eleventh hour, Beth, another group member, speaks. As she begins to weep, Rogers (the facilitator) notices that Jerry seems touched.

Rogers: Without knowing it she must be talking to you Jerry.

Jerry: Well, I am pretty choked up. I wouldn't be able to say much.

Beth continues to speak and Jerry's distress grows. Finally, Roz, another member of the group, crosses the circle of 10 chairs and puts her arms around Jerry. He begins to cry.

Jerry weeps a long time. Roz holds him and cries also.

Roz (crying): All along I really felt he didn't feel deeply about anything. We accused him of that last night.

Beth: He hadn't been able to express his feelings.

(This example illustrates not only Jerry's deepening focusing ability, following his experiencing, but also, at the right moment, the caring and facilitative effect of Roz, who is not a designated facilitator. Rogers, the facilitator, listens with sensitive concern to Beth and to Jerry. A climate has been created that allows persons and relationship to be organized into simplifying complexity.)

The second protocol is taken from the first session of a group counseling series with a group of underachieving high school students. The leader is Dr. Walter Lifton (1976), an experienced group therapist/counselor. The session started with an introduction of Dr. Lifton and a request for each student to identify himself or herself. The group then moved off almost immediately into their feelings about how teachers rejected them. Notice the leader's attempt to help the group discover the many answers and resources they already possess.

Dr. Lifton: Teachers are more comfortable with people who can understand what they're saying than with those that don't. Is that what you're trying to say?

Girl: Yeah, and they more or less, I mean, don't ignore, but they don't really pay too much attention to people who don't.

Dr. Lifton: So you kind of feel that if you don't master the stuff, they don't give you the attention. You don't feel that they care and you don't care. And so it sort of goes on like that.

Girl: I guess so.

Dr. Lifton: Well, we're saying some things about teachers that are very real, and I'm sure you have some teachers that click and others that don't. The chances are that you're going to have some more teachers that you're not going to click with. What then? Are you doomed? (pause) How do you cope with it? Suppose you have a teacher who doesn't seem to really act toward you the way you'd like him or her to act toward you. He really isn't warm, interested. Is there anything you can do about it?

Karen: Pay attention.

Dr. Lifton: Paying attention will change his attitude?

Karen: Well, if you just work up to your ability and show him what you can do.

Dr. Lifton: Yes, but you know, Karen, it's kind of a booby trap. If I understand what Gail is saying, she is saying, "If you don't care about me, I say 'the hell with you.' " And so it's sort of, you know, a cycle, and I'm not sure that I'm on the track.

Boy: If you don't like the teacher, you're not going to be able to do very well in the work.

Dr. Lifton: Bill's saying something interesting. He's saying if you don't like the teacher, why should you try?

Girl: (Inaudible comment.)

Boy: Well, the teacher's not the one who's got to get along.

Dr. Lifton: (Noticing a boy's attempt to contribute, but hesitant to talk) You seem to want to say something, Bill.

Bill: I don't know.

Boy: The teacher's got to be interested in the class—if the teacher don't like you, he's going to make it hard for you.

Girl: Not always.

Boy: But one of my teacher's did.

Girl: Who are you referring to? (giggling)

Dr. Lifton: (recognizing concern over confidentiality) Don't worry about mentioning names. We can wipe this tape. So don't worry about it. But I think the question is an important one because no matter who the person is, you're likely from here on in to get other teachers, or bosses, that you may not like and so the real question is what do you do about these characters? Are you just stuck or, of course, one way of doing it, is to do as Bill suggested, to say "Go peddle your papers. I don't want anything to do with you." You can't always do that.

Boy: Try to get them to like you. Show interest.

Karen: It happened to my brother last year. He just worked up to his ability to show the teacher what he could do. And that helped.

Dr. Lifton: So this would be one way to prove the teacher was wrong, by being something different than what he thought. Suppose you had a friend that you'd like to have with you. How would you get this person to see you in a way that she would want to be your friend? What would you do about it? (pause)

Girl: Nothing.

Gail: If a person doesn't like you, you can't make them.

Dr. Lifton: There's no way of hoping people see you differently than they see you at first? You're stuck with the first impression?

Girl: Oh, no.

Dr. Lifton: How do you change people's ideas about you?

Gail: Well, you can't just be perfect when you're near them, be different. You are what you are. You can't put on fronts in front of people because I think that would make them like you least.

Dr. Lifton: So you've got to be true; you can't be false to them. But do we act the same—are you the same person to Diane as you are to your mother or as you might be to Tom?

Girl: No.

Dr. Lifton: So that there's more than one "you" too. (laughter) That's kind of a funny idea, isn't it—that there really isn't one you. There are several different "you's."

Girl: Well, I think people are like her, she . . . I mean I'd show my personality to her. When I'm home, I'd be showing my—there's a word for it but I can't think of it—

Dr. Lifton: Just try.

Girl: Myself.

Boy: Another character. In other words, you have a different front.

Girl: Yes, everybody does. I mean you're different when you're home. You're more relaxed and . . .

Boy: You wouldn't treat your mother like a girlfriend, in other words.

Girl: That's right—I'd be uncomfortable. (laughter)

Dr. Lifton: We're also saying that the people that we feel very comfortable with, we're able to let them see more of us than others; that the more we feel comfortable in letting a person know who we really are, the easier it is for us to talk to them and to begin to work with them.

Girl: That's why you really never know a person until you see them in their home.

Dr. Lifton: You see, that's one of the problems that we've really got to understand. For this group to be most helpful, we have to find a place where we can be comfortable with each other, because until we feel able to say what we really feel, we're just playing games. We have to begin to say under what conditions would we be willing to share things with each other. How can we help each other feel that the other guy cares, or that he won't misuse what we're saying, or won't think less of us? That's the real problem that we've got to face. If we could have with this group, what you have with some of your girlfriends, except that here you have different kinds of people, you might have a chance to think through some ideas that you wished you had a chance to talk to somebody about, but don't know if they could manage it. This is really what the problem of this group is. This is why I was trying to have us see ways in which we could get comfortable with one another. (long pause)

Dr. Lifton: Kind of scares you, huh? Not always sure that you do want to share things with other people. Some things that maybe you don't feel you want to talk about. (long pause)

Gail: We all don't want to talk. When we do we get in trouble.

Dr. Lifton: Interesting, isn't it, Gail? Have you any idea why we got caught up? I have an idea. I said something that I think some people didn't like and they pulled away in a hurry. They're letting me know that they're not sure that they like this and so the best way of getting away from me is just being quiet because that's safest. Isn't that somewhat like the classroom then? I don't like the teacher; so I'm just going to keep my mouth shut and then she can't know what I'm thinking and I can't get into trouble. That doesn't quite solve it though, does it?

Tom: (Inaudible reply.)

Dr. Lifton: Can't hear you, Tom.

Tom: Keep your mouth shut and they give you a bad mark because you don't do anything in class.

Dr. Lifton: It's a funny thing, isn't it? If you do something, then they hear what you're saying. If you don't say something, then you're in trouble anyway. So that it sort of (interruption by boy)—

Boy: That you're doing something.

Dr. Lifton: For the public?

Boy: Yeah.

Dr. Lifton: Kind of odd though, isn't it? No matter what we do, if we keep our mouth shut or if we open it, we still are doing something. Gail pointed this out very nicely. You're bound to do something. (long pause)

Dr. Lifton: You know it's an interesting thing. Part of what we're saying is that sometimes the exams don't measure what we study. We're saying some of the teachers don't teach what we're being tested on. We're saying some of the teachers don't like us—what's the use of trying? We're saying some of the courses, we wish we weren't in them in the first place. And all these answers are real, and there's no question that for many of you this is one of the problems involved. But is this going to solve it for you if we come up with this as answers? Is it going to solve it? Is this going to make it easier? For example, this summer, is this going to make it easier for you this summer when you go to school if we come up with these answers?

Girl: Yes, I believe so.

Boy: Maybe.

Girl: Because if you walk into a room with the right attitude, then . . . I don't know.

Girl: Then you can do better. If you walk in with the wrong attitude, then you hate it. (pause)

Karen: Oh, I know why I worked the way I work in school, I mean, why I'm working for a goal. Well, I'm planning to go to college. I think if you have a goal set, I think you work harder.

Dr. Lifton: I'm wondering, would any of the rest of you be willing to share with us what it is you see as your purpose in school? Karen has suggested that she sees a goal that seems to be very clear to her. What about some of the rest of you? Can you see any purpose in returning?

Gail: We have no choice.

Dr. Lifton: Beg your pardon?

Gail: We haven't got any choice.

Dr. Lifton: You have no choice?

Gail: You have to go to school. It's compulsory. I think if you didn't have to, I think more people would take an interest in it. There might not be as many going to school but there would be a better attitude in school.

Dr. Lifton: In a sense, I think what you're saying is that you're kind of not liking it because you have to.

Girl: It's true.

Dr. Lifton: So you'll prove to them they can't make you do something, huh? (pause)

Boy: If you could pick your own subjects, that would be better.

Dr. Lifton: Just for kicks, what would you take if you had your own way?

Boy: Math.

Dr. Lifton: You would take only math? (inaudible comments and laughter)

Dr. Lifton: Do you want to tell us about it? Why math?

Boy: I just like math. I don't know why. It just came to me easy. I like numbers better than I do words. (pause)

Girl: I'd take all English.

Dr. Lifton: You'd take all English.

Boy: Science.

Dr. Lifton: You'd take all science.

Girl/Boy: Science.

Dr. Lifton: You'd take science, too.

GROUP LOGOTHERAPY

Techniques

The founder of logotherapy, Viktor Frankl, is credited with the contribution of the techniques of *paradoxical intention* and *dereflection* to the therapy armamentarium. The therapist employs paradoxical intention when the therapist encourages a client to *intensify* his or her neurotic symptoms. Frequently when asked to consciously magnify the symptoms, clients are unable to do so. The technique has been found to be effective for persons with phobias, obsessions, and compulsions.

Dereflection is the second major technique of logotherapy. Clients are encouraged to cease focusing on their symptoms (hyperreflecting) and instead to focus on meaning potentials. Frankl believed that people are able to forget themselves only if they give of themselves, and Williams and Patrick (1980) have contended that forgetting of oneself in dereflection is antithetical to narcissism.

Logophilosophy that teaches the acceptance of pain, guilt, and death is a necessary step all people must take, and this philosophy in and of itself is considered to be a therapeutic intervention. Books on logotherapy are used as a form of bibliotherapy. Some group leaders even spend the first few minutes of each session giving a minilecture on some aspect of logotherapy. Frankl coined the term *last aid* to describe the need to accept guilt and death rather than neurotically struggling to deny them. He believed that acceptance of one's own death can lead to authentic decisions and decisive actions in the here and now and help a person widen his or her perspective by differentiating those activities that are relatively meaningless from those that are meaningful.

Another aspect of logophilosophy considered to have therapeutic effects is its emphasis on individual uniqueness. For example, to help individuals discover otherwise unseen meanings in their lives, a logotherapist will often draw their attention to certain relationships in which they are irreplaceable.

In addition to the basic techniques and interventions described here and in the section titled The Role of the Therapist in the preceding chapter, group leaders are expected to be familiar with a variety of supplementary methods or techniques that they can apply by improvisation when they seem relevant. For example, humor is frequently employed to neutralize anticipatory anxiety.

Group Protocols

Martha (cf. Williams & Fabry, 1982) came to the group in distress about what had happened that day in the home she shared with three other women, two of them mutual lovers. The third one had expressed the desire to find a suitable psychologist, and one of the lesbians had recommended the one Martha had been seeing for the past few months. Martha had found it inappropriate to share the psychologist with someone living in the same household. She had talked this over with the psychologist, who had agreed with her. When she herself informed the three other women of this decision (which, she now realized, should have been done by the psychologist), a fierce fight broke out in which the three women attacked Martha and insisted that she move out. The incident left Martha deeply disturbed and confused.

Leader: (after listening for several minutes to Martha's account and numerous details that in her opinion were entangled in the present blow-up): What are your options?

Martha: I have no options. I have to move out. I've moved six times since my divorce, and you should have seen the crummy places I've lived in. This is the first decent place, and now these three bitches . . . How can I change my attitude in this? How can I find meaning here?

Leader: This is not a situation in which you have to change your attitude!

Martha: What do you mean?

Leader: You remember what we said about facing a meaningless situation? As long as you can change your situation, you need not accept it by moving out.

Another woman: But Martha's attitude is highly defeatist. It would be good to find a healthy attitude.

Leader: A healthy attitude, yes. But when we speak about finding a meaningful attitude in a meaningless situation, we're talking about situations that cannot be changed. You will have options about what to *do*.

Martha: No, I don't. You should have heard them tear into me. They want to get me out and I love that place (crying). Oh, how did I get into this mess?

Leader: Never mind how you got in. How will you get out?

Martha: I don't know.

Leader: Yes, you do. You have just given your answer. You said you want to stay. Would you stay even if you'd have to share your therapist?

Martha: I guess so.

Leader: Even if you'd have to give up your therapist?

Martha: Yes.

Leader: All right, then. We know where you are. We know where you want to be. How do you get from here to there? What would you choose as your first step?

(The group spent the next 20 minutes supporting Martha's decision. They talked about various ways to discuss the situation with the other women and shared similar experiences that had worked for them. They suggested that Martha face the other three women in a logodrama within our group.)

Martha called the leader the next evening and said she had left the group with a clear mind. She had fallen asleep, but awakened around two in the morning in great anxiety. She then thought over what had been said within the group and wrote down notes about her options. She felt calm again and had slept until it was time to go to work. While preparing breakfast, she spoke with the woman who owned the lease of the house and said to her what she had practiced in the logogroup: "We'll have to talk about all this later." The same evening, they had a four-hour talk, which cleared the air.

In recent years, logotherapists have become increasingly aware of the usefulness of dereflection. Regardless of whether a problem is current (as was Martha's dilemma) or whether it has been on the participant's mind for a long time (as the one in the following example), the problem occupies the client's mind; in other words, the client is "hyperreflecting" about it. It is in the nature of the group process (as it is in the nature of any therapeutic process) to get the client to talk about the problem, to think about it, to observe the problem between sessions, and this attention to the problem will increase the client's reflecting on it. This seems to be an inescapable dilemma of all therapies, especially in their diagnostic stage. You cannot diagnose and deal with a problem unless you pay attention to it and paying attention to it may make it worse (cf. Frankl, 1978).

A zigzag approach of paying attention to the problem and alternately dereflecting from it has been found useful.

Evelyn suffered from insomnia. She would fall asleep, then after two hours wake up without being able to fall asleep for hours. A medical examination had shown no organic reason for her sleeplessness. Whenever it was Evelyn's turn in the group to discuss anything that troubled her, she spoke about the agony of lying in bed, trying to fall asleep.

Leader (interrupting her tale):   Is there anything you'd like to do and don't have the time?

Evelyn: Lots of things. That's what's so infuriating. There are all these things I want to do, and I am too tired to do them.

Leader: What, for instance?

Evelyn: Two months ago I bought a pattern of needlepoint, a lovely Alpine scene. I haven't had the time to work on it for more than a couple of hours.

Leader: What other things would you like to do?

Evelyn: When we were married and did some entertaining, I enjoyed gourmet cooking. I hardly have time for that now. Another thing I meant to do ever since my father died is to sort out the stamps he left in boxes, and put them in an album the way I did when I was a child.

Henry (another group member): I did that, some years ago. I started collecting stamps again and began corresponding with people in India and Brazil. The man from Brazil came to visit me. We don't exchange stamps any more but we correct each other's letters. I am learning Portuguese that way.

Evelyn: I like that. I've always wanted pen pals in far-away countries. (Tells about a pen pal she had in Japan when she was in high school.)

Leader: You seem to have quite a few interests you have no time to follow up.

Evelyn: It's not so much the time. It's the strength. I feel exhausted all day. Especially after I have trouble with my boss, and even more so with Doris, his secretary.

Leader: Do you have more difficulties sleeping after having trouble at work?

Evelyn: I think that's probably true.

Leader: Tell us more about Doris.

Evelyn: She's terrible. (Tells about Doris's spying on people, her pettiness, her vindictiveness.) Nobody in the office likes her. She works all the time, even during coffee breaks.

Al (another group member): I had that situation once. I quit.

Evelyn: But I like my job. It's well paid, interesting. At my age I couldn't find something like that again. Why should I let that bitch make me quit?

Al: Would you rather be sleepless the rest of your life?

Evelyn: Oh, I don't know if it's all Doris's fault. I also have trouble sleeping on weekends. There's always somebody who upsets your applecart.

Leader: Are there people who have a soothing influence on you?

Evelyn: Oh sure. My granddaughter, for instance. With her I become a four-year-old again.

Leader: After you are with your granddaughter, do you sleep better?

Evelyn: Not necessarily. There's something basically wrong with me.

Leader: Let's find out a few things that are basically right with you. Would you be willing to make a list of things you'd like to do if you had the time? Like needlepoint or stamp collecting. See if you can find 10 such activities.

(Evelyn promised to make such a list for the next meeting but didn't do it. Instead, she reported an upsetting dream. She had found herself in bed with Doris, both nude. There was great gentleness between the two women.

Evelyn had gently embraced Doris and a feeling of great serenity had come upon her.)

Evelyn: Is it possible that I have lesbian feelings? And toward Doris, of all people? And at my age? No, that couldn't be true.

Leader: You recall what we said about logotherapeutic dream interpretations. Dreams are not necessarily a message from the psychological unconscious about repressed sex drives. They can also be a message from the noëtic unconscious about repressed meanings.

Henry: A message from your conscience?

Leader: What would your conscience have to say to you about your relationship with Doris?

Evelyn (startled, after a moment of reflection):   Be nice to Doris, and she'll be nice to you.

Leader: Could that be the message?

Evelyn (in great excitement):   Yes, that must be it! I didn't know I was going to say that; it just came out. And when I said it I felt as good as I felt in my dream when I hugged Doris.

Leader: What are you going to do about it?

Evelyn: Do?

Leader: Yes. We talked about this in our very first session. You don't change by thinking about it, or dreaming, but by doing. What would you say you could do as a first step toward getting closer to Doris?

Evelyn: I don't know. She is a hard person to get close to. I'll think about it.

Leader: I am sure you can think of something. You are a resourceful person. (Gives an example when Evelyn had shown resourcefulness in the group.) Tell us next week what you did.

(Next week Evelyn reported that she had asked Doris to have coffee with her. It was the first time she had done this. In fact, hardly anyone had done it. During this coffee break, Evelyn, also for the first time, had talked to Doris about things other than office matters. They found out that they had a common interest in the theater and discussed plays they both had seen. They went to coffee several times and others joined them. Nevertheless, Evelyn's insomnia persisted. She had made up a list of activities she liked to do and the leader suggested an experiment.)

Leader: You like to prepare a gourmet meal. Tomorrow, after work, buy all the ingredients, go to bed as usual, but then when you wake up, instead of trying to fall asleep again, get up and do your cooking.

Evelyn: But then I'll never get any sleep.

Leader: You can't sleep anyway, so you might as well get something done. It's a waste of time to lie there doing nothing.

Henry: You can invite Doris and the people from your office to your gourmet meal.

Evelyn: Oh no, I couldn't do that.

Leader: Well, then some other friends. And also buy some silk and patterns for your needlepoint project. Christmas is only three months away. You can make a lot of nice Christmas presents during all those sleepless nights.

Evelyn: I'll never survive these three months without sleep.

Leader: Tiredness is something your body does to you. We'll have to show your body who is master in the house. We'll tire out that body until it will fall asleep and stay that way all night. You have a perfectly healthy body, the checkups have shown that. And when your body needs sleep it knows how to get it.

Evelyn: How will I be able to go to work in the morning? I'm exhausted even now. At least, when I'm lying in bed I'm getting some rest, even if I don't sleep.

Leader: What kind of gourmet meal do you have in mind?

Evelyn: I cut out a recipe a few months ago. I'd like to try it some day.

Henry: Or some night.

Evelyn (laughing):   All right, some night. It starts out with lobster soup. (She went into some detail about the menu and its preparation.)

(The next session Evelyn reported that she had invited three friends for Friday night, had done all the shopping Thursday after work, set up everything for the preparation of food before going to bed at 11. But she never woke up till morning and had to cancel the dinner invitation.)

Evelyn: It's very embarrassing.

Leader: We can't let this happen again. Invite them for tomorrow evening but set the alarm at 2 A.M. so you are sure to wake up in time to do the cooking.

Evelyn: You're kidding.

Leader: Well, don't you want to cook your gourmet meal?

Evelyn: Yes, but I like my sleep better.

Leader: There are other choices. Instead of falling asleep and then waking up in the middle of the night, you can do the cooking before you fall asleep in the first place.

Evelyn: But I hear the best sleep comes before midnight.

Leader: All right, you can go to bed at eight, set your alarm at midnight. Or at 5 A.M. and do your cooking before you go to work.

Evelyn: This is crazy.

Leader: No crazier than lying in bed every night, doing nothing.

Next week, Evelyn reported that she had taken one of her father's stamp boxes to her bedside and started sorting them out. She didn't get very far the first night because she had fallen asleep during the sorting. She received the support of the group for her achievements, although she laughingly said that everything she tried (cooking, sorting stamps) ended in failure. The group at every opportunity pointed out to her that she had succeeded in showing herself that she was not the helpless victim of her sleeplessness, that she could change her attitude toward a disagreeable situation, that she was able to break a strangling behavior pattern—that she, in short, was able to arouse the defiant power of her human spirit. She was able to sleep most nights right through, and when she did wake up and have trouble falling asleep again, she didn't worry. She had her needlepoint at her bedside "just in case," but she hardly got to it at night.

GESTALT GROUP THERAPY

Techniques

Experiment.   The experiment is the primary technique used by Gestalt therapists. It is structure that is introduced by the therapist based on the ongoing therapy experience. It is intended to increase self-awareness and self-expression and intensify contact. There are three basic experiments in the Gestalt therapists armamentarium: boundary, enactment and reenactment, and exploratory.

Boundary experiments provide the primary method for helping the group member explore who he or she is and how he or she contacts the environment. Melnick (1980) defined a boundary experiment as any work in Gestalt therapy in which a person risks being awkward and insecure to explore one's being. For example, the therapist may ask a timid or shy group member to be assertive with the therapist or another group member and even repeat the assertive response several times with greater and greater emphasis each time.

Enactment and reenactment experiments are employed when an event has never occurred, such as a possible future event or when there is unfinished business of a past event and the past event is reenacted in the here and now. The enactment or reenactment allows the group member to complete the Gestalt and master the feelings that may be or have been associated with the event. Although the most important reenactments usually are of unfinished childhood experiences, current unfinished business constitutes much of the therapy.

Exploratory experiments are used as the title suggests to explore areas of the group member's physical and psychological being when there may be no clear starting point. For example, if the member seems to be blocking a great deal when describing his or her self, the therapist might suggest rapid free association and analysis.

Exercises.   The experiment should not be confused with structured *exercises* used in Gestalt therapy. Structured exercises or therapist directives are tasks given to the member (or usually the group) that do not emerge from the here-and-now group interaction. The structured exercise has been associated with questionable practices by Gestalt therapists in the past.

Rules.   In addition to Gestalt therapy experiments and exercises, there are games. Levitsksy and Perls (1970) described six rules.* First, *the principle of the now* is intended for the group member to present how he or she feels in the immediate moment. To facilitate "now awareness," members are encouraged to use the present tense.

I and the is the second rule. It is intended to convey that true communication includes a sender and receiver. The sender is encouraged to use the message recipient's name in the communication.

It language and I language, the third rule, is related to responsibility and involvement. Instead of using it to refer to one's behavior or bodily functions, the communicator is asked to substitute *I.* For example, instead of saying, "It is frightening," say, "I am afraid." Other applications of semantics of responsibility include the substitution of verbs for nouns and frequent use of the interpretative mode of speech.

Use of Awareness Continuum. Levitsky and Perls (1970) contended that the frequent reliance on the awareness continuum is one of the major innovations in techniques contributed by Gestalt therapy. For example, the therapist directs the group member to describe everything in his or her immediate awareness. This fourth rule maximizes focusing on one's experiences versus one's verbalizations and intellectualizing—emphasizing the *what* and *how* of behavior rather than the *why.*

No gossiping, the fifth rule, refers to talking directly to another person in the group rather than *about* that person. The speaker is asked to look at and speak directly to the person rather than to the group as a whole.

Asking questions is a sixth rule employed to discourage asking questions for information that members already possess. The therapist simply asks the questioner to change the question to a statement. The purpose of this rule is to help the group members accept responsibility.

Games.[†] Games represent a basic metacommunication by Perls inasmuch as games represent much of social behavior. For Perls, the message was not to stop playing games but to be free to substitute satisfying games for nonsatisfying games (Levitsky & Perls, 1971).

Games of dialogue are used as an integrative function whenever a "split" is detected. One of the most frequent splits is between the so-called top dog and underdog. The top dog acts like the super ego and is bossy and controlling, whereas the underdog is passive and prone to excuses and delays. The person with this split is asked to dialogue between these two aspects of himself or herself.

*From A. Levitsky and F. S. Perls, "The Rules and Games of Gestalt Therapy," in J. Fagan and I. L. Shepherd (Eds.), *Gestalt Therapy Now* (Los Altos, CA: Science and Behavior Books, 1970), Chapter 11. Reproduced with permission.

†From A. Levitsky and F. S. Perls, "The Rules and Games of Gestalt Therapy," in J. Fagan and I. L. Shepherd (Eds.), *Gestalt Therapy Now* (Los Altos, CA: Science and Behavior Books, 1970), Chapter 11. Reproduced with permission.

Making the rounds is asked for when the therapist feels that a particular theme or feeling of a group member should be faced by everyone in the group. The theme or feeling is expressed by words, touch, observing, and so on.

Unfinished business is the conceptual analogue of the incomplete task of Gestalt psychology. The group member is expected to complete the unresolved feeling with the significant other, such as parent or sibling. The most common and important, according to Perls, is resentments.

"I take responsibility" is employed to help group members increase awareness. For each statement they make, they are asked to add "I take responsibility for it."

"I have a secret" permits exploration of guilt and shame. Each group member thinks of a secret and imagines how others would react if they learned of it but they are not to reveal the secret.

Playing the projection is when the therapist asks a group member to play the role of the projected behavior or the like and then later is asked if that could be his or her own behavior.

Reversal is used when the therapist suspects that a member's overt behavior or feelings is the reverse of his or her underlying behavior or feeling. For example, a very inhibited person may be asked to play an exhibitionist.

The rhythm of contact and withdrawal is viewed as natural and the group member who is withdrawing may be encouraged to do it more completely before reengaging the group.

Rehearsal refers to one's internal rehearsal in preparation for playing one's accustomed social roles. The game is to share each other's rehearsals and thus become more aware of them.

Exaggeration represents an attempt to increase awareness of one's body language. The therapist asks a member to exaggerate a movement to make it more apparent. The verbal analogue is the repetition game in which one is asked to repeat an expression over and over with increasing emphasis.

"May I feed you a sentence" is used when the therapist wants to try out an idea on a group member but the therapist avoids interpretation, per se.

Group Protocols

Following are two protocols of Gestalt training workshops by Jim Simkin (1982). Although they are both workshops, they both illustrate very well the same techniques and dynamics that might occur in Gestalt therapy groups.

The following excerpt is an example of how one of Simpkin's workshops started. Following a short introduction, a suggested exercise involved each of the participants and very quickly one of the participants asked to work.

> Good evening. I'd like to start with a few sentences about contracts and then suggest an exercise. I believe that there are no "shoulds" in Gestalt therapy. What you do is what you do. What I do is what I do. I have a preference. I prefer that you be straight with me. Please remember, this is a preference, not a should. If you feel that you *should* honor my preference, then that's

your should! When I ask you, "Where are you?" and the like, my preference is that you tell me—or tell me that you're *not* willing to tell me. Then our transaction is straight. Any time that you want to know where I am, please ask me. I will either tell you, or tell you I am unwilling to tell you—so that our transaction will be straight.

Now for the exercise. Please look around the room and select someone you don't know or don't know well—whom you would like to know or know better. O.K.? Now here are the rules. You may do anything you like to "know" the other person better, except talk! John?

John: The lady with the brown sweater.

Therapist (T):   Marilyn, are you willing to be "known" by John?

Marilyn: Yes.

T: Elaine, please select a partner.

Elaine: That man—I believe he said his name was Bert.

T: Are you willing, Bert?

Bert: My pleasure!

T: Nancy?

Nancy: I would like to know Agnes better.

Agnes: That's fine with me.

Jonathan: Well, that leaves me to Phil.

T: Yes, unless you're willing to include me.

Jonathan: No thanks. I'd rather get to know Phil! (group laughter)

(The group breaks into dyads and for several minutes the person who has asked to know the other is the aggressor, "exploring" the other with his sensory modalities [touch, taste, smell, etc.], lifting, pulling, dancing with, and so on. Then the partners in the dyad are asked to switch and the "aggressor" becomes the "aggressee" as the exercise is repeated.)

T: O.K. I am interested in knowing more about your experience. If you have made any discovery about *yourself* and are willing to share, please tell the rest of us what you found out.

Bert: I discovered that I felt very awkward and uncomfortable when Elaine was the aggressor!

Elaine: I sensed your discomfort and found myself concerned with what you thought of me.

Bert: I would like to work on my always having to be "masculine"—my avoidance of my passivity.

T: When?

Bert: Now! (At this point, Bert leaves his chair in the circle and sits in the empty chair across from the therapist.) I feel anxious. My heart is pounding and my hands feel sweaty, and I'm very aware of all of the others in the room.

T: Is there anything you would like to say to the others?

(For the next 15 to 20 minutes, Bert worked. When he finished, the therapist turned his focus [awareness] back to the group.)

The next protocol is taken from Simkin's training film, *In the Now*.

After introductory comments, Al moved from the group circle to the "hot seat." He was very eager to start. His work with Simkin is presented verbatim from the film. It concludes with the last several minutes of the film, which involved primarily an exchange between Al and Colman, another participant.

Therapist (T): O.K., now I would suggest we start with getting in touch with what we're doing in this situation now. Most people are interested, or at least they say they are interested, in changing their behavior. This is what therapy is all about. In order to change behavior, you have to know what you're doing and how you do what you do. So, let's start with your examining, focusing your awareness, and saying what you're in touch with at this moment. Say where you are, what you're experiencing.

(Al gets up and moves to the hot seat across from therapist.)

Al: I feel as though I got the catastrophe by sitting over there suffering, and I still feel it at intervals. But I really haven't felt so much like a patient in all the time I've been a psychologist. I think it's for this special occasion. Last night at four o'clock in the morning I awoke . . . well, it started at nine . . . I started blushing in the groin, you know. I thought it was flea bite 'cause we got five new dogs . . . pups. I couldn't find the flea. By four o'clock in the morning, I was blushing here and here, in my head, and I couldn't sleep, I was itching so. And I got an antihistamine. By nine or ten in the morning the itching went away and then coming here and I get this chest . . . my chest hurts.

T: How about right now?

Al: I'm sweating. I sweat and I'm warm.

T: What happened to your voice?

Al: It got low and warm and I wiggle a little.

T: And now?

Al: I feel a tension I carry around a good deal up here—a band that grabs my head like that and pulls me together like I'm puzzled.

T: Play the band that's pulling on Al. "I am Al's band and I . . . "

Al: I am Al's band containing him. I'm his crazy megalomania—want to run the world his way.

T: Tell Al what your objections are to his running the world his way.

Al: He's a nut . . . to think he can run the world his way—or a child.

T: Now give Al a voice and let Al talk to the band.

Al: I know how to run it as well as anybody else. Why shouldn't I?

T: You sounded like a fairly reasonable nut or child at that moment. . . . And now?

Al: Back to my gut. I make myself suffer to recognize I can't take what I want.

T: Okay, what is it that you want that you're not taking at this moment?

Al: Well, I very reluctantly thought of the milk and the world as one.

T: You're reluctantly not taking the milk and the world at this moment.

Al: I'm sure that's not what I said. I reluctantly *thought* of the milk. I didn't want to talk about that. I'd rather be a megalomaniac than an infant asking for warmth (mother's milk).

T: Can you imagine anything in between those two—the infant and the megalomaniac?

Al: It's a long way, yeah. You know I'm an extremist. Let's see a bite-size. Yeah, how about just writing an article on art therapy, which I've scheduled for the last three years? I haven't done that. I would like to just flow and to come out without any pain, without giving up anything else.

T: So you want to be the breast.

Al: I want to be the breast! To be the giver, to flow. Oh, well, I hadn't thought of it that way.

T: Well, think of it that way. Take a couple of hours. Imagine yourself a big tit.

Al: It's a very feminine thing to be, a breast.

T: Yeah.

Al: Give a little.

T: Yeah.

Al: Give a lot.

T: Yeah.

Al: You get . . . you capture your son with that milk. You hold onto him.

T: Al?

Al: Yeah.

T: Would you be willing to be as tender, soft, feminine as you know how?

Al: It's a threat.

T: What's a threat?

Al: To follow your suggestion would be a threat . . . of what? Makes no sense.

T: O.K. Do the opposite. Whatever the reverse of being soft, tender, loving, feminine is for you.

Al: Be masculine.

T: Show me.

Al: It's something like *"practice"* . . . you know fatherly, uh, *"shut-up!"*

T: Yeah, do a little scowling with it. That's it.

Al: *"Shut-up!"* So it's not puzzling, it's uh, it's father. *"You burnt the soup! Leave the table,"* and then a kind of fantasy of mother crying. I sort of regret that my father died before I became friendly with him again.

T: Say this to him.

Al: I'm sorry. (Sigh) Well, inside I said I'm sorry you died.

T: Outside.

Al: I'm sorry.

T: Say this to him outside.

Al: I'm sorry you died too soon (for me).

T: Give him a voice.

Al: I haven't the slightest idea what he would say. I thought of his excusing me. He says, "You, you didn't know any better. You were young and angry."

T: Your father sounds tender.

Al: He may be the father I wanted. I never, I don't think of him as a tender man but . . .

T: It's the voice you gave him.

Al: Yeah. I may have underestimated him.

T: Say this to him.

Al: Dad, I guess I did, I underestimated you.

T: Say this to Al.

Al: Al, you underestimated me. You could have been closer . . .

T: (Interrupts) No, No. Say this sentence to Al: "Al, I underestimate you."

Al: Al, I underestimate you. You can do a good deal more than you're doing. Then I put myself down and say, "You're crazy to expect so much from yourself," and don't do anything . . . like going from do everything to do nothing. Just sit and don't create it. I feel a little phony to accept your interpretation so easily.

T: You see what you just did?

Al: I puzzled myself?

T: You said, "I feel a little phony." There came your band.

Al: And it hurts here (points to stomach). It didn't hurt there for a long time. Now it's back. What happened? I'm supposed to know? So I've got a blind spot. I'm entitled.

T: Your blind spot happens to be Al.

Al: A total blind spot?

T: You're not entitled to that blind spot. What are you doing?

Al: Puzzling. You're playing God and telling me I'm not. I'm not God? That was a . . . I didn't expect to say that at all, really.

T: What just happened?

Al: I exposed something, I guess. It was quite unintended.

T: Yeah.

Al: I was just going to argue with you, and I came out with my manic side. I don't often do that.

T: You just did.

Al: It slipped. I'm sorry. . . . I'm sorry; I'm glad; I'm glad. Whew!

T: What do you experience right now?

Al: Warmth. I love having people laugh, especially with me. So I guess everybody wants it. Wants warmth and love.

T: God never makes excuses or gives reasons.

Al: No?

T: *I* know.

Al: I give you permission to be God. I understand. Yeah, you have warmth. I give you . . . I give you warmth. What else do you want? The world? You can have the world, just be sure to give it back . . . in ten minutes. God is an imposter, because I'm God. And that other one is a fake. I really could do the whole thing myself.

T: Yeah. Now you're catching on.

There's quite a bit of . . . unfinished business that sometimes accumulates during a workshop—especially in the area of resentments and appreciations. Now you don't have to have any appreciations or resentments, you may have some other unfinished business. If you have any unfinished business, now is the time to bring this out.

Coleman: I want to talk to Al.

Al: Go ahead.

Coleman: I left last night and you bothered me. And I feel that you're haunted, you're a . . . mezepah (warlock) and you came here looking and you saw what happened to me. And you asked me a question which was really a statement. You've done that animal trainer bit before, is what your question stated. This guy showed you, and you wouldn't believe. And last night when I came to you . . . to relate to you, you almost took it.

Al: I pulled away because you damn near broke my glasses.

Coleman: Yeah.

Al: That's why.

Coleman: O.K. Go ahead. Still with the mezepah.

Al: With your hug. No, you're perceiving it . . . badly. I bought it; I did not have any notion whatsoever as to whether you had created that idea, the trainer, on the spot.

Coleman: I don't want . . . don't give me that. When I came to you last night . . . and I tried to convey to you my feeling, it wasn't your glasses. O.K., your glasses were incidental, but you turned to me and you said: "Oh, yeah, now I see why you do that."

Al: I said I had no idea . . .

Coleman: Better late than never. You couldn't take it that I felt for you . . . you had to put it off on me that I had to do it . . . you can't eat it, you can't taste it.

Al: O.K., I feel its unfinished business . . .

Coleman: And I still like you.

Al: Let's, let's hear what's behind it, then.

T: Oh, shut up!

Coleman to T: I don't mind crying; it makes it hard to talk. I . . . I did come . . . entirely as . . . I say, I think, a scoffer. Go ahead, do me. But I think it's beautiful, and I do appreciate it. Thank you, and all you beautiful people.

T: Could you add one more sentence, Coleman? Remember that the "it" in gestalt therapy is "I." Your sentence was "It's beautiful."

Coleman: I think I'm beautiful.

T: I do too.

SUMMARY

This chapter supplemented the preceding chapter by providing sample protocols of therapy groups led by therapists representing person-centered therapy, logotherapy, and Gestalt therapy. In addition, the major techniques or intervention strategies for each of the three existential-humanistic models presented were described.

R E F E R E N C E S

Coulson, W. R. (1970). Major contribution: Inside a basic encounter group. *The Counseling Psychologist, 2,* 1–34.

Frankl, V. E. (1978). *The unheard cry for meaning: Psychotherapy and humanism.* New York: Simon & Schuster.

Levitsky, A., & Perls, F. S. (1970). The rules and games of Gestalt therapy. In J. Fagan & I. L. Shepherd (Eds.), *Gestalt therapy now.* Los Altos, CA: Science and Behavior Books.

Lifton, W. M. (1976). Group-centered counseling. In G. M. Gazda (Ed.), *Theories and methods of group counseling in the schools* (2nd ed.). Springfield, IL: Charles C. Thomas.

McGaw, W. H. (Producer). (1968). *Journey into self* (documentary film). La Jolla, CA: Western Behavioral Science Institute.

Melnick, J. (1980). The use of therapist-imposed structure in Gestalt therapy. *Gestalt Journal, 3,* 4.

Raskin, N. J., & Rogers, C. R. (1995). Person-centered therapy. In R. J. Corsini & D. Wedding (Eds.), *Current psychotherapies* (5th ed.). Itasca, IL: F. E. Peacock.

Rogers, C. R. (1970). *On encounter groups.* New York: Harper and Row.

Rogers, C. R., & Wood, J. K. (1974). Client-centered theory. In A Burton (Ed.), *Operational theories of presonality.* New York: Bruner/Mazel.

Simkin, J. S. (1982). Gestalt therapy in groups. In G. M. Gazda (Ed.), *Basic approaches to group psychotherapy and group counseling.* Springfield, IL: Charles C. Thomas.

Williams, D. A., & Fabry, J. (1982). The existential approach: Logotherapy. In G. M. Gazda (Ed.), *Basic approaches to group psychotherapy and group counseling* (3rd ed.). Springfield, IL: Charles C. Thomas.

Williams, D. A., & Patrick, S. (1980). A new remedy for narcissism. *The International Forum for Logotherapy, 3,* 41–43.

CHAPTER NINE

COGNITIVE-BEHAVIORAL GROUP THEORIES

Cognitive-behavioral group treatments have become more popular in the last decade, in part as a function of changes occurring in the way mental health services are being provided. Today, there is a greater emphasis on having a demonstrated outcome for mental health treatments, and cognitive-behavioral approaches have long had measurement and evaluation of treatment effects as a cornerstone of the treatment model. Further, managed care programs often require intervention treatments that are consistent across settings and persons served; careful description and replication of behavioral interventions has been featured since the beginning of behavioral treatments. Finally, there is an increased emphasis on group treatments and behavioral models that lend themselves effectively to the delivery of group counseling and therapy, particularly in behavioral interventions techniques such as behavior rehearsal, modeling, social reinforcement, feedback, and structured learning activities.

Behavioral approaches to group work begin with the assumption that most people enter counseling or therapy because they are *doing* things that make them unhappy or are *behaving* in a way that bring problems into their lives. The presenting sentiment may be offered as an emotional statement ("I'm depressed" or "I lose my temper and get really angry") or may be presented as a fear ("I can't stand to go out in public" or "I'm so afraid my spouse will leave me"). Cognitive-behavioral models of intervention, though, assume that the emotional conditions come about because of what people *do* and *what they think or believe.* People are born with certain traits, such as eye color, sex, intellectual capability, and temperament. Subsequently, once in their social environment, they learn to behave in particular ways, and how they behave influences how they think and feel about their lives. Cognitive-behavioral approaches take the position that it is because people think and behave as they do that their lives are adaptable and satisfactory, or maladaptive and unsatisfactory.

Structured or behavioral approaches to group counseling and therapy take many forms and models, and have existed since the beginning of group work. One of the most common forms of cognitive-behavioral group work is the psychoeducational group model, which is particularly relevant for providing learning and skills development for people. The psychoeducational model is presented in Chapter 15, Life-Skills Training: A Psychoeducational Model. The current chapter addresses behavioral and cognitive-behavioral approaches to group counseling and therapy.

HISTORY AND DEVELOPMENT

Behavioral approaches to helping people have been a part of therapeutic interventions for mental health treatment since the 1920s. Psychoanalytic/psychodynamic theory is often considered the first force in psychology because of its early contributions to the understanding of the psyche and the developmental issues people experience, as well as for the therapeutic interventions developed for treating mental health concerns. Behavioral psychology, though, is considered the second force because of its emergence, in the 1920s, shortly after psychoanalytic theory. Contrary to the first force model that assumed biological needs and subconscious motivation could explain behavior, the behavioral approach is a way of understanding how maladaptive learning patterns may lead to a variety of emotional states.

John Watson has often been identified as the earliest espouser of the behavioral approach in the United States, but methods resembling behavioral interventions were around considerably before Watson's writing. Spiegler and Guevremont (1998), for example, have described how Pliny the Elder, a first-century Roman scholar, developed an intervention that closely resembles the current behavioral strategy known as *aversion therapy.* He attempted to treat alcohol abuse problems, for instance, by placing dead spiders in the bottom of the glass of a drinker. Although today's aversion techniques generally are not so drastic, they closely resemble Pliney's method in intention. Spiegler and Guevremont (1998) also described a tenth-century Icelandic treatment for depression in which a daughter helped her father overcome his despondency by having him engage in more and more active pursuits, including writing poetry, until he eventually felt better. And in the eighteenth century, the treatment program developed for a child who grew up without human contact, the "Wild Boy of Aveyron," incorporated shaping, prompting, modeling, and time-out methods for helping him to become socialized. These interventions today are common elements of behavioral treatments.

John Watson, the earliest writer on behaviorism in the United States, and later one of his students, Mary Cover Jones, primarily focused on respondent, or *classical, conditioning,* to explain the development of behaviors. They explained that people were not born with innate fears of objects and animals, but become conditioned to fear them. Consequently, if the fear was learned, it could be unlearned, or deconditioned. Mary Cover Jones demonstrated this when she successfully treated a young child who had an intense fear of rabbits. She gradually introduced a caged rabbit while the child ate, and over a period of sessions moved the rabbit closer and closer while the child continued to eat comfortably. Eventually, the child was able to accept the rabbit out of the cage and to even play with it. Watson, Jones, and others of this period believed all human responses, both positive and negative, are learned through a process of association of events in people's lives.

In the 1950s, B. F. Skinner challenged the work of earlier behaviorists' theory, indicating he thought it was too passive, and that people had to be actively engaged in the environment for learning to occur. He developed the model of *operant conditioning,* in which he posited that behavior is a function of its consequences—for example, the child who is reinforced for a particular behavior will tend to continue that behavior.

Skinner relied on observable actions and eschewed mentalistic or nonobservable explanations for the development of behavior.

In the years since Watson and Skinner, the sophistication of behavioral approaches to the treatment of emotional and behavioral problems has expanded and the intervention approach has continued to grow in popularity. In the 1950s, Albert Ellis introduced rational emotive psychotherapy, now referred to as *rational-emotive-behavioral therapy (REBT)*. From the early beginnings of Ellis's work, group treatment has been a core element of his approach. In the 1960s, Albert Bandura extended the learning models of Watson and Skinner and the cognitive components of Ellis by including social modeling, the concept that people could observe behaviors and that much learning occurs through this observational method. From Bandura's (1969) social learning theory, now called *social cognitive therapy*—which included the premise that people learn by observing others, engaging in imitation, and mentally processing the experience—a cognitive-social-modeling component came to be added to the traditional behavioral model of understanding human behavior. Other cognitive behaviorists have continued to explore the contributions of thoughts to learning, and cognitive-behavioral therapy has emerged as a major form of therapy, with contributions from theorists such as Aaron Beck and Donald Meichenbaum.

Initially, behavioral interventions focused on the individual delivery of clinical treatment, or in the treatment of several individuals in a group setting, yet the focus of all early behavioral intervention was on individual, not group, change. Whereas the theory and strategies of behavioral work lend themselves well to working in a group format, there has been less discussion of the importance of the use of the group as a therapeutic medium than might be expected. Initially, group applications of behavioral interventions focused on treating patients with similar problems (Rose, 1993) and was seen as an expedient method of treatment. The goal was to use the group more as a class and teach a larger number of people at once, similar to the aforementioned psychoeducational approach. Modeling and social-skills training were also recognized as being done more efficiently in a group setting. There has been less discussion of using behavioral techniques within the group modality than might be expected, despite its easy adaptability to this setting.

In the 1970s, there was considerable interest in teaching assertiveness skills, and the group format lent itself well to this process. Group members could practice with each other, role-playing and behavioral rehearsals could occur, and group feedback was established to help members learn to be more assertive. During this time period, there was little discussion of how the dynamics of the group functioned; rather, the focus was on the specific learning intervention. Although a large number of research publications of the time used groups to carry out the interventions, little of the focus was on the group itself.

In the late 1970s and early 1980s, several books were published on behavioral and cognitive-behavioral group therapy. Yet, the primary focus remained on the strategies of change from a behavioral perspective, not on the group's interactions, members, or leadership characteristics. In the 1970s, social-skills training, particularly centering on assertiveness training, was the focus of group work. In the 1980s, behavioral treatments expanded to include more sophisticated interventions, including cognitive restructuring and training in coping skills. Stress management and anger control interventions became more prevalent (Rose, 1993) while Ellis's (1974) Beck's (1976) and Meichenbaum's (1977) focus on cognitive restructuring became much more common. There was a continued emphasis on systematic approaches to problem solving and the use of relaxation training as a major component in addressing stress and anger. Further, Lewinsohn and his associates developed a major behavioral group treatment program for depression (Hoberman, Lewinsohn, & Tilson, 1988). Also in the 1980s there was considerable research completed on applying behavioral treatments in groups to other specific problems, including parenting groups, pain management, and the treatment of health and life-style concerns such as eating disorders.

In the 1990s, these group applications continued to be developed and refined, and today complex treatment descriptions are available. Many of the programs have become "manualized"—that is, written up in a manual format so that others may see the precise procedures described (see, for example, Meichenbaum, 1985, and Rose, 1998). Although the manuals are able to describe in detail the behavioral intervention, what is less evident in the descriptions are group process and dynamics. Rose and his collaborators (Rose, Tolman, & Tallant, 1985) have indicated in their review that group process was almost totally ignored in the outcome studies carried out in groups involving the treatment of anxiety and depression. Further, while Ellis conducted extensive treatment in group settings, he placed less emphasis on the relationship of the group leader to the members, or of the members to one another, than on the importance of covering and understanding the philosophical and practical aspects of rational-emotive-behavioral therapy in the group.

The development of behavior therapy coincided with the emergence of group counseling and therapy. Behavioral treatments have been applied in a group format as they have become more sophisticated and effective. Today, behavioral group counseling and therapy is one of the primary forms of treatment in schools and mental health settings. The use of groups for behavioral applications is reasonable both for the more general reasons of doing group work, such as cost and time efficiency, and because the premises of behavioral interventions correspond to the group format. As will be seen in this chapter's discussion of behavioral interventions and strategies, the group format allows a better opportunity to use the strategies than do individual interventions.

PREMISES OF BEHAVIORAL GROUP COUNSELING AND THERAPY

There are a number of characteristics of behavioral group counseling that are core to understanding how to use the method.

Focusing on the Here and Now

Behaviorists assume that people are the way they are as a result of the learning experiences they have had. Their behavior may be inappropriate or dysfunctional, but people continue to engage in the behavior because it continues to provide some positive outcome in the present, or because they have not recognized the importance of learning more adaptive ways of behaving. So, while some orientations will explore in detail how or why the behavior developed, behaviorists are more interested in exploring what is maintaining the behavior in the present. It may be useful to have some sense of how inappropriate or ineffective ways of behaving developed, but that understanding is not necessary for change to occur. In fact, understanding of causality is seen by some as counterproductive because people may begin to use the explanation as a justification for not changing. The behavioral approach poses that insight occurs as a result of learning new ways of being, of behaving, rather than the opposite belief that insight leads to behavioral change.

In a group setting, more attention is spent on addressing how a person wants to change and what more adaptive skills are desired and needed than on why the person does not currently have the skills. A series of questions is helpful in demonstrating to the group members the importance of the here-and-now focus:

> **Leader:**   What is your goal—what is it you want to happen?
>
> **Client:**   I want to understand why I keep getting in trouble in class.
>
> **Leader:**   Is it that you want to understand, or is it that you want to learn more effective ways to get along in class?
>
> **Client:**   Yeah, I guess that's right, I'm tired of the hassles I get in class.
>
> **Leader:**   So your ultimate goal is to get along better in class—to learn the skills others seem to have to do well in class?
>
> **Client:**   Yeah, that's it.
>
> **Leader:**   Let's talk about ways to do that. O.K., let's begin.

Defining Specific Goals

Behavioral approaches emphasize that until group members can clearly identify where they want to go, they are not likely to get there. The first step is to define the destination, then explore ways of getting there. Thus, considerable attention is paid to helping clients be very specific in what they want to accomplish. In earlier times, behaviorists were criticized—sometimes justly so—for focusing on symptoms of deep problems rather than addressing the real problem. This is less of an issue today for two reasons:

1. Substantial research over the last two decades has demonstrated that the presenting problems of clients often really are the problems they are experiencing, not just symptoms of a subconscious problem. For example, members of a parent group who are seeking better parenting skills for managing children's inappropriate behavior usually really do simply need skills training.

2. Although accepting that the problems people present with for counseling or therapy are problems they are having, behaviorists have gotten much more adept at exploring the issues and identifying the problem that needs to be addressed. At times, there are problems other than what is initially presented. Parents in a parent group, for example, may be experiencing child-rearing difficulties because of circumstances other than lack of knowledge of child management, such as marital conflict. If that is the case, then the focus is put on addressing the marital conflict, not teaching parenting skills and avoiding the more important problem.

Evaluating Results

Behaviorists are able to assess the extent to which they are having an impact on the problem by identifying specific goals, conducting a pretreatment evaluation of the extent to which a problem exists, and tailoring the treatment approach to the goals. More than any other intervention model, the behavioral approach has consistently focused on being a *science*. There is the expectation that pretreatment assessments will occur, that the treatment strategies or techniques selected will correspond to the identified problem, and that there will be an ongoing evaluation of movement toward goals.

Selecting Strategies Consistent with Learning Theory

Although learning theory is quite complex, a core premise is that behavior is learned, and the learning occurs through the reinforcement or punishment of behaviors. Those activities that people find pleasing, for example, tend to continue and recur, whereas those that people find aversive tend to be discontinued or avoided.

Behaviorists assume that there are factors within the environment or the person that contribute to the maintenance of dysfunctional behaviors. Within the environment, there may be reinforcers that influence the person to continue to engage in activities that are not functional. Workaholics, for example, often experience enormous reinforcement from the environment to continue unhealthy work schedules. Heavy smokers or drinkers often have environments that encourage or support the continued unhealthy life-style. Learning theory would posit that the workaholic, and the heavy smoker or drinker are reinforced for this behavior and that the behavior is likely to continue until either the reinforcers are reduced or alternative behaviors and reinforcers are identified to replace the unhealthy ones. Thus, the strategies that are selected must be consistent with the paradigm that promotes the development of alternative living skills.

Learning Social Living Skills

Social learning theory indicates that there is an interactional effect among people and their environment. Learning may occur through vicarious observations (watching others). Also, learning may occur as a result of interactions with others. Thus, a primary reason to conduct behavioral treatments in a group format is that the most powerful learning experiences are those that develop from interpersonal interactions. By interacting with other group members, by modeling and role-playing intermember support, and by giving and receiving feedback, people are able to move toward their goals through successive approximations to their expected way of being.

Developing and Maintaining Behavior

Ellis (1986, 1987, 1991) has identified a number of areas in which the cognitive processes of people influence their behavior and emotions. He has advocated that group leaders as well as group members must understand these concepts and then use the group to take action to bring about change. These include:

- There is an interactional relationship of thoughts, behaviors, and feelings, and each element continually affects, and is affected by, the others.
- Beyond the internal aspects of thoughts, behavior, and feelings, people also are influenced by their surroundings, and people likewise affect their surroundings.
- Irrational beliefs that people have contribute to their unhappiness. People's beliefs about having other people and the rest of the world conform to their expectations is irrational and is bound to lead to disappointment and emotional stress.
- The events of one's life are not what cause emotional disturbance; rather, it is one's interpretation—thoughts about—those events. The event does not make a person feel awful; instead, it is the irrational belief that the event should not have occurred or should have been different, or that the event was personally aimed at us, that leads to the emotional discomfort.
- All people have the capacity to develop more fulfilling and enjoyable lives, but the process requires an awareness of the possibility of thinking and behaving differently, assiduously applying rational thinking processes, and using cognitive, behavioral, and emotive methods to maintain the change.
- Although our early life incidents do influence people, it is the continued interpretation and indoctrination of those events that cause people concern in the present. The event is passed; it is the replaying of the incident in one's thoughts that maintains the discomfort. New levels of emotional reaction require new ways of thinking of past events.

STAGES OF COGNITIVE-BEHAVIORAL GROUPS

Sheldon Rose has been one of the primary writers on cognitive-behavioral treatments used in groups (1972, 1977, 1987, 1989, 1998). Rose (1998) has described the following stages of a cognitive-behavioral approach to group counseling or group therapy.

Planning for Group Treatment

During the planning stage, the group therapist identifies the purpose of the group, conducts a needs assessment to be certain there is a need for the group, specifies the structure of the group in terms of time and place, and begins recruiting group members. The process of recruiting members is a twofold activity: (1) select those who will most benefit and contribute to the group and (2) deselect those who are not likely to benefit or contribute, and refer them to more appropriate services. This process occurs through intake interviews that the group leader conducts with each member before the group begins.

During the intake interview, potential group members meet individually or in pairs with the leader(s), who helps potential members explore the expectations each has regarding the group. The purpose and content of the group will be presented. During the process, the leader interviews the group member and works to help clearly define the goal(s) the person has for joining the group, and how the person's goals might be operationally defined. An operational definition is one in which the behavior is specified sufficiently and that all persons involved (e.g., the client, group leader, and group members) will have a common understanding of what is expected as an outcome of the group. Clearly defining goals makes it possible to know the extent of the problem before the group begins, and will allow the group to be able to evaluate change and progress toward achieving the goal. Further, during the intake interview, the prospective group member has an opportunity to determine what he or she might expect from the group leader.

Cognitive-behavioral groups often use contracts that specify what each member may expect from the group and what the group leader may expect from the members of the group. The purpose of the contract, which is often written but sometimes only agreed on verbally, is to provide a statement of the expectations of both the client and the group leader. Generally, the contract will include an agreement on the part of the client to attend sessions, share treatment goals with the remainder of the group members, participate in group exercises and experiences, and track or record behavioral incidents (such as a homework assignment to practice social skills in a new setting) to share with the group. The member also agrees to abide by group guidelines, such as attendance, timeliness, payment of fees if applicable, and acceptable group behavior. The contract also calls for the member agreeing to be of assistance to other members of the group, and to participate in role-plays, behavioral rehearsals, problem-solving discussions, and other activities that will be helpful to the other members of the group. An aspect of the contract also specifies the points of evaluation or measurement of change, for assessment of progress, which is a core component of cognitive-behavioral group work.

Starting the Group

The group leader begins the session by providing an overview to the group. He or she will review the purpose of the group as well as prior agreements about meeting times and attendance, and will introduce group members to one another. Generally, there is an explanation that each member of the group shares with other group members a common area of concern and that the focus of the group will be to address that issue. The basic components of the treatment approach are specified and the groups participate in a discussion of how the group will serve to facilitate change. During the intake interview, the leader and each individual had reviewed individual expectations and developed contracts to specify how the member, the leader, and the group would work to help the member. During the initial session, any additional contracting that is necessary as a group activity is included. Group contracts might include having each member agree to seek and to offer help, to participate in group activities and functions, and to share treatment effects with the other group members.

During the starting stage, the therapist focuses on enhancing the cohesion of the group. Group cohesiveness involves having a broad level of participation from members, members finding attraction to the other group members and the group leader, and members feeling safe enough within the group to share. Steps are taken to facilitate the commitment of group members to change and grow. The leader listens empathically and supportively, and appreciates the ambivalence experienced by group members as they consider life changes. The verbal and nonverbal behavior of the leader facilitates group cohesiveness. Also a number of activities will contribute to group cohesiveness, including describing the relevance of each member to the group and having the group leader engage in socially reinforcing activities with all group members (attending, reflecting, shaping, and facilitating cohesiveness through verbal responding and positive feedback).

Attention is paid to how the group may be made more attractive to the members, as a way of facilitating commitment and cohesiveness. This may include providing food at meetings (a particularly powerful component with adolescents and children) and providing incentives for attending the sessions. (For a parenting program with low-income families, fast-food restaurants contributed coupons for free meals, which were given to members who attended each week. A school-based anger-control group for elementary school children provided smiley stickers for each student at the end of the session.) Other activities that add to the cohesiveness of the group include having a number of active interactions, such as role-plays, behavior rehearsals, and other group activities.

Assessing the Presenting Problems and Resources

Assessment, a core component of cognitive-behavioral groups, begins during the individual intake or initial interview the leader has with each group member. The assessment process focuses on identifying whether group therapy in general, and this group in particular, is appropriate for the level and type of concern being presented. The leader interviews each member to determine the cognitive, behavioral, and affective components of the problem areas being presented. From this process, the leader is able to clarify whether the goals of the particular group are consistent with the needs of the client. Also important is examining whether the most appropriate intervention would be one on one or in a group in which the dynamics of the group would facilitate change and growth.

During the intake interview, the leader explores the prospective group member's readiness for change: Is the person actively seeking help or is this an involuntary member? Has the person had experiences in the past that would indicate he or she would work well in a group? What are the resources available, both personal and situational? That is, is the person mature enough to work cooperatively in a group? Does the person have the situational resources necessary to participate (e.g., substance abusers may need other help to address their addiction before joining an advanced anger-control group, parents from housing projects may need transportation to get to group meetings, etc.)?

Often, the intake interview will include role-play exercises to evaluate the person's ability to address problems. Also, checklists and inventories are frequently used to evaluate specific components of problems. Anger checklists, substance abuse inventories, parent stress measures, test-anxiety reports, and other paper-and-pencil measures are often used. Although many therapeutic approaches use psychological evaluations aimed at personality assessment, behavioral approaches are much more likely to use evaluation instruments that specifically focus on the cognitive and behavioral problem areas being addressed by the proposed group.

Behavioral assessment will include an interview that attempts to specify the ABCs. This model examines three facets of a problem. The *B* is the *behavioral* problem—what has caused the person to agree to consider counseling or therapy. The behavior may be fighting, arguing, having panic attacks, procrastinating, or any other dysfunctional behavior. The *A* is the *antecedent*—what is happening before a person gets to the *B,* the behavioral problem. The majority of members of cognitive-behavioral groups are unable to identify what led up to the behavioral conflict, but they are good at describing what happened, or the behavioral incident. The *C* is the *consequence*—what happened as a result of the behavioral situation. For instance, when the person got angry and started fighting, what was the result? If the person experienced an anxiety reaction, what happened afterwards? Remember, the *C,* the consequence, may be positive or negative. If a person experiences a high rate of anxiety and is unable to perform well on an examination, that may result in failure of a course. On the other hand, a person who gets angry or pouts about not getting to manage a television remote control might be rewarded for the behavior by having the remote given up. Likewise, a child who has a temper tantrum in a store might actually benefit by getting the snack he or she wanted at the checkout counter. Generally, tracking the ABCs becomes an early homework assignment. Members will be asked to begin observing and recording the behavioral sequence: What happened that led up to the behavioral problem, and what happened as a consequence?

In cognitive-behavioral group work, a cognitive component is added to the ABC format and the letters take on different levels of meaning. A number of examples have been developed by Ellis (see, for example, Ellis, 1980, 1982, 1991) in which he explores the role of cognitions on behavior. We offer a modified version:

A = What happened? What was the event (antecedent)?
B = What were the beliefs? What did the person think, believe, or perceive?
C = What was the affective state? What did the person feel or experience?
D = How did the person behave? What was the behavioral result of the incident?
E = What was the consequence? What happened as a result of the behavior?
F = What would have been a better outcome?

This model is generally not covered during the initial intake session because it takes time for the leader to present the model—time that may be better spent working with all the members of the group at once. Further, the model is more detailed than most prospective group members have worked with regarding understanding their behavior. The group leader, though, may explore the topics, generally by starting with *E* and going backwards to *A* during the intake interview:

E = "What brought you here? What happened that made you aware this group might be helpful for you?" Or "What happened that convinced you there is a problem?"

D = "What did you do that caused that to happen?" Or "What did you do to contribute to this happening?"

C = "You must have been quite angry to have done that."

B = "What were you thinking then? What do you think was going through your head at the time?"

A = "What was it that happened that you got so angry and upset about?"

Summarization statement: "So you were sent to the office [*E*] for being belligerent [*D*] in class because you got so angry [*C*], thinking 'He shouldn't talk that way to me' [*B*] when he yelled at you in front of the whole class [*A*]. Is that the order of events?"

This model is very helpful as an exercise in groups, because it teaches people to track the sequence of events that led to their problem behavior. An advantage of this model is that it may be used to teach group members how to challenge their current pattern of responding. By examining how they wish *E* could be different, and by recognizing that *A* cannot change because it was the event, they are able to explore with the support of members of group how to challenge the *B*, cognitions, that led to *C*, the upsetting feelings. To have a different outcome, they need to be able to change *B*, *C*, and *D*. As an assessment tool, group members use this process in teams or pairs to help other members examine their patterns of thought behavior.

During the first session, the group as a whole reviews goals that members have established and reviews how to state the problems in specific behavioral terms. Complex problems are broken into smaller components, with the goal having specific targets of intervention amenable to a group model of treatment. During this stage of group work, the leader evaluates each group member's strengths and resources and explores possible barriers to achieving established goals. Part of the time for the assessment and goal-setting stage is used to be certain that group members are compatible enough to provide support for one another and to work on similar or related goals, while at the same time offering sufficient diversity to be able to serve as resources to one other.

A number of writers have described specific assessment procedures for (1) evaluating group members' goals and (2) assessing change as it occurs within the group setting (Rose, 1998; Smead, 1995). One method that was described by Ohlsen, Horne, and Lawe (1988) is called *idiosyncratic goal setting.* In this process, each member of the group specifies the goals he or she has as an outcome for participation in the group. The group then reviews each person's goals and discusses how those goals are similar or different from others' goals. The group then develops the group idiosyncratic goal scale comprised of the goals of each person, which are then incorporated into a group measure. Group members then use a 5-point Likert scale to indicate the degree to which the goal (problem area) is similar or dissimilar to each member of the group. From this scale, members are able to identify their specific goals and to see what the goals of the entire group are. When this scale is then used on a regular basis, say every two sessions of the group, it is possible to see how each individual is progressing on his or her goals, and to see how the group at large is progressing.

Another assessment process that has been used by Rose (1998) as an in-session evaluation is the *critical moment*. Rose has group members identify a troublesome situation they have experienced recently. They do an analysis to define what was happening, who was involved, and where it occurred. They then describe which aspect was the most troublesome for them, which is called the critical moment. The group member describes, in the critical moment, his or her behavior, affect, and cognitions. He or she explores his or her satisfaction with their cognitions, affect, and behavioral responses. If the group member is satisfied with his or her responses, then the incident is not pursued further in the group. If, on the other hand, the group member reports that he or she does not know how to respond in the critical moment, then the group engages in developing problem-solving and social-skills training. For self-criticism or rapprochement, rational emotive challenges to irrational beliefs or other cognitive-restructuring techniques may be used. Practice in reframing and coping-skills training may also be used, particularly in situations in which the group member may have no control of the situation, such as being in an aversive class or having a demanding boss.

The group membership is a tool to help throughout the assessment process. The group reviews each member's progress, serves to encourage continued growth and change, and offers suggestions as well as participates with the leader in developing recommendations for change if no progress is evident. Members often assist each other in providing observational data, evaluating the effectiveness of group learning exercises such as behavioral rehearsals or role-plays, and providing feedback for continued growth and change.

Selecting and Applying Interventions to Effect Change

The assessment and evaluation process continues throughout cognitive-behavioral group treatments. In the stage of selecting and applying interventions, the group assessments of individual concerns continue in order to be certain that appropriate interventions are being selected for the members of the group.

At the beginning of the group, usually in the initial meeting, members of the group present their concerns and issues to other members of the group. As this process unfolds, the group leader identifies commonalties and themes of the members and illustrates the universality of the general problem area to all members. Once all members have presented their goals and perspectives, and the leader has summarized the themes of each member's concerns, the group identifies the core theme of the problem area and discusses its relevance to each of them. Also, if several themes develop, the group members work to develop a hierarchy of themes and propose an order in addressing the various themes.

Once the theme of the group is endorsed, the group members discuss the outcomes they would like to achieve as a function of being in the group. Behavioral outcomes are specified and each person attempts to individualize the theme and outcome to address his or her specific concerns. The group leader then discusses intervention strategies that seem relevant and appropriate for the specific themes developed and provides the group with pros and cons regarding the various methods. This facilitates members taking ownership of the problems and the group.

The selection of interventions must be consistent with the stated purpose of the group when the initial description of the group offering was presented. The intake interviews with individual members, as well as the initial group meeting with all members, will affect which interventions are to be considered. Developmental issues also impact selection of treatment interventions. For example, children too young to understand cognitive restructuring would not be offered that model, and adults would not be provided with stickers to reinforce their attendance at group sessions.

Identifying and Dealing with Group Problems

Assessment and evaluation of the group itself is carried out to determine the extent to which the group is meeting the needs and interests of the members, to identify emerging group interactional problems or concerns, and to evaluate the impact of each behavioral strategy.

Planning for Generalization and Preparing for Termination

Throughout the group experience there is an attempt to focus on the generalization of things learned within the specific group to life outside the group. In-session behavioral rehearsals and role-plays are designed to be reflective of out-of-group concerns presented by group members. During sessions, the leader will encourage members to think about how their out-of-group life will be affected by the activities of the group. Further, regular homework assignments are a core part of cognitive-behavioral treatments.

As the group approaches termination, the group leader will engage in more verbal encouragement and support for discussions about behavior change that reflect generalization from the group to the outside. Also, some group leaders schedule meetings to occur less frequently, moving toward a fading of group support as the members apply their skills with fewer and fewer meetings. As a corollary to this fading process, group members are encouraged to identify other nontherapeutic groups that may be attractive to them so that the members look to other groups to fulfill their social interests rather than become counseling/therapy group dependent. These might include social support elements within their current lives, family relationships, and school or agency connections, or may include examining ways of extending and expanding to other avenues of interest.

Although some behavioral group leaders do not specify follow-up sessions as a component step of their treatment program in cognitive-behavioral group work, some do include "booster sessions" as part of the generalization phase of the group. Scheduling follow-up sessions as an integral part of the expectation of cognitive-behavioral group work emphasizes the importance of follow-up sessions. Follow-up provides the opportunity to bring group members back together at a specified period following group termination. The purpose is to review and discuss achievements group members have accomplished and to give the positive affirmation of continued change. There is also the opportunity to discuss new problems that may have arisen and to decide whether there is a need to reconvene the group for a few sessions to address the new problems, to refer members to other groups, or to continue in individual sessions to address specific concerns one or two of the members may have. The fine-tuning that occurs with a booster session is often just what group members need to stay on track with their changes.

THERAPIST'S ROLE

Changing Roles

In cognitive-behavioral group treatments, the therapist's role changes as the group progresses. During the pregroup assessment phase, the therapist is both a promoter of the group and a gatekeeper, making certain that those wishing to participate in the group meet the expectations and requirements of the group and that the group is the most appropriate intervention model for the client. In this regard, the therapist must have carefully thought out the need and purpose of the group, the possible participants and what their characteristics will be, the legal and ethical issues involved in offering the group, and the structural components (time, day, location, length number of participants).

Once potential group members have been notified of the group and intake interviews have been completed, the group begins. In cognitive-behavioral group therapy, the leader initially begins by providing structure and organization. During the intake interviews, there is an explanation of how the group will function and what ground rules will be necessary for the group. These expectations include a willingness on the part of each participant to share with the other members of the group what his or her respective goal is, what the expectation for change is, and a request from the group to facilitate the changes. Another expectation for each group member is a willingness to provide help and assistance to others—to give as well as to receive support and assistance within the group setting.

During the initial session, the leader provides quite a bit of structure. In addition to the expectations just cited, other ground rules for the group are explained. This includes agreements regarding attendance, payment for services, and ethical/professional guidelines for breaking confidentiality. Confidentiality would be broken, for example, if a member threatens to hurt either self or others, such as with child or spouse abuse. Although members should already understand the importance of tracking behavior change, it will be presented again during the initial session with examples and guidelines. Tracking means observing, counting, and recording targeted behavior. Besides structure, another primary role of the leader in this phase is to serve as a teacher, helping members learn to define change expectations and to understand how behavior change occurs. Frequently, the teaching role includes explaining that behavior is learned, detailing the process for establishing new behaviors, and discussing how the group format will be used for developing and incorporating a new behavioral repertoire. Early in the life of the group, the leader takes considerable responsibility for the content and process of the group.

The leader slowly shifts from the teacher role to the coach role as the group moves from the initial stage into a more developed stage of group work. As they begin to develop a new behavioral repertoire, group members practice their skills both within the group and during homework assignments outside the group. As a coach, the members are doing the work within the group. Just as in a football or basketball game in which the coach is on the sidelines calling signals and recommending plays while the players do the actual work, the group leader moves from having primary responsibility to coaching those who are taking on more of the burden of the learning. As a coach, the leader is encouraging and recommends changes and methods to be considered, but the group members have primary responsibility for carrying out the learning.

In later stages of the group, the leader transitions from the coach role to more of a consultant role. In this capacity, the goal is to have the members be somewhat independent and autonomous in their learning and skills applications. At this stage, the members describe the changes they are working on, try the new skills out both in and outside the group, and come back to their fellow group members for consultations about how to refine their new learning. The consultant is there to assist and offer recommendations and suggestions, but the primary responsibility for change at this point rests with the group members. It is at this latter stage of the group that the leader attempts to assist group members in generalizing what they have learned from their specific group setting into their lives beyond the group. A goal is to foster independence and generalization, with the expectation that change will maintain more effectively if it is under the control of the group member rather than the group leader. At this stage, the leader moves the group toward termination and schedules future "booster sessions" to help maintain the changes beyond the group.

The leader has transitioned from group promoter/gatekeeper to teacher, to coach, and to consultant in the life of the group. This is an intentional transition that is necessary to illustrate the differing roles the leader has as the group evolves. Some group leaders have difficulty in assuming some of these roles—the authority figure of the teacher, for example, if the leader has been trained in a more psychodynamic therapy role, or the consultant role if the leader has been trained to assume major responsibility for the entire life of the group. Yet, these differing roles are highly consistent with the cognitive-behavioral premise of learning new skills and behaviors.

Use of Language

Language is very important to all group leaders, but within a cognitive-behavioral framework the leader has to be aware of the impact language has in maintaining fidelity between treatment and theory. Many of the developments in solution-focused group work had their beginnings in cognitive-behavioral treatments, and the use of words to facilitate the direction of therapy is very important. The leader must be cognizant of a number of premises regarding the use of language.

Expect Change.   Cognitive-behavioral group leaders are optimistic regarding the possibility of change. There is a belief that people with dysfunctional behavior patterns really are less happy and less satisfied with their lives than they would be without the dysfunctional behavioral characteristics. People who complain of being depressed or sad or angry or even stressed not only would be happier without these problems, but it is possible to help people achieve these changes. Certainly there are no simple answers to addressing pathology or problem situations, but there is an optimism that behaviors that were learned and that are distressful can be replaced with new learned behaviors that are not as distressful or maladaptive and may even be highly positive and reinforcing.

The group leader will select words that reflect this positivity. He or she attempts to understand the parameters of the problem (When does this happen? Who is there? Where are you when it happens? How often? etc.), but there is also an attempt to know the other side (When does this not happen? Who is there when you are doing well? Where are you when you don't have this situation? How often does this problem not show? etc.). Behavioral approaches have as a premise that it is more effective to increase positive experiences than it is to reduce negative ones. Therefore, there is a strong focus on what works—an attempt to increase the strengths rather than focus on weaknesses.

Reinforce Change.   A group model we developed in the 1970s was called *model-reinforcement* counseling groups (Horne & Matson, 1977). In that work—which focused on anxiety in the form of test, speech, or social stress—members were randomly assigned to either the model-reinforcement counseling group or to an alternative model of a counseling group. The model-reinforcement counseling group started each week by playing a 5- to 10-minute audiotape of a role-played group that had been developed to be at the same stage as the current group and to be discussing topics that would be expected to parallel the current group. On the tape, the role-playing members would talk about their ability to use the new skills they had learned the week before and to discuss ways they had even extended the use of specific techniques. After the tape was completed, the leader would turn to the group members and ask them to discuss how their experiences had been for the week. The tape served as the modeling component of the model-reinforcement counseling group.

The leader of the model-reinforcement counseling group was trained to acknowledge or respond primarily to statements that were neutral or that reflected change and to ignore or to redirect all negative statements in the group. Thus, if a group member said, "I tried this relaxation stuff but it didn't work," the group leader would look at other members of the group and say, "I'm wondering who was able to have a successful experience with the relaxation assignment this week?" or "Although we never expect complete success with any new technique, I'm sure some of you had some positive results with the relaxation. Who would share how you used it to help you manage your stress?" or "Jim indicated he had some difficulty applying the relaxation skills; let's get back to him in a minute to see if we can figure what he could do to make it work more effectively; in the meantime, though, who was able to use the process effectively?" Not only were words carefully selected to reinforce those who had been successful but they were also selected to encourage others to identify ways of applying the knowledge and skills.

The group leader used verbal leads as well as nonverbal reinforcement to elicit participation and to encourage positive applications of the new skills. The leader would use head nods, smiles, eye contact, and physically turning the body toward participants who were heavily involved and engaged in skills development. Further, the leader attempted to have group interactions foster participation by saying such things as, "Kim, I noticed that as Jim talked about having difficulty with relaxation, you looked surprised. I'm wondering if you had a different experience, and if so, could you tell the group about it?"

Each week new skills were introduced to the group and the leader would explain why the skill was important, demonstrate it, and have participants role-play or practice it, and then give each other feedback on how well each seemed to master the skill. The group ended each week with all members describing how they would be able to use this skill before returning again. Usually a technique we called *pre-problem solving* would be used. This technique calls for having group members identify what problems could arise during the week that would prevent them from effectively using the new skill. A person may indicate, for example, she anticipated having difficulty remembering the steps of relaxation training, so the group would work together to help identify ways of solving the problem before it happened. One solution offered was to tape-record the group leader giving the instructions and then have the group members play the audio-tape rather than trying to remember the steps.

At the end of the treatment program, the model-reinforcement counseling group members demonstrated significantly greater reduction of anxiety and stress. This was witnessed both on general anxiety inventories and on specific measures related to their concern, such as test anxiety. They also reported a greater generalization of benefits and were more likely to recommend similar counseling to their friends and others. The only concern that developed with the model was that some group leaders felt manipulative in their behavior, but concluded that they were, in fact, doing what effective group leaders do—attending to those aspects of behavior they want to reinforce, while trying to extinguish or ignore the behaviors that were not productive or facilitative.

Emphasize Positive Motivation and Positive Expectations for Change.   Some models of group work assume that resistance to change will occur and that group leaders must constantly be prepared to deal with resistance, but cognitive-behavioral group leaders assume that people really do want to change and that they are open to learning new ways of managing their lives. This may involve reframing some of the concerns that members bring to the group (e.g., "Some of you have expressed doubts about the group being able to help you learn to manage your depression and you may be wondering if you might end up worse than you started. It is good to question how this group can help you, and I want to be sure that you have your questions answered before we go any further. Just by raising the questions, you are demonstrating that you are taking care of yourself, not so depressed that you are unable to examine how to make this work for you").

Group leaders establish positive expectations regarding treatment outcome and express confidence both in the group as well as in their personal ability to facilitate change. Ethically, group leaders can never promise change will occur, but they can share their experiences from previous groups and other members (e.g., "Although no group works all the time for all people, the anger-management group we will be following is based on a model that has been quite effective with a large number of people.

I believe that if we conscientiously apply the new skills we will be learning, we can bring about better anger management for our members as well").

Some group models identify group members as resistant when they challenge the group leader or when they fail to follow through on a homework assignment, but cognitive-behavioral group leaders are more likely to reframe the situation. Rather than label group members resistant, group leaders from a behavioral orientation are more likely to share the responsibility for change not occurring. They would take the position that clients are experiencing problems in their lives and that they would be happier without the problems. Therefore, it is assumed that clients will have the motivation to change if the counselor is able to identify the problem and offer a program that may be effective for bringing about change. If a client does not participate and begin to make changes, it is believed that the client is most likely communicating that the group is moving too quickly for the member, the member does not feel understood, or the problem being addressed may not be the primary issue for the member. It is then the responsibility of the group leader to view resistant behavior as a message that there is a need for further refinement of the goals and process of the group. If the treatment does not seem relevant to members of the group, they will not be motivated to participate and facilitate the movement of the group.

Normalize Problems.   Whereas some models of group counseling and therapy focus on pathology and illness, cognitive-behavioral group leaders are more likely to focus on strengths and learning processes. If one sees aggressive behavior in a group as a form of psychopathology and treats group members as though they are sick, the members will be more likely to conform to that expectation. The leader reframes the behavior as follows: "You have been doing the best you could under the circumstances, but the circumstances meant you had not learned better ways of handling problems in the family. In this group we are clear that you cannot use abuse and violence in the group or in the family. Having said that, though, the purpose of this group is to help you learn more adaptive skills for managing your anger, to help you learn the skills of withdrawing from the conflict long enough to calm yourself and have control over your emotions before trying to resolve the conflict. All people have problems, but not all people hurt others. The anger is normal; the aggression, though, is not acceptable, and that's what we do here; that is, we teach people more effective ways of managing that anger." Since learning theory is the core premise of behavior therapy, it is assumed that people can learn more adaptive ways of being, and that is a normal thing to do.

Normalizing does not mean making light of a problem, because the concerns of the members of the group are very important to them. Nor does it imply that all forms of deviance or pathology are normal. But normalizing does mean helping put the concerns into a context that provides motivation for change. In terms of the conditions of therapeutic change identified by Yalom (1995), the sense of universality is important— to know that having problems is universal and that the other members of the group share in emotional and behavioral conflicts. The goal of normalizing is to move from group members thinking of themselves as unique and sick and having maladaptive ways of handling the conflicts and problems of life, to learning new cognitive-behavioral methods and more adaptive ways of coping and living.

Match the Communication Style to Group Members.   The language counselors and therapists use is crucial. Although cognitive-behavioral group counseling has some sophisticated language and specific explanations for the interventions selected, group leaders use the language that fits with their group members. When working with parent groups made up of psychologists or counselors or other people used to or accustomed to the language of psychology, counselors may speak about the Premack Principle of having the more reinforcing event follow the less likely event. In most groups, though, the group leader would simply talk about "Grandma's Law," which is exactly the same as the Premack Principle, only this time the counselor would say, "Make sure your child eats the peas before he gets the dessert." This way of speaking is consistent with modeling: All models may be positive, but the models that are most similar to the group member are the ones that are the most reinforcing, the more likely to be imitated. And competency models, those that are competent but not exceptional, are more likely to be imitated than the expert model that does everything right but that is seen as unrealistic to most group members.

Use Paraphrasing and Summarizing with Reinforcing Statements.   Structuring and repeating are steps that are taken when counselors want group members to learn new skills. Counselors who take the time to paraphrase and summarize what is being said and present the information in a solution-focused manner will be more effective:

> So, Kim, you were able to use the relaxation exercises several times this week and they seemed to help you manage your concern over the test you had to take. That's great. Tell the group a few things you did to adapt the exercise to fit your busy schedule."

> "Jim, you said earlier you were not able to use the relaxation program very effectively this week. You've had a chance to hear a few others talk about it now, and Kim discussed how she adapted the program to fit her schedule. Tell me some ideas you have now on how you might use the process differently during the coming week."

Gather Information about Cognitive and Emotional Reactions.   As the group leader listens to the group members talk, the leader is continually filing away information he or she is receiving about how the group is thinking and feeling, as well as what the group is doing. Counselors know more about the behaviors—what people do—than what the group members think. Usually, group members do not process their thinking patterns either, and so the group leader listens to them as they talk, and identifies what they are thinking so that this information may be used later in the group:

Client: I put him to bed but he screamed and demanded water and a kiss.

Leader: What things are going through your head when he does this?

Client: Not again; I can't stand it again.

Leader: And after you have thought that, you start feeling hopeless. Is that when you start losing control?

Gather Information about Sequences and Patterns.   As the leader listens to group members talk about their experiences, attention is paid to their cognitive processes and emotional reactions to situations. In the process, the leader is filing away sequences and patterns about how the group members experience problems. Often, having people role-play the sequence sheds even more understanding on the sequence of events and how those lead to conflict.

Break Problems into Manageable Tasks.   One characteristic for members of counseling groups is that they often enter treatment with a host of complex problems and do not see a way to manage these enormous concerns. A group leader's task includes breaking the larger concerns into more manageable pieces and modeling effective problem-management skills. This process will also help the group leader identify where to start and what intervention strategy is the most appropriate for the beginning stage of counseling.

Personalize the Sessions.   When some group leaders initially begin doing cognitive-behavioral counseling and therapy groups, they assume that since some of the models have very detailed manuals guiding the group leader through the steps of the process, or the protocol for the group model is so clearly defined, the group leader merely walks participants through the steps. This becomes a "canned" program and lacks the cohesiveness that is so essential in effective counseling and therapy groups. One way to address this problem is to personalize the group throughout the experience. So, rather than say, "I am now going to teach relaxation skills. Does anyone have a question? Fine, then close your eyes . . . ," the group leader might say instead, "We are now going to go over the relaxation skills. How many of you have heard of this procedure? Good, Kim; and Jerry, it's good to see you've heard of it as well. Do you have any questions? Okay, will each of you close your eyes? Thank you Jim, and Raphael, and you too. . . ."

Interpret Change from a Cognitive-Behavioral Perspective.   When explaining what will happen in the group, or what has happened, it is very helpful to use the language of the cognitive-behavioral model:

> **Jim:**   Wow, this stuff worked this week. It was great.
>
> **Leader:**   Jim, that's great. You practiced the skill last week in the group, made a plan for using it each evening to really learn it well, and then you used it just as you had planned. You found that it was quite rewarding to do this homework well. Let's once more review the steps you followed.

Give Credit to Group Members for Change.   All people like credit for work well done. It is important to recognize that the group members are the ones doing the work and carrying out the exercises, and so group leaders should conscientiously credit change and growth to the group members.

> **Jim:**   Boy you were right, you said you could help master this school stuff and it's really working—you are the man!'
>
> **Leader:**   Jim, that's great that it worked so well for you this week. Let's talk about what you did, what was it about how you used the relaxation skills that seemed to work, and what might you do to keep that happening?

OTHER COGNITIVE-BEHAVIORAL GROUP COUNSELING AND THERAPY PROCEDURES

In addition to the preceding discussion of cognitive-behavioral approaches premises, stages, counselor or therapist role, leader characteristics and use of language, there are other procedures to be considered. These procedures are considered within the topics already discussed, but are detailed further here.

Goals and Objectives

Goals and objectives are considered in two ways: the goals and objectives of the individual members and the goals and objectives of the counseling or therapy group. For individuals, the leader will go into detail during the intake interview to help define goals in such a manner that there is specificity and clarity about the expectations of what is to be addressed within the group and what will be achieved as a result of being in the group.

In behavioral terms, the goals become operationally defined, or defined in such a manner that objective observers could agree that the goal has or has not been achieved. A goal to "feel better about myself" would not suffice, for objective observers would not be able to agree on achievement. The leader, though, would work with the person to help define that goal more operationally:

Client: I want to feel better about myself.

Leader: What would it take for that to happen?

Client: Well, I don't like that I'm so overweight and I'm eating horribly. Plus, I get so stressed from classes and then gorge myself, then sit around feel depressed and stupid.

Leader: You think you would feel better about yourself if you identified ways in which to manage the stress of school and work better. Then you might engage in less gorging, which would again help you feel better about yourself. That could lead to better eating habits, which could translate into a healthier body. If we want to come up with an emotional goal, it will be to feel better about yourself. The behavioral goal would be to demonstrate effective time-management skills, learn some stress-management techniques, which could include relaxation training and positive imagery, and find a pattern of eating that is healthy. We can examine each of these further, and to do that, we would need a baseline, a measure of what and when you are now eating, a stress barometer giving some indication of the extent of stress in your life today so that we would know what the cues are for you to become stressed, and some measure of how you would define healthy eating, for to increase the rate of that happening, we need to know the beginning level. Does that sound like a goal you have? If it is, we can get more specific on how to do these things.

Objective observers would be able to examine weekly reports of stress, a diary measuring steps taken to reduce stress, such as relaxation training, and changes in eating patterns that are recorded in a daily or weekly eating chart. They could examine weight measures as well as physical fitness and body image. All of these are objective measurements that may be agreed on by others, whereas only the client can tell whether she feels better. Be aware that this process often leads to developing other additional goals, for when potential clients examine their goals and what is contributing to the maladaptive life-style they have, they recognize additional contributing factors. For the present example, it may be that a contributing factor could be how time is spent, poor study habits resulting in academically related stress, or hanging with peers who also engage in a nonproductive use of time and have poor eating habits, which could lead to a need to influence current friends or find a new friendship base.

There are also group goals that are established, and these are always related to the purpose of the group. A group focusing on assertiveness training, for example, may have as a goal that by the end of the training session, all, or some percentage (6 out of 8, for example), will be able to increase their scores on an assertiveness skills paper-and-pencil measure, demonstrate through videotaped role-plays how to use assertiveness skills in a variety of settings, and be able to discuss the components of cognitive self-challenges. The point is, there is an objective measure at the end of the group, with a clear answer to whether goals were achieved and behavior change occurred. Rather than focus on how good the leader felt about the quality of the interactions and how positively he or she feels about the people in the group, the bottom line is: Was measurable change accomplished?

Selection and Group Composition

Selection of members and the composition of the group have been discussed in Chapter 3. Selection for a cognitive-behavioral counseling or therapy group is made easier by having a clear goal for the group (a definition of what is to happen and what the outcome will be for the members) and by having an organizing theme that potential members will need to fit. The leader will conduct intake interviews and identify members whose goals are consistent with the group goals.

For some cognitive-behavioral groups, homogeneity is good; for others, leaders will want heterogeneity. For students needing assistance with study skills of help in learning how to manage specific anxieties such as test, speech, or social skills, a homogeneous group would be appropriate. This group would have all members functioning at about the same level, needing approximately the same skills and about equally able to benefit from the group experience. On the other hand, heterogeneous groups function better for some other concerns, such as substance abuse, working with bullying behavior in school, or students having trouble with teachers. In these situations, a homogeneous group would likely be supportive of each other not making change, instead wanting to blame the behaviors and activities on the situations and circumstances outside of themselves. Members can become very reinforcing of each other: "No one gets along with these teachers; they're all jerks" could lead to affirmation from all the members, thus preventing the leader from having an effective entry to dealing with change. By having a mixed group, the leader has the possibility of members of the group disagreeing, thus allowing for the exploration of how the complaining member is contributing to the situation.

Group Size

The size of the cognitive-behavioral group influences the activities that occur within the group. Since cognitive-behavioral groups generally are more active than other approaches to group work, there is a need to have sufficient room in the setting to engage in activities the leader will want the members to practice. For example, if relaxation training becomes a focus of the group, the leader will not want more members of the group than can fit comfortably in a reclining or resting position. Also, when conducting role-plays and behavioral rehearsals, it is important to have sufficient room to move about and to walk. Cognitive-behavioral groups at times cover didactic material, and so a setting that is conducive to members taking notes or the leader using a chalkboard or other teaching medium is important.

A small group, three or four members, is often problematic in cognitive-behavioral groups because there is generally considerable interacting. Members are asked to describe problems they have, perhaps give a demonstration of the difficulties, and then practice new skills. For counseling a group comprised of boys who have been victimized by school bullies, for example, it is better to have more than three members, because there will be considerable practice on new skills, and having a wider range of members with whom to practice the skills is a very positive aspect of group work.

On the other hand, large groups prevent the level of skills development and practice that is desired with cognitive-behavioral groups. Trying to individualize treatment effects with more than 10 people leads to difficulty, and members may not feel they are having the opportunity of getting the level of personal attention and consideration they desire. When there is a large group, the leader has more difficulty getting around to subgroups when he or she breaks them into pairs to role-play or practice skills they have been discussing. On the other hand, some leaders like to work with larger groups in order to make more efficient use of their time, and will justify the larger groups by using other aids, such as video role-modeling tapes, co-leaders who can share in the efforts to give feedback to dyads who are role-playing activities, and using handouts and homework that allow members to practice beyond the group setting.

Frequency, Length, and Duration of Group Sessions

Cognitive-behavioral treatment groups have a broad range of treatment length, but typically are more proscribed than other approaches. They may be as short as one session, as in the case of a university counseling center offering a one-session group on a highly defined topic, such as managing stress during final examination periods. They may go on as long as several years, such as a group focusing on life-style change in which a core of group participants meet twice monthly to identify areas of change they want to work on. The members find support from the group for practicing the new skills and developing plans for applying the new behaviors outside the group. One such group we work with has been going on for more than five years. New members join as some members drop out, but all former members are invited to return as they reach a new area in which they want the resources of the group to help them address additional concerns or life-style changes.

In his review of cognitive-behavioral groups, Rose (1993) reported that intensive therapy groups generally run 14 to 18 weeks and include booster sessions at one to six months to ensure maintenance of change. Short-term, skills-focused groups are more likely to be 6 to 12 sessions.

The length of the group is likely to be determined by the nature of concerns for the group members, with time-limited group treatments being more homogeneous in group membership makeup. The short-term groups generally focus on specific topics, such as social-skills training for shy students, anxiety-management groups or anger-control methods for abusive partners, and marital communication training. Open-ended cognitive-behavioral groups are more likely to have members addressing more varied and intense problems and represent a heterogeneous mix of concerns.

Theme-oriented groups are generally closed. That means all members commit to participate the entire length of the group and no new members are added once the group has begun. This is particularly important in cognitive-behavioral skills-focused groups, such as with assertiveness or stress-management training. The process is clearly delineated and follows a program that is cumulative, with each week building on the material covered in the previous week. Adding new members is prohibited, since it would require going over all the material each time a new group member joined. Since skills-specific training groups are thought of as a "building blocks" developmental model in which mastery of one stage of skills is necessary before moving on to the next, the group does not lend itself to open membership.

The more ongoing, intensive cognitive-behavioral group, on the other hand, often has open membership and, as one client completes his or her treatment goals and exits the group, another member is added. In the ongoing, intensive treatment group, members who have been in the group for a while serve as models and co-facilitators with the group leader to help new members understand the behavioral principles involved. The ongoing members are likely to take an important role in helping acclimate the new member to the group.

The length of the treatment group is often determined by the setting in which the service is offered. University counseling centers and public schools often have 10- to 12-session groups because of their academic schedule. In the first couple weeks of a semester, information about the group is provided and members are recruited. Then the group runs for approximately 10 weeks, at which it terminates to coincide with the end of the academic term. Cognitive-behavioral groups in hospitals often are open ended and allow members to join or leave the group as their treatment program within the hospital dictates.

SUPPLEMENTS EMPLOYED

Cognitive-behavioral group counseling and therapy often rely on a number of supplemental materials, devices, and activities.

Bibliotherapy

There are numerous books and manuals available that are particularly relevant for cognitive-behavioral counseling and therapy groups. For addressing erroneous thinking Albert Ellis has written dozens of books that range in complexity from easy reading for children to professional books for therapists. Many of his books are available in popular bookstores and on the World Wide Web. Another author who has written popular books addressing cognitive restructuring is Wayne Dyer, whose books are readily available in paperback. Other books on assertiveness training, relaxation skills, stress management, and life-coping skills are common in public bookstores. There are texts targeted to specific areas of concern, such as parenting, marital communication, anger and anxiety management, physical conditions (e.g., weight management), and addressing type-A heart problems. Additionally, many group leaders develop their own handouts and readings for group members to use as homework or stimulus material to be covered from one session to the next.

Audiotaping

Audiotapes are often used just as books are—to provide homework exercises between sessions. Some of the skills that are covered are best reviewed between sessions by listening to audiotapes of the group session to help members review what was presented and in what activities the group participated. Often, members provide their own tape recorders and tapes to record the session, which, of course, raises questions of confidentiality and the possible misuse of tapes. This may be addressed by taping only sections of the group that do not address a specific person's concerns, such as when a group is participating in group training for the relaxation response or when the leader is presenting the ABCs of irrational thinking. Another use of audiotapes, though, is for the group leader to prepare a set of tapes in advance that may be loaned out to group members. These might include some that are commercially available, such as for relaxation training or parenting groups, but may be made by the group leader specifically for the particular group.

Videotaping

Cognitive-behavioral group leaders often videotape their sessions both for their own review and for use within the group. At times, two sets of recording may occur: one used by the group leader for review and supervision (and maintained in his or her files) and the other used specifically within the group itself. Since there is a strong emphasis within behavioral group counseling and therapy on feedback, modeling, behavioral rehearsal, and role-playing, videotaping the group when they engage in these exercises and then playing the segment back in the group may be very powerful. In this process, the members of the group see themselves engaging in the exercises and are able to provide frame-by-frame feedback on what was done well and what may need improvement. Participants see themselves as others see them, and are able to get more concrete and immediate feedback on how they present themselves to others.

The use of videotaping is very useful for preevaluation as well as postevaluation. By having members engage in role-played scenarios early in the group, they are able to see changes they have been made when later tapes are played that demonstrate the mastery of skills covered in the group.

SPECIAL ETHICAL CONSIDERATIONS

As with all therapeutic approaches, the leader must be cognizant of the ethical and legal considerations that go with conducting cognitive-behavioral group treatments. The ethical considerations that apply to all groups apply to this theoretical orientation, but there are other considerations that are made as well.

First and foremost is to make certain that the leader is working with the *right problem*. This is usually determined through the intake interview and the initial assessment procedures that are used. In addition, group leaders should attend to physical problems that may manifest themselves in behavioral conditions. Anxiety and depression may both be exacerbated by chemical imbalances in the body. Anger-management problems and hyperactivity may also be related to biological conditions. The group leader needs to be aware of possible physical causes of behavioral problems and require members to have physician check-ups to rule out medical causes of the behaviors.

Another aspect of being certain the group leader is attending to the right problem is in determining whether the behavior of the referred member is the problem or whether there are other issues that must be addressed. Often, people seek counseling for a specific issue, when in fact there may be other issues in the background. An example of that occurred during a weight-management group when one of the members continued to gain weight, even though the group was reviewing and discussing effective weight-management strategies. When the member was queried about why she wanted to lose weight, she explained she would feel healthier, would be able to buy more attractive clothes, and she would look better in a swimsuit—at which time she broke out crying and said, "And then my husband would want sex all the time and I can't stand it!" Clearly, the focus of the group was wrong for the concerns she had. She and her husband were interviewed outside the group and identified troubles in couples communication and sexual activities. They were referred to a group for couples on couple's communication skills and participated in individual couples sessions addressing sexual issues within the relationship, resulting in a successful outcome.

A second ethical issue for cognitive-behavioral group leaders is the issue of *preparation*. It is understood that all counselors and therapists are ethically bound to practice within their realm of expertise. At times, the cognitive-behavioral model can be deceptive, for it appears to be easy to learn—simply open a manual and follow the directions, leading group leaders to offer groups in which they have little knowledge or expertise, and often without professional supervision. Cognitive-behavioral group treatments require that the leader have training in the model and with each of the intervention approaches used, such as cognitive restructuring. Those without such training should seek supervision from more experienced practitioners.

A third area of concern is related to the second: Group leaders are expected to be *familiar with the literature* on the efficacy of cognitive-behavioral treatments and to be aware that often *several methods may be used* to treat the same problem. The Association for the Advancement of Behavior Therapy (AABT) has taken the position that when selecting treatment interventions, the least aversive method should be selected. A behaviorally oriented group in a school may treat children referred for bullying behavior by providing corporal punishment for every bully incident—a highly aversive intervention—or may elect to conduct a group that models problem solving, conflict resolution, and empathy training—a much less aversive approach.

A fourth area of concern is to be certain that participants have discussed the possible *negative ramifications of change.* Although group counselors and therapists are certain the services they are offering are beneficial, they need to explore with potential members that change often goes beyond the behavioral skills that develop in the group. In the 1970s, when assertiveness training was so popular, there were early casualties of groups that did not adequately prepare members for the possible reactions of others to the newly acquired assertive behavior. Not all spouses wanted more assertive mates; not all managers wanted more assertive employees, and not all parents wanted more assertive children. Although in the long run it was most likely healthier for the individuals involved to become more assertive, it is the professional responsibility of the group leader to review possible negative outcomes of change resulting from group participation.

APPLICATIONS TO VARIOUS AGE GROUPS

Cognitive-behavioral groups are applicable to all age levels and are used in a variety of settings. Psychoeducational groups as well as skills-specific learning groups are available in elementary, middle, and high schools. Cognitive-behavioral groups are offered in a variety of educational settings, ranging from use with young children (e.g., "think-aloud" type groups for elementary-aged children to learn to address their attention deficit problems), bully behavior management groups for aggressors and victims in middle schools, and more intensive group counseling and therapy programs for high school and college students. Outside the school setting, cognitive-behavioral groups are also used with children and adolescents in private practices, community services, and institutional settings, such as hospitals and correctional centers. With younger children, there is a greater focus on behavioral skills learning, whereas with older children and adolescents, the focus expands to include cognitive interventions.

Cognitive-behavioral treatments are also used with adults, ranging from young adulthood to the elderly. Groups are most likely to incorporate both the cognitive and behavioral components, and are offered in private practices, agencies within the community, inpatient and outpatient treatment in hospitals, and correctional facilities. The focus of cognitive-behavioral group treatment is determined by the developmental level of the potential membership, the relevance of the group to the problems of potential members, and the expectations of the setting in which the service is offered.

RESEARCH

The evaluation of treatment success is a core element of cognitive-behavioral group treatment. Considerable research supports the finding that cognitive-behavioral interventions are as powerful and as effective, if not more so, than other treatments (Dies, 1994). Having said that, it is important to recognize that few studies have attempted to parse out the role of the group leader, the dynamics of the membership, and the level of disturbance when accounting for the effectiveness of the model. Rose and colleagues (Rose, Tolman, & Tallant, 1985) have reported that behavioral group treatments are effective, but that considerably more attention needs to be devoted to understanding what components of group dynamics and group function lead to the positive changes. Previous research has focused more on outcome, as measured by behavioral changes of membership. Less attention has been paid to the leader's use of the group as a model of intervention, or to the interactional dynamics that may account for the changes that occur.

MULTICULTURAL ISSUES

The focus of cognitive-behavioral group work is on changes from dysfunctional to functional behaviors. This approach has appeal to many persons of diverse cultural backgrounds. Some people have difficulty with some group treatments in which insight and personal exploration are key elements. When individuals are reared in families that emphasize the wisdom of the elders, respect of authority and parents, and obedience to family and cultural mores, it may be difficult to participate in a group that focuses on relationships. When college students are experiencing the pain of fear of failure or the inability to develop fulfilling social relationships, they often find the direct learning focus of cognitive-behavioral treatments appealing. The group leader assumes the role of authority and takes responsibility for helping group members identify problem areas, select appropriate alternative skills and behaviors to master, and then practice the new methods in a supportive environment. This is appealing to many people.

Multicultural issues are likely to arise, however, when working with group members who are engaging in cognitive processes that are self-defeating, but in accordance with family tradition and family rules. The assumption that students should select the college major of their choice because they are most comfortable and interested in the subject may be in defiance of the family that wants a different college major, regardless of the stress on the student. Teaching group members to engage in cognitive-restructuring exercises that may lead to a challenge of parents and cultural beliefs may be very threatening and result in the termination of treatment. With other multicultural groups, the directness of cognitive-behavioral treatments may be offensive. There are groups who value more of an exploratory approach to addressing problems rather than the concrete and direct teaching method of cognitive-behavioral interventions.

SUMMARY

Cognitive-behavioral counseling and therapy groups have demonstrated excellent outcome results, and have grown in popularity as greater accountability for change has become part of the practice of mental health service delivery. Cognitive-behavioral groups are based on principles of learning theory—that people learn to behave the way they do in social settings by having some behaviors reinforced while other behaviors are extinguished or punished. The reinforced behaviors are maintained and extended, whereas the punished behaviors decrease. At times, the reinforced behaviors are appropriate for one setting but not another (e.g., rough and tumble play), may be appropriate for one age or stage of development but not for other ages or stages (e.g., talking back to parents in early childhood may be seen as cute but at a later age be seen as rebellious), or may have been maintained through habits that are unhealthy (e.g., being required to "clean the plate" of food in the family of origin may result in unhealthy eating as an independent adult). Cognitive-behavioral approaches to group counseling and therapy use the social components of the group to help members examine the need for behavioral change, identify cognitive and environmental forces that sustain the inappropriate or painful behaviors, and help design a program for change that will result in changing both cognitive and behavioral components of how members experience life.

Compared to other models, cognitive-behavioral approaches are action oriented, include instruction and specific learning steps, and focus on measurable, observable change. There is considerable interaction among members and it is expected that action methods such as role-plays, behavioral rehearsals, modeling of desired behaviors, and challenging of cognitive belief systems will occur. The approach has considerable face validity, meaning that participants can see the direct connection between the maladaptive behaviors they have and the exercises and programs implemented in the group setting. Additional resources are used for group change, including homework, bibliotherapy, the use of video- and audiotaped role models, and handouts that provide data and skills information.

REFERENCES

Bandura, A. (1969). *Principles of behavior modification*. New York: Holt, Rinehart and Winston.

Beck, A. (1976). *Cognitive therapy and emotional disorders*. New York: International Universities Press.

Bodine, R. J., & Crawford, D. K. (1999). *Developing emotional intelligence: A guide to behavior management and conflict resolution in schools*. Champaign, IL: Research Press.

Dies, R. R. (1994). Therapist variables in group psychotherapy research. In A. Fuhriman & G. Burlingame (Eds.), *Handbook of group psychotherapy: An empirical and clinical synthesis*. New York: Wiley.

Ellis, A. (1974). The group as agent in facilitating change toward rational thinking and appropriate emoting. In A. Jacobs & W. W. Spradlin (Eds.), *The group as agent of change*. New York: Behavioral Publications.

Ellis, A. (1980). Overview of the clinical theory of rational-emotive therapy. In R. Grieger & J. Boyd (Eds.), *Rational-emotive therapy: A skills approach*. New York: Van Nostrand Reinhold.

Ellis, A. (1982). Rational-emotive group therapy. In G. Gazda (Ed.), *Basic approaches to group psychotherapy and group counseling* (3rd ed.). Springfield, IL: Charles C. Thomas.

Ellis, A. (1986). Rational-emotive therapy and cognitive behavior therapy: Similarities and differences. In A. Ellis & R. Grieger (Eds.), *Handbook of rational-emotive therapy: Vol. 2.* New York: Springer.

Ellis, A. 1987. The evolution of rational-emotive therapy (RET) and cognitive behavior therapy (CBT). In J. K. Zeig (Ed.), *The evolution of psychotherapy.* New York: Brunner/Mazel.

Ellis, A. (1991). Using RET effectively: Reflections and interview. In M. E. Bernard (Ed.), *Using rational-emotive therapy effectively.* New York: Plenum.

Goldstein, A. (1999). *The prepare curriculum: Teaching prosocial competencies.* Champaign, IL: Research Press.

Hoberman, H., Lewinsohn, P., & Tilson, M. (1988). Group treatment of depression: Individual predictors of outcome. *Journal of Consulting and Clinical Psychology, 56,* 393–398.

Horne, A., & Matson, J. (1977). A comparison of modeling, desensitization, flooding, study skills, and control groups for reducing text anxiety. *Behavior Therapy, 8,* 1–8.

Meichenbaum, D. (1977). *Cognitive-behavior modification.* New York: Plenum.

Meichenbaum, D. (1985). *Stress inoculation training.* New York: Pergamon.

Ohlsen, M. M., Horne, A., & Lawe, C. (1988). *Group counseling.* New York: Holt, Rinehart and Winston.

Rose, S. (1972). *Treating children in groups.* San Francisco: Jossey-Bass.

Rose, S. (1977). *Group therapy: A behavioral approach.* Englewood Cliffs, NJ: Prentice-Hall.

Rose, S. (1987). *Working with adolescents and children in groups.* San Francisco: Jossey-Bass.

Rose, S. (1989). *Working with adults in groups: Integrating cognitive behavioral and small group strategies.* San Francisco: Jossey-Bass.

Rose, S. (1993). Cognitive-behavioral group psychotherapy. In H. Kaplan & B. Sadock (Eds.), *Comprehensive group psychotherapy* (3rd ed.). Baltimore: Williams & Wilkins.

Rose, S. (1998). *Group therapy with troubled youth: A cognitive-behavioral interactive approach.* Thousand Oaks, CA: Sage.

Rose, S., Tolman, R., & Tallant, S. (1985). Group process in cognitive-behavioral therapy. *Behavior Therapy, 8,* 71.

Smead, R. (1995). *Skills and techniques for group work with children and adolescents.* Champaign, IL: Research Press.

Spiegler, M., & Guevremont, D. (1998). *Contemporary behavior therapy* (3rd ed.). Pacific Grove, CA: Brooks/Cole.

Yalom, I. D. (1995). *Theory and practice of group psychotherapy* (4th ed.). New York: Basic Books.

CHAPTER TEN

COGNITIVE-BEHAVIORAL GROUP THEORIES

Applications

The purpose of this chapter is to provide an example of cognitive-behavioral group work—how it is developed, organized, presented, conducted, and evaluated. Since there are literally hundreds of different ways that a cognitive-behavioral group may be done, this chapter provides more of a snapshot rather than the full and in-depth picture. At the same time, the principles and practice of cognitive-behavior group work are illustrated.

CONDUCTING GROUPS FROM A COGNITIVE-BEHAVIORAL ORIENTATION

Cognitive-behavioral group counselors and therapists start with the premise that people change—it is an inevitable part of living. Most people who enter counseling or therapy want to change because they have found their lives as either painful or not as fulfilling as they wish and as they see others experiencing. Since change is occurring, the group is used to help members achieve change that is in a positive direction. It is expected that there will be movement toward getting better (a direction of change) rather than having a so-called cure (magnitude of change). There will be a focus on parsimony—seeking the smallest change that is acceptable—for from there, people may continue their growth and development.

Usually, cognitive-behavioral groups occur in a limited time period, for most people do not have the time, resources, or inclination to engage in long-term treatments. They may be open or closed, with open groups allowing members to join at any time, and closed groups admitting no new members once the groups have begun. The intake procedure may be brief or extended, but serves the purpose of identifying those for whom a cognitive-behavioral group intervention will be most beneficial. Once the group has begun, there is the expectation that all involved will be in the group to work on their personal change goals and to help others move toward accomplishing the changes they seek. It is also expected that the leader, as well as the members, will be in a continual state of examining their progress and the extent to which the goals of the group are being achieved.

A key concept that is discussed throughout this chapter is *setting up for success.* Behaviorally oriented group leaders believe that when behaviors are reinforced, they tend to be maintained or increased, whereas behaviors that are punished tend to decrease or extinguish. Therefore, we encourage group leaders to engage in behaviors that are reinforcing, including having successful experiences with their group work. Some beginning counselors and therapists seem to set themselves up for failure in a number of ways, including selecting members who might be unable to do the early group work, not being prepared with an understanding of group dynamics and procedures that influence groups to work well, and not providing for sufficient supervision of their early work. When a group experience is not successful, it often discourages people from continuing with group work; we encourage group leaders to set themselves up for success by clearly defining their goals, understanding the model of work they are proposing to offer, selecting members who are amenable to the treatment offered, having a way of measuring progress and success, and arranging for supervision to increase skill knowledge and abilities. When these steps of setting up for success are followed, a reinforcing group experience will result.

Organizing and Initiating the Group

The first step of setting up for success with a cognitive-behavioral group is to conduct an assessment of the need for the group (Smead, 1995). This may be informal or formal, but there must always be a consideration of why the group is being offered. If there is a need for the group, it is a good idea to write out a proposal or description of the group. The proposal would include the description and rationale, objectives, logistics, procedures, and how evaluation will occur. When the group is announced or advertised (see Figure 10.1), pregroup interviews are conducted and members are selected. Pregroup evaluations of goals should be conducted, then it is time for the group to begin. Following the group, posttest evaluations should be conducted as well as closure interviews with participants. Examples of these steps follow in the remainder of this chapter.

Preparing for the Group

Two counselors, Sharon and Stan, decided to offer a cognitive-behavioral group as a community service offering through a university departmental practicum center, and they wanted a successful experience. They surveyed counselors in the center and practitioners in the community to determine whether a sufficient referral base would exist and to explain to the practitioners of the community the purpose of the group. They determined from the responses that there would be a sufficient number of potential members to offer the group, and so they provided information to area practitioners to distribute to potential members. It is important to remember that, when offering a service such as this, if there are more applicants than spaces available, it is the professional responsibility of the group leader to identify alternative sources to assist people in need

FIGURE 10.1   Example of a Cognitive-Behavioral Group Announcement Recruiting Members

---

**CHANGE
A Group for People Interested in
Bringing about Changes in Their Lives**

A new group is being offered at the Center for Counseling at the University. The purpose of the group is to help participants identify areas of their lives that are not to their satisfaction, to provide group support, and to develop skills to make changes that will lead to greater satisfaction in their lives.

Members of the group will complete an intake interview then participate in weekly sessions for 10 meetings. After that time, the group may continue, depending on the interests of the group members. All members are expected to work on identifying areas of their lives they would to change, and are also expected to work with other members of the group to help them make the changes they desire.

For information and registration, call 555-1234.

---

of service. Therefore, it is wise to not be too broad in the initial invitation to participate as a group member.

The Intake Interview

The intake interview serves several very important purposes for developing a success-ful group experience. It allows the leader the chance to present again the purpose of the group and to describe the expectations for group members. It also allows the leader to hear the potential member describe how he or she sees the group meeting their needs. The leader has the opportunity of deselecting a member if the person's issues do not conform to the goals or style of the group. Finally, the intake interview provides the opportunity to provide a motivational nudge to the member interviewed, encouraging him or her to commit to actively working with the group, the leader, and the other mem-bers to bring about positive change. All of these activities provide structure to the development of the group and provides the leader with important information about what to expect when the group actually begins.

An advantage of knowing practitioners in the community is that it is possible to rely on them to make referrals that are consistent with the group offering, thereby requiring less need for the intake interview. Or, if the intake interview is conducted, it will likely be more concise, since those referred are apt to have already discussed the relevance and applicability of the group with the referring practitioner. Still, the intake interview is important to establish the need for the person to be in the group and to facilitate a "readiness for change":

Sharon (Leader):   Thank you for coming in to discuss the group we are offering. I know you have discussed this with your career counselor, and he thought this group might be helpful for some of the issues you have been dealing with. The group will meet for 10 weeks, one evening a week, and will focus on helping participants make changes in their lives that are important to them. What change have you considered working on if you join the group?

John (Applicant):   Well, I've been seeing the counselor here at the university about problems I'm having selecting a major. He said this group might be good for me. Actually, the problem I'm having isn't just choosing a major; I'm so nervous about being here at the university that I have trouble with my classes.

Sharon: Give me an example. What kind of trouble?

John: I have a hard time listening in class because I'm always thinking everyone else there is so much smarter than me, and when we have a test, my mind just goes blank. I have literally had to run from the room and throw up, I get so upset when we have a test.

As they talk further, Sharon explores other areas, such as pressure from family or friends, finances related to getting an education, goals for what to do when finished with school, subjects that have more interest than others, whether the problem existed in high school, and any medical information that might be related.

Sharon: Okay, John, it sounds as though this group may be very helpful for you in your goal to examine the problems you are having paying attention and managing your anxiety related to testing as well as to explore issues related to your choice of career and the pressure your parents are putting on you to select a major they approve of. It sounds as though the group would be right on target for what you are wanting to do. When the group begins, are you willing to attend regularly and share your concerns with other members in the group, and allow them to provide assistance as you work on these issues? Also, will you be willing to help others as they struggle with their concerns in the group?

Part of the setting up for success in a cognitive-behavioral group is to establish the group expectations of sharing the problem, helping others, and volunteering to jump right in with the first session of the group.

Another part of the intake procedure is to establish the extent to which a potential member is ready for change. Prochaska (1979, 1992, 1994) has investigated people entering therapy to identify their readiness for change or to assess what stage of change readiness they are in. He and his colleagues have identified five stages:

1. *Precontemplation.* People at the precontemplation stage are not aware they need to make change, or deny that the need for change rests with them. They have no plans of their own to change. A person who smokes and does not believe smoking is dangerous or harmful would be an example. In a cognitive-behavioral group, the focus would be on educating the member to become more familiar with the risks involved in his or her current behavior, and to be aware that there may be a need for change. The focus will be on examining and challenging belief patterns related to the maladaptive behavior (e.g., believing smoking does no harm) and providing a group support for exploring other possibilities (e.g., gathering information about the potential harms of smoking and discussing with others who have successfully stopped smoking some of the advantages of stopping).

2. *Contemplation.* Those at the contemplation stage are aware that a problem exists but they have not seriously considered any action. They may be experiencing ambivalence. A person who knows smoking is damaging to one's health in the long run and thinks he or she should stop smoking some day, but has not taken action to do so now, would be an example. A cognitive-behavioral group would focus exploring both sides of the ambivalence and encouraging the exploration of possible actions that may be taken to help with the ambivalence. This may include, again, group support, discussions with people who have successfully stopped smoking, talking to a physician, and examining aspects of the social environment that facilitate or maintain the smoking behavior.

3. *Preparation.* People at the preparation stage recognize that something needs to change, that something they are doing requires action, and they make plans to initiate that action in the very near future. A person who hears about a change group and calls to inquire about whether the group would help in stopping smoking would be an example. Within the group, the leader and other members would help the member evaluate the thoughts he or she has that still contribute to the ambivalence, identify specific goals they have for the problem, and develop a way of evaluating steps toward success as well as final measures of determining success in change. The group would be used for encouragement and support as well as suggestions and recommendations for how to initiate the changes.

4. *Action.* The person at the action stage is engaged in change. Steps are being taken to change the behavior, experiences, or the environment to facilitate overcoming the problem. The person has made a commitment of time and energy and is actively working to reduce the problem. Joining a group to work on the smoking problem and using the group members as a social support system to encourage and reinforce steps taken to stop smoking would be an example. Further, members of the group would be used for role-plays in such situations as having to refuse a friend's insistence on smoking, taking an assertive stance on where to eat so that there would be less influence of the environment on smoking behavior, and identifying positive alternative behaviors that may be engaged in that do not include smoking.

5. *Maintenance.* At the maintenance stage, change has occurred and the efforts expended now are on making certain the changes last. There is an effort to prevent relapse and to continue taking the steps necessary to make certain the change is permanent. The focus of the group at this stage is to provide continued reinforcement for change that has occurred in both thinking and behaving as well as to assist the member in identifying ways of avoiding relapse.

It is important to consider the stage potential members are in as they are inter-viewed for the group. Members do not have to be at the action stage, for people at any stage may benefit from a group experience aimed at helping them change unhealthy or unsatisfactory ways of living. On the other hand, those at the precontemplation stage are likely entering the group at the urging of someone else and will have a lower level of commitment to carry out the activities of the group. For all members of the group, it is important to consider their stage of change and to accommodate the activities of the group to be consistent with the expectations of the members.

Although Prochaska and colleagues (1979, 1992, 1994) have developed fairly sophisticated measures for evaluating members' readiness for change, potential mem-bers may also simply be asked during the intake interview, as they describe their prob-lem or concern, "Do you want to do anything about this problem?" If the answer is yes, they could be asked, "Now?" If yes, they are likely to be in the action stage, but if they answer, "Soon," then they are more likely to be in the preparation stage. If potential members are in the action stage, they are ready to be in the group and move toward addressing their concerns with the support of the group. If they are in the preparation stage, the question might be asked, "What would need to happen to help you move toward change or to consider change?" The answer provides direction for deciding whether they would be appropriate for the group now or in the near future.

Initial Group Meetings

First Session.   As with all group work, it is important to get off to a good start, to set the stage for success for the members from the beginning. This includes having reviewed notes to know who is in the group, what their presenting concerns are, an esti-mation of where they are on their readiness for change, and some specific ideas about interventions (activities) that may be appropriate. It is often useful to provide another structuring element—a phone call or a card in the mail reminding members of the group session, including day, time, place, and any other relevant information that makes attendance and participation more likely to occur.

The first session begins with a welcome and a brief overview of the purpose of the group and the agreements made regarding group norms or structure: attend regularly, seek help with concerns and problems related to the group theme, be supportive of the work others are doing, and assist in facilitating change for others. A brief reminder about professional and ethical issues is also important: what will happen if a member threatens to harm self or others, the importance of confidentiality and the development of trust among members, and what would need to happen if a member decides to leave the group.

The leader aspires to develop a group environment that is inviting and that sets the stage for sharing and helping. This is aided by having the group leader provide a description of his or her background and training as well as reasons for offering the group. The leader's openness and willingness to disclose facilitates members' expecta-tions for positive change and serves to put members at ease. While these leader behav-iors may be described as basic curative factors in group work (Yalom, 1995), from a behavioral orientation they are providing for a reinforcing environment, furnishing modeling of open disclosure and an illustration of how to share thoughts and feelings, thereby setting up the group for a successful transition from a gathering of strangers to a working group.

Sharon: I'm very pleased to see all of you here tonight, and I welcome you to our group. Your being here demonstrates a commitment to work on some issues you have identified and represents a major step toward change. As you recall, the name of our group is The Change Group—and it was established to help members identify issues or concerns in their lives that are either problematic or that are preventing us from experiencing life as richly and fully as we'd like.

Although we aren't about changing total personalities or making the world drastically different, we are here to help all members of the group clearly recognize goals they would like to have for themselves, and then use the group to develop a plan to achieve those goals over the next 10 weeks. To do this, we've agreed that each member will share openly with others ways in which they would like to change, and will invite others of the group to help in the process. Similarly, each member will help other members with the changes they are seeking.

We will meet weekly, and as we discussed at the intake, what is said and done in the group stays in the group—we respect one another to the point that we don't break the confidences that we share here. Although you may talk about what you do in the group to others, such as family members, we don't talk about the other members of the group by name or action, for it's a small world out there and we respect each other's privacy in the group. We are quite open to working on many areas of problems here, but we also need to be aware that if anyone describes a situation in which he or she may hurt another person, or self, then as a professional counselor, I'm obligated by law to intervene, even if that means breaking group confidentiality.

I have been a licensed counselor for 10 years and in that period have worked with many groups, for I believe group interactions and processes allow people to use a more realistic approach to change—in a social setting, not tucked away in individual meetings. I believe most of our problems are learned in the group or social setting, and they occur and repeat themselves within a group setting, so it is important to use a group to help us bring about the changes necessary. A group allows us the opportunity of describing our problems, getting feedback from other group members about how they see the problem for others and for themselves, and to use the group to help learn new skills and behaviors. This includes having us do some role-playing, where one of us demonstrates the problem he or she is having, and then in the group setting we role-play it, act it out, and then use the group to see how we might improve on what we're doing.

Another technique we use is called modeling. One person may have better skills at an activity than others, and we can use the group members to model the kinds of behaviors we think are important, and then we learn from each other in the process.

Another way we use the group is to explore the thinking we do that gets us in trouble. A quote from Shakespeare is "Nothing is, but thinking makes it so." Sometimes we think terrible thoughts or unhealthy thoughts that get us into trouble. We can use the group to help us examine those thoughts, to replace them with more helpful ways of thinking.

As I told you during the intake meeting, there are never any guarantees of success in counseling or therapy, but over the years we have had good success with members of our groups accomplishing most of the goals they have established for themselves. This comes about from establishing clear and attainable goals, working on the problem, having an encouraging and supportive group to help us, and having the strength to carry our changes from the group to the outside world. I am looking forward to working with you, and I'd like us to begin, to get started. Now that I've welcomed you, and told you briefly about myself and my orientation to group work, I'd like for you to introduce yourself and briefly describe what you would like to work on changing in your life, what desired changes have brought you to The Change Group. When we met for intake, I provided you with a form to sketch out some ideas (see Figure 10.2). If you have that, you might refer to it as you introduce yourself.

As the group leader listens, there will be several themes Sharon will be listening and watching for. How clearly are the problems presented? Vague descriptions are problematic, for it implies the person either doesn't know how to be clear in the description or hasn't committed sufficient time to the process. How amenable to change is the problem, and does the counselor have experience with this area? If not, where might she learn more about the needed intervention, and who might provide supervision if it is needed? The counselor may elect to use redirecting and summarizing statements to help focus the presentation:

John: So, I guess I'd like to change but I don't know. The doctor said it wasn't a physical problem, me throwing up when I have to take a test. But I've done that ever since being at the university and I just don't know what to do. I guess it's a big problem for me because I look stupid and others even laugh at me, and sometimes the professor just rolls his eyes and I know he doesn't like me.

Sharon: John, as I recall, you said you did well in high school, that this wasn't a problem; it is only since being here that the problem has developed. It seems you'd like to stop reacting with such anxiety and tension when you have a test, but just haven't figured out how. The good news is that we are interested in helping you figure what stimulates the anxiety, how to manage it better, and how to develop some alternative ways of thinking about the problem. Is that what you'd like to have happen?

John: Sure, but I just don't know. It just seems stupid.

Sharon: It may seem that way now, but that's because you don't know what else to do. I noticed Ellen nodding her head in agreement as you talked. Ellen, I'm wondering if you were able to identify with what John was describing.

FIGURE 10.2   The Need for Change

1. Describe a behavior or a characteristic that is problematic for you—one that you would like to be different for you in your life at this time.

2. Describe an example of when this has been a problem for you.

3. Describe how you would like for it to be different—what do you wish you could do or say instead?

4. Think of a ladder that has 10 rungs or steps. The first step represents no problem at all, the fifth step represents considerable problems, but not so bad as to stop your daily activities, and the tenth rung is so serious that it impacts your life a lot. The other rungs represent levels of the problem in between.

   For the problem you have described, what rung would you be on? That is, how much discomfort or how great a problem does this behavior or characteristic cause for you?

   1   2   3   4   5   6   7   8   9   10

   For others in your life, what rung would they say your behavior or characteristic puts them on? That is, how much discomfort or how great a problem does this cause for them?

   1   2   3   4   5   6   7   8   9   10

   For the behavior or characteristic you have described, what is your level of commitment to change the problem?

   1   2   3   4   5   6   7   8   9   10

   Describe a few things you think may be helpful for you as you move toward changing the problem.

Ellen: I'll say. I used to get so nervous when I had to meet people. I still have trouble with it, but at least I'm not getting sick any more. I feel for John because I know it's a lousy way to be.

Sharon: So, John, first of all, it isn't stupid—it's the best you know how to do right now, but as Ellen has said, we can learn new ways of addressing the problem. Second, you're not alone. Ellen has identified that the problem may be somewhat common; in fact, we'll find that some anxiety about new situations can be a universal concern. Right? [Others nod in agreement]. So the goal is to address the test anxiety, identify some of the things [environmental influences] that may be leading to the anxiety, and explore some ways of thinking about the situation differently so that you still care enough about your courses to study, but not enough to throw up over them, right? So at the end of 10 weeks, you'd like to be able to identify what is happening in your world and what you are thinking about that leads to such tension, reconsider how much you are going to let those outside things influence you, and develop some new skills for managing the anxiety and developing a more positive approach to studying. That's the goal?

As each member presents, the counselor looks for "recognition responses" or signs from other members that they are understanding and appreciating what the others are saying. This is used later as a way of making connections within the group, identifying members to pair up for role-plays, for developing challenges of irrational beliefs, and for providing support and encouragement.

During these interchanges, the counselor was attempting to do several things:

- Welcome and encourage each member as he or she presented, developing an alliance or tacit understanding of support and understanding for each.
- Model good attending behavior, and ways of moving toward developing a respectful and valuing interaction with each member.
- Help move toward clearly defining specific behaviors that are problematic, and establish goals to be accomplished while in the group.
- Link the behavioral descriptions of the problem to thoughts, beliefs, and attitudes held by the person, recognizing that most people do not attend to the connection between how they think, how they feel, and how they behave. The counselor several times linked the thinking to the behaving, and will return to this theme throughout the group.
- Provide some sense of hope or positive expectation that change is possible and that with the benefit of the group, it is likely to occur (a reinforcing belief).

One thing the counselor attempted *not* to do was dwell on the behavior problem as the sole topic of treatment. Based on the intake interview with John, it is likely that there are several contributing factors leading to his test anxiety, including the expectations of his family, the sensitivity he has to feeling unprepared or inferior to other students in the class, and his pattern of blaming thinking [I'm just stupid], which leads to a downward spiral of personal self-valuing. It is likely that within the first three sessions,

FIGURE 10.3   Tracking

> Tracking means keeping track of situations that are problematic for us. Your goal is to track yourself for the coming week in order to help understand when the problem occurs, what you do, and what the consequences are. Please keep the following diary and bring it to group next week. Use a separate copy of the form for each day.
>
> *Day: Describe a problem*
>
> What was the behavior or the problem?
>
> What happened before the behavior; what led up to it?
>
> What happened after the behavior; what was the consequence?
>
> How do you wish it had been different?
>
> What would need to happen for it to be different?

the focus of the problem will drift from the physical problem of test anxiety to understanding better the contributions to that anxiety and then what might be done. Still, a cognitive-behavioral approach will be used, but the focus will be more on family interactional patterns, relationships with other students, irrational thinking that is nonproductive, or some combination. Too often, counselors attend to the presenting issue as the problem to be treated rather than examining what is happening in the person's world that has created the problem.

After each member has had an opportunity to share with the group, the counselor identifies themes that exist among the members' problems and discusses again the relationship of the influences of the outside world, the thoughts people have about the situations they are in, and how they behave in relation to the feelings and circumstances. At the end of the session, the cognitive-behavioral group counselor usually gives homework assignments, for it is believed that learning new ways of managing problems requires working on the problems well beyond the once-a-week group meeting. Homework may include readings (bibliotherapy), listening to audiotapes, or engaging in some activity that is clearly defined. Often, the assignment the first week addresses learning to track behavior—that is, recognize a problematic behavior as it occurs, identify what preceded it, examine the behavioral response, and then consider what might have been done differently (see Figure 10.3).

Many group leaders use contracts with group members. Contracts have the advantage of clearly defining the behavior to be changed, the goal to be achieved, and the consequences of completing the contract. At times, goals are offered as levels to be achieved, as in goal attainment scaling. In this process, the leader helps the member identify where he or she is starting, what would be an ideal change, and what would be an acceptable change:

- *Current Behavior:* Extremely anxious when thinking about or taking an examination; can't think straight or clearly; and must leave the room several times to go to the restroom and be sick.
- *Minimal Acceptable Change:* Still anxious and nervous, but can study for sufficient time to learn the material; and can stay in room most of the time and not be ill.
- *Better than Minimal Change:* Able to study without worrying too much about the examination situation; able to be in the room and concentrate well enough to pass the examination; and able to stay in the room without being sick.
- *Best Change:* Able to study without being concerned about examinations; able to concentrate well on the examination; and comfortable talking with others about my performance and what I thought about the examination.

Early in the life of the group, the cognitive-behavioral group leader will introduce members to the cognitive connection to behaviors and feelings. This information, explained in the previous chapter, posits that situations do not cause the problems people experience. Rather, there are connections between the environment and situations, how people think and feel about those situations, their behavior, and the consequences that occur. There have been extensive discussions of these connections, primarily offered by Ellis (1994, 1996, 2000; Ellis & Dryden, 1997), whose contributions to cognitive-behavioral therapy have spanned almost five decades. Recently, Budman and Villapiano (1999) have adapted the model to a brief form of group work in which they teach group members the relationship of events, thoughts, feelings, and behaviors, and how those four components may influence one another. Their material encourages participants to examine their interpretation of an event, describe the emotional and physical reactions they have to the even, and then explore their behaviors in relation to the event and emotional/physical reactions. Another approach to examining the relationship among the cognitive-behavioral components is presented in Figure 10.4. The self-analysis form presented is based on the work of Maxie Maultsby (1975).

TECHNIQUES ASSOCIATED WITH THE COGNITIVE-BEHAVIORAL APPROACH

Literally hundreds of techniques have been developed for use in cognitive-behavioral treatment programs. A focus of the cognitive-behavioral model is to identify the specific problems that group members have and then to use or develop an intervention that is specifically relevant to the particular problem. In the group format it is assumed that there are common concerns and problems and therefore interventions appropriate for the entire group are selected. If individual members of the group do not share the specific problem area, they may be encouraged to participate regardless in order to develop new skills. Another alternative is for the intervention to be adapted for them. Following is a discussion of several of the more frequently used treatment intervention procedures.

FIGURE 10.4   A Self-Analysis

> The purpose of a rational self-analysis is to help you examine the relationship between events that happen and what you do. Start with an event (#1) that occurred. Then, describe how you felt in relation to that event (#3). Then how did you behave (#4) because you felt that way? Next, what was the consequence (#5) of how you behaved? Finally, what consequence would you have preferred to have happened (#6)? For now, leave #2 blank.
>
> **1.** Describe an event that happened.
>
> **2.** What did you think in regard to the event?
>
> **3.** How did you feel in regard to the event?
>
> **4.** How did you behave in regard to the event?
>
> **5.** What was the consequence of the behavior—what happened?
>
> **6.** What do you wish had happened—how could events have turned out that would have been satisfactory to you?
>
> Now, imagine that a video camera had taken a film of the entire event. All that you have described was captured on film. As an objective observer, maybe as another member of our group watching the film—how would you describe the event? Have the group members work with you to develop an objective description of the event.

Source: Based on Maultsby (1975).

What would the video show happening? Remember that a video cannot show intent or feeling. It is objective and doesn't show a "mean" person, or a "stupid thing," or whether someone "meant to hurt." Objectively describe the event.

Now, let's go back through the process, recognizing that sometimes our interpretation of the event may not be exactly as it happened—and that even if the event was exactly the same, an event cannot make us feel a particular way or do a particular thing. This time, the exercise is completed in reverse:

1. What do you wish had been the outcome of the event? What do you wish had happened?

2. To get the outcome you would have preferred, how would you have had to behave instead of the way you described in the sequence above?

3. To have behaved the way you would like to have in #2 above, how would you have needed to be feeling? Remember, we generally behave consistently with how we feel, and so if you feel angry, you will likely act angrily, whereas if you feel calm, you will likely act calmly. How would you have needed to feel, or preferred to have felt?

4. To have felt the way you would have preferred in #3, what would you need to be thinking? Remember, people generally feel consistently with what they are thinking, so that people who think angry thoughts usually feel angry, whereas those who think calm thoughts feel emotionally calm. What thoughts would have led to you having a calmer feeling?

5. To have the calm thoughts you would prefer to have in #4, how would you need to think differently about the event that occurred? That is, how could you think about the event differently than you did in the first situation described above?

(continued)

FIGURE 10.4   Continued

For the tracking sheet from your first week of homework, identify a situation in which you may conduct a rational self-analysis with the group.

1. The event that occurred. Describe it objectively.

2. What were your thoughts about the event? Did they influence you to become upset or did they help you remain calm? What thoughts would have benefited you in your goal to remain calm, to not become angry or anxious or depressed?

3. How did you feel in relation to the event and your thoughts about the event? How would you have preferred to feel? Remember, our goal is not to do away with feelings, but to help them be manageable and motivational for change. Describe feelings you would prefer to have that will lead to you behaving in a more appropriate or desired manner.

4. How did you behave? How do you wish you had been in that situation? Describe what you think would have been an acceptable and desirable way of behaving under the circumstances.

5. What were the consequences of your behavior? Is that what you wanted or wish had happened? If not, what would be a consequence you would prefer?

6. In order to get the consequences you prefer, go through the steps again, identifying what you would have needed to think or feel, or how you would have needed to behave, in order to get the outcome you desire.

Social-Skills Training

A careful analysis of each member's adequate level of social-skills development upon entering a group is important, for the group intervention must begin at the level of competence of the members. There are a number of reasons that group members may lack appropriate social skills, but social learning theory indicates that social skills are learned in a social setting. Group members may not have had sufficient opportunity to learn appropriate social skills in their families of origin or in the environment in which they grew up. A large number of people with social-skills deficits simply have not had adequate learning opportunities and effective models in their lives; fortunately, the group experience can address this directly.

Social skills are situationally relevant; thus, a person may have very appropriate skills in one setting but be skill deficient in another. Students may experience this situation when moving from one school to another or when moving from school to work situations. Cultural and societal norms also determine what behavior is appropriate in particular situations. People's behavior and thoughts are influenced by their cultural and environmental situations. Group members may be very proficient at thinking and behaving appropriately in one situation, but they may need considerable skill development in other areas.

When potential group members are successful in developing some new behavior, perhaps a new social skill such as meeting new friends, the process is very reinforcing and encourages the person to continue using the skill, reaching out to make even more friends. On the other hand, when the person is skills deficient and fails in efforts to make new friends, he or she is likely to withdraw and find the experience punishing and humiliating.

Rose (1998) has identified several skills as being core components of social-skills training: listening, getting clarification, maintaining relevancy, timing, and understanding emotions. Recent work examining emotional intelligence (Bodine & Crawford, 1999) has underscored research on the importance of social skills. Persons who scored higher on emotional intelligence were more likely than those who scored low to establish contact with other people, be aware of what others were thinking and feeling, and be able to maintain a positive relationship with others. Emotional intelligence seems to include each of the components Rose has identified as core elements of social skills.

Group counseling and therapy is especially suited to social-skills training, due to the opportunity to practice and receive feedback. In the group, the leader presents an overview of how social skills are learned, why they are so important, and the rationale for learning new skills. Members review specific situations in which they have felt either skilled or incapable and discuss the comfort level they felt in such situations. It is important to help members address questions about the appropriateness of social behavior (e.g., the appropriate and inappropriate ways of meeting new people), how the skills fit with each individual's personal style (e.g., the temperament of the person), and the impact of the situational context.

The group leader generally attempts to break the skills down into small learnable units and discusses why each component is important. Communication skills, for example, are necessary to learn names, provide introductions, and maintain talk. The group leader, or a member of the group, models the behavior in a role-played situation and the group critiques the performance. As the group discusses the modeled behavior, members are asked to discuss how it would be for them to use the skill, again attending to cultural influences, their personal styles of interacting, and how important the skill may be to each member. Then each group member has the opportunity of practicing the skill, either by using the whole group and having one member at a time practice or by having group members team up with three to a team (one practicing the skill, another the role-play partner, and the third a feedback observer).

Generally, it is expected that the initial role-play exercise will be quite simple and easily mastered. As the group continues to practice the skills, however, the tasks should become more difficult. Coaching by other members of the group is encouraged, and the leader models support and positive feedback. The group feedback process is very important to help each member obtain information about his or her level of performance, recommendations for improvement, and acknowledgment for the accomplishment of new skills. Homework assignments are usually used, and each week the group reviews the accomplishments of each member.

Chapter 15, Life-Skills Training, offers a more detailed presentation of a social-skills training program. In addition, there are numerous programs developed to assist leaders in the development of social skills. Goldstein (1999) developed a series of training manuals on skillstreaming for children and adolescents.

Systematic Problem Solving

All people have problems; many learn effective ways of managing the problems of their lives, but others are very ineffective at developing problem-solving skills. The group leader will need to work with group members to help identify the nature of each member's problem-solving ability. For example, some may react impulsively to how to solve problems and fail to reflect on the steps—particularly the consequences—involved in making good decisions. Some fail to adequately solve problems because others unduly influence them, such as peers or family members. Others have simply never learned the steps of problem solving.

Members of the group bring examples of situations in which they were not satisfied with their decision-making ability, were dissatisfied with the outcome of the decision, or failed to be able to recognize better ways of managing problems. As the problems are presented, the group shares in going through the steps of decision making, including identifying the problem, developing alternative ways of solving the problem, selecting a solution that seems reasonable, and evaluating the effectiveness of the decision. It is important for the members to recognize the significance of analyzing the problem, brainstorming ways of addressing the situation, and carrying out the best solution in a real-world experience.

The following questions have been modified from a reality therapy model to use when teaching problem-solving skills:

What is my problem?
What am I doing?
Is what I'm doing working?
If not, what can I do differently?

It is important to model the appropriate process. Group members are encouraged to apply the steps during homework assignments and to come back to the next session with tracking information on several decision-making experiences. Social-skills training usually requires other elements of behavioral interventions, including practicing ineffective and effective interpersonal skills, relaxation training, and cognitive restructuring.

Cognitive Restructuring. Cognitive restructuring was addressed earlier in discussing an assessment process that examines the emotional and behavioral responses group members have to situations (A = situation; B = cognitions; C = affect; D = behavior; E = consequence). Group members often engage in self-defeating thoughts that then influence their behavior as they experience distressful situations ("I never do anything right," "Everyone else is better than me") or they have erroneous beliefs that lead to inappropriate behavior ("I must get all my work done, even though it is impossible to do," "I cannot make mistakes!"). The more group members engage in self-defeating thoughts or erroneous beliefs, the more dysfunctional their behavior is likely to be. Often, the thoughts themselves prevent people from taking care of themselves or from engaging in effective problem solving.

Cognitive restructuring is a process of helping group members recognize and understand their thought patterns and the role of the thoughts in influencing their actions. It involves helping members identify the thoughts they have as being self-defeating or based on irrational or erroneous concepts. The procedure described in the assessment phase for cognitive influence on behavior is very helpful for this component of group work.

Once members have identified their thought patterns, they are taught to evaluate whether the thoughts are productive or counterproductive for achieving the goals they have established. The role of thoughts in affecting a person who has accomplished behavioral skills in assertiveness is powerful. Although people may have the skills in their behavioral repertoire, if they have beliefs that restrict them from using the skills, they will continue to have problems. In a group we conducted for assertiveness training, we found that members learned the skills very well but had not continued to use their new abilities in being assertive at a three-month follow-up. They explained that though they knew they could demonstrate the skills, they still had not revised their thinking about why they should not follow through. They reported thoughts, for example, like the following:

> "I know I had a right to use the car because I had reserved it, but when John came and said he wanted to use it at my reserved time I figured he must need it more than I did."

> "I knew I should just refuse to do the extra work but then I thought if I didn't do it then someone else would have to and so I just went ahead and did it even though I had to change all my plans."

We then conducted a three-session booster group in which we introduced the cognitive-restructuring exercises, combined with a review of the assertiveness skills. At three- and six-month follow-ups, the group members were continuing to use their assertiveness skills and reported considerable satisfaction with their new system of challenging self-defeating or erroneous thinking. Helping group members see the relationship between their thoughts, beliefs, and perceptions is primary to helping them initiate new, more effective, behavioral patterns.

When using cognitive restructuring in a group setting, the first step is to present a rationale for the process and to emphasize its importance in establishing and maintaining the changes desired. Both the leader and group members provide examples of the relationship of erroneous thinking to the feelings members have and how the feelings then impact members' behavior. An assignment to find quotations that demonstrate the link between thinking and behavior ("Nothing is, but thinking makes it so"—Shakespeare) and examples of erroneous thinking-behavioral links in popular music ("I can't stand to live without your love") often leads group members to understand how prevalent self-defeating/erroneous beliefs are in U.S. culture.

The group is then used to examine the particular self-defeating/erroneous thoughts of each group member by having each present a situation in which he or she experienced problems and then conduct the analysis presented earlier to see the relationship from thoughts to feelings, behavior, and consequences. By exploring the erroneous belief patterns of each member in the group setting, members help identify the long-term consequences of continuing to rely on the faulty cognitive belief system. The group provides feedback to each individual member on how the beliefs seem to be impacting their lives and provides encouragement to examine and replace self-defeating/erroneous thought patterns.

One technique that is useful in the process of challenging beliefs is to have each group member describe a problematic scenario and then to imagine that the situation had been videotaped. The group then examines whether the videotape would have shown the same episode that is described by the group member. Since videotapes don't show values ("That was a horrible thing that happened") or emotions ("He made me so mad"), it becomes clear that it is the perception and interpretation of the scenario, rather than the scenario itself, that led to problematic behavior. A questions such as the following could be asked: "Would the videotape show this person making you feel humiliated, or would it have shown the person talking to you in a way you wish had not happened, but over which you had some choice in deciding how to respond?"

Early in the process of teaching the cognitive-restructuring process, the leader helps members understand the differences in faulty and/or erroneous cognitive patterns and the benefits of effective coping cognitions. The goal of cognitive restructuring is not to do away with feelings, but to help people adapt the most effective cognitive process to achieve the behavioral goals they have established. The leader teaches members how to replace faulty/erroneous cognitions with more effective coping statements:

Faulty: I can't stand this!

Coping: I don't like this but I can stand it—that's what I'm in group for—to learn better skills at managing this type of situation.

Faulty: He's the most insensitive jerk in the world and he infuriates me!

Coping: He's insensitive to others, but he doesn't get to determine how I'm going to feel.

Coping statements are not meant to be "power of positive thinking" thoughts (i.e., if a person only thinks positively, all good things will come to pass). Instead, the goal is for members to have greater control over how they think about the situations they encounter and to choose to replace formerly upsetting thoughts and emotions with coping thoughts that lead to more neutral affect. The goal is not to have people feel good about every situation they encounter, but to be able to respond calmly by using coping thoughts and moving toward affective responses that promote behaving in ways that are more satisfying.

Conducting cognitive analyses with the group requires that the leader be quite familiar with the process and that he or she attend closely to the assistance each member is providing. It is possible for members to misunderstand the process and not provide the level of help to fellow members that is needed. Since faulty belief patterns generally represent a lifetime of learning, it will take considerable practice to master the new way of thinking, feeling, and behaving, and that experience may be provided both through the group interaction and through homework assignments. Group support and encouragement is very important during this period, and the use of the group to help each individual generate coping thoughts and rational challenges to irrational beliefs leads to stronger group cohesion.

In the process of practicing cognitive restructuring in the group, generally it is important to go through the steps slowly, working as a team to identify each of the components of the process, and to develop ideal outcomes in scenarios that are practiced. Once practice has led to proficiency in identifying the steps of challenging self-defeating/erroneous thinking and establishing an ideal outcome, the next step is to practice moving toward less than ideal outcomes and still maintaining control over the cognitions and behaviors.

A recent example was with a restaurant server who had a fear of spilling drinks on customers. She continually visualized herself being humiliated, yelled at by her boss, fired from her job, losing her house because of no income, and finally being homeless on the streets. The group first worked with her to challenge the chain of erroneous thoughts she had regarding the situation. She then practiced visualizations in which she was able to perform her job successfully. She "talked aloud" as she described the situation, identifying thoughts about performing the job well, while maintaining a positive affective state. The group contributed successfully with hints for the night. The group then helped her, in stages, to develop increasingly difficult imaginary scenarios in which she made mistakes, including eventually having a scenario in which she did spill drinks on a customer, but was still able to maintain coping cognitions that allowed her not to be as critical of herself and as fearful as she had been in the past. She moved from debilitating anxiety over her job to becoming calm and collected. She even began to lose the fear of failure and to begin replacing that response with a sense of humor and playfulness about picturing herself as a "fallible human being"—seeing herself as one who could make mistakes—and found humor in her life rather than "awfulizing."

Group members are taught how to move from the group setting to their broader lives in carrying out the process of cognitive restructuring. From tasks within the group, members begin recording their experiences in diaries. They then bring these back to group for group analysis of how to perform better, and they receive reinforcement for their successes. Assignments then move toward identifying the steps that are necessary to identify their successes and develop improved behavior plans for themselves before coming to the group. The group is used for review and support purposes. The goal is for the member to be able to identify the self-defeating/erroneous thinking as it is occurring and to replace the thoughts with more functional self-statements, then report these accomplishments back to the group.

SUMMARY

Cognitive-behavioral interventions are limited only by the knowledge and training experiences of the leader. Interventions range from straight behavioral change programs that focus on the application of principles of learning, to straight cognitive interventions focusing on mental schemas engaged in by people, but mostly combining the two approaches. There are books, training tapes, and institutes and programs available for those interested in learning more. The Association for the Advancement of Behavior Therapy (AABT) is the organization most involved with the training and practice of behavior therapy.

REFERENCES

Bodine, R. J., & Crawford, D. K. (1999). *Developing emotional intelligence: A guide to behavior management and conflict in schools.* Champaign, IL: Research Press.

Budman, S., & Villapiano, A. (1999). *Disturbance specific group therapy.* Providence: Manisses Communications Group.

Ellis, A. (1994). *Reason and emotion in psychotherapy.* Secaucus, NJ: Birch Lane Press.

Ellis, A. (1996). *Better, deeper, and more enduring brief therapy.* New York: Brunner/Mazel.

Ellis, A. (2000). Rational-emotive behavior marriage and family therapy. In A. Horne (Ed.), *Family counseling and therapy* (3rd ed.). Itasca, IL: Peacock.

Ellis, A., & Dryden, W. (1997). *The practice of rational-emotive behavior therapy* (rev. ed.). New York: Springer.

Goldstein, A. (1999). *Low-level aggression: First steps on the ladder to violence.* Champaign, IL: Research Press.

Maultsby, M. (1975). *Help yourself to happiness through rational self-counseling.* New York: Institute for Rational Living.

Prochaska, J. O. (1979). *Systems of psychotherapy: A transtheoretical analysis.* Homewood, IL: Dorsey.

Prochaska, J. O., & DiClemente, C. C. (1992). The transtheoretical approach. In J. C. Norcross & E. M. Goldfried (Eds.), *Handbook of psychotherapy integration.* New York: Basic Books.

Prochaska, J. O., Norcross, J., & DiClement, C. C. (1994). *Changing for good.* New York: William Morrow.

Rose, S. (1998). *Group therapy with troubled youth: A Cognitive-behavioral interactive approach.* Thousand Oaks, Ca: Sage.

Smead, R. (1995). *Skills and techniques for group work with children and adolescents.* Champaign, IL: Research Press.

Yalom, I. (1995). *The theory and practice of group psychotherapy* (4th ed.). New York: Basic Books.

CHAPTER ELEVEN

PSYCHOANALYTIC-BASED GROUP THEORIES

The full extent of Sigmund Freud's contribution to group therapy and group counseling is difficult to assess, but it is indisputable that Freud's decades of theory construction established much of the theoretical and practice agenda that followed. During the 1930s, 1940s, most of the 1950s, and part of the 1960s, psychoanalytic beliefs dominated many aspects of the therapeutic landscape for both group and individual therapies.

Throughout its long history, psychoanalysis has rested on three fundamental theoretical tenets, which endure to this day, since they represent psychoanalysis's defining features. First, and most important, a dynamic unconscious exists, which affects one's thoughts and behaviors in an observable manner. The qualifier *dynamic* is what distinguishes Freud's conceptualization of the unconscious mind from precursors to psychoanalysis (see Boring, 1950). Even sleep does not provide escape from the dynamic unconscious's influence, since dreams represent layer upon layer of latent meaning. Second, characteristics comprising the adult personality are irrevocably tied to common developmental events that occurred during early childhood. Disruption of the natural unfolding of these common events leads to dysfunctional thoughts and behaviors. Third, patterns of thought and behavior that restrict a person's potential to "love and do productive work" will become evident in the form of transference episodes, especially if certain therapeutic conditions are fostered and maintained. The hallmark of a genuine transference reaction is the person's inability to simply stop repeating the dysfunctional pattern. These three guiding tenets and other principles established by Freud served to stimulate further theory building within and outside psychoanalytic circles.

Early associates of Freud—such as Alfred Adler, Carl Jung, and Otto Rank—developed divergent theories leading to new types of therapies. Other theorists, more inspired by Freud's ideas than opposed to them, brought attention to themes not fully developed by Freud. Erich Fromm and Karen Horney drew attention to both cultural and interpersonal factors comprising human existence. The latter theme, interpersonal factors, has come to play a central role in contemporary psychoanalytic formulations and is not necessarily seen today as representing a significant departure from Freudian theory. Rather, this theme is seen as part of the logical evolution of Freud's intrapsychic theory (Alonso & Rutan, 1984; Ginter & Bonney, 1993a, 1993b). But even those who remained loyal to a traditional psychoanalytic approach were actively expanding and extending basic Freudian theory.

Anna Freud, Erik Erikson, and Heinz Hartmann were able to combine earlier psychoanalytic notions such as the id with an ever-expanding role for the ego. "Conflict-free" ego functions that were adaptive in nature were being discussed. Ego defenses were seen not only as maladaptive attempts to cope with reality but also as a means of dealing with everyday events that had no link to pathology (A. Freud, 1936/1946). Erikson deserves special recognition for extending Freud's view of human development so as to cover the entire life span of humans. Erikson's (1950a) theory of human development had universal appeal to both psychoanalytic and nonpsychoanalytic thinkers. In the area of group psychotherapy, several key developments were unfolding. Bion, Burrow, Ezriel, Foulkes, Schilder, Slavson, Wolf, and others were applying, redefining, and expanding the use of basic therapeutic concepts (e.g., interpretation, dream analysis, free association, transference, working through) to group therapy.

Recognizing the complexity of psychoanalytic theory because of its many extensions and modifications since Freud's early efforts, a brief psychoanalytic history of theoretical developments is presented. This history is organized around four theoretical perspectives: drive, ego, object relations, and self-psychology. This chapter devotes attention to the contributions of S. H. Foulkes (see "Group Analysis" in Gazda, 1982) as they relate to theory and practice (e.g., selection of group members, group size, group setting, parameters of group sessions, function of the therapist, and ground rules).

HISTORY AND DEVELOPMENT

Drive Theory

Shortly after Freud received his M.D. in 1881, he established a private practice and subsequently a close professional relationship with Joseph Breuer, who shared many of Freud's interests. The professional relationship resulted in a number of collaborative efforts, one of which was their 1895 publication *Studies on Hysteria,* a foreshadower of psychoanalysis.

During Freud's years of theory building and modifications, many theoretical components were introduced, altered, refined, and in some cases abandoned by him. The unconscious, preconscious, and conscious functions; id, ego, superego structures; psychogenetic basis for behavior; psychosexual stages of development; types of anxiety; and transference and resistance are key elements of Freudian theory that endure to this day in various forms.

Freud's theory is known as a *drive theory* because of his unwavering conviction that drives could serve as the explanatory cornerstone of psychoanalysis. For Freud, drives were the urges or beginnings of bodily stimulation that bridged the gap between the body and mind—both the conscious and unconscious mind. Drives are what motivate and lead one to action. According to Freud, any drive could be understood in terms of three qualities: source, aim, and object. *Source* refers to the actual organic origin. The *aim* of a drive is to seek gratification and thus reduction in tension. The *object* is what fulfils the aim. For example, an oral drive for nourishment could be fulfilled via the mother's breast, which represents the object of the drive. During a person's early development, the various drives, of which there are two broad categories (life and death, Eros and Thanatos), mutate and undergo changes of expression and means of fulfillment. The normal progression of these changes is captured in Freud's theory of psychosexual stages of development (oral, anal, phallic, latency, and genital) and his explanations as to how the normal progression of drive expression can be thwarted, leading to certain neurotic or psychotic behaviors.

Over time, two aspects of Freudian theory began to take center stage. First, *increasing emphasis was placed on the ego,* a mental structure postulated by Freud, which functions to overcome the unavoidable disparity between the irrational perspective of the id and the real world. While the id (a manifestation of pure, basic drives) may be temporarily satisfied with an hallucinatory image of food (i.e., pleasure principle governs the id and represents the push to seek reduction of tension), ultimately the oral drive for nourishment can only be satisfied by consuming real food (i.e., reality principle governs intervention by the ego). Eventually, theorists began to depict the ego as more than just a creation of the id whose sole purpose was to serve the id. At times, even Freud's own comments about the aim of therapy supported the theoretical shift taking place—for instance, "Where id is there shall ego be." Second, *increasing emphasis was placed on understanding the object of drives.* It was thought that if a more thorough understanding of mental disorders was to be achieved, the key was to be found in comprehending the full range of what is meant by the concept *object.* How a child "sees" the breasts of a mother who deprives the child of nourishment will significantly differ from that of a child whose mother forces nourishment on the child to meet her own set of unconscious needs. Such a perceptual difference represents a developmental stepping stone to explain ever-increasing sophistication of drive expression and maturing behaviors, especially in relation to how other people are perceived and responded to during interactions.

Ego Psychology

The ego psychology of Hartmann (1958, 1964) greatly broadened the concept of ego functioning beyond the Freudian reality principle as applied to internal conflict and as a compromise of the pleasure principle with external demands. Hartmann thought that the contrast between reality and pleasure principles was misleading. Many activities can be both pleasurable and reality based, such as intellectual curiosity and athletic performance. The autonomous ego represents preformed ego structures derived from genetic endowments, such as intelligence, memory, and talents. These attributes of ego helped regulate the struggle between reality and pleasure and were only minimally or rarely involved in the conflict between the id, external reality, or the internally housed voice of significant others—that is, the superego. Hartmann also argued that the mature person was not just the passive recipient of either internal or environmental forces but, rather, an active agent in a process of adaptation. The person did not merely adjust to reality but could alter it. The capacity for choice was strongly implied by Hartmann but never explicitly stated, perhaps in deference to Freud's stature. Because other people represent a significant aspect of external reality, Hartmann's argument also implies an interactive process of influence in both directions—that is, back and forth between people who are interacting.

Object Relations

Hartmann and others contributed to an atmosphere conducive to the development of object relations theory. St. Clair (1986) wrote, "Object relations theorists such as Melanie Klein, W. R. D. Fairbairn, Edith Jacobson, D. W. Winnicott, Margaret Mahler, and Otto Kernberg . . . stand out because their original and influential ideas greatly helped people understand relationships" (p. 11). Basically, the focus of object relations theory is on how the child unconsciously and consciously views his or her interpersonal world. Of special interest is how encountered relationships are internalized into the mind (internalization involves an evaluative quality, i.e., good, bad, neutral). The child's mind represents the encountered object as a mental impression. These internalized relationship impressions are what explain subsequent interpersonal interactions. Instead of Freudian drives mutating over time to explain behavior, there are mental representations that change over time as explanations for subsequent behaviors. Specifically, the mental representations held by an infant would not be "whole" in nature; that is, the "good breast" or "bad breast" is seen as an entity that stands alone, not as something attached to mother. Later in a child's development, "parts" of people coalesce into essentially whole people representations. Just as with drive theory, early experiences set the stage for the type of representations that follow and serve to motivate behavior. Interestingly, while ego theorists such as Erikson extended human development to the end of life, and Freud placed great importance on the period coinciding with the Oedipal complex, object relations theorists tended to focus on earlier preoedipal developmental factors that they believed explained adult behavior.

Self-Psychology

Kohut's works, such as *The Analysis of the Self* (1971), *The Restoration of the Self* (1977), and *How Does Analysis Cure?* (1984), introduced a sort of a topsy-turvy reevaluation of Freudian drive theory. For Freud, the term *narcissism* was relegated to pregential stages of self-satisfaction; it was sublimation and accompanying mental processes that allowed the person to be transformed from a pleasure-seeking infant to a reality-oriented, mature being if developmental challenges were met. Narcissism in Freud's world denoted arrested development, an intense self-focus related to unhealthy drive development. To the contrary, in Kohut's world, narcissism was a necessary ingredient for full, healthy, mature development and satisfying interpersonal involvement. Kohut saw narcissism as a developmental precursor leading to a genuine love of others. The question for Kohut was how could one love others without first loving the self? Early self-love motivates one to establish links to others; healthy, mature narcissism is evident in empathic encounters.

Kohut's position is referred to as *self-psychology* (the self takes on unparalleled importance), a theoretical tenet that served to further shift the emphasis away from the Freudian conceived body-mind link (i.e., drives) toward a view of mental life dominated by the mind itself (i.e., self). Because the self is now presented as the "center of the individual's psychological universe" (Kohut, 1977, p. 311), Kohut had afforded theorists and practitioners an opportunity to understand and explain behavior in terms other than drives and ego functions. For example, Kohut's term *selfobject* was used to refer to other people and things external to the infant that interacted with and provided for the infant and were internalized into the mind. The rudimentary self of the infant is eventually comprised of both a "grandiose self" (essentially the child's self-centered mechanism resulting in how the child perceives the outside) and the "idealized self-object" (e.g., the caregiver mother who is internalized via cognitively primitive processes). The responsive, or "mirroring," parent will, inadvertently through hers or his characteristic actions, play a primary role in transforming the initial grandiose self into a healthy personality. This transformation, facilitated by the mirroring other, is accompanied by the internalized idealized self-object being changed into something more complex (e.g., an internal felt sense of the moral goodness of one's own behavior and thoughts), which serves to guide the individual's behavior and thoughts.

Although Kohut's theory on the surface may seem somewhat similar to other psychoanalytic theories, in actuality the theory is radical in nature. His treatment of traditional concepts—such as drive, object, mental structures, human development, and transference (and how it was to be confronted via therapy)—are frequently viewed as being contrary to acknowledged standards. In the eyes of some, his views represent heterodoxy. The rich theoretical tapestry created by Freud, Hartmann, Klein, Kernberg, Kohut, and others provided a conceptual background from which a number of group therapy approaches were to develop.

GROUP PSYCHOTHERAPY AND COUNSELING

Although Freud himself was interested in group behavior and offered various psychoanalytic explanations to account for certain group actions and the role of leaders in groups (see *Group Psychology and the Analysis of the Ego,* 1921/1955), and although parallels have been drawn between Freud's weekly meetings with fellow analysts and actual group sessions, it was essentially left to others to apply psychoanalytic derived theories to group therapy. This is not to say Freud did not point the way. He asked three pivotal questions that still resonate: (1) What is a group? (2) How does the group come to exert such a strong influence over the individual? and (3) What psychological changes does the group bring about in the individual? These are questions contemporary group therapists and counselors still address.

The writings of Bion, whose therapeutic focus was on the group rather than any single individual comprising the group, were influential in the early days of psychoanalytic group work. Bion's approach to interacting with a group—comments were directed to the group-as-a-whole—represented an intriguing and radical departure from working with individual clients and served to draw attention to a new avenue for treatment. Another early figure in group work was Foulkes, who trained in psychoanalytic techniques and was influenced by Gestalt psychology (Foulkes, 1948, 1964, 1971, 1975). Although Foulkes viewed group sessions as offering something beyond what could be obtained during individual sessions, he differed from Bion in important ways.

Foulkes assumed that a therapy group represented something different from the sum of its parts. To work with a client individually was simply to co-create an artificial world atypical of the client's membership and experiences in various groups or systems outside of therapy (the family represents just one example)—therapy served as a powerful means to achieve a deep understanding of each member. Although the client-therapist dyad was useful in a group context, it was the group itself that added a much needed ingredient to facilitate a deeper abiding change in a client. In group therapy, each member's pattern of dysfunctional behavior will emerge and portray itself in a much more realistic form, realistically depicting what occurs outside the boundaries of group therapy. Furthermore, these realistic dysfunctional behaviors can be expected to fade in and out of group interactions. These dysfunctional behaviors reflect the unique psychodynamic histories of group members, histories that are to be brought to the forefront by the therapist who is responsible for helping shed light on how certain here-and-now moments in a group session are manifestations of a past that negatively impact everyday interactions.

Interestingly, although there was considerable agreement among group theorists and practitioners concerning the value of group therapy, there was notable disagreement concerning what actually constituted that value. In fact, Bion and others rush to embrace a group-as-a-whole approach was not accepted by all at the time nor since. Bion's perspective has caused others to pause and point out the danger in forgetting about the individual. Wolf and Schwartz (1962) stated that the group therapist is concerned about the "emerging wholesome individual ego. [The therapist] is not preoccupied with how the mystique of the group feels . . . but how the individual within the group, thinks, feels, fantasizes, dreams and behaviors" (p. 246). As pointed out by Shaffer and Galinsky (1989), attention paid to the individual member is reflected in the title of Wolf and Schwartz's work *Psychoanalysis in [emphasis added] Group* (1962). It becomes clear, even after a cursory review of different psychoanalytic group theories, that a continuum is present, illustrating whether the therapist selects to focus on each individual member, the group-as-a-whole, or both to varying degrees.

THEORETICAL RATIONALE

Features

In addition to the advantages already mentioned, other common features of psychoanalytic groups support their use. The following six features of psychoanalytic groups not only contribute to a group therapy rationale but also help provide answers to the three questions originally raised by Freud.

The Group as a Transitional Object.   The group itself can serve in the role of a transitional object (Koseff, 1975). Although the term was applied by Kernberg to reflect the comfort and security sought and obtained by a child through something (e.g., blanket, teddy bear) to help the child move from one level of emotional development to another level, a parallel event occurs when a group member achieves insight and gains new psychological ground with an accompanying shift in emotions and thoughts. The transitional quality allows the member to try new behaviors outside the group and receive supportive and secure feedback from members and the therapist when the "new me" is tested. Finally, Ormont (1995) contributed further to the understanding of the transitional quality of the group by stating that the group functions as a temporary "observing ego" (without risk of serious consequences) until the member receiving group feedback develops this capacity himself or herself.

Ricocheting Techniques and the "Ripple Effect."   A therapeutic technique applied to one particular member frequently has a therapeutic affect on another member or even several members of the group. An interpretation concerning a member's dream made by the therapist may prove to be meaningful for another member with a similar or overlapping psychodynamic history. The ricocheting of the technique creates insight in another member sometimes because it is simply not directed toward that person by the therapist. The third person's typical matrix of psychological defenses are not enacted, as they may have been otherwise, and this allows for the interpretation to have more of an effect than it would have if the interpretation had been directed toward the third party.

Opportunities for Bilevel Interventions.   Group therapy provides an opportunity for techniques to be "owned" and "used" by all members, not just the therapist. Having two potential sources (therapists and other members) from which an intervention may originate provides for multiple perspectives or differing levels of understanding concerning an issue under consideration in the group. A helpful interpretation rendered by a member of the group may not only prove more beneficial than a well-crafted interpretation by the therapist, but the helpful contribution can have a secondary benefit for the initiator of the interpretation by his or her gaining in ego strength and thus increasing skill for future self-analysis.

Intensification of Affects.   Group therapy creates an environment for an intensification of affect not typically found in individual therapy. Although a therapist is generally expected to maintain a degree of emotional equilibrium, members of the group may respond strongly to the behaviors or comments of another member during a group session. An unconscious transference reaction may elicit a strong emotional response from the recipient of the transference reaction. The therapist, to hasten insight and growth in the client who projected thoughts and feelings onto another member, can use the "affective storm" to the projector's advantage.

Mirror Phenomena.   The group allows for each member to see himself or herself through the reflections that come back. These reflections of how a member interacts with others can come back as true and accurate or as distortions of whom the person is. The task of the group therapist is to keep the group mirror "polished and free of dust." A therapist's knowledge about common defense mechanisms—such as rationalization, displacement, conversion, isolation, overcompensation, undoing, introjection, projection, and denial—enables the therapist to identify false mirroring events.

Multiple Transference Reactions.   Because within-group differences will exist even in what are considered homogeneous therapy groups, each member can serve as an object for different types of transference reactions. Thus, the potential depth and range of transference issues occurring outside of therapy in the member's life have higher probability of manifesting themselves during group sessions and, as a result, create a true panorama of the member's real world conflicts. Certainly, adding a co-therapist to the group (especially if the therapists are of different genders) can further enhance the probability for such occurrences.

As pointed out earlier, three tenets guide all psychoanalytic therapy: dynamic unconscious, developmental determinants, and transference reactions. Since the eventual goal of psychoanalytic group therapy is confrontation of the transference reaction, special attention will be devoted to this Freudian concept. Freud placed transference at the hub of treatment, and it still holds this position in current practice.

TRANSFERENCE

The importance of the relationship between the therapist and the client was recognized very early by Freud, primarily through his discovery of the phenomenon of transference (Freud, 1912/1959; 1915/1958). The transference of feelings toward people from the client's childhood onto the therapist provided a powerful avenue for the exploration of the origins of psychological problems. The therapist was expected to present himself or herself as an unidentifiable blank screen on which the client could freely project hidden or repressed fears and wishes as well as relationship issues from previous developmental stages. The unconscious of the client thus became accessible to the therapist. It was considered totally unacceptable for the analyst to project any of his or her feelings onto the client (i.e., countertransference). When countertransference occurred, Freud believed it had to be corrected immediately; otherwise, therapy would be adversely affected. For example, the therapist's control over the treatment process would be jeopardized. Interestingly, in spite of Freud's great insights into the therapeutic process, Ginter and Bonney (1993a, 1993b) have argued there is evidence that suggests Freud failed to completely recognize certain aspects of the therapeutic potential of unconscious communication. Further theoretical developments made by Klein and others led to a change in how transference and contertransference were viewed and confronted in therapy.

Klein (1946) coined the term *projective identification* and defined it as "a combination of splitting off parts of the self and projecting them onto another person" (p. 108). It was as if portions of the self—that is, feelings and/or images—that were associated with anxiety were psychologically cut from one's mind and projected outward. Klein (1957) later expanded the concept to include "the feeling of identification with other people, because one has attributed qualities or attitudes of one's own to them" (p. 311). As a result of this elaboration, the processes of identification and projection began to represent flip sides of the same psychological coin.

Klein's expansion of the term was significant because it allowed other theorists to broaden the concept to include the reactions of the person who is the recipient of these projections (St. Clair, 1986); that is, the recipient can also "identify" with what has been projected. Thus, what starts as an intrapsychic event ends with being an interpersonal event that psychologically involves both individuals (Kernberg, 1980; Scharff, 1989). Simply stated, projective identification occurs when one person, via primarily unconscious processes, elicits a certain behavior, thought, and/or feeling in someone else who unknowingly accepts the projection and unknowingly responds to it. This co-determination of behaviors was recognized by Wachtel (1977) who stated,

> The signals we emit to other people constitute a powerful force field. The shy person does many (sometimes almost invisible) things to make it difficult for another person to stay open to him very long. Even a well-intentioned person is likely . . . to help confirm his views that others aren't really very interested. (p. 52)

Zinner and Shapiro (1989) argued that there are many events discussed in the professional literature that actually represent instances of projective identification: scapegoating, irrational role assignments, symbiotic relationships, family projection processes, and so forth. According to these authors, such labels depict events that have common features that denote the occurrence of projective identification. The common features summarized by Zinner and Shapiro (1989) are as follows:

1. The subject perceives the object as if the object contained elements of the subject's personality.
2. The subject can evoke behaviors or feelings in the objects [sic] that conform with the subject's perceptions.
3. The subject can experience vicariously the activity and feelings of the object.
4. The participants in close relationships are often in collusion with one another to sustain mutual projections—that is, to support one another's defensive operations and to provide experiences through which the other can participate vicariously. (p. 114)

Instances of projective identification sometimes define the most significant content of interactions in and out of group therapy. For example, many dysfunctional parent-child relationships rest on a foundation of projective identification. The child who becomes the family scapegoat may be the recipient of "bad" projections. Unacceptable parts of the self are made to "disappear" from the parent's psyche and are recognized only as qualities of the child. Zinner and Shapiro (1989) suggested that psychological pain can be externalized by a parent and manifested in the scapegoated child. The child's psychological acceptance of the projected element (e.g., "stupidity") can even be manifested in the child's own contribution to the projected role (e.g., "I am stupid and deserve to be punished"). The child's psychological acceptance of the projected role allows the parent to more easily transfer bad elements *onto* and *into* the child. This process, once entrenched, may partly account for the abused child's love for the abusive parent, who may be viewed as correct because the parent seems to lack the bad quality the child possesses. From a developmental perspective, it should be pointed out that children might be especially susceptible to projective identification because of their developmental level—that is, dependency and cognitive immaturity. In extreme cases, the child can become the object of severe physical and psychological abuse. The pathological aim in cases of severe abuse is to destroy and not take back the projected elements ("You are a worthless child and I wish you were dead").

According to Ginter and Bonney (1993b), a transference reaction induced by a projective identification process significantly differs from the transference reaction as conceptualized by Freud. By way of Freud's conceptualizations, one would assume a group member simply projects his or her past emotional attachments to the therapist or another member of the therapy group (countertransference occurs when the therapist is the initiator of a projection). In classic psychoanalytic theory—that is, drive theory—the recipient of the projection becomes a parental figure and the projection represents previous emotional attachments. In such a situation, skillful therapeutic interpretations made during a series of group sessions will eventually alter the projecting member's behavior.

Ginter and Bonney (1993b) have argued that transference reactions resulting from a projective-identification process start as an intrapsychic event that has the potential to alter the behavior, thoughts, and perceptions of both the group member initiating the process and someone else in the group (a member, the therapist, several members, or even the entire group). The recipient of initial projection enacts a special role dictated primarily by the initiator's unconscious projections. Psychological boundaries between the projector and the recipient become amorphous and are distorted in such a dramatic and profound fashion that distinctions become blurred, boundaries collapse, and a special type of unity occurs. Such manifestations of transference represent a complex of mental, emotional, and social mechanisms and has been termed a *Möbius interaction.* Because several terms have been applied to psychologically based events of this type (e.g., scapegoating), because the term *countertransference* now lacks exactness, and because the type of transference under discussion is analogous to a geometric shape labeled the *Möbius strip* (a Möbius strip appears to have two sides but actually has one, i.e., what is seen by one's own eyes as boundaries in reality do not exist), Ginter and Bonney (1993a, 1993b) selected to use the term *Möbius interaction* to help differentiate among the types of transference reactions possible.

Compared to the classic type of transference reaction (and countertransference reaction) hypothesized by Freud, Ginter and Bonney (1993a) are careful to point out that the power of a Möbius interaction should not be underestimated. Prior to effective confrontation of the Möbius interaction itself, the therapist must isolate factors related to his or her own contributory role (Colson, 1985). Leary (1957) illustrated the level of difficulty involved in identifying one's own contribution to maintaining a group member's dysfunctional behavior.

> The more extreme and rigid the person, the greater the person's interpersonal "pull"—that is, the stronger his or her ability to shape the relationship with others. The withdrawn catatonic, the irretrievable criminal, the compulsively flirtatious charmer can inevitably provoke the expected response from a better balanced "other."

The flexible person can pull a greater variety of responses from others, depending on his or her conscious or unconscious motives at the moment. He can get others to like him, take care of him, obey him, lead him, envy him, and so on.

The "sick" person has a narrow range of interpersonal tactics, but these are generally quite powerful in their effect. (Leary, 1957, p. 126)

THERAPIST'S ROLE

Although approaches differ, it can be generally expected that the group therapist will adopt the following role. As a leader, he or she puts the group as a whole into the center of his or her attention; the leader tries to let the group speak, to bring out agreements and disagreements, repressed tendencies, resistances, and transference reactions. The therapist activates and mobilizes that which is latent in the group and helps in the analysis and interpretation of process and content as well as interpersonal relationships. The therapist encourages the active participation of members of the group and uses the contribution of the members in preference to his or her own. He or she emphasizes the *here-and-now* aspect of the situation and conveys an attitude of tolerance and appreciation of individual differences. The therapist helps the members of the group become active participants in the process of group maturation through which the individuals' changes take place.

Inevitably, the leader has a powerful effect on the group dynamics. Frequently, group members will first look to the therapist as being an omniscient and omnipotent figure from whom they expect magical help. In that sense, the group may experience the therapist as an all-knowing and physically powerful authority figure (e.g., the classic father figure), or, when in a regressed state, even as the primordial mother who "holds" and "nurtures." It is generally held that careful attention be paid to the process of maturation that occurs as the group is gradually weaned from its dependence on the therapist as leader. According to Foulkes, one cannot be weaned from something that has not previously been there or been powerfully established. To begin with, adopting Foulkes's perspective, therapists should accept the "exalted" position into which the group puts them, not because it gratifies their own wishes for power but because it is from this position that they can lead the group into a process of analysis, insight, and appropriate adult behavior. In other words, therapists use the projected position to the benefit of the group members. Group therapists accept the position the group chooses to confer on them at first, realizing this gives the group security. It is a position they accept but eventually relinquish—to change from leader *of* the group to being leader *in* the group. Eventually, the group replaces the therapist's authority by that of the group itself. Gradually, as the group weans itself from dependence on the therapist, who does not use his or her power destructively or coercively, leadership becomes an ego-based activity rather than a superego one.

In helping the group mature, the therapist fosters the group members' abilities to understand and interpret their own situations, reactions, and behavior and to develop the self-analytic functions of the group. The therapist waits until he or she has evidence that the group is not able on its own to understand the dynamic processes and unconscious meanings of events of the session. However, if the therapist waits sufficiently long, he or she will, more often than not, find that the group members can themselves resolve the dynamic issues of the session.

Rather than offer an endless string of interpretive remarks aimed at revealing core issues, what the therapist says is intended to elucidate what is near the surface of consciousness of what any one member of the group has not yet said. This rather humble activity, which often does not rank as "interpretation," infuses a crucial element into a group therapy session. The therapist's actions may include simply a reflecting on group events; bringing events from background into foreground of the group's attention; linking communications, clarifications, and confrontations with individuals; drawing the group's attention to events that are being ignored, such as the silence or withdrawal of a previously active member; or pointing out the configurations that are developing within the group, such as subgroupings, pairing, and scapegoating (Möbius interactions). Sometimes, the therapist will feel that his or her appropriate role is to remain silent, thereby becoming the projective and containing element of the group situation. Many group therapists use interpretation sparingly, which reflects a guiding principle: *Interpretation is used when analysis fails.*

Complementing this activity, the therapist may provide his or her understanding of the unconscious processes to the group-as-a-whole or to individuals within the group. As the group develops and as the modes of communication that the group members make with each other become more sensitive and deeper, so the therapeutic process proceeds *pai passu* with these processes. Thus, the process of therapeutic change is in a sense pursued quietly; that is, it is not solely based on interpretations. What may be fundamental for the individuals in the group is the way in which their relationships to each other alter and develop over time. The members of the group are extremely sensitive to this and they develop keen awareness and insight into these often very subtle developments. Frequently, group members will comment that they are now able to say things to each other that they would not have been able to say previously. The alteration in these role relationships and interpersonal relationships in the group provides the "moveable context" of the group therapy situation that de Mare (1972) has contrasted to the "unchanging context" of the psychoanalytic situation. In individual psychoanalysis, the therapist's relationship to the client is kept constant so that transference will appear against the unchanging context.

When interpretation is used, the therapist allows the interpretation to come to him or her from the here-and-now contributions of the group members. Basically, the therapist's interpretative activities can be differentiated into the following three types: (1) interpretation that enables unconscious processes to become more conscious, (2) interpretation of resistance and defense, and (3) interpretation of transference reactions. The group members' interpretive contributions as co-therapists to one another can be viewed as essential components of the therapeutic processes, although if and when this type of interactive activity becomes a manifestation of resistance, it has to be dealt with as such. Resistance is anything that impedes therapy—any type of opposition, whether the member is aware or not of his or her efforts to block recovery of unconscious material. (Resistance can be anything from "forgetting" about a group session to complex sets of behaviors displayed in a group session that are unconsciously intended to block the therapist's ability to uncover hidden elements of a Möbius reaction.)

The group therapist is free to make interpretations to individuals as well as to the group-as-a-whole, as interpretations always hold significance for the group and for the individual. Thus, they can be addressed to any particular individual, any configuration of relationships within the group, or between the group and the therapist. Interpretations should preferably be based on the available experience of the moment and on the level at which the emotion is most active.

The therapist directs his or her interpretation toward the following:

- Ongoing group interactive processes, such as group regressions, fantasies, subgroupings, pairings, mirroring, and so on.
- Repetitive conflict situations
- An understanding of the past experiences that spring to mind of a member in association to the group situation
- Current experiences in the life of a member both within and without the group
- Boundary incidents (i.e., events taking place that interface between the ongoing group and the outside life of individuals comprising it)

GOALS AND OBJECTIVES

The main aim of therapy is obtaining insight and adaptation (Hartmann, 1958). At the heart of group therapy's aim, one discovers a commonality shared by all the varying approaches that comprise psychoanalytic group therapies. The aim is a deep and lasting change in internal object constellations (whether conceived of in terms of ego or object representations) and the resulting external relationships and perceptions of the environment. In the group transference, relationships are explored and analyzed in order to free the individual from the transference-bound repetition, thereby enabling him or her to develop more sensitive, less distorted, and mature forms of relationships. What has been termed *ego training in action* represents working through, in the group situation, previous pathological and unresolved conflicts. Of course, these goals and objectives are simple to state; the reality is that achieving them becomes very difficult and time consuming.

Finally, as alluded to by Freud, the goal of therapy is to achieve "common unhappiness." The end result is not a promise of bliss but rather a significant breaking away from the psychological shackles that a person has dragged behind him or her into the present—the unconscious shackles that have prevented the person from living a life of love and productive work. Although effective therapy does lead to a fuller and richer life (the group member has developed powerful new skills that can be used in dealing with universal problems of everyday living), psychoanalysis is intended to help troubled individuals with their journey through life, to clear the road ahead, but it promises no panacea.

SELECTION AND GROUP COMPOSITION

Selection of Members

A wide range of persons and problems can be accommodated, provided they meet the minimal requirements of the psychoanalytic approach. The prospective group member will be required to reflect on and react to the interventions made by the therapist and the manifold communications emanating from the group members. The person under consideration must possess an ability to tolerate confrontation, the forced interaction of a relatively closed environment, and the frustration of gradual and oscillating change toward meeting his or her therapeutic goals. There must be a willingness and ability to enter into the treatment contract—that is, attend regularly (e.g., twice weekly over a two-year period) and keep the rules (e.g., confidentiality) established for the group.

In selecting a member, the therapist will probably attach less significance to traditionally psychiatric categories, such as neurosis or personality disorders, and pay more attention to the ability to communicate in a group and the capacity to develop insight and determine whether motivation exists for change (Foulkes, 1964). (However, sometimes even the apparently unmotivated client who nevertheless is placed in the group may derive considerable benefit from it [Bonney, 1965].)

Certainly, client characteristics may serve as a contraindication for group membership. Generally speaking, the earlier and deeper the developmental trauma and the more disorganized the personality, the more cautious the group therapist will be when considering such a client's inclusion. Also, severe early deprivations—such as a prolonged hospitalization, early maternal depression, institutional upbringing, and so on—warrant prolonged individual preparation or a combination of individual and group therapy. Introduced to the group prematurely, such an individual may perceive the group as yet another depriving experience and profit little from being a member (Wolff & Solomon, 1973). Finally, Yalom (1975) has indicated that narcissistic group members create special challenges for the therapist and group because of their lack of empathy for others. According to Yalom, "In short, the narcissist is a solipsist who experiences the world and other individuals as existing solely for" him or her (p. 394).

Group Composition

Wolf and Schwartz (1962) have suggested that heterogeneous groups possess an advantage over homogeneous groups. It is generally safe to assume that heterogeneous groups are closer approximations of real-world encounters, and change in the client ultimately must be transferred to future real-world encounters. According to Foulkes (1975), the widest possible span between personality types, "a mixed bag of diagnoses and disturbances" (p. 66), will best promote and elicit an ever-widening and increasing communication process that leads to greater psychological maturity. The benefit each person receives from working toward a free expression of his or her conflict in a group is closely linked with the level of communication such a group can comprehend. The heterogeneous group seems best suited to allow for this to occur. In the atmosphere of lively diversity, the all-important transference reactions, mirror reactions, and other group-specific phenomena occur and manifest themselves freely and clearly. A potential limiting factor is the therapist's and the group's ability to effectively contain the tensions created in such a group, without endangering its cohesion and integrity. Furthermore, it appears that the more diverse the group composition, the more necessary it becomes for at least one variable to be held in common—such as intelligence or education background (Foulkes, 1975).

In composing a group with optimal diversity, it is important to foresee the possibility of isolation, for whatever reason, of any one of its members. For example, the inclusion of a 65-year-old into an existing group with an age span of between 25 to 35 years of age would not be indicated; similarly, a person who holds extreme religious or political convictions probably would be isolated in a group of people with broader-based views.

If the therapist works with the model of a closed group, the decisions as to composition will be accomplished at the group's formation. If, on the other hand, the model is the open group, the important challenges of the group's composition remains throughout its life. The therapist's aim is to hold the size fairly steady, to synchronize carefully both departures and arrivals of members, and thus maintain the richness and diversity of the group's experience and the highest degree of flexibility.

The composition of specialized, more homogeneous groups—such as adolescents, adoptive parents, psychotic patients, phobic patients, alcoholics, and sexual masochists—follows similar principles. These groups, although homogeneous in the diagnostic sense, should allow for wide latitude in variables such as personality attributes, modes of expression of conflict, and defensive organization. But even if diagnostic considerations are deemed important, if a potential member possesses sufficient ego strength and initiative for change, it may be better to place him or her in a heterogeneous group because of the benefits derived for both the member and other group members. For example, because of diversity, there is some evidence that inclusion of one or two members with borderline personality in a group of neurotic members has mutual benefit for both parties. The borderline members activate strong responses in the neurotic members, and the neurotic members help the borderline members modulate the intensity of their affective swings and strengthen their capacity for secondary processes—that is, develop appropriate sets of behaviors to satisfy urges (Pines, 1975, 1978).

GROUP SETTING

The group setting is the physical environment within which the group's therapeutic task takes place. The therapist supplies, creates, and maintains the setting throughout the group's life. He or she guards the group boundaries and negotiates between the group and the wider, immediate social environment. The setting provided will contrast with the wider system within which the group functions: a hospital, a clinic, or a private practice. It is important to point out that in hospital settings, the maintenance of the group room and its availability for sessions on the appointed day and hour, are signs of the nature of the external forces surrounding the group that can work toward its integrity or destruction. Again, it is the task of the therapist to guard the physical boundaries of the group and to negotiate between the group and its environment.

In every case, the therapist should, if possible, provide a reasonably sized, quiet room free from outside interference, with an identical chair for each member arranged in a circle. The chair should be comfortable and allow for a full view of the occupants. At times, the group prescribes that the therapist's seat is fixed, and the group members themselves seat themselves in a more or less permanent order every time. In other groups, the therapist and the group members choose different positions in the circle each session. Seating changes (the choice of neighbor or the proximity to the therapist) are significant behavioral communications that are subject to translation from the nonverbal into the verbal, the unconscious into the conscious modality of experience. By keeping the setting as steady as possible, significant changes within it become available for processing.

The room itself should be entirely free of interruption from extraneous sources for the duration of each session. It is surprising how often this is difficult to achieve, yet it is vital for the success of psychoanalytic-based therapy. Colleagues and staff have to be worked with and their understanding and cooperation won. The wider network in which the therapy takes place is potentially enriching as well as diminishing of the therapeutic process. A closed group meeting held regularly in an institutional setting generates its own institutional dynamics, and the therapist has to ensure that the wider network accepts the existence of the group. It is the therapist's responsibility to create the venue for the group, prepare it for sessions, and protect it from intrusions.

GROUP SIZE

Most therapists report that they work comfortably and most effectively with six to eight members in a group, since both member and therapist are able to encompass eight persons within their visual field (Foulkes, 1964). Thus, group members can remain a face-to-face group, which helps to facilitate projective processes (i.e., transference reactions). Too large a group militates against intimacy and the feeling of containment and reduces the impact of each individual contribution. Face-to-face contact becomes more difficult in a larger group, and the constraints of time may not allow each member sufficient opportunity for self-presentation. Also, from the therapist's point of view, a group of six to eight makes it possible for him or her to pay attention to the group-as-a-whole aspects of the communication process and at the same time attend to each individual's unique contributions.

Too small a group—one with of four or five participants, for example—usually lacks the vital function of representing the social norm and emotional normalcy from which each individual in the group deviates. Typically, also a sense of weakened group identity is present. In fact, therapy in very small groups of three and four members takes on the quality of individual psychotherapy *in* the group (Gosling, 1981).

FREQUENCY, LENGTH, AND DURATION
OF GROUP SESSIONS

It is not unusual to find group sessions of 90 minutes being held once or twice a week over an extended period of two to three years, sometimes longer. Thus, psychoanalytic group therapy is prolonged, thorough, and demanding of the group members as well as the group therapist, since reliability and continuity are essential factors. It is important to note that the group dynamic of this therapeutic approach introduces a danger of group addiction—that is, "group analysis interminable" with resulting loss of independence and self-reliance and a psychologically encapsulated group. This suggests there is an advantage to the open-group format where individuals leave when goals and objectives are met and new members are introduced.

Finally, it is also important to note that brief formats have been increasingly introduced and utilized in psychoanalysis (Bauer & Kobos, 1987). For example, Sifneeo (1987) uses a type of confrontational-supportive approach and limits sessions to 12 to 15 meetings. Confrontation, clarification, and interpretation are directed toward a common theme (e.g., specific Oedipal issues) rather than a wide range of issues. Such an approach, when applied to group therapy, would seem to lend itself to groups that are more homogenous than heterogeneous simply because of the narrow focus. But psychoanalytic-based therapies are typically tied to achieving pervasive change in a person's life; it is difficult to image that brief approaches would become the norm.

TECHNIQUES AND INTERVENTIONS

A number of techniques or intervention strategies arrived at by Freud are used in psychoanalytic group therapy. Free association has been applied to group therapy by Wolf and Schwartz (1962) and was referred to as the *go-around technique*. Each member was instructed to look at other members and say, without filtering thoughts or emotions, the first thing that came to mind. Of course, the technique was used in groups to provide greater access to each member's unconscious mind and thus repressed memories. In a similar fashion, Foulkes (1964) used what was termed *free-floating discussion* or *free group association*. But beyond such applications, it is essential to keep in mind that a particular therapist's theoretical orientation and his or her focus point for a technique will profoundly affect a group therapist's use of well-established techniques. Specifically, is the focus on an individual member, the group-as-a-whole, or a combination of these (or, as is warranted at times, the self, i.e., the therapist's own thoughts and feelings)? Differences in the way a dream may be analyzed can be used to illustrate this concern.

Mitchell (1988) has discussed how the same dream will be analyzed differently by therapists, depending on their theoretical orientation. Assume that an adult female group member reports the following dream: "I had a vivid dream last night. In my dream, a person—a male person whose face kept changing during the dream—stole a jewelry box of mine in which I kept things that I felt were part of me. The box contained a set of colors and a photograph of me as a child with a red heart drawn on it. I woke up once the theft occurred with a terrible sense of having lost something."

Adopting a *drive* perspective, the dream seems to reveal a sexual encounter, possibly the loss of the person's virginity, since boxes or containers are universal symbols representing the womb, which, in turn, represents one aspect of a woman's creative potential. (Following up with having the member free associate to the dream elements will clarify the possible meaning of the various individualized symbols and check the therapist's reliance on what appears to be a universal symbol.) An *ego* interpretation might reveal that the dreamer's early curiosity and creative urges were "boxed up" and never allowed to fully develop due to parents nurturing only certain aspects of achievement, causing the child's raw creative ability to hibernate. The stolen box itself and the changing figure, from an *object relations* perspective, may be interpreted to mean the group member perceives that close relationships are ultimately untrustworthy, since allowing herself to be close to a male makes her vulnerable to having the male hurt her by taking or using for himself what she cherishes or creates. This perspective, formed very early in life by this group member, has resulted in the inability to see males as complex beings with a wide range of motives. And finally, from the *self-psychology* perspective, the dream may be symbolic of a self-love that was hindered from fully developing into an ability to create an empathic adult to adult love relationship because of certain innate potentialities not being accepted by her parents. Her parents only "reflected" back qualities consistent with their views of what comprised "a pretty little girl."

In responding to the possible meaning of this dream, the therapist obviously could have focused attention only on the group member reporting the dream, but even in the case of an individual's dream, it may be appropriate to relate latent content of the dream to something occurring within the group-as-a-whole. For example, something that may have prompted the dreamer to dream this particular dream is the unconscious realization by her that others in the group do not appreciate her genuinely "creative and insightful contributions." Whether the therapist should focus at any given time on an individual member, the group-as-a-whole, or even himself or herself has generated considerable discussion. It can be argued that overreliance on any one type of focus probably inhibits full use of the inherent advantages provided in group therapy.

In general, it appears that maintaining a balanced approach may be best, recognizing that several theorists and practitioners have commented on factors that need to be weighed before a focus point is chosen. Individual interpretations, according to Horwitz (1977), are easier for group members to understand or profit from than group-as-a-whole interpretations because of the interpersonal complexity inherent in group-as-a-whole interpretations. Also, one should keep in mind that such interpretations can generate numerous points of psychological resistance. Of course, eliciting such a level of resistance could be effectively used by a skillful therapist, since analysis of resistance, especially transference resistance, is a basic goal confronting all group therapists. Finally, Foulkes (1973) suggested that it is not so much a question of which interpretation is right but that each offers a different perspective and brings forth a hidden truth.

Point of focus and theoretical orientation are intertwined in subtle and complicated ways that can at times affect members in an unanticipated manner. For example, if a therapist were to devote a sizable portion of a group session to one member, the therapist could observe that another member later displays behaviors that reflect resentment for the attention given to the member of focus. When this is brought to the attention of the member acting out, the member may respond by saying, "I no longer trust you—I don't even think you are any good at what you do." The acting out and the comment about distrust and incompetence could be interpreted from an object relations perspective to mean that the offended member has just reproduced a set of forgotten conflicts by action and then by words without being conscious of how early psychodynamic history has contributed. The offended member is relying on a "splitting" mechanism, resulting in the therapist being perceived as "all bad" because of a perceived betrayal of attention. Kernberg has argued that if such a reaction is widespread in the sense that the whole group is now perceived as "all bad," it denotes an early preoedipal injury. Theoretically, one-to-one reactions (e.g., transference to only the therapist) represent a developmental injury of later origin.

Supplements Employed

Group psychoanalytic therapy typically employs no other medium than the verbal and nonverbal interaction of the group members. Structured exercises, play, video feedback, and so on, are not intrinsic parts of the approach. The introduction of such parameters, although they might activate and focus certain process within the group, could interfere with the gradual evolution and unfolding of the group developmental processes and various therapeutic factors. Similar to the "blank screen" approach advocated by Freud, the basic approach involves creating an atmosphere where transference reaction will manifest unencumbered by artificial structuring.

There are exceptions to this general principle. Developmentally related activities are appropriate if they facilitate the group process in a way that is compatible with psychoanalytic treatment aims. For example, play is a natural interest of the child, as might be a game activity for the preadolescent or music for the adolescent. Music brought in and played by members, for example, could be used to elicit group discussion and serve the purpose of pulling out projective responses.

SPECIAL ETHICAL CONSIDERATIONS

The therapist is ethically responsible for establishing ground rules of which the prospective group members are expected to adhere. Members are expected to attend every session, arrive on time, stay for the entire session unless unavoidable circumstances arise that prevent this, and not fraternize with other members. Individuals are expected to inform the group of their intended absence in advance, or in the case of unexpected absences, they should let the therapist know. The therapist is responsible for preparing the individual at the outset for the possibility of the individual's departure from the group, by imposing the expectation that he or she should give advance notice of intention to leave the group (e.g., a member is informed by his or her company of an upcoming transfer). This allows for a period of working through the termination of therapy and preempts a disruptive departure that may have negative repercussions for both the group and departing member. Issues of separation and individuation will differ, depending on whether the termination is planned, forced, or premature (Fieldsteel, 1996).

Finally, strict confidentiality and respect for privacy of disclosed material is asked of all the members; it is only in an atmosphere of mutual trust that therapy can take place. Violation of the confidentiality or ground rules is brought to the group. For example, when members socialize with one another outside the group, they are encouraged to examine the significance of such extra-group contact by telling of it in the group and reflecting on its meaning. Breaking the ethics of a psychoanalytic group always should be assessed in terms beyond the "surface"—both latent intrapyschic and extrapsychic meanings abound.

APPLICATIONS TO VARIOUS AGE GROUPS: THE DEVELOPMENTAL PERSPECTIVE

At times, age is a primary concern in establishing a psychoanalytic therapy group. Older individuals, adolescents, and children each introduce a different set of considerations than is found with adult groups (Colarusso, 1999). Erikson carefully delineated developmental concerns related to stagnation and despair confronting the older adult. Such concerns may not be fully appreciated or could be seen as essentially irrelevant for younger adults. Furthermore, the psychological reversal of the Oedipal complex (the parent takes on the role of child and must now be parented by his or her own children) encountered by some older adults because of the sudden onset of a physical disability or lasting illness also demands consideration. Certainly, in working with older individuals, certain illnesses such as dementia should be determined, and if evident, render the potential member as unsuitable for this form of group treatment. In fact, ego strength is an important consideration in terms of age across all age levels.

Not only are certain issues and concerns for adolescents (reactivation of Oedipal issues after the latency stage, independence and a new identity) and young children (still in the process of traversing early developmental stages) different from those of adults, but their style of interacting in a group can differ in significant ways. Adults can be expected to be verbal, whereas adolescents and children may be resistant to opening up in a therapy context. In groups of young adolescents, introducing paper and drawing or modeling materials often facilitates the group process. The way in which these materials are used provides additional opportunities for communication and gives young people who may have difficulty verbalizing the chance to become actively involved in the group process. Children's groups typically have play materials built into their structure. Also, a circular table can be introduced to simulate the circle of chairs found in an adult group. The table is divided into parts; each part becomes the child's own territory. In this way, the autistic play of a child can progress into shared play, providing a suitable substitute for the adult group process.

Finally, achieving insight (awareness) for an adult and achieving insight (awareness) for a child are qualitatively different (Ferro, 1997). Whereas awareness has a strong cognitive component for the adult, the child's awareness is much more primitive, intuitive, and experientially grounded. In many cases, evidence that therapeutic awareness has occurred is provided by what the child *does* rather than what the child *says.* Thus, in play therapy, the therapist may think in psychoanalytic terms without identifying for a child the dynamics involved in his or her actions.

MULTICULTURAL CONSIDERATIONS

Although some psychoanalytic theorists maintained a multicultural perspective in their writings (e.g., Erikson, 1950b), multiculturalism as a primary consideration lagged behind other psychoanalytic interests. (The same is historically true of other major therapeutic approaches.) Serrano and Ruiz (1991) were critical of therapists who overlooked the role that multicultural factors can play. Clients "often drop out of treatment when cultural and ethnic issues are not dealt with in treatment and they feel misunderstood by the therapist. [While] this is not to suggest that a successful therapeutic relationship can only be achieved with someone of similar ethnic or cultural background or that minority patients can only be treated by therapist of the same minority group" (p. 325), it is essential to be culturally sensitive (Serrano & Ruiz, 1991).

A therapist who fails to be cognizant of cultural and ethnic issues and as a result does not address them in group is at best less effective and at worst harmful. Recently, Robinson and Ginter (1999) called attention to the profound effects of racism and how racism permeates U.S. society, including therapy sessions, and that understanding racism is necessary if a therapist hopes to practice in an increasingly diverse society. In reviewing the role that culture and ethnicity play in working with clients, Robinson (1999) concluded, a guiding principle is that therapists "must avoid the attribution of certain occupations, attitudes, and experiences to their clients due to the visibility of their race, gender, and other identities. Making judgments about people's humanity and its quality due to established criteria is to rely on tired but extremely powerful discourses steeped in oppression" (p. 78).

In psychoanalytic circles, just as in therapy in general, greater attention is being devoted to how cultural factors play a role in therapy (e.g., Castairs, 1965; English, 1984; Locke & Kiselica, 1999; Maldonado-Sierra & Trent, 1960; Richman, 1985; Serrano & Ruiz, 1991; Yamamoto, James, & Palley, 1968). Above all else, it is crucial that theory and research lead to establishing a set of tested multicultural competencies pertaining to the practice of group psychoanalytic therapy competencies that enable the therapist to handle the challenging interplay of culture, ethnicity, and the transference reaction. A group therapist certainly should expect to find that cultural or ethnic factors in at least some cases serve as a key or core component of members' transference reactions (Comas-Diaz & Minrath, 1985; Tang & Gardner, 1999). Such transference reactions can only be therapeutically filtered and distilled via the group process if they are first recognized for what they are and not mistaken for something else. As pointed out by Brantley (1983), cultural sensitivity allows the therapist to consider the significance of cultural and ethnic aspects of a client as well as to bring to the forefront his or her own thoughts and behaviors related to racism (i.e., countertransference).

Serrano and Ruiz (1991) were able to succinctly capture the therapeutic advantage provided the therapist who is culture sensitive: "Recognition of the cultural and ethnic dimensions in our clinical work expands our field of observation and offers us more resources in our efforts at understanding [clients] and ourselves" (p. 333).

RESEARCH

Kubie (1953) stated the following in relation to scientifically validating psychoanalytic theory:

> In general, they [the limitations] can be summarized by saying that the basic design of the process of analysis has essential scientific validity, but that the difficulties of recording and reproducing primary observations, the consequent difficulty in deriving the basic conceptual structure, the difficulties in examining with equal ease the circular relationship from unconscious to conscious and from conscious to unconscious, the difficulties in appraising quantitatively the multiplicity of variables, and finally the difficulty of estimating those things which increase and those which decrease the precision of its hypotheses and the validity of its predictions are among the basic scientific problems which remain to be solved. (pp. 143–144)

In spite of these challenges, the scientific validity of psychoanalysis has been tested. Fisher and Greenberg (1977) analyzed the findings of nearly 2,000 reports across an array of disciplines. They abstracted data that was based only on procedures that could be replicated, thus excluding case study data. They found support for certain personality types, such as oral and anal; tension reduction due to dreaming; and aspects of the Oedipal complex as it pertained to males. Specifically in relation to groups, researchers have studied borderline defenses and countertransference (Greene, Rosenkrantz, & Muth, 1986); effects of early child-caregiver interactions on subsequent adult behavior (Kilmann et al., 1999); treatment approaches with anaclitic and introjection clients (Blatt, 1992); transference reactions (Burrows, 1981a, 1981b; Chance, 1952; Klein, 1977); group-as-a-whole transference (MacKenzie et al., 1987); and splitting, self-representations, and boundary phenomena (Greene, Rosenkrantz, & Muth, 1985). Again, support was found for psychoanalytic concepts.

Even though psychoanalytic theory and therapy have received extensive, prolonged scrutiny since their introduction (e.g., Cohen & Nagel, 1934; Nagel, 1959; Vaughan, 1997), the accumulation of evidence supports the use of psychoanalysis. Although other approaches may possess advantages over psychoanalytic-based therapies because of the unique factors surrounding a particular client or mental disorder, in general, it can be concluded that psychoanalytic therapy, as with other major treatment approaches, has proven itself a valuable treatment modality (Ginter, 1988).

SUMMARY

This chapter provided an overview of the theoretical and practical developments that represent psychoanalytic-based group therapies. Many of the concepts introduced by psychoanalysis—such as resistance, transference, ego, superego, defense mechanisms, developmental stages, interpretation, repression, and unconscious factors—have proven useful to therapy and counseling in general and are not solely confined to psychoanalysis. Since Freud's early publications more than 100 years ago, psychoanalysis has continued to play an influential role in individual and group approaches to treatment. A measure of the persistence of psychoanalysis was indicated by Cioffi (1973), who stated that as early as 1916, New Yorkers could select from among 500 analysts.

Even contemporary critics of the psychoanalytic approach must admit that Freud provided a basic theoretical outline that has retained its significance into the twenty-first century. When one considers the approaches that multiplied after early drive theory formulations, it appears that Freud's influence will be felt for many years to come. Finally, in summarizing what Bion, Foulkes, Hartmann, Kernberg, Klein, Kohut, and others contributed to psychoanalysis since Freud's early dominance, one could reasonably claim their contributions led to a subtle paradigm shift, but one of significant proportions. Psychoanalysis as a therapeutic approach has moved from its heavy intrapsychic focus on the individual toward an extrapsychic focus including others; a theoretical bridge has been constructed to span the inner and outer world of human existence (Ginter & Bonney, 1993a, 1993b).

REFERENCES

Alonso, A., & Rutan, J. S. (1984). The impact of object relations theory on psychodynamic group therapy. *American Journal of Psychiatry, 141,* 1376–1380.

Bauer, G. P., & Kobos, J. C. (1987). *Brief therapy: Short-term psychodynamic intervention.* Northvale, NJ: Aronson.

Blatt, S. J. (1992). The differential effect of psychotherapy with anaclitic and introjective patients. *Journal of the American Psychoanalytic Association, 40,* 691–724.

Bonney, W. C. (1965). Pressures toward conformity in group counseling. *Personnel and Guidance Journal, 43,* 970–973.

Boring, E. G. (1950). *A history of experimental psychology* (2nd ed.). New York: Appleton.

Brantley, T. (1983). Racism and its impact on psychotherapy. *American Journal of Psychiatry, 140,* 1605–1608.

Breuer, J., & Freud, S. (1955). Studies on hysteria. In *Standard Edition* (Vol. 2). London: Hogarth. (Original work published in 1895)

Burrows, P. B. (1981a). The family connection: Early memories as a measure of transference in a group. *International Journal of Group Psychotherapy, 31,* 3–23.

Burrows, P. B. (1981b). Parent orientation and member-leader behavior: A measure of transference in group. *International Journal of Group Psychotherapy, 31,* 175–191.

Castairs, G. M. (1965). Cultural elements in response to treatment. In A. V. Reuck & R. Porter (Eds.), *Transcultural psychiatry.* London: Churchhill.

Chance, E. (1952). A study of transference in group psychotherapy. *International Journal of Group Psychotherapy, 2,* 40–53.

Cioffi, F. (1973). *Freud: Modern judgments.* London: Macmillan.

Cohen, M., & Nagel, E. (1934). *An introduction to logic and scientific method.* New York: Harcourt & Brace.

Colarusso, G. A. (1999). The development of time sense in middle adulthood. *Psychoanalytic Quarterly, LXVIII,* 52–83.

Colson, D. B. (1985). Transference-countertransference in psychoanalytic group therapy: A family systems view. *International Journal of Group Psychotherapy, 35,* 503–518.

Comas-Diaz, L., & Minrath, M. (1985). Psychotherapy with ethnic minority borderline clients. *Psychotherapy, 22,* 418–426.

de Mare, P. B. (1972). *Perspective in group psychotherapy.* London: George Allen and Unwin.

English, R. (1984). *The challenge for mental health minorities and their worldviews.* Austin, TX: The Hogg Foundation for Mental Health, University of Texas.

Erikson, E. H. (1950a). *Childhood and society.* New York: Norton.

Erikson, E. H. (1950b). Childhood in two American Indian tribes. In E. H. Erikson (Ed.), *Childhood and society*. New York: Norton.

Ferro, A. (1997). *The child and the psychoanalyst: The question of techniques in child psychoanalysis*. (P. Faugeras & D. Faugeras, Trans.). Ramonville, Saint-Agne: Editions Eres.

Fieldsteel, N. D. (1996). The process of termination in long-term psychoanalytic group therapy. *International Journal of Group Psychotherapy, 46*, 25–39.

Fisher, S., & Greenberg, R. P. (1977). *The scientific credibility of Freud's theories and therapy*. New York: Basic Books.

Foulkes, S. H. (1948). *Introduction to group-analytic psychotherapy*. London: William Heinemann Medical Books.

Foulkes, S. H. (1964). *Therapeutic group analysis*. New York: International Universities Press.

Foulkes, S. H. (1971). Access to unconscious processes in group analytic group. *Group Analysis, 4*, 4–14.

Foulkes, S. H. (1973). The group as a matrix of the individual's mental health. In L. R. Wolberg & E. K. Schwartz (Eds.), *Group therapy 1973*. New York: Stratton Intercontinental Medical Books.

Foulkes, S. H. (1975). *Group-analytic psychotherapy, method and principles*. London: Gordon and Breach Science Publishers.

Freud, A. (1946). *The ego and the mechanisms of defense*. New York: International Universities Press. (Original work published 1936)

Freud, S. (1955). *Group psychology and the analyses of the ego*. In J. Stachey (Ed. and Trans.), *The standard edition of the complete psychological works of Sigmund Freud: Collected papers* (Vol. 2). London: Hogarth. (Original work published 1921)

Freud, S. (1958). Observations on transference. In J. Stachey (Ed. and Trans.), *The standard edition of the complete psychological works of Sigmund Freud: Collected papers* (Vol. 2). London: Hogarth. (Original work published 1915)

Freud, S. (1959). The dynamics of the transference. In E. Jones (Ed.), *Sigmund Freud: Collected papers* (Vol. 2). New York: Basic Books. (Original work published 1912)

Gazda, G. M. (1982). *Basic approaches to group psychotherapy and group counseling* (3rd ed.). Springfield, IL: Charles C. Thomas.

Ginter, E. J. (1988). Stagnation in eclecticism: The need to recommit to a journey. *Journal of Mental Health Counseling, 10*, 3–8.

Ginter, E. J., & Bonney, W. (1993a). Freud, ESP, and interpersonal relationships: Projective identification and the Mobius interaction. *Journal of Mental Health Counseling, 15*, 150–169.

Ginter, E. J., & Bonney, W. (1993b, January). *Inexplicable classroom behavior: The Möbius interaction*. Presentation made at the annual conference of the American Association for Specialists in Group Counseling, Athens, GA.

Gosling, R. H. (1981). A study of very small groups. In J. S. Grotstein (Ed.), *Do I dare disturb the universe? A memorial to Dr. Wilfred Bion*. London: Maresfield.

Greene, L. R., Rosenkrantz, J., & Muth, D. Y. (1985). Splitting dynamics, self-representations and boundary phenomena in the group psychotherapy of borderline personality disorder. *Psychiatry, 48*, 234–245.

Greene, L. R., Rosenkrantz, J., & Muth, D. Y. (1986). Borderline defenses and countertransference: Research findings and implications. *Psychiatry, 49*, 253–264.

Hartmann, H. (1958). *Ego psychology and the problem of adaptation*. (D. Rapaport, Trans.). New York: International Universities Press.

Hartmann, H. (1964). *Essays on ego psychology*. New York: International Universities Press.

Horwitz, L. (1977). A group centered approach to group psychotherapy. *International Journal of Group Psychotherapy, 27*, 423–440.

Kernberg, O. F. (1975). A systems approach to priority setting of interventions in groups. *International Journal of Group Psychotherapy, 25*, 251–275.

Kernberg, O. F. (1980). *Internal world and external reality: Object relations theory Applied*. New York: Aronson.

Kilmann, P. R., Laughlin, J. E., Carranza, L. V., Downer, J. T., Major, S., & Parnell, M. M. (1999). Effects of attachment-focused group preventive intervention on insecure women. *Group Dynamics: Theory, Research, and Practice, 3*, 138–147.

Klein, E. B. (1977). Transference in training groups. *Journal of Personality and Social Systems, 1*, 53–64.

Klein, M. (1946). Notes on some schizoid mechanisms. *International Journal of Psycho-Analysis, 27*, 99–110.

Klein, M. (1957). On identification. In M. Klein, P. Heimann, & R. E. Money-Kyrle (Eds.), *New directions in psychoanalysis: The significance of infant conflict in the pattern of adult behavior*. New York: Basic Books.

Kohut, H. (1971). *The analysis of the self.* New York: International Universities Press.

Kohut, H. (1977). *The restoration of the self.* New York: International Universities Press.

Kohut, H. (1984). *How does analysis cure?* Chicago: University of Chicago Press.

Koseff, J. W. (1975). The leader using object-relations theory. In Z. A. Liff & J. Aronson (Eds.), *The leader in the group.* New York: Aronson.

Kubie, L. S. (1953). Psychoanalysis as a basic science. In F. Alexander & H. Ross (Eds.), *20 years of psycho-analysis.* New York: Norton.

Leary, T. (1957). *Interpersonal diagnosis of personality: A functional theory and methodology for personality evaluation.* New York: Ronald Press.

Locke, D. C., & Kiselica, M. S. (1999). Pedagogy of possibilities: Teaching about racism in multicultural counseling courses. *Journal of Counseling and Development, 77,* 80–86.

MacKenzie, K. R., Dies, R. R., Coche, E., et al. (1987). An analysis of AGPA institute groups. *International Journal of Group Psychotherapy, 37,* 55–74.

Maldonado-Sierra, E., & Trent, R. (1960). The sibling relationship in group psychotherapy with Puerto Rican schizophrenics. *American Journal of Psychiatry, 117,* 239–244.

Mitchell, S. A. (1988). *Relational concepts in psychoanalysis: An integration.* Cambridge, MA: Harvard University Press.

Nagel, E. (1959). Methodological issues in psychoanalytic treatment. In S. Hooke (Ed.), *Psychoanalytic, scientific method and philosophy.* New York: New York University Press.

Ormont, L. R. (1995). Cultivating the observing ego in group setting. *International Journal of Group Psychotherapy, 45,* 489–506.

Pines, M. (1975). Group psychotherapy with "difficult" patients. In L. Wollberg, M. Aronson, & A. R. Wolberg (Eds.), *Group therapy: An overview.* New York: Stratton Intercontinental Medical Books.

Pines, M. (1978). Contributions of S. H. Foulkes to group-analytic psychotherapy. In L. R. Wolberg, M. L. Aronson, & A. R. Wollberg (Eds.), *Group therapy: An overview.* New York: Stratton Intercontinental Medical Books.

Richman, J. (1985). Social class and mental health revised: Sociological perspective on the diffu-

sion of psychoanalysis. *Journal of Operant Psychiatry, 16,* 2–6.

Robinson, T. L. (1999). The intersections of dominant discourses across race, gender and other identities. *Journal of Counseling and Development, 77,* 73–77.

Robinson, T. L., & Ginter, E. J. (1999). Introduction to the *Journal of Counseling and Development*'s special issue on racism. *Journal of Counseling and Development, 77,* 3.

Scharff, J. S. (Ed.). (1989). *Foundation of object relations family therapy.* Northvale, NJ: Aronson.

Serrano, A. C., & Ruiz, E. J. (1991). Transferential and cultural issues in group Psychotherapy. In S. Tuttman (Ed.), *Psychoanalytic group theory and therapy* (No. 7). American Group Psychotherapy Association Monograph Series. Madison, CT: International Universities Press.

Shaffer, J., & Galinsky, M. D. (1989). *Models of group therapy.* Englewood Cliffs, NJ: Prentice-Hall.

Sifneos, P. E. (1987). *Short-term dynamic psychotherapy: Evaluation and technique* (2nd ed.). New York: Plenum.

St. Clair, M. (1986). *Object relations and self psychology: An introduction.* Pacific Grove, CA: Brooks/Cole.

Tang, N. M., & Gardner, J. (1999). Race, culture, and psychotherapy: Transference to minority therapists. *Psychoanalytic Quarterly, LXVIII,* 1–20.

Vaughan, S. G. (1997). *The talking cure: The science behind psychotherapy.* New York: Putnam's.

Wachtel, P. L. (1977). *Psychoanalysis and behavior therapy: Toward an integration.* New York: Basic Books.

Wolf, A., & Schwartz, E. K. (1962). *Psychoanalysis in group.* New York: Grune & Stratton.

Wolff, H. H., & Solomon, E. C. (1973). Individual and group psychotherapy: Complementary growth experience. *International Journal of Group Psychotherapy, 23,* 177–184.

Yalom, L. D. (1975). *The theory and practice of group psychotherapy* (2nd ed.). New York: Basic Books.

Yamamoto, J., James, G., & Palley, N. (1968). Cultural problems in psychiatric therapy. *Archives in General Psychiatry, 19,* 45–49.

Zinner, J., & Shapiro, R. L. (1989). Projective identification as a mode of perception and behavior in families of adolescents. In J. S. Scharff (Ed.), *Foundations of object relations family therapy.* New York: Aronson.

CHAPTER TWELVE

PSYCHOANALYTIC-BASED GROUP THEORIES

Applications

It has been suggested that groups move through developmental stages that are symbolic of the cycle of life—that is, birth, infancy, childhood, adolescence, adulthood, and death (Mann, Gibbard, & Hartman, 1967; Mills, 1964). On the surface, the suggestion that a group, on some level, follows the universal cycle of human development might seem too simplistic to serve a useful purpose, but a closer look at this suggestion indicates it possesses merit. For example, a careful study of Erikson's (1950) stages of development reveals that many of the issues individuals struggle with along their developmental journey (e.g., fear, self-doubt, sense of unworthiness, incompetence, uncertainty, and meaninglessness) are the same issues of concern that clients enter group psychotherapy with, or at least are issues that seem to surface from time to time during the life of a psychoanalytic group.

Certainly, many group practitioners would agree that the early stage of a group's development is a time when issues of *trust* and exploration of *freedom* are highlighted. Middle stages are devoted to taking *initiative* and *industry* (getting to work), and *intimacy, identity, generativity* (caring for others) and *integrity* (finding a reliable meaning and self acceptance) are characteristic of the mature, functioning group. It appears many of Erikson's developmental terms are similar to the terms used by others to describe what occurs during different stages of group development (see Bonney, 1969; Lacoursiere, 1980; Mahler, 1969; Tuckman, 1965; Tuckman & Jensen, 1977). Of course, it should be pointed out that unlike the sequential patterns found in maturational processes, developmental factors contribute in a much less direct fashion to what actually occurs in a psychoanalytic group, yet these developmental factors are of most interest to psychoanalytic oriented therapists.

It is important to highlight that although a degree of correspondence (varying from high to relatively low) probably exists between *actual, observable developmental histories* and *psychodynamic histories,* one would be mistaken to assume an exact correlation is present. The person's psychodynamic interpretation (means of making sense) of any event at a particular point in that person's development is what affects later behavior and thoughts. This is why two children in the same family exposed to the same horrific event (e.g., sexual maltreatment) can experience radically different psychological outcomes. Thus, while knowledge of the developmental stages that groups move through is important for the therapist to possess, it is a necessity for the therapist to understand each member's unique psychodynamic history (Allen, 1992; Bascal & Newman, 1990; Patton & Meara, 1992; Scharfman, 1992). It should be noted that this chapter reflects a contemporary approach to psychoanalytic-based group therapy, an approach that pulls primarily from object relations theory.

PSYCHODYNAMIC HISTORIES

Each member's psychodynamic history accounts for his or her dysfunctional behavior, which, in turn, has resulted in the person entering a psychoanalytic group. The group should be viewed as a microsociety that also represents the "displaced" family for each member (i.e., each member will see reflected in the faces of others present in the group his or her own mother, father, sibling, stepfather, stepmother, stepsibling, uncle, aunt, etc.). Various psychoanalytic writers have provided models of psychodynamic development (e.g., Winnicott's [1958] concepts of integration, personification, and object relating) that allow for greater insight into members' dysfunctional behaviors and a retrospective glimpse of each group member's psychodynamic history. Although Winnicott's model (or some other model, i.e., Fairbairn, 1941/1954; Foulkes, 1971, 1973, 1975; Jacobson, 1964; Kernberg, 1976; Klein, 1932/1975; Kohut, 1977; Mahler, Pine, & Bergman, 1975) helps the group therapist hypothesize causes and possible intervention remedies for a particular member's interpersonal difficulties, it is important to emphasize that psychoanalytic theory never provides the group therapist a simple "cookbook approach" to group therapy. Freud (1913/1958) concluded during the early years of the twentieth century that psychotherapy is similar to a game of chess. One might know some of the opening and closing moves of the chess game, but for the most part all the moves that fall between the opening and closing of the game rest on what Luborsky (1984) termed "intuitively applied guidelines" (p. 13).

TECHNIQUES: A PERSPECTIVE

A number of well-known techniques and technique-related concerns are associated with psychoanalytic-based approaches. Examples are free association (e.g., Wolf and Schwartz's [1962] "go around"), group-as-a-whole–based interpretations, dream sharing and analysis, recognition of the affect of defense mechanisms on the group, confrontation of members' resistance, and transference analysis of members' group behavior. Effective application of psychoanalytic-based group techniques can be expected to produce several therapeutic outcomes, such as the realization of the "universalization of issues, insight, mind-body holism, and working through normal stages of human development" (Ettin, 1992, p. 74). The last outcome, working through stages of development, can only be fully achieved by therapeutically "attacking" a member's transference-related issues. In a sense, the group member goes back through early events and (with the assistance of the group therapist) undoes what went wrong earlier. Transference reactions represent the therapeutic "heart" of psychoanalytic-based group therapies because transference psychologically replicates early events and provides an opportunity to "correctly" work through stages of one's development and thus create a so-called new psychodynamic history. Simply stated, the central task of the psychoanalytic-oriented therapist is to effectively confront transference reactions, enabling each member to overcome the unique transference issues that support his or her dysfunctional thoughts and behaviors. The advantage group psychotherapy offers over individual therapy is the multiple possibilities (i.e., therapist and group members) onto which psychodynamic histories can be psychologically pasted (e.g., unconsciously the therapist's face has become one's mother and each member has donned the mask of some significant other from the past or present).

Although many nonpsychoanalytic counselors and therapists possess a general knowledge of psychoanalytic-based techniques, the area that is probably least understood by them, in terms of its key role in psychoanalytic group work, is the transference reaction. The remainder of this chapter will be devoted to illustrating and understanding the role of transference and the process of projective identification.

ILLUSTRATION OF A GROUP SESSION

Excerpts from an "emotionally deprived mothers" group (see Gazda, 1982) are used to illustrate several aspects of a psychoanalytic approach. The group, comprised of five mothers, represents a group that is entering its second year of group psychoanalysis. Two sessions prior to the session, abstracted from and reported here, the therapist draws the group's attention to the imminent summer break. The members had been given the year's timetable at the beginning of the treatment year. This sample was selected because it provides examples of transference (i.e., specifically, a type of Möbius reaction). Transference issues are discussed in detail following the illustration. Finally, although interpretations are offered following certain segments in the group dialogue, these are "silent" interpretations, which are not shared with the group. (See Chapter 11 for a discussion of interpretation timing, i.e., when interpretations are made by the therapist.)

Group Session

Wendy is five minutes late, which is out of character for her. As a rule, she is half an hour early, sitting in the waiting room. She now sits herself in an empty chair, with the entire group present. The chairs are always put out in a circle and are left there, whether a group member is absent with or without notification. Wendy does not greet anyone.

- *Interpretation:* Wendy is acting in a manner that reflects omnipotent control of the group meeting. Her absence of five minutes "pulls" the group to take up the "pain" of the imminent summer break.

Jessy: (with a deep sigh) I thought you had gone for good.

Sylvia: (with a little contemptuous laugh) Gone where? She has nowhere to go. I am going to my mum this summer. (She talks at length about the fantasized stay with her mother, with whom she has not been in touch for years. The group listens to her intently, yet no one tells her what the group and she know—that Sylvia is not in touch with her mother and does not know for sure where she lives.)

■ *Interpretation:* In response to feelings of abandonment displaced on Wendy from the therapist's and the group's break, the group retreats with Sylvia to the fantasy life with the "good" mother who never leaves.

Mary: It will be nice in the country—nice for the kids—out in the sun and all those animals, they'll like it. (There is no reason to assume that Sylvia's mother lives in the country. She last lived in East London.)

Sylvia: Perhaps I'll stay . . . what's there here for me?

■ *Interpretation:* The anguish of the nonsustaining environment is verbalized.

Wendy: I couldn't make it . . . early, I mean. . . . I get a bit tired. . . . I got up late. Anyway, I am here now, aren't I? (with some anger). (Wendy had to substitute for a depressed hospitalized mother when Wendy was still quite young; there were three younger siblings.)

■ *Interpretation:* Wendy resonates to the group's agony of abandonment. From her past, she relives the burden of mothering her young siblings with inadequate means at her disposal.

Therapist: Wendy is tired of looking after the group when I leave the group for my own holidays, with my own family.

Sylvia: (shouts at the therapist) There you have it—that's what happens when one is late. One can't always be on time to please you . . . it's awful here . . . cold . . . what's the matter with the heating? . . . I won't sit here like that. I didn't have anything (to eat) before I came—they (the children) had it all (jumps up as to leave the room). The therapist gets up and puts her hand on Sylvia's arm and pushes her into the chair, keeps her hand on her arm for a while, then goes back to her chair and sits down. Sylvia sits back in her chair.

■ *Nonverbal Intervention:* Physical intervention and support are provided to help Sylvia "hold" the experience of psychological emptiness (manifested as sensations of cold and hunger).

Mary: (pale with agitated hand movements) We have other things to do than coming here . . . it's not the only place . . . it's like all the others, anyway . . . you (therapist) lock it up good and proper when you go—or we shall break in and break your inside up? And keep it safe from us. (The group becomes very noisy; there is confused cross-talk, much shouting, and some pushing of chairs. The therapist cannot follow the talk. The impression is of shaking, banging, and stomping. The therapist feels anxious, alone, and worried that her clinic colleagues will be disturbed and angry with her. This lasts some five minutes or so, but it feels much longer.)

- ■ *Comment:* The group and the therapist feel the meaning of the verbal assault. A transference reaction (i.e., Möbius interaction; see preceding chapter for theoretical discussion) occurs as Mary pours out her feelings and thoughts related to fear of abandonment and destruction into the therapist (the reaction of the group helps "fuel" the transference, i.e., Möbius interaction).

Doris: (silent so far) We can meet alone—without her (therapist). (No one takes this up, and Doris, a fairly silent member of the group, does not try to develop this and sinks back in her chair.)

- ■ *Interpretation:* A flicker of self-help is in the group, but it seems to be too early in the desperate affective experience to be taken up by the group.

Wendy: (to the therapist) John (her eldest son) is going camping with the school—it's not far. . . . I'll see him on Sunday in the camp; they are waiting on the bus for us (the mothers of the campers). (The group is listening carefully, looking at the therapist.)

- ■ *Interpretation:* The substitute mother in the group challenges the therapist on behalf of the group as well as herself.

Therapist: (first looks at Wendy and then at the others in turn) Yes, I am going away on holiday with my family, and I shall not see you. There is no way that you can visit me and see what I am doing with my family. I am far away from the clinic. I am looking after myself only.

Doris: I have been away all alone too. (Tells of an outing as a schoolgirl. The group gets impatient, and there is much shifting about in chairs.)

- ■ *Interpretation:* Doris represents denial of impotence and dependency needs. The group's reaction represents a rejection of this potential solution.

Jessy: What did I do last time? (meaning in the Easter break). (The group, one member after another, including Doris, recounts in great and accurate detail, what she, Jessy, had told them she had done during the break. The therapist inwardly marvels at this feat of memory, which she herself does not possess over this event.)

- ■ *Interpretation:* The "mothering" function of "holding for and holding together" is demanded by one member of the group, which, in face of the unreliable therapist-mother, is now required to take on this function—and does so well and with satisfaction. It seems to give back to the group members a belief in their own mothering ability.

Doris: I think it is time to go. (Makes as if to get up. No one gets up with her, and she sits down again.)

- *Interpretation:* Symbolic solution is presented—"I leave you before you leave me"—a solution that provides control only for the member.

Wendy: We can meet in my place. Is it all right with you? (to the therapist). (It seems that no one thinks of meeting in the group room without the therapist, although she suggested this on previous occasions.)

- *Interpretation:* The group room is a "part" of the therapist—possibly symbolic of a mother's womb or a mother's embrace (i.e., a protected place that nourishes those it contains).

Therapist: How was it last time (Easter break)? It was all right then, wasn't it, and it is all right now?

Sylvia: This time is not last time, so is it or isn't it?

- *Interpretation:* For this member, this is reminiscent of the unreliable, arbitrary mother, who is suspected of taking away things for her own use.

Therapist: (repeats that it is all right) I think it feels as if one could not rely on me to be the same, to want the same, to come back after the break; because I go away and leave you, it all feels very dangerous and new. It seems what was all right last time may not be this time.

Wendy: It was in my place last time. (The group starts to work out a time for the meeting at Wendy's place, and the usual "group day" and time is not mentioned. The situation once more becomes confused and anger arises.)

- *Interpretation:* Group time and place are seen as belonging to the therapist.
- *Intervention (not presented here):* The therapist recognizes the group's need for assistance. The therapist concludes the session by helping settle the day and time of the meeting during the summer break.

UNDERSTANDING THE ROLE OF TRANSFERENCE

Central to the preceding illustration are transference reactions (the therapist is seen as the mother who withdraws her support). A type of Möbius transference reaction (Ginter & Bonney, 1993) occurs when the therapist "feels anxious, alone, and worried that her colleagues will be disturbed and angry with her." In this case, the therapist experiences the member's (Mary's) psychological fear that is linked to the issue of being abandoned (i.e., "I am not worth loving—I must deserve to be left behind"). But an important distinction can be made; although the therapist was "pulled" into this transference reaction, she was able to "contain" it and then "revert" the situation back to a therapeutic one. (The therapist did not move to next level, which would have resulted in "abandoning" the member(s) in some manner, e.g., ignoring.) Specifically, the therapist regained her position as the therapist of the group to whom the members looked for assistance in finding a solution to the group concern, which she did (at the end of the session) by offering suggestions about meeting while she was absent. (Also, returning after the break is strong proof that this "mother" will not "abandon her children.")

Since transference is the key factor that marks psychoanalytic-based group therapy as different from other types of group therapies, it will be discussed under the next chapter heading; specifically, Ginter and Bonney's (1993) conceptualization of transference reactions will be discussed in detail. According to Ginter and Bonney, transference reactions fall into three basic categories: client-only transference reactions (the client projects onto the therapist [or other member(s)] "images" from the past, e.g., the client sees the therapist [member(s)] as her own mother); therapist-only transference reactions (originally labeled *countertransference* by Freud, e.g., the therapist sees the group member as her own father); and Möbius reactions, where the projections are identified with by the recipient (e.g., the client sees the therapist as her abandoning mother and the therapist accepts this projected role and acts as the mother did in the past). Finally, projective identification may be thought of as an extrapsychic-intrapsychic *process* (Moxnes, 1999) that produces the *outcome* labeled the *Möbius interaction.*

During Möbius reactions, the psychological boundaries between the group member and the therapist (or other member[s]) become amorphous and are distorted in such a dramatic way that the interaction is one where distinctions become blurred, boundaries disappear, and a unique type of unity occurs. Such events represent a complex of mental, emotional, and social mechanisms. This type of projective identification process produces a form of reciprocal interweaving that hinders a true awareness of the projective identification occurrence in both the member and the group therapist.

Returning to and abstracting a segment of the group session (alluded to earlier) provides an opportunity to visually illustrate the distinctive nature of a Möbius type of transference reaction.

Mary: (pale with agitated hand movements) We have other things to do than coming here . . . it's not the only place . . . it's like all the others, anyway . . . you (therapist) lock it up good and proper when you go—or we shall break in and break your inside up? And keep it safe from us. (The group becomes very noisy; there is confused cross-talk, much shouting, and some pushing of chairs. The therapist cannot follow the talk. The impression is of shaking, banging, and stomping. The therapist feels anxious, alone, and worried that her clinic colleagues will be disturbed and angry with her. This lasts some five minutes or so, but it feels much longer.)

Figure 12.1 graphically illustrates both a classic Freudian transference reaction and a Möbius reaction based on the content of the preceding segment. The drawing labeled " 'Classic' Transference Reaction" is a type of interaction that is analogous to a strip of paper forming a circle. One side represents the flow of the group member's projections (e.g., fear of abandonment by the therapist who is seen as "mother"); the opposite side represents the group therapist's reactions (e.g., an objective interpretation

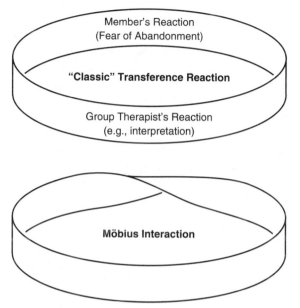

Fear of Abandonment Accepted by Group Therapist
and She Psychologically Abandons the Member

FIGURE 12.1   Differentiating Types of Transference Reactions

such as, "When you are confronted with a stressful situation you feel like I will not be supportive—you are afraid I will abandon you like your mother did years ago—you are afraid I will lock up what you need and deprive you. [pause of several seconds] This also seems to happen to you in other relationships during period of stress"). In this case, the therapist and member maintain a collocated interaction in which the therapist maintains a unique, distinct identity. The drawing labeled "Möbius interaction" (Figure 12.1) illustrates where the therapist unconsciously accepts the projection and experiences anxiety, loneliness, and worry, and senses that others will be disturbed and angry with her. As long as these feelings and thoughts are "held," the therapist will not be capable of rendering an objective interpretation of what has occurred. If held and contained too long, the therapist is likely to have a reaction that results in rejecting (abandoning) the group member.

This type of interaction is analogous to a Möbius strip. The Möbius strip is a special type of circle that can be illustrated by taking a strip of material such as paper and giving the material a half twist and then connecting the two ends together. After being formed, if a person placed his or her finger on what appears to be one side of the Möbius strip and then followed this side with his or her finger, the person would discover that the Möbius strip is literally one sided, not two sided. If the Möbius strip was cut in half following an imaginary line drawn down the middle of the strip, the cut would result in a large single band of material, not two separate strips.

Practice Considerations

It is important for the group therapist to *recognize* signs of a possible Möbius interaction. (Möbius reactions have the potential to stall therapeutic progress as well as further strengthen a member's dysfunctional interpersonal behavior, e.g., the group therapist now becomes the abusive father and the member once again responds in a subservient, emotionally starved manner.) A number of possible intrapsychic and extrapsychic markers exist during a group session that may denote a Möbius interaction:

- The group therapist consistently treats a particular member in an atypical manner compared to other members with similar complaints.
- Persistent and recurring feelings and/or thoughts are experienced by the group therapist that do not match events during a session.
- A prolonged series of vivid or unusual images are experienced by the group therapist that do not correspond to the overt content of what the group member is saying.
- The group therapist interacts with the member in a manner that matches the pattern of other relationships reported by the group member.

Again, as pointed out in the previous chapter, these occurrences differ from the experience of countertransference as originally hypothesized by Freud, because the "psychological spark" for the group therapist's transference experience originates with the member, not the therapist.

The primary task of the group therapist is to disrupt the Möbius interaction and prevent himself or herself from enacting the role created for him or her by the member's psychodynamic history. In the group illustration, the therapist "contained" the projections ("feels anxious, alone, and worried") and did not play the role of the mother who abandons the daughter. Such short-term containment without moving into the stage of role enactment is far from easy, but the difficulty associated with identifying and disrupting the Möbius interaction is certainly overshadowed by the therapeutic gains that can be made. The Möbius interaction corresponds to a central conflict of the group member that has taken on a tangible manifestation in the group—it can be observed and experienced by others. Thus, the member's conflict is no longer confined solely to the intrapsychic areas, but traverses both inner and outer realities.

The question becomes: What steps can be taken to invert the interpersonal "twist" of a Möbius interaction? It requires a four step process: *recognition* of a Möbius interaction occurring, *probing* the transference interaction, *confronting* the Möbius interaction and restructuring the member-therapist relationship, and *assessing* future group (and out-of-group) relationships for change. The three steps of probing, confronting, and assessing will be discussed next.

Probing.   During this phase, it is important to keep in mind the defensive nature of the projective identification. Although projective identification can be viewed as a front-line defense to protect the group member from some perceived threat in the group, it is often supplemented and supported by various defense mechanisms (e.g., denial, undoing, reaction formation, conversion, isolation, displacement, and rationalization). These latter defenses can precede, follow, or coincide with the projective identification occurrence. In relation to a Möbius interaction, these defenses can be viewed as a secondary means to maintain or reestablish stability between conflicting forces. In many instances, their occurrence can serve as an important clue, because they expose intrapsychic oppositional forces that fuel the projective identification process. Once the oppositional forces are identified and their presence validated by a genuine understanding of the member-group therapist interactions, the understanding can be used to guide various therapeutic interventions (e.g., refusal to play out the role of the mother who abandons).

Confronting. Group sessions should be structured in a manner to decrease the frequency that transference interactions will repeat themselves. Confronting the member by specifically pointing out tactics (e.g., helplessness, angry outburst) that the member relies on to pull and/or push the therapist (or other group members) into a Möbius interaction can be a means of facilitating client change. Because it can be assumed that the tactics relied on by the member can also occur outside the group sessions, the group therapist must explore with the member, at some point, how the identified tactics are manifesting themselves in other relationships, as well.

Transference-specific confrontation is defined as an interaction (verbal and/or nonverbal) initiated by the group therapist that draws the member's attention to his or her contributions to and reliance on a particular transference pattern. Furthermore, it is recommended that the group therapist not initially use self-disclosure to elicit insight in the member. The reason for this recommendation is that self-disclosure is more likely to create a strong emotional response that interferes with the type of basic insight needed for greater and deeper understanding of a transference interaction (Fitzpatrick, 1999). For example, let us say that a member's Möbius pattern typically results in being rejected by others (or eventually abandoned by others as in the group illustration). The therapist indicates that during most group sessions, he or she has felt distant and uncaring and wonders why. Such a response poorly orchestrated may be too intense for the member to achieve meaningful insight (and in this case could result in the member's decision to leave group therapy—a decision that would enhance the existence of this particular transference pattern).

Several comments made by Tansey and Burke (1989) are pertinent to the issues at hand. For instance, "an unfavorable outcome will be much less likely, though still possible, if the therapist has separated himself [or herself] sufficiently from the induced identification to intervene in a calm and evenhanded manner" (p. 144). Thus, it may be concluded that self-disclosure should be avoided initially; instead, a type of confrontation should be used that is not viewed by the member as representing an attack on the member's person. Finally, when self-disclosure is considered, its use must be carefully weighed in light of the therapeutic gains that have been achieved—keeping in mind that it is possible that self-disclosure may never be necessary or that its use may even be contraindicated for the remainder of therapy.

Although confrontation is one means to restructure the member-therapist relationship, another means is to resist identifying with a member's projection, as alluded to earlier. Kiesler (1982) provided one example of a procedure based on Leary's (1957) studies on interpersonal behavior that might enable a therapist to interpret interpersonal behaviors that occur between people. This procedure might also be used to ascertain how the therapist might counter the "pull" of a member. Kiesler's (1982) procedure allows for understanding a member's interpersonal behavior as part of an ongoing diagnosis process and allows for a prediction of what responses made by the therapist would be complementary (or noncomplementary) in relation to a member's projection. Operating from such a procedural base as Kiesler's may enable the therapist to optimize efforts.

Finally, when the group therapist is using confrontation, it is important to recognize that the transference interaction is not only a means to deal with conflictual threat but also an avenue for the member to feel connected with others in and outside the group. This need for connecting is basic and universal—a need that is experienced in some form by essentially everyone. (If the need were absent, group therapy would be impossible.) Although the Möbius interaction can denote a type of perverted connectedness (i.e., maladaptive interactions), its dynamics still serve to motivate the member to maintain relationships with others, including the group therapist. The implication is that during the early stages of group therapy, certain responses (i.e., misinterpretation of the dynamics of the transference interaction) will not only fail to invert the Möbius interaction but also could result in premature termination by the member or unnecessary referral by the group therapist.

Assessing Change: The Final Step.   The most effective type of assessment has elements that are process and outcome oriented as well as qualitative and quantitative oriented. This assessment must be ongoing. Kiesler (1982) astutely observed "that the therapist's prepotent assessment tool involves his or her own internal responses to the client" (p. 15). This remark highlights the importance that a group therapist can play as an assessment tool, a use of one's self that is certainly congruent with the arguments presented in this chapter and other sources (Ginter, 1989a, 1989b).

In addition to assessment of the member's psychological environment, there should be planned assessment of the member's interpersonal environments outside the group. The hallmark of successful psychoanalytic group therapy is that therapeutic change transfers beyond the confines of the in-group relationships (member to therapist, member to members). The significance of this last statement cannot be overemphasized, for it is generally recognized that outside relationships can sabotage in-session therapeutic gains achieved.

From an interpersonal perspective (Ginter, 1999), member change always has a ripple property that fans out to all current and future interactions. For example, Zinner and Shapiro (1989) wrote that a common phenomenon in family therapy occurs when "a previously asymptomatic parent becomes emotionally disturbed following independent activity and improvement in the clinical status of the adolescent" (p. 118) who had been in treatment. It should be assumed that even after the member has achieved significant movement, this achievement can be upset by preexisting transference patterns that the member has established with significant others. In the example just presented, familial pressures to return to the unhealthy status quo may serve to undo therapeutic gains unless the member himself or herself can avoid the pull of the intrapychic-extrapsychic residuals that remain from a previously established Möbius pattern—a pattern that has acquired a "life of its own" in the very fabric of the group member's interpersonal world established outside the group. (In some cases, these "pulls" from outside the psychotherapy group may very well have greater power than anything learned in the group, resulting in relapse in some cases. Effective intervention may have to extend beyond the four walls of the group room if gains are to persist.) Thus, it appears that a comprehensive assessment should include an evaluation of the client's interpersonal environment.

SUMMARY

The role that developmental histories play in a member's dysfunctional behavior was briefly discussed. Techniques were presented, with special attention paid to transference reactions. Following an excerpt from a psychoanalytic-based group therapy session, a detailed presentation was made concerning transference reactions—specifically, the type of transference reaction labeled a Möbius interaction. The importance of understanding the Möbius interaction is central to understanding contemporary psychoanalytic-based group work. In addition to representing a core element of therapeutic change, the Möbius interaction represents psychoanalytic-based therapy's long journey from using an intrapsychic approach to the contemporary state that recognizes the therapeutic necessity of an extrapsychic approach to group work. Finally, practice considerations (probing, confronting, and assessing intervention effects) were discussed in terms of transference.

REFERENCES

Allen, D. W. (1992). Hysterical patients and the obsessive personality. In M. J. Aronson & M. A. Scharfman (Eds.), *Psychotherapy: The analytic approach.* Northvale, NJ: Aronson.

Bacal, H. A., & Newman, K. M. (Eds.). (1990). *Theories of object relations: Bridges to self psychology.* New York: Columbia University Press.

Bonney, W. C. (1969). Group counseling and developmental processes. In G. M. Gazda (Ed.), *Theories and methods of group counseling in schools.* Springfield, IL: Charles C. Thomas.

Erikson, E. H. (1950). *Childhood and society.* New York: Norton.

Ettin, M. F. (1992). *Foundations and applications of group psychotherapy: A sphere of influence.* Boston: Allyn and Bacon.

Fairbairn, W. R. D. (1954). A revised psychopathology of the psychoses and psychoneuroses. In W. R. D. Fairburn (Ed.), *An object-relations theory of*

personality New York: Basic Books. (Original work published 1941)

Fitzpatrick, K. (1999). Term of endearment in clinical analysis. *Psychoanalytic Quarterly, LXVIII,* 119–125.

Foulkes, S. H. (1971). Access to unconscious processes in group analytic group. *Group Analysis, 4,* 4–14.

Foulkes, S. H. (1973). The group as a matrix of the individual's mental health. In L. R. Wolberg & E. K. Schwartz (Eds.), *Group therapy 1973.* New York: Stratton Intercontinental Medical Books.

Foulkes, S. H. (1975). *Group-analytic psychotherapy, method and principles.* London: Gordon and Breach Sciences Publishers.

Freud, S. (1958). *On the treatment (further recommendations on the technique of psychoanalysis).* In J. Strachey (Ed.), Standard edition (Vol. 12).

London: Hogarth Press and the Institute of Psychoanalysis. (Orginal work published 1913)

Gazda, G. M. (1982). *Basic approaches to group psychotherapy and group counseling* (3rd ed.). Springfield, IL: Charles C. Thomas

Ginter, E. J. (1989a). Slayers of monster-watermelons found in the mental health patch. *Journal of Mental Health Counseling, 11,* 77–85.

Ginter, E. J. (1989b). If you meet Moses/Jesus/Mohammed/Buddha (or associate editors of theory) on the road, kill them! *Journal of Mental Health Counseling, 11,* 335–344.

Ginter, E. J. (1999). David K. Brooks' contribution toward establishing a developmentally based life-skills approach to mental health counseling. *Journal of Mental Health Counseling, 21,* 191–202.

Ginter, E. J., & Bonney, W. (1993). Freud, ESP, and interpersonal relationships: Projective identification and the Möbius interaction. *Journal of Mental Health Counseling, 15,* 150–170.

Jacobson, E. (1964). *The self and the object world.* New York: International Universities Press.

Kiesler, D. J. (1982). Interpersonal theory for personality and psychotherapy. In J. C. Anchin & D. J. Kiesler (Eds.), *Handbook of interpersonal psychotherapy.* New York: Pergamon.

Kernberg, O. (1976). *Object relations theory and clinical psychoanalysis.* New York: Aronson.

Klein, M. (1975). *The psycho-analysis of children.* New York: Delta Books. (Original work published 1932)

Kohut, H. (1977). *The restoration of the self.* New York: International Universities Press.

Lacoursiere, R. (1980). *The life cycle of groups: Group development stage theory.* New York: Human Sciences Press.

Leary, T. (1957). *Interpersonal diagnosis of personality: A functional theory and methodology for personality evaluation.* New York: Ronald Press.

Luboborsky, L. (1984). *Principles of psychoanalytic psychotherapy: A manual for supportive-expressive treatment.* New York: Basic Books.

Mahler, C. A. (1969). *Group counseling in the schools.* Boston: Houghton Mifflin.

Mahler, M. S., Pine, F., & Bergman, A. (1975). *The psychological birth of the human infant.* New York: Basic Books.

Mann, R. D., Gibbard, G., & Hartman, S. (1967). *Interpersonal styles and group development.* New York: Wiley.

Mills, T. (1964). *Group transformation: An analysis of a learning group.* Englewood Cliffs, NJ: Prentice-Hall.

Moxnes, P. (1999). Understanding roles: A psychodynamic model for role differentiation in groups. *Group Dynamics: Theory, Research, and Practice, 3,* 99–113.

Patton, M. J., & Meara, N. (1992). *Psychoanalytic counseling.* New York: Wiley.

Scharfman, M. A. (1992). The treatment of eating disorders. In M. J. & M. A. Scharfman (Eds.), *Psychotherapy: The analytic approach.* Northvale, NJ: Aronson.

Tansey, M. J., & Burke, W. F. (1989). *Understanding countertransference: From projective identification to empathy.* Hillsdale, NJ: Analytic Press.

Tuckman, B. (1965). Developmental sequence in small groups. *Psychological Bulletin, 63,* 384–399.

Tuckman, B., & Jensen, M. (1977). Stages of small-group development revisited. *Group Organizational Studies, 2,* 419–427.

Winnicott, D. W. (1958). *Maturational processes and the facilitating environment.* New York: International Universities Press.

Wolf, A., & Schwartz, E. (1962). *Psychoanalysis in groups.* New York: Grune & Stratton.

Zinner, J., & Shapiro, R. L. (1989). Projective identification as a mode of perception and behavior in families of adolescents. In J. S. Scharff (Ed.), *Foundations of object relations family therapy.* New York: Aronson.

CHAPTER THIRTEEN

DEVELOPMENTAL GROUP COUNSELING

An Integrated Approach

Thus far, no systematic attempt has been made to provide an approach to group *counseling* applicable to all age levels. Previous attempts have singled out methods of group counseling with children, with adolescents, or with adults. Slavson (1945), however, long ago recognized the need for differential treatment for different age groups in group *therapy.* "Group therapy," he said, "is practiced on different levels, and in discussing its functions in therapy, it is necessary that these levels be kept in mind" (p. 201).

Experience also demonstrated the need for a position that especially allows for and accommodates a different emphasis with different age groups in group counseling. The developmental approach to interview group counseling, activity-interview group counseling, and play group counseling therefore uses the developmental task concept (Havighurst, 1948, 1952, 1953) with subsequent coping behaviors to serve as broad guidelines for the group counselor and life-skills leader. Havighurst (1952) defined *developmental task* as follows:

> A developmental task is a task which arises at or about a certain period in the life of the individual, successful achievement of which leads to his happiness and to success with later tasks, while failure leads to unhappiness in the individual, disapproval by society, and difficulty with later tasks. (p. 2)

Havighurst (1952) also cited two reasons why the concept of developmental task is useful to educators. His reasons seem equally applicable to counselors and life-skills trainers: "First, it helps in discovering and stating the purpose of education [group counseling] in the schools. . . . The second use of the concept is in the timing of educational [group counseling] efforts" (p. 5). He described timing to mean *teachable moment* (p. 5). Readiness for group counseling is determined by the dissonance between the developmental task and its subsequent coping behavior.

Zaccaria (1965) gave a more comprehensive interpretation of developmental tasks than did Havighurst. His interpretation included Havighurst's (1952) "bio-socio-psychological" emphasis, the "vocational development" emphasis of Super and colleagues (1957, 1963), and Erikson's (1950, 1959, 1963) "psychosocial crises."

In addition to accepted classification of human development along psychosocial and vocational domains, there are well-defined developmental stages in the physical-sexual area (Gesell, Ilg, & Ames, 1956; Gesell, Ilg, Ames, & Bullis, 1946), the cognitive area, à la Piaget (Flavell, 1963; Wadsworth, 1971; Zigler & Child, 1973), the moral area, according to Kohlberg (Duska & Whelan, 1975; Kohlberg, 1973; Kohlberg & Turiel, 1971), the ego developmental stages of Loevinger (1976), and the affective stages of Dupont (1978, 1979). When individuals are viewed along these seven areas of human development, one can obtain a rather complete picture of them. Using these developmental parameters to gauge normal progress in one's total development puts one in a unique position to provide timely assistance in the area(s) (tasks) where mastery is lagging.

Cognitive, moral, ego, and affective developmental *stage* theorists differ from the physical-sexual, psychosocial, and vocational *age* developmental theorists insofar as they do not generally relate stage development in these areas to age development. Therefore, using the developmental models places certain interpretive restrictions on the counselor, since he or she cannot evaluate stage development based on age development. Nevertheless, certain general classifications can be made. Research by Brooks (1984) showed that the developmental tasks could be classified according to the developmental age group: childhood, adolescence, and adulthood. Furthermore, Figure 13.1 illustrates that the seven areas of human development could be collapsed into four generic life-skill areas: interpersonal communication/human relations, physical fitness/ health maintenance, identity development/purpose in life, and problem solving/ decision making. In turn, these generic life skills are utilized and developed in four settings: home and family, school, work, and the community at large.

The United States and much of the rest of Western culture is organized on the basis of expected progressive development in the biological, intellectual, vocational,

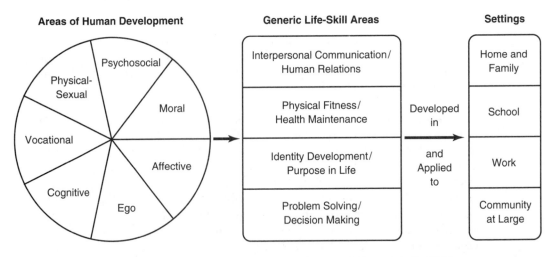

FIGURE 13.1   A Model for the Development and Application of Generic Life Skills

sociological, and psychological realms of its citizens, and as such, the concept of developmental task has general applicability. For example, schools are organized on a preschool and kindergarten, early elementary school, middle school, and high school basis; state laws govern marriageable ages of its citizens; federal laws govern legal retirement age; and so forth (Muuss, 1962).

Although there are variations in individual biological, social, intellectual, vocational, and psychological development, there are classifiable periods between and within age groups. Several individuals (Blocher, 1974; Brammer & Shostrom, 1960; Erikson, 1950; Havighurst, 1952; Super et al., 1957, 1963) have developed various classification schemes for the developmental phases. For group counseling purposes, the phases can be divided into (1) early childhood or preschool and early school, ages 5 to 9; (2) preadolescent, ages 9 to 13; (3) adolescent, ages 13 to 20; and (4) adult. That there is sometimes considerable overlap between age groups is well documented. There is also a special discrepancy between the sexes at the end of the latency period and the beginning of pubescence—beginning from ages 8 to 13 for girls and 10 to 15 for boys.

Group counselors therefore must be alert to individual differences and organize their groups to accommodate them. The emphasis of our approach begins with the kindergarten child of age 5.

THEORETICAL FOUNDATIONS: BASIC ASSUMPTIONS OF THE DEVELOPMENTAL GROUP COUNSELING MODEL FOR ALL AGES

The position taken in the developmental group counseling model for all ages is that humans are endowed with *free will* and therefore have the capacity to make choices, for "good or evil." Certain people who are brain-damaged, severely retarded, or acutely disturbed may be exempted from this hypothesis to varying degrees. Even "normals," because of their condition of birth, may have varying degrees or spheres within which they can exercise free will. However, a further assumption is made that humans have a conscience that cannot be reduced to the consequences of learning father images, or anything else. This conscience lies in what may be called tensions of the human spirit (Fabry, 1980). Frankl (cited in Fabry, 1980) put it this way: "To be human means to be caught in the tensions between what we are and what we are meant to be, to be aware that we do not need to remain the way we are but can always change" (pp. 84–85).

In his book *Life after Life,* Moody (1975) contended that persons clinically dead experienced a powerful need to respond to an out-of-body experience that urged them to strive "to know and to love." Assuming that this "healthy" human tension exists, humans would appear to possess an innate need to know and to understand. This need, then, provides a basis for many of the *educational* and *insight*-generating assumptions underlying this model. The remainder of this chapter will describe the rationale for the application of the model to each of three specific age groups. The next chapter contains examples of applications and techniques.

GROUP COUNSELING FOR THE PRESCHOOL
AND EARLY SCHOOL CHILD: THE PLAY GROUP

Although much has been written about *play* therapy, only one book, according to Landreth (1991), has been devoted entirely to *group* play therapy: Ginott's (1961) *Group Psychotherapy with Children: The Theory and Practice of Play Therapy.* Actually, Schiffer (1969) also published a book devoted to the play therapy group, titled *The Therapeutic Play Group.* Both Ginott and Schiffer were influenced by Slavson, and therefore these books present a similar rationale and methodology.

For the purposes of group treatment, preschool and early school includes the ages from approximately 5 to 9. "Little is known as to what the values of a group to a child of 3 or 4 may be," according to Slavson (1945, p. 203). Schiffer (1969) went further than Slavson and stated that "children up to the age of four years, approximately, who have emotional disturbances of a functional type, are best treated by female therapists through individual therapy, because their disturbances are reactive to faults in experience and errors in parent management especially involving the mother" (p. 99).

Play Techniques

The primary mode of group counseling for children ages 5 to 9 involves play and action. Schiffer (1969) and Slavson (1945, 1948) have advocated play group therapy for young children less than 12 years of age, and we concur with them. (O'Connor [1991] has recommended structured activity oriented group therapy for children 6 to 12 years.)

We prefer to refer to group play therapy as *group play techniques* or *play group counseling* when it is applied to basically normal children who are not hospitalized. Although the basic rationale for emphasizing play and action techniques for this age group is the same, whether it be play therapy or play techniques or play group counseling, the degree of disturbance of the child, the training of the therapist (counselor), and the setting are different. We discourage school personnel from working with seriously disturbed children and from doing "therapy" in the school setting unless they are sufficiently trained at the doctoral level in school counseling, counseling psychology, school psychology, or clinical psychology. Nevertheless, when one considers the various processes of therapy that are currently practiced—save for psychopharmacological, electroshock, and surgical therapies—there is probably very little reason to insist that a therapist be required to receive training in medicine, or for that matter, at the doctoral level in other disciplines, although doctoral-level training should provide the therapist or counselor with greater sophistication of techniques and, it is hoped, with higher-level ethical practices. In other words, there is no reason why most group play therapy techniques cannot be modified for use by counselors in the school and community mental health settings, providing the group members are not seriously disturbed and the counselor is trained in group counseling and play techniques and has the appropriate playroom facilities and play media available.

Lebo (1955) has credited Rosseau as the first to recommend that children be educated through play, although Klein (1955) has taken credit for the development in 1919 of psychoanalytic play techniques.

Harms (1948) has referred to play as the "language of childhood" (p. 237), and Frank (1955) has stated that "in play we . . . observe various themes or schemes in which this [child's] immediate concerns are focused and more or less symbolically played out" (p. 585). Frank also has referred to play as "learning to learn: [coping] with life tasks" (p. 583). It is generally agreed that all psychotherapy constitutes some form of learning. Axline (1955) has succinctly conveyed our feelings on this issue in the following assertion regarding learning and psychotherapy: "It [psychotherapy] seems to be a cumulative, compound, integrative, effective experience that can be used to illustrate many learning theories. At the same time, it raises many questions as to the adequacy of any existing theory to explain conclusively the learning experience that occurs during psychotherapy" (p. 622).

Axline (1969) has explained the value of play therapy as follows: "Play therapy is based upon the fact that play is the child's natural medium of self-expression. It is an opportunity which is given to the child to 'play out' his feelings and problems just as in certain types of adult therapy, an individual 'talks out' his difficulties" (p. 9).

In regard to therapeutic play, Conn (1951) has stated, "Every therapeutic play method is a form of learning process during which the child learns to accept and to utilize constructively that degree of personal responsibility and self-discipline necessary for effective self-expression and social living" (p. 753).

Lowrey (1955) has argued that "we should be more accurate if we spoke of 'activity' (or activities) instead of 'play' with reference to therapy. For it is the activity with its release of fantasy, imagery, fears, hostility, and other feeling and thoughts which give us quick insights into the problems besetting our child patients" (p. 574). Until now, we have been speaking of play therapy without regard to its use in groups. What are the unique features or values that play in a group setting offers? Slavson (1945) has claimed that the function of the group in the treatment of young children lies in three areas: "(1) play and activity; (2) association with other children of the same age; [and] (3) the role of the worker [therapist]" (p. 208). The play and activity, according to Ginott (1961), should facilitate contact with the child, catharsis, insight, reality testing, and sublimation.

Slavson (1945) also has stated that in all instances the value of a group to children

> lies in the fact it supplies a field in which the child may relate himself to others, thus helping him to break through isolation, withdrawal, and aggressive rejection of people . . . to go out . . . into the human environment, thus leading from egocentricity and narcissism to object relationships . . . to test himself against others and discover the boundaries of his ego. . . . [Group therapy] offers the possibility of developing patterns of relationship with human beings of the same intellectual, emotional, and social development, in which the feeling of sameness and therefore of comfort and security is greatest. (p. 209)

The role of the group leader or "worker," according to Slavson (1945), varies with the age of the children. Leaders are more active with the young child who is dependent on them for support, and, of necessity, for young children, much of the authority must come from the therapist. The leader's role changes both with the ages of the children and their changing personalities. "While [the leader] functions at first as a source of security and support, his role changes to one of guidance and authority" (Slavson, 1945, p. 209).

Some specific values attached to play therapy are suggested by Solomon (1955). It is his belief that through

> the use of play, the child is able to express his own regressive tendencies, thereby lessening the need to act out such forms of behavior in his real life situation . . . and the release of aggression or hostility with its appropriate emotion, that of anger, and the lessening of fears through the amelioration of the catastrophic results from the expression of the primitive impulses of gains which accrue from the judicious use of play therapy. (p. 594)

Solomon (1940) has summarized the therapeutic values of play therapy as follows: "(1) release of hostility toward parents, siblings, etc.; (2) alleviation of guilt feelings; (3) opportunity to express freely all love fantasies; (4) incorporation of therapeutic suggestions in direction of growth; and (5) desensitization by means of repetition" (p. 763).

Amster (1943) succinctly conveyed part of our purpose for advocating the use of play and action techniques when she stated:

> Essentially play is an activity a child comprehends and in which he is comfortable, an integral part of his world, his method of communication, his medium of exchange, and his means of testing, partly incorporating and mastering external realities.
> . . . Provision of play materials means the provision of a natural means of communication, through which the child's problems may be expressed more readily and the treatment more likely to succeed.
> In treatment of children, play is always a medium of exchange and it is comparable to words, the adult's medium of exchange. It is not a therapy in itself any more than words can be. All therapies require a therapeutic relationship and a medium of exchange. The purpose of the play activity determines its role and importance in treatment. Therefore, play as a medium differs from play as a technique even as words differ from any purposive use of them. Play is a technique when it is used in treatment for definite diagnostic and therapeutic purposes. (p. 62)

Amster (1943)* has listed and defined six uses of play:

1. Play can be used for diagnostic understanding of the child. . . . We can observe the child's capacity to relate himself to others, his distractibility, his rigidity, his areas of preoccupation, his areas of inhibition, the direction of his aggression, his perception of people, his wishes, and his perception of himself. In the play, his behavior, ideas, feeling, and expressions help our understanding of his problem and how he sees it. (p. 63)
2. Play can be used to establish a working relationship. This use of play is helpful with the young child who lacks the adult's facility for verbal self-expression and with the older child who shows resistance or inability to articulate. (p. 64)

*From F. Amster, "Differential Uses of Play in Treatment of Young Children," *American Journal of Orthopsychiatry, 13,* no. 1 (1943): 62–68. Copyright © 1943 by the American Orthopsychiatric Association, Inc. Reproduced by permission.

3. Play can be used to break through a child's way of playing in his daily life and his defenses against anxiety. This use is helpful as an additional way of treating distortions in a child's way of playing. (p. 65)
4. Play can be used to help a child verbalize certain conscious material and associated feelings. This use is helpful when a child blocks in discussing certain materials and an impasse in treatment is created. (p. 65)
5. Play can be used to help a child act out unconscious material and to relieve the accompanying tension. This cathartic use of play deals with symbolic material which has dangerous significance to the child. The therapist must be aware of how much release in play the particular child can tolerate without panic and must be aware of the kind of participation and interpretation in which to engage. (p. 67)
6. Play can be used to develop a child's play interests which he can carry over into his daily life and which will strengthen him for his future life. This use of play has particular importance because of the correlation between the play and work capacities of an individual. (p. 67)

O'Connor (1991) addressed the curative elements in play therapy as follows:

> Within the play therapy, it is the experiential aspect of the play sessions that is viewed as the essential aspect of the treatment process. Without corrective experiences, the activities in the session become therapeutic play at best and repetitions of the child's dysfunctional past at worst. The therapist must be able to conceptualize the type of experiences that will foster the correction of those of the child's: past experience, present assumptions about the workings of the world, patterns of behavior and social interaction, and, finally, the child's developmental lags. (p. 101)

As applied to group setting, O'Connor (1991) emphasized, "For a child to try a new behavior and be reinforced by peers is a more powerful and curative experience than any amount of discussion in which he might engage with you as either an individual therapist or even as the group leader" (p. 330).

(For a presentation of the major theoretical positions of *play* therapy—not group play therapy—see O'Connor and Braverman's [1997] *Play Therapy Theory and Practice.*)

On the other side of the ledger, Bender (1955) wrote:

> If the play technique used is important to the adult and gives him a tool with which he can understand the child and relate to him with confidence and warmth, the play setup will undoubtedly contribute to the relationship. Beyond this I doubt if there is any specific therapeutic value to the play procedures. (p. 785)

Nelson (1972) has cautioned that play activities may distract the child who is ready to deal directly with a problem and thus interfere with communication.

Principles of Learning Related to Play
and Action Methods: Modeling

A small group represents a slice of society. Its composition determines how closely it will represent the society of a given member. Group counseling provides an opportunity for social learning or behavior change that is maximized by the presence (modeling) of other individuals. Whether the group setting is the preferred mode for assisting a given individual's behavior and feelings of self-worth depends on many factors discussed later in this chapter. The topic of import at this point is how to maximize opportunities for behavioral change for the young child from the ages of 5 to 9. Play and action-oriented techniques such as sociodrama, child drama, and psychodrama are natural media or modes through which young children communicate and express themselves; therefore, following the emphasis on developmental group procedures, the group counselor is encouraged to take advantage of these media. In addition to maximizing the relationship-engendering procedures through the use of play and action methods, group counselors must also use relevant learning principles if their counseling armamentarium is to be complete. In the following paragraphs, a model will be developed that will assist practicing group counselors in their understanding and treatment of young children in groups. Young children have not developed their verbal facility to a high level, and thus verbally loaded (interview-type) group treatment is of limited value. Young children in particular are dependent on the imitation (modeling) of others for much of their learning. It is because of their relatively low verbal facility and also because of their relatively undeveloped behavioral repertoires, that combinations of modeling and operant conditioning models may be used in modifying their behavior.

Modeling, sometimes referred to as *no-trial learning* or *observational learning* (Bandura, 1965, 1986), can be a very efficient method for changing the behavior of the young child. A model can exhibit a preferred way of behaving, relating, or problem solving. This real-life model can be a peer or the adult group counselor or both. It is apparent that the peer and adult models must be capable of providing exemplary behavior; peers must be chosen with care to ensure mutual helpfulness. The group counselor, too, must be able to model appropriately. (Peer selection will be discussed later in this chapter.)

Rose (1973) described the modeling procedure as "a set of therapist activities designed to increase the observer's probability of matching behavior" and listed eight procedures for the simulated modeling sequence (1998):

1. Orientation of the group members to the modeling sequence
2. Determination of a set of interactive behaviors in which one or several members of the group are deficient
3. Modeling (or demonstration) of a behavior or given sequence of behaviors
4. Behavioral rehearsal (or practice by the client of the modeled behaviors)
5. Coaching (the giving of hints or prompts to the target person while he or she is rehearsing)
6. Group feedback (after the rehearsal, the evaluation of what the target person did well and could consider doing differently)
7. Re-rehearsal (repeating the practice until the given client is comfortable and correcting for feedback)
8. The negotiation of an extra group task (in which the client designs a task and tries out in the real world what he or she has learned in the group). (p. 225)

Rose may use each of these procedures independently of each other and with other procedures not included in the sequence. (According to Rose, modeling procedures lend themselves especially to group treatment because the group contains an abundance of potential models, new models can be introduced without seriously disrupting the existing social patterns, multiperson role-playing can be used, and group pressures can be stimulated to encourage imitation.)

In addition to modeling opportunities made available through group peers and the counselor, symbolic models can be presented in the playroom in the form of dolls and puppets and verbally through counselor-read stories, counselor-led puppet plays, and psychodrama. Structured play settings will give the counselor the greatest control over modeling, since the counselor will be able to recreate the setting, character, and other factors responsible for precipitating and maintaining the child's problem behavior (Hambridge, 1993). (Structured play and modeling may be the equivalent of simulation or gaming techniques applied to older groups.) Since the structured problem situation may be anxiety producing for the young child, it should be introduced only after the group counselor has developed a strong base of mutual trust and understanding in the free-play situation used in the early stages of treatment. Free play can also provide the group counselor an opportunity to validate a diagnosis of the child's problem based on interview and case history data.

Research studies such as those of Chittenden (1942), Bandura, Ross, and Ross (1963), Beach (1967), Hansen, Niland, and Zani (1969), and Liebert, Sprafkin, and Davidson (1982) demonstrated that symbolic or vicarious modeling can produce change similar to real-life models. In vicarious modeling, the counselor or someone in a story, in a movie, on TV, or in puppet play rewards certain characters for prosocial behaviors and punishes the characters in pantomime, verbally, or both ways for asocial and antisocial behavior. Through the use of vicarious modeling, the group counselor can structure the kind and amount of modeling opportunities that seem necessary to modify a child's behavior.

Psychodrama or role-playing can also be used to involve all the members in the counseling or play group in minimally structured areas of problem behaviors. In the psychodrama, the group counselor is the director, one of the children is the protagonist or the person with an avowed problem, and the other children become the auxiliary egos. A vicarious psychodrama can be created from puppet characters, with the counselor assuming all roles and structuring the problem and its resolution as he or she chooses.

Modeling as described here is, first of all, a method for producing new learning. Bandura (1965) explained this occurrence by postulating the existence of component responses in the person's behavioral repertoire of prior learning that are reproduced in unique combinations by new stimuli. Second, he postulated that

> exposure to models may also strengthen or weaken inhibitory responses in the observer. . . . Reinforcers administered to a model undoubtedly serve a discriminative function signifying the probably reinforcement contingencies associated with the modeled classes or responses. In addition, rewarding consequences may result in vicarious extinction of inhibitory responses. Conversely, observed aversive outcomes tend to establish conditioned emotional responses . . . that help to support avoidant and inhibitory repertoires. (p. 321)

A third effect of modeling, according to Bandura (1965), is that

> the behavior of models may elicit previously learned responses that match precisely or
> bear some resemblance to those exhibited by the model. This response facilitation
> effect can be distinguished from disinhibition when the behavior in question is not
> likely to have incurred punishment and, therefore, any increase in responsivity is not
> attributable to the reduction of inhibitory responses. (p. 321)

It is not our intention to portray modeling (real-life or vicarious) as the only
method or learning principle applicable to the young child treated in a play group setting. Modeling and various conditioning procedures should be viewed as complementary methods for modifying or shaping behavior. Illustrations of the combined use of
modeling and social reinforcement procedures to increase the assertiveness of relatively inhibited children are provided in early studies by Jack (1934) and Page (1936).
Also, the acquisition of psychomotor skills governed largely by proprioceptive stimuli
that are not observable or easily described verbally requires more than modeling. Varying amounts of overt practice in addition to modeling are usually necessary in the
acquisition of psychomotor skills (Bandura, 1965, 1986).

Since "self-administered primary and conditioned rewards may frequently over-
weigh the influence of external stimuli in governing social behavior" (Bandura, 1965,
pp. 331–332), children's self-concept or feelings of worth may very well be a significant determinant of the ease and/or degree to which they can learn from a good model.
Thus the necessity of "relationship therapy" or, as Carkhuff (1969a, 1969b) would
describe it, building a strong facilitative base through the use of empathy, respect, and
warmth, cannot be ignored in treatment. Otherwise, the more action-oriented principles, such as modeling and conditioning, will prove to be of limited applicability.
Arnold Lazarus (1968), a well-respected behavioral therapist, has stated that "there is
nothing in modern learning theory to justify withholding the combined advantages of
interpretation and desensitization, or any other method or technique which seems to
have beneficial effects" (p. 155).

Prerequisites for Effective Modeling

In order to assure that modeling is effective, certain conditions need to be satisfied.
Rose (1982a, Chapter 15; 1998, Chapter 4) has succinctly summarized these prerequisite conditions. Some of the attributes that may increase the effectiveness of the model
include demonstrated competence in areas highly regarded by the observer; possession
of general renown as perceived by the observer; possession of some of the observer's
population attributes (such as race, sex, age, and experience); possession of skill status
that the observer could realistically expect to achieve; and possession of power as perceived by the observer. If most of the prerequisite conditions have been observed during one or more modeled interactions and if these modeled behaviors are practiced in a
supportive group or in the real world, the likelihood of the modeled behaviors being
performed in the real world is increased (Bandura, 1977).

Bandura (cited in Rose, 1972) has shown that dependency on the model by the
counselee increases the probability of imitation. Therefore, Rose suggested that the

therapist can foster counselee dependency early in the relationship through maintaining a high degree of structure, providing physical assistance, and providing direct advice. However, as the counseling or therapy progresses, one would reduce the dependency-inducing behaviors. Bandura also discovered that reinforcement of the model increased the likelihood that the counselee would match the model's behavior, especially when the reward was given in the presence of the counselee. He found, furthermore, that the frequency of the matching response is reduced when the model is directly or vicariously punished. "Far more powerful than any of the above characteristics, however, is the incentive control of observing behaviors" (Bandura, 1969, p. 137). "For this reason, whenever possible, models should be reinforced in the presence of the observer and observers should be reinforced for successful duplication of the modeled behavior" (Rose, 1982a, p. 475).

Another prerequisite for achieving successful modeling appears to be worth citing. Bandura (1969) found that "modeled characteristics that are highly discernible can be more readily acquired than subtle attributes, which must be abstracted from homogeneous responses differing on numerous stimulus dimensions" (p. 136). In other words, Bandura's (1986) research suggests that complex behaviors will need to be simplified or divided into related parts to ensure ease and success of imitation.

Even though young children acquire much of what they learn through imitation, Rose (1973) called attention to the difficulty that younger children (ages 4 to 8) have with imitation. In order to ensure greater success, he suggested the use of matching games in the first meeting (e.g., the members imitating a social or task role such as father, mechanic, or baseball player or the leader telling a story with words and actions that the group repeats).

Bandura (1986) and Rose (1982a, 1998) have posited that the modeling effect is enhanced by three other procedures: behavior rehearsal, coaching, and group feedback.

Behavior Rehearsal.   *Behavior rehearsal* is defined by Rose (1982a) as "the simulated reproduction or role play of modeled or conceptually described behavior by the client" (p. 475).

Sturm (1965) suggested that behavioral rehearsal in comparison to other techniques has "a far greater potential to (1) generate vivid lifelike behavior and cues, thereby maximizing the utility of response and stimulus generalization; (2) condition a total behavioral response—physiological, motoric, and ideational—rather than merely verbal; and (3) dispense the powerful reinforcements of enacted models and other characters, who in real life or in fantasy have already dispensed reinforcements" (p. 57). Behavior rehearsal approximates a real-life experience and appeals to the young child who enjoys role-playing, thus facilitating new learning.

Coaching.   According to Rose (1982a), Oden and Asher (1977) have described *coaching* "as a training method that relies heavily on the verbal transmission of cues, concepts, and rules in the performance of a target behavior in a simulated or real stress situation" (p. 475). Rose (1982a) has pointed out that in groups, the " 'coach' (the group therapist or a group member) sits behind the actor in a role-play and whispers behaviors, rules, or principles that the actor needs to consider during the role-play. Occasionally, cue cards are used instead of coaches. When coaching is used, it is generally faded in subsequent role plays" (pp. 475–476).

Group Feedback.   Rose (1982a) defined *group feedback* as "a set of verbal responses by group members to a given individual about his or her overt or covert behavior and effectiveness, or other characteristics of handling a given situation" (p. 476). According to Rose, feedback is likely to be facilitative if it provides adequate, but not excessive, amounts of information; if it helps to identify other responsibilities and alternatives; if effective components of performance are pointed out prior to discussing ineffective components; and if clients are trained in the giving and receiving of constructive feedback in practice exercises.

Group feedback usually follows behavioral rehearsal, and occasionally it follows modeling. Group feedback may be used in later sessions to provide counselors with peer impressions of their achievements both in and out of the group (Rose, 1982a, 1998).

Application of a Developmental Approach to Group Counseling for Children 5 to 9 Years of Age

The following descriptors (see Gazda, 1989) in the problem-solving/decision-making life-skills area have been used in selecting three children for inclusion in play group counseling: "is able to be goal-directed, understands cause-and-effect relationships, is able to work independently on a task, and tries new methods of problem solving." These children have been assessed by their teachers and counselors, and appear to have deficits and strengths in one or more of these tasks. Each child was selected to serve as a model in one or more of these tasks; in addition, each child also required help in developing age-appropriate skill levels in one or more of the tasks.

Mark is an 8-year-old boy who has difficulty working independently; however, he is goal directed and is receptive to trying different methods of problem solving. Elaine is an 8-year-old girl who has difficulty understanding the cause-and-effect relationship of her behavior but she is able to work independently. Richard is an 8-year-old boy who is fearful of the future and reluctant to take risks by using creative problem-solving procedures; however, he is goal directed.

The counselor uses a free-play setting for the first three or four sessions. She meets the group for 45 minutes and holds the session in a playroom. During this time, the children can play with a variety of toys and materials. The counselor shows an interest in each child and makes every effort to establish rapport or build the base or mutual trust and liking for one another. After the base has been established, the counselor begins to structure the last half of each play session. At first, she does this through story reading and telling and through the use of puppets. She introduces vicarious models in this way and verbally rewards appropriate behavior. Moving from puppets to dolls, she structures situations and asks the children to use the dolls to work out solutions. She rewards appropriate solutions verbally and asks for replays of inappropriate solutions until they approach appropriate coping behavior for dealing with the tasks.

As the children show progress with vicarious modeling, the counselor also sets up sociodramas and psychodramas revolving around school and family situations for the group to use in modifying their behavior. Finally, the counselor moves into the realm of the here-and-now relationship between herself and each child and those between the children. She models for the children by encouraging their appropriate independence from her and also by rewarding appropriate dependence.

The play and action-selected media are used to promote relationship development and problem resolution and are not, therefore, in themselves the primary focus of the treatment. The counselor is always conscious of the timing of her moves and of the purpose of her techniques. She moves from the least threatening situations in the beginning to the more threatening, but more relevant, procedures as the children show signs of growth. The preceding procedure or model provides ample opportunity for vicarious and real-life modeling and numerous opportunities for implementing other learning principles of desensitization, shaping, operant conditioning, discriminate and assertive training, and reciprocal inhibition. The deliberate use of these principles represents the science of play group counseling, whereas the when and how of implementing them represent the art of this form of treatment.

Although the position in this illustration (and in this text) is that play group counseling held in a playroom is the method of choice for children of approximately 5 to 9 years of age, various skills training groups are also encouraged. Most of these groups are structured and time limited, especially when held in the school setting, but also when held in out-of-school clinics. Success has been demonstrated using structured groups, for example, in elementary school children of divorce in grades 3 to 6 (Anderson, Kinney, & Gerler, 1984), for 8- and 9-year-old boys with learning and behavior problems (Mishne, 1971), sexually abused 11- and 12-year-old inner-city girls (Kitchur & Bell, 1989), and for children with social-skills deficits (Edleson, 1981; Rose, 1982b), to cite only a representative sample. Often, concurrent parent counseling or family counseling groups are held in conjunction with these skills-training groups, especially in the case of divorce. (See Chapter 15 for a comprehensive presentation of social/life-skills training.)

Selection and Group Composition

As with other age groups, there is virtually no sound research on preferred ways of selecting and composing a counseling group for the child from 5 to 9 years old. During this period of development, except for the more mature children in the 8- to 9-year-old bracket, children rely heavily on the adult or older siblings as their model(s). For this reason, the group counselor has more direct control over what happens in a counseling group with 5- to 9-year-olds than with other age groups. Nevertheless, careful selection and grouping for maximum positive mutual influence is still of prime importance.

The following suggestions are given as guidelines for selecting children for play group counseling:

1. The best predictor of what children will do in a play group is what they in fact do in a similar group, such as a trial group similar to the treatment or play group. The best combinations or those who show the greatest mutually therapeutic interactions should be selected a soon as they can be identified for the permanent group. (Schiffer [1969] recommended two or three preplacement sessions with children who have been tentatively selected for a play group to reveal potential selection problems.)

2. When open-ended groups are conducted, the counselor must try to replace children who have completed treatment with those who can fill the role being vacated. This choice should be based on previous group behavior of the prospective group member, but actual behavior may require removing children from the group if their behavior is detrimental to themselves and the group. (Schiffer [1969] recommends a *closed* group for children or removal or replacement soon after the group has started to avoid fear of removal by the remaining children or psychological dislocation for a "new" or added child.)

The concept of role balancing (Schiffer [1969] called it *psychological balance*) is suggested as a rule of thumb to follow. This means that one should avoid overloading a group with a particular behavior type, such as aggressive, hyperactive children, but rather include a hyperactive or aggressive child in a group, including a calm, self-reliant child as well as a withdrawn child and perhaps one other child of a behavioral type that will provide a model for one of the other three. With respect to composition and group balance, Schamess (1993) had this to say:

> Functional balance is achieved by selecting group members who differ in diagnosis, defensive organization, and pattern of interpersonal interaction. Corrective peer interaction is most likely to take place in groups that contain inhibited, superego-bound children who are constricted affectively and behaviorally and children with conduct disorders and impulse disorders. A ratio of two constricted children for each child who acts out seems to be optimal. (p. 583)

In support of this procedure, Ginott (1968) has stated:

> An effeminate boy needs to identify with more masculine playmates. The dependent child needs the example of more self-reliant groupmates. . . . Aggressive youngsters need groupmates who are strong but not belligerent. Fearful children need to be placed in a group of more mature youngsters. (p. 177)

3. Slavson (1943) and Ginott (1968) both considered the basic prerequisite for admission to a therapy group as the presence or capacity for social hunger within the child. This concept would help the play group counselor in screening out only the most antisocial children. Usually, these kinds of children are obvious potential "wreckers of groups" and would not be considered for group treatment unless it could be rigidly controlled in a mental hospital or child guidance clinic. Nevertheless, children who show little self-restraint, shallow feelings toward others, and little conscience should be considered lacking in social hunger and poor risks for play group counseling.

4. Age and sex constitute two additional categories that the group counselor must consider when composing a group for treatment by play and action techniques. Ginott (1968) has recommended that preschool children can be placed appropriately in mixed sex groups, whereas school-age children should be separated by sexes. This procedure may prove more appropriate for a clinic population served by Ginott; however, we have found little need to separate the sexes until they approach latency, or roughly the age of 9 or 10. At this point, the girls are beginning to mature more rapidly than the boys, and their flirtations and advanced psychosexual behavior interfere with treatment when they are placed with less mature boys. According to O'Connor (1991), the ability to mix the sexes within a group varies with the age of the children, the type of group, and the goals of the intervention. He has contended that there is no fixed rule but it is a dimension that should be considered.

For the most part, children of the same age constitute the most therapeutic grouping. Exceptions are made deliberately to place more aggressive children in older age groups and some immature children in groups with children who are younger than themselves, but not immature. A general practice to follow would be to compose groups in which there is no more than a year's range in the chronological age. O'Connor (1991) stated that there should be no more than a three-year age spread, especially among younger children.

5. Differences in ethnic backgrounds, race, and intelligence do not pose serious problems for young children. However, grouping those with gross differences in intelligence, such as inclusion of retarded youngsters with those of average to better than average intellectual ability, should be avoided. According to O'Connor (1991), children should all be within 15 IQ points of one another.

6. Children who have been labeled "unsuitable for group therapy," according to Ginott (1961, p. 27), are children who as infants were deprived of close contacts with their mothers, children with murderous attitudes toward their siblings, sociopathic children, children who have shown accelerated sexual drives, children who have been exposed and/or involved in perverse sexual experiences, those who habitually steal, extremely aggressive children, and the children who suffer from severe or acute trauma leading to the development of gross stress reactions, such as inappropriate terror to a family pet (following being bitten by a dog) or refusal to enter an automobile (following a recent auto mishap).

7. Schiffer (1969) recommended co-therapists (a male and a female) for "children whose emotional disturbance can be attributed to traumatic deprivation caused by the loss or extended separation from one or both parents; or, when the family is intact, children whose problems are caused by parents whose sex-role functions are poorly defined" (p. 107).

Group Size

The size of a group of young children composed for the purpose of play group counseling should be considered in the light of counselor control. Young children have not developed to any large degree such social graces as listening while others are talking, taking turns, or being considerate of others who may be suffering emotional stress. Since fewer built-in controls exist within each child at this age, the counselor must be prepared to exercise control so that the group does actually function as a facilitative group. In addition to lacking social controls, young children lack adequate controls for their own and others' safety. The counselor must therefore be alert to the safety needs of each child. The fearful child especially requires this kind of safety assurance.

To focus intently on what each child attempts to communicate requires eternal vigilance on the part of the counselor. Since young children depend on their play and nonverbal means for much of their communication, the counselor must control the number of such stimuli so as to be in touch with each child in the group and with the group as a whole. When the counselor moves to structured play and sociodrama and psychodramatic techniques, it is vital to maintain the kind of control over these media that will serve the purpose of counselee growth.

The larger the number in a play group, the fewer the opportunities for the development of close, intimate relationships among the children and between a child and the counselor. Therefore, the larger the number, the slower the development of group cohesiveness; and group cohesiveness appears to be critical in the development of a growth group (Goldstein, Heller, & Sechrest, 1966). Among young children, cohesiveness is especially difficult to achieve, since each child is quite self-centered. In fact, it often appears that in play group counseling, the counseling is individual counseling within the group setting rather than group counseling per se.

Another factor that could increase or delimit counselor control is the nature of the counselees in the group. This problem should be controlled through role balancing, one or two rather aggressive and/or hyperactive youngsters in a group of less aggressive or hyperactive children. When all the preceding considerations are given to group size, a good practice to follow is not to exceed five (Schiffer [1969] considered six to be the maximum, and O'Connor [1991] recommended four to six for a single counselor and six to ten with co-counselors), regardless of experience and competence, and to include no more than two or three children if one is just beginning to practice play group counseling. (If co-counseling is practiced, one or two additional children may be added to these groups.)

Frequency, Length, and Duration of Group Sessions

Play group counseling (technique) is both prevention and remediation oriented. It is prevention oriented to the degree that a child is having some difficulty acquiring adequate coping behaviors to master successfully a given developmental task. It is remedial to the degree that a child has failed to develop appropriate coping behaviors for a given developmental task and therefore is beginning to experience difficulty in intra- and interpersonal relationships. The counselor, in setting up a play group, should determine the degree to which the group is composed of children who require preventive or remedial treatment. The former usually do not require as intensive treatment or as much counselor intervention as the latter.

When combined with a supportive life-skills training program, preventive play group counseling could be effective on a 40- to 60-minute weekly basis over a period from 3 to 12 months. Play group counseling that is primarily remedial requires greater intensity of treatment, all other variables being equal, and varies directly with length and frequency of group sessions. Therefore, two group sessions of 40 to 60 minutes equally spaced throughout the week are recommended. Schiffer (1969) recommended one session of 60 to 90 minutes (depending on the age of the children—under age 7, 60 minutes, and over age 7, up to 90 minutes). Early termination is suggested when needed to stop uncontrolled behavior, but cancellation of sessions is highly discouraged.

The duration of treatment is difficult to predict; however, periodic evaluations should be made with parents, teachers, and significant others to appraise the child's progress. Usually, too much is expected by teachers, parents, and even counselors. Counselors often terminate treatment at the first sign of progress, thus creating a real possibility of a relapse on the part of the child. No minimum time can be set for remedial treatment in play groups, but the counselor should consider six months a reasonable treatment period. At least three months should be allowed for any play group.

For those children who may be able to set their own goals/contracts, the time required for meeting their goals/contracts would determine their length of stay in the group when open-ended groups are used. However, contracting with this age group, other than the upper level of 8-year-olds, is of rather limited value, especially since their presence in the group may not be entirely voluntary.

Media

The purposes for the use of play- and action-facilitating media are as follows:

1. To facilitate relationship building or to establish the facilitative base between the children and the counselor
2. To increase the potential for communication between the child and counselor and among the children themselves by capitalizing on the natural medium of child play
3. To assist the child in recognizing and/or understanding the difference between appropriate and inappropriate coping behavior—thus providing an opportunity for reality testing
4. To protect the child's degree of self-disclosure through encouraging a certain degree of vicarious expressiveness and experiencing
5. To provide occasions for symbolic or vicarious modeling
6. To facilitate the occurrence of responses that can be rewarded by the counselor— that is, to maximize the opportunity to use the principles of operant conditioning and shaping
7. To maximize the controlled use of "release therapy" when appropriate

Much has been written regarding the use of play- and action-producing media with the young child, but virtually no carefully controlled investigations have been done that have demonstrated the superiority of one toy over another or one action technique over another. Nor can one expect to find this kind of exacting information, since different toys are likely to be preferred for different problem types.

Certain toys and materials are provided for "release therapy." These usually include plastic inflatable figures for punching, pop guns for releasing hostility, finger-paint for smearing and messing, and pounding tools and boards for releasing aggression.

These media should be used with caution, since aggressive children may be stimulated to greater aggression, hostility, and destructiveness if the use of the toy or medium reinforces these qualities within them rather than serves as cathartic release.

Pupil personnel workers of the Baltimore County (Maryland) School System (Board of Education, 1963) have categorized play media under these three areas: (1) *toys for release of aggression* (bop bags, guns, soldiers, rubber puppets, fingerpaints, clay, and play dough); (2) *real-life toys* (doll house, family dolls, animals, medical kits, play money, cars, trucks, chalkboard, and telephones); and (3) *toys for enhancement of self-concept* (play logs, erector set, puzzles, and maps). Ginott (1961, 1968) has advocated the use of specific toys for the development of the objectives of a therapeutic relationship (catharsis, insight, reality testing, and sublimation). To convey the permissiveness of counselors in their attempt to establish a good therapeutic relationship, counselors make heretofore forbidden toys available to the child, such as noise-making toys, including drums, pegboards, xylophones, air rifles, and cap guns. Other forbidden toys—such as a typewriter, flashlight, and tool kit—according to Ginott, serve the purpose of establishing a good relationship. A doll family also serves this end.

Materials included in the playroom for release or catharsis must be carefully chosen to fit the child's basic problem. Care should be taken not to include materials that lead to diffuse hyperactivity. Ginott (1961, 1968) cautioned that catharsis in children almost always leads to mobility and acting out and that acting out in and of itself has no curative effects aside from pleasure and release. For hyperactive children, Ginott recommended materials that will focus their energies, such as pegboards, building blocks, rifles for shooting, nails for driving, wood for sawing, construction boxes, and the like. For fearful and fragile children, Ginott recommended materials that can be handled without the aid of tools, such as water, paint, sand, play dough, dolls, chalk, and crayons. These materials also have the added advantage of permitting children to conceal certain feelings and to erase or to remake or refine certain products.

Toys alone do not provide the child *insight;* therefore, Ginott (1968) suggested that the counselor structure play situations that will enable children to gain insight into the dynamics of their behavior. This can be done, for example, by providing only one gun, which will likely bring out a conflict. The counselor also might structure a task that requires cooperation of all the children if it is to be accomplished. This might include, for example, preparing puppets for a puppet show. Ginott cautioned the counselor to avoid treating the child suffering from a character disorder with insight methods.

For *reality testing,* toys should be chosen so that the playroom is furnished with those of graded difficulty. Complex puzzles and toys should be excluded from the playroom, especially for the child whose self-image and ego strength are low.

> In order for play therapy to be an experience in social learning, children should be provided with situations and materials that demand exploration of others as well as them. Most children at times in their therapy, should be exposed to peers, resistive materials, and planned scarcity of tools, so that they can test themselves in relation to social actualities. (Ginott, 1961, p. 60)

Finally, Ginott recommended sand, water, paint, and clay as essential media for *sublimation* of children's urethral and anal drives. A variety of outlets to promote sublimation have been suggested by Ginott. He cited the need for sublimating anger through the punching of dolls or plastic bounce-back toys, as well as the possibility of destroying clay figures or composing critical poems and writing murder mysteries.

In addition to the usual toys included in a typical playroom, consideration should be given to the use of other action-oriented media, including sociodrama, child drama, and psychodrama; storytelling and books for the child's use and for the group when read by the counselor; the construction and use of puppets for symbolic or vicarious sociodrama and psychodrama; and short films and filmstrips, music, and tape recording. These media offer the counselor the opportunity to introduce models vicariously through puppet shows, stories, audiotapes and videotapes, and films or filmstrips, which the children can use to imitate. These vicarious models are especially useful when the group is lacking in appropriate peer models. The sociodrama and psychodrama are action techniques that the counselor can structure for the playroom in which the models or participants (protagonist and auxiliary egos) are the group members themselves.

For the mature 8-year-old child, media and techniques appropriate for the preadolescent may be more appropriate than those suggested for the young child. The reader should refer to the media section for preadolescents in this chapter (pages 286–287) for a discussion of appropriate media and to Landreth (1991) and Schaefer and Cangelosi (1993) for additional suggestions of playroom equipment and rationale for use of playroom materials.

The Playroom

The playroom should be located in an area of the school or clinic where the noise will not distract other adults or children. It should be designed so there is complete privacy from onlookers (except for authorized adult observers who are behind a one-way mirror) and it should be soundproof (Meeks, 1967). The playroom should be neither too small nor too large, since cramped quarters force children into continuous close contact, which creates occasions for irritation as well as lack of privacy, and a room that is too large engenders running and roughhousing. With these considerations in mind, Ginott (1961) and Schiffer (1969) recommended a room of 300 to 400 square feet. Speers and Lansing (1965) used a room 280 square feet for play therapy with autistic children.

The room should be furnished with certain permanent or at least semipermanent facilities. The room itself and all its furnishings should be constructed with the physical safety of the children and the counselor in mind. The room should be well lighted and ventilated. Any glass in the windows and light fixtures should be protected by wire mesh. The walls should be easily cleaned and repaintable and the floor also should be easily cleaned, but not treated with wax or other types of polish that would make it slippery. Indoor-outdoor carpeting may be suitable in some cases where safety factors are preeminent.

Each playroom should be equipped with at least one study table and a long wooden bench for use as a table or work area. A chalkboard should be fastened to a wall, and a sturdy easel should be fastened so that it will not fall or collapse. Chairs should be of wood or plastic and noncollapsible. A small area should be set aside for a floor sandbox, including seating space on the edges. A sink with running water should be included in one area of the room. A young child should easily be able to control the faucets. A large doll house should be part of the permanent facilities in a playroom, although it could be portable and stored in a cabinet. Bathroom facilities must be in an easily accessible adjoining room. A large, sturdy cabinet should be set against one wall or in a corner for the storage of supplies and toys, or an adjoining closet should be available for storage. Finally, electrical outlets should be placed above the reach of the children, but accessible to the counselor for the use of items such as tape reorders, slide projectors. and record players.

GROUP COUNSELING FOR THE PREADOLESCENT: ACTIVITY-INTERVIEW AND ACTIVITY GROUP COUNSELING

The preadolescent is the child in the latency period, with an age range from 9 to 13 years old. During this four-year span, the developmental gap between boys and girls is most noticeable, with the normal girl developing secondary sexual characteristics in advance of the normal boy by one to two years. Thus, girls in the latter years of the latency period may be better described as early adolescents. The same holds true for more rapidly developing boys. Any of the classifications used to differentiate age groups and developmental levels must be considered only as a norm, with exceptions especially prominent at either end of the age group. Nevertheless, to understand and better assist a given age group, it will be necessary to employ what is known about the *typical* child in a particular age group.

Because boys and girls do vary greatly within the developmental levels, group leaders are encouraged to make use of the guidelines of developmental tasks and appropriate coping behaviors for the age group preceding and also for the age group immediately above the one in which they work. Hence, group leaders of preadolescents would need to appraise themselves of the developmental levels of the child 5 to 9 years of age as well as the adolescent above the age of 13.

Children in latency are often neglected children because they have entered into a period of quiescence. Their natural group consists of peers of the *same sex*. They are in the so-called homosexual age of development, wherein boys prefer to be with boys and girls prefer to be with girls. Cub Scouts and Boy Scouts become important for boys, and girls' clubs, Brownies, and Girl Scouts are important to girls.

The school grades most representative of latency or preadolescence are grades 4, 5, and 6, or the middle school. Junior high school overlaps at least in the seventh grade, but for the early-maturing boys and especially for the girls, eighth grade finds them in the early adolescent phase of development. When working with 13-year-olds, therefore, the group leader must use developmental guidelines and group techniques for both the preadolescent and the early adolescent.

The knowledge and skills appropriate to the following seven developmental areas—psychosocial, physical-sexual, cognitive, vocational, moral, ego, and affective—have been incorporated into the four generic life-skills areas described in Chapter 15. The skills appropriate to the child of ages 9 to 13 are listed by age level in *Group Counseling: A Developmental Approach* (Gazda, 1989). Readers are encouraged to use these skills as guides for assessing the appropriateness of including a child in the activity-interview group counseling described in this chapter.

One of the first psychotherapists, if not the first, to recommend the use of activity as a means of creating a therapeutic climate was Moreno (1946), whose activity-oriented approach led to the development of sociodrama and psychodrama. Slavson (1954), however, pioneered and expanded the application of media such as arts and crafts, table games, and outdoor activities (e.g., field trips and excursions) in the treatment of adolescents and preadolescents. He referred to this treatment procedure as *activity group therapy* and *activity-interview group therapy*. Gabriel (1939), along with Slavson, was one of the first to use activity group work in the treatment of behavioral disorders. She also used field trips, clay, painting, and related activities in treating preadolescents in groups.

Slavson (1945) made the following comment related to the value of activity groups for the preadolescent:

> What little children gain through play and acting out, young children in their latency period and early adolescence achieve through manual activity, creative expression, and free play and interaction with one another. Older adolescents and adults require verbal expression and insight to gain the same results. (p. 202)

Galkin (1937) and Hallowitz (1950) also contributed to the field of activity group therapy. They used the natural medium of outdoor play and a camp environment of the preadolescent and adolescent in activity group therapy. Activity and play therapy models have been adapted for schools (Gaines, 1986), private practice (MacLennan, 1986), and inpatient psychiatric units (Stearns, 1991).

Ginott (1961, 1968) followed the lead of Slavson and added additional activity media to the treatment of preadolescents. In addition to the usual arts and crafts, table games, and such, he introduced penny arcade-type machines, such as rifle galleries and electric bowling tables, and modern communication devices, such as the walkie-talkie and typewriter.

An activity group approach within the context of *counseling* has been described by Blakeman and Day (1969). They have borrowed from the activity group therapy literature "the need for communication through a natural and spontaneous activity" and combined this with counseling within a group setting. Their process is defined as follows: "Activity group counseling refers to the group process which improves communication through natural spontaneous activity whereby peers participate in the developmental, behavioral, and attitudinal concerns of the individual members of the counseling group" (Blakeman & Day, 1969, p. 61). Thus activity group therapy has been used as the model for the development of activity-oriented procedures for counseling; had they followed Slavson's (1964) lead, they might have more appropriately named it *activity-interview group counseling* à la Slavson's *activity-interview group psychotherapy,* its forerunner. Actually, Blakeman and Day used activities such as darts, basketball, swimming, rifle shooting, table games (e.g., chess), and various card games to generate interaction among the preadolescent boys with whom they worked. The activity was then followed by group discussion of the personally relevant interactions. This method is similar to Slavson's activity-interview group psychotherapy approach.

No single "activity" approach to group counseling seems to include the several options possible. In view of this situation, we have proposed two activity-oriented approaches to group counseling for the preadolescent. Each is developed on the hypothesis that group games, both highly physical and sedentary, are the most natural media and means through which the preadolescent communicates freely and spontaneously.

Activity-Interview Group Counseling

Activity-interview group counseling is a composite of activity group therapy à la Slavson and interview group counseling. In essence, an activity, such as darts, is used to involve the group and to lower the inhibitions and defenses of the group members. The activity itself may provide an opportunity for physical catharsis or a nonsystematized desensitization. It serves the same purpose as systematic desensitization practiced by behaviorally oriented counselors and therapists. In addition to providing a means for tension reduction through physical catharsis, the activity provides an opportunity for interpersonal interactions, which are the concern of the counselor and members in the group "interview" period following the games or activity.

Activity-interview group counseling, like all other variations of developmental group counseling described in this chapter, is a combination of prevention and remediation. Thus, it is intended for preadolescents in particular, but also for adolescents and some adults who are not suffering from debilitating emotional problems.

The activities may be many and varied. They should be chosen by the group counselor according to the needs of the group members. Care should be taken to vary the games or activities in order to provide some success experiences to all members of the group. Athletic preadolescents should have the opportunity to demonstrate their talents in team sports, such as basketball, touch football, and volleyball. In like fashion, less athletic preadolescents should have an opportunity to experience success in table games, such as electric bowling, table tennis, chess, checkers, video games, and the like. Still other activities—such as dancing, swimming, and arts and crafts—should be used for those who may have talents apart from the physical or intellective.

Since the activity itself in activity-interview group counseling represents only part of the treatment, those activities that involve simultaneously several if not all the group members should be most used. The discussion or interview group counseling session following the game or activity constitutes the second part of the treatment. During this period, the counselor helps the group members focus on the nature of the interactions that occurred during the activity phase of the treatment. The behavior that occurred during the activity is related to the life-style of a given group member in the following sequence: The counselor builds a strong facilitative base with high levels of empathy, respect, and warmth; only after having established a feeling of mutual trust and caring does the counselor move the group member into the planning and action phase of the treatment through appropriate self-disclosure, genuineness, concreteness, confrontation, and immediacy, à la Carkhuff (1969a, 1969b).

The interview or discussion phase need not be held in a formal setting such as a conference room, although such a room should be available when movement from an activity setting is required. The conference room can also be set up as a dual-purpose room, including equipment and materials for group activities as well as chairs for the interview phase. (See the activity-interview group protocol in the next chapter for an illustration of its application.)

Activity Group Counseling

Activity group counseling is akin to Slavson's activity group therapy. Activity group counseling is different from activity-interview group counseling to the extent that the counselor is much less active on a verbal level. (There is no separate interview phase following a structured activity.) The counselor is present as a catalyst and source of safety or control, but the composition of the group and activities, materials, and other media are chosen more carefully than would be necessary for activity-interview group counseling. Activity group counseling requires a greater skill in social engineering because the group members and the media must be relied on more heavily as agents of change.

The setting and media must accommodate in particular the needs of the overinhibited and the belligerent preadolescent (Ginott, 1968). The engineering requires a careful balance of group members, including some overinhibited and some belligerent with some who fall between these two extremes. If the balance is incorrect, the hyperactive and belligerent preadolescents threaten the overinhibited and cause them to withdraw even further. If a group is composed totally of overinhibited preadolescents, there are no assertive peer models for them to imitate, and thus the counselor would be the only model for positive change. Since preadolescents are separated by sex for group treatment, we are describing all-male and all-female groups.

The overinhibited, shy, withdrawn, sexually inadequate preadolescent boy will require media such as fire-for-fire play, walkie-talkies, tape recorders, video games, and various penny arcade-type machines—rifle gallery, electric bowling table, and the like (Ginott, 1961, 1968). These media are captivating and serve to involve indirectly the overinhibited preadolescent boy with others until he can progress to direct personal confrontations. In addition, some of these media will permit him to release latent hostility.

On the other hand, the aggressive and belligerent preadolescent boy needs to learn how to sublimate and control his hostile feelings. Fire play, rifle galleries, boxing machines, and the like provide him with acceptable media to release his aggression without infringing on the rights of others. Shop materials include hard substances such as wood for sawing and hammering and similar substances that serve as media for sublimation for the belligerent preadolescent (Slavson, 1955). Slavson recommends clay, water colors, appropriate molds for making ashtrays, large sheets of paper, and equipment for cooking simple refreshments for the less belligerent. Ginott (1961, 1968) has found it necessary to add to the traditional facilities pioneered by Slavson. He has found that the aggressive and acting-out preadolescent in particular requires media cited earlier such as fire-for-fire play, rifle galleries, boxing machines, and the like. These kinds of media appeal to the masculine identification of the aggressive, hostile, and acting-out preadolescent who tends to view water colors, clay, and fine arts material as sissy and to avoid them.

The great attraction of video and computer games (such as Nintendo with suggested use by Gardner [1993]) for preadolescents and adolescents opens an entirely new medium for use in activity and activity-interview group counseling. Friendly competition among group members may be used productively. Currently, the games are not group oriented. Johnson (1993), however, reported on the adaptation of the computer for play media by utilizing painting with a *Power Pad* and *Leo's 'lectric Paintbrush* software as well as computer art therapy with graphics.

Although less is known regarding the media that is suited for aggressive, belligerent, and shy, withdrawn preadolescent girls, some will be comfortable with many of the media used for their counterparts among the boys. Others will prefer to engage in more traditional feminine pursuits, such as styling and setting one another's hair, sewing, cooking, listening to music and dancing, table games, swimming, painting, and handicrafts. It would appear that a balance between sedentary games and active physical games would be preferred. Just as with the preadolescent boys, the use of a variety of activities will permit each girl to be successful at one or more activities.

Selection and Group Composition

The preadolescent age group is the one age group that definitely calls for separation of the sexes in the group treatment plan. There also might be some reason to separate the sexes in the age group from 5 to 9; however, this would most likely be true for those reaching the latency period around age 9. The preadolescent age represents the time when boys prefer to be with boys and girls prefer to be with girls; their natural choices are for members of the same sex. This preference should be respected when placing preadolescents in counseling groups.

Activity and activity-interview groups, we contend, are the preferred modes of treatment for the preadolescent. The majority of counselees in the age group are boys, and games and activities are their most comfortable ways of relating. This tends to be a *masculine* preference, however, and activities, though relevant, are not as necessary in the group counseling of preadolescent girls. Except for the more aggressive preadolescent girls, interview group counseling, without activities—the preferred mode of counseling for adolescents and adults—may be used effectively with preadolescent females.

As with other age groups, role balancing and the provision of models for mutual imitation are of prime importance in activity-oriented group counseling. Hansen, Niland, and Zani (1969), in a study of model reinforcement group counseling with elementary school children of low sociometric ratings, had this comment on group composition:

> When none of the students exhibit successful classroom behavior, it is difficult to learn acceptable behavior from each other. This may be true of other group counseling stud-

ies using different criteria in which all persons in the group share a common problem. Thus, group composition may be a major reason why so many group counseling studies report null results. (p. 744)

Although proper group composition is important in *activity-interview* group counseling, it is even more critical in the engineering of therapeutic elements for *activity* group counseling because of the greater emphasis of the peer groupmates on each other and the less active role of the group counselor. The best predictor of the performance or functioning of a preadolescent in a group is some observable behavior during a trial or preliminary group placement (Gazda, 1968).

The preadolescent can be placed in an oversized newly formed group for a trial period of three or four sessions. The best participant combinations, based on direct observation of interaction, can be retained for the duration of the group. The others can be continued on an individual counseling basis until an opening in an open-ended group becomes available or until enough counselees are available for the formation of a new group.

Certain preadolescents do not make good candidates for group treatment. Ginott (1968) has labeled as unsuitable for group treatment (1) preadolescents with accelerated sexual matters; (2) preadolescents who have actively engaged in homosexual activities; (3) psychopathic preadolescents; (4) destructive preadolescents whose aggressiveness is deep rooted in hostility toward self (masochism) or others (homicidal); (5) preadolescents with long histories of stealing outside the home (preadolescents who steal only at home may be bidding for affection or a temporary act of revenge; these preadolescents may be placed in a group treatment setting); (6) preadolescents who have been involved in a recent trauma or catastrophe; and (7) preadolescents suffering from *intense* sibling rivalry.

Schiffer (1969) cited the following problem children in advanced latency (9 years to puberty) for whom activity therapy is contraindicated: the "characterologically narcissistic, psychopaths (sociopaths), children with severe rivalry problems, and psychotic children" (p. 103). Schiffer has contended that psychoneurotic children are not contraindicated for activity forms of group therapy but has cautioned that they can be helped only to a limited extent.

The chronological age difference of preadolescents in group treatment should not exceed two years (Ginott, 1968). The social age and the intellectual age of the group members must also be considered in the composition of a group. Since both types of activity-oriented group counseling approaches use the physically active games as well as sedentary games with neither predominating, the socially mature but physically small preadolescents are guaranteed some game or activity in which they have a chance to compete and excel.

The greater the emphasis on activities in the treatment plan (e.g., activity group counseling versus activity-interview group counseling), the less the importance of intellectual differences. Nevertheless, "normals" should not be placed in groups with mental retardates, and vice-versa.

Some chronologically younger preadolescents are often deliberately placed in a group with older preadolescents when the younger preadolescent is overly aggressive and requires the control of older groupmates. Similarly, some chronologically older but immature preadolescents are sometimes placed in groups with younger groupmates.

Generally, siblings and close relatives and friends should not be placed in the same group. When siblings are present in the same group, they sometimes feel compelled to look after each other and thus reduce their independent participation. Also, there is the greater possibility of one telling on another, especially when angered or hurt in a family quarrel. The presence of close friends and/or relatives poses the problem of trying to maintain the image that had been developed. This image-maintenance behavior interferes with the counselee's freedom to be real and spontaneous rather than role dominated.

Setting and Media

Consistent with the developmental emphasis of this chapter, all settings, insofar as possible, should be "natural" to the counselee. Activity group approaches to counseling require large rooms and open outdoor areas where a variety of activities by several counselees may be engaged in simultaneously. Schiffer, for example, suggested that a room of approximately 600 square feet is of optimal size (cited by Ginott, 1961). The room should be of sufficient size to accommodate workbenches and tables, table tennis, penny arcade-type machines, space for crafts, a meal table, and perhaps facilities to play recorded music. The typical school does not have rooms of this sort. The typical school, however, does have an industrial arts shop, recreation areas, and a home economics suite. These rooms, with their media and materials, can be adapted to the preadolescent.

In addition to the school shop and home economics suite, the gymnasium, swimming pool, and athletic fields and various game courts all provide areas that can be used by the activity group counselor. A small conference room capable of comfortably accommodating six or seven people should be available to the activity group counselor, especially when the activity-interview approach is being used. This room would serve as a place to which to retire for the interview phase following a physical activity. The dual-purpose room described earlier in this chapter could serve equally well for a conference-activity room.

The activity group counselor should view the entire community as the treatment setting. Camping and field trips should be included whenever possible. The therapeutic use of fire building by the preadolescent has been cited by Ginott (1961, 1968), and the camp with its campfire would provide a more natural means of using fire as a treatment medium than the artificial setting of fire building in a sink. Visits to community fairs, penny arcades, and video game rooms may also be more naturally used as treatment media than would be their use in a school setting. Nevertheless, these types of games should be available in one setting or the other and preferably convenient for repeated use.

Gump and Sutton-Smith (1955) hypothesized that certain behaviors (respondent behaviors) were made more likely by given physical settings or, more specifically, that the *amount* and *kind* of social interaction is significantly affected by variation of activity settings. Their subjects were 23 boys, ages 9½ to 11½ years, who had adjustment difficulties. They had been sent to the University of Michigan Fresh Air Camp. They found that amount and kind of interaction differed significantly between swimming and crafts. Swimming produced significantly *greater interactions;* however, when compared to counselor involvement, crafts produced significantly *greater involvement* than swimming.

The researchers concluded, "The general implication for recreational and thera- peutic work with children is that choice of activities per se is very important; this choice will markedly affect the children's relations to one another and to the leader or therapist" (Gump & Sutton-Smith, 1955, p. 759). For example, in the swim setting, the counselor was more often called on to admire and recognize assertive actions and to settle or supervise conflict interactions and less often asked to be involved in helping interactions, whereas in crafts, the opposite tended to be true. According to Gump and Sutton-Smith,

> The counselor learns from such data that a "prescription" of swimming will send a child to a "robust" social climate in which total interaction is high and in which assertion and attacking are highly likely. A crafts "prescription," on the other hand, will place a child in a "mild" social climate in which total interaction is low, assertive and conflict interaction minimal, and dependency (helping—being helped) interaction high. (1955, p. 759)

Obviously, then, the choice of setting *as well as choice of media used* within the setting should be made carefully to accommodate the needs of the group members. Set- tings as well as media should be varied to meet the needs of *all* group members.

For the more sedentary games—such as card games, chess, and simulator games like the Family Game—small tables should be available to permit the group to divide into subgroups and to spread out the materials included in the game kit. A sufficient number of chairs should be available for the number involved in the group. With more and more simulation games being produced and with their inclusion of filmstrips and sound films, a filmstrip projector and a movie projector with screens and a TV monitor and VCR would be appropriate accessories.

Group Size

Many of the considerations discussed in the section for children from 5 to 9 years of age apply to preadolescent children from ages 9 to 13. Although average children from 9 to 13 years old have become more socialized than children from 5 to 9 years of age, they still do not have the same degree of self-control that adolescents and adults have mastered. For this reason, group counselors need to limit the number of group partici- pants in this age group so that they can control the therapeutic group processes.

Another consideration given to group size for activity groups is the nature of the activity itself and the possible controlling and/or safety conditions of the activity. Activities such as touch football, softball, and basketball permit physical movement over a wide range or area and detract from the control and resultant safety extended by a group leader, whereas table games (e.g., cards and table tennis) localize the group and make it possible for the group counselor who uses activities to retain more overall con- trol of the group members as well as control the safety factor. Activities such as touch football and softball are difficult to play with a small group, and unless another group can be obtained to serve as the opposition, some of the larger team sports would prove inappropriate for activity-oriented group counseling.

Providing models for each member in the group is another condition of group counseling that must be considered when determining size for activity groups. If each preadolescent has a model in the group, it is easy to see that each time a person is added, one is in fact adding that person plus a model (unless certain individuals are serving as models for more than one group member, which is quite feasible).

No systematic research has been completed regarding size of preadolescent activity groups; however, we have found 5 to 7 members to be an optimum number. Under certain circumstances, especially if a co-counselor is employed, as many as 10 may be included in an activity-type counseling group.

Frequency, Length, and Duration of Group Sessions

The degree of disturbance of the group participants is probably the best indicator of the frequency and duration of treatment through activity-interview group counseling. As with other types of group counseling, activity-interview group counseling, in our opinion, is both prevention and remediation oriented. The degree to which remediation is necessary or the degree to which coping behaviors must be varied or initiated will determine how often and how long a group should meet.

Both activity-interview group counseling and activity group counseling require approximately six months to one year of meeting one-and-a-half to two hours a session at least once a week. Twice-a-week sessions of approximately one-and-a-half hours are recommended, especially in the beginning of a group until cohesiveness or *esprit de corps* has developed. These time periods are only rough guidelines for closed activity groups. Open-ended groups should be employed with great care if at all, and if employed, member turnover should be very gradual.

GROUP COUNSELING FOR THE ADOLESCENT AND ADULT

This section of the chapter deals with group counseling for adolescents and adults beginning with age 13 through old age. The typical adolescent and adult have achieved a stage in their development where the most natural and efficient communication medium is language, or verbalizing. Thus, with this age group, *interview group counseling* is the preferred mode of treatment. Unquestionably, the needs and coping behaviors of differing age groups will vary, as illustrated in the knowledge and skills appropriate to different age groups found in Appendix A of the fourth edition of *Group Counseling: A Developmental Approach* (Gazda, 1989). Group leaders are directed to this Appendix A for knowledge and skills appropriate to adolescents and adults.

The counseling/therapy model that is perhaps most consistent with the developmental group counseling model and that describes the process of change that occurs in a counseling intervention focusing on counselee verbalization is the cognitive-behavior model of Meichenbaum (1977, 1985). Meichenbaum describes his model as an integrative approach inasmuch as he considers insight development as involving both cognitive and affective domains and that frequently the coping response mediated through these domains must be taught. He summarizes his position as follows: "In short, I am proposing that behavior change occurs through a sequence of mediating process involving the interaction of inner speech, cognitive structures, and behavior and their resultant outcomes" (Meichenbaum, 1977, p. 218).

The change process consists of three phases, according to Meichenbaum. These phases, he has cautioned, are not lockstep, but are interwoven. Phase 1 is *self-observation*. In this first step, the counselee becomes an observer of his or her own behavior. (In the developmental model, this phase is called *self-exploration*.) Meichenbaum has also referred to this phase as *raised consciousness*, which is the purpose of self-exploration. Typically, the counselee is in a kind of "mental rut" when he or she comes for counseling; his or her thoughts and behaviors are frequently maladaptive and lead to a sense of helplessness and despair. In order to change the maladaptive thoughts and behavior, the counselee must learn to produce thoughts and behaviors incompatible with maladaptive ones. Thus, according to Meichenbaum, the counselee must discover that he or she is no longer a victim of such thoughts and feelings, but an active contributor to his or her own experience.

The counselee usually comes to counseling with some conceptualization of his or her problems. This conceptualization must undergo change if he or she is to change. This change is mediated by the interaction between counselee and counselor and other counselees. The reconceptualization that takes place is one in which the individual redefines the problem and as a result gains a sense of control and hope, both necessary if change is to occur. In short, says Meichenbaum, the counselee is changing what he or she is saying to himself or herself about the maladaptive behavior. According to Mendel (1968) the assignment of meaning is part of every therapist-patient interaction, independent of the therapist's theoretical rationale, and, as Lieberman, Yalom, and Miles (1973) discovered, that "meaning attribution" (adding an explanation for behavior or events) was an element significantly related to positive change in their research on small-group treatment modalities.

Admittedly, the manner that a counselor uses to prepare a counselee to accept a particular conceptualization varies considerably from "hard sell" to varieties in between. He, as do we, recommends that the counselee and counselor evolve a common conceptualization; that is, that the counselee is an active participant in reaching a reconceptualization of his or her problems. "With skill, the therapist has the client come to view his problem from a different perspective, to fabricate a new meaning or explanation for the etiology and maintenance of his maladaptive behavior" (Meichenbaum, 1977, p. 223).

Phase 2 concerns the counselee's *initiating cognitions and behaviors that interfere with the maladaptive ones*. Meichenbaum (1977) summarized this process as follows: "As the client's self-observations become attuned to incipient low-intensity aspects of his maladaptive behavior, the client learns to initiate cognitions and behaviors that interfere with the maladaptive ones. The self-observation signals the opportunity for producing the adaptive thoughts and behaviors" (p. 223).

Meichenbaum hypothesized that the recognition of the maladaptive behavior triggers an internal dialogue. "However, if the client's behavior is to change, then what he says to himself and/or imagines, must initiate a new behavioral chain, one that is incompatible with his maladaptive behaviors" (Meichenbaum, 1977, p. 224). This new behavioral chain is guided by the translation that has evolved in the counseling process—the counselee's reconceptualization of the cause of his or her problems and his or her part in their continuance. When the counselee uses the new conceptualizations, he or she can follow with different (coping) behaviors, which then serve to consolidate his or her emerging structures.

"In summary, the refocusing of the client's attention, the attention in appraisal, and physiological reactions will help change the internal dialogue that the client brought into therapy. In turn, the internal dialogue comes to guide new behavior, the results of which have an impact on the individual's cognitive structures" (Meichenbaum, 1977, p. 224). Meichenbaum's Phase 2 is similar to the *understanding phase* in the developmental group counseling model. However, Phase 2 appears to go further insofar as it appears to involve some trial responses.

Phase 3 of Meichenbaum's model has to do with the counselee's emitting *coping behaviors* in vivo and what the counselee says to himself or herself about the outcomes of these "experiments." Meichenbaum has referred to this third phase as *cognitions concerning change.*

Meichenbaum emphasized that in this phase, it is not enough to produce adaptive acts such as through skill training; rather, what the counselee says to himself or herself about these acts or behaviors and their consequences, especially reactions from others, will determine whether the behavior will persist and generalize. According to Meichenbaum, therapy is not successful until both the counselee's behavior and internal dialogue change.

Insofar as the developmental group counseling model (see Gazda, 1989) also includes teaching new attitudes and behavior based on a consistent model for given life-skills areas, these two models do not appear to be inconsistent with each other. The major difference, in our opinion, is the contribution that Meichenbaum makes to explaining the verbalization process that takes place during counseling and therapy, especially the constructs of internal dialogue and cognitive structures and how the interview counseling process contributes to the formation of these mediating constructs. The developmental model operates on the assumption that the counselee can accept the rationale offered for a given life-skill area. For example, if the life-skill deficit area is interpersonal communication/human relations, the model that the group leader chooses to teach the counselee in this area must be logical and meaningful to the counselee before he or she will learn it. If it is too esoteric or appears unrelated to the counselee's deficit, he or she will not expend the necessary effort to learn the model. Once the model is learned, it has within it generalizability.

Although the authors use the descriptors of knowledge and skills in Appendix A of Gazda (1989) as broad indicators of counselee strengths and deficits, it is unlikely that Meichenbaum would use a similar diagnostic approach. Nevertheless, how one organizes one's thinking about these deficits is related to the interview process that prepares a counselee to accept a new model of behavior with its rationale and reject the old nonproductive model with its rationale.

Selection and Group Composition

The characteristics of a group's composition have been shown to affect the performance and outcome of the group. Shaw (1981) found that groups composed of heterogeneous personalities and member abilities tended to function more effectively. Heslin (1964) reviewed group member characteristics and also showed that the members' ability and adjustment were consistently related to how well the group performed. Jacobs (1974) reported that groups composed of friendly, expressive, and person-oriented members were more productive than groups composed of members lacking these characteristics. Reitan and Shaw (1964) found greater conformity in mixed-sex groups, whereas Schmitt and Hill (1977) found that racially mixed groups produced greater interpersonal tension than groups composed of one race. Zimpfer and Waltman (1982) observed that expressions of warmth in adolescent groups occurred more often when the groups were socioeconomically and heterogeneously composed. Kennedy (1989) recommended that *early* adolescent groups be composed of patients of the same sex, whereas Leader (1991) observed that mixed-sex *adolescent* groups have advantages over same-sexed groups.

When selecting patients for group therapy, Piper and McCallum (1994) listed the following general criteria:

- Minimum level of interpersonal skill
- Motivation for treatment
- Positive expectations of gain from therapy
- Current psychological discomfort
- An interpersonal problem
- Commitment to changing interpersonal behavior
- Succeptibility to the group influence (moderate approval-dependency)
- Willingness to be of help to others (p. 3)

When composing interview counseling groups of adolescents and adults, we have found that one should be careful not to mix high school freshmen and sophomores with juniors and seniors. Occasionally, there can be groupings across more than two grade levels, but this arrangement should be made with care.

Kymissis (1993) recommended grouping adolescents for treatment according to age as early adolescent 12 to 14 years, middle adolescents 14 to 16 years, and late adolescents 16 to 18 years. If not enough are available according to these age groups, early adolescent groups could include 12 to 15 years and late adolescents 15 to 18 years. The number of group members can range from five to eight. Within the college-age population, there is less problem in mixing lower- and upper-division students than there is in the high school setting; however, undergraduates are not usually easily absorbed into counseling groups of graduate students.

Outside of a school or college setting, we have worked successfully with age ranges of over 40 years. Increasingly, though, the generation gap has made it somewhat difficult to include the young adult of college age with adults over 30 years of age. Careful screening should be given if exceptions are to be made where the generation gap exists, since the primary goal is to provide each individual with co-helpers and models that would best facilitate his or her problem resolution.

Table 13.1 represents an adaptation of a rating system developed by Rose (1973) for selecting individuals for interview group counseling. The adaptation involves using the tentative generic life-skills developed in the Delphi study (Brooks, 1984). By this system, prospective counselees are ranked according to their life-skills strengths and weaknesses. The ranking is done based on an interview with each prospective counselee. The interviewer uses 5 as the criterion of the average adolescent's developmental stage. Each prospective counselee is compared to this assumed mean; 1 represents the lowest point on the scale and 9 represents the highest point.

Table 13.1 illustrates the rankings for the nine prospective counselees. Because Bob was too different from the other group prospects, he would not be selected for placement in this proposed group.

One should look to the life-skills development model as a gross indicator of the type of problems that a person might be experiencing in this age group. Once the nature of counselee X's problem (perhaps the absence of an appropriate coping behavior) has been classified, the counselor is in a position to select a person of approximately the same age (counselee Y) who has developed a successful coping behavior for the specific task of counselee X. In like fashion, the counselor would try to find another counselee who can model for counselee Y, and so on. Matching for purposes of providing at least one good model other than the counselor should be the goal of the group counselor. Selecting two counselees who are having similar coping problems for placement in the same group would be acceptable, so long as at least one person in the group could model appropriate coping behavior in the task area where the other one is deficient.

TABLE 13.1 Life-Skills Criteria and Rating Scheme for Selecting Adolescents for a Counseling Group

POTENTIAL COUNSELEES	FITNESS/HEALTH MAINTENANCE	INTERPERSONAL COMMUNICATIONS/ RELATIONSHIPS	IDENTITY DEVELOPMENT	PROBLEM-SOLVING/ DECISION-MAKING
David	7	4	7	6
Paul	8	6	5	3
Mike	3	5	3	7
James	4	3	5	3
Bob	4	1	1	2
Karen	7	4	5	5
Sharon	3	5	3	4
Jill	8	6	3	6
Jane	4	3	7	4

Source: Gazda (1989), Chapter 6. Reprinted by permission.

In addition to selecting counselees on the basis of their adequate or inappropriate coping behavior for a specific generic life-skill, the pretesting of each prospective counselee (especially adults) on the indexes of perceiving and responding (Gazda et al., 1999) would provide the counselor with levels of counselee functioning on these two dimensions. Since these indexes are loaded on the verbal dimension, they would be especially appropriate for use in predicting a counselee's potential in interview group counseling. The Index of Responding, in particular, is a very good predictor of the ease or difficulty with which a person can be trained systematically in human relations skills. These skills are essentially the ability to implement the core dimensions in relating to others. High-level (helpful) responses beget high levels. Thus, counselees will be in a better position to be heard in depth (helped) by both the counselor and other group members if they can communicate at rather high levels in terms of their ability to be concrete or specific about the nature of their problems, if they can self-disclose in depth (high levels), and if they can be genuine in talking about their troubles. In other words, if a group member self-discloses genuinely and concretely, the counselor and other counselees are more likely to respond with high levels of the core dimensions of empathy, respect, warmth, concreteness, genuineness, appropriate self-disclosure, confrontation, and immediacy. Conversely, if a counselee can discriminate (perceive) at relatively high levels and can respond at helpful levels as shown on the Global Scale (Appendix D in Gazda [1989]), that group member is likely to be a good counselee and model for other counselees. The higher the communication level of the total group members and counselor, the better the opportunity for the group to receive help and to receive it most efficiently.

Group Setting

The settings for interview group counseling will vary with the age group involved. For the high school and college groups, a comfortable conference room for seating with 8 to 10 individuals is all that is required. As a rule, the group should not sit around a table, since the table frequently is a barrier to closeness and the resultant opportunity for healthy intimacy. If the room has a rug on the floor, the group may even choose to spend part of the time sitting on the floor as they become more informal and comfortable with each other. Especially important is the necessity for complete privacy and freedom from interruptions.

The setting for adult groups may range, depending on the purpose of the group, from a room in a clinic or industrial setting to a room in a home for the aged. In all cases, the room should be large enough to accommodate 8 to 10 individuals, and the chairs should possess the degree of comfort necessary for the physical condition of the counselee—usually padded or upholstered chair or couches that can be arranged in a circle. Tables provide the group with an initial feeling of security, but their ultimate effect is to serve as a barrier and therefore they usually should not be included. A rug on the floor makes the room more adaptable to sitting on the floor if the members prefer—especially in the case of marathons.

Ideally, the setting for interview group counseling should have a small anteroom adjacent to it as well as a bathroom and a small dining area so that it could easily be adapted for a marathon session. The marathon approach is compatible with the framework of the developmental model.

Group Size

Our clinical experience has led us to the development of a rule of thumb for group size based on the type of counselee in the group and the duration and frequency of group sessions. If the duration and frequency is short, such as three months, we prefer small groups of 5 to 7, since this allows for greater intensity of interaction and greater opportunity for growth. If we have from three to six months or a year, we prefer groups of 7 to 10. (With groups running beyond six months, one must allow for attrition, for various reasons, of 1 or 2 members. Therefore, it would be prudent to begin with at least 7 members—with other considerations, such as degree of life-skills deficits of counselees, taken into account.)

The nature of the counselees' problems or degree of deficits and duration and frequency of group sessions have a direct bearing on the size of a counseling group. Also, as a rule, the smaller the group, the more frequently it meets; and the longer it meets, the greater the opportunity for intensity of group involvement and growth.

Frequency, Length, and Duration of Group Sessions

The frequency and the duration of the group sessions are directly related to the intensity of group involvement and growth. In addition to group size, frequency and duration of the group sessions cannot be considered apart from the nature of the counselees' problems or number and degree of deficits, and also whether a group is open (continues to admit new members as old members complete their treatment) or closed (retains all its original members until some agreed-upon termination date). The more severe the counselees' deficits, in general, the more frequently and the longer duration they would meet.

In educational settings, the quarter, semester, and academic school year are natural division points that must be considered in composing groups. Group counselors may therefore be guided somewhat by the likelihood that their group composition might change radically at any one of these division points and thus choose to set termination dates around them. In this regard, a quarter arrangement would call for at least two group sessions interspersed during a week, whereas a semester arrangement might call for one session per week of approximately one-and-one-half to two hours, and the same would be true for an academic school year. When faced with a short duration for treatment, we have used one or more marathon sessions in addition to the weekly group sessions to intensify the group involvement and potential for growth.

Media

The primary media employed in *interview* group counseling are, as the name implies, counselee and counselor talk—verbal communication. Of course, this is only complete when nonverbal behaviors are observed in conjunction with verbal communications.

Any media, however, that improve communication and lead to increased self-understanding of counselees and improved interpersonal communication are suitable for use in interview group counseling.

Focused feedback (Stroller, 1968) using the videotape recorder (VTR) is recommended as an auxiliary medium to be employed in interview group counseling. When it is employed, the counselor, co-counselor, or group member who is operating the camera and VTR must be selective in focusing on both discrepant and nondiscrepant feedback. In other words, the decision to view and to play back a certain segment or interaction must be made on the basis of whether the interaction helps the counselees understand where they are incongruent with themselves and thus discourage or, if congruent, reinforce their responses.

The VTR adds extraneous elements to a group and is not recommended for general application to interview group counseling until the counselor has had practice using the equipment and is very comfortable with it. An audiotape recorder can also be used in a group in much the same manner as the VTR; however, it lacks the quality of visual cues that are often very revealing to the counselees and group counselor.

MULTICULTURAL ISSUES

Developmental group counseling would be subject to the same multicultural issues as the other basic theoretical models described in this text. Insofar as the group leader uses the coping knowledge and behavior, described by age group in Appendix A of *Group Counseling: A Developmental Approach* (Gazda, 1989) as normative knowledge and skills to be achieved by group members, there will be a White, middle-class bias. Forewarned, the counselor can make some logical adjustments.

Most multicultural issues will involve race, gender, socioeconomic status, and language. Race may enter as an issue especially in the games and activities engaged in during activity-interview group counseling. Some African American group members may be more interested in and more skillful in the physically active games. Likewise, females in general may be somewhat more interested in the more sedentary games/ activities. Play by children of some racial groups and some lower socioeconomic groups may be naturally more aggressive.

In play group counseling, care must be taken to provide play material representative of the group membership; for example, doll families should represent all racial members in the play group.

Language could be a problem with immigrants who have not yet gained command of English. This would be more prevalent with the young child but could be equally difficult for adults who are recent immigrants. It would be helpful to include a co-facilitator of the minority race even if the individual is not fully trained in counseling skills.

As with other models of interview group counseling/therapy, members of certain races, cultures, and economic groups may be less willing to self-disclose and seek self-direction in a counseling group but instead defer to the group leader for guidance. Counselors must walk a fine line between resisting succumbing to the temptation to advise and direct but yet give enough useful information and assistance that will maintain the interest and involvement of these members.

SPECIAL ETHICAL CONSIDERATIONS

Developmental group counseling poses no special ethical problems beyond any other model of group counseling or therapy. In fact, if the model for selecting group members and the ground rules for groups (see Chapter 14) are followed, ethical breaches may be even fewer.

Most ethical breaches occur, however, because the group counselor is not adequately trained and lacks the degree of professionalism to protect group members from himself or herself and each other. Group counseling/therapy requires greater vigilance and expertise than individual counseling/therapy, because there are many more and different interactions to track and monitor. Also, when confrontive behaviors occur in a group setting, the impact is multiplied by the number present who witness it; therefore, the impact on the recipient can be much greater than that in a one-to-one situation.

SUMMARY

This chapter is itself a summary of the developmental group counseling model that is presented in detail in *Group Counseling: A Development Approach* (Gazda, 1989). The chapter gave a brief description of the rationale for a developmental model and then separate treatment of specific models applied to three age groups: children from 5 to 9 years of age, preadolescents of ages 9 to 13, and adolescents and adults of ages 13 through old age.

The theoretical approach is based on the hypothesis that both prevention and remediation of problems across the age span can best be served if considerations are given to the developmental stages and coping behaviors appropriate to the given age group. A universe of coping behaviors has been arrived at and each has been classified under one of four generic life-skills areas: interpersonal communication/human relations, problem solving/decision making, physical fitness/health maintenance, and identity development/purpose in life.

A theory and a method of play group counseling consistent with the developmental needs of young children have been described in some detail. Play and action techniques are considered the media most consistent with the natural interests and inclinations of young children. The values and limitations of toys and play materials have been documented from theoretical and research literature and from personal clinical experiences.

The chapter discussed the interventions that appear to be most applicable to changing behavior in the young child. Modeling, behavior rehearsal, coaching, and group feedback were presented as interventions most applicable to young children. Sociodrama and psychodrama or role-playing and action-oriented procedures were also described.

Selection and group composition, group size, media, and the playroom were separate topics dealt with in this chapter. Each section was developed to be consistent with the theoretical rationale outlined for developmental group counseling.

Two types of group counseling for the preadolescent were outlined. Activity-interview group counseling incorporates aspects of activity group therapy à la Slavson, Ginott, and Schiffer, plus interview group counseling. Activity group counseling is a modification of Slavson's activity group therapy. It emphasizes the activity or game part of the treatment procedure more than the combined use of games followed by discussion (activity-interview group counseling). These methods were described as most appropriate for preadolescents, who are game and activity oriented at this age level.

The various types of games, simulations, and media used in the activity approaches were given, and suggestions were made for their utilization within the total treatment program. Both sedentary and more physically active games are recommended.

A defense was provided for separating the sexes in the activity approaches to group counseling and a rationale for selection and group composition was outlined. Essentially, the groups are homogeneous with regard to sex, but heterogeneous with regard to problems of coping behaviors. The behavioral types for whom the activity group approaches are indicated were listed.

Group size for optimum conditions was recommended at between five and seven members, depending on the severity of disturbance, appropriate models available for inclusion in the group, and counselor skills. Frequency, length, and duration of group treatment were all related to the same variables considered when determining the size of a preadolescent activity and activity-interview groups. For closed groups, six months to one year of one to two sessions of one-and-one-half hours per week were given as rough guides for the prospective practitioner of activity group approaches.

Since the activity group approaches call for settings both within the school and within the community, considerable emphasis was place on this section. Suggested media were also included in this discussion. Examples of the settings included swimming pools, athletic fields and courts, gymnasiums, conference rooms, and parks. Examples of media included arts and crafts, card and table games, simulation games, physical activities, and, of course, counselee verbal participation in the interview phase.

Interview group counseling is the approach most suitable for adolescents and adults. Within this form variations such as marathons and focused feedback can be adapted to strengthen the treatment program. Deemed consistent with the relationship and *behavioral* (life-skills training) features of developmental group counseling is the cognitive-behavior model of Meichenbaum. An overview of Meichenbaum's model was given to provide further explanation of the process of change for developmental interview group counseling.

The concepts of role balancing and the provision of models for each group participant are the key elements stressed for proper selection and group composition. Identifying inadequate coping behaviors of prospective group members is a guideline also recommended to the group counselors for the selection procedure.

The recommended setting for interview group counseling is a conference-type room with comfortable chairs and a rug on the floor (for sitting on the floor when appropriate) capable of seating 10 people comfortably in a circle. The setting should guarantee privacy and freedom from interruptions. Also, it should include adjacent bathroom facilities and a small dining area that would be suitable for adapting to a marathon session. Space and electrical outlets suitable for videotaping and playback are recommended facilities.

Group size for interview group counseling ranges from 5 to 10 members; however, optimum size is dependent on member interaction, leadership, and intermember relations. Odd-numbered groups seem to be least subject to polarization according to group dynamics research reports.

As a general rule, the severity of the counselees' problems will determine the frequency and duration of treatment. The more frequently a group meets and the longer the sessions (up to about two hours), the more rapid the development of group cohesiveness and positive therapeutic results. Closed groups of a quarter, a semester, or even an entire academic year are quite feasible in educational settings, whereas open groups with no specified group termination date are more practical for clinical settings.

The media most used in interview group counseling are counselee and counselor verbalizations. Nonverbal expressions are basic to full communication, and therefore the group counselor must also be proficient in reading nonverbal messages or expressive movements.

REFERENCES

Abramowitz, C. V. (1976). The effectiveness of group psychotherapy with children. *Archives of General Psychiatry, 33,* 320–326.

Amster, F. (1943). Differential uses of play in treatment of young children. *American Journal of Orthopsychiatry, 13,* 62–68.

Anderson, R. F., Kinney, J., & Gerler, E. R., Jr. (1984). The effects of divorce on children's classroom behavior and attitudes toward divorce. *Elementary School Guidance and Counseling, 19,* 70–76.

Axline, V. M. (1955). Play therapy procedures and results. *American Journal of Orthopsychiatry, 25,* 618–626.

Axline, V. (1969). *Play therapy* (rev. ed.) New York: Ballantine.

Bandura, A. (1965). Behavioral modifications through modeling procedures. In L. Krasner & L. P. Ullman (Eds.), *Research in behavior modification.* New York: Holt, Rinehart and Winston.

Bandura, A. (1969). *Principles of behavior modification.* New York: Holt, Rinehart and Winston.

Bandura, A. (1977). *Social learning theory.* Englewood-Cliffs, NJ: Prentice-Hall.

Bandura, A. (1986). *Social foundations of thought and action.* Englewood Cliffs, NJ: Prentice-Hall.

Bandura, A., Ross, D., & Ross, S. (1963). Imitation of film-mediated aggressive models. *Journal of Abnormal and Social Psychology, 66,* 3–11.

Beach, A. I. (1967). *The effect of group model-reinforcement counseling on achievement behavior of seventh and eight grade students.* Doctoral dissertation, Stanford University.

Bender, L. (1955). Therapeutic play techniques: Discussion. *American Journal of Orthopsychiatry, 25,* 784–787.

Blakeman, J. D., & Day, S. R. (1969). Activity group counseling. In G. M. Gazda (Ed.), *Theories and methods of group counseling in the schools.* Springfield, IL: Charles C. Thomas.

Blocher, D. H. (1974). *Developmental counseling* (2nd ed.). New York: Ronald Press.

Board of Education of Baltimore County, Maryland, Guidance Department. (1963). *Elementary school counseling.* Mimeograph.

Brammer, L. M., & Shostrom, E. L. (1960). *Therapeutic psychology.* Englewood Cliffs, NJ: Prentice-Hall.

Brooks, D. K., Jr. (1984). *A life-skills taxonomy: Defining the elements of effective functioning through the use of the Delphi technique.* Doctoral dissertation, University of Georgia.

Carkhuff, R. R. (1969a). *Helping and human relations. Vol. 1. Selection and training.* New York: Holt, Rinehart and Winston.

Carkhuff, R. R. (1969b). *Helping and human relations. Vol. 2. Practice and research.* New York: Holt, Rinehart and Winston.

Chittenden, G. E. (1942). An experimental study in measuring and modifying assertive behavior in young children. *Monograph of Social Research and Child Development, 7*(1, Whole No. 31).

Conn, J. H. (1951). Play interview therapy of castration fears. *American Journal of Orthopsychiatry, 25,* 747–754.

Dagley, J. C., Gazda, G. M., Eppinger, S. J., & Stewart, E. A. (1994). Group psychotherapy research with children, preadolescents, and adolescents. In A. Fuhriman & G. M. Burlingame (Eds.), *Handbook of groups psychotherapy.* New York: Wiley.

Dupont, H. (1978). *Affective development: A Piagetian model.* Paper presented at the UAP-USC Eighth Annual Interdisciplinary International Conference: Piagetian Theory and the Helping Professions, February 3–4, Los Angeles.

Dupont, H. (1979). Affective development: Stage and sequence. In R. L. Mosher (Ed.), *Adolescents' development and education.* Berkeley, CA: McCutchon.

Duska, R., & Whelan, M. (1975). *Moral development: A guide to Piaget and Kohlberg.* New York: Paulist Press.

Edleson, J. E. (1981). Teaching children to resolve conflict: A group approach. *Social Work, 26,* 488–493.

Erikson, E. H. (1950). *Childhood and society.* New York: Norton.

Erikson, E. H. (1959). Growth and crises of the healthy personality. *Psychological Issues, 1,* 50–100.

Erikson, E. H. (1963). *Childhood and society* (2nd ed.). New York: Norton.

Fabry, J. A. (1980). *The pursuit of meaning.* New York: Harper and Row.

Flavell, J. H. (1963). *The developmental psychology of Jean Piaget.* Princeton: Van Nostrand.

Frank, L. K. (1955). Play in personality development. *American Journal of Orthopsychiatry, 25,* 576–590.

Gabriel, B. (1939). An experiment in group treatment. *American Journal of Orthopsychiatry, 9,* 146–170.

Gaines, T. Jr. (1986). Application of child group psychotherapy. In A. E. Riester & I. A. Kraft (Eds.), *Child group psychotherapy: Future tense.* Madison, CT: International University Press.

Galkin, J. (1937). The possibilities offered by the summer camp as a supplement to the child guidance center. *American Journal of Orthopsychiatry, 7,* 474–483.

Gardner, J. E. (1993). Nintendo games. In C. E. Schaefer & D. M. Cangelosi (Eds.), *Play therapy techniques.* Northvale, NJ: Aronson.

Gazda, G. M. (1968). Group counseling: A functional approach. In G. M. Gazda (Ed.), *Basic approaches to group psychotherapy and group counseling.* Springfield, IL: Charles C. Thomas.

Gazda, G. M. (1989). *Group counseling: A developmental approach* (4th ed.). Boston: Allyn and Bacon.

Gazda, G. M., Asbury, F. R., Balzer, F. J., Childers, W. C., Phelps, R. E., & Walters, R. P. (1999). *Instructor's manual with test bank and transparency masters for human relations development: A manual for educators* (6th ed.). Boston: Allyn and Bacon.

Gesell, A., Ilg, F. L., & Ames, L. B. (1956). *Youth: the years from ten to sixteen.* New York: Harper.

Gesell, A., Ilg, F. L., Ames, L. B., & Bullis, G. E. (1946). *The child from five to ten.* New York: Harper.

Ginott, H. G. (1961). *Group psychotherapy with children: The theory and practice of play therapy.* New York: McGraw-Hill.

Ginott, H. G. (1968). Group therapy with children. In G. M. Gazda (Ed.), *Basic approaches to group psychotherapy and group counseling.* Springfield, IL: Charles C. Thomas.

Goldstein, A. P., Heller, K., & Sechrest, L. B. (1966). *Psychotherapy and the psychology of behavior change.* New York: Wiley.

Gump, P., & Sutton-Smith, B. (1955). Activity-setting and social interaction: A field study. *American Journal of Orthopsychiatry, 25,* 755–760.

Hallowitz, E. (1950). Camping for disturbed children. *Mental Hygiene, 34,* 406.

Hambridge, G., Jr. (1993). Structured play therapy. In C. E. Schaefer & D. M. Cangelosi (Eds.), *Play therapy techniques.* Northvale, NJ: Aronson.

Hansen, J. C., Niland, T. M., & Zani, L. P. (1969). Model reinforcement in group counseling with elementary school children. *Personnel and Guidance Journal, 47,* 741–744.

Harms, E. (1948). Play diagnosis: Preliminary considerations for a sound approach. *Nervous Child, 7,* 233–246.

Havighurst, R. J. (1948). *Developmental tasks and education.* Chicago: University of Chicago Press.

Havighurst, R. J. (1952). *Developmental tasks and education* (2nd ed.). New York: Longmans, Green.

Havighurst, R. J. (1953). *Human development and education.* New York: David McKay.

Heslin, R. (1964). Predicting group task effectiveness from members' characteristics. *Psychological Bulletin, 63,* 248–256.

Jack, L. M. (1934). An experimental study of ascendant behavior in preschool children. *University of Iowa Studies in Child Welfare, 9,* 3–5.

Jacobs, A. (1974). Affect in groups. In A. Jacobs & W. Spradlin (Eds.), *The group as agent of change.* New York: Behavioral Publications.

Johnson, R. G. (1993). High tech play therapy. In C. E. Schaefer & D. M. Cangelosi (Eds.), *Play therapy techniques.* Northvale, NJ: Aronson.

Kennedy, J. F. (1989). The heterogeneous group for chronically ill and physically healthy but emotionally disturbed children and adolescents. *International Journal of Group Psychotherapy, 39,* 105.

Kitchur, M., & Bell, R. (1989). Group psychotherapy with preadolescent sexual abuse victims: Literature review and description of inner city group. *International Journal of Group Psychotherapy, 39,* 285–310.

Klein, M. (1955). The psychoanalytic play technique. *American Journal of Orthopsychiatry, 25,* 223–237.

Kohlberg, L. (1973). Continuities and discontinuities in childhood and adult moral development revisited. In P. B. Baltes & K. W. Schaie (Eds.), *Life-span development psychology: Research and theory.* New York: Academic Press.

Kohlberg, L., & Turiel, P. (1971). Moral development and moral education. In G. Lesser (Ed.), *Psychology and educational practice.* New York: Scott, Foresman.

Kymissis, P. (1993). Group psychotherapy with adolescents. In H. I. Kaplan & B. J. Sadock (Eds.), *Comprehensive group psychotherapy* (3rd ed.). Baltimore: Williams & Wilkins.

Landreth, G. L. (1991). *Play therapy: The art of the relationship.* Muncie, IN: Accelerated Development.

Lazarus, A. (1968). Behavior therapy in groups. In G. M. Gazda (Ed.), *Basic approaches to group psychotherapy and group counseling.* Springfield, IL: Charles C. Thomas.

Lazarus, A. A. (1982). Multimodal group therapy. In G. M. Gazda (Ed.), *Basic approaches to group psychotherapy and group counseling* (3rd ed.). Springfield, IL: Charles C. Thomas.

Leader, E. (1991). Why adolescent group therapy. *Journal of Child Adolescent Group Therapy, 1,* 81.

Lebo, D. (1955). The development of play as a form of therapy. *American Journal of Psychiatry, 12,* 418–442.

Lieberman, M. A., Yalom, I. D., & Miles, M. (1973). *Encounter groups: First facts.* New York: Basic Books.

Liebert, R. M., Sprafkin, J. N., & Davidson, E. S. (1982). *The early window: Effects of television on children and youth* (2nd ed.). Elmsford, NY: Pergamon.

Loevinger, J. (1976). *Ego development.* San Francisco: Jossey-Bass.

Lowery, L. G. (1955). Therapeutic play techniques: Introduction. *American Journal of Orthopsychiatry, 25,* 574–575.

MacLennan, B. W. (1986). Child group psychotherapy in special settings. In A. E. Reister & J. Kraft (Eds.), *Child group psychotherapy: Future tense.* Madison, CT: International Universities Press.

Meeks, A. (1967). Dimensions of elementary school guidance. *Elementary School Guidance and Counseling, 1,* 163–187.

Meichenbaum, D. (1977). *Cognitive-behavior modification.* New York: Plenum.

Meichenbaum, D. (1985). *Stress innoculation training.* New York: Pergamon.

Mendel, W. (1968). The non-specifics of psychotherapy. *International Journal of Psychiatry, 5,* 400–402.

Mishne, J. (1971). Group therapy in an elementary school. *Social Casework, 52,* 18–25.

Moody, R. (1975). *Life after life.* Atlanta: Mockingbird Books.

Moreno, J. L. (1946). *Psychodrama. Vol. 1. The principle of spontaneity.* Beacon, NY: Beacon House.

Muuss, R. E. (1962). *Theories of adolescence.* New York: Random House.

Nelson, R. (1972). *Guidance and counseling in the elementary school.* New York: Holt, Rinehart and Winston.

O'Connor, K. J. (1991). *The play therapy primer: An integration of theories and techniques.* New York: Wiley.

O'Connor, K. J., & Braverman, L. M. (Eds.). (1997). *Play therapy theory and practice: A comparative presentation.* New York: Wiley.

Oden, S., & Asher, S. (1977). Coaching children in social skills for friendship making. *Child Development, 48,* 495–506.

Page, M. L. (1936). The modification of ascendant behavior in preschool children. *University of Iowa Studies in Child Welfare, 9,* 3–65.

Pescosolido, F. J., & Petrella, D. M. (1986). The development, process and evaluation of group psychotherapy with sexually abused preschool girls. *International Journal of Group Psychotherapy, 36,* 447–469

Piper, W. E., & McCallum, M. (1994). Selection of patients for group intervention. In H. S. Bernard & K. R. MacKenzie (Eds.), *Basics of group psychotherapy.* New York: Guilford.

Reitan, H., & Shaw, M. (1964). Group membership, sex, composition of the group, and conformity behavior. *Journal of Social Psychology, 64,* 45–51.

Rose, S. D. (1973). *Treating children in groups: A behavioral approach.* San Francisco: Jossey-Bass.

Rose, S. D. (1982a). Group counseling with children: A behavioral and cognitive approach. In G. M. Gazda (Ed.), *Basic approaches to group psychotherapy and group counseling* (3rd ed.). Springfield, IL: Charles C. Thomas.

Rose, S. D. (1982b). Promoting social competence in children: A classroom approach to social and cognitive skill training. *Child and Youth Services, 5,* 43–59.

Rose, S. D. (1998). *Group therapy with troubled youth: A cognitive-behavioral interactive approach.* Thousand Oaks, CA: Sage.

Schaefer, C. E., & Cangelosi, D. M. (Eds.). (1993). *Play therapy techniques.* Northvale, NJ: Aronson.

Schamess, G. (1993). Group spychotherapy with children. In H. I. Kaplan & B. J. Sadock (Eds.), *Comprehensive group psychotherapy* (3rd ed.). Baltimore: Williams & Wilkins.

Schiffer, M. (1969). *The therapeutic play group.* New York: Grune & Stratton.

Schmitt, N., & Hill, T. E. (1977). Sex and race composition of assessment center groups as a determinant of peer and assessor ratings. *Journal of Applied Psychology, 62,* 261–264.

Shaw, M. E. (1981). *Group dynamics: The psychology of small group behavior.* New York: McGraw-Hill.

Slavson, S. R. (1943). *An introduction to group therapy.* New York: Commonwealth Fund and International Universities Press.

Slavson, S. R. (1945). Differential methods of group therapy in relation to age levels. *Nervous Child, 4,* 196–210.

Slavson, S. R. (1948). Group therapy in child care and child guidance. *Jewish Social Service Quarterly, 25,* 203–213.

Slavson, S. R. (1954). *Re-educating the delinquent.* New York: Harper.

Slavson, S. R. (1955). Group psychotherapies. In J. L. McCarey (Ed.), *Six approaches to psychotherapy.* New York: Dryden.

Slavson, S. R. (1964). *A textbook in analytic group psychotherapy.* New York: International Universities Press.

Solomon, J. C. (1940). Active play therapy: Further experiences. *American Journal of Orthopsychiatry, 10,* 763–781.

Solomon, J. C. (1955). Play techniques and the integrative process. *American Journal of Orthopsychiatry, 25,* 591–600.

Speers, R., & Lansing, C. (1965). *Group therapy in childhood psychosis.* Chapel Hill: University of North Carolina Press.

Stearns, F. A. (1991). Inpatient group treatment of children and adolescents: In R. L. Hendren & I. A. Berlin (Eds.), *Psychiatric inpatient care of children and adolescents.* New York: Wiley.

Stoller, F. H. (1968). Focused feedback with video tape: Extending the group's function. In G. M. Gazda (Ed.), *Innovations to group psychotherapy.* Springfield, IL: Charles C. Thomas.

Sturm, I. E. (1965). The behavioristic aspects of psychodrama. *Group Psychotherapy, 18,* 50–64.

Super, D. E., Crites, J., Hummel, R., Mosher, H., Overstreet, C. B., & Warnath, C. (1957). Vocational development: A framework for research. *Monograph No. 1.* New York: Bureau of Publications, Teachers College, Columbia University.

Super, D. E., Starishevesky, R., Matlin, N., & Jordan, J. P. (1963*). Career development: Self-concept theory.* New York: College Entrance Examination Board.

Wadsworth, B. J. (1971). *Piaget's theory of cognitive development.* New York: McKay.

Zaccaria, J. S. (1965). Developmental tasks: Implications for the goals of guidance. *Personnel and Guidance Journal, 24,* 372–375.

Zigler, E. F., & Child, I. L. (Eds.). (1973). *Socialization and personality development.* Reading, MA: Addison-Wesley.

Zimpfer, D., & Waltman, D. (1982). Correlates of effectiveness in group counseling. *Small Group Behavior, 13*(3), 275–290.

CHAPTER FOURTEEN

DEVELOPMENTAL GROUP COUNSELING

Applications

This chapter contains sample protocols and intervention techniques for the three different levels of developmental group counseling: children (ages 5 to 9), preadolescents (ages 9 to 13), and adolescents and adults. Inasmuch as this theoretical model includes the entire age range, except for infancy, settings will ranges from playroom to activity space to conference/office group room. (A video demonstration of developmental group counseling with adults is available through Part 1 of "Gazda on Groups" and can be obtained from Microtraining Associates, Inc., Box 9641, North Amherst, MA 01059-9641. See Instructor's Manual for details.)

PLAY THERAPY

Techniques

Inasmuch as almost all children come involuntarily to play therapy, parents need to be advised on how to respond to the child's anticipated fear of and resistance to separation from the parent to enter the playroom. Since a small group of children and parents will be in the waiting room, the group counselor/therapist will usually ask the parents, especially the first time, to follow him or her to the playroom with his or her child and to leave immediately with a comment such as, "I'll wait for you in the waiting room." If a child resists separation from the parent(s), it is recommended that the counselor avoid forcible separation, but rather, as a temporary measure, arrange to see the child and parent(s) in the playroom as a family unit until such time that the child trusts the counselor enough to join the playgroup.

How the counselor structures the playroom experience for the children is crucial to the receptivity to the experience. Structuring is a continuous process but the counselor begins with a brief introduction, such as, "You may play with the things in this room in any way you want to." Later, as certain children "test the limits," the counselor shows understanding, but sets a limit. For example, if a child wishes to leave early, the counselor says, "You want to go now, but do not leave the playroom until time is up."

Ginott (1961) listed several limits that are conducive to effective play therapy:

1. *Situational Limits.* The physical setting of the playroom should be arranged to prevent undesirable behavior in advance by not including toys or materials that can be used by the children to hurt themselves or others.
2. *Time Limit.* Children should not be permitted to leave the playroom until the time is up. The child's desire to leave should be recognized, but the limit should be enforced. The counselor should alert the children to the impending end of the session to permit them to prepare to end their play activity. Attempts to prolong the session should be recognized but the time limit should be firm.
3. *Taking Toys/Materials from Playroom.* Toys may not be taken from the playroom. However, objects such as paintings or clay figures may be taken home.
4. *Breakage.* Room equipment or expensive toys are not to be broken. For example, inflated plastic clowns and the like may be punched but not punctured.
5. *Physical Attacks on the Counselor.* No therapeutic benefits accrue from physical attacks on the counselor.
6. *Physical Fighting among Children.* Although some therapists permit fighting, aggression should be directed toward toys in the playroom, except for a light slap or mild fight.

The preferred time to introduce limits with young children (ages 5 to 9) is when the need arises. There seems to be little advantage to beginning treatment by citing prohibitions that may never occur.

Sample Protocol

Limit Setting

Tim: I'm going to hit Alice.

Counselor: You're angry with Alice, but our rule says you cannot hurt anyone in the playroom.

Alice: (crying) Tim slapped at me.

Tim: But I didn't hit you; you're a crybaby.

Counselor: Tim, you don't like this rule and want to find out if we really mean it.

Tim: When I get mad at my brother, I hit him.

Counselor: So you think you can do the same thing here.

Tim: We don't have any stupid rules at my house.

Counselor: We *have* rules in this playroom and everyone must obey them.

Tim: I don't like Alice.

Counselor: You don't have to like Alice, but you cannot hit her.

Tim: I just won't play with her.

The preceding interaction includes a combination of empathic reflection and a firm insistence on obeying the rules. It is important that the counselor not get into debates with the children. He or she should make the point and turn to other issues.

Reisman and Ribordy (1993) cited four important questions that the counselor/therapist addresses early in the relationship with children: "(1) What is your understanding of why you are here, and how do you feel about it? (2) What do you believe are your problems, and how do you feel about them? (3) What do you plan to do about your problems? (4) How can I be of help to you?" (p. 145). The directness in which the counselor approaches the children in gaining answers to these questions depends on the age and maturity of the children. Typically, the younger the child, the less direct the approach.

ACTIVITY-INTERVIEW DEVELOPMENTAL GROUP COUNSELING

Techniques

Activity-interview group counseling is a composite of activity group therapy à la Slavson and interview group counseling. In essence, an activity (e.g., darts) is used to involve the group and to lower the inhibitions and defenses of the group members. The activity itself may provide an opportunity for physical catharsis or a nonsystematized desensitization. It serves the same purpose as systematic desensitization practiced by behaviorally oriented counselors and therapists. In addition to providing a means for tension reduction through physical catharsis, the activity provides an opportunity for interpersonal interactions, which are the concern of the counselor and members in the group "interview" period following the game or activity.

Activity-interview group counseling, like all other variations of group counseling described in this model, is a combination of prevention and remediation. Thus, it is intended for preadolescents in particular, but also for adolescents and some adults who are suffering from debilitating emotional problems.

The activities may be many and varied. They should be chosen by the group counselor according to the needs of the group members. Care should be taken to vary the games or activities in order to provide some success experiences to all members of the group. Athletic preadolescents should have the opportunity to demonstrate their talents in team sports such as basketball, touch football, and volleyball. In like fashion, less athletic preadolescents should have an opportunity to experience success in table games such as electric bowling, table tennis, chess, checkers, nonviolent video games, and the like. Still other activities—such as dancing, swimming, and arts and crafts—should be used for those who may have talents apart from the physical or intellective.

Since the activity itself in activity-interview group counseling represents only part of the treatment, those activities that involve simultaneously several if not all the group members should be most used. The discussion or interview group counseling session following the game or activity constitutes the second part of the treatment. Dur-

ing this period, the counselor helps the group members focus on the nature of the interactions that occurred during the activity phase of the treatment. The behavior that
occurred during the activity is related to the life-style of a given group member.

The counselor builds a strong facilitative base with high levels of empathy,
respect, and warmth. Only after having established a feeling of mutual trust and caring
does the counselor move the group member into the planning and action phase of the
treatment through appropriate self-disclosure, genuineness, concreteness, confrontation, and immediacy, à la Carkhuff (1969a, 1969b).

The interview or discussion phase need not be held in a formal setting such as a
conference room, although such a room should be available when movement from an
activity setting is required. The conference room can also be set up as a dual-purpose
room, including equipment and materials for group activities as well as chairs for the
interview phase.

The following protocol illustrates the dual-purpose setting used with a group of
Black preadolescent "problem students" ranging in age from 10 to 14. The protocol
includes portions taken from the sixth group session. The setting is a dual-purpose
room in which six Black boys are milling around. Some are reading; others are drawing; one is throwing darts. Jerry (the subject of discussion) is very active. The counselor
is a White male in his early thirties.

Sample Protocol

Jerry: I'm not gonna' tell anything in the meeting today because every time I
do, Roger tells Mr. Andrews.

Roger: I did not tell!

Counselor: Let's hear about this.

Jerry: I am not going to say anything.

Roger: He went and shot off his big mouth, and because I told Mr. Andrews,
now he is mad at me.

Jerry: Ah, Peanut, that isn't either what happened. That isn't the first time
you've done this, Peanut. I've been playing with you all day and you've been
doing it all along. Every time you touch him, he gets mad. Just touch him a little bit and he gets mad; he's a baby.

Counselor: How about that, group? How would you handle this?

Walt: Jerry is to blame; he is always to blame. He's a great big bully.

Jerry: I didn't touch him. I know what I'm gonna' do about it! I'm just not
gonna' associate with anybody in this group any more.

Roger: Don't worry; it will pass over.

Mike: I think we ought to put them together and let them fight it out.

Counselor: It seems to be a lot of buzzing, but no one wants to say anything
directly to Jerry or Roger about the situation. I get the idea that all of you
would like to, but you're kinda' frightened of what they might say back.

Jerry: I think the way to settle this whole thing is if I don't associate with Roger anymore. When he gets tired of not associating with me, he'll come around and say, "Let's make friends again"; then we'll be friends.

Counselor: I'm still puzzled about your saying Roger is responsible for all your problems.

Jerry: Yes, he is. And even though you want me to say something, I'm not gonna' say nothing different. He is responsible for all my problems. Let's do something different; I'm tired of this. I don't want to be talking all day long. I'm mad at this group.

Counselor: It seems like Jerry doesn't feel like the group is satisfying him any more. How do the rest of you feel?

Group: It's great; it's what we want. Let's do it.

Walt: Let's get Jerry out of the group if he doesn't like it.

Harry: If he wants out, let's get him out.

Leo: Yeah, let's get him out, if he doesn't want to be in the group; let's get him out.

Counselor: I guess the boys are saying, Jerry, that the door is open.

Ernie: Well, one thing about this group is that when we do play basketball or football, we got a sorry bunch of players. None of them really want to play ball. They're just a bunch of goof-offs. We got a sorry bunch of players.

Mike: That's what you say. You shoot all the time anyway, how would you know? You never pass it to anyone. Why don't you try to teach some of the boys how to play, rather than chewing at them all the time?

Roger: Well, I'd like to say something, I tell you this. When Jerry has the ball, even if you're wide open, he won't pass it to you. He won't pass it to any little boys. All he wants to do is shoot or pass it to one of the big boys. He keeps on dribbling like he don't even hear. All he does is shoot.

Mike: I think Jerry and I are the best basketball players in here and I think Jerry doesn't like the other boys. He never passes. I try at least to be good to them.

Jerry: Yeah, Walt, Leo, and Tim, they're no good. They won't even play. They lose interest in the game, and if you don't keep on them all the time, they won't even play. No sense to pass to them, anyway. They just dribble and lose it. They're no good anyway.

Leo: The group wasn't formed just for basketball. There are other reasons, too. Someone else might be good in football. You just want to be the hog in everything you do, Jerry.

Counselor: It seems like some of you boys felt like being good in basketball was the main purpose in the group, while others seem to think that there are other purposes in the group.

Sam: Yeah, keep us out of trouble.

Jerry: I'd like to talk now. Now, you say I don't pass the ball, but who in here does pass the ball? Every time I pass to Tim or Walt, they lose the ball. Every time. So why pass to them? Just lose it if I pass it to them.

Walt: What are you talking about, boy? You don't even know what you are talking about.

Jerry: Now you answer that, Walt. Why should I pass it to you? Now, if you see somebody that ain't gonna' do no good with something that is given to them, why give it to them? Why do it? Why give it to them?

Counselor: It seems like Jerry sees a different purpose for the group. He wants to be a good basketball player and have a basketball team. Some of the rest of you don't feel that way.

Mike: Well, I think anybody that don't know how to play ought to learn, and I think that this is a good place to learn to do things. I think Jerry is wrong. I think we ought to be teaching boys to learn.

Jerry: The time to learn is not while you're playing the game. The time to learn is on your own in your own yard. Besides that, you can't teach boys that don't want to learn. Some of these boys would rather play dodge, so go let them play dodge, but when they come on a basketball floor, they ought to play basketball and they ought to try to be good. If they don't show a lot of interest, they shouldn't ought to be out there.

Walt: I'm no good at basketball, but I think I'd have a lot of fun playing basketball if Jerry weren't there.

Roger: Jerry always shoots the ball so when we get back to this meeting, he can just talk all the time and brag about what he did during the game.

Counselor: Let's take a look now, boys, at what we are doing. It seems as though everybody is ganging up against Jerry, and it seems like we're trying to tell him that he's not a very good sport when it comes to playing basketball. I think maybe we're being a little hard on him.

Jerry: Don't worry about me. I don't feel bad.

Mike: I think this is good because I think Jerry needs help. I think he needs help badly not only in basketball but all over.

Jerry: I don't think I need no help.

Mike: Yes, you do need some help. You need lots of help.

Jerry: You can't help me.

Counselor: Mike, what do you see he needs help in?

Mike: He needs to learn how to keep his mouth shut, and he needs help to learn how to act.

Jerry: I don't need no help from none of you. I don't want any help from anybody.

Counselor: You don't want any help, from any of us?

Roger: That's his main problem. When somebody tries to help him, he won't let them. It is the same thing he was saying. If he won't help himself, how can we help?

Jerry: Be quiet. Oh, shut up, Peanut. Peanut, will you shut up! I'm leaving this group. I'm through with this group. This group can't help me. I don't like any of you, and I'm not gonna' be in this group. I am through with you, and I don't want anything to do with you or anybody in this group.

Counselor: Sorry you feel that way, Jerry. It sounds like we have been a little hard on you today. It seems like the boys had a lot on their minds.

Harry: Yes, it's true.

Jerry: I'm quitting. I don't want anything more to do with you. I don't want to come to any more of the group meetings. Count me out.

Counselor: We'll leave it up to you, Jerry. Whatever you decide is all right with us. I think, though, that we should leave it open if you would like to come back.

Jerry: I won't come back, and I won't have any more to do with it.

Mike: I hope you do come back, Jerry. I like you. I just think there are some things you need to work on.

Walt: Yeah, we like you, Jerry. I'm sorry that you are so mad.

Roger: I like you, too, Jerry, even if you are mad at me. And if you don't want to be in the group, I don't think you should have to be.

As the meeting ends, Jerry says that he is quitting and is very angry. Jerry comes back to the counselor during the week, however, and apologizes for getting angry. He comes back to the group and is a model group member.

The protocol illustrates a very action-oriented approach on the part of the counselor. He assumed that he had a good base built with Jerry and the rest of the group. The counselor and the group members showed empathy, warmth, respect, self-disclosure, genuineness, concreteness, immediacy, and confrontation—with a rather heavy emphasis on confrontation. If Jerry had not previously experienced the counselor and group members as helpful individuals, the result of this session would not have been so positive.

The confrontations of the peer group, though appearing hurtful, were genuine and mixed with expressions of caring. Jerry was rewarded for his positive behavior and physical attributes, but he was confronted (verbally) for his inappropriate attitudes and behavior. One must be reminded that without a strong base to begin with, confrontation would produce unhealthy responses rather than the healthy response by Jerry.

PROTOCOL ILLUSTRATIVE OF INTERVIEW DEVELOPMENTAL GROUP COUNSELING FOR ADOLESCENTS AND ADULTS

The protocol that follows illustrates the development of the phases through which a given counselee progresses when the group counselor and the group members use the core conditions of a helping relationship. The core conditions represent the essence of the process goals of the developmental group counseling model and of interview group counseling, in particular.

The following protocol was taken from a group session very early in the life of a group. It illustrates the application of the core conditions by the senior author to a problem introduced by a group member in interview group counseling. Since there was no facilitative base built with the counselee, the group counselor and members were careful to begin with interchangeable responses, especially of empathy. The interaction covered only 10 minutes of group time and yet led to a decision that the counselee felt was necessary and appropriate.

The counselee was in her mid-twenties. The group was composed of male and female members from their early twenties to their late fifties. Each statement is numbered to permit easy identification.

PROTOCOL

Counselee: (1) Every time the phone rings, my heart jumps. I stay worried all the time.

Counselor: (1) You're really pretty sure then that you're going to get some bad news every time the phone rings.

Counselee: (2) Yes, it seems like that I just wait to hear some upsetting new from home.

Group Member A (female): (1) Something then is going on at home that makes you think that something bad is going to happen.

Counselee: (3) Yes, my sister is ill, and they're trying to find out what's wrong with her but they tell me they don't know exactly what it is yet. I feel like maybe I should be there instead of 84 miles away, living my own life.

Counselor: (2) You feel kind of guilty that in this time of crisis in your family that you're not there to help out.

ANALYSIS

Counselee: (1) Stimulus 1 was the counselee's initial statement of her problem.

Counselor: (1) Response 1 by the group counselor was an attempt to convey an interchangeable response of empathy in that the basic concern of the counselee was communicated regarding the problem at hand.

Counselee: (2) The counselee's response showed that she felt understood at least at a minimal level.

Group Member A (female): (1) The group member simply gave another interchangeable level of response conveying understanding at the level the counselee was communicating. Now the counselor and Group Member A had both begun to build a facilitative base with the counselee.

Counselee: (3) At this point, the counselee feels it is safe to be more concrete or specific about her problem.

Counselor: (2) Here, the counselor detects guilt expressed by the counselee and he responds to it seeking to move to a level beyond what the counselee is revealing explicitly.

Counselee: (4) Yes, it seems like that every time they've needed me, I was either away at school or not available. This really has me upset!

Group Member B (male): (1) It is not the first time that they couldn't depend on you to be around. You've been away quite a bit sometimes.

Counselee: (5) Yes. Maybe it wouldn't affect me so badly if this were the first crisis, but it seems like it's just been one a minute in the last five years, and I'm really feeling guilty. I'm married now, but I still feel like I have commitments to Mom and Dad.

Counselor: (3) You feel that during these five years away from home you weren't doing enough to help your Mom and Dad. Now you are married and you're in less position to help them than you were before.

Counselee: (6) Yes. This is it, and then this is the point that confuses me. They wanted me to go away to school and get an education and get a good job. But then being away from home and getting a good education caused me not to be there when they needed me. Now, I've got a good education and am working and I feel like I should be there with them.

Counselor: (4) After they sacrificed for you, you stayed away and now you feel like you owe them something in return, but you haven't been able to pay them back in some way or other.

Counselee: (4) The counselee confirms the feeling of guilt and tells why she feels that way.

Group Member B (male): (1) Another group member responds. He attempts to give an interchangeable-level response, but his choice of words could be perceived as confrontive by the counselee.

Counselee: (5) The counselee does not misread group member B's response, but uses it to expand on her reasons for her feeling of guilt.

Counselor: (3) Here, the counselor reenters the interaction and tries to identify the conflict that he perceives regarding the counselee's married state and the dual commitments it introduced. He was trying to go beyond an interchangeable response to get at a source of counselee conflict.

Counselee: (6) The counselee feels understood and so introduces another source of her conflict and confusion.

Counselor: (4) Now the counselor shows how well he understands by being concrete and specific about the source of her conflict and feeling of guilt.

Counselee: (7) I guess that's getting to the point. Just marrying and getting your own life, job, house—just how much can you participate in family situations when you are out of school, out of the house, without really feeling like you are giving them less than you really should?

Group Member C (male): (1) You just wish you knew what was a fair return to them . . . (interrupted here by counselee response)

Counselee: (8) Yes.

Group Member C (male): (2) . . . after you're married, and what married people owe their parents.

Counselee: (9) Yes, especially after they've made sacrifices for me.

Counselor: (5) I get the feeling that you feel that you do need to do more than you have done.

Counselee: (10) Yes, but then on the other hand, I'm wondering if I really should.

Counselor: (6) Sometimes you think you should, and other times you don't know what a fair return is.

Counselee: (7) The counselee senses that the counselor is very closely in tune with her. It is a little threatening, perhaps, since she comes back trying somehow to justify her current position.

Group Member C: (1) Group member C picks up the counselee's struggle over what is fair on her part. He helps her concretize her conflict while still feeling accepted unconditionally.

Counselee: (8) The counselee feels the accuracy of group member C's response and interrupts him with a "Yes."

Group Member C: (2) Group Member C simply finishes what he intended to say.

Counselee: (9) The counselee goes back to the counselor's use of the word *sacrifice* in his fourth response. She accepts the fact that her parents did sacrifice for her.

Counselor: (5) At this point, the counselor makes the decision to move the counselee into more action levels and introduces for the first time a degree of conditionality. Heretofore, as the base was being built, all counselor and other helper responses were unconditional.

Counselee: (10) The conditionality is sensed by the counselee, and she backtracks slightly as she seeks to justify not doing anything about her guilt feelings—not taking action.

Counselor: (6) The counselor senses the threat felt by the counselee and temporarily moves back to an interchangeable response (unconditionality).

Counselee: (11) Yes, so if I could just work out this problem of not being so—so I wouldn't be so concerned with what's going on at home. If it just wouldn't occupy my mind so much. It really is upsetting me! It seems if I could adjust to the fact that Mom and Dad and my sister have a life, Jack (husband of counselee) and I have a life, and we can just do so much and then function normally.

Counselee: (11) The counselee points up (concretizes) the essence of her conflict once more.

Group Member D (female): (1) Somehow if you can just get settled in your own mind that there has to be this separation and that you can feel comfortable about whether you've been fair to your parents.

Group Member D (female): Group member D gives an interchangeable-level response showing empathy and unconditionality.

Counselee: (12) Do you think that it's normal to worry about a sister that is sick and ill, and is it normal to the point that you think about it 80 percent of the time, moping and wondering if something is deadly wrong with her? I just don't know what will becomes of me, nor would I know how to help Mom and Dad.

Counselee: (12) Here, the counselee is moving to action by asking if she is normal having the feelings that she does have. She is also indicating a readiness for conditionality on the part of the helpers.

Group Member C (male): (3) You really don't think it's normal to spend that much time worrying about her. You're also feeling quite a bit of guilt about her illness and the fact that you can't do more for her and your parents.

Group Member C (male): (3) The group member interprets the counselee's earlier responses as meaning that the counselee felt her concerns to be at the abnormal level. He also aims for an additive level response by an interpretation of guilt feelings over the counselee's sister's illness and then he comes back to her concern with her parents at an interchangeable level.

Counselee: (13) That's why I'm coming and asking for help, because I don't know whether or not it's normal. I kind of feel it is normal, since I do have close ties, and I really do love them—love her and

Counselee: (13) Group Member C's response forces the counselee to be more explicit in her feelings toward her sister; otherwise, she reiterates what she has been saying. She also corrects the group member's misin-

my family. But then I don't have guilt feelings about her illness, 'cause this is something that I did not have anything to do with. I do have a guilt feeling about whether or not I really did help them [parents] enough, or if I'm committing myself to home (when I say home, I mean to Mom and Dad and family) as much as I should. That is the essence of my problem. And then it seems like that because I do have these guilt feelings, and it stays on my mind—like I'm always wondering about if something is going to happen. If it is, I say well I should be there. Then if I were there, I wonder how much I really could do.

terpretation of the abnormality of her feelings and the fact that she does not feel guilt about her sister's illness.

Counselor: (7) What could you do? You're kind of torn between the feeling that you need to be there on the one hand, and realistically if you were there, you couldn't do anything anyway to change your sister's health, but you might in some ways be a comfort to your parents.

Counselor: (7) The counselor simply tries to communicate at an interchangeable level the nature of her feelings and conflict.

Counselee: (14) Yes. Now what are your views on this?

Counselee: (14) Counselee senses her base with the counselor and risks action or a counselor conditional response.

Counselor: (8) I guess all I can tell you, Marilyn, is what I hear you telling me—that you're pretty miserable right now the way things are, and it is not getting any better, and that you need to take some kind of action to feel better about this relationship between you and your parents, that you need to do something more than you have done. I don't know what's possible, but that is what I heard you telling me—that you feel like you owe more than you've been giving them back.

Counselor: (8) The counselor, not prepared to give specific advice, tries to respond by summarizing for the counselee the overriding message that he had been receiving throughout the short interaction, with the confidence that the counselee could translate the message to specific action. Here, the counselor showed respect for the counselee's potential for arriving at specific behavioral responses.

Counselee: (15) I do feel that I have to do more. I guess now my next move must be to talk to my husband about my feelings and make plans to do something more for my parents but that will be acceptable to him.

Counselee: (15) The counselor was on target, and this was confirmed by the counselee's response. Something that was not known heretofore, the husband's role, was introduced and apparently this was as far as the group could take the counselee until she took the action she herself decided on.

INTERVENTION STRATEGIES AND TECHNIQUES

Group members should be selected through a screening interview to determine the appropriateness of a group counseling experience for them and to motivate them for the experience. In addition, the counselor uses this time to present the ground rules and contract to the prospective group members and obtain their commitment. The following ground rules are geared toward use with adolescent and adult groups. They can be modified or abbreviated for preadolescent and children's groups.

Ground Rules/Contract

These ground rules are repeated during the first meeting of the group. In essence, they serve as a contract and, as such, can be put in writing and signed.

1. Set a goal or goals for yourself before you enter the group, or at the very latest, as early as you can isolate and define your direction of change. Revise these goals as clarification and/or experience dictates.
2. Discuss as honestly and concretely as you can the nature of your trouble, including the successful and unsuccessful coping behaviors you have employed.
3. When you are not discussing your own concerns, listen *intently* to the other group members and try to help them say what they are trying to say and to communicate your understanding, caring, and empathy for them.
4. Maintain the confidentiality of all that is discussed in the group. (There are no exceptions to this rule other than those that pertain to you only.)
5. Be on time and attend regularly until termination of the group (if a closed group) and until you have met your goals (if the group is open ended).
6. Give the counselor the privilege of removing you from the group if he or she deems it necessary for your health and for the overall benefit of the group.
7. Concur that all decisions affecting the group as a whole will be made by consensus only.
8. Inform the group counselor in private, before the group is constituted, of individuals who, for various reasons, would constitute a serious impediment to your group participation. (We feel that the "cards should be stacked in the counselee's favor" as much as possible; therefore those individuals who could inhibit the counselee should be excluded from the group if at all possible.)

9. You may request individual counseling interviews, but what is discussed in these interviews should be shared with the group at the appropriate time and at the discretion of the counselor and yourself.
10. When fees are involved, agreement on amounts and payment schedules is made with the counselor before counseling begins.

Stages in Group Development and Counselor or Counselee Involvement*

During the first meeting of the group, it is important for the group counselor to introduce himself or herself and if there is a co-counselor for that person to introduce himself or herself. A brief introduction, including name, qualifications for leading the group, and some comments indicating eagerness to work with the group, may be all that is necessary. Following the self-introduction by the counselor(s), the counselor asks for volunteers to introduce themselves and state why they came to the group and what they hope to gain from it. After everyone has voluntarily introduced themselves, the counselor may cite similarities and differences with respect to the group members' presenting problems. Sometimes the counselor makes these comparisons as the introductions are in process.

When everyone has been introduced, the counselor again asks for a volunteer to go into greater detail about his or her presenting problem. If no one volunteers following a wait period that is not so long as to generate group anxiety, the counselor may ask the person who appears most willing to talk to "say more about his or her situation." As the counselee begins to describe the situation, the counselor responds with empathy, respect, and warmth. In the first session in particular the counselor is quite active in responding to counselees' feelings and emotions. The counselor attempts to model what he or she expects the counselees to initiate in their responses to each other. The counselor avoids evaluative or judgmental responses and discourages group members from making such responses. If they do occur, the counselor softens their impact by identifying the feeling created in the recipient, thereby supporting the recipient.

The *exploratory stage* may last for one or several sessions. There is no clear-cut period when that stage ends and is followed by a *transition stage,* during which several, and eventually all, members begin to disclose in greater depth than the somewhat superficial levels presented in the exploratory stage. The *action stage* follows the transition stage. It is during this stage that counselees really become very specific about their problems and associated feelings and search for workable solutions, trying out different ways of contending with their problems. Members not only become more specific but in doing they also become more genuine and are more appropriately self-disclosing. Members challenge each other, but also offer high levels of respect and encouragement.

The *termination stage* usually involves members reviewing how they have benefited and acknowledging each other's progress. Frequently, efforts are made to hold a follow-up session at some prearranged date and location. As the termination date approaches, members begin to tie up loose ends and avoid opening up new issues.

*See Chapter 3 for a more detailed discussion of the stages in group development.

Some, however, may seek to extend the number of sessions to avoid losing the group support.

The group counselor should provide a mechanism for follow-up of members as a means of evaluating his or her effectiveness and to give members a chance to reenter another group if warranted. The follow-up could be by a mailed questionnaire or a follow-up interview.

Although we have been describing the stages through which group members progress over the life of the group, counseling groups also tend to go through these same stages in a given session. These stages may be very brief and often go from exploratory (warm-up) directly to action as the group matures, and briefly a termination (closing-down stage) as the time for ending the session arrives.

Use of Games or Structured Exercises in Group Counseling*

There are certain advantages and disadvantages in the use of games or structured exercises to facilitate group counseling. First, we suggest that exercises can be useful only when the group leader has had considerable experience with them and can predict their effects at a certain juncture in the group's development. The exercise can serve as a catalytic agent to increase cohesiveness, self-disclosure, and trust. Our observations of the use of exercises, however, suggest that they are used in lieu of the counselor's interpersonal or helping skills; when they are used in this way, one exercise after another is introduced to activate the group. Frequently under these conditions the exercises become recreational at best because there is no coherent theoretical rationale or encompassing plan for their use.

Group counselors may also find exercises to be a problem when they lose control of the pacing mechanism of the group as a result of the use of an exercise. The exercise has the quality of a foreign substance placed into a chemical compound, the reaction of which is unknown to the group leader and often may be explosive, uncontrollable, and harmful to the participants.

Some exercises also lead to questionable ethical practices. For example, the "trust fall" (having group members stand in a circle and catch members as they fall backward into one another) can result in physical injury if a member is dropped. Even the use of arm wrestling has been known to result in shoulder dislocation.

The frequent employment of exercises also has the potential of reducing the counselor's sensitivity and responsibility to the group. Counselors take the risk of depending too much on the exercise activities and too little on their own skills. In addition to the potential of exercises leading to counselor apathy and reduction of effort, there is the distinct possibility that the group members will also assume less responsibility for their own behavior because of the opportunity to hide behind the rules of the exercises. The exercise becomes the safe scapegoat.

More research on the effective use of games and structured exercises is needed, but until it is forthcoming they should be used cautiously. See Duncan's (1976) discussion of this issue for a more complete treatment.

*See Chapter 3 for additional discussion of the use of games and exercises.

Coping with Problem Members

For a comprehensive discussion of coping with problem members, see the topic Roles in Chapter 3.

SUMMARY

This chapter supplemented the preceding chapter on developmental group counseling by providing sample protocols of play group counseling, activity interview group counseling, and interview group counseling. In addition, strategies for preparing prospective members for group counseling with ground rules and contracts were provided. Techniques or intervention strategies for dealing with special problem types and situations were included, along with a description of the four stages of group development.

REFERENCES

Carkhuff, R. R. (1969a). *Helping and human relations: A primer for lay and professional helpers: Vol. 1. Solution and training*. New York: Holt, Rinehart and Winston.

Carkhuff, R. R. (1969b). *The development of human resources: A primer for lay and professional helpers: Vol. 2. Practice and research*. New York: Holt, Rinehart and Winston.

Duncan, J. A. (1976). Games people play in groups. *Together: ASGW, 1,* 54–62.

Ginott, H. G. (1961). *Group psychotherapy with children*. New York: McGraw-Hill.

Reisman, J. M., & Ribordy, S. (1993). *Principles of psychotherapy with children* (2nd ed.). New York: Lexington Books.

■ ■ ■ ■ ■ ▬▬▬▬▬▬▬▬▬▬▬▬▬▬▬▬▬▬▬▬▬▬▬▬▬

CHAPTER FIFTEEN

LIFE-SKILLS TRAINING

A Psychoeducational Model

Life-skills is defined as all the skills and knowledge a person experiences, apart from the academic skills, that are necessary for effective living. Obviously, this is a very general definition, and it does not imply that academic skills are not very important for effective living. Rather, the focus of the definition is on separating those skills that have been the primary domain of educational institutions from those that have been, at best, a secondary concern and, at worst, no concern at all.

Whereas the academic curriculum involves reading, writing, arithmetic (mathematics), and more, the life-skills curriculum encompasses four generic life-skills determined in a national Delphi study (Brooks, 1984): interpersonal communication/human relations, problem solving/decision making, physical fitness/health maintenance, and identity development/purpose in life. Even though theoretically separated, there is some overlap between what could be considered the life-skills curriculum and the academic curriculum in educational institutions. For example, interpersonal communication/human relations obviously contains some elements of reading, writing, speech, and civics. Elements of problem solving/decision making can be found in virtually all of the academic skills. Physical fitness/health maintenance includes health education and more. Identity development/purpose in life incorporates philosophy, religion, psychology, and the like.

As an additional point, it is important to note that the term *life-skills* is deliberately hyphenated. This is to distinguish it from other uses of the term that are somewhat similar yet have different origins and different meanings. In this text and as used elsewhere by the senior author, *life-skills* connotes (and is related to a training model involving) application in both *prevention* and *remediation* of human problems.

Life-skills training (LST) is multifaceted. It refers to the application of the LST model to prevention and remediation of problems as well as to the training of trainers. In this context, the life-skills paradigm represents an innovation in the rapidly developing field of mental health "training" models.

OVERVIEW OF LIFE-SKILLS TRAINING PARADIGM

The genesis of training models in helping (and their resulting training methods) can be traced to (1) education where actual teaching skills were incorporated into the models,

(2) psychology where the impact of behavior modification and social learning theory is obvious, and (3) the group counseling and group dynamics literature. The training model is an educational approach that directly attacks deficits through skills training. This approach is deemed more efficient and more effective (Adkins, 1984b; Goldstein, Sprafkin, & Gershaw, 1976; Lazarus, 1976) but represents a shift from the traditional treatment approach. Traditional helping approaches in psychiatry, psychology, and social work have emphasized understanding *causes* of deficit behavior through exploring the past, talking about the present, and planning changes for the future. In contrast, training approaches are concerned with learning. Founded on the belief that there are certain generic life-skills that are important for effective human functioning, these models deemphasize historical information and propose an educational approach to train others in needed skills. It is on this basis that the many training models have developed (see Table 15.1).

Model Development

It is apparent from an examination of the 13 models in Table 15.1 that the evolution of the skills training approach in mental health has a relatively short history. Despite the relative newness of the approach, skills training models have progressed from having a very narrow focus to having a strong and broadly based program.

The initial narrow focus was manifested in two ways: in the skills the models addressed and in the populations to be served. Early skills training models and research were confined mostly to the area of interpersonal relationship development (Carkhuff, 1969a, 1969b; Gazda et al., 1973; Pierce, Schauble, & Wilson, 1971). In the early to mid-1970s, more comprehensive models that moved beyond interpersonal communication skills and advocated training in more than one dimension began to appear. Of the multidimensional models, the ones with the most complete taxonomies are the Canadian, Life-Skills Training, People in Systems, Multimodal Behavior Therapy, and Developmental Therapy (see Table 15.1). The Canadian and Life-Skills models appear to be the most comprehensive, although the Canadian model is more focused on career development.

During this period, when models were progressing from focus on a particular skill toward focus on a taxonomy of skills, there was a great deal of parallel development that resulted in a number of researchers and practitioners proposing similar programs directed at a variety of populations. Notice in Table 15.1 that many of the training models in use today were narrowly focused in the sense that they were developed for specific populations. However, with few exceptions, either the original developer, his or her students or colleagues, or others have adapted the material for use with additional groups.

The life-skills training (LST) model developed by George Gazda (Gazda, Childers, & Brooks, 1987) has not been adapted. However, this model departs from the focus on a narrow population; LST is designed for general use with two exceptions: those who are actively psychotic and those whose reasoning abilities are impaired by organic brain syndrome.

In summary, the populations served by training models tend to be very general and in some cases limited only by decisions made by the users. Accordingly, many of

TABLE 15.1   Skills Training Models

MODEL	ORIGINATOR(S)	PRIMARY REFERENCE
Structured Learning Therapy	Arnold Goldstein, Robert Sprafkin, N. Jane Gershaw	Goldstein, A., Sprafkin, R., Gershaw, N. J. (1976). *Skill training for community living.* New York: Pergamon.
People in Systems	Gerard Egan, Michael Cowan	Egan, G., & Cowan, M. A. (1979). *People in systems.* Monterey, CA: Brooks/Cole.
Canadian	Saskatchewan Newstart	Smith, P. (1982). *The development of taxonomy of the life skills required to become a balanced self-determined person.* Ottawa, Canada: Employment and Immigration Canada.
Multimodal Behavior Therapy	Arnold Lazarus	Lazarus, A. A. (1976). *Multimodal behavior therapy.* New York: Springer.
Life Skills Education	Winthrop R. Adkins	Adkins, W. R. (1984a). Life skills education: A video-based counseling/learning system. In D. Larson (Ed.), *Teaching psychological skills: Models for giving psychology away.* Monterey, CA: Brooks/Cole.
Developmental Therapy	Mary Margaret Wood	Wood, M. M. (1975). *Developmental therapy.* Baltimore: University Park Press.
Relationship Enhancement	Bernard Guerney, Jr.	Guerney, B. G., Jr. (1977). *Relationship enhancement.* San Francisco: Jossey-Bass.
Structured Groups for Facilitating Development	David J. Drum, Jr. Eugene Knott	Drum, D. J., & Knott, J. E. (1977). *Structured groups for facilitating development.* New York: Human Sciences Press.

PRIMARY POPULATION	TRAINING METHODS	PREVENTIVE OR REMEDIAL	TAXONOMY DEVELOPMENT
Persons with psychological disturbances, skill-deficient adolescents, police, managers, teachers	Modeling, role-playing, feedback, transfer training	Developed as remedial	59 "modeling tapes" developed
Anyone	No specific methods developed; references given for recommended existing programs	Developed as preventive	Packages of skill needed to face developmental tasks and crises completely
Economically disadvantaged adults	61 lessons, all following 5-phase plan of stimulus evolution, objective skill, practice inquiry, skill application, and evaluation	Developed as remedial	Product objectives
All persons with psychological disturbances	Technical eclecticism; primarily didactic; each of 7 modalities requires attention	Remedial	Complete taxonomy has been developed around 7 modalities
Disadvantaged adolescents and adults	Instruction, audiovisual demonstration, discussion (problem-centered structured inquiry model)	Developed as remedial	"Sets" of prevocational, motivational, and social problems in living
Emotionally disturbed young children	Psychoeducational classroom approach	Developed as preventive	Complete development of 144 developmental therapy curriculum objectives in 4 curriculum areas: behavior, communication, socialization, and academic
Anyone who is able to master the relationship enhancement skills	Intellectual explanation discussion of concepts and teaching skills	Preventive and remedial	Confined to interpersonal relationship skills (developed for improving relationships between family members—now expanded to others)
Anyone	Educational experiential groups that provide procedures, methods, and systematic techniques	Preventive and remedial	Three areas: acquiring life skills, resolving life themes, and making life transitions; each has a series of workshop topics

(continued)

TABLE 15.1   Continued

MODEL	ORIGINATOR(S)	PRIMARY REFERENCE
Human Resources Development	Robert R. Carkhuff & Associates	Carkhuff, R. R. (1969). *Helping and human relations: A primer for lay and professional helpers. Vols. 1 & 2.* New York: Holt, Rinehart and Winston.
Psychosocial Adjustment Skills	Robert L. Akridge, Bob L. Means	Akridge, R. L., & Means, B. L. (1982). Psychosocial adjustment skills training. In B. Bolton (Ed.), *Vocational adjustment of disabled persons.* Baltimore: University Park Press.
Deliberate Psycho-logical Education	Ralph L. Mosher, Norman A. Sprinthall	Mosher, R. L., & Sprinthall, N. A. (1971). Psychological education: A means to promote personal development during adolescence. *The Counseling Psychologist, 2*(4), 3–82.
Changes	Eugene Gendlin, Kathleen McGuire Boukydis	Gendlin, E. T. (1981). *Focusing.* New York: Bantam.
Life-Skills Training	George M. Gazda	Gazda, G. M., Childers, W. C., & Brooks, D. K., Jr. (1987). *Foundations of counseling and human services.* New York: McGraw-Hill.

PRIMARY POPULATION	TRAINING METHODS	PREVENTIVE OR REMEDIAL	TAXONOMY DEVELOPMENT
Anyone	Helpees go through sequence of involvement, exploration, understanding, and action	Developed as remedial	Primarily interpersonal relationships; also developed a physical fitness/ health maintenance program
Vocational rehabilitation clients	Training group	Remedial	3 competency areas: self-management, interpersonal relations, and life planning "Spheres" of functioning: physical, intrapersonal, ideological, financial, and technical
Adolescents	Group and classroom instruction by teachers and counselors	Preventive	
Anyone interested in talking about his or her situation in a supportive group of listeners and who is willing to serve also as a listener to others	Weekly 2- to 3-hour meeting for participating to learn listening and focusing skills; Egalitarian peer-helping takes place in pairs, triads, or small groups; no distinction is made between "helpers" and "helpees"	Can be preventive or remedial	Based on the client-centered model as developed by Carl Rogers
All except actively psychotic or those whose reasoning abilities are impaired by organic brain syndrome	Instruction in skill-deficit areas using wide variety of materials and methods according to following sequence: brief instruction, trainee role-play and practice, feedback, and homework	Developed with preventive and remedial dimensions; multiple impact training is the name given to remedial part of the model	"Families" of life skills suggested; generic life skills (GLS) empirically derived are: ■ Fitness/health maintenance ■ Identity development ■ Interpersonal communication/human relations ■ Problem solving/ decision making GLS are applied in family, work, school, and community

the original models that were developed to meet the needs of specific populations were quickly adapted for use with other groups. Adaptation was possible because the skills training methodology, derived from related disciplines, is a consistent process, flexible enough to accommodate various skills and populations.

There are similar elements in the training methods of each of the models examined in Table 15.1 in the sense that they all contain some combination of cognitive and experiential components. The differences lie in the extent to which each component is used in the training and in the specific topics included in the model. Also, there is a tendency in these models to use existing intervention strategies in the experiential phase rather than strategies that are unique to the particular model.

As has been demonstrated in this overview, skills training models have progressed from a focus on a particular skill and/or a particular population to programs that encompass a comprehensive taxonomy of skills applicable to a very general population. The commonality tying these models together is the educational approach evident philosophically and in the training methodology used to implement these programs as helping approaches. In a very brief period of time, there has been successful development of a new approach to mental health. The popularity and rapidly increasing application of the skills training procedures for the prevention and remediation of human problems suggests that the field is in the midst of the development of a "fourth force" in mental health prevention and treatment. Life-skills training is a comprehensive contribution to this fourth force.

The Development and Rationale of the Life-Skills Training Model

The LST model has been a progressive development, the product of many years of professional experience of the senior author, George Gazda. The earliest influence on this model was during the 1960s and 1970s when Gazda was actively engaged in the development of group counseling and therapy (Gazda, 1968a, 1968b, 1971, 1978). During this period, Gazda and his students conducted groups with several different populations, including juvenile delinquents, professional educators, psychiatric patients, recovering alcoholics, convicted felons, and adults seeking personal growth, among others. Contact with the developing groups procedures for implementing therapeutic intervention and different kinds of contact—such as with experimental research, especially in the form of doctoral dissertations—further influenced Gazda's thinking and accounted for his ideas changing.

The result of this experience, of particular relevance to the LST model, was the gradual development of a theory of developmental group counseling. This developmental model for group counseling was especially influenced by the work of developmental theorists such as Erickson (1950, 1963), Havighurst (1953, 1972), Tryon and Lilienthal (1950), Super (1963), Gesell, Ilg, Ames, and Bullis (1946), Piaget (Flavell, 1963; Wadsworth, 1971), Kohlberg and Turiel (1971), Loevinger (1976), and Dupont (1978). A comprehensive framework for the application for developmental group counseling included the holistic view of development of individuals across ages and stages.

Concurrent with Gazda's development of a comprehensive groups counseling model, he and his students and colleagues were influenced by the human resources development model of Robert Carkhuff and associates (1969a, 1969b). From this model, Gazda and colleagues developed human relations/communications training applications for educators (Gazda et al., 1973, 1977, 1984, 1991, 1995, 1999), health care practitioners (Gazda, Childers, & Walters, 1982; Gazda, Walters, & Childers, 1975), criminal justice personnel (Sisson, Arthur, & Gazda, 1981), and secondary school students (Gazda, Walters, & Childers, 1981).

Two decades of experience in the application of communication and problem-solving skills training to psychiatric patients in a veterans administration hospital led Gazda and a clinical nurse specialist, Mildred Powell, to introduce a holistic treatment model—multiple impact training (Gazda, 1981). This approach introduced the idea of providing simultaneous training interventions of multiple generic life-skills. In evaluating this approach, May (1981) found a significant improvement in trained patients over controls in two out of three of the generic life-skill areas in which they were trained. Additional research by Illovsky (1985) also found significant improvement in trained patients over controls on two life-skills variables.

Following this experience with a remedial life-skills approach, Gazda and his students developed life-skills training modules that have been applied to elementary and secondary schools for preventive purposes. Research on these programs is promising (Kavkewitz, 1983; Spalding, 1985).

The final development leading to the model proposed in this text was the Delphi dissertation study (Brooks, 1984). Using descriptors of knowledge/skills necessary for successful coping behavior consonant with age and/or stage of development, theorists achieved consensus on the basic life-skills for each age group: childhood, adolescence, and adulthood. These experts also classified the life-skills by generic area, producing the four generic life-skills described earlier.

Theoretical Rationale for Life-Skills Training

The viewpoint expressed in the LST model, of an age-progressive developmental framework, is consistent with U.S. society and with Western culture in general, since the cultures are organized on the basis of expected increments of mastery in the biological, intellectual, vocational, sociological, and psychological realms of their citizens.

When building the LST model, we began with how the whole person is constituted developmentally (see Figure 13.1 in Chapter 13). Notice that there are seven areas of human development represented. It is the theories associated with these seven areas that are the source from which descriptions of skills have been determined. Through the Brooks (1984) Delphi study, these descriptors have been grouped by age and rated as to their importance in human development. Additional descriptors were added by the developmental experts. Each expert classified the descriptors into generic life-skills areas, or families of related knowledge and skills by age groups (see Figure 13.1 in Chapter 13).

The life-skills taxonomy admittedly represents compromises and certain liberties in interpretations of developmental theoretical models. The greatest liberty assumed was the classification of knowledge/skills descriptors of *stage* theorists into the three general *age* groupings of childhood, adolescence, and adulthood. Essentially, these were the theories of intellectual, ego, moral, and affective development. Even those theories of human development that are age related—namely, psychosocial, physical-sexual, and vocational—contain various gaps, especially at the upper end of the age scale. Even with these weaknesses, the life-skills taxonomy represents the first comprehensive attempt using a developmental rationale.

Basic Assumptions

The following list briefly discusses the basic assumptions underlying the life-skills training model:

1. *There are at least seven well-defined areas of human development: psychosocial, physical-sexual, vocational, cognitive, ego, moral, and affective (see Figure 13.1 in Chapter 13).* Although others may have developed models for areas of human development, seven theorists were selected for the life-skills model. These, together with their developmental area, are as follows: Erikson (1950, 1963), Havighurst (1953, 1972), and Tryon and Lilienthal (1950) (psychosocial); Gesell, Ilg, Ames, and Bullis (1946) (physical-sexual); Super (1963) (vocational); Piaget (cf. Flavell, 1963; Wadsworth, 1971) (cognitive); Loevinger (1976) (ego); Kohlberg and Turiel (1971) (moral); and Dupont (1978) (affective).

2. *From the seven well-defined areas of human development, coping behaviors (life-skills) can be determined that are appropriate to age or stage.* Each of the theorists who has developed models included as the seven areas of human development has also specified certain attitudes and behaviors that seem to be necessary for individuals to achieve mastery of a given age or stage. For example, Havighurst (1953, 1972) pointed out that during middle age (between ages 30 and 60), the man and woman must abandon the more strenuous leisure-time activities and develop leisure-time activities that are meaningful, satisfying, and applicable to the physical limitations of their age.

Using the attitudes and behaviors specified by the theorists, Gazda identified approximately 300 life-skills from the seven areas of human development. These 300 life-skills and others contributed by selected developmental experts contacted in the Delphi questionnaire (Brooks, 1984) can be classified into three general age groups: childhood, adolescence, and adulthood. Furthermore, a consensus of developmental experts can be obtained for each life-skill by age grouping. In essence, a taxonomy of life-skills by three general age groupings can be constructed (Brooks, 1984).

3. *There are identifiable stages in each of the seven areas of human development through which individuals must progress if they are to achieve mastery of later, more advanced stages.* This assumption can be illustrated by reference to a specific area—moral development. According to Duska and Whelan (1975), stage development is invariant in moral development. In reference to Kohlberg's moral stage development theory, they state, "Moral development is growth, and like all growth, takes place according to a pre-determined sequence" (p. 48).

4. *Accomplishment of developmental tasks is dependent on mastery of* life-skills— *that is, coping behaviors appropriate to stage and task.* This concept may be illustrated by citing a psychosocial developmental task of early childhood followed by the coping behaviors necessary to achieve this task. "Achieving an appropriate dependence-independence pattern" represents the developmental task. The coping behaviors necessary to complete this task require "adjusting to less private attention and becoming independent physically while remaining strongly dependent emotionally." Examples of this would be a child's ability to share parents with his or her new teacher, with peers, and with others while simultaneously learning rules of safety to give greater mobility and physical independence.

5. *In general, there are certain age ranges when certain coping skills (life-skills) are optimally learned.* A developmental model, whether age- or stage-related, assumes that mastery of concepts and skills at an earlier level is prerequisite to mastery of more advanced concepts and skills. Much of the remedial instruction in education is also based on this assumption. For example, before one is able to master long division, one must first be able to master the multiplication process. In career development, before one achieves the highest position on a career ladder, one must achieve mastery of successive lower positions on the ladder. In achieving a positive self-concept, one must struggle with moments of self-doubt and various degrees of insecurity.

Havighurst (1972) supported this assumption of an optimal learning period with two related concepts: the "teachable moment" and the "developmental task." Concerning the first, he stated, "When the body is ripe, and society requires and the self is ready to achieve a certain task, the teachable moment has come" (p. 7). In defense of his concept of this teachable moment, Havighurst (1972) referred to Palmer's introduction to a conference on critical periods of development sponsored by the Social Science Research Council:

> In their respective ways, von Sendon, Lorenz, Spitz, and Piaget have observed phenomena which suggest that there may be critical periods in the development of the child—points or stages during which the organism is maximally receptive to specific stimuli. Such stages may exist in the development of fundamental sensory processes, such as conceptions about size, shape, distance, and in the development of social behavior as well. The critical periods hypothesis asserts that those stages are of limited duration: there may be a finite period of increased inefficiency for the acquisition of experience, before which it cannot be assimilated and after which the level of receptivity remains constant. (p. 6)

Havighurst's (1953) description of the developmental task carried the readiness concept one step further:

> A developmental task is a task which arises at or about a certain period of life of the individual, successful achievement of which leads to happiness and success with later tasks, while failure leads to unhappiness in the individual, disapproval by society, and difficulty with later tasks. (p. 2)

The position taken in this text is that the coping skill(s) necessary to complete a given developmental task or series of developmental tasks that may constitute a *stage* of development can be determined across the seven areas of human development cited earlier. In the LST model, these constitute a life-skill or a group of life-skills.

6. *Individuals achieve optimal functioning when they attain operational mastery of fundamental life-skills.* This assumption is dependent on future research. Before comprehensive research can be initiated, however, instruments and other means for assessing life-skills mastery must be developed. Some promising self-report instruments are described by Darden, Gazda, and Ginter (1996) and Darden, Ginter, and Gazda (1996).

In the meantime, life-skill mastery must be shown empirically to be necessary and sufficient for optimal functioning; there is some argument on this issue, stemming from an alternate, more "traditional" frame of reference. Bellack (1979) acknowledged that insofar as the skill model ascribes *some* interpersonal difficulties to specific response deficits, these deficits are conceptually responsive to skills training programs. He cautioned, however, that there are a variety of other factors that could cause the same pattern of social failures. For instance, anxiety has been shown to interfere with many types of behavior patterns and to serve as an inhibitory function over others (Bellack, 1979; Martin, 1971). In addition, research (Arkowitz, Lichtenstein, McGovern, & Hines, 1985; Wolpe & Lazarus, 1966) indicates that interpersonal anxiety can interfere with effective social performance even in the absence of social skills deficits. Further, cognitive disturbances, such as ones associated with schizophrenia, can interfere with or distort interpersonal communication as well as produce bizarre behavior that results in interpersonal failure (Bellack, 1979; Bellack & Hersen, 1978). Faulty attributions have also been shown to affect the course of interpersonal behavior independent of skill level (Eisler, Frederiksen, & Peterson, 1978; Warren & Gilner, 1978). And finally, Bellack suggested that people can have response capabilities in their repertoires but fail to emit the response because they have not been reinforced (or have been punished).

7. *Neuroses and functional psychoses frequently result from failure to develop one's life-skills.* Kazdin (1979) acknowledged the importance of social behavior in psychotic patients in the following statement:

> Social behaviors occupy an important role in the definition of behavior of psychotic patients as evidenced by withdrawal, irrational statements, blunted affect, and difficulty in communication skills. These behaviors do not begin to exhaust the symptoms of psychiatric patients but illustrate the role of social behavior in identifying psychopathology. (p. 54)

Citing the research of Fairweather, Sanders, Maynard, and Cressier (1969), Freeman and Simmons (1963), and Staudt and Zubin (1957) encompassing several somatic, pharmacological, and psychotherapeutic treatments, Kazdin (1979) showed the treatment provided in the hospital had little relationship to community adjustment of psychiatric patients. Research by Greenberg and colleagues (1975), Linn, Caffey, Klett, and Hogarty (1977), and Paul and Lentz (1977), on the other hand, suggested more favorable results for specific treatments, such as *social learning* programs and foster home care:

The problems in social behaviors that psychiatric patients evidence apparently do not simply emerge immediately preceding their entrance into the career of a patient. Persons later seen in treatment have often shown a history of prior [poor] social relations and withdrawal from interpersonal social relationships. Possibly, there would be value in identifying individuals with such interpersonal deficits prior to the point at which this is compounded with additional problems of pathology in order to intervene early. (Kazdin, 1979, p. 65)

Zubin and Spring (1977) have suggested that improvements in *coping skills* in general, and particularly in the area of *social interaction,* are possible factors that might decrease a susceptibility to schizophrenia. The evidence reviewed by Kazdin that persons diagnosed as psychotic have had a long history of interpersonal problems, particularly those with a poor prognosis, suggests the value of training in social skills early in life as an attempt to decrease the risk of psychiatric treatment later in life.

With regard to neurotics, Bryant and colleagues (1976) found that 28 percent of a sample of neurotic outpatients were regarded as socially unskilled. Argyle (1981) reported that these same neurotic outpatients were low in components of control (assertiveness) and rewardingness and were extremely bad conversationalists. They often suffered acutely from social anxiety and avoided many social situations altogether. Argyle concluded that neurotic patients suffer from all the main kinds of social inadequacy:

I conclude that SST [social skills training], of various kinds, is useful for neurotics, especially those with social behavior problems, and I believe that it will be most effective if use is made of the principles of social interaction. A valuable recent development, especially in North America, is the administration of SST by nurses, social workers, probation officers, and so on, as well as by psychologists. (Argyle, 1981, p. 283)

8. *Instruction and/or training in life-skills that is introduced when a person is developmentally ready to learn given concepts and skills serves the role of preventive mental health.* The position taken in the LST model is that if individuals are taught the subskills of the four generic life-skills during the optimum period for them to be learned, and if in fact they are learned, the cumulative effect would be to enable them to contend effectively with life's problems and therefore be less subject to mental and emotional disturbances. This assumption represents the basis for the preventive mental health contention of this model. Obviously, only long-term, longitudinal studies can validate this assumption. Until such time as a comprehensive LST program can be initiated through the age span, this assumption will remain unvalidated.

9. *Instruction and/or training in life-skills that is introduced when a person is suffering from emotional or mental disturbance, of a functional nature, serves the role of remediation in mental health.* If one assumes that persons suffering from emotional or mental disturbances that are not the result of organic origin are so affected because they lack appropriate coping skills in one or more of the generic life-skills areas, then instruction and/or training that develops coping skills will result in a remediation of these skill deficits, and the person will be able to cope effectively. This assumption can be tested more readily than the previous one because the effects of remedial interventions can be determined immediately following the training.

10. *The greater the degree of functional disturbance, the greater the likelihood that the individual will be suffering from multiple life-skill deficits.* Consultation and research by Gazda in a psychiatric hospital over a period of more than 20 years has suggested that hospitalized patients suffer from *multiple* life-skill deficits. Furthermore, remediation of these patients requires multiple life-skill training interventions. These multiple life-skill interventions have been shown by May (1981) to result in improvement by psychiatric patients.

The basic assumptions of the LST model provide the elements that permit the operationalization of the model when combined with the more than 300 specific life-skill descriptors determined from the national Delphi study (see Gazda, 1989). Our concern now, in the next section, is with outlining the process through which the LST model is implemented.

ISSUES IN ESTABLISHING TRAINING GROUPS

Selection of Members

Since there are two basic types of training groups—training for prevention and training for remediation—the initial question is whether groups will be composed of prevention or remediation candidates. Although there are situations when two groups are required for effective training, sometimes prevention and remediation candidates will be mixed in the same group. Consider, for example, a population of all ninth-graders in a particular school who are being trained in physical fitness and health maintenance skills. Some students would likely be obese or deficient in some physical exertion measure, whereas others would be in the normal or average range but could benefit from the skill training by applying the principles or adopting the life-style that will maintain their status as they move through life. Those who are in the remedial category can also benefit from the same information by applying the principles to their lives in a way that allows them to move toward the average and then continue to apply the principles to maintain the position once acquired. In this case, it is not as important to segregate prevention candidates from remediation candidates, since both groups could benefit from the information. Making the decision to segregate the two groups can generally be determined by whether separation is logistically possible, by the way in which the curriculum is written, and by whether the two groups could benefit equally from the experience.

An important factor in member selection is whether the potential member is volunteering or is asked to participate by someone else. If practical, groups composed of persons who volunteer to participate are most desirable. The advantage to this arrangement is obvious. A training group can be quickly sabotaged by members who tune out the trainer and training.

Another approach to selection, particularly of reluctant members, is a trial membership in a training group. This is a technique that tends to decrease a negative response and gives a group member the option of either staying or leaving after a certain number of hours or sessions. A good rule of thumb is to ask the person to stay for the first one-third of the sessions. This allows ample time to understand the nature of the group, the style of the leader, the other participants, and the potential benefit of the training to the person's life. If, after the trial period, the individual decides to drop out of the group, the decision is based on facts rather than assumptions. In reality, many times, the most resistant member initially becomes the strongest supporter later.

Training Group Composition

There are pros and cons concerning heterogeneity and homogeneity along a number of variables when considering group composition. From experience with hundreds of training groups, though, we have developed some guidelines that work most of the time. At times there are budgetary or logistical constraints that dictate a different composition, or a group is preidentified, as in a work group or a school class. When selection for grouping is a possibility, the following guidelines are advocated:

1. In training groups conducted at worksites, keep groups homogeneous with regard to level of position. For example, training groups for hospital personnel work best if all members are functioning at essentially the same level—*supervisors* in nursing, housekeeping, and business office could be trained together. This arrangement tends to decrease threat and increase verbalization of all members. This also avoids the situation of supervisors in the same training group with their supervisees.

2. Mixing departments in the group representation allows rapport and thus better understanding to develop interdepartmentally. This is a positive residual spin-off of training groups that address a frequent problem, especially in larger organizations. We have found that by forcing interaction through participation in the same group, group members frequently develop an appreciation for the problems that departments other than their own experience, resulting in an increase in interdepartmental cooperation and esprit de corps.

3. In many organizations there are employees who respond negatively to any changes or innovations that are introduced. These persons should be spread out over several groups to prevent sabotage of the training group. This guideline, in fact, applies generally across groups of various ages and settings.

4. Mix sexes and races in training groups to approximate the real world.

5. Grouping children in elementary and high school depends to some extent on the training topic, and since there are so many individual differences from school to school, a *rough* guideline is to avoid mixing children with preadolescents and preadolescents with adolescents. However, these categories frequently overlap within the same grade, and so sometimes the decision about mixing these categories must be made at the time of the training, taking into consideration all of the existing factors mentioned in this chapter as well as the trainer's "intuition." One approach in the school setting is to assign training groups tentatively with the understanding that changes might be made after the training begins. If all students understand this from the outset, changes that are made will be more readily accepted.

6. When grouping individuals who require significant remedial training, such as community mental health patients and psychiatric patients, the primary criteria are that they have deficits in the same generic life-skill areas and that they are in contact with reality.

Training Group Setting

A typical classroom that seats 30 students is adequate for training school-age children and adolescents, assuming that desks/chairs can be moved to create smaller groupings of two to eight or less. Units for training are developed so that the teacher/leader gives instructions or a minilecture to the entire class and then subgroups are formed with peer leaders to work on the training exercises while the adult teacher or leader moves from group to group, monitoring the process. A similar setting can be used for adult training groups, but since training with adult groups is not usually done in an academic setting, conference rooms are usually more appropriate. Also, groups usually are 10 to 12 in size, so options for subgroupings into pairs or triads are possible. Regardless of physical location, the setting should be free from disruption and extraneous noise.

Training Group Size

Since the success of training groups depends on active participation of group members in the exercises, size is very important. There might very well be a constraint in a particular situation that would dictate either a group too large or too small to be effective. However, when given a choice, a group size of 10 to 18 members seems to be optimal. Fewer than 10 might not allow as much peer feedback as desired and might encourage 1 or 2 to monopolize the group time. A group larger than 18 gets unwieldy in terms of controlling the situation and getting everyone involved in the exercise. In our experience, 12 members is optimal because of the possible subdivision available (two groups of six, six groups of two, three groups of four, four groups of three). Also, when working with the entire group, 12 persons can easily participate in each exercise without delaying the process.

At times, large groups of individuals (50 or more people) with minimal deficits are trained by using co-trainers or assistants, or peer helpers who distribute themselves throughout the group to answer questions, aid in role-playing or other experiential activity, or simply observe. This model can be effective; the key to its successful implementation seems to be skilled assistants. This way, a trainer can present didactic information as well as model desired behavior, then give assignments to the group, and let the assistants aid in the skill acquisition process. The drawback of this model, in addition to problems associated with weak assistants, is that rapport does not develop as quickly, so participants are likely to be reluctant to become personally involved in the training setting. This could possibly impede gain in skill development.

The Training Group Trainer

The skill and personal qualities of the trainer are of paramount importance to the success of the training experience. Although generalists do exist in the training field, it is more common that a trainer will be proficient in one or two skills that thus establish him or her as an "expert" in those areas. However, an additional expertise is required for the LST model. The array of roles the trainer assumes include teacher, model, evaluator, motivator, encourager, facilitator, protector, and training media developer (Gazda et al., 1987). Trainers must be competent to fulfill these roles across skill areas. The process during which this achievement occurs can be viewed as a *pyramid of training.*

The first step in the process is training the prospective trainer in the skills to be taught. This includes essentially putting prospective trainers through an experience similar to the one that they will be expected eventually to lead. The systematic training allows achievement of skills at points along the way in training, thus developing the ability to model the skill effectively. This ability is of paramount importance in training. Included in the training at this stage of trainer instruction is the ability to transfer successfully the modeling of the skills from the training group to everyday life.

The second stage of trainer instruction involves co-leadership of a training group with an experienced, effective trainer. This phase allows the neophyte trainer's way of being with people to be incorporated with proven training exercises.

The third step in trainer instruction involves allowing the neophyte trainer to train alone under the supervision of an experienced trainer. This can be accomplished in a number of ways, including observation through a one-way mirror, videotape or audiotape recordings of the group that are evaluated later, or having the experienced leader participate as a naive group member in the training group. The key here is genuine feedback that will allow the neophyte trainer to fine-tune his or her skills.

The last stage is when the neophyte trainer trains alone. At this point, *neophyte* may be a misnomer, even though this is an anxiety-inducing experience for some trainers. The anxiety is generally short-lived, however, since only the most effective persons progress to this point. Along the way, the trainers are taught to encourage group members, give effective feedback in a nonhurtful manner, evaluate the progress of each group member, motivate members to practice the skills outside the group, protect sensitive members from hurt or verbal attack of stronger members, and listen closely to identify barriers, hidden agendas, inadequacies, strengths, fears, or other items that might affect group process or skill achievement.

In addition to the skills mentioned, one important quality of effective trainers is that they allow disagreement or even confrontation without becoming defensive or feeling that their own position needs to be defended. If the trainer is comfortably confident with himself or herself, it is possible to listen to disagreement or confrontation without personalizing it. This difficult stance in a group setting is one of the tests that expert trainers have to pass when implementing the training sequence with groups.

Sequence of Training

The training process takes place in roughly the following sequence:

1. *Theoretical Instruction.* This part of training is kept to a minimum in order to devote the majority of time to skill development. However, the extent to which a theoretical rationale and documentation of the technique takes place depends on particular members and the level of the group. Brighter, more articulate group members demand and should receive more communication of the theoretical underpinning of the process, whereas less aware groups will spend the majority of their time in the experiential mode.

2. *Leader Modeling.* One of the first experiential activities is initiated by the group leader, who models what he or she considers to be appropriate behavior (based on the skill being taught). Group members are thus able to visualize the process. An alternative at this stage is a videotape illustrating the skill in a controlled setting. This is a valuable supplement to a training group, since the tape can be designed to communicate some very specific teaching points. It also allows the trainer to focus more on the group without having to do specific modeling at this point.

3. *Demonstration Using Simulations.* The group leader has a number of options, beginning with using paper-and-pencil responses as a nonthreatening group activity. Other options include a variety of role-playing arrangements, from a group role-play involving everyone, to a role-play demonstration in front of the group, or various configurations of the group in role-play practice. The simulations comprise the heart of the training process and allow members to begin feeling comfortable with the process and with the new skills. It is important when designing the simulations to begin with the least threatening situation and move with each new activity to an increasing level of threat. The threat is induced by being put on the spot in front of others to exhibit a new skill; thus, the trainer might move from anonymous to personal and from hypothetical to real.

4. *Personally Relevant Interactions.* Toward the end of the training process, the leader, by virtue of skill development and rapport among group members, should be in a position to ask the group to discuss real or personally relevant situations with each other. This is the step immediately preceding generalization of the skill outside the group setting. The trainer can determine readiness at this point by observing the extent to which group members are willing to disclose their feelings and are committed to transferring the information or insight they have gained to a specific situation outside the group.

5. *Transfer of Training.* The ultimate effects of training are the degree to which the training transfers to dealing with the problems of daily living. In one sense, this stage is a part of each of the four previous stages as well as a separate or final stage. It is part of each stage insofar as homework assignments given during each of the stages relate to transfer of the skill being developed to relevant issues in one's life. And, of course, the final goal/stage of training is transferability of laboratory-learned skills to real-life situations.

Techniques Used

In the preceding section of this chapter, we described the basic training model employed in skills training. Typically, the sequence for training begins with the leader providing an intellectual explanation or rationale for the training unit. The second phase provides trainees the opportunity to discuss and react to the leader's rationale underlying the unit. Following the discussion and clarification, the third phase is practice, which involves leader modeling of the concept/skill to be learned, role-playing by the leader and trainees, feedback by the leader and trainees, and finally homework to be done by trainees between training sessions.

Supplements Used

The number and variety of supplements employed are limited only by the ingenuity of the trainer. Nevertheless, there are some basic media employed that have proven effective in enhancing training in certain skills. Especially valuable is audio-video feedback when training individuals in interpersonal communication skills. It is best if the video operator is operating from a studio-type room adjoining the training room. This allows the trainer to communicate directly with the operator as the tapes are reviewed.

Other supplements include bibliotherapeutic reading assignments, homework (practice) assignments, paper-and-pencil tests and exercises, personal journals and record keeping, among others. Any supplement that would facilitate a better understanding of the skill to be learned and increased practice of the skill would be appropriate.

Special Ethical Considerations

Inasmuch as some skills training sessions resemble group counseling/therapy, there is a need to advise trainees of the importance of maintaining confidentiality of self-disclosures made in training sessions. Personally relevant self-disclosure is especially pertinent when training in the areas of interpersonal communication and problem solving/decision making; and trainees need to be cautioned to maintain confidentiality of these disclosures.

When trainees are encouraged to volunteer to role-play and practice certain skills, there is a risk of poor performance that could be embarrassing. Trainees should therefore be given options of "passing" when their turn comes up.

Sometimes trainees are in therapy with the trainer. In these cases, much caution must be taken by the therapist not to divulge content from a therapy session during a training session.

Often, training includes groups of people who work closely together. In such cases, supervisors should not be trained with supervisees. Training of homogeneous work groups also strains confidentiality. Screening for training groups is typically not as rigorous as for therapy groups. Thus, there is the possibility that some members will need to be deselected if they do not fit with their co-trainees.

Constant vigilance is needed on the trainer's part not to mix therapy with training. This is an easy mistake to make.

Multicultural Issues

Insofar as life-skills training and other related models of social skills training are used in prevention as well as remediation of psychosocial and behavioral deficits, there will always be the need to monitor the relevance of the training for a given culture, race, gender, ethnic group, and so on. If one uses the developmental descriptors for the four generic life-skills of the Gazda model in Gazda, Childers, and Brooks (1987, Appendixes D through G), the user should be aware that the population from which these descriptors of knowledge and skills were derived were mostly middle-class Caucasians and that the data in the area of physical-sexual development were obtained in the 1940s.

Regardless of which model of skills training that the trainer might employ, he or she will need to allow trainees the opportunity to question the knowledge/skill that is being taught/trained. Trainees will resist or reject training that cannot be assimilated into their system of values and beliefs.

Sample Training Sessions

Two samples of training sessions for children (ages 5 to 9) (Example 1) and adolescents (ages 13 to 18) (Example 2) are included to illustrate how life-skills training can be incorporated into the school curriculum. A third example is given to illustrate how training can be provided for adults in a community mental health center. Each example is for one training session only and is preceded and followed by related training sessions. (A videotape demonstration of life-skills training with adults is available through Part 2 of "Gazda on Groups" and can be obtained from Microtraining Associates, Inc., Box 9641, North Amherst MA 01059-9641. See Instructor's Manual for details.)

IDENTITY DEVELOPMENT/PURPOSE IN LIFE-SKILLS TRAINING: EXAMPLE 1
   I. *Setting:* School/Children
  II. *Life-Skill Objectives:* Ability to obey rules in the absence of authority, to face problems with confidence in one's ability to solve them, to understand one's place within one's immediate environment, to understand that one's perspective is often different from that of others.
 III. *Activity:* Give children this situation: An extraterrestrial being wants to attend their school for awhile. Parents agree, but only if children take the responsibility for teaching the extraterrestrial earth manners.
   A. Procedure:
      1. Let children discuss this novel situation among themselves for awhile.
      2. Ask children to brainstorm what manners they would teach the extraterrestrial. Then ask them to discuss why they chose the particular manners they did.
      3. Ask children how they would teach the extraterrestrial the manners identified.
      4. Contract with the children to practice no more than three of the chosen manners for the coming week.
      5. Ask children at week's end to evaluate how well the extraterrestrial would have learned manners during the preceding week.

6. Identify new sets of manners to be taught to the extraterrestrial during the following week.

PROBLEM-SOLVING/DECISION-MAKING SKILLS TRAINING: EXAMPLE 2

I. *Setting:* School/Adolescents

II. *Life-Skill Objectives:* Ability to analyze multiple variables in problem solving, to learn to use an effective approach to decision making, to do critical task analysis as an initial step in problem solving.

III. *Activity:* Curriculum in problem solving. Present students with a fictitious newspaper article. For example:

Singer Jay Geally has been fired from the title role in the hit Broadway musical *Rowing Along the Mississippi.* Apparently no one told him the show must go on, and he had missed twelve performances since taking over the role on November 2—and he also missed his originally scheduled opening performance in September. Understudy Dan Dickson will perform until a new star is found. Absenteeism also cost Jay a TV series, "Hard Rock." The reason given was emotional problems because of the breakup of his marriage to superstar Brenda Beaconson.

A. Procedure:
   1. Have students identify the problem.
   2. Ask students to define the problem and delineate any subproblems.
   3. Students can generate possible solutions.
   4. Ask students to role-play and decide which of the solutions would be most appropriate.
   5. As a group, students can discuss their individual decisions and "imaginatively" assess the possible outcomes of the various solutions.

INTERPERSONAL COMMUNICATION/HUMAN RELATIONS SKILLS TRAINING: EXAMPLE 3

I. *Setting:* Community/Adults

II. *Life-Skill Objectives:* Ability to establish and enjoy relationships within social groups; recognize and respect the individual's rights, personal worth, and uniqueness of others; tolerate and respect those of different backgrounds, habits, values, and appearance.

III. *Activity:* Through a program in the mental health center, learn the components of effective listening skills and practice effective listening skills.

A. Procedure:
   1. Generate list of good listening characteristics
      a. The group will discuss the characteristics of a good listener and generate a list. Write these on the chalkboard.
   2. Interviewing in dyads
      a. Have persons choose a partner whom they do not know well. Each partner is to take about five minutes to tell the other about himself or herself using items such as: how long he has lived here, where she was born, information about his family, outside interests, one behavior she values

in herself, and so on. The listener then repeats the information, which the speaker corrects if necessary. Then roles are reversed.

3. Introducing a person to the group
   a. Bring the group back together and ask each person to introduce his or her partner to the group. When all persons have participated, discuss the activity, starting with the question, "What did you find out about others in the group?" or "What did you learn about your listening skills?"
4. Homework: Instruct persons to observe the nonverbal listening behaviors of others and be prepared to share this with the group at the next session.

Research

Gazda's (Gazda et al., 1987) life-skills training model has been the subject of numerous research studies for over 20 years. The earliest studies concentrated on interpersonal communication training with teachers and prospective teachers (see Gazda et al., 1999). Improved interpersonal communication skills were demonstrated with as little as 20 hours of training. Similar studies of trainees occurred in church work (McCurdy, 1975), corrections (Chishom, 1975), medical units (Seidenschnur, 1974), houseparent roles (Layser, 1974), and psychiatric patients (Illovsky, 1985; May, 1981; Powell, Illovsky, O'Leary, & Gazda, 1988) who showed significant gains in interpersonal communication skills. Additional life-skills changes in health maintenance and vocational development were found in trained psychiatric patients by Illovsky (1985), May, Powell, Gazda, and Hauser (1985), and Powell and colleagues (1988). Instruments for assessing life-skills changes are described in articles by Darden, Gazda, and Ginter (1996), Darden, Ginter, and Gazda, (1996), and Picklesimer, Hooper, and Ginter (1998).

Hundreds of *studies* have been completed on skills training. In the period from 1970 to 1981 alone, Marshall and Kurtz (1982) cited 141. The ERIC database listed 342 social skills/psychoeducation *articles* for the period of 1990 to 1998. Research, however, does not confirm the unequivocal superiority of one skills training model over another (Marshall, Charping, & Bell, 1979; Schneider & Byrne, 1985). Matarazzo (1978) reported, however, that skills training models seem to produce results superior to control group results.

Schneider and Byrne (1985) investigated through meta-analysis the comparative effectiveness of the primary models of social skills training. No single intervention was found to be uniformly effective. Effectiveness varied among subjects and settings. Nevertheless, when mean effect sizes were compared across all studies with various subjects and problems, operant interventions were more effective than modeling and coaching, and modeling and coaching were likewise more effective than social cognitive methods. Coaching and operant interventions were most effective with aggressive children, whereas modeling methods were highly effective for withdrawn children.

Schneider and Byrne attempted to interpret the differing intervention effects by suggesting that withdrawal-related problems may be the result of skill deficits and that modeling is an effective intervention strategy for alleviating the deficit. They suggested that aggression may be related to the inability to appropriately use skills that have already been learned. They, therefore, suggested further that aggressive children may learn to use appropriate behaviors in social situations through coaching and appropriate reinforcement.

Jones, Sheridan, and Binns (1993) recommended that a combination of social skills training techniques be utilized because of the complexity of interpersonal behaviors:

> In general, coaching, modeling, behavioral rehearsal, cueing, and positive reinforcement are potent components of social skills programs for students at risk. To maximize treatment effectiveness and increase potency of social skills interventions, these procedures should be implemented as a package and not in isolation. (p. 66)

A large body of literature now exists that documents the effectiveness of social skills training as a therapeutic intervention for a large variety of populations. These include children and adolescents (Cummings & Haggerty, 1997; DuPaul & Eckert, 1994; Kutnick & Marshall, 1993; O'Reilly & Glynn, 1995; Thompson, Bundy, & Wolfe, 1996), and especially children and adolescents with autism and learning disabilities (Conte, 1995; Elksnin, Elksnin, & Sabornie, 1994; Forness & Kavale, 1996; Gonzalez-Lopez & Kamps, 1997), as well as at-risk and behavioral-disordered children and adolescents (Jones, Sheridan, & Binns, 1993; Lockman, Coie, Underwood, & Terry, 1993; Neel & Cessna, 1993), working mothers (Morgan & Hensley, 1998), obese individuals (Harvey & Powers, 1998), and many other populations.

Especially obvious is the limited application of social skills training in *prevention*. Where it exists, it is found with children and adolescents in the school setting. (See for example, Cummings [1997]; DuPaul & Eckert [1994]; and Jones, Sheridan, & Binns [1993].) The vital importance of life/social skills training is expressed in the following quotation: "Social-emotional development seems to have more impact on determining success or failure, adaptation or maladaptation in school, as well as society at large" (Black, Downs, Bastien, Brown, & Wells, 1987, p. vi).

SUMMARY

This chapter was intended primarily to present the theoretical rationale for the life-skills training (LST) model and to illustrate methods for its operationalization. We began with a definition of life-skills and life-skills training and then proceeded to place LST in perspective by comparing it with the other major skills training models.

The historical development of LST is traced to Gazda's early work in developing a group counseling model in the late 1960s and early 1970s, followed by a model for interpersonal communication skills training in the1970s, and finalized with the development of the LST taxonomy from seven theories of human development. The rationale for LST is developed around the following 10 basic assumptions:

1. There are at least seven well-defined areas of human development: psychosocial, physical-sexual, vocational, cognitive, ego, moral, and affective.
2. From the seven well-defined areas of human development, coping behavior (life-skills) can be determined that are appropriate to age or stage.

3. There are identifiable stages in each of the seven areas of human development through which individuals must progress if they are to achieve mastery of later, more advanced stages.

4. Accomplishment of developmental tasks is dependent on mastery of life-skills—that is, coping behaviors appropriate to stage and task.

5. In general, there are certain age ranges when certain coping skills (life-skills) are optimally learned.

6. Individuals achieve optimal functioning when they attain operational mastery of fundamental life-skills.

7. Neuroses and functional psychoses frequently result from failure to develop one's life-skills.

8. Instruction and/or training in life-skills that is introduced when a person is developmentally ready to learn given concepts and skills serves the role of preventive mental health.

9. Instruction and/or training in life-skills that is introduced when a person is suffering from emotional or mental disturbance, of a functional nature, serves the role of remediation in mental health.

10. The greater the degree of functional disturbance, the greater is the likelihood that the individual will be suffering from multiple life-skill deficits.

Implementation of the LST model was outlined through describing the selection of trainees, grouping trainees for training, training setting, size of training groups, role of the trainer, sequence of training, techniques employed, supplements used, ethical considerations, multicultural issues, and three sample training sessions. The chapter closed with a brief description of research on the LST model and references to research on social skills training in general.

REFERENCES

Abridge, R. L., & Means, B. L. (1982). Psychosocial adjustment skills training. In B. Bolton (Ed.), *Vocational adjustment of disabled persons.* Baltimore: University Park Press.

Adkins, W. R. (1984). Life skills education: A video-based counseling/learning system. In D. Larson (Ed.), *Teaching psychological skills: Models for giving psychology away.* Monterey, CA: Brooks/Cole.

Argyle, M. (1981). The contribution of social interaction research to social skills training. In J. D. Wine & M. D. Smye (Eds.), *Social competence.* New York: Guilford.

Arkowitz, H., Lichtenstein, E., McGovern, K., & Hines, P. (1985). The behavioral assessment of social competence in males. *Behavior Therapy, 7*, 3–13.

Bellack, A. S. (1979). Behavioral assessment of social skills. In A. S. Bellack & M. Hersen (Eds.), *Research and practice in social skills training.* New York: Plenum.

Bellack, A. S., & Hersen, M. (1978). Chronic psychiatric patients: Social skills training. In M. Hersen & A. S. Bellack (Eds.), *Behavior therapy in the psychiatric setting.* Baltimore: Williams & Wilkins.

Black, D. W., Downs, J., Bastien, J., Brown, L., & Wells, P. (1987). *Social skills in the school.* Omaha, NE: Boys Town.

Brooks, D. K., Jr. (1984). *A life-skills taxonomy: Defining the elements of effective functioning through the use of the Delphi technique.* Unpublished doctoral dissertation, University of Georgia, Athens.

Bryant, B. M., Tower, P., Yarkley, K., Urbieta, H., & Letemendia, F. (1976). A survey of social inadequacy among psychiatric outpatients. *Psychological Medicine, 6,* 101–112.

Carkhuff, R. R. (1969a). *Helping and human relations: A primer for lay and professional helpers: Vol. 1. Selection and training.* New York: Holt, Rinehart and Winston.

Carkhuff, R. R. (1969b). *Helping and human relations: A primer for lay and professional helpers: Vol. 2. Practice and research.* New York: Holt, Rinehart and Winston.

Chishom, A. J. (1975). *Some effects of systematic human relations training on offenders' ability to demonstrate helping skills.* Unpublished doctoral dissertation, University of Georgia, Athens.

Conte, R. (1995). A classroom-based social skills intervention for children with learning disabilities. *Alberta Journal of Educational Research, 41*(1), 84–102.

Cummings, C., & Haggerty, K. P. (1997). Raising healthy children. *Educational Leadership, 54*(8), 28–30.

Darden, C. A., Ginter, E. J., & Gazda, G. M. (1996). Life-Skills Development Scale—Adolescent Form: The theoretical and therapeutic relevance of life-skills. *Journal of Mental Health Counseling, 19*(2), 142–163.

Darden, C. A., Gazda, G. M., & Ginter, E. J. (1996). Life-skills and mental health counseling. *Journal of Mental Health Counseling, 18*(2), 132–141.

Drum, D. J., & Knott, J. E. (1977). *Structured groups for facilitating development.* New York: Human Sciences Press.

DuPaul, G. J., & Eckert, T. L. (1994). The effects of social skills curricula: Now you see them, now you don't. *School Psychology Quarterly, 9*(2), 113–132.

Dupont, H. (1978, February). *Affective development: A Piagetian model.* Paper presented at the UAP-USC Eighth Annual Interdisciplinary conference "Piagetian Theory and the Helping Professions," Los Angeles.

Duska, R., & Whelan, M. (1975). *Moral development: A guide to Piaget and Kohlberg.* New York: Paulist Press.

Egan, G., & Cowan, M. A. (1979). *People in systems.* Monterey, CA: Brooks/Cole.

Eisler, R. M., Frederiksen, L. W., & Peterson, G. L. (1978). The relationship of cognitive variables to the expression of assertiveness. *Behavior Therapy, 9,* 419–427.

Elksnin, L. K., Elksnin, N., & Saborine, E. J. (1994). Job-related social skills instruction of adolescents with mental retardation. *Journal for Vocational Special Needs Education, 12*(1), 1–7.

Erikson, E. H. (1950). *Childhood and society.* New York: W. W. Norton.

Erikson, E. H. (1963). *Childhood and society* (2nd ed.). New York: W. W. Norton.

Fairweather, G. W., Sanders, D. H., Maynard, A., & Cressler, D. L. (1969). *Community life for the mentally ill.* Chicago: Aldine.

Flavell, J. H. (1963). *The developmental psychology of Jean Piaget.* Princeton, NJ: Van Nostrand.

Forness, S. R., & Kavale, K. A. (1996). Treating social skills deficits in children with learning disabilities: A meta-analysis of the research. *Learning Disabilities Quarterly, 19*(1), 2–13.

Freeman, H. E., & Simmons, O. G. (1963). *The mental patient comes home.* New York: Wiley.

Gazda, G. M. (Ed.). (1968a). *Basic approaches to group psychotherapy and group counseling.* Springfield, IL: Charles C. Thomas.

Gazda, G. M. (Ed.). (1968b). *Innovations to group psychotherapy.* Springfield, IL: Charles C. Thomas.

Gazda, G. M. (Ed.). (1969). *Theories and methods of group counseling in the schools.* Springfield, IL: Charles C. Thomas.

Gazda, G. M. (1971). *Group counseling: A developmental approach.* Boston: Allyn and Bacon.

Gazda, G. M. (1978). *Group counseling: A developmental approach* (2nd ed.). Boston: Allyn and Bacon.

Gazda, G. M. (1981). Multiple impact training. In R. J. Corsini (Ed.), *Handbook of innovative psychotherapies.* New York: Wiley.

Gazda, G. M. (1989). *Group counseling: A developmental approach* (4th ed.). Boston: Allyn and Bacon.

Gazda, G. M., Asbury, F. R., Balzer, F. J., Childers, W. C., Deselle, E., & Walters, R. P. (1973). *Human relations development: A manual for educators.* Boston: Allyn and Bacon.

Gazda, G. M., Asbury, F. R., & Balzer, F. J., Childers, W. C., Phelps, R. E., & Walters, R. P. (1995). *Human relations development: A manual for educators* (5th ed.). Boston: Allyn and Bacon.

Gazda, G. M., Asbury, F. R., Balzer, F. J., Childers, W. C., Phelps, R. E., & Walters, R. P. (1999). *Human relations development: A manual for educators* (6th ed.). Boston: Allyn and Bacon.

Gazda, G. M., Asbury, F. R., Balzer, F. J., Childers, W. C., Phelps, R. E., & Walters, R. P. (1999). Instructor's manual with test bank and transparency masters for *Human relations develop-

ment: A manual for educators (6th ed.). Boston: Allyn and Bacon.

Gazda, G. M., Asbury, F. R., Balzer, F. J., Childers, W. C., & Walters, R. P. (1977). *Human relations development: A manual for educators* (2nd ed.). Boston: Allyn and Bacon.

Gazda, G. M., Asbury, F. R., Balzer, F. J., Childers, W. C., & Walters, R. P. (1984). *Human relations development: A manual for educators* (3rd ed.). Boston: Allyn and Bacon.

Gazda, G. M., Asbury, F. R., Balzer, F. J., Childers, W. C., & Walters, R. P. (1991). *Human relations development: A manual for educators* (4th ed.). Boston: Allyn and Bacon.

Gazda, G. M., Childers, W. C., & Brooks, D. K., Jr. (1987). *Foundations of counseling and human services.* New York: McGraw-Hill.

Gazda, G. M., Childers, W. C., & Walters, R. P. (1982). *Interpersonal communication: A handbook for health professionals.* Rockville, MD: Aspen Systems.

Gazda, G. M., Walters, R. P., & Childers, W. C. (1975). *Human relations development: A manual for health sciences.* Boston: Allyn and Bacon.

Gazda, G. M., Walters, R. P., & Childers, W. C. (1981). *Realtalk: Exercises in friendship and helping skills.* Atlanta, GA: Humanics.

Gendlin, E. T. (1981). *Focusing.* New York: Bantam Books.

Gesell, A., Ilg, F. L., Ames, L. B., & Bullis, G. E. (1946). *The child from five to ten.* New York: Harper.

Goldstein, A. P., Sprafkin, R. P., & Gershaw, N. J. (1976). *Skill training for community living: Applying structured learning therapy.* New York: Pergamon.

Gonzalez-Lopez, A., & Kamps, D. M. (1997). Social skills training to increase social interactions between children with autism and then typical peers. *Focus on Autism and Other Developmental Disabilities, 12*(1), 2–14.

Greenberg, D. J., Scott, S. B., Pisa, A., & Friesen, D. D. (1975). Beyond the token economy: A comparison of two contingency programs. *Journal of Consulting and Clinical Psychology, 43,* 498–503.

Guerney, B. G., Jr. (177). *Relationship enhancement.* San Francisco: Jossey-Bass.

Harvey, K. H., & Powers, P. S. (1998). The "Free to Be Me" psychoeducational group: A conceptual model for coping with being overweight. *Journal for Specialists in Group Work, 23*(3), 312–325.

Havighurst, R. J. (1953). *Human development and education.* New York: Longmans, Green.

Havighurst, R. J. (1972). *Developmental tasks and education* (3rd ed.). New York: David McKay.

Illovsky, M. (1985). *The therapeutic effects of two life-skill components in the treatment of psychiatric patients.* Unpublished doctoral dissertation, University of Georgia, Athens.

Jones, R. N., Sheridan, S. M., & Binns, N. R. (1993). Schoolwide social skills training: Providing preventive services to students at-risk. *School Psychology Quarterly, 8*(1), 57–80.

Kavkewitz, M. (1983). *Assessment of life skills training in communication, appearances, physical fitness, and health maintenance as a substance abuse prevention program for secondary school students.* Unpublished doctoral dissertation, University of Georgia, Athens.

Kazdin, A. E. (1979). Sociopsychological factors in psychopathology. In A. S. Bellack & M. Hersen (Eds.), *Research and practice in social skills training.* New York: Plenum.

Kohlberg, L., & Turiel, E. (1971). Moral development and moral education. In G. Lesser (Ed.), *Psychology and educational practice.* New York: Scott, Foresman.

Kutnick, P., & Marshall, D. (1993). Development of social skills and the use of the microcomputer in the primary school classroom. *British Educational Research Journal, 19*(5), 17–33.

Layser, G. R. (1974). *The effects of human relations training with houseparents and perceived effects of boys in student houses.* Unpublished doctoral dissertation, University of Georgia, Athens.

Lazarus, A. A. (1976). *Multi-modal behavior therapy.* New York: Springer.

Linn, M. W., Caffey, E. M., Klett, J., & Hogarty, G. (1977). Hospital vs. community (foster) care for psychiatric patients. *Archives of General Psychiatry, 34,* 78–83.

Lockman, J. E., Coie, J. D., Underwood, M. K., & Terry, R. (1993). *Journal of Consulting and Clinical Psychology, 61*(6), 1053–1058.

Loevinger, J. (1976). *Ego development.* San Francisco: Jossey-Bass.

Martin, B. (1971). *Anxiety and neurotic disorders.* New York: Wiley.

May, H. J. (1981). *The effects of life-skill training versus current psychiatric methods on therapeutic outcome in psychiatric patients.* Unpublished doctoral dissertation, University of Georgia, Athens.

May, H. J. Powell, M., Gazda, G. M., & Hauser, G. (1985). Life skill training: Psychoeducational training as a mental health treatment. *Journal of Clinical Psychology, 41*(3), 359–367.

Marshall, E. K., Charping, J. W., & Bell, W. J. (1979). Interpersonal skills training: A review of the research. *Social Work Research and Abstracts, 15,* 10–16.

Marshall, E. K., & Kurtz, P. D. (1982). *Interpersonal helping skills.* San Francisco: Jossey-Bass.

Matarazzo, R. G. (1978). Research on the teaching and learning of psychotherapeutic skills. In S. L. Garfield & A. E. Bergin (Eds.), *Handbook of psychotherapy and behavior change.* New York: Wiley.

McCurdy, M. E. (1975). *Application of systematic human relations training in churches.* Unpublished doctoral dissertation, University of Georgia, Athens.

Morgan, B., & Hensely, L. (1998). Supporting working mothers through group work: A multimodal psychoeducational approach. *Journal for Specialists in Group Work, 23*(3), 298–311.

Mosher, R. L., & Sprinthall, N. A. (1971). Psychological education: A means to promote personal development during adolescence. *The Counseling Psychologist, 2*(4), 3–82.

Neel, R. S., & Cessna, K. K. (1993). Replacement behavior: A strategy for teaching social skills to children with behavior problems. *Rural Special Education Quarterly, 12*(1), 30–35.

O'Reilly, M. F., & Glynn, D. (1995). Using a process social skills training approach with adolescents with mild intellectual disabilities in a high school setting. *Developmental Disabilities, 30*(3), 187–198.

Paul, G. L., & Lentz, R. J. (1977). *Psychosocial treatment of chronic mental patients: Milieu versus social learning programs.* Cambridge, MA: Harvard University Press.

Picklesimer, B. K., Hooper, D. R., & Ginter, E. J. (1998). Life skills, adolescents, and career choice. *Journal of Mental Health Counseling, 20*(3), 272–282.

Pierce, R., Schauble, P. B., & Wilson, R. R. (1971). Employing systematic human relations training for teaching constructive helper and helpee behavior in group therapy situations. *Journal of Research and Development in Education, 4,* 97–109.

Powell, M., Illovsky, M., O'Leary, W., & Gazda, G. M. (1988). Life-skills training with hospitalized psychiatric patients. *International Journal of Group Psychotherapy, 38*(1), 109–117.

Schneider, B. H., & Byrne, B. M. (1985). Children's social skills training: A meta-analysis. In B. H. Schneider, K. Rubin, & J. E. Ledingham (Eds.), *Children's peer relations: Issues in assessment and intervention.* New York: Springer-Verlag.

Seidenschnur, P. P. T. (1974). *The effects of human relations training upon the work atmosphere and communication skills of a medical unit's staff.* Unpublished doctoral dissertation, University of Georgia, Athens.

Sisson, P. J., Arthur, G. L., & Gazda, G. M. (1981). *Human relations for criminal justice personnel.* Boston: Allyn and Bacon.

Smith, P. (1982). *The development of a taxonomy of the life skills required to become a balanced self-determined person.* Ottawa, Canada: Employment and Immigration Canada.

Spalding, J. (1985). *A comparative evaluation of an Adlerian based program, individual education, with a traditional program.* Unpublished doctoral dissertation, University of Georgia, Athens.

Staudt, V. M., & Zubin, J. (1957). A biometric evaluation of the somato-therapies in schizophrenia. *Psychological Bulletin, 54,* 171–196.

Super, D. E. (1963). Vocational development in adolescence and early adulthood: Tasks and behaviors. In D. E. Super (Ed.), *Career development: Self-concept theory.* New York: College Entrance Examination Board.

Thompson, K. L., Bundy, K. A., & Wolfe, W. R. (1996). Social skills training for young adolescents: Cognitive and performance components. *Adolescence, 31*(123), 505–521.

Tryon, C., & Lilienthal, J. W. (1950). Developmental tasks: I. The concept and its importance. In *Fostering mental health in our schools: 1950 yearbook of ASCD.* Washington, DC: Association for Supervision and Curriculum Development.

Wadsworth, B. J. (1971). *Piaget's theory of cognitive development.* New York: David McKay.

Warren, N. J., & Gilner, F. H. (1978). Measurement of positive assertive behaviors: The behavioral test of tenderness expression. *Behavior Therapy, 9,* 179–184.

Wolpe, J., & Lazarus, A. A. (1966). *Behavior therapy techniques.* New York: Pergamon.

Wood, M. M. (1975). *Developmental therapy.* Baltimore: University Park Press.

Zubin, J., & Spring, B. (1977). Vulnerability—A new view of schizophrenia. *Journal of Abnormal Psychology, 86,* 103–126.

CHAPTER SIXTEEN

SELF-HELP/MUTUAL SUPPORT GROUPS

The title of this chapter reflects the blurring of the slight differences in how self-help and mutual support groups are defined. A recent review of research and development of self-help/mutual support groups by Goodman and Jacobs (1994) also used both descriptors. Mutual support is such a key feature of self-help groups that many writers use the terms *self-help* and *mutual support* interchangeably. However, some (Pearson, 1986) differentiate between the two on the basis of who they are *led* by rather than who they are *for*. Mutual support is used to denote those groups that, because of age, for example, are *not* led by peers, such as support groups for children of divorce. In support groups such as this, the group resembles a counseling or therapy group as much as a self-help group. Self-help is used to denote groups led by *peers*. Goodman and Jacobs (1994) have suggested that

> it is useful to conceive a continuum of all help-oriented interventions, bounded on one end by everyday acts of social support (like friends or family trying to help someone ill or hurt) and on the other end by the methods of group therapy. The difficulty lies in the fact that MSGs [mutual support groups] exist throughout the space between the two poles. (pp. 489–490)

For simplicity sake, we shall use *self-help* to refer to self-help/mutual support groups (MSGs).

In 1982, Katz estimated that well over a half million self-help groups existed and that at least 14 million people were members of such groups (Katz, 1982). As of 1993–1994, Goodman and Jacobs (1994) estimated that 11.4 million individuals were members of mutual support groups in 1993—"easily outnumbering all forms of therapy" (p. 498). "Our prediction is that the MSG will become the nation's de facto 'treatment of choice' for many psychopathologies and nonpsychiatric life predicaments by the year 2010 or 2020" (Goodman & Jacobs, 1994, p. 497).

In the largest reported survey of the roles played by professionals in mutual support (self-help) groups, Lotery (1985) confirmed earlier findings in studies by Burstein (1985) (cited in Goodman & Jacobs, 1994) that professionals (primarily mental health) were involved in 83 percent of the 426 responding mutual support groups of the 3,000 listed in the California Self-Help Center. These studies call for a revision of the heretofore prevailing belief that mental health professionals were excluded from self-help group involvement. Based on the important role self-help groups currently play and the predicted role they are expected to play in the future, this chapter is included in this text.

HISTORY AND DEFINING CHARACTERISTICS

Self-help is by no means a new phenomenon. In the broadest sense, the activity of self-help is as old as human society (Pancoast, Parker, & Froland, 1983). In the early twentieth century, Kropotkin (1914/1972) traced cooperative groups to prehistoric times and suggested that the very condition of civilization lay in the early development of habits of cooperation through food gathering and the maintenance of group safety. In the narrower sense of groups formed for mutual aid in dealing with a specific issue, self-help can be traced to two different roots. One is economic and is typified by the emergence of the English Friendly Societies, an early form of trade unions (Katz & Bender, 1976a). The other is religious and was first expressed in the Methodist group founded by John Wesley in the 1700s (Rodolfa & Hungerford, 1982).

Self-help has developed expressions that have been responsive to the demands of the times. The early part of the twentieth century saw the growth of unions and ethnic self-help associations. The first anonymous groups were formed in the early 1930s, coinciding with the Depression and the repeal of Prohibition, and continued to develop through the 1950s. Some of these groups, such as Alcoholics Anonymous (A.A.) and Gamblers Anonymous, established national organizations that still exist today. In the 1950s, self-help became increasingly politicized with the emergence of the civil rights movement, the women's movement, and consumer groups (Pancoast, Parker, & Froland, 1983). Throughout the century, and continuing to the present, self-help groups have become less economic and more personal in emphasis (Remine, Rice, & Ross, 1984).

Defining and classifying a phenomenon with such a long history and such diverse forms of expression is not a simple task. Killilea (1976) has suggested that self-help might not be a single, unitary movement. According to her, self-help groups could be seen as support systems, as social movements, as spiritual movements and secular religions, as systems of consumer participation, as alternative care-giving systems adjunct to professional helping systems, as intentional communities, as subcultural entities that represent a way of life, as supplementary communities, as expressive social influence groups, and as organizations of the deviant and stigmatized.

Katz and Bender (1976b) proposed a classification of self-help groups that includes the whole range of the phenomenon. Their classification consists of the following categories: (1) groups that focus primarily on individual self-fulfillment or personal growth (e.g., Recovery, Inc.); (2) groups that focus primarily on social advocacy (e.g., the Committee for the Rights of the Disabled); (3) groups whose primary focus is to create alternative patterns for living (e.g., gay rights and women's liberation groups); (4) groups that provide refuge (usually residential) for desperate people who are seeking protection from the pressures of life and society (e.g., addicts or ex-addicts); and (5) mixed types of groups that arise from shared life situations (e.g., bereavement, divorce, or Vietnam veterans).

Katz (1972) made a distinction between groups whose primary purpose is to change society and those that work for adjustment of their members within the existing framework. Gay rights organizations and women's rights groups have a political and societal orientation, whereas groups such as A. A. and Parents Without Partners focus on individual adjustment. Katz and Bender (1976b) labeled the societal orientation as an *outer* focus and the individual orientation as an *inner* focus.

Within the context of the self-help group with an inner focus, we find different systems of classification. Bean (1975) suggested three types of groups: crisis, permanent, and addiction. Crisis-oriented groups address problems resulting from major life transitions. The focus of these groups is to provide emotional support and educational information. Membership may be temporary. Permanent self-help groups focus on long-term problems that carry a stigma and mark the individual as different. Groups for dwarfs, former prisoners, or mental patients fall into this category. The goals of these groups are to improve members' self-esteem and to combat prejudice. Addiction-oriented self-help groups are geared toward people with destructive habits, such as drugs, alcohol, gambling, overeating, and smoking. The focus is on helping member learn new behaviors.

Borman (1979) categorized self-help groups with an inner focus according to how they deal with change. One type of group works toward effecting change within its members. The other type seeks to help members adapt to life changes. The first type of group centers on the need to modify member behavior and attitude. The anonymous groups and Recovery, Inc., are examples of this type. These groups often specify clear and concrete guidelines through which to obtain the desired change. The second type of group focuses more on adapting to and coping with life changes. These groups provide a variety of helping methods for their members, but do not specify concrete guidelines. Parents Without Partners, Widowed Persons Service, and Survivors of Suicide Victims are examples of this category.

It is the self-help group oriented toward helping the individual, rather than changing society, that is of interest to the mental health professional. The groups whose primary role is social advocacy (e.g., National Organization of Women and National Gay Task Force) tend to have large, powerful national organizations. The individual-oriented groups may have national organizations that perform some advocacy functions, but the heart of these lies in the face-to-face interaction of the individual members at the local level. These groups provide services similar to those provided by the mental health professional and could be considered to be adjuncts or alternatives to psychotherapy (Levy, 1976).

Despite their diversity, self-help groups share underlying characteristics that embody the essentials of the self-help phenomenon. Katz and Bender (1976b) suggested a definition that has gained widespread acceptance:

> Self-help groups are voluntary, small group structures for mutual aid and the accomplishment of special purpose. They are usually formed by peers who have come together for mutual assistance in satisfying a common need, overcoming a common handicap or life-disrupting problem, and bringing about desired social and/or personal change. The initiators and members of such groups perceive that their needs are not, or

cannot be, met by or through existing social institutions. Self-help groups emphasize face-to-face social interactions and the assumption of personal responsibility by members. They often provide material assistance, as well as emotional support; they are frequently "cause"-oriented, and promulgate an ideology or values through which members attain an enhanced sense of personal identity. (p. 9)

The definition suggests that self-help groups share the following characteristics: a peer orientation, a problem focus, an estrangement from societal norms, and an ideological base. Peer orientation is the central characteristic of the self-help groups. Most self-help groups are organized and maintained by persons who share a common condition, situation, symptom, or experience. It is the fact of sharing a problem that defines membership status in the groups. A peer in a self-help group thus has a commonality or mutuality of problems with other members.

The problems faced by members of self-help groups differentiate them from society as a whole. At times, individuals faced with particular problems have not been able to get help within the existing system. The emergence of the present self-help group movement occurred in the 1930s when two groups with stigmatizing conditions—mental retardation and alcoholism—began to create mechanisms for those affected by the conditions to help one another, as opposed to relying on professional help (Steinman & Traunstein, 1976). The self-help movement is based on an outsider orientation. The degree of this orientation differs among the particular groups. Some groups are composed of members who are stigmatized by society and considered deviant (e.g., alcoholics, addicts, gamblers, transvestites, ex-convicts, dwarfs, and mental patients) (Sagarin, 1969). Other groups deal with conditions which, although not considered stigmata, are not shared by other members of society (e.g., serious illnesses, disabilities, and losses).

Perhaps because members of self-help groups are out of step with society, these groups develop ideologies to counteract the stigma and isolation. The groups have teachings about the causes and cures of the particular problem. These teachings, or ideologies, are guidelines that serve to sustain and inspire the person afflicted with the problem. Ideologies can be written and specific, as in the case of the 12-step program of Alcoholics Anonymous, or an informal oral tradition passed on from member to member (Borman, 1982).

Although self-help groups possess unique characteristics, they also share characteristics with other helping groups. They are similar to counseling groups in structure and broad goals. Both types of groups emphasize face-to-face interaction among their members. The overall goal of both is to bring about personal change. Lakin (1985) has suggested a number of characteristics that self-help groups share with traditional therapy groups. According to him, both emphasize emotional expression and catharsis, encourage support among their members, and work toward implementing behavior change and more effective coping strategies.

A study by Toro, Rappaport, and Seidman (1987) suggests some possible differences between self-help groups and psychotherapy groups. Members of the self-help group studied (GROW International) perceived that their group had more active leaders, greater group cohesion, more structure and task orientation, and more independence than did members of the psychotherapy groups. Members of psychotherapy groups perceived that their groups encouraged more expression of negative and other feelings and showed more flexibility in changing the group's activities than did members of the self-help groups. However, since little research has been done comparing self-help and psychotherapy groups, the results need to be interpreted cautiously.

The most significant difference between self-help and counseling groups is in the leadership patterns. Most self-help groups are still organized and led by nonprofessionals. Distrust of the professional is not uncommon (Back & Taylor, 1976). In fact, assumption of responsibility for change by the members is the essence of the self-help group. From their perspective, the know-how and expertise lies with those who have struggled with and overcome the problem. Thus, peer leadership is an important aspect of the helping power of the self-help group.

THEORETICAL RATIONALE

The issue of how self-help groups function—or to put it simply, how self-help groups help—is still very much an open question. Some rudimentary attempts have been made to develop theories specific to self-help groups (Antze, 1979; Levy, 1976). Most theoretical approaches derive from existing sociological and psychological theory (Katz, 1981). The following change mechanisms have been proposed: mutual support (Katz, 1981; Silverman, 1980); helper therapy (Riessman, 1965); the role of ideology (Antze, 1979); and essential parameters toward a formal model (Goodman & Jacobs, 1994).

The role of mutual support in self-help groups seems almost axiomatic. Self-help is often termed *mutual aid*. Self-help groups are alternately called *support groups*. There seems to be a tacit assumption in the literature on self-help groups that a mutual support process is operating and that this process is positive. Silverman (1985) suggested that it might be important to look at the specific type of mutual support at work in the groups.

There is a body of considerable research that indicates that social support buffers the adverse psychological impact of stressful life events and ongoing life strains (Thoits, 1986). Thus, the value of social support is recognized as a positive force for individuals under stress. Since self-help is directed at people in stress, social support is likely to be one of the helping processes in the self-help group (Silverman, 1985).

Recent writings and research on social support have stressed the variety that exists in social support because there is increasing evidence that differing types of support have varying effects (Kessler, Price, & Wortman, 1985). The source of the social support seems to be crucial in the effectiveness of the support. For instance, women with breast cancer may be more likely to accept emotional support from someone who has had the same experience than from an uninformed friend (Dunkel-Schetter & Wortman, 1982).

The self-help groups may provide a particularly effective form of social support for individuals experiencing unique situations or problems. Schacter (1959), reporting on a study of affiliative tendencies of college students during periods of anxiety, observed that students first chose to be with others in the same situations. Silverman and Smith (1984), in a study of three self-help groups, found that people who joined the groups did so out of a need to find someone else who had a similar experience. Peers who have gone through a similar experience seem to be unique sources of help for people in stress.

Not only may the opportunity to find someone like oneself be central to learning to cope with stress, but also the opportunity to change roles and become a helper may be important as well. Riessman (1965), who has called this "the helper therapy principle," suggested several ways in which helping might be beneficial to the helper. Doing something worthwhile to help someone in need may give the helper a sense of adequacy and effectiveness. The helper may also benefit from the status associated with the role. In addition, in the process of helping, the helper may be learning through teaching and acquiring a broader perspective of his or her predicament. Rappaport (1985) has called this process *empowerment:* gaining psychological control over oneself and extending the positive influence to others.

There is some evidence for the positive effects of the helping process. In a study of Mended Hearts, a self-help group for heart surgery patients, Lieberman and Borman (1979) found significant differences between two groups of men who had undergone open-heart surgery. Only those who were active in the organization and could be considered helpers made better adjustments than nonmembers. In a study of groups of multiple sclerosis sufferers, Compassionate Friends, and Overeaters Anonymous, Rappaport (1985) found that the individuals who both provided and received social support obtained more benefits and satisfaction from their participation.

Both mutual aid and helper therapy are helping processes that operate to a greater or lesser extent in other types of groups. Antze (1979) has proposed a theory of how self-help groups work, based on a unique feature of the groups. According to him, each group has an ideology—a specialized system of teachings that members consider to be the key to recovery. These teachings are the cumulative wisdom of member experiences. Ideology may be explicit or implicit, but in all cases it guides the purpose of the group and structures the self-help process (Suler, 1984).

It is Antze's belief that ideologies are systems of meaning that function as a "cognitive antidote" to the basic features of a condition shared by everyone who joins the group. The ideology of the group counteracts the maladaptive beliefs of the members, undermining the problematic aspects of their life-style. In time, new attitudes and values replace the dysfunctional ones. Suler (1984) suggested that "the groups construct a social reality that acts as a shared basis for perceiving and acting in the world" (p. 30).

Antze developed his theory from observation of groups whose objectives are behavioral control of members: Alcoholics Anonymous, Recovery, Inc., and Synanon. These groups have explicit, well-developed ideologies. However, the concept has also been applied to the groups that emphasize adaptation and coping with stressful situations (Sherman, 1979; Suler, 1984). The goal of most behavioral control groups is to eliminate or control problematic behavior. The ideology attempts to counteract habitual self-destructive attitudes and beliefs held by an individual that contribute to the behavior. Stress-coping groups, on the other hand, do not seek to eliminate behavior, but to reconceptualize it and place it in an adaptive perspective (Sherman, 1979).

The ideology of these groups is not as carefully delineated as that of the behavioral control groups.

Each group, whether oriented toward behavioral change or coping, develops its own unique ideology based on the problem shared by its members. As an illustration, Antze (1979) contrasted the ideology of Alcoholics Anonymous and Recovery, Inc. According to him, alcoholism is perpetuated by the alcoholics' belief that they are omnipotent. The ideology of A.A. encourages the individual to accept alcoholism as a disease that is beyond his or her control and to rely on a "higher power." The former psychiatric patients of Recovery, Inc., tend to prolong their symptoms by attributing them to sickness beyond their control. Recovery's ideology encourages them to believe that they can overcome their symptoms if they try hard enough to act as if they are healthy. The various stress-coping groups encapsulate and transmit the essence of what has worked for others who have previously faced that specific problem or situation.

In emphasizing the role of ideologies, Antze (1979) is arguing for the existence of another helping process in the self-help group. He has called this the *persuasive function* of the group. According to him, the process works because the groups are fixed communities of beliefs. The beliefs are perpetuated by activities characteristic of the groups: sharing of experience and offering of advice. Both can be subtle forms of indoctrination. Because self-help groups deal with specialized problems, members tend to be alike in some ways. Festinger (1954) has suggested that individuals are more likely to be influenced by groups of persons whom they perceive as similar to themselves.

Goodman and Jacobs (1994) reviewed the self-help/mutual support literature and concluded:

> It lacks a psychology of its intimate method. However, there are frequent *indirect,* incidental, and partial descriptions of communication behavior described in competing definitions and research findings. These help us to create an initial picture of a generic MSG [mutual support group] process. The following two propositions are intended to isolate essential parameters and serve as a "starter kit" toward a formal model. (p. 500)

The first proposition is: "Each member will give and get help for similar life-disrupting predicaments" (Goodman & Jacobs, 1994, p. 500). Self-help groups (mutual support groups) (the term used by Goodman and Jacobs) universally use the term *member* rather than *client* or *patient* to reflect their egalitarian setting compared to psychotherapy patients and to reflect a widespread experience of mutuality, fidelity, or constituency somewhat similar to club or team member.

Give and get refers to the expectation of members to provide help as well as to receive help, and *similar life-disrupting predicaments* "means that members are intimate with many aspects of the group's designated problem" (Goodman & Jacobs, 1994, p. 500). According to Goodman and Jacobs, members often attribute their common life-disrupting experience as the reason for their extreme openness and empathic understanding leading to a feeling of psychological safety and eventual personal change.

The second proposition of Goodman and Jacobs (1994) is: "Group process is characterized by *less skeptical response to each other's disclosures; fewer interpretations of character;* and *more empathic responses*" when compared with group or individual therapies" (p. 501). *Less skeptical response to each other's disclosures* occurs because members have a "de facto acceptance of each other's application" (p. 501). According to Goodman and Jacobs, this de facto acceptance diminishes the typical denial and resistance stages of the self-discovery process in psychotherapy, resulting in limited group criticism of any member's resistance to trying new coping strategies. Members tend to be instructive and patient with each other.

Fewer interpretations of character than found in psychotherapy groups means that members do not focus on broad self-disclosures of life histories but rather on details of a particular addiction, medical condition, loss, and the like, sometimes to the point of obsessing. Groups do not focus on a member's personal neurosis but on interpretations about the generic aspects of the group's common concern, such as "People who have not lost a spouse do not have a clue as to how we feel."

More empathic responses, according to Goodman and Jacobs, are of three forms: (1) "me too" self-disclosures that display parallel experience, (2) questions based on empathic understanding, and (3) "reflections" that mirror an expressed emotion. Members describe their feelings of empathic understanding as "talking to someone in the same boat."

In addition to the two propositions toward a formal model, Goodman and Jacobs (1994) outlined five additional essential processes that occur in a typical mutual support group that could be expanded toward a generic model:*

1. The typical group compensates for the lack of full-time professional leadership by "overprotecting" the psychological vulnerability of its members. . . . They "take care of their own" in the absence of a professional caretaker.
2. The frequent generalizations (general interpretations) about common concerns that MSGs use are generated by at least six measurable sources: (a) lessons learned by actually coping with the group's problem and experiencing success and failure, (b) ideas, attitudes, and techniques gleaned from television and print mass media (c) direct experience with a professional care-giver, (d) familiar customs and practices learned in an ethnic or other subculture, i.e., folk wisdom, (e) special self-help programs purchased as books, audio tapes, and pamphlets, and (f) the group's idiosyncratic ideology evolved through an amalgam of member contributions.
3. Because the basis of MSG membership is clear acknowledgement, i.e., admission, self-diagnosis, confession, etc. of a personal problem, not much group time is devoted to this subject. . . . The typical group's process centers on tension relief, special problem solving, and sometimes advocacy. Discussion of individual pathogenesis is uncommon.
4. MSG process is characterized by a more active coping style, a greater display of personal agency, more emotionally expressive talk, and more resource exchange when compared to their matched cohorts in a typical therapy group.
5. MSC ideologies, methods, and frequent use of general interpretations stimulate cognitive restructuring in members. (Goodman & Jacobs, 1994, p. 502)

*B. Goodman and M. K. Jacobs, "Self-Help, Mutual-Support Groups," in A. Fuhriman & G. M. Burlingame (Eds.), *Handbook of group psychotherapy: An empirical and clinical synthesis* (New York: Wiley, 1994). Reprinted by permission of John Wiley & Sons, Inc.

Leader's Role and Professional's Involvement

The helping processes that seem to be most central to the effectiveness of self-help groups—mutual aid, helper therapy, and the role of ideology—are processes in which the professional plays a peripheral role. When professionals take a primary role in self-help groups, they run the risk of tampering with the intrinsic helping process of the groups. There are roles for the professional in the self-help group, but they are not the traditional roles that the professional has assumed in other helping groups (Silverman, 1986).

As long as the professionals screen members, convene the groups, and retain responsibility for running the program, the process is not a self-help experience. Aspects of mutual help exist in any group therapy experience (Yalom, 1985), but not to the degree found in self-help groups. The therapy group leader does not relinquish his or her control and authority. Maintaining dependence on the professional in a self-help setting limits the effectiveness of helper therapy and interferes with the "empowerment" of the individual (Rappaport, 1985).

Antze (1979) has suggested that professional involvement runs the risk of tampering with group ideologies. The mere presence of a professional may weaken the meaning of certain teachings (e.g., "Only a drunk can help another drunk"). If the professional points out that a belief runs against medical or psychological knowledge, the effect is certain to be negative. Antze has recommended that the first rule for a professional working with a self-help group should be a scrupulous respect for its teachings.

Most, although not all, writers in the self-help area stress the need for collaboration between the groups and professionals. However, they also note the obstacles to collaboration. For example, self-help groups have been observed to have a strong bias against professional help (Barish, 1971) and to distrust professionals (Back & Taylor, 1976).

Nevertheless, Lotery's (1985) research on leadership structure of a sample of the California Self-Help Center's list of groups produced a surprising finding. She found that professionals participated in at least 13 roles. Surprisingly, about 14 percent of the groups frequently had professionals as the sole leader and about 35 percent of the groups used them as co-leaders. Some other leadership roles assumed by professionals included referring new members (57 percent), speakers (35 percent), consultants and advisors (35 percent), procurers of resources (29 percent), organizers and coordinators of groups (25 percent), group observers (17 percent), and evaluators (12 percent). Thirty-eight percent of the groups reported professionals as regular members.

Lotery also found that most of the roles assumed by professionals were welcomed, and there was even a desire for more involvement in the roles of referral sources, teacher, speaker, student, and co-leader. The groups surveyed were least interested in professionals serving as sole leaders or coordinators/organizers. Although Lotery's research suggests many roles for professionals in self-help groups, the actual number of hours contributed per month was small: less than 2 hours for 37 percent of the group, between 2 and 10 hours for 20 percent, and over 10 hours for 10 percent.

In spite of the difficulties, professionals are becoming involved in self-help groups, and most groups welcome the involvement (Wollert, Knight, & Levy, 1980).

One of the factors in effective collaboration seems to be a knowledge of the specific goals and workings of the self-help group. Another is the establishment of rapport. In their report on the development of a collaborative model between professionals and Make Today Count, a self-help group for individuals dealing with life-threatening illness, Wollert, Knight, and Levy (1980) have suggested that professionals need to convey respect for the group in order for the alliance to work. Mutual referral between self-help groups and professionals can be beneficial to the individual in need of help. The self-help group can provide valuable information and affiliation that can serve to augment professional services. When making a referral to a self-help group, a professional should have an awareness of the goals and workings of the group (Rodolfa & Hungerford, 1982). Some individuals who join a self-help group may be functioning at a significantly lower level of adaptation than other members and might need more than the group is able to offer. The self-help group can refer the individual to professional sources of help in the event that participation in the group becomes too stressful (Rodolfa & Hungerford, 1982).

Yoak and Chesler (1985) suggested shared leadership as a method of collaboration. In a study of 43 self-help and support groups for parents of children with cancer, they found three forms of leadership: the professionals as primary leaders, the parents as primary leaders, and leadership shared between parents and professionals. The shared leadership groups had a greater longevity, tended to retain parents of deceased children, and had more varied approaches to organizational structure and activities. Yoak and Chesler suggested that the shared leadership model may incorporate both a lack of dependence on the professional and the continuing access to professional resources.

The type of service that professionals have most commonly provided to self-help groups is some form of organizational assistance during the early stages of development (Wollert & Barron, 1983). In a study of 10 well-known self-help groups—including Alcoholics Anonymous, Recovery, Inc., and Parents Anonymous—Borman (1979) found professional encouragement in the formative stages of all the groups. The type of services provided by professionals varies widely in terms of their level of assumed responsibility. The positive outcomes for this type of collaboration include learning group interaction skills from observation of the professional and bolstering of confidence, which comes from the interaction (Wollert & Barron, 1983).

Consultation is another service that professionals may render to self-help groups. Consultative services are typically time limited and intermittent. They may have either an organizational focus or a case focus. The case focus is useful when questions arise concerning issues of psychological diagnosis, medical screening, or crisis intervention (Wollert & Barron, 1983).

Professionals may also adapt roles of an ongoing nature. Sponsorship is one of these roles. Sponsorship provides professional acknowledgment of the group and contributes to the group's credibility in the community. Sponsors, however, ideally leave the leadership of meetings to a group member, although they may influence the process through advice to the leaders or through emergency intervention. Wollert and Barron (1983) suggested the advocator-mediator role for the professional. The responsibilities of the advocator-mediator are to observe the group, identify conflicts, clarify alternatives for resolution, and negotiate compromises acceptable to all those involved.

Goodman and Jacobs (1994) concluded:

> Conceptual work on the meaning of leadership for the MSG method is needed to differentiate between activities that (1) actually guide group conversation, (2) develop procedures for training facilitators, (3) provide influential consultation, (4) develop media programs, and (5) speak only to the group's common concern as someone else contrives group process. (p. 505)

Goodman and Jacobs's description of the problems in the conceptualization of leadership in self-help groups encompasses the reasons why research on the subject is so difficult to perform. Nevertheless, a few studies have provided results that at least can give some guidance for further research. Stewart (1990) analyzed 19 studies on leader activities and concluded that group members described professionals as making inappropriate referrals, failing to follow up, not giving enough time and energy, and being naïve about self-help group methods and values. Professionals saw their roles as group trainers, initiators of group process, networkers, referral resources, and speakers. Professionals were concerned about self-help groups providing false information to their members. Stewart concluded that both group members and professionals wanted some interaction, but there were also barriers related to the professionals' lack of information about self-help groups and preparation for helping them. Group members were seeking nonauthoritarian help from professionals not typical of the professionals' usual role.

Some group process differences in leadership by group therapy professionals compared with self-help group member-leaders were obtained by Toro, Rappaport, and Seidman (1987). Self-help group members perceived their leaders to be more active and their groups to be more structured, cohesive, independent, and task oriented than did members of therapy groups. Therapy patients, on the other hand, perceived their groups to be more flexible and to encourage more expressions of negative feelings.

In another study of group process, Toro and colleagues (1988) compared professional-led groups to member-led groups of mental patients. Member-led groups viewed themselves as having more emotional expression, cohesion, and self-discovery and less small talk and mutual agreements. Members of professional-led groups perceived themselves as giving fewer self-disclosures, having less small talk and information, and having fewer agreements.

In terms of long-term effectiveness of member-led and professional-led mutual support (self-help) groups, Toseland, Rossiter, Peak, and Hill (1990) found no difference with caregivers of elderly persons. They also found that groups led by professionals as well as peers reduced stress and increased interpersonal competence over no-treatment controls.

GOALS AND OBJECTIVES

Lakin (1985) cited the rapid development of self-help groups in recent years as one of the most striking developments in mental health services:

Those who join self-help groups include sufferers from addictions or physical illnesses, lonely or depressed persons, formerly hospitalized individuals trying to maintain themselves in the community, as well as people who feel disadvantaged socially or politically. . . . In short, those groups are composed of individuals who share common afflictions, adjustment problems, psychological symptoms, social convictions, life experiences or life circumstances. (p. 179)

The goals and objectives, in general, are aimed at the members' resumption of active coping. The ideology of the particular self-help group will determine the route to active coping. Lakin classified the ideologies as secular and spiritual or religious. He cited Antze's (1979) claims "that the ideologies of self-help organizations serve to break some link in the maladaptive cognitive chain of events and to provide viable defenses against its renewal" (Lakin, 1985, p. 193). Lakin used three types of self-help groups to illustrate Antze's thesis. Alcoholics Anonymous groups attempt to deal with the alcoholic's problems by countering the presumed assertiveness of alcoholics by teaching surrender. In A.A., one's aim is to reduce feelings of omnipotence in favor of reliance on a "higher power" for guidance and faith. Recovery, Inc., a self-help group for former mental patients, attempts to block their premature surrender by promoting willpower in order to change their views of themselves as active and self-responsible. Synnanon, a self-help group for addicts, attempts to keep them drug free by reversing the addicts' social and emotional detachments through a process that demands expression of feelings and strengthening of social engagement. Synnanon self-help groups use provocative interpersonal confrontations to provoke a discharge of emotions considered necessary to counter the characteristic avoidance patterns of the addict.

Not all self-help groups are as systematized in their approach to alleviating the affliction of their members as those of A.A., Recovery, Inc., and Synnanon. Nevertheless, according to Antze (cited in Lakin, 1985):

Each self-help group claims a certain wisdom concerning the problem it treats, and each has a specialized system of teachings that its members venerate as the secret of recovery. Each self-help ideology develops characteristic rituals, rules of behavior, slogans, and favorite expressions to describe important feelings, attitudes, and behaviors. All of these reflect the group's explicit and implicit beliefs about the disabilities that have brought the members to the group and how to overcome them. (p. 192)

SELECTION AND COMPOSITION

The selection process for self-help groups cannot be as formal and controlled as for counseling groups. Open access is a key characteristic of self-help groups. Membership is available to anyone suffering from the particular condition addressed by the group. Self-help groups typically do not screen members. New groups often have to campaign actively for members in order to continue to function. Established groups depend on both professional referrals and informal word-of-mouth networks.

Since the sole requirement for membership in a self-help group is a particular problem or characteristic, the groups tend to be both homogeneous and heterogeneous.

The shared problem provides a common identity for a membership that often varies greatly in age and socioeconomic status.

Group Size

Silverman (1985) suggested that a typical self-help group has between 10 and 20 members. However, this figure does not give the complete picture. The range of group size is extensive, from the few members of a beginning group to more than 50 in some well-established groups. The larger groups tend to have a formal structure and emphasize information dissemination, whereas the smaller ones offer more opportunities for interaction among members. Some groups with large memberships split into smaller segments during parts of their meeting time in order to encourage member-to-member interaction.

Group Setting

Typically, self-help groups hold meetings in church halls, public buildings, or other no-rent or low-rent facilities. Many small groups meet in members' homes. Since most self-help groups are financed by minimal dues or voluntary contributions, economy often becomes the primary consideration in choosing a setting.

Frequency and Duration of Sessions

Frequency of sessions depends on the goals of the self-help group. Addiction groups tend to have more frequent meetings than crisis groups. These groups may meet more than once a week, whereas a typical life-transition group might meet once a month, although the senior author has found that weekly meetings for bereavement support groups to be optimal. In addition, most self-help groups also offer services to supplement group sessions. Newsletters published by both national organizations and local groups offer information about the group's concerns. Some groups maintain a hotline service so that those in need have constant access to information and to an understanding listener. Others, particularly those dealing with addictive behavior, use a "buddy system" so that members can count on one-to-one encouragement between meetings.

Theoretically, a self-help group can continue to function indefinitely. The group is always open to new members. In fact, recruiting new members is an important function of the group. As older members leave, they are replaced by the new ones. In actuality, some self-help groups are not successful in maintaining continuity. It is Borman and Lieberman's (1979) belief that the less successful groups fail to recruit new members, thus becoming closed systems and eventually dying out.

Supplements Employed

Self-help groups seem to be bound by few rules in their use of media. Most of the groups allow for member-to-member interaction for some portion of the meetings, but also include a variety of educational and therapeutic components. Programs for meetings can include visiting speakers, group discussions, study groups, films, and skills training.

Information is highly valued by self-help groups and is delivered through a variety of media. Groups often maintain lending libraries of books and pamphlets dealing with the issue they address. Newsletters published by the group are also used to disseminate information.

Special Ethical Considerations

Inasmuch as most self-help groups are led by nonprofessionals, there is no professional ethical code of conduct to guide and regulate self-help leaders and groups. However, when professionals lead self-help groups, they are usually bound by their own profession's code of conduct. Lakin (1985) has pointed to incidents such as the shocking deaths of 900 members of the People's Temple and internal turmoil of Synnanon traceable to ideologies that became misguided by unhealthy leaders. It is Lakin's belief that the absence of professional leadership in self-help groups leads to the following dangers:

> (1) less control over the influence of strongest members, (2) programmatic or overly ideological interpretation of group processes, and (3) an authoritarian, or even totalitarian, outlook on the group's processes which can result in significant harm to some members. (p. 197)

Goodman and Jacobs (1994) have cited criticism of professionals who have expressed concern about the blind leading the blind in mutual support groups and their lack of helping skills as well as the need for ethical guidelines, professional consultation, and responsibility for damaged dropouts. Goodman and Jacobs have referred to Reissman's (1990) article (cited in Goodman & Jacobs, 1994) on the new "self-help backlash" in which he summarized the critique as follows:

> (1) participants can become addicted to attending meetings to the point of disabling other aspects of their lives, (2) some MSGs have become brazenly profit oriented, (3) MSG professionals exaggerate the numbers of people that need them, (4) spontaneous remission and self-controlled recovery is disregarded by many MSGs, (5) MSGs overestimate their success rate, and (6) the focus of some MSGs diverts members from addressing community and social factors that cause or contribute to their predicament or illness. (Goodman & Jacobs, 1994, p. 509)

Although the need for ethical guidelines for self-help groups has been voiced by professionals, the great variety and numbers of self-help groups pose a serious obstacle for their development in the near future. Perhaps a first step in protecting group members would be for self-help groups to retain the consultation services of qualified professional group leaders.

Multicultural Issues

Sidron, Chesler, and Chesney (1991) found some evidence that support groups of parents of mentally ill children and children with cancer in Israel and the United States showed some parallel processes and outcomes. It is their belief that universal characteristics of self-help/mutual support groups would be identified through international research.

Lakin (1985) has pointed out that groups such as A.A. and Recovery, Inc., tend to appeal to individuals with limited education who are relatively psychologically unsophisticated. On the other hand, he uses SAGE, for the elderly, as an example of a self-help group that attracts a well-educated and relatively sophisticated group of older clients.

Goodman and Jacobs (1994) have referred to the small, private, free-standing, self-help groups about which little is known, but it is believed that they might exist in numbers equal to the more recognized public groups. It is quite possible that the small, private self-help groups are operating privately to restrict membership for prejudicial reasons.

Although self-help groups recruit members with a common problem or issue, and, by nature of the purpose of their existence, are homogeneous and are exclusive, there is room for heterogeneity within the common condition, which is the basis for the establishment of the particular group. For example, there would be no reason to restrict group members to a bereavement support group based on gender, race, age, and so forth.

Insofar as self-help groups develop to meet specific needs of the membership and their origination is from the "grass roots" or those with need, there is great flexibility in accommodating any of the multicultural conditions that might call for self-help or mutual support. A bias reflecting some multicultural condition could still exist in an established self-help group based on its location, referral, recruitment area, and the nature of the group leadership.

RESEARCH

The rapid growth of self-help groups would seem to be a testimony to their effectiveness. However, the research on their efficacy and how they function has been limited (Powell, 1985; Toro, Rappaport, & Seidman, 1987).

Research on self-help groups presents some particular difficulties. Self-help groups vary in focus, type, structure, meaning to participants, member characteristics, ideology, and so on. Research designs and methods are complicated by the need to study the groups in their natural settings (Katz, 1981). In addition, few self-help groups have any doubts about their effectiveness and thus find no need to collaborate in research (Levy, 1984). Those that might be willing to collaborate often question the appropriateness of outcome criteria set by outsiders.

In his review of studies on autonomous self-help organizations, Powell (1987) concluded that they showed positive effects. However, he cautioned that these findings come from quasi-experimental designs and thus are not as powerful as they would be if experimental designs had been employed. Moreover, the positive evaluations are related to active participation over an extended period of time. There seem to be few benefits for the occasional or passive participants.

Barlow, Burlingame, Nebeker, and Anderson (1999) performed a meta-analysis of 29 medical self-help groups that were reported in the literature from 1970 to 1997. Posttreatment analysis showed no significant differences between experimental and control conditions; however, pre-to-posttreatment analysis showed that self-help groups had higher member improvement when compared to control group members. When between-subject versus within-subject error terms for the experimental and control groups were studied, the conclusion was reached that there were no significant differences between self-help groups and nontreated controls. Although these results differ from meta-analyses of psychotherapy groups where treated groups tend to show improvements over nontreated controls, many more questions were raised than answered. This study suggested many variables that need to be investigated when researching the effectiveness of self-help groups.

According to Goodman and Jacobs (1994), "Overall, outcome research on MSGs generally paints a positive picture" (p. 507). They refer to Medvene's (1987) "Selected Highlights of Research on Effectiveness of Self-Help Groups" to support their contention (Medvene, cited in Goodman & Jacobs, 1994). Medvene sampled 22 positive outcome studies completed for the California Self-Help Center. These studies included such groups as people coping with chronic physical problems, smokers, surgical patients, cancer patients, parents of premature infants, widows, bereaved parents, discharged mental patients, children of parents with drinking problems, child abusers, and young drug and alcohol abusers. Some reported gains/benefits were that smokers had higher quit rates than nonparticipating controls; scoliosis support group members, compared to similar nonparticipating patients, had fewer psychosomatic symptoms, higher self-esteem, a more positive outlook, and better patient-physician relationships; women with metastasized breast cancer in a support group had fewer maladaptive coping responses, were less phobic, and had lower mood disturbances than a comparable group who did not join a support group; widows who were paired with other widows for support compared to nonpaired widows felt better, made new friends, and began more new activities, among other improvements; and patients discharged from a state psychiatric hospital who were in a self-help group required less rehospitilization and for less time than nonparticipating discharged patients.

Levy (1984) suggested that self-help group research has a unique contribution to make to psychotherapy. According to him, self-help groups have much to recommend as sources of information about the nature of therapeutic process, social support systems, and small groups. The groups are characterized by a pragmatic attitude toward their operation. Group procedures are likely to reflect what has been found to be effective. Levy believes that "by observing the operation of self-help groups, we have a unique opportunity to gain insight into the natural psychotherapeutic processes of everyday life" (1984, p. 159).

Various authors have stressed the positive contributions of self-help groups to the mental health field. Some consider the growth of self-help a revolution in mental health services (Gartner & Riessman, 1984). They view the formal service structure as too big, bureaucratized, inaccessible, costly, and often ineffective. For them, self-help represents a major shift in health care from an emphasis on the professional service giver to an emphasis on consumer. Others (Lieberman & Borman, 1979) view self-help as a welcome addition to the existing mental health delivery system that can be used to alleviate some of the strain on the system. In spite of the differences in philosophic orientation, writers in the field agree that self-help has important practical implications. It is inexpensive, highly responsive, and accessible. The positive quality of self-help groups cited most by proponents is *empowerment*. According to them, self-help groups do not encourage dependency, as does the traditional model of professional service delivery.

Self-help groups have not escaped criticism, however. Lakin (1985) has suggested that the procedures of certain behavioral control groups (e.g., Recovery, Inc., A.A., and Synanon) may be inappropriate and even harmful for some people. It is Frew's (1986) belief that because of a lack of professional leadership, self-help groups do not progress past the initial, inclusion phase of their development and thus cannot reach their full potential as therapeutic groups. Powell (1987) cited the problems that plague self-help groups: the tentative and uncertain goals and activities of the beginning group; leadership struggles within groups that sap their effectiveness; and the groups' continued need to struggle for resources.

SUMMARY

Self-help/mutual support in groups is one of the oldest forms of care for human problems. Yet, its power and potential have only recently been rediscovered by scholars and mental health professionals. Today, it is an increasingly utilized and rapidly growing mental health service.

The self-help groups that interface with the mental health profession are those oriented toward helping the individuals achieve either behavioral change or adjustment to a life change. The groups are characterized by the following: a peer orientation, a problem focus, an estrangement from societal norms, and an ideological base. These characteristics distinguish self-help groups from other psychotherapy groups and contribute to their unique effectiveness. Individuals who share a common, often stigmatizing, problem come together and find support and hope. Peer leadership provides opportunities for "helper" therapy and member empowerment. Group ideologies serve as powerful, persuasive systems that provide a "cognitive antidote" to the condition addressed by the group.

The optimal role for professionals in self-help groups seems to be one that will preserve their unique helping processes. Some of the roles played by professionals ("professionals" are not just trained counselors or "therapists") include sole leader, co-leader, referring new members, speakers, consultants and advisors, procurers of resources, organizers and coordinators of groups, group observers, and evaluators.

Consistent with other chapters dealing with specific theoretical models, this chapter also included a presentation of the theoretical rationale, goals and objectives, selection and composition, group size, group setting, frequency and duration of sessions, supplements employed, special ethical considerations, multicultural issues, and research.

Recent research is beginning to delineate the effectiveness of the self-help process. Further research has the potential of increasing our understanding of how humans attempt to help each other cope with the stresses of everyday life.

REFERENCES

Antze, P. (1979). The role of ideologies in peer psychotherapy groups. In M. A. Lieberman & L. D. Borman (Eds.), *Self-help for coping with crisis.* San Francisco: Jossey-Bass.

Back, K. W., & Taylor, R. C. (1976). Self-help groups: Tool or symbol? *Journal of Applied Behavioral Science, 12*(3), 295–309.

Barish, H. (1971). Self-help groups. In *The encyclopedia of social work* (16th ed.). New York: The National Association of Social Workers.

Barlow, S. H., Burlingame, G. M., Nebeker, R. S., & Anderson, E. (1999). Meta-analysis of medical self-help groups. *International Journal of Group Psychotherapy, 50,* 53–70.

Bean, M. (1975). Alcoholics anonymous, part I. *Psychiatric Annals, 5,* 7–61.

Borman, L. D. (1979). Characteristics of development and growth. In M. A. Lieberman & L. D. Borman (Eds.), *Self-help groups for coping with crisis: Origins, members, processes, and impact.* San Francisco: Jossey-Bass.

Borman, L. D. (1982). Kalmuk resettlement in America. In G. H. Weber & L. M. Cohen (Eds.), *Belief and self-help.* New York: Human Sciences Press.

Borman, L. D., & Lieberman, M. A. (1979). Conclusion: Contributions, dilemmas, and implications for mental health policy. In M. A. Lieberman & L. D. Borman (Eds.), *Self-help groups for coping with crisis: Origins, members, processes, and impact.* San Francisco: Jossey-Bass.

Burstein, B. (1985). *Needs assessment of California mental support groups.* Unpublished manuscript, California Self-Help Center, Department of Psychology, University of California, Los Angeles.

Dunkel-Schetter, C., & Wortman, C. B. (1982). The interpersonal dynamics in cancer: Problems in social relationships, and their impact on the patient. In H. S. Friedman & M. R. Dimatteo (Eds.), *Interpersonal issues in health care.* New York: Academic.

Festinger, L. (1954). A theory of social comparison processes. *Human Relations, 7,* 117–140.

Frew, J. E. (1986). Leadership approaches to achieving maximum therapeutic potential in mutual support groups. *Journal for Specialists in Group Work, 11*(2), 93–99.

Gartner, A., & Riessman, F. (Eds.). (1984). *The self-help revolution.* New York: Human Sciences Press.

Goodman, G., & Jacobs, M. K. (1994). The self-help, mutual support group. In A. Furhiman & G. M. Burlingame (Eds.), *Handbook of group psychotherapy: An empirical and clinical synthesis.* New York: Wiley.

Katz, A. H. (1972). Self-help groups. *Social Work, 17,* 120–121.

Katz, A. H. (1981). Self-help and mutual aid: An emerging social movement. *Annual Review of Sociology, 7,* 129–155.

Katz, A. H. (1982). Self-help and human services. *Citizen Participation, 3*(3), 22–23.

Katz, A. H., & Bender, E. I. (1976a). Self-help groups in western society: History and prospects. *The Journal of Applied Behavioral Science, 12*(3), 265–282.

Katz, A. H., & Bender, E. I. (1976b). *The strength in us: Self-help groups in the modern world.* New York: Franklin Watts.

Kessler, R. C., Price, R. H., & Wortman, C. B. (1985). Social factors in psychopathology: Stress, social support and coping processes. *Annual Review of Psychology, 36,* 531–572.

Killilea, M. (1976). Mutual help organizations: Interpretations in the literature. In G. Caplan & M. Killilea (Eds.), *Support systems and mutual help: Multidisciplinary explorations.* New York: Grune & Stratton.

Kropotkin, P. (1972). *Mutual aid: A factor of evolution.* New York: New York University Press. (Original work published 1914).

Lakin, M. (1985). *The helping group.* Reading, MA: Addison-Wesley.

Levy, L. H. (1976). Self-help groups: Types and psychological processes. *The Journal of Applied and Behavioral Science, 12,* 311–322.

Levy, L. H. (1984). Issues in research and evaluation. In A. Gartner & F. Riessman (Eds.), *The self-help revolution.* New York: Human Sciences Press.

Lieberman, M. A., & Borman, L. D. (Eds.). (1979). *Self-help groups for coping with crisis: Origins, members, processes, and impact.* San Francisco: Jossey-Bass.

Lotery, J. L. (1985). *A review of self-help/mutual support group theory and research with an emphasis on the role of mental health professionals.* Unpublished doctoral dissertation, University of California, Los Angeles.

Medvene, L. (1987). *Selected research highlights on the effectiveness of self-help groups.* Unpublished manuscript. California Self-Help Center, Department of Psychology, UCLA.

Pancoast, D., Parker, P., & Froland, C. (Eds.). (1983). *Rediscovering self-help: Its role in social care.* Beverly Hills: Sage.

Pearson, R. E. (1986). Guest editorial. *Journal for Specialists in Group Work, 11*(2), 66–67.

Powell, T. J. (1985). Improving the effectiveness of self-help. *Social Policy, 16,* 22–29.

Powell, T. J. (1987). *Self-help organizations and professional practice.* Silver Springs, MD: National Association of Social Workers.

Rappaport, J. (1985). The power of empowerment language. *Social Policy, 16,* 15–21.

Remine, D., Rice, R. M., & Ross, J. (1984). *Self-help groups and human service agencies: How they work together.* New York: Family Service America.

Riessman, F. (1965). The "helper" therapy principle. *Social Work, 10,* 27–32.

Riessman, F. (1990). The new self-help backlash. *Social Policy, 21*(1), 42–48.

Rodolfa, E. R., & Hungerford, L. (1982). Self-help groups: A referral resource for professional therapists. *Professional Psychology, 13*(3), 345–353.

Sagarin, E. (1969). *Odd man in: Societies of deviants in America.* Chicago: Quadrangle Books.

Schacter, S. (Eds.). (1959). *The psychology of affiliation.* Stanford, CA: Stanford University Press.

Sherman, B. (1979). Emergence of ideology in peer psychotherapy groups. In M. A. Lieberman & L. D. Borman (Eds.), *Self-help groups for coping with crisis: Origins, members, processes, and impact.* San Francisco: Jossey-Bass.

Sidron, B., Chesler, M. A., & Chesney, B. K. (1991). Cross-cultural perspectives on self-help groups. Comparison between participants and nonparticipants in Israel and the United States. *American Journal of Community Psychology, 19*(5), 667–681.

Silverman, P. (1980). *Mutual help groups: Organization and development.* Beverly Hills: Sage.

Silverman, P. (1985). Tertiary/secondary prevention: Preventive intervention, the case for mutual self help groups. In R. K. Conyne (Ed.), *The group worker's handbook: Varieties of group experience.* Springfield, IL: Charles C. Thomas.

Silverman, P. (1986). The perils of borrowing: Role of the professional in mutual help groups. *Journal for Specialists in Group Work,11*(2), 68–73.

Silverman, P., & Smith, D. (1984). Helping in mutual help groups for the physically disabled. In A. Gartner & F. Riessman (Eds.), *The self-help revolution.* New York: Human Sciences Press.

Steinman, R., & Traunstein, D. M. (1976). Redefining deviance: The self-help challenge to the human services. *Journal of Applied Behavioral Science, 12*(3), 347–361.

Stewart, M. J. (1990). Professional interface with mutual-aid self-help groups: A review. *Social Science and Medicine, 31,* 1143–1158.

Suler, J. (1984). The role of ideology in self-help groups. *Social Policy, 14,* 29–36.

Thoits, P. A. (1986). Social supports as coping assistance. *Journal of Consulting and Clinical Psychology, 54,* 416–423.

Toro, P. A., Rappaport, J., & Seidman, E. (1987). Social climate comparison of mutual help and psychotherapy groups. *Journal of Consulting and Clinical Psychology, 55*(3), 430–431.

Toro, P. A., Reischl, T. M., Zimmerman, M. A., Rapport, J., Seidman, E., Luke, D. A., & Roberts, L. J. (1988). Professionals in mutual help groups: Impact on social climate and members' behavior. *Journal of Consulting and Clinical Psychology, 56,* 631–632.

Toseland, R. W., Rossiter, C. M., Peak, T., & Hill, P. (1990). Therapeutic processes in peer led and professionally led support groups for caregivers. *International Journal of Group Psychotherapy, 40,* 279–303.

Wollert, R., & Barron, N. (1983). Avenues of collaboration. In D. Pancoast, P. Parker, & C. Froland (Eds.), *Rediscovering self-help: Its role in social care.* Beverly Hills: Sage.

Wollert, R. W., Knight, B., & Levy, L. H. (1980). Make today count: A collaborative model for professional and self-help groups. *Professional Psychology, 11,* 130–138.

Yalom, I. (1985). *The theory and practice of group psychotherapy* (3rd ed.). New York: Basic Books.

Yoak, M., & Chesler, M. (1985). Alternative professional roles in health care delivery: Leadership patterns in self-help groups. *Journal of Applied Behavioral Science, 21,* 427–444.

PROFESSIONAL STANDARDS FOR THE TRAINING OF GROUP WORKERS

Association for Specialists in Group Work

Revision Approved by the Executive Board, January 22, 2000
Prepared by F. Robert Wilson and Lynn S. Rapin, Co-Chairs,
and Lynn Haley-Banez, Member, ASGW Standards Committee
Consultants: Robert K. Conyne and Donald E. Ward

PREAMBLE

For nearly two decades, the Association for Specialists in Group Work (herein referred to as ASGW or as the Association) has promulgated professional standards for the training of group workers. In the early 1980s, the Association published the ASGW Training Standards for Group Counselors (1983) which established nine knowledge competencies, seventeen skill competencies, and clock-hour baselines for various aspects of supervised clinical experience in group counseling. The focus on group counseling embodied in these standards mirrored the general conception of the time that whatever counselors did with groups of individuals should properly be referred to as group counseling.

New ground was broken in the 1990 revision of the ASGW Professional Standards for the Training of Group Workers with (a) the articulation of the term, *group work,* to capture the variety of ways in which counselors work with groups, (b) differentiation of core training, deemed essential for all counselors, from specialization training required of those intending to engage in group work as part of their professional practice, and (c) the differentiation among four distinct group work specializations: task and work group facilitation, group psychoeducation, group counseling, and group psychotherapy. Over the ten years in which these standards have been in force, commentary and criticism has been elicited through discussion groups at various regional and national conferences and through published analyses in the Association's journal, the *Journal for Specialists in Group Work.*

In this Year-2000 revision of the ASGW Professional Standards for the Training of Group Workers, the foundation established by the 1990 training standards has been preserved and refined by application of feedback received through public discussion and scholarly debate. The Year-2000 revision maintains and strengthens the distinction between core and specialization training with requirements for core training and aspirational guidelines for specialization training. Further, the definitions of group work specializations have been expanded and clarified. Evenness of application of training standards across the specializations has been assured by creating a single set of guidelines for all four specializations with specialization specific detail being supplied where necessary. Consistent with both the pattern for training standards established by the Council for Accreditation of Counseling and Related Educational Programs accreditation standards and past editions of the ASGW training standards, the Year-2000 revision addresses both content and clinical instruction. Content instruction is described in terms of both course work requirements and knowledge objectives while clinical instruction is articulated in terms of experiential requirements and skill objectives. This revision of the training standards was informed by and profits from the seminal ASGW Best Practice Guidelines (1998) and the ASGW Principles for Diversity-Competent Group Workers (1999). Although each of these documents have their own form of organization, all address the group work elements of planning, performing, and processing and the ethical and diversity-competent treatment of participants in group activities.

PURPOSE

The purpose of the Professional Standards for the Training of Group Workers is to provide guidance to counselor training programs in the construction of their curricula for graduate programs in counseling (e.g., master's, specialist, and doctoral degrees and other forms of advanced graduate study). Specifically, core standards express the Association's view on the minimum training in group work all programs in counseling should provide for all graduates of their entry level, master's degree programs in counseling, and specialization standards provide a framework for documenting the training philosophy, objectives, curriculum, and outcomes for each declared specialization program.

Core Training in Group Work

All counselors should possess a set of core competencies in general group work. The Association for Specialists in Group Work advocates for the incorporation of core group work competencies as part of required entry level training in all counselor preparation programs. The Association's standards for core training are consistent with and provide further elaboration of the standards for accreditation of entry level counseling programs identified by the Council for Accreditation of Counseling and Related Educational Programs (CACREP, 1994). Mastery of the core competencies detailed in the ASGW training standards will prepare the counselor to understand group process phenomena and to function more effectively in groups in which the counselor is a member.

Mastery of basic knowledge and skill in group work provides a foundation which specialty training can extend but does not qualify one to independently practice any group work specialty.

Specialist Training in Group Work

The independent practice of group work requires training beyond core competencies. ASGW advocates that independent practitioners of group work must possess advanced competencies relevant to the particular kind of group work practice in which the group work student wants to specialize (e.g., facilitation of task groups, group psychoeducation, group counseling, or group psychotherapy). To encourage program creativity in development of specialization training, the specialization guidelines do not prescribe minimum trainee competencies. Rather, the guidelines establish a framework within which programs can develop unique training experiences utilizing scientific foundations and best practices to achieve their training objectives. In providing these guidelines for specialized training, ASGW makes no presumption that a graduate program in counseling must provide training in a group work specialization nor that adequate training in a specialization can be accomplished solely within a well-rounded master's degree program in counseling. To provide adequate specialization training, completion of post-master's options such as certificates of post-master's study or doctoral degrees may be required. Further, there is no presumption that an individual who may have received adequate training in a given declared specialization will be prepared to function effectively with all group situations in which the graduate may want to or be required to work. It is recognized that the characteristics of specific client populations and employment settings vary widely. Additional training beyond that which was acquired in a specific graduate program may be necessary for optimal, diversity-competent, group work practice with a given population in a given setting.

DEFINITIONS

Group Work: is a broad professional practice involving the application of knowledge and skill in group facilitation to assist an interdependent collection of people to reach their mutual goals which may be intrapersonal, interpersonal, or work-related. The goals of the group may include the accomplishment of tasks related to work, education, personal development, personal and interpersonal problem solving, or remediation of mental and emotional disorders.

Core Training in Group Work: includes knowledge, skills, and experiences deemed necessary for general competency for all master's degree prepared counselors. ASGW advocates for all counselor preparation programs to provide core training in group work regardless of whether the program intends to prepare trainees for independent practice in a group work specialization. Core training in group work is considered a necessary prerequisite for advanced practice in group work.

Specialization Training in Group Work: includes knowledge, skills, and experiences deemed necessary for counselors to engage in independent practice of group work. Four areas of advanced practice, referred to as specializations, are identified: Task Group Facilitation, Group Psychoeducation, Group Counseling, and Group Psychotherapy. This list is not presumed to be exhaustive and while there may be no sharp boundaries between the specializations, each has recognizable characteristics that have professional utility. The definitions for these group work specializations have been built upon the American Counseling Association's model definition of counseling (adopted by the ACA Governing Council in 1997), describing the methods typical of the working stage of the group being defined and the typical purposes to which those methods are put and the typical populations served by those methods. Specialized training presumes mastery of prerequisite core knowledge, skills, and experiences.

SPECIALIZATION IN TASK AND WORK GROUP FACILITATION:

- The application of principles of normal human development and functioning
- through group-based educational, developmental, and systemic strategies
- applied in the context of here-and-now interaction
- that promote efficient and effective accomplishment of group tasks
- among people who are gathered to accomplish group task goals.

SPECIALIZATION IN PSYCHOEDUCATION GROUP LEADERSHIP:

- The application of principles of normal human development and functioning
- through group-based educational and developmental strategies
- applied in the context of here-and-now interaction
- that promote personal and interpersonal growth and development and the prevention of future difficulties
- among people who may be at risk for the development of personal or interpersonal problems or who seek enhancement of personal qualities and abilities.

SPECIALIZATION IN GROUP COUNSELING:

- The application of principles of normal human development and functioning
- through group-based cognitive, affective, behavioral, or systemic intervention strategies
- applied in the context of here-and-now interaction
- that address personal and interpersonal problems of living and promote personal and interpersonal growth and development
- among people who may be experiencing transitory maladjustment, who are at risk for the development of personal or interpersonal problems, or who seek enhancement of personal qualities and abilities.

SPECIALIZATION IN GROUP PSYCHOTHERAPY:

- The application of principles of normal and abnormal human development and functioning
- through group-based cognitive, affective, behavioral, or systemic intervention strategies
- applied in the context of negative emotional arousal

- that address personal and interpersonal problems of living, remediate perceptual and cognitive distortions or repetitive patterns of dysfunctional behavior, and promote personal and interpersonal growth and development
- among people who may be experiencing severe and/or chronic maladjustment.

CORE TRAINING STANDARDS

I. Coursework and Experiential Requirements

A. Coursework Requirements

Core training shall include at least one graduate course in group work that addresses such as but not limited to scope of practice, types of group work, group development, group process and dynamics, group leadership, and standards of training and practice for group workers.

B. Experiential Requirements

Core training shall include a minimum of 10 clock hours (20 clock hours recommended) observation of and participation in a group experience as a group member and/or as a group leader.

II. Knowledge and Skill Objectives

A. Nature and Scope of Practice

1. *Knowledge Objectives.* Identify and describe:
   a. the nature of group work and the various specializations within group work
   b. theories of group work including commonalties and distinguishing characteristics among the various specializations within group work
   c. research literature pertinent to group work and its specializations
2. *Skill Objectives.* Demonstrate skill in:
   a. preparing a professional disclosure statement for practice in a chosen area of specialization
   b. applying theoretical concepts and scientific findings to the design of a group and the interpretation of personal experiences in a group

B. Assessment of Group Members and the Social Systems in Which They Live and Work

1. *Knowledge Objectives.* Identify and describe:
   a. principles of assessment of group functioning in group work
   b. use of personal contextual factors (e.g., family-of-origin, neighborhood-of-residence, organizational membership, cultural membership) in interpreting behavior of members in a group
2. *Skill Objectives.* Demonstrate skill in:
   a. observing and identifying group process
   b. observing the personal characteristics of individual members in a group
   c. developing hypotheses about the behavior of group members
   d. employing contextual factors (e.g., family of origin, neighborhood of residence, organizational membership, cultural membership) in interpretation of individual and group data

C. Planning Group Interventions

1. *Knowledge Objectives.* Identify and describe:
   a. environmental contexts, which affect planning for group interventions
   b. the impact of group member diversity (e.g., gender, culture, learning style, group climate preference) on group member behavior and group process and dynamics in group work
   c. principles of planning for group work
2. *Skill Objectives.* Demonstrate skill in:
   a. collaborative consultation with targeted populations to enhance ecological validity of planned group interventions
   b. planning for a group work activity including such aspects as developing overarching purpose, establishing goals and objectives, detailing methods to be used in achieving goals and objectives, determining methods for outcome assessment, and verifying ecological validity of plan

D. Implementation of Group Interventions

1. *Knowledge Objectives.* Identify and describe:
   a. principles of group formation including recruiting, screening, and selecting group members
   b. principles for effective performance of group leadership functions
   c. therapeutic factors within group work and when group work approaches are indicated and contraindicated
   d. principles of group dynamics including group process components, developmental stage theories, group member roles, group member behaviors
2. *Skill Objectives.* Demonstrate skill in:
   a. encouraging participation of group members
   b. attending to, describing, acknowledging, confronting, understanding, and responding empathically to group member behavior
   c. attending to, acknowledging, clarifying, summarizing, confronting, and responding empathically to group member statements
   d. attending to, acknowledging, clarifying, summarizing, confronting, and responding empathically to group themes
   e. eliciting information from and imparting information to group members
   f. providing appropriate self-disclosure
   g. maintaining group focus; keeping a group on task
   h. giving and receiving feedback in a group setting

E. Leadership and Co-Leadership

1. *Knowledge Objectives.* Identify and describe:
   a. group leadership styles and approaches
   b. group work methods including group worker orientations and specialized group leadership behaviors
   c. principles of collaborative group processing
2. *Skill Objectives.* To the extent opportunities for leadership or co-leadership are provided, demonstrate skill in:
   a. engaging in reflective evaluation of one's personal leadership style and approach

    b. working cooperatively with a co-leader and/or group members

    c. engaging in collaborative group processing.

F. Evaluation

    1. *Knowledge Objectives.* Identify and describe:

        a. methods for evaluating group process in group work

        b. methods for evaluating outcomes in group work

    2. *Skill Objectives.* Demonstrate skill in:

        a. contributing to evaluation activities during group participation

        b. engaging in self-evaluation of personally selected performance goals

G. Ethical Practice, Best Practice, Diversity-Competent Practice

    1. *Knowledge Objectives.* Identify and describe:

        a. ethical considerations unique to group work

        b. best practices in group work

        c. diversity competent group work

    2. *Skill Objectives.* Demonstrate skill in:

        a. evidencing ethical practice in planning, observing, and participating in group activities

        b. evidencing best practice in planning, observing, and participating in group activities

        c. evidencing diversity-competent practice in planning, observing, and participating in group activities

SPECIALIZATION GUIDELINES

I. Overarching Program Characteristics

A. The program has a clearly specified philosophy of training for the preparation of specialists for independent practice of group work in one of the forms of group work recognized by the Association (i.e., task and work group facilitation, group psychoeducation, group counseling, or group psychotherapy).

    1. The program states an explicit intent to train group workers in one or more of the group work specializations.

    2. The program states an explicit philosophy of training, based on the science of group work, by which it intends to prepare students for independent practice in the declared specialization(s).

B. For each declared specialization, the program specifies education and training objectives in terms of the competencies expected of students completing the specialization training. These competencies are consistent with

    1. the program's philosophy and training model,

    2. the substantive area(s) relevant for best practice of the declared specialization area, and

    3. standards for competent, ethical, and diversity sensitive practice of group work

C. For each declared specialization, the program specifies a sequential, cumulative curriculum, expanding in breadth and depth, and designed to prepare students for independent practice of the specialization and relevant credentialing.

D. For each declared specialization, the program documents achievement of training objectives in terms of student competencies.

II. Recommended Coursework and Experience

A. Coursework. Specialization training may include coursework which provides the student with a broad foundation in the group work domain in which the student seeks specialized training:

1. *Task/Work Group Facilitation:* coursework includes but is not limited to organizational development, management, and consultation, theory and practice of task/work group facilitation

2. *Group Psychoeducation:* coursework includes but is not limited to organizational development, school and community counseling/psychology, health promotion, marketing, program development and evaluation, organizational consultation, theory and practice of group psychoeducation

3. *Group Counseling:* coursework includes but is not limited to normal human development, health promotion, theory and practice of group counseling

4. *Group Psychotherapy:* coursework includes but is not be limited to normal and abnormal human development, assessment and diagnosis of mental and emotional disorders, treatment of psychopathology, theory and practice of group psychotherapy

B. Experience. Specialization training includes

1. *Task/Work Group Facilitation:* a minimum of 30 clock hours (45 clock hours recommended) supervised practice facilitating or conducting an intervention with a task or work group appropriate to the age and clientele of the group leader's specialty area (e.g., school counseling, student development counseling, community counseling, mental health counseling)

2. *Group Psychoeducation:* a minimum of 30 clock hours (45 clock hours recommended) supervised practice conducting a psychoeducation group appropriate to the age and clientele of the group leader's specialty area (e.g., school counseling, student development counseling, community counseling, mental health counseling)

3. *Group Counseling:* a minimum of 45 clock hours (60 clock hours recommended) supervised practice conducting a counseling group appropriate to the age and clientele of the group leader's specialty area (e.g., school counseling, student development counseling, community counseling, mental health counseling)

4. *Group Psychotherapy:* a minimum of 45 clock hours (60 clock hours recommended) supervised practice conducting a psychotherapy group appropriate to the age and clientele of the group leader's specialty area (e.g., mental health counseling)

III. Knowledge and Skill Elements

In achieving its objectives, the program has and implements a clear and coherent curriculum plan that provides the means whereby all students can acquire and demonstrate substantial understanding of and competence in the following areas:

A. **Nature and Scope of Practice**

The program states a clear expectation that its students will limit their independent practice of group work to those specialization areas for which they have been appropriately trained and supervised.

B. **Assessment of Group Members and the Social Systems in Which They Live and Work**

All graduates of specialization training will understand and demonstrate competence in the use of assessment instruments and methodologies for assessing individual group member characteristics and group development, group dynamics, and process phenomena relevant for the program's declared specialization area(s). Studies should include but are not limited to:

1. methods of screening and assessment of populations, groups, and individual members who are or may be targeted for intervention

2. methods for observation of group member behavior during group interventions

3. methods of assessment of group development, process, and outcomes

C. **Planning Group Interventions**

All graduates of specialization training will understand and demonstrate competence in planning group interventions consistent with the program's declared specialization area(s). Studies should include but are not limited to:

1. establishing the overarching purpose for the intervention

2. identifying goals and objectives for the intervention

3. detailing methods to be employed in achieving goals and objectives during the intervention

4. selecting methods for examining group process during group meetings, between group sessions, and at the completion of the group intervention

5. preparing methods for helping members derive meaning from their within-group experiences and transfer within-group learning to real-world circumstances

6. determining methods for measuring outcomes during and following the intervention

7. verifying ecological validity of plans for the intervention

D. **Implementation of Group Interventions**

All graduates of specialization training will understand and demonstrate competence in implementing group interventions consistent with the program's declared specialization area(s). Studies should include but are not limited to:

1. principles of group formation including recruiting, screening, selection, and orientation of group members

2. standard methods and procedures for group facilitation

3. selection and use of referral sources appropriate to the declared specialization

4. identifying and responding constructively to extra-group factors which may influence the success of interventions

5. applying the major strategies, techniques, and procedures

      6. adjusting group pacing relative to the stage of group development

      7. identifying and responding constructively to critical incidents

      8. identifying and responding constructively to disruptive members

      9. helping group members attribute meaning to and integrate and apply learning

      10. responding constructively to psychological emergencies

      11. involving group members in within-group session processing and on-going planning

E. Leadership and Co-Leadership

All graduates of specialization training will understand and demonstrate competence in pursuing personal competence as a leader and in selecting and managing the interpersonal relationship with a co-leader for group interventions consistent with the program's declared specialization area(s). Studies should include but are not limited to:

      1. characteristics and skills of effective leaders

      2. relationship skills required of effective co-leaders

      3. processing skills required of effective co-leaders

F. Evaluation

All graduates of specialization training will understand and demonstrate competence in evaluating group interventions consistent with the program's declared specialization area(s). Studies should include but are not limited to methods for evaluating participant outcomes and participant satisfaction.

G. Ethical Practice, Best Practice, Diversity-Competent Practice

All graduates of specialization training will understand and demonstrate consistent effort to comply with principles of ethical, best practice, and diversity-competent practice of group work consistent with the program's declared specialization area(s). Studies should include but are not limited to:

      1. ethical considerations unique to the program's declared specialization area

      2. best practices for group work within the program's declared specialization area

      3. diversity issues unique to the program's declared specialization area

IMPLEMENTATION GUIDELINES

Implementation of the Professional Standards for the Training of Group Workers requires a commitment by a program's faculty and a dedication of program resources to achieve excellence in preparing all counselors at core competency level and in preparing counselors for independent practice of group work. To facilitate implementation of the training standards, the Association offers the following guidelines.

Core Training in Group Work

Core training in group work can be provided through a single, basic course in group theory and process. This course should include the elements of content instruction detailed below and may also include the required clinical instruction component.

Content Instruction.   Consistent with accreditation standards (CACREP, 1994; Standard II.J.4), study in the area of group work should provide an understanding of the types of group work (e.g., facilitation of task groups, psychoeducation groups, counseling groups, psychotherapy groups); group development, group dynamics, and group leadership styles; and group leadership methods and skills. More explicitly, studies should include, but not be limited to, the following:

- principles of group dynamics including group process components, developmental stage theories, and group member's roles and behaviors;
- group leadership styles and approaches including characteristics of various types of group leaders and leadership styles;
- theories of group counseling including commonalties, distinguishing characteristics, and pertinent research and literature;
- group work methods including group leader orientations and behaviors, ethical standards, appropriate selection criteria and methods, and methods of evaluating effectiveness;
- approaches used for other types of group work, including task groups, prevention groups, support groups, and therapy groups; and,
- skills in observing member behavior and group process, empathic responding, confronting, self-disclosing, focusing, protecting, recruiting and selecting members, opening and closing sessions, managing, explicit and implicit teaching, modeling, giving and receiving feedback

Clinical Instruction.   Core group work training requires a minimum of 10 clock hours of supervised practice (20 clock hours of supervised practice is recommended). Consistent with CACREP standards for accreditation, the supervised experience provides the student with direct experiences as a participant in a small group, and may be met either in the basic course in group theory and practice or in a specially conducted small group designed for the purpose of meeting this standard (CACREP, 1994; Standard II.D). In arranging for and conducting this group experience, care must be taken by program faculty to assure that the ACA ethical standard for dual relationships and ASGW standards for best practice are observed.

Specialist Training in Group Work

Though ASGW advocates that all counselor training programs provide all counseling students with core group work training, specialization training is elective. If a counselor training program chooses to offer specialization training (e.g., task group facilitation, group psychoeducation, group counseling, group psychotherapy), ASGW urges institutions to develop their curricula consistent with the ASGW standards for that specialization.

Content Instruction.   Each area of specialization has its literature. In addition to basic course work in group theory and process, each specialization requires additional coursework providing specialized knowledge necessary for professional application of the specialization:

- *Task Group Facilitation:* coursework in such areas as organization development, consultation, management, or sociology so students gain a basic understanding of organizations and how task groups function within them.
- *Group Psychoeducation:* coursework in community psychology, consultation, health promotion, marketing, curriculum design to prepare students to conduct structured consciousness raising and skill training groups in such areas as stress management, wellness, anger control and assertiveness training, problem solving.
- *Group Counseling:* coursework in normal human development, family development and family counseling, assessment and problem identification of problems in living, individual counseling, and group counseling, including training experiences in personal growth or counseling group.
- *Group Psychotherapy:* coursework in abnormal human development, family pathology and family therapy, assessment and diagnosis of mental and emotional disorders, individual therapy, and group therapy, including training experiences in a therapy group.

Clinical Instruction.   For Task Group Facilitation and Group Psychoeducation, group specialization training recommends a minimum of 30 clock hours of supervised practice (45 clock hours of supervised practice is strongly suggested). Because of the additional difficulties presented by Group Counseling and Group Psychotherapy, a minimum of 45 clock hours of supervised practice is recommended (60 clock hours of supervised practice is strongly suggested). Consistent with CACREP standards for accreditation, supervised experience should provide an opportunity for the student to perform under supervision a variety of activities that a professional counselor would perform in conducting group work consistent with a given specialization (i.e., assessment of group members and the social systems in which they live and work, planning group interventions, implementing group interventions, leadership and co-leadership, and within-group, between-group, and end-of-group processing and evaluation).

In addition to courses offering content and experience related to a given specialization, supervised clinical experience should be obtained in practica and internship experiences. Following the model provided by CACREP for master's practica, we recommend that one quarter of all required supervised clinical experience be devoted to group work:

- *Master's Practicum:* At least 10 clock hours of the required 40 clock hours of direct service should be spent in supervised leadership or co-leadership experience in group work, typically in Task Group Facilitation, Group Psychoeducation, or Group Counseling (at the master's practicum level, experience in Group Psychotherapy would be unusual) (CACREP, 1994; Standard III.H.1).
- *Master's Internship:* At least 60 clock hours of the required 240 clock hours of direct services should be spent in supervised leadership or co-leadership in group work consistent with the program's specialization offering(s) (i.e., in Task Group Facilitation, Group Psychoeducation, Group Counseling, or Group Psychotherapy).

- *Doctoral Internship:* At least 150 clock hours of the required 600 clock hours of direct service should be spent in supervised leadership or co-leadership in group work consistent with the program's specialization offering(s) (i.e., in Task Group Facilitation, Group Psychoeducation, Group Counseling, or Group Psychotherapy).

REFERENCES

Association for Specialists in Group Work. (1998). ASGW Best Practice Guidelines. *Journal for Specialists in Group Work, 23,* 237–244.

Association for Specialists in Group Work. (1999). ASGW Principles for Diversity-Competent Group Workers. *Journal for Specialists in Group Work, 24,* 7–14.

Association for Specialists in Group Work. (1983). ASGW Professional Standards for Group Counseling. Alexandria VA: Author.

Association for Specialists in Group Work. (1990). Professional Standards for the Training of Group Workers. Alexandria VA: Author.

Council for Accreditation of Counseling and Related Educational Programs (CACREP). (1994). *CACREP accreditation standards and procedures manual.* Alexandria, VA: Author.

BEST PRACTICE GUIDELINES FOR GROUP WORKERS

Association for Specialists in Group Work

Revision Approved by the Executive Board, March 29, 1998
Prepared by Lynn S. Rapin and Linda Keel, ASGW Ethics Committee Co-Chairs

PREAMBLE

The Association for Specialists in Group Work (ASGW) is a division of the American Counseling Association whose members are interested in and specialize in group work. We value the creation of community; service to our members, clients, and the profession; and value leadership as a process to facilitate the growth and development of individuals and groups.

The Association for Specialists in Group Work recognizes the commitment of its members to the Code of Ethics and Standards of Practice (as revised in 1995) of its parent organization, the American Counseling Association, and nothing in this document shall be construed to supplant that code. These Best Practice Guidelines are intended to clarify the application of the ACA Code of Ethics and Standards of Practice to the field of group work by defining Group Workers' responsibility and scope of practice involving those activities, strategies and interventions that are consistent and current with effective and appropriate professional ethical and community standards. ASGW views ethical process as being integral to group work and views Group Workers as ethical agents. Group Workers, by their very nature in being responsible and responsive to their group members, necessarily embrace a certain potential for ethical vulnerability. It is incumbent upon Group Workers to give considerable attention to the intent and context of their actions because the attempts of Group Workers to influence human behavior through group work always have ethical implications. These Best Practice Guidelines address Group Workers' responsibilities in planning, performing and processing groups.

SECTION A: BEST PRACTICE IN PLANNING

A.1. Professional Context and Regulatory Requirements

Group Workers actively know, understand and apply the ACA Code of Ethics and Standards of Best Practice, the ASGW Professional Standards for the Training of Group Workers, these ASGW Best Practice Guidelines, the ASGW diversity competencies, the ACA Multicultural Guidelines, relevant state laws, accreditation requirements, relevant National Board for Certified Counselors Codes and Standards, their organization's standards, and insurance requirements impacting the practice of group work.

A.2. Scope of Practice and Conceptual Framework

Group Workers define the scope of practice related to the core and specialization competencies defined in the ASGW Training Standards. Group Workers are aware of personal strengths and weaknesses in leading groups. Group Workers develop and are able to articulate a general conceptual framework to guide practice and a rationale for use of techniques that are to be used. Group Workers limit their practice to those areas for which they meet the training criteria established by the ASGW Training Standards.

A.3. Assessment

    a. *Assessment of self.* Group Workers actively assess their knowledge and skills related to the specific group(s) offered. Group Workers assess their values, beliefs and theoretical orientation and how these impact upon the group, particularly when working with a diverse and multicultural population.

    b. *Ecological assessment.* Group Workers assess community needs, agency or organization resources, sponsoring organization mission, staff competency, attitudes regarding group work, professional training levels of potential group leaders regarding group work; client attitudes regarding group work, and multicultural and diversity considerations. Group Workers use this information as the basis for making decisions related to their group practice, or to the implementation of groups for which they have supervisory, evaluation, or oversight responsibilities.

A.4. Program Development and Evaluation

    a. *Group Workers identify the type(s) of group(s) to be offered and how they relate to community needs.*

    b. *Group Workers concisely state in writing the purpose and goals of the group.* Group Workers also identify the role of the group members in influencing or determining the group goals.

    c. *Group Workers set fees consistent with the organization's fee schedule, taking into consideration the financial status and locality of prospective group members.*

    d. *Group Workers choose techniques and a leadership style appropriate to the type(s) of group(s) being offered.*

    e. *Group Workers have an evaluation plan consistent with regulatory, organization and insurance requirements, where appropriate.*

    f. *Group Workers take into consideration current professional guidelines when using technology, including but not limited to Internet communication.*

A.5. Resources

Group Workers coordinate resources related to the kind of group(s) and group activities to be provided, such as: adequate funding; the appropriateness and availability of a trained co-leader; space and privacy requirements for the type(s) of group(s) being offered; marketing and recruiting; and appropriate collaboration with other community agencies and organizations.

A.6. Professional Disclosure Statement

Group Workers have a professional disclosure statement which includes information on confidentiality and exceptions to confidentiality, theoretical orientation, information on the nature, purpose(s) and goals of the group, the group services that can be provided, the role and responsibility of group members and leaders, Group Workers' qualifications to conduct the specific group(s), specific licenses, certifications and professional affiliations, and address of licensing/credentialing body.

A.7. Group and Member Preparation

    a. *Group Workers screen prospective group members if appropriate to the type of group being offered.* When selection of group members is appropriate, Group Workers identify group members whose needs and goals are compatible with the goals of the group.

    b. *Group Workers facilitate informed consent.* Group Workers provide in oral and written form to prospective members (when appropriate to group type): the professional disclosure statement; group purpose and goals; group participation expectations including voluntary and involuntary membership; role expectations of members and leader(s); policies related to entering and exiting the group; policies governing substance use; policies and procedures governing mandated groups (where relevant); documentation requirements; disclosure of information to others; implications of out-of-group contact or involvement among members; procedures for consultation between group leader(s) and group member(s); fees and time parameters; and potential impacts of group participation.

    c. *Group Workers obtain the appropriate consent forms for work with minors and other dependent group members.*

    d. *Group Workers define confidentiality and its limits (for example, legal and 0ethical exceptions and expectations; waivers implicit with treatment plans, documentation and insurance usage).* Group Workers have the responsibility to inform all group participants of the need for confidentiality, potential consequences of breaching confidentiality and that legal privilege does not apply to group discussions (unless provided by state statute).

A.8. Professional Development

Group Workers recognize that professional growth is a continuous, ongoing, developmental process throughout their career.

   a. *Group Workers remain current and increase knowledge and skill competencies through activities such as continuing education, professional supervision, and participation in personal and professional development activities.*
   b. *Group Workers seek consultation and/or supervision regarding ethical concerns that interfere with effective functioning as a group leader.* Supervisors have the responsibility to keep abreast of consultation, group theory, process, and adhere to related ethical guidelines.
   c. *Group Workers seek appropriate professional assistance for their own personal problems or conflicts that are likely to impair their professional judgement or work performance.*
   d. *Group Workers seek consultation and supervision to ensure appropriate practice whenever working with a group for which all knowledge and skill competencies have not been achieved.*
   e. *Group Workers keep abreast of group research and development.*

A.9. Trends and Technological Changes

Group Workers are aware of and responsive to technological changes as they affect society and the profession. These include but are not limited to changes in mental health delivery systems; legislative and insurance industry reforms; shifting population demographics and client needs; and technological advances in Internet and other communication and delivery systems. Group Workers adhere to ethical guidelines related to the use of developing technologies.

SECTION B: BEST PRACTICE IN PERFORMING

B.1. Self Knowledge

Group Workers are aware of and monitor their strengths and weaknesses and the effects these have on group members.

B.2. Group Competencies

Group Workers have a basic knowledge of groups and the principles of group dynamics, and are able to perform the core group competencies, as described in the ASGW

Professional Standards for the Training of Group Workers. Additionally, Group Workers have adequate understanding and skill in any group specialty area chosen for practice (psychotherapy, counseling, task, psychoeducation, as described in the ASGW Training Standards).

B.3. Group Plan Adaptation

a. *Group Workers apply and modify knowledge, skills and techniques appropriate to group type and stage, and to the unique needs of various cultural and ethnic groups.*
b. *Group Workers monitor the group's progress toward the group goals and plan.*
c. *Group Workers clearly define and maintain ethical, professional, and social relationship boundaries with group members as appropriate to their role in the organization and the type of group being offered.*

B.4. Therapeutic Conditions and Dynamics

Group Workers understand and are able to implement appropriate models of group development, process observation and therapeutic conditions.

B.5. Meaning

Group Workers assist members in generating meaning from the group experience.

B.6. Collaboration

Group Workers assist members in developing individual goals and respect group members as co-equal partners in the group experience.

B.7. Evaluation

Group Workers include evaluation (both formal and informal) between sessions and at the conclusion of the group.

B.8. Diversity

Group Workers practice with broad sensitivity to client differences including but not limited to ethnic, gender, religious, sexual, psychological maturity, economic class, family history, physical characteristics or limitations, and geographic location. Group Workers continuously seek information regarding the cultural issues of the diverse population with whom they are working both by interaction with participants and from using outside resources.

B.9. Ethical Surveillance

Group Workers employ an appropriate ethical decision making model in responding to ethical challenges and issues and in determining courses of action and behavior for self and group members. In addition, Group Workers employ applicable standards as promulgated by ACA, ASGW, or other appropriate professional organizations.

SECTION C: BEST PRACTICE IN GROUP PROCESSING

C.1. Processing Schedule

Group Workers process the workings of the group with themselves, group members, supervisors or other colleagues, as appropriate. This may include assessing progress on group and member goals, leader behaviors and techniques, group dynamics and interventions; developing understanding and acceptance of meaning. Processing may occur both within sessions and before and after each session, at time of termination, and later follow up, as appropriate.

C.2. Reflective Practice

Group Workers attend to opportunities to synthesize theory and practice and to incorporate learning outcomes into ongoing groups. Group Workers attend to session dynamics of members and their interactions and also attend to the relationship between session dynamics and leader values, cognition and affect.

C.3. Evaluation and Follow-Up

   a. *Group Workers evaluate process and outcomes.* Results are used for ongoing program planning, improvement and revisions of current group and/or to contribute to professional research literature. Group Workers follow all applicable policies and standards in using group material for research and reports.
   b. *Group Workers conduct follow-up contact with group members, as appropriate, to assess outcomes or when requested by a group member(s).*

C.4. Consultation and Training with Other Organizations

Group Workers provide consultation and training to organizations in and out of their setting, when appropriate. Group Workers seek out consultation as needed with competent professional persons knowledgeable about group work.

PRINCIPLES FOR DIVERSITY-COMPETENT GROUP WORKERS

Association for Specialists in Group Work

Revision Approved by the Executive Board, August 1, 1998
Prepared by Lynn Haley-Banez, Sherlon Brown, and Bogusia Molina
Consultants: Michael D'Andrea, Patricia Arrendondo,
Niloufer Merchant, and Sandra Wathen

PREAMBLE

The Association for Specialists in Group Work (ASGW) is committed to understanding how issues of diversity affect all aspects of group work. This includes but is not limited to: training diversity-competent group workers; conducting research that will add to the literature on group work with diverse populations; understanding how diversity affects group process and dynamics; and assisting group facilitators in various settings to increase their awareness, knowledge, and skills as they relate to facilitating groups with diverse memberships. As an organization, ASGW has endorsed this document with the recognition that issues of diversity affect group process and dynamics, group facilitation, training, and research. As an organization, we recognize that racism, classism, sexism, heterosexism, ableism, and so forth, affect everyone. As individual members of this organization, it is our personal responsibility to address these issues through awareness, knowledge, and skills. As members of ASGW, we need to increase our awareness of our own biases, values, and beliefs and how they impact the groups we run. We need to increase our awareness of our group members' biases, values, and beliefs and how they also impact and influence group process and dynamics. Finally, we need to increase our knowledge in facilitating, with confidence, competence, and integrity, groups that are diverse on many dimensions.

Definitions

For the purposes of this document, it is important that the language used is understood. Terms such as "dominant," "nondominant," and "target" persons and/or populations are used to define a person or groups of persons who historically, in the United States, do not have equal access to power, money, certain privileges (such as access to mental health services because of financial constraints, or the legal right to marry, in the case of a gay or lesbian couple), and/or the ability to influence or initiate social policy because of unequal representation in government and politics. These terms are not used to denote a lack of numbers in terms of representation in the overall U.S. population. Nor are these terms used to continue to perpetuate the very biases and forms of oppression, both overt and covert, that this document attempts to address.

For the purposes of this document, the term "disabilities" refers to differences in physical, mental, emotional, and learning abilities and styles among people. It is not meant as a term to define a person, such as a learning disabled person, but rather in the context of a person with a learning disability.

Given the history and current cultural, social, and political context in which this document is written, the authors of this document are limited to the language of this era. With this in mind, we have attempted to construct a "living document" that can and will change as the sociopolitical and cultural context changes.

THE PRINCIPLES

I. Awareness of Self

A. Attitudes and Beliefs

1. Diversity-competent group workers demonstrate movement from being unaware to being increasingly aware and sensitive to their own race, ethnic and cultural heritage, gender, socioeconomic status (SES), sexual orientation, abilities, and religion and spiritual beliefs, and to valuing and respecting differences.
2. Diversity-competent group workers demonstrate increased awareness of how their own race, ethnicity, culture, gender, SES, sexual orientation, abilities, and religion and spiritual beliefs are impacted by their own experiences and histories, which in turn influence group process and dynamics.
3. Diversity-competent group workers can recognize the limits of their competencies and expertise with regard to working with group members who are different from them in terms of race, ethnicity, culture (including language), SES, gender, sexual orientation, abilities, religion, and spirituality and their beliefs, values, and biases. (For further clarification on limitations, expertise, and type of group work, refer to the training standards and best practice guidelines, Association for Specialists in Group Work, 1998; and the ethical guidelines, American Counseling Association, 1995.)
4. Diversity-competent group workers demonstrate comfort, tolerance, and sensitivity with differences that exist between themselves and group members in terms

of race, ethnicity, culture, SES, gender, sexual orientation, abilities, religion, and spirituality and their beliefs, values, and biases.

B. Knowledge

1. Diversity-competent group workers can identify specific knowledge about their own race, ethnicity, SES, gender, sexual orientation, abilities, religion, and spirituality, and how they personally and professionally affect their definitions of "normality" and the group process.
2. Diversity-skilled group workers demonstrate knowledge and understanding regarding how oppression in any form—such as, racism, classism, sexism, heterosexism, ableism, discrimination, and stereotyping—affects them personally and professionally.
3. Diversity-skilled group workers demonstrate knowledge about their social impact on others. They are knowledgeable about communication style differences, how their style may inhibit or foster the group process with members who are different from themselves along the different dimensions of diversity, and how to anticipate the impact they may have on others.

C. Skills

1. Diversity-competent group workers seek out educational, consultative, and training experiences to improve their understanding and effectiveness in working with group members who self-identify as Indigenous Peoples, African Americans, Asian Americans, Hispanics, Latinos/Latinas, gays, lesbians, bisexuals, or transgendered persons and persons with physical, mental/emotional, and/or learning disabilities, particularly with regard to race and ethnicity. Within this context, group workers are able to recognize the limits of their competencies and: (a) seek consultation, (b) seek further training or education, (c) refer members to more qualified group workers, or (d) engage in a combination of these.
2. Group workers who exhibit diversity competence are constantly seeking to understand themselves within their multiple identities (apparent and unapparent differences), for example, gay, Latina, Christian, working-class and female, and are constantly and actively striving to unlearn the various behaviors and processes they covertly and overtly communicate that perpetuate oppression, particularly racism.

II. Group Worker's Awareness of Group Member's Worldview

A. Attitudes and Beliefs

1. Diversity-skilled group workers exhibit awareness of any possible negative emotional reactions toward Indigenous Peoples, African Americans, Asian Americans, Hispanics, Latinos/Latinas, gays, lesbians, bisexuals, or transgendered persons and persons with physical, mental/emotional, and/or learning disabilities that they may hold. They are willing to contrast in a nonjudgmental manner their own beliefs and attitudes with those of Indigenous Peoples, African Americans, Asian Americans, Hispanics, Latinos/Latinas, gays, lesbians, bisexuals, or transgendered persons and persons with physical, mental/emotional, and/or learning disabilities who are group members.

2. Diversity-competent group workers demonstrate awareness of their stereotypes and preconceived notions that they may hold toward Indigenous Peoples, African Americans, Asian Americans, Hispanics, Latinos/Latinas, gays, lesbians, bisexuals, or transgendered persons and persons with physical, mental/emotional, and/or learning disabilities.

B. Knowledge

1. Diversity-skilled group workers possess specific knowledge and information about Indigenous Peoples, African Americans, Asian Americans, Hispanics, Latinos/Latinas, gays, lesbians, bisexuals, and transgendered people and group members who have mental/emotional, physical, and/or learning disabilities with whom they are working. They are aware of the life experiences, cultural heritage, and sociopolitical background of Indigenous Peoples, African Americans, Asian Americans, Hispanics, Latinos/Latinas, gays, lesbians, bisexuals, or transgendered persons and group members with physical, mental/emotional, and/or learning disabilities. This particular knowledge-based competency is strongly linked to the various racial/minority and sexual identity development models available in the literature (Atkinson, Morten, & Sue, 1993; Cass, 1979; Cross, 1995; D'Augelli & Patterson, 1995; Helms, 1992).

2. Diversity-competent group workers exhibit an understanding of how race, ethnicity, culture, gender, sexual identity, different abilities, SES, and other immutable personal characteristics may affect personality formation, vocational choices, manifestation of psychological disorders, physical "dis-ease" or somatic symptoms, help-seeking behavior(s), and the appropriateness or inappropriateness of the various types of and theoretical approaches to group work.

3. Group workers who demonstrate competency in diversity in groups understand and have the knowledge about sociopolitical influences that impinge upon the lives of Indigenous Peoples, African Americans, Asian Americans, Hispanics, Latinos/Latinas, gays, lesbians, bisexuals, or transgendered persons and persons with physical, mental/emotional, and/or learning disabilities. Immigration issues, poverty, racism, oppression, stereotyping, and/or powerlessness adversely impacts many of these individuals and therefore impacts group process or dynamics.

C. Skills

1. Diversity-skilled group workers familiarize themselves with relevant research and the latest findings regarding mental health issues of Indigenous Peoples, African Americans, Asian Americans, Hispanics, Latinos/Latinas, gays, lesbians, bisexuals, or transgendered persons and persons with physical, mental/emotional, and/or learning disabilities. They actively seek out educational experiences that foster their knowledge and understanding of skills for facilitating groups across differences.

2. Diversity-competent group workers become actively involved with Indigenous Peoples, African Americans, Asian Americans, Hispanics, Latinos/Latinas, gays, lesbians, bisexuals, or transgendered persons and persons with physical, mental/emotional, and/or learning disabilities outside of their group work/counseling setting (community events, social and political functions, celebrations, friendships,

neighborhood groups, etc.) so that their perspective of minorities is more than academic or experienced through a third party.

III. Diversity-Appropriate Intervention Strategies

A. Attitudes and Beliefs

1. Diversity-competent group workers respect clients' religious and/or spiritual beliefs and values, because they affect worldview, psychosocial functioning, and expressions of distress.

2. Diversity-competent group workers respect indigenous helping practices and respect Indigenous Peoples, African Americans, Asian Americans, Hispanics, Latinos/Latinas, gays, lesbians, bisexuals, or transgendered persons and persons with physical, mental/emotional, and/or learning disabilities and can identify and utilize community intrinsic help-giving networks.

3. Diversity-competent group workers value bilingualism and sign language and do not view another language as an impediment to group work.

B. Knowledge

1. Diversity-competent group workers demonstrate a clear and explicit knowledge and understanding of generic characteristics of group work and theory and how they may clash with the beliefs, values, and traditions of Indigenous Peoples, African Americans, Asian Americans, Hispanics, Latinos/Latinas, gays, lesbians, bisexuals, or transgendered persons and persons with physical, mental/emotional, and/or learning disabilities.

2. Diversity-competent group workers exhibit an awareness of institutional barriers that prevent Indigenous Peoples, African Americans, Asian Americans, Hispanics, Latinos/Latinas, gays, lesbians, bisexuals, or transgendered members and members with physical, mental/emotional, and/or learning disabilities from actively participating in or using various types of groups, that is, task groups, psychoeducational groups, counseling groups, and psychotherapy groups or the settings in which the services are offered.

3. Diversity-competent group workers demonstrate knowledge of the potential bias in assessment instruments and use procedures and interpret findings, or actively participate in various types of evaluations of group outcome or success, keeping in mind the linguistic, cultural, and other self-identified characteristics of the group member.

4. Diversity-competent group workers exhibit knowledge of the family structures, hierarchies, values, and beliefs of Indigenous Peoples, African Americans, Asian Americans, Hispanics, Latinos/Latinas, gays, lesbians, bisexuals, or transgendered persons and persons with physical, mental/emotional, and/or learning disabilities. They are knowledgeable about the community characteristics and the resources in the community as well as about the family.

5. Diversity-competent group workers demonstrate an awareness of relevant discriminatory practices at the social and community level that may be affecting the psychological welfare of persons and access to services of the population being served.

C. Skills

1. Diversity-competent group workers are able to engage in a variety of verbal and nonverbal group-facilitating functions, dependent upon the type of group (task, counseling, psychoeducational, psychotherapy), and the multiple, self-identified status of various group members (such as Indigenous Peoples, African Americans, Asian Americans, Hispanics, Latinos/Latinas, gays, lesbians, bisexuals, or transgendered persons and persons with physical, mental/emotional, and/or learning disabilities). They demonstrate the ability to send and receive both verbal and nonverbal messages accurately, appropriately, and across/between the differences represented in the group. They are not tied down to one method or approach to group facilitation and recognize that helping styles and approaches may be culture-bound. When they sense that their group facilitation style is limited and potentially inappropriate, they can anticipate and ameliorate its negative impact by drawing upon other culturally relevant skill sets.

2. Diversity-competent group workers have the ability to exercise institutional intervention skills on behalf of their group members. They can help a member determine whether a "problem" with the institution stems from the oppression of Indigenous Peoples, African Americans, Asian Americans, Hispanics, Latinos/Latinas, gays, lesbians, bisexuals, or transgendered persons and persons with physical, mental/emotional, and/or learning disabilities, such as in the case of developing or having a "healthy" paranoia, so that group members do not inappropriately personalize problems.

3. Diversity-competent group workers do not exhibit a reluctance to seek consultation with traditional healers and religious and spiritual healers and practitioners in the treatment of members who are self-identified Indigenous Peoples, African Americans, Asian Americans, Hispanics, Latinos/Latinas, gays, lesbians, bisexuals, and transgendered persons and/or group members with mental/emotional, physical, and/or learning disabilities when appropriate.

4. Diversity-competent group workers take responsibility for interacting in the language requested by the group member(s) and, if not feasible, make an appropriate referral. A serious problem arises when the linguistic skills of a group worker and a group member or members, including sign language, do not match. The same problem occurs when the linguistic skills of one member or several members do not match. This being the case, the group worker, should (a) seek a translator with cultural knowledge and appropriate professional background, and (b) refer to a knowledgeable, competent bilingual group worker or a group worker competent or certified in sign language. In some cases, it may be necessary to have a group for group members of similar languages or to refer the group member for individual counseling.

5. Diversity-competent group workers are trained and have expertise in the use of traditional assessment and testing instruments related to group work, such as in screening potential members, and they also are aware of the cultural bias/limitations of these tools and processes. This allows them to use the tools for the welfare of diverse group members following culturally appropriate procedures.

6. Diversity-competent group workers attend to as well as work to eliminate biases, prejudices, oppression, and discriminatory practices. They are cognizant of how

sociopolitical contexts may affect evaluation and provision of group work and should develop sensitivity to issues of oppression, racism, sexism, heterosexism, classism, and so forth.

7. Diversity-competent group workers take responsibility in educating their group members to the processes of group work, such as goals, expectations, legal rights, sound ethical practice, and the group worker's theoretical orientation with regard to facilitating groups with diverse membership.

CONCLUSION

This document is the "starting point" for group workers as we become increasingly aware, knowledgeable, and skillful in facilitating groups whose memberships represent the diversity of our society. It is not intended to be a "how to" document. It is written as a call to action and/or a guideline and represents ASGW's commitment to moving forward with an agenda for addressing and understanding the needs of the populations we serve. As a "living document," the Association for Specialists in Group Work acknowledges the changing world in which we live and work and therefore recognizes that this is the first step in working with diverse group members with competence, compassion, respect, and integrity. As our awareness, knowledge, and skills develop, so too will this document evolve. As our knowledge as a profession grows in this area and as the sociopolitical context in which this document was written, changes, new editions of these Principles for Diversity-Competent Group Workers will arise. The operationalization of this document (article in process) will begin to define appropriate group leadership skills and interventions as well as make recommendations for research in understanding how diversity in group membership affects group process and dynamics.

REFERENCES

American Counseling Association. (1995). *Code of ethics and standards.* Alexandria, VA: Author.

Association for Multicultural Counseling and Development. (1996). *Multicultural competencies.* Alexandria, VA: American Counseling Association.

Association for Specialists in Group Work. (1991). Professional standards for training of group workers. *Together, 20,* 9–14.

Association for Specialists in Group Work. (1998). Guidelines for best practice. *Journal for Specialists in Group Work, 23,* 237–244.

Atkinson, D. R., Morten, G., & Sue, D. W. (Eds.). (1993). *Counseling American minorities* (4th ed.). Madison, WI: Brown & Benchmark.

Cass, V. C. (1979). Homosexual identity formation: A theoretical model. *Journal of Homosexuality, 4,* 219–236.

Cross, W. E. (1995). The psychology of Nigrescence: Revising the cross model. In J. G. Ponterotto, J. M. Casas, L. A. Suzuki, & C. M. Alexander (Eds.), *Handbook of multicultural counseling* (pp. 93–122). Thousand Oaks, CA: Sage.

D'Augelli, A. R., & Patterson, C. J. (Eds.). (1995). *Lesbian, gay and bisexual identities over the lifespan.* New York: Oxford University Press.

Helms, J. E. (1992). *A race is a nice thing to have.* Topeka, KS: Context Communications.

GUIDELINES FOR ETHICS

American Group Psychotherapy Association

INTRODUCTION

The American Group Psychotherapy Association is a professional multidisciplinary organization whose purpose is to: "provide a forum for the exchange of ideas among qualified professional persons interested in group psychotherapy and to publish and to make publications available on all subjects relating to group psychotherapy; to encourage the development of sound training programs in group psychotherapy for qualified mental health professionals; to encourage and promote research on group psychotherapy and to establish and maintain high standards of ethical, professional group psychotherapy practice."

Membership in the American Group Psychotherapy Association presumes strict adherence to standards of ethical practice. As a specialty organization, AGPA supports the ethical codes of the primary professional organizations to which our members belong. Providing guidelines for the ethical behavior of group psychotherapists serves to inform both the group psychotherapist and public of the American Group Psychotherapy Association's expectations in the practice of group psychotherapy.

GENERAL GUIDELINES

Ethical complaints about AGPA members will be directed to the primary professional organization of the members. AGPA's response as to sanctions will parallel that of the primary organization. For example, if the primary organization concludes that an individual's membership should be suspended for one year, AGPA will suspend membership for one year. Should an ethical complaint be received regarding a member of AGPA who does not belong to a primary professional organization, the complaint will be directed to the state licensing board and/or the state or federal legal system. If the member is found guilty, AGPA's sanctions will parallel the sanctions of the state licensing board, other governmental agencies or courts of law as to the person's ability to practice; the AGPA cannot parallel such sanctions as fines, penalties or imprisonment.

Reprinted by permission from American Group Psychotherapy Association.

For those members of the American Group Psychotherapy Association who are psychiatrists, the principles of ethics as applied by the American Psychiatric Association shall govern their behavior; those members who are clinical psychologists shall be expected to comply with the principles of ethics laid down by the American Psychological Association; those members who are clinical social workers shall be expected to comply with the ethical standards established by the National Federation of Societies for Clinical Social Work; those members who are clinical specialists in nursing shall be expected to comply with the principles of ethics of the American Nurses' Association; those members who are pastoral counselors shall be expected to comply with the ethical standards of the American Association of Pastoral Care; and those members of other professional disciplines having published principles of ethics shall follow those principles. Members of the Association who do not belong to one of the above professional groups having a published standard of ethics shall follow the principles of ethics laid down by the American Psychological Association.

GUIDELINES OF GROUP PSYCHOTHERAPY PRACTICE

The following guidelines of group psychotherapy practice shall serve as models for group therapists' ethical behavior.

Responsibility to Patient/Client

1. The group psychotherapist provides services with respect for the dignity and uniqueness of each patient/client as well as the rights and autonomy of the individual patient/client.

    1.1 The group psychotherapist shall provide the potential group patient/client with information about the nature of group psychotherapy and apprise them of their risks, rights and obligations as members of a therapy group.

    1.2 The group psychotherapist shall encourage the patient/client's participation in group psychotherapy only so long as it is appropriate to the patient/client's needs.

    1.3 The group psychotherapist shall not practice or condone any form of discrimination on the basis of race, color, sex, sexual orientation, age, religion, national origin or physical handicap, except that this guideline shall not prohibit group therapy practice with population specific or problem specific groups.

2. The group psychotherapist safeguards the patient/client's right to privacy by judiciously protecting information of a confidential nature.

    2.1 The group shall agree that the patient/client as well as the psychotherapist shall protect the identity of its members.

    2.2 The group psychotherapist shall not use identifiable information about the group or its members for teaching purposes, publication or professional presentations unless permission has been obtained and all measures have been taken to preserve patient/client anonymity.

2.3 Except where required by law, the group psychotherapist shall share information about the group members with others only after obtaining appropriate patient/client consent. Specific permission must be requested to permit conferring with the referring therapist or with the individual therapist where the patient/client is in conjoint therapy.

2.4 When clinical examination suggests that a patient/client may be dangerous to himself/herself or others, it is the group psychotherapist's ethical and legal obligation to take appropriate steps in order to be responsible to society in general, as well as the patient/client.

3. The group psychotherapist acts to safeguard the patient/client and the public from the incompetent, unethical, illegal practice of any group psychotherapist.

3.1 The group psychotherapist must be aware of her/his own individual competencies, and when the needs of the patient/client are beyond the competencies of the psychotherapist, consultation must be sought from other qualified professionals or other appropriate sources.

3.2 The group psychotherapist shall not use her/his professional relationship to advance personal or business interests.

3.3 Sexual intimacy with patients/clients is unethical.

3.4 The group psychotherapist shall protect the patient/client and the public from misinformation and misrepresentation. She/he shall not use false or misleading advertising regarding her/his qualifications or skills as a group psychotherapist.

Professional Standards

The group psychotherapist shall maintain the integrity of the practice of group psychotherapy.

1. It is the personal responsibility of the group psychotherapist to maintain competence in the practice of group psychotherapy through formal educational activities and informal learning experiences.

2. The group psychotherapist has a responsibility to contribute to the ongoing development of the body of knowledge pertaining to group psychotherapy whether involved as an investigator, participant or user of research results.

3. The group psychotherapist shall accept the obligation to attempt to inform and alert other group psychotherapists who are violating ethical principles or to bring those violations to the attention of appropriate professional authorities.